Canadian School
DICTIONARY

usage, gra
idioms, examp
word history
illustrati   be
Cana
conf
pronu
usage, g
exar.ples
parts of sp
appendix, usa
word history,
pronunciati

D1213634

gage EDUCATIONAL PUBLISHING COMPANY
A DIVISION OF CANADA PUBLISHING CORPORATION
Vancouver · Calgary · Toronto · London · Halifax

Copyright © 2000 Gage Educational Publishing Company
A Division of Canada Publishing Corporation

We acknowledge the financial support of the Government of Canada
through the Book Publishing Industry Development Program for our
publishing activities.

PAGE DESIGN AND ILLUSTRATION: ArtPlus Limited
PAGE MAKE-UP: Heather Brunton/ArtPlus Limited
COVER DESIGN: Campbell Sheffield Design Inc.

Canadian Cataloguing in Publication Data

Main entry under title:
    Gage Canadian school dictionary

ISBN 0-7715-1999-0

1. English language—Dictionaries, Juvenile

PE1628.5.G33 1998   j423   C98-932860-0

We hope you find this dictionary helpful, easy-to-use, and
enjoyable to browse through. If you have any comment to
make, please let our editorial team know. Perhaps you have a
suggestion that we should add to our database.

Gage Educational Publishing Company
164 Commander Blvd.
Toronto, ON M1S 3C7

Phone   416-293-8464 X 271
Fax   416-293-0757
e-mail   info@gage.canpub.ca

Errata   page 196 Kwanzaa:
        The date should be December 26, not 6.
page 367 map:
        There should be lines from Malecite (Maliseet)
        to Québec and New Brunswick, and from
        Mi'kmaq to Québec, Prince Edward Island,
        Nova Scotia, and New Brunswick.

ISBN 0-7715-1999-0

 2 3 4 5 FP 04 03 02 01 00

Written, printed, and bound in Canada

Editorial Team

Reviewers and Consultants

Gage Canadian Reference Series

General Editor T. K. Pratt
      Professor, Department of English
      University of Prince Edward Island

Gage Canadian Dictionary
Gage Canadian Thesaurus
Gage Canadian Intermediate Dictionary
Gage Canadian Junior Dictionary
Gage Canadian School Dictionary
Gage Canadian School Thesaurus

Contents

A Challenge

There are features in this dictionary that you may not have seen in a dictionary before. Can you find the following?

1. A word that first came into the English language in Canada.

2. Two words that are often confused with each other.

3. An activity that helps you pronounce words correctly.

4. A picture that tells you how tall an elephant is.

5. A situation where "for good" doesn't have to be a good thing.

6. The Roman numeral for eight.

7. The correct places to use capital letters.

You can find out even more by doing the activities on pages 7 to 18. Try them!

1. There's one on page 72, **cat-train**. You can find more of these words by looking for a picture of a tiny maple leaf.

2. There's **accept** and **except**, on page 20. You can find more of these words by looking for boxes titled CONFUSABLES. There are also different boxes that tell you about grammar, using words, and word history. Just open the dictionary almost anywhere!

3. There's one on page 15. You can find more activities to help you improve your dictionary skills on pages 7 to 18.

4. Look at page 126. You can find many other pages with pictures that give you useful information about animals, plants, ships, people, etc.

5. There's one on page 158. You can find more of these phrases that have special meanings (they're called idioms) on almost every page of this dictionary.

6. Look at page 373. You can find many more useful facts about numbers, Canada, abbreviations, countries of the world, etc. by looking at pages 365-376.

7. Look at page 377. You can find more information about grammar and using words in the rest of the pages of this Mini-Guide.

Getting to Know Your Dictionary

This dictionary contains facts about nearly 15 000 words that you are most likely to use when you speak, write, listen, or read. The following pages provide information and activities that will help you to find and use these words.

LOOKING UP A WORD YOU CAN'T SPELL ....

How do you look up a word you can't spell?

Suppose, for example, that you want to find the spelling and meaning of a word that you heard as **kaos**. You look up *kaos* in the dictionary, and there's no such word. So, use the chart *Common Spellings of English Sounds*, shown on pages 8 and 9. Here's what to do.

- Look at the first column (*Sound*) and find *k*.
- Look to the right and you can see some possible spellings for the sound *k* at the *beginning of a word*: **c**oat, **ch**emistry, **k**ind, **qu**ick, **qu**ay. This means the word you heard could be *caos, chaos, kaos* (no good, you've tried that) *qaos*, or *quaos*. Check these out, and you will find the word *chaos*.

For some words, you may have to go to the other columns for *middle of word* or *end of word* spellings.

It also helps to know the symbols used for sounds. Here they are. The symbol ə is called the schwa (pronounced shwȧ).

a	bat	e	bed	i	bid	o	pot	u	cup	th	thin
ā	cake	ē	me	ī	bite	ō	go	ū	rude	ᴛʜ	then
ȧ	bar	ə	about	ər	over	ȯ	for	u̇	put	zh	measure

TRY IT

Use the *Common Spellings of English Sounds* chart to find the spellings of words that sound like these.

1. sī′əns
2. shō fər′
3. ō′shən
4. ə kwīr′
5. nā′bər
6. thrū

Common Spellings of English Sounds

Sound	Beginnings of words	Middles of words	Ends of words
a	and, aunt	hat, plaid, half, laugh	—
ā	age, aid, eight	face, fail, straight, payment, gauge, break, vein, neighbour	say, weigh, bouquet, they, café, matinée
ȧ	art	barn, bazaar, heart	hurrah
b	bad	table, rabbit	rub, ebb
ch	child	cappuccino, richness, nature, watching, question	much, catch
d	do	lady, ladder	red, used
e	any, aerial, air, end	many, said, says, let, bread, leopard, friend, bury	—
ē	equal, eat, either	metre, team, need, receive, people, keyhole, machine, believe	algae, quay, acne, flea, bee, key, Métis, loonie, pity
f	fat, phone	after, coffee, often, laughter, gopher	roof, sniff, cough, half, epitaph
g	go, ghost, guess	ago, giggle, catalogues	bag, egg, rogue
h	help, who	ahead	—
i	enamel, in	message, been, pin, sieve, women, busy, build, hymn	—
ī	aisle, aye, either, eye, ice, island	height, line, align, might, buying, type	aye, eye, lie, high, buy, sky, dye
ē	gem, jam	educate, badger, soldier, adjust, tragic, exaggerate, enjoy	bridge, rage, hajj
k	coat, chemistry, kind, quick, quay	record, account, echo, lucky, acquire, looking, liquor, extra	back, seek, walk, tuque
l	land, llama	only, follow	coal, fill
m	me	coming, climbing, summer	calm, hum, comb, solemn
n	gnaw, knife, nut	miner, manner	sign, man, inn
ng	—	ink, finger, singer	bang, tongue
o	all, almond, author, awful, encore, honest, odd, ought	watch, palm, taut, taught, sawed, hot, bought	Ottawa, paw

Common Spellings of English Sounds

Sound	Beginnings of words	Middles of words	Ends of words
ō	open, oath, own	George, sewn, home, boat, folk, brooch, soul, flown	chateau, sew, potato, toe, though, blow
ȯ	order, oar	born, board, floor, mourn	—
oi	oil, oyster	boil, boyhood	boy
ou	hour, out, owl	bound, drought, howl	plough, now
p	pen	paper, supper	up
r	run, rhythm	parent, hurry	bear, burr
s	cent, psychology, say, science, sword	decent, loosen, muscle, massive, answer, extra	nice, marvellous, miss, lax
sh	chauffeur, sure, shirt	ocean, machine, special, unsure, conscience, nauseous, tension, issue, mission, nation	cache, wish
t	ptarmigan, tell, Thomas	doubtful, later, latter	doubt, crashed, bit, mitt
th	thin	toothache	bath
ŦH	then	mother	smooth, bathe
u	oven, up	come, does, flood, trouble, cup	—
ū	ooze	neutral, move, food, group, rule, fruit	threw, shoe, caribou, through, blue
u̇	—	wolf, good, should, full	—
yū	Europe, use, you, Yukon	beauty, feud, duty	queue, few, cue, you
v	very	over	of, love
w	will, wheat, one	choir, quick, twin	—
y	young	opinion, canyon	—
z	xylophone	raisin, scissors, exact, lazy, dazzle	has, maze, buzz
zh	—	measure, division	mirage
ə	alone, essential, oblige, upon	spaghetti, fountain, moment, pencil, bottle, criticism, button, cautious, circus	sofa
ər	early, urge	salary, term, learn, first, word, journey, turn, syrup	liar, deter, stir, actor, fur, burr, measure

FAST FIND . . . .

How do you find a word quickly? Here are two strategies to use.

Alphabetical Order

The entry words in the *Gage School Dictionary* are in alphabetical order:

A B C D E F G H I J K L M N O P Q R S T U V W X Y Z

Whenever you want to look up a word in the dictionary, decide if the first letter of the word comes in the first half (A to M) or the second half (N to Z) of the alphabet. Then **try to open the dictionary near the right part.**

TRY IT

Which half of the dictionary would you turn to if you were looking up each of the following entry words?

1. empty   2. shark   3. portfolio   4. literature

Words in the dictionary with the **same first** letter are also arranged alphabetically according to the **second letter**. Here are some **c** words, in alphabetical order: case, cease, chain, coal, cry, cycle.

When the **first two letters are the same**, words are alphabetized by the **third letter**, and so on: chair, cheer, chief, choice, choose, chum.

TRY IT

1. Arrange the following words in alphabetical order to make sentences.

   • me followed black dog a yesterday
   • clawed cat a big David
   • four wrestling them were of
   • my truck I chairs in can't rental carry

2. Find the two entry words between which your name would go.

Guide Words

At the top of each page of the dictionary are two words. For example:

adequate   23   adverb

These words are called **guide words**. The guide word on the left is the first entry word to appear on the page; the guide word on the right is the last. All the entry words on that page will fall between the two guide words alphabetically. **Looking at guide words helps you find the entry that you want more quickly.**

TRY IT

By looking at the guide words shown for page 23, decide which of the following will appear as entry words on page 23:

admire, adjective, adopt, adventure, advantage, advertise, address, advise

DEFINITIONS...

A definition explains the meaning of a word. If a word has more than one definition, each definition is given a different number. Usually the most common meaning is given first. For example, *beam* has three definitions:

beam (bēm) **1** *n* a large, long piece of wood, concrete, or steel used to support buildings. **2** *n* a ray or rays of light: *The beam from the flashlight made the cat's eyes shine.* **3** *v* look or smile brightly: *Her face beamed with delight.*

TRY IT

Do you know the meanings of the words in italics below? Look up each word in the dictionary and write down the definition that makes sense.

1. My brother and his friends play in a *band*.
2. I must *enter* the information in the computer.
3. The firefighter directed a *jet* of foam at the burning airplane.
4. Please don't turn down the corner of the *page*.

Examples

Many definitions are followed by one or more examples, printed in italics. Examples show how the word is used in sentences or phrases. Look at the entry for *deliver*.

de·liv·er (di liv′ər) **1** *v* carry something to the proper place: *Moina delivers newspapers every morning.* **2** *v* give: *to deliver a speech.* **–de·liv′er·er**, *n*, **–de·liv′er·y**, *n*.

Write your own example sentences for the following definitions:

1. **bottom** (def. 1) the deepest or lowest part:....
2. **graze** (def. 2) scrape:....
3. **hamper** (def. 1) get in the way of:....
4. **part** (def. 2) a share:....

With a partner, check your examples to make sure they fit the definitions and make good sense. Then compare them with the examples in the dictionary. In each case, decide whether your example, your partner's example, or the one in the dictionary is best. Be prepared to say why.

ROOT WORDS..

Sometimes a word you want to look up is not a main entry. In such cases, you should **find the root word** of the one you want to look up.

Related Words

Some entries in the dictionary are in the same paragraph as a main entry.

op·pose (ə pōz′) *v* be against: *Many people opposed the widening of the street.* **op·posed, op·pos·ing.** –**op′po·si′tion,** *n.*
op·po·nent (ə pō′nənt) *n* a person who is on the other side in a fight, game, or argument.
op·po·site (op′ə sit) **1** *adj* as different as can be: *North and south are opposite directions.* **2** *n* a thing as different as can be: *North is the opposite of south.* **3** *prep* directly across from: *There is a bus stop opposite the school.*

Here you can see the words **opposition, opponent,** and **opposite.** These words are related to the word **oppose,** that is, they all come from the same roots.

Endings

Sometimes a word you want to look up is a different form of a main entry. Again, you should **find the root word** of the one you want to look up.

- **Verb forms** made by simply adding *-ed* or *-ing* to the root word are not given as entries in the dictionary. If you look for *watched* or *watching* you will find only the root word *watch*. You will find entries like **magnified**, **magnifying**, where the spelling of the root word **magnify** has changed.

- **Adjective forms** made by simply adding -er or -est to the root word are not given as entries in the dictionary. If you look for *longer* or *longest* you will find only the root word *long*. You will find entries like **happier**, **happiest**, where the spelling of the root word **happy** has changed.

- **Plural forms** made by simply adding *-s* or *-es* to the root word are not given as entries in the dictionary. If you look for *cars* or *buses* you will find only the root word *car* or *bus*. You will find entries like **hobbies**, where the spelling of the root word **hobby** has changed.

Write down the entry word you would look up to find the meaning of each word in italics:

1. Marilou is *giving* me chocolates for my birthday.
2. I was *terrified* by that movie.
3. She *knew* the answer all along.
4. The cook baked the *largest* cake we'd ever seen.
5. We saw the *funniest* clown at the party!

In each of the following sentences, replace the word in italics with its correct plural form.

6. I've been to three *party* this month.
7. There were several *child* in the driveway.
8. Three *goose* were blocking the road.

IDIOMS ....

Suppose you read the sentence *Michael asked his sister to lend a hand with the snow shovelling.*

You know the meaning of *lend*. But do you know the meaning of *lend a hand*? If not, you will find the phrase explained at the end of the entry for *lend*:

lend (lend) *v* let someone have for a while: *Will you lend me your bike for an hour? Banks lend money to people.* **lent, lend·ing. –lend′er,** *n.*
lend a hand, help: *He lent a hand with the dishes.*

Lend a hand is an idiom. It has a special meaning that you could not guess from the meanings of the separate words. Michael does not want his sister to lend him one of her hands!

Rewrite each of the following sentences, using an idiom in place of the words in italics. The key word of the correct idiom is in parentheses after each sentence.

1. After he has heard a song once, he can play it *without reading the music.* (**ear**)
2. She is a sensible person, and her ideas are always *practical.* (**earth**)
3. My mother gave me a *scolding* for being late for supper. (**piece**)
4. The job won't take long if we all *work hard.* (**pitch**)

PRONUNCIATION ....

The way a word sounds is shown in parentheses ( ) immediately after the entry word. Since English words are often not pronounced the way they are spelled, the pronunciations are marked using special symbols.

Pronunciation symbols

On the next page is a pronunciation key. You will find a copy of this on the inside of the covers of the dictionary. The symbol ə is called the schwa (pronounced shwȧ).

a	bat	e	bed	i	bid	o	pot	u	cup	th	thin
ā	cake	ē	me	ī	bite	ō	go	ū	rude	ᴛʜ	then
à	bar	ə	about	ər	over	ȯ	for	u̇	put	zh	measure

TRY IT

1. Pronounce each of the following words, and look carefully at the special vowel symbols used.

   game (gām) **put** (pu̇t) **yolk** (yōk) **hurt** (hərt)
   war (wȯr) **mark** (màrk) **view** (vyū) **line** (līn)
   town (toun) **leap** (lēp) **toy** (toi) **zoom** (zūm)

2. Say each of the following words aloud. Then write them down, underlining the syllables that are pronounced with schwa.

   bottom, buffalo, corral, button, gorilla, command

3. Use the pronunciation key to write down the pronunciation for each of the following words. Say each word aloud to yourself, then put down one symbol for each sound that you hear.

   climb, creep, forge, great, learn, leave, love, pale, stone, thick, then, write

   When you have finished, look up these words in the dictionary and check the pronunciations you have written.

Stress

In most words of two or more syllables, one syllable is spoken with more stress than any of the others. The stressed syllable is shown by a heavy raised mark (′) placed after it. For example, in these words the stress is on the first syllable:

cotton (kot′ən), **nephew** (nef′yū), **paper** (pā′pər).

In the following words the stress is on the second syllable:

delight (di līt′), **excite** (ek sīt′), **prefer** (pri fər′).

TRY IT

Say each of the words that follow and decide which is the stressed syllable.
Then copy the pronunciation of each word and add the stress mark.

decide (di sīd)   survive (sər vīv)   pursue (pər sū)
pattern (pat ərn)   image (im ij)   terrible (ter ə bəl)

In addition to the main stress, many words have one or two syllables with a lighter
stress. This is shown by means of a lighter mark (′) placed after the syllable.
Say the following examples and listen for the lighter stress:

demonstrate (dem′ən strāt′)
hippopotamus (hip′ə pot′ə məs)

The main stress is called **primary stress** and the lighter is **secondary stress**.

PART-OF-SPEECH LABELS......................

Words like *noun*, *adjective*, and *verb* are names for parts of speech. The eight
parts of speech used in the dictionary, together with their abbreviations, are
listed below.

noun	*n*	pronoun	*pron*
verb	*v*	preposition	*prep*
adjective	*adj*	conjunction	*conj*
adverb	*adv*	interjection	*interj*

TRY IT

Look up the following words and write which part of speech they are.

1. basic   3. lightly   5. or   7. they
2. cape   4. munch   6. ouch   8. toward

USAGE LABELS ....

Informal and Slang

Some words are labelled *Informal*. These words may be all right to use in ordinary
speech, in written conversation, or in a letter to a close friend, but should not be
used in formal writing.

Some words are labelled *Slang*. These words are not yet considered part of the general language. Slang may be all right to use in ordinary speech but should not be used in written work.

Canadianisms

The entry **outport** is labelled with a tiny maple leaf. This means that the word or meaning is used mainly in Canada and that it first came into the English language in Canada. Such words are called *Canadianisms*.

TRY IT

Look up the following Canadianisms in the dictionary. Then write a sentence for each one.

1. bateau
2. break-up
3. lobstick
4. muskeg
5. slapshot
6. toonie
7. tuque
8. umiak

FEATURE BOXES ....

There are four kinds of feature boxes in the *Gage School Dictionary*. They are titled **Word History, Using Words, Confusables,** and **Grammar Check.**
These boxes give extra information about one or more of the entry words above them.

Word History

These feature boxes tell about the history of words.

TRY IT

Look up the *Word History* boxes for the following and read the box. Then answer the question.

1. **deca-**   How many events are in a pentathlon?
2. **digit**   What is another English word that comes from the Latin *dicitus*?
3. **expert**   From which language did this word come into English?
4. **graph**   What is an English word that ends in *graph*, meaning "writing"?

Using Words

These boxes give advice on how to use a particular word. Some boxes will tell about words that have similar, but not identical, meanings; other boxes explain when it is (or is not) all right to use a particular word.

Look up the *Using Words* boxes for the following, and write an example sentence to illustrate the information in the box.

1. data   2. fish   3. interested   4. less

Confusables

These boxes highlight words that can get confused with one another, often because they are spelled, or sound, almost the same.

Choose the correct word from inside the parentheses that will complete the sentence. If you are unsure which word to use, look up the *Confusables* box for that word.

1. (Lay, Lie) down on the bed and have a rest.
2. I (new, knew) that trick was not (new, knew)!
3. The (principal, principle) of the school is in her office.
4. That dog over (their, there, they're) belongs to (their, there, they're) son.

Grammar Check

Important information about grammar, writing, or punctuation is highlighted in the *Grammar Check* boxes. If you need more detailed information, look at the *Grammar and Usage Mini-Guide* at the end of the dictionary.

Find answers to the following questions in the *Grammar Check* boxes for the words in italics.

1. Write today's *date* in five different ways.
2. Write a sentence using the words *good* and *well* correctly.
3. What are three examples of irregular *past tense* verbs?
4. What is one way to avoid *repetition* in your writing?

a or **A** (ā) *n* the first letter of the English alphabet, or any speech sound that it stands for. The sound of *a* in *mat* is different from the sound of *a* in *mate*. *pl* **a's** or **A's.**

aard·vark (ärd′vàrk′) *n* an animal from southern Africa that eats ants and termites.

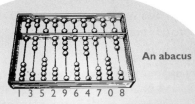

An abacus

The beads above the bar count 5 each when lowered to the bar. The beads below the bar count 1 each when raised to the bar. In the picture, the beads are set for 1 352 964 708.

ab·a·cus (ab′ə kəs) *n* a frame with rows of beads used for counting. *pl* **ab·a·cus·es** or **ab·a·ci** (ab′ə sī′ *or* ab′ə sē′).

a·ban·don (ə ban′dən) *v* give up completely: *They finally abandoned the idea as hopeless.* –**a·ban′doned,** *adj.*

ab·bey (ab′ē) *n* the building where a group of monks or nuns live.

ab·bre·vi·ate (ə brē′vē āt′) *v* make a word or phrase into a shorter form: *We can abbreviate the word Doctor to Dr.* **ab·bre·vi·at·ed, ab·bre·vi·at·ing. ab·bre·vi·a·tion** (ə brē′vē ā′shən) *n* a short form, such as *MP* for *Member of Parliament.*

ab·di·cate (ab′də kāt′) *v* give up a position of authority: *When the king abdicated, his daughter became queen.* **ab·di·cat·ed, ab·di·cat·ing.** –**ab′di·ca′tion,** *n.*

ab·do·men (ab′də mən) *n* the part of the body that contains the stomach, the intestines, and other important organs; the belly. –**ab·dom′i·nal,** *adj.*

ab·duct (ab dukt′) *v* take a person away by force or trickery; kidnap. –**ab·duc′tion,** *n.*

ab·hor (ab hòr′) *v* think of as disgusting and horrible. **ab·horred, ab·hor·ring.** –**ab·hor′rent,** *adj.*

a·bil·i·ty (ə bil′ə tē) **1** *n* power to do: *A horse has the ability to pull heavy loads.* **2** *n* skill or talent: *She has great ability as a hockey player.* *pl* **a·bil·i·ties.**

a·blaze (ə blāz′) *adv* or *adj* on fire.

a·ble (ā′bəl) *adj* having power or skill: *Little kids are able to walk, but they're not able to drive.* **a·bler, a·blest.** –**a′bly,** *adv.*

ab·nor·mal (ab nòr′məl) *adj* very different from what is normal, especially in a bad way. –**ab·nor′mal·ly,** *adv.*

a·board (ə bòrd′) *adv* or *prep* on a ship, train, etc.

a·bol·ish (ə bol′ish) *v* do away with: *I wish that we could abolish war.* –**ab′o·li′tion,** *n.*

a·bom·i·na·ble (ə bom′ə nə bəl) *adj* disgusting; hateful.

ab·o·rig·i·ne (ab′ə rij′ə nē′) *n* one of the people who first lived in a country. **ab·o·rig·i·nal** *adj* having to do with the people who first lived in a country, or their descendants. In Canada, the aboriginal peoples are the First Nations, the Inuit, and the Métis. Another form is **Aboriginal.**
►See Appendix.

a·bout (ə bout′) **1** *prep* having to do with: *a story about pioneers.* **2** *adv* around: *Look about and tell me what you see.*
about to, ready to: *The plane is about to take off.*

a·bove (ə buv′) **1** *adv* in a higher place: *The sky is above.* **2** *prep* over: *Can you hear above the noise? She is above average in height.* **3** *adv* above zero on a temperature scale: *The high today is five above.*

a·bridge (ə brij′) *v* shorten something written. **a·bridged, a·bridg·ing.**

a·broad (ə brod′) *adv* outside your own country, especially overseas.

a·brupt (ə brupt′) **1** *adj* sudden: *Her speech came to an abrupt end.* **2** *adj* gruff; rude: *He had an abrupt way of speaking.* –**a·brupt′ly,** *adv.*

ab·scess (ab′ses) *n* a pocket of pus in some part of the body.

ab·sent (ab′sənt) *adj* away; not in the expected place; not existing: *Three members of the class were absent. Trees are almost absent in some parts of the Prairies.* –**ab′sence,** *n.*

ab·sen·tee (ab′sən tē′) *n* a person who is away.

ab·sent-mind·ed *adj* forgetting or not noticing things: *I'm so absent-minded that I went to the fridge and put in my books instead of my lunch!*

ab·so·lute (ab′sə lūt′) *adj* complete; perfect; certain: *absolute silence, absolute proof.* –**ab′so·lute′ly,** *adv.*

ab·sorb (ab zòrb′) *v* take in and keep: *A sponge absorbs water.* –**ab·sorp′tion,** *n.*

ab·sorb·ent *adj* able to absorb much: *Towels are absorbent.* **ab·sorb·ing** *adj* extremely interesting: *an absorbing story.*

ab·stain (ab stān′) *v* choose not to do or use something: *Most athletes abstain from smoking.* –**ab′sti·nence** (ab′ stə nəns), *n.*

ab·stract (ab′strakt) *adj* not real or concrete: *A sugar cube is a real thing; sweetness is abstract.*

ab·surd (ab zərd′ *or* ab sərd′) *adj* plainly not true; foolish. –**ab·surd′i·ty,** *n,* –**ab·surd′ly,** *adv.*

a·bun·dant (ə bun′dənt) *adj* more than enough; very plentiful: *There are abundant gas reserves in Western Canada.* –**a·bun′dance,** *n,* –**a·bun′dant·ly,** *adv.*

a·buse (ə byūz′ *for 1 and 2,* ə byūs′ *for 3 and 4*) **1** *v* use wrongly: *The officer abused his authority by arresting a harmless onlooker.* **2** *v* treat badly: *to abuse a pet.* **3** *n* bad treatment: *abuse of a helpless prisoner, child abuse.* **4** *n* insulting language. **a·bused, a·bus·ing.** –**a·bu′sive** (ə byū′ siv), *adj.*

An abyss can be very narrow, but is always deep.

a·byss (ə bis′) *n* a very deep crack or hole.

ac·a·dem·ic (ak′ə dem′ik) *adj* having to do with school or schoolwork: *Linda's academic program included math, science, and social studies.*

A·ca·di·a (ə kā′dē ə) *n* that part of old French Canada which included present-day Nova Scotia and New Brunswick: *Acadia was a French colony from 1604 to 1713.* –**A·ca′di·an,** *n* or *adj.*

ac·cel·er·ate (ak sel′ə rāt′) *v* speed up. –**ac·cel′er·a′tion,** *n.*

ac·cel·er·a·tor *n* the pedal that the driver presses to make a vehicle go faster.

ac·cent (ak′sent) **1** *n* a special way of pronouncing words: *She speaks with an Ontario accent.* **2** *n* emphasis or stress on a particular syllable of a word: *In the word* abundant, *the accent is on the second syllable.*

ac·cept (ak sept′) *v* take what is offered or given; welcome: *He accepted our gift. She was soon accepted by her new classmates.* –**ac·cept′ance,** *n.* **ac·cept·a·ble** *adj* good enough.

CONFUSABLES .... accept

accept means "receive":
   Will you accept this prize?

except means "other than":
   Everyone smiled, except me.

ac·cess (ak′ses) **1** *n* the right to use: *All children have access to the library.* **2** *v* reach a place or get at something: *You can access the computer files now.* –**ac·ces′si·ble,** *adj.*

ac·ces·so·ry (ak ses′ə rē) **1** *n* something extra: *He bought a mirror and some other accessories for his bicycle.* **2** *n* a person who helps another commit a crime: *The person who drives the getaway car for a bank robber is an accessory.* pl **ac·ces·so·ries.**

ac·ci·dent (ak′sə dənt) *n* something that happens unexpectedly and by chance. It is sometimes a bad thing but not always: *He was injured in a car accident. Their meeting while on holiday in Corner Brook was an accident.* –**ac′ci·den′tal,** *adj,* –**ac′ci·den′tal·ly,** *adv.*

ac·com·mo·date (ə kom′ə dāt′) *v* have room for; lodge: *Can you accommodate a group of five for two weeks?* **ac·com·mo·dat·ed, ac·com·mo·dat·ing.** –**ac·com′mo·da′tion,** *n.* **ac·com·mo·dat·ing** *adj* helpful; kind: *She was accommodating enough to lend me a quarter.*

ac·com·pa·ny (ə kum′pə nē) **1** *v* go along with: *May we accompany you on your walk?* **2** *v* in music, play or sing along with: *She accompanied him on the guitar.* **ac·com·pa·nied, ac·com·pa·ny·ing.** –**ac·com′pa·ni·ment,** *n.*

ac·com·plice (ə kom′plis) *n* a person who helps another to commit a crime.

ac·com·plish (ə kom′plish) *v* carry out; complete: *Did you accomplish your task? He can accomplish a lot in a day.* **ac·com·plished** *adj* expert; skilled: *an accomplished dancer.* **ac·com·plish·ment** *n* something done with knowledge and skill: *The teacher was proud of his students' accomplishments.*

ac·cord (ə kòrd′) *n* agreement: *The two friends were in complete accord.* –**ac·cord′ance,** *n.* **ac·cord·ing·ly** *adv* in agreement with something stated: *These are the rules. You can act accordingly or leave the club.* **of one's own accord,** without being asked.

ac·count (ə kount′) **1** *n* an arrangement with a bank or company for saving money or paying for things. **2** *n* a report or explanation: *The newspaper published an account of the trial.* **ac·count·ant** *n* a person who looks after or checks business accounts. **on account of,** because of: *The game was cancelled on account of rain.* **on no account,** under no circumstances; no way: *On no account should you tell him everything.* **take into account** or **take account of,** make allowance for; consider: *When planning a vacation, you have to take travelling time into account.*

ac·cu·mu·late (ə kyū′myə lāt′) *v* collect little by little: *We accumulated lots of junk in our garage.* **ac·cu·mu·lat·ed, ac·cu·mu·lat·ing.** –**ac·cu′mu·la′tion,** *n.*

ac·cu·rate (ak′yə rit) *adj* exactly right; correct. –**ac′cu·ra·cy** (ak′yər ə sē), *n,* –**ac′cu·rate·ly,** *adv.*

ac·cuse (ə kyūz′) *v* say that someone has done something wrong: *They accused him of being a liar.* **ac·cused, ac·cus·ing.** –**ac′cu·sa′tion,** *n,* –**ac·cus′er,** *n,* –**ac·cus′ing·ly,** *adv.*

ac·cus·tomed (ə kus′təmd) *adj* usual: *By Monday he was back in his accustomed place.* **accustomed to,** used to; in the habit of: *She was accustomed to hard work.*

ace (ās) **1** *n* a playing card with one spot. **2** *n* an expert: *Peter is an ace at basketball.* **3** *v* *Informal.* do something perfectly or extremely well: *Siu-Wah aced the math test.* **aced, ac·ing.**

ache (āk) **1** *n* an ongoing pain, such as a headache or toothache. **2** *v* feel this kind of pain: *My back aches.* **3** *v* *Informal.* wish very much: *During the hot days we ached to go swimming.* **ached, ach·ing.**

a·chieve (ə chēv′) **1** *v* get done: *I achieved very little today.* **2** *v* reach a goal by one's own efforts: *She achieved fame as a swimmer.* **a·chieved, a·chiev·ing.** –**a·chieve′ment,** *n.*

ac·id (as′id) **1** *n* a chemical that works against bases. Acids eat away at metal or flesh. **2** *adj* sour or bitter; sharp and biting: *Rhubarb has an acid taste. His acid remarks hurt my feelings.* –**a·cid′ic,** *adj.*

acid rain rain or snow that is polluted by acids formed in the air after waste chemicals are released into the air by factories, cars, etc.

ac·knowl·edge (ak nol′ij) **1** *v* admit or recognize: *He acknowledges his faults. She was acknowledged to be the best player on the team.* **2** *v* show that one has received or noticed something: *He acknowledged the gift with a pleasant letter.* **ac·knowl·edged, ac·knowl·edg·ing.** –**ac·knowl′edg·ment** or **ac·knowl′edge·ment,** *n.*

ac·ne (ak′nē) *n* a very pimply condition of the skin, common among teenagers.

a·cous·tics (ə kûs′stiks) *n* the qualities of a room that affect whether you hear a sound badly or well. –**a·cous′tic,** *adj.*

ac·quaint (ə kwānt′) *v* make familiar: *"Let me acquaint you with the facts,"* she said. **ac·quaint·ance 1** *n* a person known to you but not a close friend: *The actor had many acquaintances but few friends.* **2** *n* knowledge or experience of someone or something: *I have some acquaintance with computers, but I'm no expert.*

ac·quire (ə kwīr′) *v* gain or get: *In a few years she acquired a store of her own.* **ac·quired, ac·quir·ing.** **ac·qui·si·tion** (ak′wə zish′ən) *n* something acquired: *Our most recent acquisition is a colour printer.*

ac·quit (ə kwit′) v declare not guilty: *The jury acquitted the man accused of stealing.* **ac·quit·ted, ac·quit·ting.** –**ac·quit′tal,** n.

a·cre (ā′kər) n a non-metric unit for measuring land area, equal to about half a hectare.

ac·ro·bat (ak′rə bat′) n a person who can dance on a rope or wire, swing on trapezes, etc. –**ac′ro·bat′ic,** adj.

ac·ro·bat·ics pl.n tricks of an acrobat.

ac·ro·nym (ak′rə nim′) n a word made up of the first letters of the full name of something: *DOS is an acronym for Disk Operating System.*

a·cross (ə kros′) **1** adv or prep from one side to the other: *What is the distance across (adv)? She drew a line across the page (prep).* **2** prep on the other side of; beyond: *I live in Ottawa and my grandparents live across the river in Hull.*

ℕORTH
𝔼AST
𝕎EST   **An acrostic of NEWS**
𝕊OUTH

a·cros·tic (ə kros′tik) n a poem or piece of writing in which the first or last letter of each line spells out a word if you read them one after another.

a·cryl·ic (ə kril′ik) **1** n a clear, tough plastic. **2** n a kind of paint made with this plastic as a base.

act (akt) **1** n something done; a deed: *an act of kindness.* **2** v do something: *The firefighters acted quickly.* **3** v behave: *to act like a fool.* **4** v perform in a play, musical, etc. **5** n a main division of a play or opera: *This play has three acts.* **6** n a law or decree. An Act of Parliament is a law that has been passed by Parliament. **7** v do the work of: *This thick, folded towel can act as a sponge.*

ac·tion (ak′shən) **1** n something done; an act: *Giving food to the dog was a kind action.* **2** n battle or a part of a battle: *My grandparents know someone who was wounded in action in the Second World War.* **ac·tor** n a person who acts on the stage, in movies, or on television or radio. Some people use the word **actress** for a girl or woman.

act up, *Informal.* be troublesome: *The knee I hurt last summer is acting up again. He's acting up because he didn't get his way.*

ac·tive (ak′tiv) adj doing or moving a lot; lively: *She was a very active child.* –**ac′tive·ly,** adv.

ac·ti·vate v make active: *You can activate dried yeast by mixing it with warm water.* **ac·tiv·ist** n someone who works hard to make changes in society: *Karen was an activist for animal rights.*

ac·tiv·i·ty (ak tiv′ə tē) **1** n liveliness: *The kitchen hummed with activity as they prepared the dinner.* **2** n an action: *The suspect's activities were being closely watched by the police.* **3** n something to do, usually planned: *outdoor activities, classroom activities.*

ac·tu·al (ak′chū əl) adj real. –**ac′tu·al·ly,** adv.

a·cute (ə kyūt′) adj sharp: *Dogs have an acute sense of smell.* –**a·cute′ly,** adv.

acute angle an angle less than 90°.

A.D. abbreviation for the Latin words *anno Domini,* meaning "in the year of our Lord," that is, after the birth of Jesus Christ: *From 200 B.C. to A.D. 500 is 700 years.*

a·dapt (ə dapt′) **1** v make fit or suitable: *Good writers adapt their words to the age of their readers. The farmer can adapt her barn for use as a garage.* **2** v change one's behaviour so as to fit in with a new situation: *He has adapted well to his new school.* –**a·dapt′a·ble,** adj, –**ad′ap·ta′tion,** n.

a·dap·ter n any device that lets something fit where it was not made to fit. **Adaptor** is another spelling.

add (ad) **1** v put together: *When you add 4 and 2 and 3, you get 9.* **2** v go on to say: *He said goodbye and added that he had enjoyed his visit.* –**ad·di′tion,** n.

ad·di·tion·al (ə dish′ə nəl) adj added; extra; more. **ad·di·tive** n a substance that is added to food to colour or preserve it: *Chocolate bars are full of additives.*

ad·dict (ad′ikt) n a person who is dependent on a harmful drug. –**ad·dict′ed,** adj, –**ad·dic′tion,** n.

ad·dress (ə dres′ or ad′res) **1** n the house number, street name, and other details that tell where someone lives. **2** v speak to: *The safety officer addressed the students.* **3** n the code telling exactly where a piece of information is stored in a computer's memory.

ad·e·quate (ad′ə kwit) *adj* enough; good enough, high enough, strong enough, etc. –**ad′e·quate·ly,** *adv.*

ad·here (ad hēr′) *v* stick; cling: *Mud adheres to shoes.* **ad·hered, ad·her·ing.**

ad·he·sive (ad hē′siv) **1** *adj* sticky; used for sticking: *adhesive tape.* **2** *n* any substance used to stick things together. Glue is an adhesive.

ad·ja·cent (ə jā′sənt) *adj* next; adjoining: *Saskatchewan is adjacent to Manitoba.*

ad·jec·tive (aj′ik tiv) *n* a word describing a person, place, or thing. In the sentence *Her little dog is hungry,* the words *little* and *hungry* are adjectives that describe the noun *dog.*

Grammar ✓*Check* **. . . . adjective**

Try to use adjectives that are clear, not vague: *The meal they served was* **mouthwatering** is more expressive than *The meal they served was* **nice.**

---

ad·just (ə just′) *v* change so as to make better: *to adjust a radio dial. You can adjust this chair to different heights.* –**ad·just′a·ble,** *adj,* –**ad·just′ment,** *n.*

ad lib (ad′ lib′) *Informal.* making it up as you go along: *Did they have a script, or did they do their skit ad lib?*

WORD HISTORY . . . . ad lib

Ad lib is short for Latin *ad libitum,* meaning "at pleasure."

---

ad·mire (ad mīr′) *v* think highly of: *Everyone admires her brave deeds.* **ad·mired, ad·mir·ing.** –**ad·mir′er,** *n.*

ad·mi·ra·ble *adj* worth admiring.

ad·mi·ra·tion *n* a feeling of wonder and approval: *I am full of admiration for your bravery.*

ad·mit (ad mit′) **1** *v* confess: *He admits now that he was wrong.* **2** *v* allow to enter: *This ticket will admit you to the play.* **ad·mit·ted, ad·mit·ting.** –**ad·mit′ted·ly,** *adv.*

ad·mis·sion (ad mish′ən) **1** *n* the act of allowing someone to enter: *admission of immigrants into Canada.* **2** *n* the price of entering: *Admission to the show is seven dollars.*

3 *n* the act of admitting that something is true: *We appreciate your honest admission of the mistake.* **ad·mit·tance** *n* the right to enter.

ad·o·les·cent (ad′ə les′ənt) *n* a person who is no longer a child but not yet an adult. –**ad′o·les′cence,** *n.*

a·dopt (ə dopt′) *v* take as your own: *I liked your idea and adopted it. The Kazowskis have adopted a baby girl.* –**a·dop′tion,** *n.*

a·dore (ə dòr′) *v* respect and love deeply: *She adores her mother.* **a·dored, a·dor·ing.** –**ad′o·ra′tion,** *n.*

a·dor·a·ble *adj Informal.* cute; attractive: *an adorable child.*

a·dult (ə dult′ *or* ad′ult) **1** *adj* mature; full-grown: *An adult frog looks very different from a tadpole.* **2** *n* a grown-up person, animal, or plant.

ad·vance (ad vans′) **1** *v or n* move forward: *The excited crowd advanced toward the city centre* (*v*). *Our advance through the checkout line was very slow* (*n*). **2** *n or v* loan: *My parents gave me an advance of $10 toward my new video game* (*n*). *They advanced me the money* (*v*). **ad·vanced, ad·vanc·ing.**

ad·vanced *adj* further forward; at a higher level.

ad·van·tage (ad van′tij) *n* something that helps a person to succeed or win: *A good education is always a great advantage.* –**ad′van·ta′geous** (ad′vən tā′jəs), *adj.*

take advantage of, make use of: *She took advantage of the cheap airfare to fly to Fredericton. People take advantage of his good nature by making him do all the work.*

ad·ven·ture (ad ven′chər) *n* an exciting experience. –**ad·ven′tur·er,** *n,* –**ad·ven′tur·ous** or **ad·ven′ture·some,** *adj.*

ad·verb (ad′vərb) *n* a word that is used to describe a verb, an adjective, or another adverb. Adverbs answer the questions "How?" "When?" or "Where?" In the sentence *She walked rapidly,* the word *rapidly* is an adverb describing how she walked.

Grammar ✓*Check* **. . . . adverb**

Many adverbs are made by adding *-ly* to an adjective: *sadly, quickly, clearly.* Sometimes the spelling is a little different: *happily, easily, miserably.*

ad·ver·tise (ad′vər tīz′) *v* let people know about: *We put a notice in the newspaper to advertise the yard sale.* **ad·ver·tised, ad·ver·tis·ing.** **–ad′ver·tise′ment** (ad′vər tīz′mənt *or* ad vər′tis mənt), *n.*

ad·vise (ad vīz′) *v* tell someone what he or she should do: *He advised me to eat more vegetables.* **ad·vised, ad·vis·ing.** **–ad·vis′er** or **ad·vi′sor,** *n.*

ad·vice (ad vīs′) *n* an opinion given to someone about what that person should do: *The doctor's advice is to get a good rest.*

ad·vis·a·ble *adj* sensible: *It's not advisable for him to go while he is sick.*

CONFUSABLES .... advice

advice is the noun: *I gave him advice.*
advise is the verb: *I advised him.*

aer·i·al (er′ē əl) **1** *n* a radio or television antenna. **2** *adj* having to do with the air. An aerial photograph is one taken from high in the air. Aerial roots are roots that grow in the air instead of the ground.

aer·o·bics (er ō′biks) *n* a very active kind of exercise that helps you breathe better. **–aer·o′bic,** *adj.*

aer·o·dy·nam·ic (er′ō dī nam′ik) *adj* able to travel fast because it is shaped so that the air can easily pass around it when it is moving. Racing cars are aerodynamic.

aer·o·sol (er′ə sol′) *n* a spray can or the mist or foam it sprays out.

aer·o·space (er′ə spās′) *n* the earth's atmosphere and the space beyond it.

af·fair (ə fer′) **1** *n* a matter of business: *The Prime Minister has many affairs to look after.* **2** *n* any thing or happening: *The street party we had on Canada Day was a most enjoyable affair.*

af·fect (ə fekt′) **1** *v* cause a change in; influence: *The amount of rain affects the growth of crops.* **2** *v* pretend to have or feel: *She affected a great knowledge of computers, but she hardly knew how to use a keyboard.* **–af′fec·ta′tion,** *n,* **–af·fect′ed,** *adj.*

CONFUSABLES .....affect

affect means "influence": *Did that affect you?*
effect means "result": *It had no effect on me.* Notice that **affect** is a verb; **effect** is usually a noun.

af·fec·tion (ə fek′shən) *n* a friendly feeling; love. **–af·fec′tion·ate** (ə fek′shə nit), *adj,* **–af·fec′tion·ate·ly,** *adv.*

af·firm (ə fərm′) *v* declare firmly: *She affirmed that the signature was hers.*

af·firm·a·tive *adj* showing agreement; saying yes: *an affirmative answer.* **–af·firm′a·tive·ly,** *adv.* **in the affirmative,** with a word or statement meaning yes: *She replied in the affirmative when asked if she would like to go bowling.*

af·flict (ə flikt′) *v* cause pain to; trouble very much: *All his life he was afflicted with poor health.* **–af·flic′tion,** *n.*

af·flu·ent (af′lū ənt) *adj* rich. **–af′flu·ence,** *n.*

af·ford (ə fòrd′) **1** *v* have enough money, time, or strength for something: *Can we afford to upgrade our computer system?* **2** *v* give: *Reading this story will afford real pleasure.* **–af·ford′a·ble,** *adj.*

a·flame (ə flām′) **1** *adj* or *adv* in flames; on fire. **2** *adj* or *adv* as if on fire; excited: *Your words have set my heart aflame (adv).*

a·float (ə flōt′) *adj* or *adv* floating on water or in air: *The children sent toy boats afloat on Lake Winnipeg (adv).*

a·fraid (ə frād′) **1** *adj* frightened; feeling fear: *She is not afraid of snakes.* **2** *adj* sorry: *I'm afraid I must ask you to leave now.*

af·ter (af′tər) **1** *prep, conj,* or *adv* following something: *Kim is after me in line (prep). Put it away after you use it (conj). Let's work now—we can play after (adv).* **2** *prep* or *conj* considering; because of: *After all her help, how can you ignore her like that (prep)? This is a pretty disappointing mark, after I studied so hard (conj)!* **3** *prep* chasing or looking for: *What is he after? That dog is always after our cat.*

af·ter·noon *n* the time from noon to evening.
af·ter·thought *n* a thought that comes after you have already finished planning. **af·ter·ward** *adv* later. **Afterwards** is another form.

a·gain (ə gen′ *or* ə gān′) *adv* another time; once more: *Come again to play. Say that again.*

a·gainst (ə genst′ *or* ə gānst′) **1** *prep* in opposition to: *He spoke against the suggestion.* **2** *prep* on: *Rain beats against the window.* **3** *prep* in defence from: *A fire is a protection against cold.*

age (āj) **1** *n* how old a person or thing is, was, or will be: *the age of ten. Turtles live to a great age.* **2** *n* a certain time in a person's life or in history: *old age, the information age.* **3** *n* Usually, **ages,** *pl*, *Informal.* a long time: *I haven't seen you for ages.* **4** *v* make or become old: *He is aging fast. Worry ages a person.* **aged, ag·ing** or **age·ing.**

a·ged (ā′jid *for 1,* ājd *for 2*) **1** *adj* having lived a long time: *The aged woman had many grandchildren.* **2** *adj* that has been left for a time, to improve the flavour: *aged cheese.*

a·gen·da (ə jen′də) **1** *n* a notebook for writing down what needs to be done: *a homework agenda.* **2** *n* a list of things to be done or discussed: *the agenda for a meeting.*

a·gent (ā′jənt) **1** *n* a person or company that acts for another: *You can get an agent to find a buyer for your house.* **2** *n* anything that accomplishes some purpose: *Yeast is an important agent in making bread.*

a·gen·cy *n* a company or group that helps people with something or does business for them: *a rental agency. The Human Rights Commission is a government agency.*

ag·gra·vate (ag′rə vāt′) *v* make worse; annoy; irritate. **ag·gra·vat·ed, ag·gra·vat·ing.** **–ag′gra·va′tion,** *n.*

ag·gres·sion (ə gresh′ən) *n* the habit of making attacks. **–ag·gres′sor,** *n.*

ag·gres·sive 1 *adj* in the habit of starting quarrels: *An aggressive person is always ready to pick a fight.* **2** *adj* active; energetic; forceful: *The police began an aggressive campaign against speeding.* **–ag·gres′sive·ly,** *adv,* **–ag·gres′sive·ness,** *n.*

ag·ile (aj′īl *or* aj′əl) *adj* moving or thinking quickly and easily: *An acrobat has to be agile.* **–a·gil′i·ty** (ə jil′ə tē), *n.*

ag·i·tate (aj′ə tāt′) **1** *v* shake: *The slightest wind will agitate the leaves of some trees.* **2** *v* disturb or upset; excite: *She was very agitated by the news of her brother's accident.* **3** *v* keep talking or writing about something you want changed: *They were agitating for a later bedtime.* **ag·i·tat·ed, ag·i·tat·ing. –ag′i·ta′tion,** *n.*

ag·i·ta·tor 1 *n* a person who keeps talking or writing about something, hoping that it will be changed. **2** *n* a device for shaking or stirring: *Most washers have an agitator in the centre for swishing the laundry around in the water.*

a·go (ə gō′) *adv* in the past: *Huge herds of bison lived on the plains of Canada long ago.*

ag·o·ny (ag′ə nē) *n* very great suffering of body or mind: *the agony of a toothache.* *pl* **ag·o·nies.**

ag·o·niz·ing *adj* very painful or difficult.

a·gree (ə grē′) **1** *v* have the same opinion: *I agree with you.* **2** *v* be alike: *Your story agrees with mine.* **3** *v* arrange: *We agreed to have supper together.* **4** *v* consent: *She agreed to go with us.* **a·greed, a·gree·ing. –a·gree′ment,** *n.*

a·gree·a·ble 1 *adj* pleasant; pleasing: *The boy had an agreeable manner.* **2** *adj* willing: *If my mother is agreeable, we could go with her to visit my aunt in Flin Flon.*

agree with, have a good effect on: *This food does not agree with me; it makes me sick.*

Some land can be used for raising cattle and also for growing corn.

ag·ri·cul·ture (ag′rə kul′chər) *n* farming; the raising of crops and farm animals. **–ag′ri·cul′tur·al,** *adj.*

a·head (ə hed′) **1** *adv* in front; before: *They told me to walk ahead.* **2** *adv* further on: *Boris was ahead of his class in reading.* **3** *adv* winning in a race or game: *The Maple Leafs shot ahead 3 to 1.*

get ahead, succeed: *You need a good education to get ahead.*

go ahead, 1 begin or continue: *Go ahead with your work.* **2** it's all right; you may do it: *Want to try it? Go ahead!*

aid (ād) **1** *v or n* help or support: *The flood victims were aided by people from all over Canada* (*v*). *I can walk now with the aid of a crutch* (*n*). **2** *n* a thing or person that helps: *Pictures are often used as teaching aids.*

aide (ād) *n* assistant; helper: *He works as a nurse's aide.*

AIDS (ādz) *n* acronym for a very serious disease caused by a virus that keeps a person's body from fighting infections. Its full name is **Acquired Immune Deficiency Syndrome.**

ai·ki·do (ī kē' dō *or* ī' kē dō') *n* a system of self-defence first used in Japan. It uses no weapons.

aim (ām) **1** *v* point or direct something: *I aimed at the target but missed. Her questions were aimed at the younger children.* **2** *n* goal; purpose: *His aim was to make at least one new friend.*

aim·less *adj* without aim or purpose.

air (er) **1** *n* the mixture of gases that surrounds the earth, which we breathe. Air is made up of nitrogen, oxygen, hydrogen, and other gases. **2** *v* make known: *Don't air your opinions too loudly.*

air bag *n* a bag built into a car that pops out and fills with air in an accident. **air·borne** (er'bôrn') *adj* in or carried through the air. **air conditioner** a machine that cools and cleans the air.

air·craft *n* any machine that can travel through the air. **air·field** *n* the landing field of an airport. **air force** the branch of the armed forces that uses aircraft. **air·line** *n* a company that operates aircraft and offers regular flights.

air·lock *n* a small, airtight room used for moving between two places that have different air pressure. **air mass** a large layer of air with a certain temperature and a certain amount of moisture: *A cold air mass moved down from Hudson Bay.* **air·plane** *n* a flying machine with fixed wings and a motor. **air·port** *n* a place where aircraft regularly land and take off.

air·tight 1 *adj* so tight that no air can get in or out. **2** *adj* with no weaknesses: *The soccer team had an airtight defence.*

in the air, going around: *Wild rumours were in the air.*

on the air, broadcasting or being broadcast on radio or TV.

up in the air, *Informal.* uncertain: *Our plans for the trip to the Calgary Stampede are still up in the air.*

aisle (īl) *n* a walkway between rows of seats or shelves.

a·jar (ə jär') *adj or adv* slightly open: *Leave the door ajar* (*adj*). *The wind blew the door ajar* (*adv*).

WORD HISTORY . . . . al-

English has borrowed many words from Arabic. A lot of these were borrowed with *al,* the Arabic word for "the," attached at the beginning. Here are some: *alcohol, alcove, alfalfa, algebra, alkali, almanac.*

---

a·larm (ə lärm') **1** *n* sudden fear when you become aware of danger: *The moose ran off in alarm.* **2** *v* make uneasy; frighten: *The breaking of a branch under my foot alarmed the deer.* **3** *n* a warning of danger: *They heard the alarm and left the building at once.* **4** *n* a bell or other thing that makes a noise to warn or waken people: *an alarm clock, a fire alarm.*

al·bum (al'bəm) **1** *n* a book with blank pages for holding things like photographs. **2** *n* a collection of songs on CD, tape, or record.

WORD HISTORY . . . . album

Album is from the Latin *albus* meaning "white." The pages of an album are blank, or white, so that you can put whatever you want on them.

---

al·co·hol (al'kə hol') *n* a colourless liquid in beer, wine, whisky, gin, and other strong drinks. Alcohol acts as a drug.

al·co·hol·ic 1 *adj* having to do with alcohol: *alcoholic drinks.* **2** *n* a person who cannot help drinking too much alcohol.

al·cove (al'kōv) *n* a small space opening off a larger room.

a·lert (ə lərt') *adj* wide awake and aware of what's going on: *The dog was alert, noticing every sound.*

al·fal·fa (al fal'fə) *n* a plant used as a food for horses and cattle.

al·gae (al'jē) *pl.n* a name for simple plants like seaweeds that grow in water and make their own food. Some algae form a scum on the top of ponds.

al·ge·bra (al'jə brə) *n* a part of mathematics that uses letters and other symbols to stand for numbers and how they are used.

a·li·as (ā′lē əs) *n* a false name: *The spy's real name was Harrison, but she sometimes went by the alias of Lee. pl* **a·li·as·es.**

al·i·bi (al′ə bī′) **1** *n* a claim made by an accused person that he or she was somewhere else when a crime was committed. **2** *n Informal.* an excuse. *pl* **al·i·bis.**

al·ien (ā′lē ən) **1** *n* a being from outer space. **2** *n* a person who is not a citizen of the country in which he or she is living. **3** *adj* strange or unfamiliar; completely unknown: *an alien language.*

al·ien·ate **1** *v* cause a person to stop caring or become unfriendly: *Her bad temper is alienating her friends.* **2** *v* cause a person to feel that he or she does not belong: *When I first came to Canada I felt alienated because I could not speak the language.*

a·lign (ə līn′) **1** *v* bring into a straight line: *We aligned the chairs in front of the stage.* **2** *v* bring into co-operation with others: *They aligned themselves with the peace movement.* –**a·lign′ment,** *n.*

a·like (ə līk′) *adj* or *adv* the same: *Joel and his father walk alike (adv).*

a·live (ə līv′) **1** *adj* not dead. **2** *adj* active; lively; brisk.
alive with, full of: *The streets were alive with people.*

al·ka·li (al′kə lī′) *n* a chemical that works against acids. Alkalis dissolve in water, and strong ones can burn flesh. **Base** is another word for alkali: *Lye and ammonia are alkalis.* –**al′ka·line′** (al′kə līn′ *or* al′kə lin), *adj.*

all (ol) **1** *adj* the whole amount or number of: *The mice ate all the cheese.* **2** *pron* everyone or everything: *All is well.* **3** *adv* completely; entirely: *He was all tired out.*
all at once, suddenly: *All at once, the cat pounced.*
all but, almost; nearly: *All but dead from hunger, she struggled on.*
all right, 1 satisfactory: *The work was not excellent, but it was all right.* **2** yes: *"Will you come with me?" "All right."* **3** in good health; well: *He said he was feeling all right.* **4** in a satisfactory way: *The engine seemed to be working all right.*
all-round, able to do many things; useful in many ways: *an all-round athlete.*
at all, in any way or at any time: *They refused to work at all.*
in all, altogether: *There were 100 people in all.*

Al·lah (al′ə *or* ä′lə) *n* the name for God in the religion of Islam.

al·ler·gy (al′ər jē) *n* sickness or discomfort such as sneezing or itching caused by something that is harmless to most people: *He has an allergy to strawberries and gets a rash when he eats them. pl* **al·ler·gies.** –**al·ler′gic** (ə lər′jik), *adj.*

al·ley (al′ē) **1** *n* a narrow back street in a city or town. **2** *n* a building where people can go bowling. *pl* **al·leys.**

al·li·ga·tor (al′ə gā′tər) *n* a large scaly, thick-skinned reptile that has big teeth, short legs, and a long body and tail.

al·lit·er·a·tion (ə lit′ə rā′shən) *n* the use of a connected series of words that begin with the same sound. *Example: Powerful panthers pushed past pigs.*

al·low (ə lou′) **1** *v* let; permit: *She is allowed one hour a day on the family computer.* **2** *v* set aside for a certain purpose: *We ought to allow an extra hour in case of delays.*
al·low·ance *n* an amount given or set aside: *My mom has a travelling allowance for business trips.*

al·loy (al′oi) *n* a mixture of two or more metals. Alloys are often harder, lighter, and stronger than the pure metals. Brass is an alloy of copper and zinc.

al·ly (ə lī′ *for 1,* al′ī *for 2*) **1** *v* join with another for support in a conflict: *Canada allied itself with several other countries in World War II.* **2** *n* a person or group on the same side as another in a conflict: *Gloria is my friend and ally.* **al·lied, al·ly·ing.** *pl* **al·lies.**
al·li·ance (ə lī′əns) *n* an agreement to help each other. **al·lied** (ə līd′) **1** *adj* united by agreement: *allied nations, allied armies.* **2** *adj* connected; related: *Cutting and pasting are allied activities.*

al·ma·nac (ol′mə nak′ *or* al′mə nak′) *n* a book updated every year, giving information on many different topics.

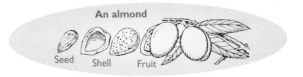
An almond
Seed   Shell   Fruit

al·mond (om′ənd, ol′mənd, *or* am′ənd) *n* a sweet, oval nut.

al·most (ol′mōst) *adv* nearly: *We're almost there.*

a·lone (ə lōn′) *adj* or *adv* without any other people or things: *She is alone in the treehouse (adj). One boy can do this work alone (adv).*

a·long (ə long′) **1** *prep* from one end of something to the other: *Trees are planted along the street.* **2** *adv* further; onward: *Move along quickly.* **3** *adv* with oneself: *He took his dog along.*
all along, the whole time: *He was here all along.*

a·loud (ə loud′) *adv* loud enough to be heard: *I read the story aloud to the others.*

al·pha·bet (al′fə bet′) *n* the set of letters used in writing a language, especially as arranged in a familiar order: *The English alphabet has twenty-six letters.*
−**al′pha·bet′i·cal** (al′fə bet′ə kəl), *adj.*
al·pha·bet·ize *v* arrange in **alphabetical order,** the order of the alphabet.

al·read·y (ol red′ē) *adv* before this time; by this time: *You are half an hour late already. The baby has already broken her new toy.*

CONFUSABLES .... already

already means "by this time":
No, he's already gone.
all ready means "completely ready":
I'm all ready to go.

al·so (ol′sō) *adv* too; in addition: *This dress is prettier than the other one; it is also cheaper.*

al·tar (ol′tər) *n* a table or stand used for religious ceremonies.

al·ter (ol′tər) *v* change: *If this coat is too big, I can alter it to fit you. Since her summer on the farm, her whole outlook has altered.* −**al′ter·a′tion,** *n.*

al·ter·nate (ol′tər nāt′ *for 1,* ol′tər nit *for 2 and 3*) **1** *v* follow each other by turns, first one and then the other: *Jolene and her brother will alternate in setting the table.* **2** *adj* every other: *I clean my room on alternate days.* **3** *n* a person chosen to take someone's place if necessary; a substitute. **al·ter·nat·ed, al·ter·nat·ing.** −**al′ter·nate·ly,** *adv.*

al·ter·na·tive *n* a choice: *We had the alternative of going to a movie or renting a video. Steve took the second alternative and rented Star Wars.*

al·though (ol ŦHō′) *conj* in spite of the fact that: *Although it had rained all morning, they went on the hike.*

al·ti·tude (al′tə tyūd′ *or* al′tə tūd′) *n* height above the earth or above sea level: *The altitude of Banff, Alberta is 1380 m.*

al·to·geth·er (ol′tə geŦH′ər) **1** *adv* completely; entirely: *The house was altogether destroyed by fire.* **2** *adv* all included: *Altogether there were ten books on the shelf.*

CONFUSABLES .. altogether

altogether means "completely":
She's altogether mean.
all together means "co-operatively":
Sing all together!

a·lu·mi·num (ə lū′mə nəm) *n* a silver-white, very light and strong metal that does not tarnish easily. It is used to make cans, foil, and many other things.

al·ways (ol′wiz *or* ol′wāz) *adv* every time; all the time: *Night always follows day. Chris is always cheerful.*

Alz·hei·mer's disease (olts′hī mərz də zēz′) Alzheimer's disease makes older people become confused and lose their memory.

a.m. *abbreviation for* the time from midnight to noon: *Classes begin at 9 a.m.*

am·a·teur (am′ə chər) **1** *n* a person who does something for pleasure, not for money or as a job: *Only amateurs used to take part in the Olympics.* **2** *n* a person without much skill: *You can tell this haircut was given by an amateur−what a mess!* −**a′ma·teur′ish,** *adj.*

a·maze (ə māz′) *v* surprise or impress very much: *She was so amazed by the surprise party that she could not think of anything to say.* **a·mazed, a·maz·ing.** −**a·maze′ment,** *n.*

am·bas·sa·dor (am bas′ə dər) *n* a representative of the highest rank sent by one government to another. An ambassador lives in a foreign country and speaks and acts on behalf of his or her government.

am·ber (am′bər) *n* a brownish yellow substance like glass, often used in jewellery. It is the fossilized resin of pine trees that grew long ago.

am·bi·dex·trous (am′bə dek′strəs) *adj* able to use both hands equally well.

am·big·u·ous (am big′yū əs) *adj* having more than one possible meaning. The sentence *After Ted hit Hari, he ran away* is ambiguous because you can't tell who ran away.

am·bi·tion (am bish′ən) *n* a goal that a person wants very much to reach: *Her ambition was to be a great writer.*

am·bi·tious 1 *adj* very eager to succeed: *My ambitious sister is training very hard in tae kwon do. "I must win!" she keeps saying.* **2** *adj* that can only be done by someone eager to succeed, because it is so difficult: *Learn to play a guitar in an afternoon? That's a pretty ambitious plan!*

am·bu·lance (am′byə ləns) *n* a van, boat, or aircraft equipped to carry sick or wounded people.

am·bush (am′bush) **1** *n* a surprise attack from a hiding place. **2** *v* attack in this way: *A group of bandits ambushed the travellers on the trail through the woods.*

a·men (ā′men′ *or* ä′men′) *interj* in some religions, a word said at the end of a prayer and meaning "may it be so."

a·mi·a·ble (ā′mē ə bəl) *adj* good-natured and friendly.

am·mo·nia (ə mōn′yə) **1** *n* a colourless gas with a strong smell. **2** *n* water with this gas dissolved in it. Ammonia is useful for cleaning.

am·mu·ni·tion (am′yə nish′ən) **1** *n* bullets, bombs, and anything else that can be shot or thrown as a weapon. **2** *n* anything that can be used to fight or argue against: *In our attack on smoking, our main ammunition was information about lung cancer.*

am·ne·sia (am nē′zhə) *n* loss of memory, caused by brain injury, disease, or shock.

a·moe·ba (ə mē′bə) *n* a tiny one-celled animal that can be seen only with a microscope. *pl* **a·moe·bas** *or* **a·moe·bae** (ə mē′bē *or* ə mē′bī).

a·mong (ə mung′) **1** *prep* surrounded by: *a house among the trees.* **2** *prep* a part of; one of: *Canada is among the largest countries of the world. His brothers were among the crowd.* **3** *prep* giving some to each of: *We divided the grapes among us.*

a·mount (ə mount′) **1** *n* quantity: *No amount of coaxing would make the dog give up the ball.* **2** *n* the total: *What is the amount of the bill for the* groceries? **3** *v* add up; be equal: *The loss from the flood amounts to a million dollars. Keeping what belongs to another amounts to stealing.*

USING WORDS . amount/number

Use **amount** when talking about things that can be measured: *Our class ate a huge amount of ice cream at the picnic.*

Use **number** when talking about things that can be counted: *Our class ate a large number of hotdogs at the picnic.*

---

am·pere (am′pēr) *n* an SI unit for measuring electric current. About one ampere of current is needed to produce 100 watts of electric power. The ampere is one of the seven base units in the SI. *Symbol:* A

am·phib·i·an (am fib′ē ən) **1** *n* an animal that lives both on land and in water. Frogs are amphibians. **2** *n* a vehicle able to travel across land or water. **3** *n* an aircraft that can take off from or land on either land or water. –**am·phib′i·ous,** *adj.*

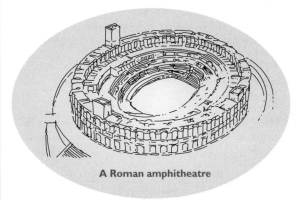

A Roman amphitheatre

am·phi·the·a·tre (am′fə thē′ə tər) *n* a round or oval building with rows of seats rising all around an open space in the middle, called an arena. **Amphitheater** is another spelling.

am·pli·fy (am′plə fī′) *v* make stronger, louder, fuller, etc.: *When sound is amplified, it can be heard over a greater distance. You can amplify your description by giving more details.* **am·pli·fied, am·pli·fy·ing.**

am·pli·fi·er *n* part of a sound system that makes the sound louder.

am·pu·tate (am′pyə tāt′) *v* to cut off a body part in a medical operation. **am·pu·tat·ed, am·pu·tat·ing.** –**am′pu·ta′tion,** *n.*

Am·rit·sar (ȧm rit′sar) *n* the location of the **Golden Temple**, the centre of the Sikh religion.

a·muse (ə myūz′) **1** *v* cause to laugh or smile: *Her tricks did not amuse the babysitter!* **2** *v* keep pleasantly interested; entertain: *The new game amused the children for hours.* **a·mused, a·mus·ing.**

a·muse·ment (ə myūz′mənt) **1** *n* enjoyment; pleasure; being amused: *We showed our amusement by laughing.* **2** *n* entertainment, such as a game, a show, or a ride. An **amusement park** has many of these.

an·a·con·da (an′ə kon′də) *n* a huge olive-green snake that kills its prey by squeezing it so it cannot breathe. The anaconda is the largest snake in the world.

an·a·gram (an′ə gram′) *n* a word that is made up by changing around the letters in another word. *Example: silent* and *listen.*

an·a·logue (an′ə log′) *adj* handling information through moving parts instead of just numbers. An analogue watch is one with hands that move around a dial. The opposite of analogue is **digital**.

an·a·lyse (an′ə līz′) **1** *v* examine all the parts or features of: *You analyse a sentence by explaining the form and use of every word in it.* **2** *v* separate something into its parts: *A chemist can analyse water into two gases, hydrogen and oxygen.* **Analyze** is another spelling. **an·a·lysed, an·a·lys·ing.** **–a·nal′y·sis** (ə nal′ə sis), *n*, *pl* **a·nal·y·ses** (ə nal′ə sēz′).

a·nat·o·my (ə nat′ə mē) **1** *n* the structure of an animal or plant: *The anatomy of an earthworm is much simpler than that of a person.* **2** *n* the science of the structure of animals or plants: *Anatomy is a part of biology.*

an·ces·tor (an′ses tər) *n* a person, animal, or thing of the past that another is directly descended from. Your great-grandparents are your ancestors; the mammoth is the ancestor of the elephant. You can even say that the typewriter is the ancestor of the computer. **–an·ces′tral,** *adj.*

an·chor (ang′kər) **1** *n* a heavy object that keeps a boat from drifting. **2** *v* fix firmly: *Pegs anchored the tent to the ground.*

an·cient (ān′shənt) **1** *adj* of times long past: *The ancient Egyptians built pyramids.* **2** *adj* very old: *An ancient maple tree stood on the corner.*

an·ec·dote (an′ik dōt′) *n* a short story about some interesting incident or event: *Many anecdotes are told about Sir John A. Macdonald.*

a·ne·mi·a (ə nē′mē ə) *n* a sickness caused when the blood does not have enough red blood cells or does not carry enough oxygen. A person who has anemia is usually pale and weak, and gets tired quickly. **Anaemia** is another spelling. **–a·ne′mic,** *adj.*

an·e·mom·e·ter (an′ə mom′ə tər) *n* a machine that measures the speed of wind.

an·es·thet·ic (an′əs thet′ik) *n* a drug that causes the body to lose its ability to feel. A **general anesthetic** puts a person to sleep. A **local anesthetic** just numbs a certain area of the body. **Anaesthetic** is another spelling.

an·gel (ān′jəl) **1** *n* in some religions, an immortal, heavenly being. **2** *n* a person who is very good, kind, innocent, or beautiful. **–an·gel′ic** (an jel′ik), *adj.*

an·ger (ang′gər) *n* the feeling you have toward someone who has done something very wrong: *In a moment of anger, I wanted to hit my brother.*

an·gry 1 *adj* feeling or showing anger: *I was angry when she borrowed my bicycle without asking.* **2** *adj* stormy: *an angry sky.* **an·gri·er, an·gri·est. –an′gri·ly,** *adv.*

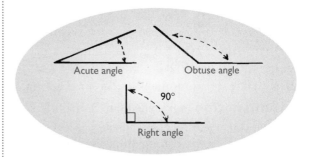

Acute angle   Obtuse angle

90°

Right angle

an·gle (ang′gəl) **1** *n* two straight lines or surfaces that meet, and the space between them. **2** *n* a slant toward a certain point of view: *Try writing your story from a different angle.* **an·gled, an·gling.**

an·gu·lar (ang′gyə lər) **1** *adj* having angles or sharp corners. **2** *adj* thin and bony; not fat.

✿ **an·glo·phone** (ang′glə fōn′) *n* a person in a bilingual or multilingual country, especially Canada, whose first or main language is English.

an·i·mal (an′ə məl) **1** *n* a living thing that is not a plant. Unlike most plants, most animals can move from one place to another and are unable to make their own food. **2** *n* any creature other than a human.

an·i·mate (an′ə māt′ *for 1 and 2*, an′ə mit *for 3*) **1** *v* make lively: *His funny stories animated the whole party.* **2** *v* make into a movie using cartoons, clay figures, etc. instead of real actors, animals, and things: *The movie* Bambi *is an animated classic.* **3** *adj* living. Plants and animals are animate. **an·i·mat·ed, an·i·mat·ing.** –**an′i·mat′ed,** *adj,* –**an′i·ma′tion,** *n.*

an·i·mism (an′ə miz′əm) *n* belief that each creature, thing, or natural event has its own spirit.

an·kle (ang′kəl) *n* the joint that connects the foot with the leg.

an·klet 1 *n* a short sock. **2** *n* a band or fine chain worn around the ankle.

an·ni·ver·sa·ry (an′ə vər′sə rē) *n* the yearly return of a certain date when people celebrate or remember something special that happened in an earlier year: *Tomorrow is my parents' wedding anniversary. pl* **an·ni·ver·sa·ries.**

an·nounce (ə nouns′) *v* make known publicly: *The principal has announced that there will be no school this afternoon.* **an·nounced, an·nounc·ing.** –**an·nounce′ment,** *n.*
an·nounc·er *n* in radio or television, a person who introduces programs, reads news, etc.

an·noy (ə noi′) *v* bother; irritate; make angry; bug. –**an·noy′ance,** *n,* –**an·noy′ing,** *adj.*

an·nu·al (an′yū əl) **1** *adj* coming once a year: *Your birthday is an annual event.* **2** *adj* for a year: *Ms. Kuzak's annual income is $45 000.* **3** *adj* living only one year or season: *Corn and beans are annual plants.* –**an′nu·al·ly,** *adv.*

a·non·y·mous (ə non′ə məs) *adj* of unknown name: *The author of this poem is anonymous.*

an·o·rak (an′ə rak′) **1** *n* an Inuit waterproof, hooded coat of animal skins, used when kayaking. Today anoraks are made of other waterproof material. The lower edge of an anorak can be fastened tightly around the opening in the kayak. **2** *n* any hooded, medium-length coat or jacket.

an·o·rex·i·a (an′ə reks′ē ə) *n* an eating disorder. People with anorexia stop eating because they are afraid of getting fat. **Anorexia nervosa** is the full name.

an·oth·er (ə nuṯн′ər) **1** *adj* one more: *Drink another glass of milk* (*adj*). **2** *pron* a different one; someone or something else: *I don't like this book; give me another.*

an·swer (an′sər) **1** *v* speak, write, or act in return: *I asked him a question, but he would not answer. We knocked on the door and Cory answered.* **2** *n* a solution to a problem: *We have found the answer at last!*
answer back, reply in a rude, saucy way.

ant (ant) *n* a small insect that lives in tunnels in the ground or in wood. Ants live together in large groups or communities called colonies. –**ant′like′,** *adj.*

ant·arc·tic (an tårk′tik *or* an tår′tik) **1** *adj* having to do with the South Pole: *an antarctic weather station, antarctic wildlife.* **2** *n* **the Antarctic,** the region around the South Pole. **Antarctic Circle** an imaginary line around the earth that marks off the south polar region.

ant·eat·er (an′tē′tər) *n* an animal that eats ants and termites, which it catches with its long, sticky tongue.

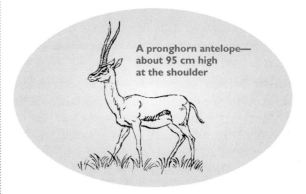
A pronghorn antelope— about 95 cm high at the shoulder

an·te·lope (an′tə lōp′) *n* a swift animal that looks like a deer but does not shed its horns. Most kinds live in the grasslands of Africa. *pl* **an·te·lope** *or* **an·te·lopes.**

an·ten·na (an ten′ə) **1** *n* a feeler on the head of an insect, lobster, etc. **2** *n* in radio or television, a wire often placed high in the air to send or receive electrical signals. *pl* **an·ten·nae** (an ten′ē *or* an ten′ī) for 1, **an·ten·nas** for 2.

an·them (an′thəm) *n* a song of praise, devotion, or patriotism. *O Canada* is the national anthem of Canada.

an·ther (an′thər) *n* the part of the stamen of a flower that produces the pollen.

an·thol·o·gy (an thol′ə jē) *n* a collection of poems, stories, or other writings by a number of different authors: *We use a Canadian anthology in language arts. pl* **an·thol·o·gies.**

an·thro·pol·o·gy (an′thrə pol′ə jē) *n* the science that deals with the origin, development, customs, and beliefs of human beings. –**an′thro·pol′o·gist,** *n*.

anti– *a prefix meaning* against. *Anti-aircraft* missiles are for fighting against *aircraft*. *Antigravity* means "against *gravity*."

an·ti·bi·ot·ic *n* a drug that can kill microbes that cause disease. Penicillin is an antibiotic.

an·ti·bod·y *n* a substance produced in the blood that fights disease-causing microbes and poisons. *pl* **an·ti·bod·ies. an·ti·dote** *n* something that acts against a poison or other bad thing; a remedy: *Milk is an antidote for some poisons. A hug is a good antidote for a bad mood.*

an·ti·freeze *n* a substance added to a liquid to lower its freezing point. Antifreeze is put into car radiators because it prevents the water in the radiator from freezing. **an·ti·sep·tic** *n* a substance that kills germs and prevents infection: *Iodine is a common antiseptic.*

an·ti·tox·in *n* a substance formed in the body that protects a person against poison made by an infection or disease.

an·tic·i·pate (an tis′ə pāt′) **1** *v* expect; look forward to: *She had anticipated a good vacation in Muskoka; but when the time came, she was sick.* **2** *v* think of and prepare for in advance: *We anticipated a cold winter.* **an·tic·i·pat·ed, an·tic·i·pat·ing.** –**an·tic′i·pa′tion,** *n*.

an·tics (an′tiks) *pl.n* funny actions and tricks: *The clown amused us by his antics.*

an·tique (an tēk′) *n* something made long ago: *That carved chest is a genuine antique.*

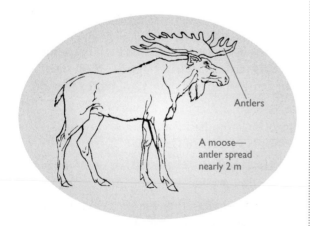

Antlers

A moose— antler spread nearly 2 m

ant·ler (ant′lər) *n* the solid horn of a deer, elk, moose, etc.: *Horns are hollow but antlers are solid.*

an·to·nym (an′tə nim′) *n* a word that means the opposite of another word. *Hot* is an antonym of *cold*.

anx·i·e·ty (ang zī′ə tē *or* angk sī′ə tē) *n* uneasy thoughts; fear or worry: *Parents feel anxiety when their children are sick. Her anxiety to succeed made her work hard.* *pl* **anx·i·e·ties.** –**anx′ious** (angk′shəs), *adj*, –**anx′ious·ly,** *adv*.

an·y (en′ē) **1** *adj or pron* one or more out of many, no matter which: *Any book will do (adj). I'm getting rid of these videotapes–take any that you like (pron).* **2** *adj or pron* some: *Do you have any fresh fruit (adj)? No, I don't have any (pron).* **3** *adj* every: *Any child knows that.* **4** *adv* at all; even a little: *If she leans over any farther, she'll fall. Has the sick child improved any?*

an·y·bod·y *pron* any person. **an·y·how 1** *adv* in any case: *I wouldn't get it finished anyhow, even if I worked all day.* **2** *adv* no matter how: *It is wrong anyhow you look at it.* **3** *adv* at least: *We must have waited an hour anyhow; maybe two.* **4** *adv Informal.* carelessly: *We had a hard time sorting the papers, because he had piled them up anyhow.* **an·y·one** *pron* any person. **an·y·place** *adv Informal.* anywhere: *I can't find my glasses anyplace.* **an·y·thing 1** *pron* any thing: *Have you had anything to eat?* **2** *adv* at all: *Is your skateboard anything like mine?* **an·y·time** *adv* at any time. **an·y·way** *adv* in any case: *I am coming anyway, no matter what you say.* **an·y·where** *adv* in, at, or to any place: *I will meet you anywhere you say.*

a·or·ta (ā ôr′tə) *n* the main artery that carries the blood from the left side of the heart to all parts of the body except the lungs. *pl* **a·or·tas** or **a·or·tae** (ā ôr′tē *or* ā ôr′tī).

a·part (ə pàrt′) **1** *adv* to pieces: *Krista took the watch apart to see what made it tick.* **2** *adv* away from each other: *Keep the dogs apart.*

apart from, besides; except for: *Apart from that one mistake, we did a very good job.*

a·part·heid (ə pàrt′hīt) *n* a system that used to be in South Africa, where blacks had fewer rights than whites and were forced to live in separate areas and go to their own schools, restaurants, etc.

a·part·ment (ə pàrt′ mənt) *n* a self-contained set of rooms to live in, in a house or larger building.

ape (āp) *n* an animal like a monkey, but with no tail. Chimpanzees, gorillas, and gibbons are apes. –**ape′like′**, *adj.*

a·pex (ā′peks) *n* the highest point: *The apex of a mountain is the mountaintop.* *pl* **a·pex·es** or **a·pi·ces** (ā′pə sēz′ *or* ap′ə sēz′).

a·phid (ā′fid *or* af′id) *n* a very small insect that lives by sucking juices from plants.

a·pol·o·gize (ə pol′ə jīz′) *v* say you are sorry. **a·pol·o·gized, a·pol·o·giz·ing.** –**a·pol′o·get′ic** (ə pol′ə jet′ik), *adj,* –**a·pol′o·get′i·cal·ly,** *adv.* **a·pol·o·gy** 1 *n* words saying you are sorry: *I owe you an apology for forgetting to phone.* 2 *n* a weak substitute: *One cracker is a poor apology for breakfast.*

a·pos·tro·phe (ə pos′trə fē) a sign (') used: 1 *n* to show that one or more letters have been left out, as in *aren't* for *are not.* 2 *n* to show the possessive forms of nouns, as in *Shanti's book, the lions' den.* 3 *n* to form certain plurals, especially of letters: *There are two o's in* apology.

Grammar ✓Check .. apostrophe

An apostrophe has two main uses:
- In contractions, to show that some letters are missing: *can't* (cannot), *she's* (she is or she has), *'99* (1999).
- To show possession, for example
  in singular: *Sulu's cat, Ross's jacket.*
  in plural: *the Ranganathans' house, the girls' bicycles, the men's washroom.*

ap·pa·ra·tus (ap′ə rat′əs) *n* equipment used for a certain activity. *pl* **ap·pa·ra·tus** or **ap·pa·ra·tus·es.**

ap·par·ent (ə per′ənt) 1 *adj* obvious; easy to see or understand: *The rockiness of the Canadian Shield is very apparent.* 2 *adj* seeming; that appears to be: *The apparent thief was innocent; we found the real thief later.* –**ap·par′ent·ly,** *adj.*

ap·pa·ri·tion (ap′ə rish′ən) *n* a ghost.

ap·peal (ə pēl′) 1 *v* ask for help: *The children appealed to their mother when they were in trouble.* 2 *v* be attractive: *That painting appeals to me.*

ap·pear (ə pēr′) 1 *v* be seen; come in sight: *One by one the stars appear.* 2 *v* seem; look: *The apple appeared sound on the outside, but it was rotten inside.* 3 *v* be presented to the public: *His latest book appeared a year ago. My favourite singer will appear on TV tonight.* –**ap·pear′ance,** *n.* **keep up appearances,** act as if everything is normal when it's not.

ap·pen·dix (ə pen′diks) 1 *n* an extra part added at the end of a book. 2 *n* a small part attached to the large intestine. *pl* **ap·pen·dix·es** or **ap·pen·di·ces** (ə pen′də sēz′). **ap·pen·di·ci·tis** (ə pen′də sī′tis) *n* an inflammation of the appendix (def. 2).

ap·pe·tite (ap′ə tīt′) 1 *n* a desire for food: *Since he had no appetite, they had to coax him to eat.* 2 *n* desire: *Amy has a great appetite for adventure.* **ap·pe·tiz·ing** *adj* giving an appetite to people who see or smell it: *appetizing food.*

ap·plaud (ə plod′) 1 *v* show approval by clapping hands, shouting, etc.: *The audience at the concert applauded my piano playing.* 2 *v* approve; praise: *My parents applauded my decision to continue piano lessons.* –**ap·plause′,** *n.*

ap·pli·ance (ə plī′əns) *n* a machine, especially an electric one that does one particular task. Vacuum cleaners and refrigerators are examples of household appliances.

ap·ply (ə plī′) 1 *v* put on: *He applied two coats of paint to the table.* 2 *v* use: *I know the rule but I don't know how to apply it.* 3 *v* ask formally: *She applied for a job.* **ap·plied, ap·ply·ing.** **ap·pli·cant** *n* a person who applies for a job, help, etc. **ap·pli·ca·tion** 1 *n* a formal request: *I have put in my application for art camp.* 2 *n* a way of using: *The application of what you have just learned will help you solve new problems.* 3 *n* a computer program that does a particular kind of work: *a word-processing application.*

ap·point (ə point′) *v* choose for a certain job or purpose: *We appointed Fatima as our captain. We met at the appointed place and time.* **ap·point·ment** 1 *n* an arrangement to see or meet someone at a certain place and time: *I have a dentist's appointment at four o'clock.* 2 *n* the choice of someone for a certain job or position: *The appointment of Lucia as president pleased her friends.*

ap·pre·ci·ate (ə prē′shē āt′) **1** *v* think highly of; value; enjoy: *Almost everybody appreciates good food.* **2** *v* be thankful for: *We appreciate your help.* **ap·pre·ci·at·ed, ap·pre·ci·at·ing.** –**ap·pre′ci·a′tion,** *n,* –**ap·pre′ci·a·tive** (ə prē′ shə tiv), *adj.*

ap·pren·tice (ə pren′tis) *n* a person who is learning a trade by working under someone already skilled at it. –**ap·pren′tice·ship,** *n.*

ap·proach (ə prōch′) *v* come near: *They quietly approached the crib and looked down at the sleeping baby. Winter is approaching.* –**ap·proach′a·ble** (ə prō′chə bəl), *adj.*

ap·pro·pri·ate (ə prō′prē it) *adj* suitable; proper: *Jeans and a sweater are appropriate clothes for the hike.* –**ap·pro′pri·ate·ly,** *adv,* –**ap·pro′pri·ate·ness,** *n.*

ap·prove (ə prüv′) **1** *v* think or say that something is good: *The teacher looked at the student's work and approved it.* **2** *v* give permission for: *Our parents approved our plans for the weekend.* **ap·proved, ap·prov·ing.** –**ap·prov′al,** *n.*

ap·prox·i·mate (ə prok′sə mit) *adj* nearly correct: *The approximate distance of the Olympic marathon is 42 km; the exact distance is 42.195 km.* –**ap·prox′i·mate·ly,** *adv,* –**ap·prox′i·ma′tion,** *n.*

ap·ti·tude (ap′tə tyüd′ or ap′tə tüd′) *n* a natural ability: *Alexander Graham Bell had a great aptitude for inventing things.*

a·quar·i·um (ə kwer′ē əm) *n* a pond, tank, or glass bowl in which living fish, water animals, and water plants are kept. *pl* **a·quar·i·ums** or **a·quar·i·a** (ə kwer′ē ə).

a·quat·ic (ə kwot′ik or ə kwat′ik) *adj* having to do with water: *Water lilies are aquatic plants. Swimming and sailing are aquatic sports.*

aq·ue·duct (ak′wə dukt′) *n* a large trough or pipe for bringing water from a distance.

a·rach·nid (ə rak′nid) *n* any of a group of small animals that have eight legs and two body parts. Like insects, arachnids have hard outer coverings; spiders, scorpions, mites, and ticks are arachnids.

arc (ärk) **1** *n* part of a circle. **2** *n* a curved line or path: *The football followed a graceful arc as it sailed between the goal posts.* **3** *n* the stream of bright light or sparks that you can see when an electric current jumps across a gap.

ar·cade **1** *n* a passageway with an arched roof. **2** *n* any covered passageway: *Some buildings have arcades with small stores along either side.* **3** *n* a place where people can pay to play video games.

arch (ärch) **1** *n* a curved structure that forms the top of a doorway, window, bridge, or tunnel. **2** *n* the part of the bottom of the foot between the ball and the heel.

ar·chae·ol·o·gy (är′kē ol′ə jē) *n* the study of the life and customs of ancient times by digging up and examining the buried remains of cities, homes, monuments, etc. **Archeology** is another spelling. –**ar′chae·ol′o·gist,** *n.*

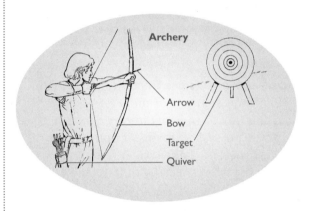

arch·er·y (är′chə rē) *n* shooting with bows and arrows. –**arch′er,** *n.*

ar·chi·pel·a·go (är′kə pel′ə gō′) *n* a sea with many islands in it or the islands themselves: *The islands in the Arctic Ocean north of Canada are called the Canadian Archipelago.* *pl* **ar·chi·pel·a·gos** or **ar·chi·pel·a·goes.**

ar·chi·tec·ture (är′kə tek′chər) **1** *n* the science and art of designing buildings. **2** *n* a special style or manner of building: *Greek architecture made use of many pillars.* **ar·chi·tect** *n* a person who designs buildings.

ar·chive (är′kīv) Usually, **archives,** *pl.n* a collection of public records or historical papers: *The Public Archives of Canada are in Ottawa.*

arc·tic (ärk′tik or är′tik) **1** *adj* having to do with the North Pole: *the arctic fox.* **2** *n* **the Arctic,** the region around the North Pole. **arctic char** a food fish of the salmon and trout family found throughout the Arctic. **Arctic Circle** an imaginary line around the earth that marks off the north polar region.

ar·e·a (er′ē ə) **1** *n* a surface: *The playing area was marked off with white lines.* **2** *n* region: *The Rocky Mountain area is the most mountainous in Canada.*

area code (er′ē ə   kōd′) a three-digit number standing for a particular area served by a telephone system: *The area code for Prince Edward Island is 902.*

a·re·na (ə rē′nə) **1** *n* a building for indoor sports: *There is a basketball game at the arena tonight.* **2** *n* in ancient times, a place for contests or shows: *Roman slaves fought with lions in the arena.*

aren't (árnt) are not.

ar·gue (ár′gyū) **1** *v* talk with someone who disagrees, sometimes angrily: *He argued with his brother about who should wash the dishes.* **2** *v* give reasons for or against something: *Laura argued for camping instead of staying in hotels.* **ar·gued, ar·gu·ing.**

ar·gu·ment **1** *n* a talk, sometimes angry, between people who disagree. **2** *n* reasons offered for or against something.

ar·id (er′id) *adj* dry and lifeless: *Desert lands are arid.*

a·rith·me·tic (ə rith′mə tik) *n* the use of addition, subtraction, multiplication, and division.

arm (árm) **1** *n* the part of a person's body between the shoulder and the hand. **2** *n* something shaped or used like an arm: *the arm of a chair, an arm of the sea.* **–arm′ful′**, *n*, **–arm′less**, *adj.*

arm·chair *n* a chair with sidepieces to rest your arms on.

an arm and a leg, *Informal.* a lot of money: *These skates cost me an arm and a leg.*

twist someone's arm, *Informal.* put strong pressure on someone: *I had to twist his arm to get him to come at all.*

A nine-banded armadillo—about 45 cm long, excluding the tail

ar·ma·dil·lo (ár′mə dil′ō) *n* a small burrowing animal with armourlike coverings and strong claws. *pl* **ar·ma·dil·los.**

ar·mi·stice (ár′mə stis) *n* an agreement to stop fighting a war.

Ar·mi·stice Day November 11, the anniversary of the end of World War 1, is now called Remembrance Day.

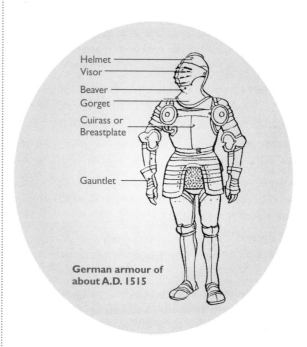

Helmet
Visor
Beaver
Gorget
Cuirass or Breastplate
Gauntlet

German armour of about A.D. 1515

arms (ármz) *n* weapons: *Arms may be used for defence or attack.*

armed forces all the groups that fight for one country in a war. **ar·mour 1** *n* a suit, often of metal, that soldiers used to wear for protection. **Armor** is another spelling. **2** *n* any protective covering: *The steel plates of a warship and the scales of a fish are armour.* **ar·my 1** *n* a very large group of soldiers trained and armed for war. **2** *n* a very large number of anything: *an army of ants.*

up in arms, very angry; in rebellion: *The students were up in arms when their class trip was cancelled.*

a·ro·ma (ə rō′mə) *n* a pleasant smell, especially of food or certain plants: *the aroma of fresh apple pie.* **–ar′o·mat′ic** (er′ə mat′ik), *adj.*

a·round (ə round′) **1** *adv* or *prep* in a circle: *spin around (adv). The moon revolves around the earth (prep).* **2** *prep* approximately; about: *around six o'clock, around $5. It was around here that I lost the key.* **3** *prep* avoiding an object or a hassle with something: *to swerve around a pothole. Can we work around that problem somehow? We plan our day around the baby's schedule.*

ar·range (ə rānj′) **1** *v* put in order; set up: *The room is arranged for a party.* **2** *v* plan: *Can you arrange to be here by six o'clock?* **ar·ranged, ar·rang·ing.** –**ar·range′ment,** *n.*

ar·ray (ə rā′) **1** *n or v* display: *an array of beautiful Inuit carvings* (n). *The dinosaur bones were arrayed on a table* (v). **2** *n* variety: *She used an array of tools for the job.* **3** *n* regular arrangement: *a square array of numbers.*

ar·rest (ə rest′) **1** *v* catch and take to jail or court: *The police arrested the bank robber as he ran down the street.* **2** *v* stop: *Filling a tooth arrests decay.*

ar·rive (ə rīv′) **1** *v* come to a particular place: *We arrived in Kingston a week ago.* **2** *v* come: *The day of the party has arrived.* **ar·rived, ar·riv·ing.** –**ar·ri·val** (ə rī′vəl), *n.*
arrive at, reach: *We have arrived at a decision.*

ar·ro·gant (er′ə gənt) *adj* very conceited and bossy. –**ar′ro·gance,** *n,* –**ar′ro·gant·ly,** *adv.*

ar·row (er′ō) **1** *n* a thin stick with a pointed tip and feathers at the other end. An arrow is made to be shot from a bow. **2** *n* anything shaped like this, such as a sign (►) used to point to something.

ar·son (àr′sən) *n* the crime of setting fire to a building or other property on purpose.

art (àrt) **1** *n* drawing, painting, or sculpture: *He is studying art and music.* **2** *n* a branch of learning or a skill, thought of as having more to do with creativity or imagination than rules: *the art of cooking, the art of making friends.* –**art′ist,** *n,* –**ar·tis′tic,** *adj.*
art·work *n* pictures and other material used in a book, magazine, bulletin board display, etc.

ar·ter·y (àr′tə rē) **1** *n* any of the tubes that carry blood from the heart to all parts of the body. **2** *n* a main transportation route: *Robson Street is one of the main arteries of Vancouver.* *pl* **ar·ter·ies.**

ar·te·sian well (àr tē′zhən wel′) a deep well made by drilling, from which water gushes up without pumping.

ar·thri·tis (àr thrī′tis) *n* any disease affecting the joints of the body, making them stiff, swollen, and painful.

ar·thro·pod (àr′thrə pod′) *n* one of a very large group of animals, including insects and spiders, that have no backbone and have legs and bodies made up of joined segments.

ar·ti·cle (àr′tə kəl) **1** *n* a piece of writing in a magazine, newspaper, or book: *This magazine has a good article on dinosaurs.* **2** *n* a thing of a specific kind: *Bread is an important article of food.* **3** *n* one of the words *a, an,* and *the,* which come before nouns: *a book, an egg, the boy.*

ar·ti·fact (àr′tə fakt′) *n* anything made by humans: *The archaeologist discovered several Stone-Age axes.*

ar·ti·fi·cial (àr′tə fish′əl) **1** *adj* made by humans; not natural: *artificial flowers, artificial ice.* **2** *adj* put on or pretended; not real: *an artificial voice.* –**ar′ti·fi′cial·ly,** *adv.*
artificial respiration a way of getting a person to breathe normally again by forcing air in and out of the person's lungs.

ar·ti·san (àr′tə zən *or* àr′tə zan′) *n* a person skilled in a trade or craft. Carpenters and weavers are artisans.

as (az) **1** *adv* equally: *Beth is as tall as Malik.* **2** *prep* in the position of: *Malik will act as teacher today.* **3** *conj* in the same way that: *Treat others as you wish them to treat you.* **4** *conj* because: *We should get going, as it is quite late.*
as of, beginning on: *As of March 31, the library will be closed for repairs.*
as to, about: *We have no information as to the cause of the riot.*

USING WORDS . . . . . as/like

As is often confused with **like.**

In comparisons, use **as** when a clause follows, complete with its own subject and verb:
She worked as she never did before.

Use **like** if just a noun follows, with or without adjectives:
She worked like a horse.

---

as·bes·tos (as bes′təs *or* az bes′təs) *n* a greyish-white mineral found in the form of fibres. Because it will not burn, it was once used to make things fireproof. Breathing its dust, however, damages the lungs.

as·cend (ə send′) *v* go up: *He watched the airplane ascend higher and higher. Few people ascend high mountains.* –**as·cent′,** *n.*

ash (ash) *n* what is left after something has been thoroughly burned: *We cleaned the ashes out of the fireplace.*

a·shamed (ə shāmd′) *adj* feeling shame; very sorry: *I was ashamed that I had been rude to them.*

a·side (ə sīd′) *adv* to one side: *Move the table aside.*

ask (ask) **1** *v* try to find out from someone by a question: *Ask him how old he is.* **2** *v* try to get by words: *Ask her to sing. Ask for what you want.* **3** *v* invite: *She asked ten friends to the party.*

a·sleep (ə slēp′) **1** *adj* sleeping: *The cat is asleep.* **2** *adv* into sleep: *The tired boy fell asleep.* **3** *adj* numb: *My foot is asleep.*

Leaves and shoots of asparagus

as·par·a·gus (ə sper′ə gəs) *n* a plant whose long, tender green shoots are used for food.

as·pect (as′pekt) *n* one side of something: *We must consider all the aspects of this plan.*

as·phalt (as′folt *or* ash′folt) *n* a black substance, heated and mixed with crushed rock, which is used for paving.

as·pire (ə spīr′) *v* have a hopeful desire for something: *Kayla aspired to be captain of the team.* **as·pired, as·pir·ing. –as′pi·ra′tion,** *n.*

As·pi·rin (as′pə rin) *n* *a trademark for* a pill used to relieve the pain or fever of headaches, colds, etc.

as·sail (ə sāl′) *v* attack violently: *The older kids assailed our snow fort.* **–as·sail′ant,** *n.*

as·sas·sin (ə sas′ən) *n* a murderer, especially of a politically important person. **–as·sas′si·nate′,** *v,* **–as·sas′si·na′tion,** *n.*

as·sault (ə solt′) *n or v* attack: *They made an assault on the enemy camp* (n). *You have assaulted my friend* (v)!

as·sem·ble (ə sem′bəl) **1** *v* gather together: *Assemble all the ingredients first. We assembled in the gym.* **2** *v* put together; build: *This model car is easy to assemble.* **as·sem·bled, as·sem·bling.**

as·sem·bly 1 *n* a gathering of people; a meeting: *The principal called an assembly of the students for Monday morning.* **2** *n* the action of putting parts together: *The label reads, "Some assembly required."*

assembly line a row of workers or machines for assembling something, such as a car, in a factory. Each one does part of the work and passes it to the next, until the product is finished. ❦ **assembly member** in Prince Edward Island, a member of the Legislative Assembly who is not a councillor.

as·sent (ə sent′) **1** *v* agree: *Everyone assented to the plan to sponsor a child.* **2** *n* agreement: *She gave a nod of assent.*

as·sert (ə sərt′) **1** *v* say firmly: *Luc asserts that he will go no matter what.* **2** *v* insist on a right, a claim, etc.: *Assert your independence.* **–as·ser′tion,** *n,* **–as·ser′tive,** *adj.*

as·sess (ə ses′) *v* decide on the value of: *The staff will assess the need for new playground equipment. We have assessed your work and found it excellent.* **–as·sess′ment,** *n.*

as·set (as′et) **1** *n* something valuable: *The ability to get along with people is an asset.* **2 assets,** *pl.n* property: *Her assets include a house, a car, and jewellery.*

as·sign (ə sīn′) **1** *v* give a share or task: *The camp director assigned a job to each cabin.* **2** *v* fix or set: *The judge assigned a day for the trial.* **–as·sign′ment,** *n.*

as·sist (ə sist′) **1** *v* help: *She assisted her mother with the yard work. She assisted in the scoring of the goal.* **2** *n* in some sports, the credit given to a player who helps score a goal, put an opponent out, etc. **–as·sist′ance,** *n.*

as·sist·ant *n* a helper; an aid.

as·so·ci·ate (ə sō′shē āt′ *for 1 and 2,* ə sō′shē it *for 3*) **1** *v* connect in thought: *We associate camping with summer.* **2** *v* join as a companion or friend; keep company: *She associates only with people interested in sports.* **3** *n* a companion or partner: *I am one of his associates on this project.* **as·so·ci·at·ed, as·so·ci·at·ing.**

as·so·ci·a·tion 1 *n* a group of people joined together for some common purpose; a society: *Artists in the local Arts Association share a studio and gallery.* **2** *n* a connection or relationship: *Anna and Jo enjoyed a close association over many years. There is a clear association between campfires and marshmallows.*

as·sort·ment (ə sȯrt′mənt) *n* a collection of various kinds: *an assortment of candies.* —**as·sort′ed**, *adj.*

as·sume (ə sūm′) **1** *v* take for granted: *Eva assumed that the bus would be on time.* **2** *v* take: *to assume a responsibility, to assume the blame.* **as·sumed, as·sum·ing.**

as·sump·tion (ə sump′shən) *n* something taken for granted: *Our assumption that we would win was wrong: we lost!*

as·sure (ə shūr) **1** *v* make sure: *The man assured himself that the bridge was safe before crossing it.* **2** *v* tell positively: *The captain of the ship assured the passengers that there was no danger.* **as·sured, as·sur·ing.**

as·sur·ance **1** *n* a statement meant to make a person more sure: *Sara gave me many assurances that she would not tell my secret.* **2** *n* self-confidence: *Hours of practice gave me assurance in singing.*

as·ter·isk (as′tə risk) *n* a star-shaped mark (*) used in printing and writing to call attention to something.

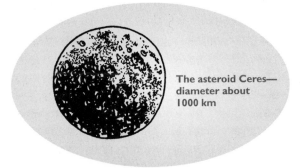

The asteroid Ceres— diameter about 1000 km

as·ter·oid (as′tə roid′) *n* any of the many very small planets that revolve around the sun, mainly between the orbits of Mars and Jupiter.

asth·ma (az′mə) *n* a long-term disease that causes coughing and difficulty in breathing. —**asth·mat′ic** (az mat′ik), *adj* or *n.*

as·ton·ish (ə ston′ish) *v* surprise very much: *The magic trick astonished the little girl.* —**as·ton′ish·ing**, *adj*, —**as·ton′ish·ment**, *n.*

as·tound (ə stound′) *v* fill with wonder: *We were astounded by the beauty of Niagara Falls.* —**as·tound′ing**, *adj.*

a·stray (ə strā′) *adv* out of the right way: *The trail was so poorly marked that hikers often went astray.*

as·tron·o·my (ə stron′ə mē) *n* the science that deals with the sun, moon, planets, stars, and other bodies in space. —**as·tron′o·mer**, *n.*

as·tro·labe (as′trə lāb′) *n* an instrument used by people long ago for finding their way by the sun and stars. **as·trol·o·gy** *n* the study of how the positions of stars and planets are supposed to influence people and events, including future events. It is not scientific. **as·tro·naut** (as′trə not′) *n* someone who travels or works in outer space.

as·tro·nom·i·cal **1** *adj* extremely large or great, like the numbers used to describe distances between stars: *an astronomical price.* **2** *adj* having to do with astronomy: *an astronomical telescope.*

a·sy·lum (ə sī′ləm) **1** *n* refuge or shelter: *Many refugees from warring countries have found asylum in Canada.* **2** *n* a place where mentally ill people used to stay in order to receive care.

ate (āt) *v* the past tense of **eat.**

ath·lete (ath′lēt) *n* a person who is active and skilled in sports. —**ath·let′ic** (ath let′ik), *adj.* **athlete's foot** a skin disease of the feet, caused by a fungus. It causes red, itchy sores.

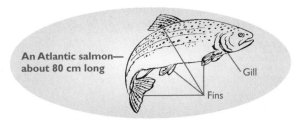

An Atlantic salmon— about 80 cm long   Gill   Fins

At·lan·tic (at lan′ tik) *adj* having to do with the Atlantic Ocean: *the Atlantic coast, Atlantic salmon.* **Atlantic Provinces** Newfoundland, Prince Edward Island, Nova Scotia, and New Brunswick.

at·las (at′ləs) *n* a book of maps.

> **WORD HISTORY** .... **atlas**
>
> The word **atlas** comes from the name *Atlas*, a character in Greek myth. The first map books used to have a picture of him holding up the world with his shoulders and hands. According to the story, he was punished in this way for rebelling against the gods.

ATM *abbreviation* for automated teller machine, a machine that lets you take out or put in money in your bank account.

at·mos·phere (at′məs fēr′) **1** *n* the layer of air that surrounds the earth. **2** *n* surrounding influence: *a friendly atmosphere. He lived in an atmosphere of poverty.*
–**at′mos·pher′ic** (at′məs fer′ik), *adj.*

An atoll in the Pacific Ocean

a·toll (at′ol *or* ə tol′) *n* a ring-shaped coral island or reef formed on top of land in the ocean. The pool in the centre is called a lagoon.

at·om (at′əm) **1** *n* the smallest part of an element, that still has all its special characteristics. An atom of an element can react with other substances, without being forever changed. Atoms are made up of protons, neutrons, and electrons. **2** *n* the tiniest bit: *There is not an atom of truth in his whole story.*
–**a·tom′ic** (ə tom′ik), *adj.*
atomic bomb a bomb that splits atoms to cause a horrific explosion. **Atom bomb** is another name for it. **atomic energy** the energy, or power, that holds atoms together; nuclear energy.

a·tri·um (ā′trē əm) **1** *n* either of the two upper parts of the heart, which receive blood from the veins. **2** *n* a high hall or court in a large building, often with a skylight. *pl* **a·tri·a** (ā′trē ə) *or* **a·tri·ums.**

a·troc·i·ty (ə tros′ə tē) *n* an extremely cruel or wicked act: *the atrocities of war. pl* **a·troc·i·ties.**
a·tro·cious (ə trō′shəs) *adj* extremely bad: *an atrocious crime, atrocious spelling.*

at·tach (ə tach′) *v* fasten or connect: *Julia attached a rope to her sled.* –**at·tach′ment,** *n.*
be attached to, like very much: *She is very attached to her cousin.*

at·tack (ə tak′) **1** *v* use force, words, or weapons to hurt or fight: *The dog attacked with its teeth bared. The newspapers attacked the new*

prime minister. **2** *v* start on something energetically: *to attack a problem.* **3** *v* act harmfully on: *Some bacteria attack tooth enamel.* **4** *n* the sudden beginning of sickness, pain, etc.: *an attack of the flu, an attack of guilt.*

at·tempt (ə tempt′) **1** *v* try: *I will attempt to get better grades.* **2** *n* a try; an effort: *They made an attempt to bike across Canada.*

at·tend (ə tend′) *v* be present at: *I attend school.*
at·tend·ance 1 *n* the act of attending: *Attendance at all classes is required.* **2** *n* the number of people present: *The attendance at the meeting was over 200.*

at·ten·tion (ə ten′shən) *n* care and thought: *The players gave the coach their full attention.*
–**at·ten′tive,** *adj,* –**at·ten′tive·ly,** *adv.*
pay attention, watch or listen carefully.

at·tic (at′ik) *n* a space just below the roof of a house.

at·tire (ə tīr′) *n* clothes of a special kind: *swimming attire, evening attire.*

at·ti·tude (at′ə tyūd′ *or* at′ə tūd′) **1** *n* way of thinking, acting, or feeling: *I like your helpful attitude.* **2** *n* a position of the body: *Ken stood in the attitude of a goalie ready to play.*

at·tor·ney (ə tər′nē) *n* a lawyer. *pl* **at·tor·neys.**
Attorney General *n* the chief law officer of Canada or of a Canadian province. The Attorney General is a member of the Cabinet.

at·tract (ə trakt′) **1** *v* pull to itself: *A magnet attracts iron.* **2** *v* be interesting to: *Bright colours attract children.* –**at·trac′tion,** *n,* –**at·trac′tive,** *adj.*

at·trib·ute (ə trib′yūt *for 1,* at′rə byūt′ *for 2*) **1** *v* think of as belonging to or caused by: *She attributes her success to hard work.* **2** *n* a quality or characteristic: *Fitness is an attribute of a good athlete.* **at·trib·ut·ed, at·trib·ut·ing.**

auc·tion (ok′shən) *n* a public sale in which each thing is sold to the person who offers the most money for it.

au·dac·i·ty (o das′ə tē) *n* boldness: *He had the audacity to go to the party without being invited. pl* **au·dac·i·ties.**

au·da·cious (o dā′shəs) **1** *adj* bold; daring: *an audacious rescue attempt.* **2** *adj* too bold; rude: *an audacious request for money.*

au·di·ence (od′ē əns) *n* the people watching or listening to something: *The students cheered their classmate's speech.*

au·di·ble *adj* loud enough to be heard. **au·di·o** *adj* having to do with sound that is recorded or broadcast: *audio equipment, the audio part of a movie.* **au·di·tion** *n* a test of the ability of a singer, actor, etc., who would like to be chosen for a certain performance. **au·di·to·ri·um** *n* a large room for an audience in a school, theatre, church, etc.; a large hall.

aunt (ant) **1** *n* the sister of a person's father or mother. **2** *n* the wife of a person's uncle.

au·ror·a bor·e·al·is (ȯ rȯ′rə bȯ′rē al′is) streamers of coloured light in the northern sky at night; the northern lights. In the southern hemisphere, a similar thing can be seen in the southern sky. It is called the **aurora australis.**

au·then·tic (o then′tik) *adj* genuine; real: *authentic Inuit carvings.*

au·thor (oth′ər) *n* a person who writes books: *Barbara Smucker is a famous Canadian children's author.*

au·thor·i·ty (ə thȯr′ə tē) **1** *n* the right to command, judge, or act: *Parents have authority over their children. A police officer has the authority to arrest careless drivers.* **2** *n* a source of correct or reliable information: *A good dictionary is an authority on the meaning of words.* *pl* **au·thor·i·ties.**

au·thor·ize 1 *v* give someone the authority or the right: *The Prime Minister authorized her to make the decision.* **2** *v* approve: *This dictionary authorizes the two spellings* traveller *and* traveler.

au·to·bi·og·ra·phy (ot′ə bī og′rə fē) *n* the story of a person's life written or told by that person. *pl* **au·to·bi·og·ra·phies.**

au·to·graph (ot′ə graf′) *n* a signature, especially as a souvenir: *I have the autographs of two of the Ottawa Senators.*

au·to·mate (o′tə māt′) *v* design or set up something to be done by computers, or by machines that run mostly by themselves, so that fewer workers are needed. **au·to·mat·ed, au·to·mat·ing.** –**au′to·mat′ed,** *adj,* –**au′to·ma′tion,** *n.*

au·to·mat·ic 1 *adj* working by itself: *an automatic lock, an automatic pump.* **2** *adj* done without thought or attention: *Breathing and* swallowing are usually automatic. **3** *n* something with parts that work by themselves, such as a car whose motor changes gear by itself. –**au′to·mat′i·cal·ly,** *adv.*

au·to·mo·bile (ot′ə mə bēl′) *n* car.

au·to·mo·tive *adj* having to do with cars, trucks, and other motorized vehicles.

au·top·sy (ot′op sē) *n* an examination of a dead body to find out the cause of death or what damage has been done to the body. *pl* **au·top·sies.**

au·tumn (ot′əm) *n* the season between summer and winter; fall.

aux·il·ia·ry (og zil′ə rē *or* og zil′yə rē) *adj* assisting: *Some sailboats have auxiliary engines.* **auxiliary verb** a kind of verb used along with the main verb in a sentence to show the time of the action and certain other things. *Examples: be, have, will.* In the sentence *I will take my camera with me,* the auxiliary verb *will* shows that the action (the main verb *take*) is in the future.

Grammar ✓*Check* .. **auxiliary verb**

Here are some examples of auxiliary verbs.

- *I will take my camera with me.* Here the auxiliary verb **will** shows that the action (*take*) is in the future.
- *We are eating supper.* Here the auxiliary verb **are** helps to show that the action (*eat*) is going on right now.
- *Have you read this book?* Here the auxiliary verb **have** helps to show that the action (*read*) happened sometime in the past.
- *The CD was stolen.* Here the auxiliary verb **was** helps to show that the action (*steal*) is not something the CD did, but something that happened to the CD.

---

a·vail·a·ble (ə vā′lə bəl) *adj* there for people to use: *The saw is not available at the moment; Bryony is using it. Some tickets are still available.*

av·a·lanche (av′ə lanch′) *n* the sudden sliding of a large mass of snow, ice, dirt, or rocks down the side of a mountain.

a·venge (ə venj′) *v* get revenge for: *The knight avenged the insult by defeating his enemy in a duel.* **a·venged, a·veng·ing.** –**a·veng′er,** *n.*

av·e·nue (av′ən yū′) *n* a wide street.

av·er·age (av′ə rij) **1** *n* in arithmetic, the quantity found by adding up several other quantities and then dividing the sum by the number of quantities: *The average of 3, 10, and 5 is 6.* **2** *adj* usual; ordinary: *average snowfall.*

a·ver·sion (ə vėr′zhən) **1** *n* a strong dislike: *Some people have an aversion to snakes.* **2** *n* a thing or person that is disliked: *Nicknames are my pet aversion.*

a·vi·a·tion (ā′vē ā′shən) *n* the designing, making, and flying of aircraft.

a·vi·a·tor *n* a person who flies an aircraft; pilot.

av·id (av′id) *adj* enthusiastic: *He is an avid reader.*

a·void (ə void′) *v* keep away from; keep from doing: *Avoid the really muddy area at the back of the schoolyard. We avoided driving through large cities on our trip.* –**a·void′a·ble,** *adj*, –**a·void′ance,** *n.*

a·wake (ə wāk′) **1** *v* wake up: *We awoke from a sound sleep. The alarm clock awoke me.* **2** *adj* not asleep: *Wanda is always awake early.* **3** *adj* on the alert; watchful: *Our government is awake to that danger.* **a·woke, a·wak·ing.**

a·wak·en·ing **1** *n* the act of waking up or becoming aware: *an awakening to danger.* **2** *adj* waking up: *the sounds of the awakening birds.*

a·ward (ə wȯrd′) **1** *v* give to a deserving person, group, etc.: *A medal was awarded to the boy who saved the child.* **2** *n* a prize for excellence: *The Stanley Cup is an award given to the top team in the NHL.*

a·ware (ə wer′) *adj* knowing: *I was too sleepy to be aware how cold it was. He is not aware of his danger.* –**a·ware′ness,** *n.*

a·way (ə wā′) *adv or adj* at or to some other place; in another direction: *Get away from the fire* (*adv*). *The sailor was far away from home* (*adj*). *She looked sad and turned away* (*adv*).

U S I N G   W O R D S . . . . . away

Away is used with many verbs that have to do with getting rid of something (*give away a book, take away pain*), using up something (*pass away the time*), or of something gradually disappearing (*The noise died away.*).
See how many more examples you can think of.

---

awe (o) *n* great wonder and fear or reverence: *We feel awe when we see huge waves crashing at Peggy's Cove.* **awed, aw·ing.**

awe·some *adj* causing awe: *The great fire was an awesome sight.* **aw·ful** *adj Informal.* very bad, great, ugly, etc.: *Your room is in an awful mess.* –**aw′ful·ly,** *adv.*

a·while (ə wīl′ *or* ə hwīl′) *adv* for a short time: *She stayed awhile.*

awk·ward (ok′wərd) **1** *adj* clumsy: *Seals are very awkward on land, but are graceful in the water.* **2** *adj* hard to use: *The handle of this cup has an awkward shape.* **3** *adj* embarrassing: *He asked me an awkward question.* –**awk′ward·ly,** *adv,* –**awk′ward·ness,** *n.*

Two awnings on a house

awn·ing (on′ing) *n* a piece of canvas, plastic, or other material spreading outward from the top of a window or door for protection from the sun or rain.

axe (aks) *n* a tool for chopping wood. *pl* **ax·es.**

ax·is (ak′sis) **1** *n* a line going through an object, on which the object seems to turn: *The earth's axis is an imaginary line through the North and South Poles.* **2** *n* either of the lines that you start with in making a graph. One is vertical, the other is horizontal. *pl* **ax·es** (ak′sēz).

ax·le (ak′səl) *n* a bar or shaft that a wheel or pair of wheels turns on.

aye (ī) *n* a *yes* vote or voter: *The ayes won when the vote was taken.*

b or **B** (bē) the second letter of the English alphabet, or any speech sound that it stands for. The sound of *b* is heard twice in *baby*. *pl* **b's** or **B's.**

bab·ble (bab'əl) *v* talk too much, too fast, or in a way that cannot be understood: *Claire babbled on and on about her adventure at Cree Lake.* **bab·bled, bab·bling.** –**babble,** *n.*

A baboon—about 80 cm tall

ba·boon (bə bün') *n* a kind of large, fierce monkey with a doglike face and a short tail. Baboons live in the rocky hills of Africa and the Arabian peninsula.

ba·by (bā'bē) **1** *n* a very young child or animal: *Some babies cry a lot.* **2** *v* treat like a baby; handle very carefully: *to baby a sick child, to baby a new car. pl* **ba·bies. ba·bied, ba·by·ing.** –**ba'by·ish,** *adj.*

baby carriage a light carriage used for wheeling a baby around. **ba·by·sit** *v* take care of a child while the parents are busy or away. –**ba'by·sit'ter,** *n.*

bach·e·lor (bach'ə lər) *n* an unmarried man.

back (bak) **1** *n* the part of a person's body opposite to the chest; the upper part of an animal's body: *She turned her back to the wind.* **2** *n* the side of anything opposite or behind the front: *the back of the room, the back of a rug.* **3** *adj* or *adv* behind in space or time: *a back issue of a magazine* (adj), *to walk back three steps* (adv). **4** *adv* to the place or person that something or someone came from: *Put the book back. I gave the money back.*

❀ **back bacon** bacon cut from the back of the pig rather than the sides: *Back bacon has little fat and tastes like ham.* **back·board** *n* a board above and behind the basket on a basketball court.

back·bone 1 *n* the spine; a series of small bones along the middle of the back in humans and many other animals. **2** *n* the courage to stand up for what you think is right.

back·fire 1 *v* explode too soon or in the wrong place. **2** *v* have an unexpected bad result: *His plan backfired, and instead of getting rich he lost all his money.* **back·fired, back·fir·ing.**

back·log *n* a number of things to be done: *The office had a backlog of orders waiting to be filled.*

back·pack *n* bag for schoolbooks, food, or other equipment, with straps for carrying it on your back. Bigger backpacks for hiking or bike trips are attached to a light metal frame for support.

back·yard or **back yard** *n* a yard behind a house.

back and forth, first one way and then the other: *He paced back and forth impatiently.*

back down, give up a claim: *When I challenged her to prove it, she backed down.*

back off, stop attacking.

back out, *Informal.* decide not to do something after all: *He was going to come on the trip to Sept Îles, but he backed out.*

back up, 1 move backward. **2** support: *If you tell your dad what happened, I'll back you up.* **3** copy from a computer onto a disk. **4** plug up so that liquid collects and overflows: *The drain is backed up.*

behind someone's back, secretly and with a mean purpose: *He seemed to be a good friend but then I found out he was talking about me behind my back.*

get off someone's back, *Informal.* stop nagging or criticizing someone: *I finally told him if he didn't get off my back I wouldn't help him at all.*

get someone's back up, *Informal.* make or become angry and stubborn: *She was only joking, so don't get your back up.*

back·ground (bak'ground') **1** *n* the back part of a picture, scene, or pattern: *Lake Nipissing is in the foreground with the cottage in the background. The material had pink flowers on a white background.* **2** *n* all the things that lead up to or explain something: *We studied the background to the news.* **3** *n* upbringing or heritage; experience and training: *a farming background. Gita's background is French Canadian.*
in the background, out of sight; not in clear view: *The shy boy kept in the background.*

back·ward (bak'wərd) **1** *adv* or *adj* toward the back or toward an earlier time: *He looked backward (adv). She gave him a backward look (adj).* **2** *adj* or *adv* with the back first: *a backward somersault (adj). Count backward from 100 (adv).* **Backwards** is another form for the adverb.

USING WORDS .... backward

You can use **backward** and **backwards** as adverbs:
Niko tumbled backward over his own gym bag.
Niko tumbled backwards over his own gym bag.
But use only **backward** as an adjective:
Niko took a backward tumble over his own gym bag.

---

ba·con (bā'kən) *n* salted and smoked meat from the back and sides of a pig.

bac·te·ri·a (bak tē'rē ə) *pl.n* very tiny and simple living things that are like plants in some ways and like animals in other ways. They can only be seen through a microscope and are found in the air, soil, water, and in the bodies of all plants and animals. *sing* **bac·te·ri·um.**

bad (bad) **1** *adj* not good; wrong, harmful, etc.: *Cheating is bad. Smoking is bad for your lungs.* **2** *adj* severe; serious: *A bad thunderstorm delayed the airplane.* **3** *adj* rotten; spoiled: *a bad egg.* **worse, worst. –bad'ness,** *n.*
bad·lands *n* a region of barren land marked by ridges, gullies, and unusual rock formations, as found in southwestern Saskatchewan and southeastern Alberta. The skeletons of prehistoric animals have been found in the badlands. **bad·ly 1** *adv* in a bad manner: *She sings badly.* **2** *adv Informal.* very much: *We badly need that money.*
not bad, *Informal.* pretty good.

badge (baj) *n* something worn on a piece of clothing to show that a person belongs to a certain school, organization, occupation, etc. Police officers wear badges.

badg·er (baj'ər) **1** *n* an animal of the weasel family with long, coarse grey fur, a wide, heavy body, and long front claws for digging. Badgers live in burrows; in Canada, they are found especially on the Prairies. **2** *v* nag or pester: *He's been badgering his sister to let him come along.*

baf·fle (baf'əl) *v* be too hard to figure out: *This puzzle baffles me.* **baf·fled, baf·fling.**

bag (bag) **1** *n* a container made of paper, plastic, cloth, leather, etc. that can be closed: *Fresh fruit is often sold in plastic bags.* **2** *v* or *n* bulge: *These pants bag at the knees (v). When I'm tired I have bags under my eyes (n).* **bagged, bag·ging. –bag'ful',** *n.*
bag·gage *n* the bags, suitcases, etc. that a person takes when travelling. **bag·gy** *adj* hanging loosely: *The clown wore baggy pants.*

ba·gel (bā'gəl) *n* a firm, doughnut-shaped bread roll.

Ba·hai (bə hī') *n* a religion based on the teachings of **Baha Ullah**, a prophet of Persia. He taught that all people are united under God, whatever their religion.

bail (bāl) **1** *n* money paid to free an arrested person until he or she is tried in court. **2** *v* scoop water out of the bottom of a boat.
bail out, drop from an airplane by parachute.

Bai·sak·hi (bī sä'kē) *n* a festival of the Sikh religion, held on April 13. It celebrates the day that the first five Sikhs were baptized.

bait (bāt) **1** *n* food used to attract fish or other animals in order to catch them: *Worms are often used as bait in fishing.* **2** *n* anything used to trick someone into doing something.

bake (bāk) **1** *v* cook by dry heat in an oven: *to bake bread. Cookies bake quickly.* **2** *v* dry or harden by heat: *to bake bricks.* **baked, bak·ing.**
bak·er *n* a person who makes and sells bread, pies, cakes, etc. **baker's dozen** thirteen.
bak·er·y *n* a baker's shop; a place where bread, cakes, etc. are made or sold. **Bake shop** is another name. **baking soda** a white powder used in baking, medicine, cleaning, etc. **Bicarbonate of soda** is the scientific name.

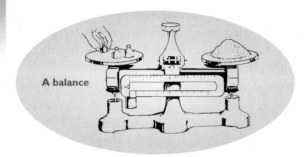

A balance

bal·ance (bal′əns) **1** *n* steadiness: *She lost her balance and fell off the ladder.* **2** *v* keep or put in a steady condition or position: *Can you balance a loonie on its edge?* **3** *n* an instrument for finding the mass of something. It works like a seesaw and looks like a bar with two pans at either end. You put the thing in one of the pans and in the other one you put objects whose mass you already know. When the bar stops seesawing and the pans are exactly even, each one is holding the same mass. **4** *n* the part that is left over; the remainder: *I'll pay $5 now and the balance later.* **bal·anced, bal·anc·ing.**
in the balance, undecided: *The result was in the balance until the last moment.*

bal·co·ny (bal′kə nē) **1** *n* an outside platform with an entrance from an upper floor of a building. **2** *n* an upper level of seats in a theatre or hall. *pl* **bal·co·nies.**

bald (bold) **1** *adj* without hair on the head. **2** *adj* bare: *a bald mountaintop.* —**bald′ness,** *n.*

bale (bāl) *n* a large bundle of hay, straw, or cotton.

ball (bol) **1** *n* a round or oval object that is thrown, kicked, knocked, bounced, or batted around in a game. **2** *n* anything round or roundish; something that looks like a ball: *a ball of string, the ball of your thumb. The earth is a ball.* **3** *n* a large, formal party with dancing. **4** *n* Informal. a very good time; a lot of fun: *We had a ball at camp.*

bal·lad (bal′əd) *n* a simple poem that tells a story, often put to music. *The Wreck of the Edmund Fitzgerald* is a ballad by Canadian **balladeer** Gordon Lightfoot.

bal·let (bal′ā) *n* an artistic dance that usually tells a story or expresses a mood, performed on stage by one or more dancers.

bal·le·ri·na (bal′ə rē′nə) *n* a female ballet dancer.

bal·loon (bə lūn′) *n* a bag filled with air or a gas lighter than air.

bal·lot (bal′ət) *n* a piece of paper for writing down or checking off your vote. When you are done, you put it in a **ballot box.**

balm (bom *or* bàm) **1** *n* a sweet-smelling oil obtained from certain kinds of trees, used to heal or to lessen pain. **2** *n* anything that heals or soothes: *My mother's kind words were a balm to my hurt feelings.*

balm·y *adj* mild; soft; gentle: *a balmy breeze.*

ba·lo·ney (bə lō′nē) **1** *n* nonsense or foolishness: *Karl thought that his uncle's story about the fish he caught was a lot of baloney.* **2** *n* another spelling of **bologna,** a kind of sausage.

bam·boo (bam bū′) *n* a treelike tropical grass with a stiff, hollow, woody stem that has hard, thick joints: *She bought a fishing rod made of bamboo.*

bam·boo·zle (bam bū′zəl) *Informal.* **1** *v* cheat or trick: *He was bamboozled into trading his best Toronto Blue Jays baseball cards for a cheap bike lock.* **2** *v* puzzle or confuse: *The computer manual had me completely bamboozled.* **bam·boo·zled, bam·boo·zling.**

ban (ban) **1** *v* make a rule against; forbid: *Smoking is banned on buses in Canada.* **2** *n* a rule against something: *There is a ban on parking in this narrow street.* **banned, ban·ning.**

ba·nan·a (bə nan′ə) *n* a long, curved tropical fruit with a yellow peel and firm, creamy flesh.

band (band) **1** *n* a group travelling, acting, or playing music together: *a band of robbers, a rock band.* **2** ❈ *n* a group of First Nations people living on a reserve and officially recognized as a unit. **3** *n* a strip of colour, or of some material such as metal, cloth, or rubber: *a blue rug with bands of grey. Put an elastic band around that package.*

band·age (ban′dij) **1** *n* a strip of cloth or other material for covering a wound or injury. **2** *v* put a bandage on. **band·aged, band·ag·ing.**

ban·dit (ban′dit) *n* a robber.

bang (bang) **1** *n* a sudden loud noise: *She popped a balloon, and the bang scared me.* **2** *v* hit, close, etc. with a sudden loud noise: *The door banged shut.*

bangs (bangz) *pl.n* a fringe of hair on the forehead: *I have short hair and bangs.*

ban·ish (ban′ish) *v* send away, especially as a punishment: *She was banished from the game because she was always cheating.*

bank (bangk) **1** *n* a long pile or heap: *There was a bank of snow over a metre deep.* **2** *v* the ground beside a river. **3** *n* a shallow place in water; a shoal. The Grand Banks are shallow places in the Atlantic Ocean off Newfoundland. **4** *n* a place for saving or borrowing money. **5** *n* a supply of anything, used as needed: *a food bank.*
bank account an arrangement for putting your money in a bank. **bank·rupt** *adj* unable to pay debts. –**bank′rupt·cy** (bangk′ rəp sē), *n.*
bank on, depend on: *I can bank on Kurt to help me.*

> **WORD HISTORY . . . . bankrupt**
>
> **Bankrupt** comes originally from the Italian word *bancarotta* = "bank" + "broken."

❈ **bank·er** (bang′kər) **1** *n* someone who fishes off the Grand Banks. **2** *n* a fishing boat of the Grand Banks.

ban·ner (ban′ər) **1** *n* flag: *a school banner.* **2** *adj* outstanding: *a banner year at the Olympics for Canada.*

❈ **ban·nock** (ban′ək) *n* a flat, round cake made of flour, salt, and water, especially if cooked over an open fire.

ban·quet (bang′kwit) *n* a formal dinner or a feast, often with speeches: *The teachers had a banquet for the principal when she retired.*

bap·tize (bap′ tīz *or* bap tīz′) *v* give a first name to a person; christen: *The baby was baptized Robert.* **bap·tized, bap·tiz·ing.** –**bap′tism,** *n.*

bar (bàr) **1** *n* a long, narrow piece of something: *an iron bar, a bar of soap, a bar of chocolate.* **2** *v* close or block; exclude; forbid: *He bars the doors every night. All talking is barred during study period.* **3** *n* in music, a unit of rhythm, from one **bar line** to another: *The accent falls on the first note of each bar.* **4** *n* a place with a counter where alcoholic drinks are served. **barred, bar·ring.**
bar code a series of printed lines of different widths that a machine can read to show how much something costs or where it is supposed to go. **bar graph** a chart showing bars of different lengths in order to compare different amounts.

bar·bar·i·an (bàr ber′ē ən) **1** *n* in ancient times, a person belonging to a tribe thought to be uncivilized: *Rome was conquered by barbarian peoples.* **2** *adj* not civilized; rude, savage, or ignorant. –**bar·bar′ic** (bàr ber′ ik), *adj.*

> **WORD HISTORY . . . . barbarian**
>
> The word **barbarian** comes originally from the Greek word *barbaros* meaning "foreigner." The Greek word with the repetition *bar-bar* was probably in imitation of the strange-sounding language that they heard foreign peoples speak.

bar·be·cue (bàr′bē kyū′) **1** *n* a grill or open fireplace for cooking food over coals or over an open flame. **2** *v* roast food over coals or open flame, or in the spicy sauce often used for this. **bar·be·cued, bar·be·cu·ing.**

> **USING WORDS . . . . barbecue**
>
> You may sometimes see this word written *barbeque,* with a *q.* This is incorrect spelling. Don't use it.

bar·ber (bàr′bər) *n* a person whose business is cutting hair and shaving or trimming beards.

bare (ber) **1** *adj* without any clothing, decoration, furniture, or anything extra: *bare legs, bare branches, bare walls, the bare facts.* **bar·er, bar·est, 2** *v* make bare; uncover or show: *The dog bared its teeth.* **bared, bar·ing.**
bare·back *adv* or *adj* on a horse's bare back.
bare·foot *adj* or *adv* without shoes or socks on.
bare·ly 1 *adv* only just; hardly: *He has barely enough money to live on.* **2** *adv* in a rather bare style: *The room was furnished barely but neatly.*
with your bare hands, without tools or weapons: *He can break bricks with his bare hands.*

bar·gain (bàr′gən) **1** *n* an agreement to trade or exchange: *Let's make a bargain: I'll do your chores if I can borrow your bike.* **2** *v* try to get a good price or make a good trade: *For ten minutes I stood bargaining with the farmer for her vegetables.* **3** *n* something good for a low price: *These skates are a bargain at $15.*
bargain for, expect; be ready for: *We expected rain, but the hail was more than we bargained for.*
into the bargain, besides; also: *I can't come; I've got piano lessons, and homework into the bargain.*

B b

barge (bàrj) **1** *n* a large, flat-bottomed boat for carrying loads. **2** *v* move clumsily: *He barged around the room, knocking things over.* **barged, barg·ing.**

barge in, *Informal.* enter rudely and without an invitation.

bark (bàrk) **1** *n* the tough outside covering of the trunk, branches, and roots of trees. **2** *v* the short, sharp sound a dog makes, or a sound like it, such as a cough. **3** *v* make this sound: *The dog barked.*

bar mitz·vah (bàr′ mits′və) *n* a Jewish boy who has reached the age of 13, the age of religious responsibility.

barn (bàrn) *n* a farm building for hay, grain, machinery, and animals.

barn·yard *n* the yard around a barn for farm animals.

bar·na·cle (bàr′nə kəl) *n* a small saltwater animal with a shell. It attaches itself to undersea things like rocks, the bottoms of ships, and docks.

ba·rom·e·ter (bə rom′ə tər) *n* an instrument that measures the pressure of the air and shows likely changes in the weather. –**bar′o·met′ric** (ber′ə met′rik), *adj.*

bar·rel (ber′əl) **1** *n* a container with round, flat ends and curved sides made of boards held together by hoops. **2** *n* the metal tube of a gun.

bar·ren (ber′ən) **1** *adj* not producing anything: *A desert is barren.* **2** ❋ *n* the Barrens, a barren stretch of land in northern Canada, west of Hudson Bay. Short grass, moss, and small wildflowers grow there in summer, but no trees. It is also called the **Barren Ground** or **Barren Lands.**

bar·ri·er (ber′ē ər) *n* something that blocks the way or separates: *Shyness can be a barrier to making friends. A barrier separated the two tennis courts.*

bar·ter (bàr′tər) *v* or *n* trade instead of using money to buy or sell: *He bartered his boat for a car* (*v*). *Barter is still used in some marketplaces* (*n*).

base (bās) *n* **1** the part that something rests on; the bottom: *The CN Tower rests on a wide base of steel and concrete.* **2** *v* build or rest something on a foundation: *Base your arguments on fact.* **based, bas·ing. 3** *n* in baseball, any of the four stations that players run to at the corners of the diamond-shaped field. **4** *n* in arithmetic, the number that is the starting point for a numbering system: *The base of the decimal system is ten.* **5** *n* a chemical that works against acids. Bases dissolve in water, and strong ones can burn flesh. **Alkali** is another word for base. **6** *adj* mean and selfish; low; cowardly: *To betray a friend is a base thing to do.* **bas·er, bas·est.**

base·ment *n* the lowest storey of a building, partly or completely below ground; cellar.

bash·ful (bash′fəl) *adj* shy and awkward around strangers: *The child was too bashful to say hello.* –**bash′ful·ly,** *adv,* –**bash′ful·ness,** *n.*

ba·sic (bā′sik) *adj* forming the base or starting point: *Addition, subtraction, multiplication, and division are the basic operations of arithmetic.* –**ba′si·cal·ly,** *adj.*

ba·sis *n* the fact, idea, feeling, etc. that something is built on: *The basis of their friendship was their interest in hockey.* pl **ba·ses** (bā′sēz).

ba·sin (bā′sən) **1** *n* a wide, shallow bowl used especially to hold water for washing. **2** *n* a low place in land, usually containing water, such as the Annapolis Basin in Nova Scotia. **3** *n* all the land drained by a river and the streams that flow into the river: *the St. Lawrence basin.*

bas·ket (bas′kit) *n* a container made of twigs, strips of wood, plastic, or metal, etc. woven together: *a clothes basket, a wastepaper basket, a fruit basket.*

baste (bāst) *v* drip or pour melted fat or butter or a sauce on meat as it is roasting: *He basted the turkey to brown it and keep it moist.* **bast·ed, bast·ing.**

A little brown bat— about 9 cm long; wingspread about 35 cm

bat (bat) **1** *n* a specially shaped wooden stick or club, used to hit the ball in baseball, cricket, etc. **2** *n* a flying animal that resembles a mouse with skinlike wings. Bats fly at night and feed mostly on insects.

right off the bat, right away.

batch (bach) *n* a quantity of anything made or handled as one lot or set: *a batch of cookies, a batch of mail.*

A bateau

❧ **ba·teau** (ba tō′) *n* a light, flat-bottomed riverboat: *Bateaux were used to carry freight and passengers between Montréal and Kingston.* *pl* **ba·teaux** (ba tōz′).

bath (bath) *n* a washing of the body. **bathing suit** (bā′ᴛʜing sūt′) a garment worn for swimming. **bath·room** *n* a room with a toilet, a sink, and often a bath or shower. A room with toilets in a public building is usually called a **washroom. bath·tub** *n* a tub to take a bath in. **bathe** (bāᴛʜ) **1** *v* take a bath: *She bathes every morning.* **2** *v* give a bath to: *We bathe our dog regularly.* **bathed, bath·ing.**

bat mitz·vah (bȧt′ mits′və) *n* a Jewish girl who has reached the age of 12, the age of religious responsibility.

ba·ton (bə ton′) **1** *n* a light, hollow metal rod twirled as an art: *She marched at the front of the Canada Day parade, twirling a baton.* **2** *n* a stick used by the leader of a band or choir to keep time and direct the performance. **3** *n* a stick passed from runner to runner in a relay race.

bat·ter (bat′ər) **1** *v* hit again and again so as to bruise, damage, or break: *The firefighter battered down the door with a heavy axe.* **2** *n* a thick liquid mixture made by beating together flour, milk, eggs, etc. –**bat′tered,** *adj.*

bat·ter·y (bat′ə rē) *n* a container holding materials that produce electricity by chemical action. A watch battery is tiny, round, and flat, while a flashlight battery is long and tube-shaped. *pl* **bat·ter·ies.**

bat·tle (bat′əl) *n* fight or struggle: *a battle with enemy soldiers, a battle of words, the battle against poverty.*

bawl (bol) *v* Informal. cry loudly: *The small boy bawled whenever he hurt himself.* **bawl out,** scold: *She bawled out her sister for denting her bicycle.*

bay (bā) **1** *n* a part of a sea or lake reaching into the land, such as Hudson Bay or the Bay of Fundy. **2** *n* a space, area, platform, etc. used for a special purpose: *The truck backed up to the loading bay of the warehouse.*

ba·zaar (bə zȧr′) **1** *n* a market. **2** *n* a sale, especially of used or homemade things, held to raise money.

B.C. *abbreviation for* before Christ. B.C. is used for times before Christ was born; A.D. is used for times after Christ was born: *From 20 B.C. to A.D. 50 is 70 years.*

beach (bēch) **1** *n* an almost flat shore of sand or little stones at the edge of a lake or ocean. **2** *v* pull up on the shore: *to beach a canoe.*

bead (bēd) **1** *n* a bit of glass, plastic, clay, etc. with a hole through it, so that it can be strung on a thread with others like it. **2** *n* a tiny ball, drop, or bubble: *beads of sweat.* **bead·y** *adj* small, round, and shiny: *That Canada goose has beady eyes.*

beak (bēk) **1** *n* the horny mouth of a bird. **2** *n* anything like this, such as the mouth of some turtles. **beak·er** *n* a glass container with a wide top and a little spout, used in laboratories.

beam (bēm) **1** *n* a large, long piece of wood, concrete, or steel used to support buildings. **2** *n* a ray or rays of light: *The beam from the flashlight made the cat's eyes shine.* **3** *v* look or smile brightly: *Her face beamed with delight.*

bean (bēn) **1** *n* a smooth, rather flat seed used as a vegetable: *pork and beans.* **2** *n* the long pod containing these seeds: *When young and fresh, green or yellow beans are good eaten raw.* **3** *n* any seed shaped like a bean: *coffee beans.* **bean·bag** *n* a small bag partly filled with dried beans or pellets, used to toss in play. A **beanbag chair** is a very large, specially shaped beanbag for sitting in.

bear (ber) **1** *v* carry: *That ice is too thin to bear your weight.* **2** *v* endure: *She can't bear the noise.* **3** *v* produce fruit: *This tree bore a lot of apples last year.* **4** *v* give birth to: *Women bear children.* **5** *n* a large, heavy animal with fur, a very short tail, and large, flat paws. The **brown bear, black bear,** and **polar bear** are all found in Canada. **bore, borne** or **born, bear·ing.** –**bear′a·ble,** *adj,* –**bear′er,** *n.*
a bear for punishment, someone who loves challenges and hard work.
bear with, be patient with.

beard (bērd) *n* the hair growing on a man's chin and cheeks.

beast (bēst) **1** *n* any animal except a human, especially a four-footed animal. **2** *n* a cruel or very rude person.
beast·ly *adj* or *adv* terrible or terribly: *Watch out, I'm in a beastly mood* (adj). *It's beastly cold in Yellowknife today* (adv).

beat (bēt) **1** *v* hit hard, again and again: *The cruel farmer beat his horse.* **2** *v* make a sound by hitting or being hit, especially according to a rhythm: *The drums beat loudly. The rain beats on the window.* **3** *v* move in and out, back and forth, up and down, etc.: *The bird beat its wings.* **4** *v* win against: *Their team beat ours by a huge score.* **beat, beat·en, beat·ing.**
off the beaten path, where few people go.

beau·ty (byū′tē) **1** *n* the quality that pleases in a person, flowers, music, pictures, etc.: *Robert Bateman's paintings capture the beauty of wildlife. There is beauty in a kind act.* **2** *n* something beautiful: *the beauties of nature.* pl **beau·ties.**
beau·ti·ful *adj* very pleasing to see, hear, experience, or think about: *a beautiful picture, beautiful music, a beautiful dream.* –**beau′ti·ful·ly,** *adv.*

A beaver—about 75 cm long excluding the tail; tail about 30 cm long and 16 cm wide

bea·ver (bē′vər) *n* a soft-furred animal with a broad, flat tail and feet adapted to swimming. It is a Canadian symbol.

be·cause (bi kuz′) *conj* **Because** is used to tell the reason for something: *Most children play tag because they enjoy it. Because we were very late, we ran.*

beck·on (bek′ən) *v* signal with the hand or head: *He beckoned me to follow.*

be·come (bi kum′) **1** *v* **Become** is used to talk about a change: *It is becoming colder. She became a mother last year.* **2** *v* seem proper for; suit; look good on: *That white dress becomes you.* **be·came, be·come, be·com·ing.**
become of, happen to: *What has become of the box of candy?*

bed (bed) **1** *n* anything to sleep or rest on. **2** *n* the bottom or base of something: *a muddy stream bed, a bed of concrete, a bed of roses.*
bed·ding *n* sheets, blankets, or anything else used to make a bed. **bed·rid·den** (bed′rid′ən) *adj* having to stay in bed; not able to be up and around: *I was bedridden with the flu for two days.*
bed·rock *n* the solid rock beneath the soil and looser rocks. **bed·room** *n* a room to sleep in.
bed·time *n* the usual time for going to bed: *His bedtime is nine o'clock.*

Bee: honeybees with a section of honeycomb

bee (bē) **1** *n* an insect with four wings that lives in large groups and makes honey and wax. Female bees can sting. **2** *n* a gathering for work and fun: *a quilting bee, a spelling bee.*
bee·hive 1 *n* a hive or house for bees. **2** *n* a busy, crowded place: *The West Edmonton Mall is a beehive in December.*

beef (bēf) **1** *n* the meat from a steer, cow, or bull, used for food. **2** *v* *Slang.* complain: *Some people are always beefing.*
beef up, *Informal.* make stronger, heavier, etc.

beep (bēp) *n* a short, sharp sound made by a machine. It is often a signal: *A beep from the microwave told us that our dinner was ready.*
beep·er *n* a small portable device that makes a beeping sound to let you know you should phone somebody, take a pill, etc.

beer (bēr) **1** *n* an alcoholic drink made from malt, water, yeast, and hops. **2** *n* a drink made from roots or plants, such as root beer or ginger beer. ❦ **beer parlour** or **parlor** a room in a hotel or tavern where beer is sold.

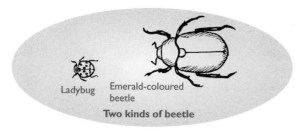

Ladybug Emerald-coloured beetle

Two kinds of beetle

bee·tle (bē′təl) *n* an insect with two pairs of wings–the hard, shiny front pair protects the soft flying pair.

be·fore (bi fȯr′) **1** *conj, prep,* or *adv* earlier than something else: *We always play games before the bell rings* (conj). **2** *adv* or *prep* in the past: *He has never been late before.* **3** *prep* or *adv* in front or ahead of someone or something: *The door opened and a little girl stood before me* (prep). **4** *conj* or *prep* rather than: *I'll give up the trip before I go with them* (conj).

beg (beg) **1** *v* ask people to give you food, clothes, or money as a gift: *The old man said that he had no way to live except by begging.* **2** *v* ask humbly or with all your heart: *She begged her brother to forgive her.* **begged, beg·ging.** –**beg′gar,** *n.* **beg off,** escape from a promise, duty, etc. by asking: *Although he had promised to go biking with me, he begged off because of a headache.*

be·gin (bi gin′) *v* start: *to begin work.* **be·gan, be·gun, be·gin·ning.**
be·gin·ner *n* a person learning to do something for the first time. **be·gin·ning 1** *n* a start: *Make a good beginning.* **2** *n* the first part: *I enjoyed this book from beginning to end.*

be·have (bi hāv′) *v* act: *She behaved very politely the whole time.* **be·haved, be·hav·ing. be·hav·iour** or **be·hav·ior** (bi hāv′yər) *n* a way of acting; actions: *His sulky behaviour turned everyone off.*

be·hind (bi hīnd′) **1** *adv* or *prep* at or toward the back of someone or something: *They walked along, the dog following behind* (adv). **2** *n* Informal. rear end; seat: *He fell on his behind.* **3** *prep* supporting: *Her friends are behind her.* **4** *adv* or *prep* late; later than someone or something else: *The buses are behind today* (adv).

be·ing (bē′ing) **1** *n* a person; a living creature: *Men, women, and children are human beings.* **2** *n* life; existence: *This world came into being long ago.*

belch (belch) **1** *v* or *n* burp. **2** *v* throw out with force: *The volcano belched fire and smoke.*

be·lieve (bi lēv′) **1** *v* think something is true or real: *Do you believe in ghosts?* **2** *v* think somebody tells the truth: *My friends believe me.* **3** *v* have faith; trust: *I'll believe in you, Cas, no matter what.* **be·lieved, be·liev·ing.** –**be·liev′a·ble,** *adj,* –**be·liev′er,** *n.*
be·lief (bi lēf′) **1** *n* what someone thinks is true; opinion: *It was once common belief that the world was flat.* **2** *n* religious faith; creed: *All are welcome here, regardless of belief.*

Bells: a handbell and a bell in a tower

bell (bel) **1** *n* a hollow metal object that rings when it is struck. It is often shaped like an upside-down cup. **2** *n* the stroke or sound of a bell: *Our teacher dismissed us before the last bell.*

bel·low (bel′ō) **1** *v* roar as a bull does. **2** *v* shout in a deep, loud voice: *The lifeguard bellowed to the swimmers to stay near the shore.* **3** *n* the sound of either of these.

bel·ly (bel′ē) **1** *n* the part of the body that contains the stomach and intestines; abdomen. **2** *n* the bulging part of anything, or the hollow in it: *the belly of a ship.* *pl* **bel·lies.**
belly button *Informal.* navel.

be·long (bi long′) **1** *v* have a proper place: *That book belongs on this shelf.* **2** *v* be accepted: *Right away, they made me feel that I belonged.*
be·long·ings *pl.n* things that belong to a person.
belong to, 1 be the property of: *Does this cap belong to you?* **2** be a part of or be a member of: *She belongs to the swim club.*

be·low (bi lō′) **1** *adv* in or to a lower place or part: *From the airplane we could see the fields below.* **2** *prep* lower than; under: *No one got below 9 out of 15 on the quiz.* **3** *adj* below zero on a thermometer: *That morning it was ten below in Winnipeg.*

belt (belt) **1** *n* a strip of leather, cloth, etc. worn around the body to tighten or hold up clothing, to hold tools, or as a decoration. **2** *n* any broad strip or band; an area or region: *a belt of trees. Wheat grows in the wheat belt of Saskatchewan.*

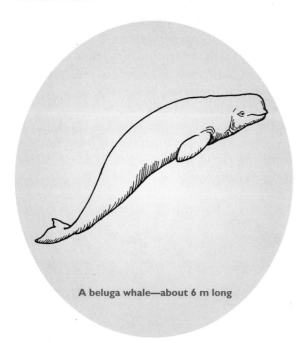

A beluga whale—about 6 m long

be·lu·ga (bə lü′gə) *n* a small white whale that lives in the Arctic and as far south as the Gulf of St. Lawrence. Like some other whales, the beluga is an endangered species.

bench (bench) **1** *n* a long seat, usually of wood or stone. **2** *n* a worktable used by a carpenter or other worker.

bend (bend) **1** *v* turn or curve out of a straight line: *The strong man bent the iron bar as if it were rubber. She bent to pick up a stone.* **2** *n* a turn or curve: *a sharp bend in the road.* **3** *v* direct: *She bent her mind to her homework.* **bent, bend·ing.**
around the bend, *Informal.* crazy: *His knuckle-cracking nearly drove me around the bend.*
bend over backward, try very hard for someone else: *We bent over backward to make him feel at home.*
bent *n* a habit or talent: *You have a bent for drawing.*
bent on, determined to do something: *She is bent on becoming a pilot.*
bent out of shape, *Slang.* angry.

be·neath (bi nēth′) **1** *adj* or *prep* below. **2** *prep* not good enough for: *The proud girl thought washing dishes was beneath her.*

ben·e·fit (ben′ə fit) **1** *n* a good, helpful thing or result: *One of the benefits of exercise is fitness.* **2** *v* be good for: *Rest will benefit a sick person.* **3 benefits,** *pl.n* money from the government to help people who need it. **ben·e·fit·ed** or **ben·e·fit·ted, ben·e·fit·ing** or **ben·e·fit·ting.**
ben·e·fac·tor *n* a person who has helped others through gifts or actions.
ben·e·fi·cial (ben′ə fish′əl) *adj* helpful: *Sunshine is beneficial to plants.* **be·nev·o·lent** *adj* kind: *Helping at the food bank is a benevolent act.*

ber·ry (ber′ē) *n* a small, juicy fruit that has two or more seeds: *Strawberries and currants are berries.* *pl* **ber·ries.**

ber·serk (bər zərk′) *adj* or *adv* in a frenzy.
go berserk, go into a frenzy: *Paul went berserk when he learned the bus had left without him.*

be·side (bi sīd′) *prep* by the side of; near; close to: *Grass grows beside the creek.*

be·sides 1 *adv* also; more than that; moreover: *He didn't want to quarrel; besides, he had come to enjoy himself.* **2** *prep* in addition to: *Others came to the picnic besides our own family.*
beside oneself, out of one's mind: *He was beside himself with worry over his lost dog.*
beside the point, not related to the topic.

best (best) **1** *adj* or *n* most excellent: *Who does the best work (adj)? We want only the best (n).* **2** *adv* in the most excellent way: *Who reads best?* **3** *adj* favourite; closest: *your best friend.* **4** *n* the most you can do or give: *I did my best to explain.*
at best, under the most favourable circumstances: *Summer is at best rather short.*
get the best of, beat; defeat.
make the best of, do as well as possible with: *Try to make the best of a bad job.*
the best part of, most of: *She worked on her project for the best part of the day.*

bet (bet) **1** *v* promise to give something to someone you disagree with if that person is right and you are wrong: *I bet you a loonie I will pass this test.* **2** *n* the money or thing promised: *A loonie is not much of a bet.* **3** *v* be very sure: *I bet they'll be late.* **bet, bet·ting.**
a safe bet, something you can be sure of.

be·tray (bi trā′) *v* be unfaithful or disloyal to: *She betrayed her friends by breaking her promise. The traitors betrayed their country.* **–be·tray′al,** *n.*

bet·ter (bet′ər) **1** *adj* more desirable or of higher quality: *We need a better computer than this.* **2** *adv* in a more excellent way: *I will plan better next time.* **3** *adj* improved in health: *Are you feeling better?*

better off, in a better condition: *Grandma is better off now that she has a job. You'd be better off with a warmer jacket.*

get the better of, beat; defeat: *The tortoise got the better of the hare.*

be·tween (bi twēn′) **1** *prep* or *adv* having to do with a space, time, or amount that has two things as its boundaries: *between the house and the barn, between three and four o'clock.* **2** *prep* to talk about a connection that involves two things or people: *You can choose between this video and that one. Jess and I went fishing; between us we caught nine fish. There is now a road between Nova Scotia and Prince Edward Island.*

between you and me, as a secret: *Let's keep this between you and me.*

USING WORDS . between/among

Use **between** when there are just two people or things involved: *Bo and I had only three dollars between us.*

Use **among** for more than two: *They divided the work among the four of them.*

bev·er·age (bev′ə rij) *n* a drink. Milk, tea, coffee, juice, and pop are beverages.

be·ware (bi wer′) *v* be careful; be on your guard: *Beware! Falling rock. Beware of strangers.*

be·wil·der (bi wil′dər) *v* confuse completely; fill with uncertainty: *The little boy was bewildered by the noise of the crowd.* **–be·wil′der·ment,** *n.*

be·yond (bi yond′) **1** *prep* past: *It is an hour beyond the time I should have gone. Daria lives beyond the edge of town.* **2** *prep* out of the reach of: *He was beyond medical help. The meaning of this story is beyond me.* **3** *prep* more than: *The price was beyond what he could pay.*

bi·as (bī′əs) **1** *n* a tendency to favour one side too much: *The writer's bias was easy to recognize.* **2** *v* to influence unfairly. **bi·assed** or **bi·ased, bi·as·sing** or **bi·as·ing.**

bi·assed or **bi·ased** *adj* giving or having an unbalanced view: *She was biassed where her children were concerned.*

Bi·ble (bī′bəl) **1** *n* the book of sacred writings of the Christian religion; the **Old Testament** and the **New Testament**. **2** *n* **bible,** a highly respected book on any subject. **–bib′li·cal** (bib′lə kəl), *adj.*

bib·li·og·ra·phy (bib′lē og′rə fē) *n* a list of books, articles, etc. about a certain subject or by a certain author. *pl* **bib·li·og·ra·phies.**

Grammar ✓*Check* .. **bibliography**

A **bibliography** is a list of all the works used in a project, or in research.

Place it on a separate page at the end.

All bibliography entries should include:
• the name of the author(s)
• the title of the work
• the publisher's name, with the date and place

Arrange the entries alphabetically, by author's name.

bi·car·bo·nate of soda (bī kȧr′bə nit əv sō′də) a white powder used in cooking, medicine, etc. **Baking soda** is the usual name for it.

bi·ceps (bī′seps) *n* the large muscle at the front of the upper arm, used to bend the elbow. *pl* **bi·ceps** or **bi·ceps·es.**

bick·er (bik′ər) *v* argue about things that don't matter: *The cousins bickered all afternoon.*

bi·cy·cle (bī′sə kəl) *n* a vehicle with two wheels, one behind the other, that support a light metal frame with handlebars and a seat for the rider. You ride it by pushing two pedals with your feet.

bike (bīk) *n Informal.* bicycle. A **mountain bike** or **all-terrain bike** (ATB) has wide tires with deep tread, and nearly straight handlebars. A **BMX bike** has similar tires but high, V-shaped handlebars with a bar connecting them across the middle.

WORD HISTORY .... bicycle

Bicycle is one of many words in English that use the prefix **bi-**. This prefix comes from Latin and means "two." In **bicycle** it is joined to **cycle,** from the Greek *kyklos* meaning "wheel." A bicycle has two wheels!

There are several other bi- words in this dictionary that have to do with *two*. See if you can find them.

bid (bid) **1** *v* offer to pay a certain price: *First she bid $5 for the tablecloth. He then bid $6.* **2** *n* an offer, a try: *My bid was $7. The prisoner made a bid for freedom.* **bid, bid·ding.** **–bid′ding,** *n*.

big (big) **1** *adj* large: *a big room, a big book. An elephant is a big animal.* **2** *adj* older or grown up: *my big brother.* **3** *adj* important: *This is big news.* **big·ger, big·gest. –big′ness,** *n*.
big deal! *Informal.* So what? It's not important!

Big·foot (big′fùt′) *n* according to legend, a very large, hairy, humanlike creature that lives wild in the mountains of the Pacific Coast: *They claimed they saw Bigfoot during a hiking trip.* **Sasquatch** is another name for this creature.

big·horn (big′hòrn′) *n* a greyish-brown wild sheep of the Rocky Mountains. *pl* **big·horn** or **big·horns.**

big·ot (big′ət) *n* a prejudiced person. Someone who treats people with contempt without even knowing them. **–big′ot·ed,** *adj*.

bi·lin·gual (bī ling′gwəl) **1** *adj* able to speak two languages. **2** ❦ *adj* able to speak both English and French.

bill (bil) **1** *n* a paper showing how much is owed or paid: *You can't return this to the store without the bill.* **2** *n* a piece of paper money: *a five-dollar bill.* **3** *n* a planned law. In Canada, a bill becomes an act if it gets a majority vote in Parliament. **4** *n* the horny part of the jaws of a bird; a beak.
bill of rights a statement of human rights and basic freedoms.
fill the bill, *Informal.* be just what is needed.
foot the bill, *Informal.* pay the bill.

bill·board (bil′bòrd′) *n* a large outdoor sign displaying an advertisement.

bil·lion (bil′yən) *n or adj* a thousand million (1 000 000 000).

bin (bin) *n* a large box for holding loose things like potatoes, toys, bulk foods, etc.

bi·na·ry (bī′nə rē) *adj* having to do with two. In math, the **binary system** uses only two digits, 0 and 1.

binary digit (bī′nə rē dij′it) either of the digits 0 or 1, that are the basic unit of information in computers. You can think of a light switch with 0 as *off* and 1 as *on*. **Binary digit** is often shortened to **bit**.

bind (bīnd) **1** *v* tie: *She bound the package with a strong cord.* **2** *v* hold by a promise, duty, law, etc.: *Signing this agreement binds you to keep it.* **bound, bind·ing.**

bind·er 1 *n* a cover with metal rings in it for holding loose sheets of paper together. **2** *n* a machine that cuts stalks of grain and ties them into bundles.

Eyepiece   Binoculars

bi·noc·u·lars (bə nok′yə lərz) *pl.n* an instrument that makes objects seem bigger and closer when you look through it.

bio– *a prefix meaning* life or living things. A *biography* is the story of someone's life. *Biology* is the study of living plants and animals.
bi·o·de·grad·a·ble (bī′ō di grā′də bəl) *adj* able to be broken down by a natural process: *The paper wrappers were biodegradable so she added them to the compost.* **bi·og·ra·phy** (bī og′rə fē) *n* the story of a person's life. **–bi·og′ra·pher,** *n*, **–bi′o·graph′i·cal** (bī′ə graf′ə kəl), *adj*.
bi·ol·o·gy (bī ol′ə jē) *n* the science of living things; the study of plants (botany) and animals (zoology).
–bi′o·log′i·cal (bī′ə loj′ə kəl), *adj*, **–bi·ol′o·gist,** *n*.
bi·on·ic (bī on′ik) **1** *adj* having to do with an artificial body part that strengthens or replaces a natural one, and works electronically: *a bionic arm.* **2** *adj* in science fiction, having superhuman powers given by this kind of body part.
bi·o·sphere (bī′ə sfēr′) *n* the parts of the earth and its atmosphere that plants and animals can live in: *Some scientists worry that our biosphere is shrinking.*

bird (bərd) *n* an animal that lays eggs and has wings, two legs, and a body covered with feathers. Most birds can fly. A **bird of prey**, such as a hawk or owl, is one that eats other birds or small animals.

birth (bərth) **1** *n* the act or fact of being born: *the birth of a baby.* **2** *n* a beginning: *the birth of a nation.*

birth·day *n* the date that a person is born.

birth·place *n* the place where a person was born or something started: *Kingston, Ontario, was the birthplace of hockey.*

bi·sect (bī sekt′) *v* in mathematics, divide something into two equal parts.

bi·son (bī′zən) *n* a large, shaggy, grass-eating wild animal of the North American prairies. **Buffalo** is another name for it. *pl* **bi·son.**

bit (bit) **1** *n* part of a tool for drilling. **2** *n* the part of a bridle that goes in the horse's mouth. **3** *n* a small piece or amount: *bits of broken glass. Could I have a bit of your orange? I am a bit tired.* **4** *n* the basic unit of information in computers; short for **binary digit.**

bite (bīt) **1** *v* grab, cut into, or cut off with the teeth: *She bit the carrot. Don't bite your fingernails.* **2** *n* a wound made by biting or stinging: *Don't scratch your mosquito bite.* **bit, bit·ten, bit·ing. bite the bullet,** bravely face something very difficult. **bite the dust,** fall dead, be defeated, or come to an end.

WORD HISTORY . . . . . bite the bullet

The expression **bite the bullet** comes from the days when wounded soldiers used to have surgery on the battlefield with no anesthetic. They were given a bullet to bite on to keep them from crying out in pain.

---

bit·ter (bit′ər) **1** *adj* having a sharp, unpleasant taste: *bitter medicine.* **2** *adj* full of pain, disappointment, anger, or grief: *a bitter defeat, a bitter cry. The death of his father was a bitter loss.* **3** *adj* very cold: *a bitter wind.* –**bit′ter·ly,** *adv,* –**bit′ter·ness,** *n.*

bi·zarre (bə zàr′) *adj* extremely strange or odd: *The bizarre scarecrow was dressed in slippers, raincoat, and a woman's hat.*

blab (blab) *v* tell secrets; talk too much. **Blabber** is another word for this. **blabbed, blab·bing.** –**blab′ber·mouth,** *n.*

black (blak) **1** *n* the colour of fresh tar. Black is the darkest colour; pure black reflects no light. **2** *n* Usually, **Black,** a person with African ancestors. –**black′ness,** *n.*
black and blue badly bruised. **black and white** writing; print: *You can read it right there in black and white.* **black·en** *v* make or become black, dark, or dirty: *Slush from traffic blackened the snow.* **black fly** a tiny black fly whose bite is itchy and painful. Black flies are most plentiful in late spring. **black·head** *n* a pore in the skin plugged with dirt, dead cells, and oil. **black hole** an area in space with such strong gravity that nothing caught in it can escape, not even light. **black ice** ice that forms on roads and sidewalks, so thin it is invisible or looks like wet pavement.
black·mail *n* get or try to get money or some other advantage from a person by saying that if he or she does not give what is asked, you will tell his or her secrets. **black·out 1** *n* a short spell of blindness or unconsciousness. **2** *n* a power failure: *The storm caused a blackout in our neighbourhood.* **3** *n* the act of holding back news or other information: *Sports blackouts are used to boost ticket sales.*
black out, become unconscious; faint: *I don't know what happened after that, because I blacked out.*

blad·der (blad′ər) *n* a soft, thin bag in the body that receives urine from the kidneys.

blade (blād) **1** *n* the cutting part of anything like a knife or sword. **2** *n* the flat part of a leaf or of anything else: *the blade of a paddle, the shoulder blade.*

blame (blām) **1** *v* say that something bad or wrong was caused by: *We blamed the fog for our accident.* **2** *n* the act of saying this about someone or something: *I missed an easy catch, so I took the blame.* **blamed, blam·ing.**
blame·less *adj* not deserving to be criticized for anything.
be to blame, deserve to be blamed: *Each person said somebody else was to blame.*

blank (blangk) **1** *n* a space left empty or to be filled in: *Leave a blank after each word.* **2** *adj* not written or printed on: *blank paper.*
draw a blank, try something and fail completely.

blan·ket (blangk′it) **1** *n* a soft, heavy covering of wool or other material to keep people or animals warm. **2** *n* anything like a blanket: *A blanket of snow covered the ground.*

blast (blast) **1** *n* a strong, sudden rush of wind or air: *the icy blasts of a Canadian winter.* **2** *v* make by blowing up with dynamite, etc.: *The miners blasted a tunnel through the rock.* **3** *n* *Slang.* a fun and exciting time: *We had a blast at the Halloween party.*
blast off, take off, as a rocket does: *Make ready to blast off.*

blaze (blāz) **1** *n* burn or shine brightly: *The house blazed with lights at Diwali.* **2** *v* burst out in anger: *She blazed at the insult.* **blazed, blaz·ing.**

bleach (blēch) **1** *v* whiten by chemicals or sunlight: *We bleached the stains out of the shirt. Bleached bones lay on the desert.* **2** *n* a chemical used to whiten.

bleach·ers *pl.n* the rows of seats at outdoor games such as baseball and football.

bleak (blēk) **1** *adj* bare and empty: *the bleak, rocky peak of Mount Robson.* **2** *adj* harsh; dreary; dismal: *A prisoner's life is bleak.* **–bleak′ly,** *adv,* **–bleak′ness,** *n.*

bleed (blēd) **1** *v* lose blood: *This cut is bleeding.* **2** *v* feel pity, sorrow, or grief: *His heart bled for the children who had lost their parents.*
bled (bled), **bleed·ing.**

blend (blend) **1** *v* mix thoroughly: *Blend these ingredients for the cake.* **2** *v* lead into each other gradually: *The colours of the rainbow blend into one another.*

bless (bles) **1** *v* cause good things and experiences to come to someone: *Our grandparents have blessed our family in many ways.* **2** *v* make holy: *The bishop blessed the new church.*
blessed or **blest, bless·ing.**
bless·ing 1 *n* a prayer of thanks or of dedication. **2** *n* a wish for happiness and success: *When she left home, she received her parents' blessing.* **3** *n* good fortune: *Peace is a great blessing.*

blind (blīnd) **1** *adj* not able to see: *The person with the white cane is blind.* **2** *v* make unable to see: *The bright lights blinded me for a moment.* **3** *n* a window covering, heavier and stiffer than a curtain, that can be closed by pulling it down or sideways. A **Venetian blind** is made of strips

going across; a vertical blind has strips going up and down. **–blind′ly,** *adv,* **–blind′ness,** *n.*
blind·fold *n* something covering the eyes: *They used a scarf for a blindfold.*

blink (blingk) *v* close and open the eyes quickly: *to blink your eyes.*

bliss (blis) *n* very great happiness; perfect joy: *For Marci, a day at Wasaga Beach is pure bliss.* **–bliss′ful,** *adj,* **–bliss′ful·ly,** *adv.*

blis·ter (blis′tər) *n* a little bubble filled with watery liquid, that forms on the skin because of burning or rubbing: *My new shoes are making blisters on my heels.*

bliz·zard (bliz′ərd) *n* a long, violent, blinding snowstorm, usually with temperatures of -10°C or colder.

bloat (blōt) *v* swell; puff up.

blob (blob) *n* a small, soft drop or lump: *Blobs of wax covered the candlestick.*

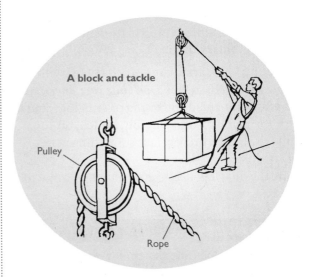

A block and tackle

Pulley

Rope

block (blok) **1** *n* a solid piece of wood, stone, ice, etc. with straight sides: *The child loved to play with blocks.* **2** *v* stop or prevent: *to block traffic.* **3** *n* the distance between two streets: *Walk one block east.*
block·ade *n* something designed to stop people from getting through: *The protesters put up a blockade on the road.* **block and tackle** a set of pulleys and ropes used to lift or pull heavy loads. **block·head** *n* a stupid person; fool.

blond (blond) **1** *adj* light in colour: *blond hair, blond furniture.* **2** *n* a person with light hair. **Blonde** is also used for this.

blood (blud) *n* the red liquid flowing through your body, that shows when you cut your skin. Blood flows through veins and arteries, or **blood vessels**, carrying oxygen and digested food to all parts of the body and taking away waste.

blood bank a supply of blood that hospitals can use for patients, given by **blood donors**.

blood·cur·dling *adj* terrifying: *We heard a bloodcurdling scream.* **blood·sucker** *n* a leech or other animal that sucks blood.

blood·thirst·y *adj* eager to kill: *the bloodthirsty pirate.* **blood·y** *adj* bleeding or covered with blood: *a bloody nose, a bloody bandage.*

in cold blood, cruelly and on purpose.

make your blood boil, make you very angry.

make your blood run cold, terrify you.

bloom (blūm) **1** *n* a flower. **2** *v* have flowers; open into a flower: *Many plants bloom in spring.* **3** *n* a look of health and beauty: *A year of country living brought the bloom back to their cheeks.* **4** *n* the powdery coating on some leaves and fruits such as grapes and plums.

blos·som (blos′əm) **1** *n* a flower, especially on a fruit tree: *apple blossoms.* **2** *v* have flowers; open into flowers. **3** *v* develop: *He blossomed into an excellent actor.*

blot (blot) **1** *n* or *v* stain or spot: *an ink blot on a piece of paper* (*n*). **2** *v* dry or soak up with paper, a cloth, etc.: *I blotted the spill with a paper towel.* **blot·ted, blot·ting.**

blouse (blouz) *n* a shirt for women and girls.

blow (blō) **1** *n* a hard hit; a knock; stroke: *I got a blow to the head from a falling branch.* **2** *n* something that causes hurt or loss; a severe shock: *His mother's death was a great blow to him.* **3** *v* move air in a stream: *The wind blew gently.* **4** *v* make a sound using a strong stream of air: *to blow a horn. The whistle blew.* **5** *v* explode, burst, burn out, or ruin in some other way: *to blow a fuse or a tire.* **blew, blown, blow·ing.**

blow·hole 1 *n* a hole for breathing in the top of the head of some sea mammals, such as whales. **2** *n* a hole in the ice where whales, seals, etc. come to breathe.

blow out of the water, *Slang.* be far better than; defeat totally.

blow over, pass by or be forgotten. *After a while the big fuss blew over.*

blow someone away or **blow someone's mind,** *Slang.* amaze or shock someone.

blow up, 1 explode. **2** fill with air: *to blow up a balloon.* **3** *Informal.* get very angry: *Mom blew up at me for getting tar on the rug.* Other expressions for this are **blow your top, blow your stack.** **4** enlarge: *We blew the photo up into a poster.* **come to blows,** start fighting.

blub·ber (blub′ər) *n* the fat of some sea mammals, such as whales.

Bluejays—about 30 cm long including the tail

blue (blū) **1** *n* the colour of the clear sky in daylight. **2** *adj* sad: *I felt blue when my best friend moved away.* **blu·er, blu·est.** **–blu′ish,** *adj.* **blue·ber·ry** *n* a small, round, blue berry that is good to eat and grows on a small bush. **blue·jay** or **blue jay** *n* a noisy, chattering North American bird with a crest and a blue back.

❀ **Blue·nose** *n* the name given to a famous boat built in Nova Scotia. It was a special kind of sailboat called a **schooner.** The *Bluenose* sailed from 1921 to 1946 and was the fastest sailing boat in the North Atlantic fishing fleets.

a blue streak, very much or very fast: *When Morgan came home from camp, he talked a blue streak for two days, telling us about it.*

once in a blue moon, very rarely: *Once in a blue moon she phones me up.*

out of the blue, completely unexpectedly: *Their visit came out of the blue.*

bluff (bluf) **1** *n* a high, steep cliff. **2** ❀ *n* a line or clump of trees on the flat prairie: *The farmhouse was sheltered from the wind by a bluff.* **3** *v* pretend to be confident in order to get others to respect you or do what you want: *She bluffed her way through the interview.* **4** *n* a threat that cannot be carried out.

blun·der (blun′dər) **1** *n* a stupid mistake. **2** *v* move or act blindly or clumsily: *Carl stumbled around, blundering into furniture in the dark.*

blunt (blunt) **1** *adj* not sharp; dull: *a blunt knife.* **2** *adj* giving your opinion without being careful of the feelings of others: *blunt criticism.*

blur (blər) *v* make fuzzy in form or outline: *Mist blurred our view of Confederation Bridge.* **blurred, blur·ring. –blur′ry,** *adj.*

blurt (blərt) *v* say suddenly or without thinking: *He blurted out the secret.*

blush (blush) *v* turn red in the face: *He was so shy that he blushed every time he was spoken to.*

blus·ter (blus′tər) **1** *v* storm or blow noisily and violently: *The wind blustered around the house.* **2** *v* talk loudly, roughly, and arrogantly: *When he was excited and angry, he blustered a great deal.* **–blus′ter·y,** *adj.*

board (bȯrd) **1** *n* a wide, thin piece of wood used for building, etc.: *We used pine boards to make the shelves.* **2** ❧ **the boards,** *pl.n* the wooden guard fence surrounding the ice of a hockey rink. **3** *n* meals provided for pay: *She charges $75 a week for board.* **4** *n* a group of people managing something; council: *a school board.* **5** *v* get on a bus, plane, etc.: *We board the school bus at the corner of Yonge Street.*

board·walk *n* a sidewalk made of boards, usually on a waterfront: *She liked to stroll along the boardwalk early in the morning.*

on board, on a train, aircraft, etc.: *When everybody was on board, the plane took off.*

boast (bōst) *v* talk too proudly; brag: *She boasts about her new car.* **–boast′ful,** *adj.*

boat (bōt) *n* a vessel for travelling on water, such as a motorboat, a rowboat, or a sailboat.

bob (bob) **1** *v* move up and down with short, quick motions: *The duckling bobbed up and down on the waves.* **2** *v* to cut short. **3** *n* a float on a fishing line. **bobbed, bob·bing.**

bob·cat *n* a wild cat closely related to the Canada lynx but having a longer tail, shorter ears, and smaller paws. **bob·sled** *n* a long closed-in sled with a steering wheel and brakes. Bobsledding is an Olympic sport.

bod·y (bod′ē) **1** *n* all the material that makes up a person, animal, or plant: *This girl has a strong, healthy body.* **2** *n* the main part of a person or animal, not including the head, arms, or legs: *He has a short body and long legs.* **3** *n* a group or mass: *The entire student body went to the play. Lake Huron is a body of water.* **4** *n* thickness or fullness: *This shampoo is supposed to add body to your hair.* pl **bod·ies.**

bod·y·check *n* in hockey, bumping into the player who has the puck. **bod·y·guard** *n* a person or group of people who guard someone: *A bodyguard goes with the Prime Minister all the time.*

bog (bog) *n* an area of wet, soft, spongy ground. **–bog′gy,** *adj.*
get bogged down, get stuck.

boil (boil) **1** *v* make or be so hot that bubbles form and steam or vapour rises: *Water boils at 100°C. Boil some water for tea.* **2** *v* be very excited or stirred up: *to boil with anger.* **3** *n* a red, painful swelling on the skin.
boil down, shorten by getting rid of unimportant parts: *He boiled down his notes to a list of the main facts.*

bois·ter·ous (boi′stə rəs) *adj* noisy and rough in a cheerful way: *a boisterous game.*

bold (bōld) *adj* brave; daring: *The bold voyageurs travelled thousands of kilometres by canoe.* **–bold′ly,** *adv,* **–bold′ness,** *n.*

bolt (bōlt) **1** *n* an object like a screw but with a flat end instead of a point. **2** *n* a sliding lock for a door, gate, etc. **3** *v* fasten with a bolt: *The two metal plates are bolted together.* **4** *n* a stroke of lightning. **5** *v* run away suddenly: *The horse bolted.* **6** *v* swallow food quickly without chewing: *Don't bolt your food.*
a bolt from the blue, something completely unexpected.
bolt upright, stiff and straight: *Awakened by a noise, he sat bolt upright in bed.*

bomb (bom) *n* a container filled with explosive that is set off by a fuse or by hitting something.
bom·bard (bom bȧrd′) **1** *v* attack with bombs or big guns, or anything that can be thrown. **2** *v* direct many questions, remarks, etc. at: *She bombarded me with suggestions.* **–bom·bard′ment,** *n.*

A Bombardier

❧ **Bom·bar·dier** (bom′bə dēr′ *or* bom bȧrd′yā) *n* a trademark *for* a large vehicle for travelling over snow and ice, usually with tracked wheels.

bond (bond) **1** *n* anything that ties or unites: *a bond of love between sisters.* **2** *v* start to love or feel close to someone: *Dad has not bonded with our new puppy yet.*

bone (bōn) *n* one of the pieces of the skeleton of an animal. –**bone'less,** *adj,* –**bon'y,** *adj.*

bon·fire (bon'fir') *n* a large fire built outdoors: *We warmed ourselves around the bonfire.*

WORD HISTORY . . . . bonfire

This word was originally *bonefire*, that is, a funeral fire for burning dead bodies.

---

bo·nus (bō'nəs) *n* something given free, as an extra: *The last question on the quiz is a bonus.*

book (bůk) **1** *n* a number of pages bound together, for reading or for writing in: *a homework book, a story book.* **2** *v* reserve; ask for something ahead of time: *We booked a table at the restaurant.* **book·case** *n* a piece of furniture with shelves for holding books. **book·let** *n* a little book with paper covers. **book·worm 1** *n* any of various insects that eat away at the bindings or pages of books: *The librarian was concerned about silverfish in her collection, one of the worst bookworms.* **2** *n* somebody who loves to read: *All the kids in that family were bookworms.*

boom (būm) **1** *n* a deep, hollow sound like the roar of thunder: *the boom of a bass drum.* **2** *n* a sudden rapid growth in business, population, etc.: *There has been a boom in computer sales in recent years.* **3** *n* a large raft of logs being towed over water.

boost (būst) **1** *v* lift or push from below or behind. **2** *v* increase: *The store has boosted its prices.*

boot (būt) **1** *n* a strong outer covering for the foot and ankle and often, the whole lower leg. **2** *v* or *n* kick: *I booted the can off the sidewalk* (*v*). **3** *v* **boot up,** start the operating system of a computer, usually by turning the computer on. **give someone the boot,** send someone away or fire a worker in an unkind way.

too big for your boots, too proud of yourself.

you can bet your boots, you can be very sure.

booth (būth) *n* a closed-in or partly closed-in space for a certain purpose. Public telephones are often in booths, and a market has booths where people show and sell their things. *pl* **booths** (būŦHz *or* būths).

bor·der (bôr'dər) **1** *n* a boundary separating two provinces, states, countries, etc.: *We reached Detroit by crossing the border at Windsor.* **2** *v* form a boundary with: *Manitoba borders Ontario.* **3** *n* an edge, or a strip on the edge: *The tablecloth had a lace border.*

bore (bôr) **1** *v* make a hole or tunnel through something: *A drill can bore through wood or cement.* **2** *v* make someone tired and uninterested: *The TV show bored me so much I turned it off.* –**bored, bor·ing.** –**bore'dom,** *n.*

born (bôrn) **1** *v* brought into life: *He was born on May 17.* **2** *adj* by birth; by nature: *a born athlete.*

bor·row (bô'rō) **1** *v* get something from another person with the understanding that it must be returned: *Are you finished with that book you borrowed from me?* **2** *v* take and use as one's own: *The word* toboggan *was borrowed from the Abenaki language.* –**bor'row·er,** *n.*

CONFUSABLES . . . . borrow

borrow means "get"
When you borrow something, you get it from someone: *Saito wants to borrow Janna's bicycle.*

lend means "give"
When you lend something, you give it to someone for a time: *Janna was happy to lend her bicycle to Saito.*

---

boss (bos) *Informal.* **1** *n* the one in charge; a person who hires workers or tells them what to do. **2** *v* give orders to: *Don't boss me around!* **boss·y** *adj Informal.* always telling others what to do and how to do it. **boss·i·er, boss·i·est.**

bot·a·ny (bot'ə nē) *n* the science of plants. –**bo·tan'i·cal** (bə tan'ə kəl), *adj,* –**bot'a·nist,** *n.*

botch (boch) *v* do a bad job of something: *They tried to make a model airplane, but they botched it.*

both (bōth) *adj, pron,* or *conj* two, when only two are thought of; the one and the other: *Both blouses are white* (*adj*). *Both belong to her, and they are both new* (*pron*). *She was both strong and healthy* (*conj*).

both·er (boŦH'ər) **1** *n* worry; fuss; trouble or extra work: *What a lot of bother about nothing.* **2** *v* spend the effort, time, or worry; take the trouble: *Don't bother to write it down, I'll remember it.* **3** *v* annoy or make uncomfortable: *The flies are bothering me.*

bot·tle (bot′əl) **1** *n* a container for holding liquids, usually made of glass or plastic, with a narrow top and no handles. **2** *v* put into bottles. **bot·tled, bot·tling.**

bot·tle·neck *n* something that makes going forward difficult or slow: *a bottleneck in traffic.*

bottle up, hold in; keep back: *He bottled up his anger and said nothing.*

bot·tom (bot′əm) **1** *n* the deepest or lowest part: *the bottom of a tree, the bottom of a hill, the bottom of my heart.* **2** *n* the underside or the floor of something: *the bottom of the sea. The bottom of that glass is wet.* –**bot′tom·less,** *adj.*

bought *v* the past tense of **buy.**

boul·der (bōl′dər) *n* a large rock.

bounce (bouns) **1** *v* fly into the air after hitting a surface, like a ball: *to bounce up and down on the bed.* **2** *n* one act of hitting a surface and flying back or up: *I caught the ball on the first bounce.* **bounced, bounc·ing.** –**boun′cy,** *adj.*

bound (bound) **1** *v* leap; jump: *The mountain goats bounded from rock to rock.* **2** *v* form the boundary of; limit: *Prince Edward Island is bounded by water on all sides.* **3** *adj* going; on the way: *Where are you bound? I am bound for home.* –**bound′less,** *adj.*

bound·a·ry *n* a line that divides two areas or forms the edge or limit of something: *Lake Ontario forms part of the boundary between Canada and the United States.*

out of bounds, outside the area allowed by rules, custom, or law: *She kicked the ball out of bounds.*

USING WORDS . . . . . bound

This word **bound** often appears in compounds meaning "stuck somewhere":
housebound = stuck in the house
snowbound = stuck somewhere because of snow
strikebound = stopped because of a strike

---

bou·quet (bū kā′ *or* bō kā′) **1** *n* a bunch of flowers. **2** *n* fragrance: *The perfume has a delicate bouquet.*

bow (bou *for 1 and 2,* bō *for 3-5*) **1** *v* bend the body or lower the head in greeting, respect, etc.: *The man bowed to his dance partner.* **2** *v* give in: *We cannot bow to their every wish.* **3** *n* a knot with loops, often for decoration: *a bow of ribbon.*

4 *n* a weapon for shooting arrows. **5** *n* a light wooden rod for playing a violin, cello, etc.

bowl (bōl) **1** *n* a hollow, rounded dish, usually without handles. **2** *v* play the game of bowling. –**bowl′ful′,** *n.*

bowl·ing *n* an indoor game where you roll a heavy ball at wooden pins to knock them down. It is played in a **bowling alley.**

box (boks) **1** *n* a usually rectangular container, with or without a lid, made of wood, metal, cardboard, etc. to pack or put things in.
2 *v* fight with the fists as a sport: *My sister and I would box in the basement to practise our skills.*

boy (boi) *n* a male child. –**boy′hood′,** *n,* –**boy′ish,** *adj.*

brace (brās) **1** *n* something that holds parts in place; a support: *We used a log as a brace for the leaning wall.* **2 braces,** *pl.n* a special set of wires worn on your teeth to straighten them.
3 *v* make firm or steady by supporting: *I braced my foot on a rock and pulled hard on the rope.* **braced, brac·ing.**

brace·let *n* a band or chain worn around the wrist or arm.

brack·et (brak′it) **1** *n* an L-shaped support sticking out from a wall, used to hold up a shelf, etc. **2** *n* any of these signs, ( ), [ ], or { }, used around words or numbers to separate them from others.

brag (brag) *v* talk very proudly: *He bragged about his new computer.* **bragged, brag·ging.**

braid (brād) **1** *n* a band or cord formed by weaving together three or more strands of hair, ribbon, straw, etc.: *a vest trimmed with gold braid.* **2** *v* weave or twine three or more strands of hair, ribbon, straw, etc. together: *She can braid her own hair.*

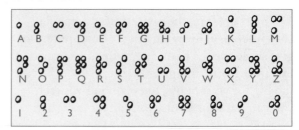

The alphabet and numerals in braille

braille (brāl) *n* a system of writing and printing for blind people. The letters in braille are made of raised dots and you read by feeling them.

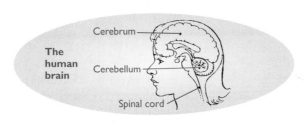

The human brain

brain (brān) 1 n the mass of nerve cells inside the skull or head of humans and animals, used in feeling and thinking. 2 Often, **brains,** *pl.n* intelligence: *A dog has more brains than a worm.* –**brain′y,** *adj.*

brain·storm 1 *n* a sudden bright idea: *Patty had a brainstorm that proved to be the answer to our problem.* 2 *v* try to solve a problem by having a meeting where everyone shares ideas: *We brainstormed all morning but nothing useful resulted.* **brain·wash** *v* use strong persuasion, repetition, and sometimes even trickery or torture to replace what is in somebody's mind with new thoughts or ideas: *They were brainwashed into buying a new car when they didn't need one.*

brake (brāk) 1 *n* something used to slow down or stop a vehicle or machine by pressing or rubbing against a moving part. 2 *v* slow or stop by using a brake. **braked, brak·ing.**

bran (bran) *n* the brown covering of a grain of wheat, rye, etc., often separated from the kernel when the grain is ground into flour.

branch (branch) 1 *n* part of a tree that grows out from the trunk. 2 *n* a division; part: *a branch of a river, a branch of a family. Geometry is a branch of mathematics.*

brand (brand) 1 *n* a certain kind, made by a particular company: *Do you like this brand of peanut butter?* 2 *n* Usually, **brand name**, a name or mark that a company uses to distinguish its products from the products of other companies; trademark. 3 *n* a mark made by burning the skin with a hot iron: *Ranchers put brands on their cattle and horses to show who owns them.* **brand-new** *adj* very new; as new as if just made: *a brand-new bicycle.*

brass (bras) 1 *n* a yellow metal made of copper and zinc. 2 *n* the metal wind instruments, such as trumpets and trombones, in a band or orchestra. They are usually made of brass.

brat (brat) *n* an annoying child. –**brat′ty,** *adj.*

brave (brāv) 1 *adj* able to face danger or difficult things even though you are afraid: *Miranda was brave; she stood up to the bully.* **brav·er, brav·est.** 2 *v* face something difficult without giving up: *The early Canadian explorers braved much danger.* **braved, brav·ing.** –**brave′ly,** *adv,* –**brav′er·y,** *n.*

brawl (brol) *n* a noisy fight involving several people. –**brawl′er,** *n.*

bread (bred) 1 *n* a food made of flour mixed with milk or water and, often, yeast. It is baked or fried in various shapes. 2 *v* cover with bread crumbs or meal before cooking: *He breaded the chicken before frying it.*

breadth (bredth) *n* how broad a thing is; the distance across; width: *He has travelled the length and the breadth of Canada.*

break (brāk) 1 *v* come apart or cause to come apart; crack; burst: *The plate broke into pieces when it fell on the floor.* 2 *v* stop working or cause to stop working: *Her radio broke.* 3 *n* a broken place; crack: *a break in the wall.* 4 *v* fail to keep; act against: *to break a promise, to break the law.* 5 *v* force one's way: *A thief broke into the house.* 6 *v* stop or interrupt something: *to break a habit. Let's break for lunch.* 7 *n* a short stop or interruption: *The coach told us to take a five-minute break.* 8 *n* Slang. chance; opportunity: *Finding the money was a lucky break.* **broke, brok·en, break·ing.** –**break′a·ble,** *adj.*
break·a·way *n* in hockey or lacrosse, an attack on goal when the defence is out of position.
break·down 1 *n* a failure to work: *Everything stopped because of a breakdown in the machinery.* 2 *n* a loss of health: *He had a mental breakdown from working too hard.* 3 *n* the separation of something into its parts: *We made a breakdown of the trip costs, including gas, food, and motels.*
break down, 1 stop working: *The car's engine broke down.* **2** begin to cry: *She broke down when she heard the bad news.* **3** separate into parts: *Big projects can be broken down into small jobs.*
break even, *Informal.* finish with the same amount one started with; not win or lose.
break out, have pimples, rashes, etc. on the skin: *Strawberries make me break out.*
break up, 1 scatter: *The fog is breaking up.* **2** end: *The Student Council broke up their meeting early.*

break·fast (brek′fəst) *n* the first meal of the day.

break–up (brā′kup′) **1** *n* the end of a friendship, marriage, or partnership. **2** ✤ *n* especially in the North, the breaking of the ice on a river or lake, the sign of the coming of spring: *We stood on the bridge and watched the break-up.* Another form is **breakup.**

breast (brest) **1** *n* either of the milk-producing organs on the chest of female mammals. **2** *n* the upper front part of the body; the chest.

breath (breth) *n* air taken into the lungs and let out again: *Hold your breath a moment.*

breathe (brēฐн) *v* take air into the lungs and let it back out. **breathed, breath·ing.**

breath·er (brē′ฐнər) *n* a short rest.

breath·less (breth′lis) **1** *adj* panting or gasping: *Running upstairs very fast made him breathless.* **2** *adj* holding one's breath because of fear, interest, excitement, etc.: *The beautiful scenery of the Cabot Trail left her breathless.*

breath·taking (breth′tā′king) *adj* thrilling; exciting: *a breathtaking ride on a roller coaster.*

catch your breath, stop for rest: *The hikers sat on a rock to catch their breath.*

take a person's breath away, amaze or thrill a person.

under your breath, in a whisper: *She was talking under her breath so we couldn't hear her.*

breed (brēd) **1** *v* have babies: *Rabbits breed rapidly.* **2** *v* raise: *The farmer breeds cattle and pigs for market.* **3** *n* kind; sort: *Terriers and spaniels are breeds of dog.* **bred, breed·ing.**

breeze (brēz) **1** *n* a light, gentle wind. **2** *v* *Informal.* move along easily or quickly: *She breezed through her homework.* **breezed, breez·ing.**

brew (brū) **1** *v* make a drink by boiling and soaking something to draw out the flavour: *to brew tea.* **2** *n* a drink that is brewed: *She gave me a brew made from herbs.*

bribe (brīb) *n* a gift offered to someone in order to get that person to do something: *The thief offered the police a bribe to let him go.* –**brib′er·y** (brī′bə rē), *n.*

brick (brik) **1** *n* a block of hard clay, used for building: *It took three loads of bricks to build the wall.* **2** *n* anything shaped like a brick: *a brick of ice cream.*

bride (brīd) *n* a woman just married or about to be married. –**brid′al,** *adj.*

bride·groom *n* a man just married or about to be married. **brides·maid** *n* a woman who stands with the bride at a wedding.

The Québec Bridge— the longest cantilever span in the world

The suspension bridge at Dunvegan, Alberta

bridge (brij) **1** *n* something built over a river, road, etc. so that people can get across. **2** *n* the upper, bony part of the nose.

brief (brēf) *adj* short: *a brief visit, a brief letter.* –**brief′ly,** *adv.*

bri·gade (bri gād′) **1** *n* a large group of soldiers; part of an army. **2** *n* any group of people organized for some job: *A fire brigade puts out fires.* **3** ✤ *n* a **fur brigade,** a group of canoes or dog sleds that used to carry furs to a trading post.

bright (brīt) **1** *adj* giving or having much light: *a bright star, a bright day.* **2** *adj* vivid; deep but not dark: *bright yellow, bright green.* **3** *adj* smart: *A bright person learns quickly.* **4** *adj* cheerful or happy: *a bright smile.* –**bright′ly,** *adv,* –**bright′ness,** *n.*

bright·en *v* become bright or brighter: *The sky brightened after the storm.*

bril·liant (bril′yənt) **1** *adj* very bright: *brilliant colours, brilliant sunshine.* **2** *adj* showing or having great ability: *He is a brilliant musician.* –**bril′liance,** *n.*

brim (brim) *n* the edge of a cup, glass, bowl, etc.: *I filled my glass to the brim.*

brine (brīn) *n* salty water: *Some pickles are kept in brine.*

bring (bring) **1** *v* carry to another place or person: *Bring me a clean plate, please.* **2** *v* persuade; convince: *I can't bring myself to eat worms.* **brought, bring·ing.**

bring about, cause: *The floods in Québec were brought about by heavy rains.*

bring off, do or get successfully: *She brought off a perfect mark in science.*

bring on, cause to start: *I think my headache was brought on by lack of sleep.*

bring out, 1 show clearly: *His paintings bring out the vastness of the North.* **2** offer to the public: *Every year car makers bring out new models.*

bring up, 1 care for and train a child: *They brought up four children.* **2** suggest or mention: *Please don't bring that up at the table!* **3** vomit.

CONFUSABLES ..... bring

bring means "carry to":
Bring me a bag from the car.

take means "carry away":
Take the dog out to the park.

---

brink (bringk) *n* a dangerous edge: *the brink of the cliff. His business is on the brink of ruin.*

brisk (brisk) *adj* quick and active; lively and sharp: *a brisk walk, a brisk "Hello!"* –**brisk'ly,** *adv.*

bris·tle (bris'əl) *n* the short, stiff hair of some animals or plants: *Brushes are often made of the bristles of hogs.*

brit·tle (brit'əl) *adj* hard but very easily broken. Thin glass and dead twigs are brittle. –**brit'tle·ness,** *n.*

broad (brod) **1** *adj* wide: *a broad road.* **2** *adj* not detailed: *Give us a broad summary of the book.*

broad·cast 1 *v* send out by radio or television: *Her speech will be broadcast tonight.* **2** *v* scatter seed, etc. over an area by hand. –**broad'cast'er,** *n.* **broad·en** *v* make or become broader: *The river broadens at its mouth.*

broad-minded *adj* respecting customs and ideas that are different from your own.

broc·co·li (brok'ə lē) *n* a vegetable with green stems and flower heads.

bro·chure (brō shūr') *n* a booklet, often with pictures, that advertises something or gives information: *I sent for a brochure on Québec; we may go there this summer.*

broil (broil) *v* cook something directly over the fire or heat on a rack, or under the heat in a pan: *to broil steaks.*

bron·co (brong'kō) *n* a western pony, often wild or only partly tamed. *pl* **bron·cos.**

bronze (bronz) **1** *n* a yellowish or reddish brown mix of copper and tin. A medal made of bronze is often the prize for a person who comes third in a contest. **2** *v* make or become brown: *The sailor was bronzed from the sun.* **bron·zed, bronz·ing.**

brooch (brōch) *n* a pin worn on the clothes as a decoration.

brood (brūd) **1** *n* a group of baby birds hatched and cared for together: *a brood of chicks.* **2** *v* think a long time about something serious or sad: *He brooded over his lost dog.*

broom (brūm) *n* a brush for sweeping, with a long handle called a **broomstick.**

broth (broth) *n* a thin soup made from the water that meat, fish, or vegetables have been boiled in.

broth·er (brutH'ər) *n* a son of the same parents: *My parents had me first, then my brother.* –**broth'er·ly,** *adj.*

brow (brou) *n* the forehead: *a wrinkled brow.*

brown (broun) **1** *n* or *adj* the colour of coffee, cinnamon, or chocolate. **2** *v* make or become brown: *Brown the onions in hot butter.* –**brown'ish,** *adj.*

brown·ie 1 *n* a small square of rich, chewy chocolate cake often containing nuts. **2** *n* **Brownie,** a member, aged six to nine, of the Girl Guides. **3** *n* in stories, a good-natured, helpful elf or fairy.

browse (brouz) **1** *v* look casually for something interesting in a book or computer file, on the Web, or in a store. **2** *v* feed on the tender parts of trees and bushes: *The deer moved through the woods, browsing on young shoots and leaves.* **browsed, brows·ing.**

bruise (brūz) **1** *n* an injury that doesn't break the skin but leaves a dark, sore spot. **2** *n* a soft spot on a fruit or vegetable where it has been pressed or dropped. **3** *v* cause or get bruises: *I bruised my leg when I fell on the step. Peaches bruise easily.* **bruised, bruis·ing.**

brunch (brunch) *n* a meal that is eaten in late morning and combines breakfast and lunch: *We met for brunch at the new restaurant.*

bru·nette (brū net′) *n* a person with dark hair.

brush (brush) **1** *n* a tool for cleaning, tidying your hair, or painting. A brush is made of bristles, hair, or wires fastened into a stiff back or handle. **2** *v* use a brush on: *She brushed her hair until it was shiny.* **3** *v* touch lightly: *Her jacket got dirty when she brushed against the car door.* **4** *n* a short fight or quarrel: *The protesters had a brush with the police.* **5** *n* small trees or bushes growing rather thickly together.
brush up on something, study; review: *I need to brush up on my French before the test.*

brute (brūt) **1** *n* an animal without power to think. **2** *n* a very cruel or stupid person.
bru·tal (brū′təl) *adj* extremely harsh or cruel: *a brutal winter. The pirates were brutal in battle.* –**bru·tal′i·ty** (brū tal′ə tē), *n.*

bub·ble (bub′əl) **1** *n* a very thin, round shell of liquid or solid with air or gas inside: *soap bubbles. I like breaking the bubbles in packing material.* **2** *n* a ball of air in a liquid or solid: *Sometimes there are bubbles in ice or glass.* –**bub·bly,** *adj.*
bubble gum chewing gum that can be blown up to form a large bubble.
bubble over, talk enthusiastically: *The campers bubbled over with ideas for the canoe trip.*

buc·ca·neer (buk′ə nēr′) *n* pirate.

WORD HISTORY ...... buccaneer

The word **buccaneer** originally referred to a person who cooks or smokes meat at a barbecue. Picture the scene, on the shore of a desert island, with pirates!

buck (buk) **1** *n* a male animal such as a deer, hare, rabbit, kangaroo, or antelope. **2** *v* jump into the air with the back arched and come down with the front legs stiff: *Her horse began to buck, but she stayed on.* **3** *v* work against: *The swimmer bucked the current with strong strokes.* **4** *n* Slang. dollar.

buck·et (buk′it) *n* a large, rounded container with a flat bottom and an arched handle, used for carrying liquids, sand, etc.; a pail.

buck·le (buk′əl) **1** *n* a catch or clasp to hold together two loose ends of a belt or strap. **2** *v* fasten with a buckle: *He buckled his belt.* **3** *v* bulge, kink, wrinkle, or give way under heavy strain or pressure: *The heavy snowfall caused the roof of the arena to buckle.* **buck·led, buck·ling.**
buckle down, begin to work hard: *She buckled down to her homework.*

bud (bud) **1** *n* a small swelling on a plant stem that will grow into a flower, leaf, or branch. **2** *n* a partly opened flower or leaf.

Bud·dha (bud′ə *or* bū′də) *n* the title of a great philosopher and teacher called Gautama, who lived in India in the 500s B.C.
Bud·dhism (bud′iz əm *or* bū′diz əm) *n* a religion based on the ideas and teachings of Buddha. –**Bud′dhist,** *adj* or *n.*

bud·dy (bud′ē) *n* Informal. a close friend. *pl* **bud·dies.**

budge (buj) *v* move or give way even a little: *The stone was so heavy that we could not budge it.* **budged, budg·ing.**

budg·et (buj′it) **1** *n* a plan showing how much money will probably be received and how it will be spent during a given time: *They've increased the music budget at our school.* **2** *v* make a plan for spending: *I budget my allowance.* **budg·et·ed, budg·et·ing.**

The buffalo of North America—about 175 cm high at the shoulder

Water buffalo of India—about 155 cm high at the shoulder

buf·fa·lo (buf′ə lō′) **1** *n* a large North American wild animal closely related to cattle. It has a big, shaggy head, a hump, and very strong front legs. Great herds of buffalo used to graze on the plains. **Bison** is another name for it. **2** *n* a large horned animal from Asia or Africa, related to cattle. The Asian water buffalo is tame but the wild water buffalo of Africa is fierce and dangerous. *pl* **buf·fa·loes, buf·fa·los,** or **buf·fa·lo.**

buff·er (buf′ər) **1** *n* something that softens or absorbs the force of something: *They planted some trees as a buffer against wind and snow.* **2** *n* in science, a substance that keeps the acid level in a solution about the same even when an acid or alkali is added.

buf·fet (bə fā′ *for 1 and 2,* buf′it *for 3*) **1** *n* a low cabinet with a flat top, for holding dishes, silver, and table linen. **2** *n* a meal at which guests serve themselves from food laid out on a table. **3** *v* knock, strike, or hurt: *The waves buffeted us.* **buf·fet·ed, buf·fet·ing.**

bug (bug) *Informal.* **1** *n* any insect or a creature somewhat like an insect. Ants, flies, spiders, beetles, and mosquitoes are all bugs. It is not a scientific label. **2** *n* a disease germ: *the flu bug.* **3** *n* a problem in a machine or computer program: *a bug in the fire alarm system.* **4** *n* a person who is very interested in something: *a camera bug.* **5** *v* annoy; bother: *Her grumbling bugs me.* **6** *v* hide a small microphone in: *This room is bugged.* **bugged, bug·ging. –bug′gy,** *adj.*

A buggy (def. 1)

bug·gy (bug′ē) **1** *n* a light open carriage pulled by one or more horses. It has a wide, benchlike seat or seats for passengers. **2** *n* a baby carriage. **3** *n* something with wheels, usually small, for transporting things or people. A grocery cart may be called a buggy. A **lunar buggy** is a small vehicle used on the moon. *pl* **bug·gies.**

build (bild) *v* make by putting materials together: *It took us a whole year to build our model boat. Birds build nests.* **built, build·ing. –build′er,** *n.*
build·ing 1 *n* something built, especially something with walls and a roof. Barns, houses, sheds, factories, and hotels are all buildings. **2** *n* the business or work of making houses, stores, bridges, ships, etc.

bulb (bulb) **1** *n* a round underground bud or stem from which certain plants grow. Onions, tulips, and lilies grow from bulbs. **2** *n* an electric light made of glass. **3** *n* a rounded part at the end of something: *the bulb of a thermometer.*

bulge (bulj) **1** *v* swell outward: *His pockets bulged with apples and candy.* **2** *n* an outward swelling: *There was a bulge where she was holding the kitten under her jacket.* **bulged, bulg·ing.**

bulk (bulk) **1** *n* large size, thickness, or heaviness: *An elephant has bulk.* **2** *n* the largest part: *The oceans form the bulk of the earth's surface.* **–bulk′y,** *adj.*
in bulk, 1 in large amounts. **2** loose in bins, not in packages. Food set out for sale in this way is called **bulk food.**

A bull walrus— about 3 m long

bull (bul) **1** *n* the adult male of cattle. **2** *n* the male of other large adult animals, such as the buffalo, moose, whale, elephant, walrus, or seal. **bull·doz·er** *n* a powerful tractor with a wide steel blade attached to its front. It is used to move dirt, rocks, etc., and to clear and level ground for building. **bull·frog** *n* a large frog of North America that makes a loud, croaking noise. **bull's-eye** *n* the centre of a target: *Robin Hood's arrows always hit the bull's-eye.*

bul·let (bul′it) *n* a piece of metal made to be shot from a rifle, pistol, or other small gun.

bul·le·tin (bul′ə tən) **1** *n* a short news report. **2** *n* a regular newsletter, such as one published by a club for its members.
bulletin board a board where people can put up notices, display artwork, etc.

bul·ly (bul′ē) **1** *n* a person who teases, frightens, or hurts smaller or weaker people. **2** *v* frighten into doing something by rough talk or threats: *He was bullied into giving away his candy. pl* **bul·lies; bul·lied, bul·ly·ing.**

bum (bum) *Informal.* **1** *n* a lazy or good-for-nothing person; loafer. **2** *v* get (food, money, etc.) by begging from other people: *She tried to bum a ride.* **3** *n* rear end; seat. **bummed, bum·ming.**
bum around, loaf around; do nothing: *He spent his whole summer bumming around.*

bump (bump) **1** *v* push or hit against something solid: *Craig bumped into me. The heavy bag of books kept bumping my leg.* **2** *v* move or proceed with bumps: *Our car bumped along the rough road.* **3** *n* a raised place: *She has a bump on her head from getting hit by a baseball. Try to avoid the bumps in the road.* **4** *v Informal.* move a person or thing out of the original position, usually in order to make room for someone or something else: *Their win bumped our curling team from second place to third in the tournament.* –**bump′y,** *adj.*

bump·er *n* the bar or bars of rubber or metal across the front and back of a vehicle that protect it from damage if it is bumped.

bun (bun) *n* a small, round piece of bread dough that has been baked. Buns are often sweet.

bunch (bunch) **1** *n* a group of things of the same kind joined together: *a bunch of grapes, a bunch of flowers.* **2** *n Informal.* any group or large amount: *a bunch of friends, a bunch of junk.*

bun·dle (bun′dəl) **1** *n* a number of things tied or wrapped together: *We recycled several bundles of old clothing.* **2** *n* wrap or tie together; make up into a bundle: *We bundled our newspapers for the blue box pickup.* **3** *v* send away in a hurry: *They bundled Ramie off to the hospital in an ambulance.* **bun·dled, bun·dling.**
bundle up, dress warmly.

bunk (bungk) *n* a bed set against a wall like a shelf, or joined in a frame to another one above or below it. The two together are called **bunkbeds.**

Buoys marking a safe channel for ships

buoy (boi *or* bū′ē) *n* an anchored object floating on the water as a warning or guide.
buoy·ant *adj* able to float: *A cork is buoyant in water; a stone is not.* –**buoy′an·cy,** *n.*

bur·den (bər′dən) *n* a heavy load: *a burden of firewood, a burden of debts.*

bu·reau (byū′rō) **1** *n* the office of a certain kind of business: *We asked about the plane fares at a travel bureau.* **2** *n* dresser; a chest of drawers. *pl* **bu·reaus.**

bur·glar (bər′glər) *n* a person who breaks into a house or other building to steal.
–**bur′glar·y,** *n,* –**bur′glar·ize,** *v.*

burn (bərn) **1** *v* be on fire: *The campfire burned all night.* **2** *v* set on fire; destroy or be destroyed by fire: *They burn wood in the fireplace.* **3** *v* hurt or mark with fire, heat, or acid: *He burned his hand on the hot iron.* **4** *n* an injury caused by fire, heat, or an acid: *The burn on her arm healed quickly.* **5** *v* make or be excited with anger, eagerness, etc.: *to burn with fury, burning with enthusiasm.* **burned** or **burnt, burn·ing.**

burn down, destroy or be destroyed completely by fire: *The barn burned down.*

burn up, 1 use up: *This car burns up a lot of gasoline.* **2** *Informal.* make angry: *Their teasing burns me up.*

burp (bərp) *v* let air up from the stomach, often with a noise.

burr (bər) *n* a prickly seedcase or flower of some plants. Burrs stick to cloth and fur.

bur·row (bər′ō) **1** *n* a hole dug in the ground by an animal for shelter: *Rabbits live in burrows.* **2** *v* dig or search with the hands: *She burrowed through the pile of clothes looking for the lost ring.*

burst (bərst) **1** *v* break open: *The balloon burst with a bang.* **2** *v* act suddenly: *to burst into tears. Don't burst into the room without knocking.* **3** *n* a sudden outbreak or increase: *There was a burst of laughter when the clown fell down. He won the race with a burst of speed.* **burst, burst·ing.**

bur·y (ber′ē) **1** *v* put in a hole in the ground and cover with soil: *The girls buried the dead bird.* **2** *v* put away; cover up; hide: *The squirrels buried nuts under the fallen leaves.* **bur·ied, bur·y·ing.**

bur·i·al (ber′ē əl) *n* the act of putting a dead body in a grave, in a tomb, or in the sea; burying.

bus (bus) *n* a large vehicle with seats inside for many passengers. *pl* **bus·es** or **bus·ses.**

bush (bu̇sh) **1** *n* a woody plant smaller than a tree, with many separate branches starting at or near the ground. **2** *n* forest or wild country.
bushed *adj Informal.* very tired. ❀ **bush pilot** someone who flies planes mostly in the bush country of the far north. **bush·y** *adj* spreading out like a bush; growing thickly: *a bushy beard.*
beat around the bush, take a long time to get to the point: *Tell me the truth right away and don't beat around the bush.*

bush·el (bùsh′əl) *n* a non-metric measure of volume for grain, fruit, vegetables, etc., usually equal to about 36 L: *a bushel of apples.*

busi·ness (biz′nis) **1** *n* work: *A carpenter's business is building with wood.* **2** *n* a matter; affair: *The whole business sounds pretty silly to me.* **3** *n* trade; buying and selling: *This store does a lot of business in summer.*

busi·ness·per·son *n* a man or woman who works for or operates a business. Businessperson can be used in place of **businessman** or **businesswoman**: *Sally joined other businesspeople for lunch on Fridays.*

mean business, *Informal.* be serious: *When my father's voice gets quiet like that, he means business!*

mind your own business, stay out of the affairs of others.

bus·y (biz′ē) **1** *adj* working; active; having plenty to do: *Mother is a busy person.* **2** *adj* full of work or activity: *Main Street is a busy place.* **bus·i·er, bus·i·est. –bus′i·ly,** *adv.*

bus·y·bod·y *n* a nosey person who interferes in the affairs of others.

butch·er (bùch′ər) **1** *v* kill animals for food: *Cattle, sheep, and pigs are butchered at the abattoir.* **2** *v* kill needlessly or cruelly. **3** *v* do very badly: *He butchers that song by singing it so fast and loud.*

butt (but) **1** *n* the end part: *the butt of a gun.* **2** *v* hit with the head: *A goat butts.*

butt in, *Informal.* meddle; interfere.

Butterfly: a tiger swallowtail— wingspread about 12 cm

but·ter (but′ər) **1** *n* the yellowish fat obtained by churning cream or whole milk. **2** *n* a spread that is like butter: *peanut butter, honey butter.*

but·ter·fly *n* an insect with a slender body and four large, often brightly coloured wings.

but·ter·milk *n* the sour, fat-free liquid left after butter has been made from cream.

❧ **butter tart** a rich, sweet tart with a firm or runny filling made from butter, brown sugar, syrup, raisins, etc.

but·ton (but′ən) **1** *n* a little piece of metal, plastic, etc. sewn on clothing and other things, to hold parts together or to decorate. **2** *n* a small part that is pushed or turned to make something work: *Push that button to start the machine.*

buy (bī) **1** *v* get by paying a price: *You can buy a bag of chips for a dollar.* **2** *n* Informal. a bargain: *That jacket was a real buy.* **bought, buy·ing. –buy′er,** *n.*

CONFUSABLES ......buy

buy means "purchase":
  Where did you buy those boots?
by means "beside":
  Put your boots by the door.

---

buzz (buz) *n* a loud humming like the sound made by flies or bees: *the buzz of a mosquito, the buzz of conversation.*

by–law (bī′lo′) *n* a law made by a city, company, club, etc.: *Our city has a by-law to control the height of buildings.*

by–prod·uct (bī′prod′əkt) *n* something produced in making or doing something else: *Buttermilk is a by-product of making butter.*

by·stand·er (bī′stan′dər) *n* a person who stands near or watches but does not take part: *Innocent bystanders are often hurt in street fights.*

byte (bīt) *n* a unit of computer memory, made up of eight bits. One letter or number keyed in on a computer takes one byte of memory.

c or **C** (sē) *n* the third letter of the English alphabet, or any speech sound that it stands for. The *c* in *cat* is different from the *c* in *city*. *pl* **c's** or **C's.**

C **1** the Roman numeral for 100. ▶See Appendix. **2** *symbol for* Celsius.

cab (kab) *n* a car that can be hired with a driver for a short trip; taxi.

cab·bage (kab′ij) *n* a vegetable with thick leaves closely wrapped to form a round head.

cab·in (kab′ən) **1** *n* a small, roughly built house. **2** *n* a room to sleep in on a ship.
❧ **cabin fever** *n* a feeling of being depressed and restless because you've been kept inside for a long time: *After two days of staying inside because of the blizzard we began to get cabin fever.*

cab·i·net (kab′ə nit) **1** *n* a piece of furniture with shelves or drawers to hold dishes, medicines, etc. **2** ❧ *n* Usually, **Cabinet,** a group of advisers to a government leader.

ca·ble (kā′bəl) **1** *n* a thick electric cord containing a bundle of wires protected from each other by insulation: *A cable connects the printer to our computer.* **2** *Informal. n* short for **cable television**: *Do you have cable?* **3** *n* a strong, thick rope, usually made of wires twisted together: *The truck used a cable to tow the car.*
cable TV a system that picks up programs from various TV stations through a very high antenna and sends them by electric cable to the TV sets of people who pay for it. A TV set that is hooked up to cable TV does not need an antenna. The full name for this system is **cable television**.

ca·boose (kə būs′) **1** *n* a small car on a freight train, usually the last car, where the train staff can work, rest, and sleep. **2** ❧ *n* a movable sleeping cabin used by loggers and other workers. **3** ❧ *n* a small cabin built on a sleigh, with benches and a stove in it: *My grandpa says he knew someone who travelled to school in a caboose during the winter.*

cache (kash) **1** *n* a place to hide things, or the things that are hidden. **2** ❧ *n* a storing place for food, furs, etc.: *The trappers made a cache to keep their food safe from bears and other animals.*

cack·le (kak′əl) *n* the shrill, broken sound that a hen makes after laying an egg, or any sound like this.

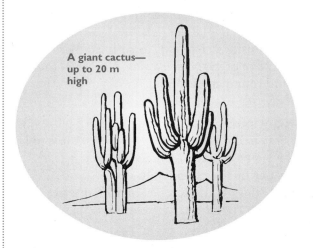
A giant cactus—up to 20 m high

cac·tus (kak′təs) *n* a plant with a thick stem that is soft, moist, and spongy inside, usually having prickles but no leaves. Most cactuses grow in dry, hot regions. *pl* **cac·tus·es** or **cac·ti** (kak′tī).

ca·fé (ka fā′) *n* a small restaurant that serves light meals, coffees and teas, pastries, etc.
caf·e·te·ri·a (kaf′ə tē′rē ə) *n* an eating place, usually inside another building such as a school, where customers serve themselves.

cage (kāj) *n* a frame or box closed in with wires or bars, for keeping animals in.

cake (kāk) **1** *n* a baked mixture of flour, sugar, eggs, and other things: *a layer cake, a fruit cake.* **2** *n* a solid, shaped mass: *a cake of soap, a cake of maple sugar.*
take the cake, 1 win first prize; be the best. **2** be the worst or last in a series of annoying things.

cal·cu·late (kal′kyə lāt′) *v* use math in order to find out something: *The lumberjack calculated how much wood he would need for the cabin.* **cal·cu·lat·ed, cal·cu·lat·ing.** —**cal′cu·la′tion,** *n.*
cal·cu·la·tor *n* a little electronic machine that calculates. It has a keypad and a tiny screen.

❀ **ca·lèche** (kə lesh′) *n* a light, two-wheeled, one-horse carriage for two passengers, with a top that can be folded down and a seat in front for the driver: *We went for a calèche ride in Québec City.*

cal·en·dar (kal′ən dər) *n* a chart showing the months of the year, with the days numbered and arranged in weeks.

calf (kaf) **1** *n* a baby cow, bull, moose, elephant, whale, seal, etc. **2** *n* the thick fleshy part of the leg below the knee. *pl* **calves.**

call (kol) **1** *v* or *n* shout: *He called from downstairs* (*v*). **2** *n* the special cry of an animal or bird: *the call of a moose.* **3** *v* a command; invitation; summons: *Every farmer in the neighbourhood answered the firefighters' call for volunteers.* **4** *v* name; describe as: *Are you calling me a liar?* **5** *v* or *n* visit or stop: *The rabbi called at our house yesterday* (*v*). **6** *v* to telephone: *Call me at this number.* –**call′er,** *n.*
call it a day, stop work or some other activity.
call off, cancel: *We called off our trip due to poor weather.*
on call, ready or available: *Some doctors are on call day and night.*

calm (kom *or* kȧm) *adj* quiet; still; peaceful; steady: *a calm sea, a calm voice.* –**calm′ly,** *adv,* –**calm′ness,** *n.*

Cal·o·rie (kal′ə rē) **1** *n* a unit measuring the energy value of foods, equal to about four kilojoules: *A medium-sized orange has about a hundred calories.* *pl* **cal·o·ries.**

cal·u·met (kal′yə met′) *n* a long decorated tobacco pipe traditionally smoked by people of the First Nations on special occasions.

ca·lyx (kā′liks) *n* the outer leaves that surround a flower bud. The individual leaves are called sepals. *pl* **ca·lyx·es** or **cal·y·ces** (kal′ə sēz).

cam·bi·um (kam′bē əm) *n* the layer of soft, growing tissue between the bark and the wood of trees and shrubs. New bark and wood grow from here.

cam·cord·er (kam′kȯr′dər) *n* a small video camera and recorder combined in one machine that can be held in your hand.

cam·el (kam′əl) *n* a large, four-legged desert animal with either one or two humps on its back. The humps store fat that the camel's body turns into water and energy.

cam·er·a (kam′ə rə) *n* a machine for making photographs, movies, or TV images, or for recording videos.

cam·ou·flage (kam′ə flȧzh′) **1** *n* an outward appearance that keeps a thing from being noticed: *The white fur of a polar bear is a natural camouflage in the snowy Arctic.* **2** *v* disguise: *The girls used branches to camouflage their fort in the woods.* **cam·ou·flaged, cam·ou·flag·ing.**

camp (kamp) **1** *n* a place outdoors used for staying overnight in a tent or trailer: *Our camp was right in Kluane National Park.* **2** *v* make a camp: *We decided to camp by the Nisling River the first night.* The spot where you do is called a **campsite.** A **campground** is a park with a lot of campsites in it. –**camp′ing,** *n.*

cam·paign (kam pān′) *n* a series of connected activities with a goal in mind: *Mount Sinai Hospital had a campaign to raise money.*

can (kan) an auxiliary verb used: **1** *v* to say that a person or thing is able or allowed to do something: *My new model train can go very fast. I cannot see because you're standing in my way. You can't go there.* **2** *n* a metal container, usually sealed so that a special tool is needed to open it: *an oil can, a pop can, a can of beans.*
past tense **could.**

canned (kand) **1** *adj* preserved by being put in airtight cans or jars: *canned soup.* **2** *adj* *Informal.* recorded so it can later be played in a performance instead of using the real thing: *canned music, canned laughter.*

> ## USING WORDS .... can/may
>
> In careful English, some people don't use **can** to mean "be allowed to." For example, they insist that: *Can I go?* means *Am I able to go?* and *May I go?* means *Am I allowed to go?*
> In informal language, people use **can** for both.

Canada Day (kan′ədə dā′) July 1st, Canada's national holiday. Canada became a nation on July 1, 1867.
Canada goose a large wild goose of North America. It has a black head and neck, a white throat, and a brownish-grey body. **Canada jay** a North American bird that has black and grey feathers. It is also known as the **whisky-jack.** It has many nicknames, including **lumberjack, moosebird,** and **camp robber.**

❧**Ca·na·darm** (kan′ə dȧrm) *n* a special mechanical arm that extends from a spacecraft so it can move things around in space. It is built in Canada.

Ca·na·di·an (kə nā′dē ən) **1** *n* a person born in Canada or living there. **2** *adj* having to do with Canada or its people.
❧**Ca·nuck** (kə nuk′) *n Informal.* a Canadian.

Canadian Charter of Rights and Freedoms (kə nā′dē ən chȧr′tər əv rīts ənd frē′dəmz) a part of our constitution that explains what rights and freedoms Canadian citizens have.

Canadian Shield (kə nā′dē ən shēld′) an area of ancient rock encircling Hudson Bay and covering nearly half the mainland of Canada. The Canadian Shield is rich in gold, copper, nickel, and iron.

ca·nal (kə nal′) *n* a waterway dug across land for ships or small boats to go through, or to carry water to places that need it.

can·cel (kan′səl) *v* stop the plans for something: *The picnic was cancelled because of the rain.* **can·celled** or **can·celed, can·cel·ling** or **can·cel·ing.** –**can′cel·la′tion,** *n.*
cancel out, balance something opposite so that both can be ignored: *The bus ticket you borrowed from me cancels out the loonie I owe you.*

can·cer (kan′sər) *n* a very harmful disease. Abnormal body cells multiply quickly and spread, destroying the healthy tissues and organs of the body.

can·di·date (kan′də dāt′) *n* a person trying to be chosen for something: *Four candidates are running for mayor in Victoria.*

can·dle (kan′dəl) *n* a stick of wax with a string in it called a wick, burned to give light: *Jewish people light candles to celebrate Hanukkah.*
can·de·la·bra (kan′ də lab′ rə) *n* a candle holder that has two or more branches.

can·dy (kan′dē) *n* a food made with sugar or syrup and flavouring: *We need sugar, milk, chocolate, and walnuts to make that kind of candy.* *pl* **can·dies.**

cane (kān) **1** *n* a stick used to lean on in walking: *I had to use a cane until my twisted ankle got better.* **2** *v* a long jointed stem, or a plant with such stems, such as sugar cane or bamboo. **caned, can·ing.**

can·ni·bal (kan′ə bəl) **1** *n* a person who eats human flesh: *Tribes of cannibals once lived on islands in the south Pacific Ocean.* **2** *n* an animal that eats others of its own kind: *Many fish are cannibals.*

Thwart

A canoe

ca·noe (kə nü′) *n* a light, narrow boat with pointed ends, moved with a paddle. *pl* **ca·noes.** –**ca·noe′ist,** *n.*

can·o·py (kan′ə pē) *n* a rooflike covering above a bed, throne, entrance to a building, etc.: *Many animals live in the shade of the forest canopy.* *pl* **can·o·pies.**

can·ta·loupe (kan′tə lōp′) *n* a kind of sweet, juicy melon with rough, greyish skin and orange flesh. **Muskmelon** is another word for it.

can·vas (kan′vəs) **1** *n* a strong, rough cloth made of cotton, flax, or hemp, used to make tents, sails, casual shoes, etc. **2** *n* a piece of canvas for painting a picture on, especially in oil paints.

can·vass (kan′vəs) *v* go around asking for subscriptions, votes, orders, etc.: *We canvassed the neighbourhood for contributions to UNICEF.*

can·yon (kan′yən) *n* a narrow valley with high, steep sides, usually with a stream at the bottom.

cap (kap) **1** *n* a soft, close-fitting covering for the head, especially one with a visor. **2** *n* anything like a cap, such as the lid of a bottle. **3** *n* the highest part; the top.

ca·pa·ble (kā′pə bəl) *adj* able or fit to do something; skilled and efficient: *Saroj is a very capable organizer–she planned a great party!* –**ca′pa·bly,** *adv.*
ca·pa·bil·i·ty *n* ability or power: *This computer system has scanning capability.*
capable of, able or likely to do: *You are capable of excellent work if you try.*

ca·pac·i·ty (kə pas′ə tē) *n* the amount a room or container can hold: *The capacity of this can is 4 L. The temple has a seating capacity of 100 people.*

cape (kāp) **1** *n* an outer garment without sleeves, falling loosely from the shoulders. **2** *n* a point of land stretching out into the water.

cap·i·tal (kap′ə təl) **1** *n* the city where the government of a country, province, or state is located: *Victoria is the capital of British Columbia.* **2** *n* Also, **capital letter**, an upper-case letter like A, G, or Y. **3** *adj* punishable by death: *Capital punishment is not legal in Canada.* **4** *n* money or property, especially in business: *A great deal of capital is needed to set up a factory.*

Grammar ✓Check .. capital letter

When writing English, you should always give a capital letter to the first word in a sentence. Look in the *Grammar and Usage Mini-Guide* pages at the end of this dictionary for more rules on capitalizing letters.

---

cap·puc·ci·no (kap′ə chē′nō) *n* a mixture of hot Italian coffee and steamed milk, often topped with powdered cinnamon or cocoa and whipped cream.

cap·size (kap′sīz′ *or* kap sīz′) *v* overturn; turn bottom side up: *The canoe capsized in the rough waters of James Bay.* **cap·sized, cap·siz·ing.**

cap·sule (kap′səl) **1** *n* a small case or covering: *Medicine in capsules is easy to swallow.* **2** *n* the front section of a rocket, made to carry instruments, astronauts, etc. into space. In flight the capsule can separate from the rest of the rocket and go into orbit or be brought back to earth.

cap·tain (kap′tən) **1** *n* a leader; chief: *I was proud that the coach chose me to be captain of the swim team.* **2** *n* a commander of a ship.

cap·tion (kap′shən) *n* an explanation or title for a picture or cartoon.

cap·ture (kap′chər) *v* take by force, skill, or trickery: *The spider captured the fly in its web.* **cap·tured, cap·tur·ing.**
cap·tive *n* a person or animal taken and held. –**cap·tiv′i·ty,** *n.*
cap·tor *n* a person who takes or holds a prisoner.

car (kär) **1** *n* a motorized passenger vehicle used on roads: *They made the trip by car.* **2** *n* any vehicle that moves on more than two wheels, such as a railway car or streetcar. **3** *n* anything that carries passengers, such as the basket on a hot air balloon: *an elevator car, a cable car, bumper cars.* –**car′ful′,** *n.*

car·a·ga·na (ker′ə gan′ə) *n* a shrub with small, light green leaves growing in pairs along a stem. People in the prairies use it for hedges, windbreaks, etc.

car·a·mel (ker′ə məl *or* kär′məl) *n* a sauce or chewy candy flavoured with browned sugar.

car·a·van (ker′ə van′) **1** *n* a group of people travelling together in separate vehicles or on separate animals: *A caravan of Arab merchants and camels moved across the desert.* **2** *n* a large vehicle that you can live in on a long trip.

car·bo·hy·drate (kär′bō hī′drāt) *n* a substance, such as sugar or starch, made up of carbon, hydrogen, and oxygen. Carbohydrates give our bodies energy.

card (kärd) **1** *n* a small, rectangular piece of stiff paper, thin cardboard, or plastic: *a credit card, a business card, a playing card, a score card.* **2** *n* a piece of stiff paper, usually folded, with a message or greeting and a picture or design, given on a special occasion: *a birthday card, a Valentine card.* **3** *n* a small board with electronic circuits on it that can be added to a computer to allow it to do certain things: *a sound card.* **4** *n* **cards,** *pl* a game played with a set of playing cards: *She enjoys cards.*
card·board *n* a fairly thick kind of stiff paper used for making cards, cartons, boxes, etc.
put your cards on the table, be completely honest about your plans and goals.

car·di·ac (kär′dē ak′) having to do with the heart. A **cardiac pacemaker** keeps the heartbeat steady. A **cardiac arrest** is a stopping of the heart, or a heart attack.

car·di·nal (kär′də nəl) *adj* a North American songbird. The male has bright red feathers marked with grey and black.

cardinal number (kär′də nəl num′bər) any of the numbers that show quantity and are used in ordinary counting. One, two, three, four, five, six, fifteen, forty-eight, eight hundred, etc. are cardinal numbers.

care (ker) **1** *v* feel strong interest: *The violinist cares deeply about music.* **2** *n* serious attention to what you are doing: *A good cook works with care.* **3** *n* love and respect shown by giving what someone needs: *The vet gave the dog the best of care.* **cared, car·ing.**

care·free *adj* without worry; light-hearted; happy. **care·ful** *adj* paying attention: *Be careful crossing the street.* **care·giv·er** *n* someone who looks after children, sick people, or anyone else who needs help. **care·less** *adj* sloppy: *careless work.* **care·tak·er** *n* a person who takes care of a building, property, etc.

care for, 1 like: *I don't care for her.* **2** watch over and give what is needed: *The nurse will care for him during the night.*

take care, be careful: *Take care on the icy path or you will slip.*

take care of, 1 watch over and give what is needed: *A babysitter takes care of children.* **2** deal with: *My mother will take care of this bill.*

ca·reer (kə rēr') **1** *n* an occupation or profession: *She chose law for her career.* **2** *v* rush along wildly: *Farley lost control of his bike and careered down the hill.*

car·go (kȧr'gō) *n* the load carried on a ship, aircraft, truck, etc.: *a cargo of wheat.* *pl* **car·goes** or **car·gos.**

Caribou—
about 130 cm high
at the shoulder

car·i·bou (ker'ə bū) *n* a North American reindeer. They live in herds on the tundra. *pl* **car·i·bou** or **car·i·bous.**

WORD HISTORY . . . . caribou

Caribou comes from an Algonquian word *xalibu* meaning "one that paws or scratches." The deer paws through snow to reach the grass underneath.

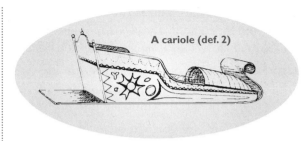

A cariole (def. 2)

❧ **car·i·ole** (ker'ē ōl') **1** *n* a one-horse sleigh. **2** *n* a dogsled that can carry one person lying down: *The sick trapper was brought to the Hudson's Bay Company trading post in a cariole.*

car·ni·val (kȧr'nə vəl) **1** *n* a fair or a travelling show with rides, food, games, etc. **2** *n* a program of events celebrating a particular sport, season, etc.: *We admired the amazing ice sculptures at the Winter Carnival in Québec City.*

car·ni·vore (kȧr'nə vȯr') *n* any animal that feeds mainly on meat rather than plants. Cats, dogs, etc. are carnivores. –**car·niv'o·rous,** *adj.*

car·ol (ker'əl) *n* a song or hymn of joy: *Christmas carols.*

car·pen·ter (kȧr'pən tər) *n* a worker who builds or repairs things made of wood. –**car'pen·try,** *n.*

car·pet (kȧr'pit) *n* Sometimes, **carpeting**, a heavy, woven covering for floors and stairs.

car·ry (ker'ē) **1** *v* take from one place to another: *Via Rail trains carry passengers across Canada.* **2** *v* support the weight of; hold up: *Those pillars carry the roof.* **car·ried, car·ry·ing.**

car·riage (ker'ij) **1** *n* a horse-drawn vehicle with wheels that was common before cars were invented. **2** *n* anything with wheels used to move or carry people or things, usually by pushing it: *a baby carriage.*

carried away, so full of strong feeling that you can't act or speak reasonably: *Arguing for your own opinion is fine, but don't get carried away.*

carry on, 1 do; manage: *She carries on a successful babysitting business.* **2** keep going; continue: *Carry on reading from where we left off.* **3** *Informal.* behave or talk wildly or foolishly: *Oh, stop whining and carrying on!*

carry out, get done: *She carried out her job well.*

cart (kȧrt) *n* a vehicle, often with only two wheels, used to carry loads by pushing or pulling: *a baggage cart, a shopping cart.*

put the cart before the horse, get things backward.

car·ti·lage (kär′tə lij) *n* a tough, elastic substance forming parts of the skeleton; gristle. The tip of the nose is made of cartilage and skin.

car·ton (kär′tən) *n* a cardboard box. Those containing drinks are usually coated with wax, and have a spout for pouring.

car·toon (kär tün′) **1** *n* a sketch or drawing showing persons, things, or events in a light-hearted way. **2** *n* a movie or TV show made from drawings: *Her favourite cartoon comes on at 4:00.* –**car·toon′ist**, *n.*

carve (kärv) *v* cut; make by cutting: *First Nations peoples carved totem poles from trees to celebrate their heritage.* **carved, carv·ing.**

case (kās) **1** *n* an instance or example: *We agreed that every case of cheating should be punished.* A **case study** is a story or situation that can be studied as a good example of something: *Our trip to New Brunswick was a case study in good vacation planning!* **2** *n* anything to hold or cover something: *Put the laptop back in its case.*
in any case, anyhow; no matter what happens: *In any case, you should prepare for the worst.*
in case, so as to be ready for what might happen: *Here's an umbrella in case it rains.*
in case of, if there is: *In case of fire walk quietly to the nearest door.*
on someone's case, *Slang.* nagging someone.

cash (kash) **1** *n* money that can be paid right away. Coins, paper money, and money paid by a bank card are all forms of cash. Cheques and credit cards are not. **2** *v* change into cash: *The bank cashed my $20 cheque.*

cas·se·role (kas′ə rōl′) *n* food cooked in a dish in the oven and served in the same dish. Usually it contains mixed ingredients.

cas·sette (kə set′) *n* an audiotape or videotape inside a small, flat, sealed plastic case. You put the whole case in the tape recorder or VCR.

cast (kast) **1** *v* throw: *to cast a stone.* **2** *n* a plaster support used to keep a broken bone in place while it is mending. **3** *n* the actors in a play: *The cast of* Romeo and Juliet *was listed in the program.* **cast, cast·ing.**

cast·a·way (kas′tə wā′) *n* a shipwrecked person.

cast·off *n* something that has been put aside as no longer useful: *You can use those brushes for painting; they're castoffs.*

cast a ballot, vote.

cast off, untie a boat or raise its anchor.

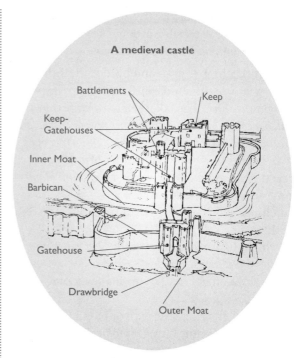

A medieval castle

Labels: Battlements, Keep, Keep-Gatehouses, Inner Moat, Barbican, Gatehouse, Drawbridge, Outer Moat

cas·tle (kas′əl) *n* a large building or fort of medieval times, protected against attack by thick walls, towers, heavy gates, etc.

cas·u·al (kazh′ū əl) *adj* relaxed and informal: *casual clothes, a casual visit.* –**cas′u·al·ly**, *adv.*

cas·u·al·ty (kazh′ū əl tē) *n* a person injured or killed in an accident or war. *pl* **cas·u·al·ties.**

cat (kat) **1** *n* a small, tame, furry meat-eating animal with short ears, a tail, long whiskers, and soft paws with claws that can be drawn in. **2** *n* any animal of the group that includes cats, lions, tigers, leopards, etc. –**cat′like**, *adj.*
let the cat out of the bag, tell a secret: *It was supposed to be a surprise party, but he let the cat out of the bag.*
rain cats and dogs, rain very hard.

cat·a·logue (kat′ə log′) *n* a list of things in a collection, with notes or descriptions and sometimes pictures: *a book catalogue in a library, a sales catalogue from a store.*

cat·a·ma·ran (kat′ə mə ran′) **1** *n* a boat with two hulls or floats joined side by side by a frame. **2** ❧ *n* a large, roughly built sled for hauling lumber, etc.

cat·a·pult (kat′ə pult′) **1** *n* a large weapon used in ancient times for shooting stones, arrows, etc. **2** *n* slingshot. **3** *v* throw or be thrown as if from a catapult: *I stopped my bike so suddenly that I was catapulted over the handlebars.*

ca·tas·tro·phe (kə tas′trə fē) *n* a sudden great disaster; a terrible event: *The forest fires in British Columbia were a catastrophe.*

catch (kach) **1** *v* grab and hold something: *to catch a ball, to catch someone's attention. The police caught the thief.* **2** *v* take; get: *to catch fire, to catch a cold. You have just five minutes to catch your train.* **3** *v* notice: *She caught me taking a cookie.* **4** *n Informal.* a hidden meaning or difficulty; trick: *There's a catch to that question; think about it carefully.* **caught, catch·ing.**

catch·ing *adj* likely to spread from one person to another.

catch on, *Informal.* understand: *They caught on when I gave an example.*

catch sight of, notice: *The cat suddenly caught sight of the bluejay.*

catch up, 1 come up level with or pass a person or thing going the same way: *My brother ran to catch up with us.* **2** make up for lost time, missed work, etc.

cat·e·go·ry (kat′ə gȯ′rē) *n* one division in a system for grouping things: *The two main categories of books are fiction and non-fiction.* *pl* **cat·e·go·ries. –cat′e·gor·ize′,** *v.*

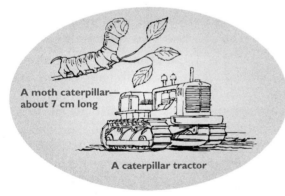

A moth caterpillar—
about 7 cm long

A caterpillar tractor

cat·er·pil·lar (kat′ər pil′ər) *n* the wormlike form that turns into a butterfly or moth.

✈ **cat-train** *n* a series of large sleds pulled by a **caterpillar tractor.** Cat-trains are used in the North for hauling goods in winter.

Cath·o·lic (kath′ə lik′) *adj* having to do with the Christian church led by the Pope. **–Ca·thol′i·cism′** (kə thol′ə siz′əm), *n.*

cat·tle (kat′əl) *pl.n* cows, bulls, and steers.

caught (kot) *v* the past tense of **catch.**

cau·li·flow·er (kol′ē flou′ər) *n* a vegetable that has a solid, white head with a few leaves around it.

caulk (kok) *v* fill up a seam, crack, or joint with a special rubbery substance called **caulking** so that it will not leak; make watertight: *We had to caulk the seams of our boat again this spring.*

cause (koz) **1** *n* a person, thing, or event that makes something else happen: *The flood was the cause of much damage.* **2** *v* make happen; make do something; bring about: *The fire caused much damage. The sound of the Labour Day fireworks caused me to jump.* **3** *n* an important goal or movement shared by many people: *World peace is a worthy cause.* **caused, caus·ing.**

cau·tion (kosh′ən) **1** *n* taking care to be safe; avoiding risks: *Use caution in crossing streets.* **2** *n* a warning: *Be sure to read the caution on the label.* **3** *v* warn; urge to be careful: *The police officer cautioned us against playing in the street.* **–cau′tious,** *adj.* **–cau′tious·ly,** *adv.*

cave (kāv) **1** *n* a hollow space underground: *He found several caves along the British Columbia coast.* **2** *v* **cave in,** *Informal.* give in: *Mom finally caved in and took us to the Canadian National Exhibition.* **caved, cav·ing. –cave′-in′,** *n.*
cav·ern (kav′ərn) *n* a large cave.
–cav′ern·ous, *adj.* **cav·i·ty** *n* a hole; a hollow place: *Cavities in teeth are caused by decay.* *pl* **cav·i·ties.**

CD (sē′dē′) *abbreviation for* compact disc, a small round plate with sounds, pictures, or words digitally stored on it in very tiny pits. A laser beam inside a compact disc player or computer finds the information on the disc and transmits it. It is changed back into images or sounds so you can hear it or see it.

CD-ROM *n* a compact disc on which huge amounts of information can be stored and later read or used on a computer. *pl* **CD-ROMs.**

cease (sēs) *v* stop: *The music ceased suddenly.* **ceased, ceas·ing. –cease′less,** *adj,* **–cease′less·ly,** *adv.*

ceil·ing (sē′ling) *n* the inside top covering of a room.

cel·e·brate (sel′ə brāt′) *v* do special things to mark a particular event: *to celebrate Canada Day with fireworks.* **cel·e·brat·ed, cel·e·brat·ing. –cel′e·bra′tion,** *n.*

cel·e·brat·ed *adj* famous: *Lucy Maud Montgomery is a celebrated Canadian author.* **ce·leb·ri·ty** *n* a famous person: *I collect autographs of celebrities such as Wayne Gretzky.* *pl* **ce·leb·ri·ties.**

cel·er·y (sel′ə rē) *n* a vegetable with long, crisp stalks that are eaten raw or cooked.

cell (sel) **1** *n* a small room in a prison. **2** *n* any small, hollow place: *Bees store honey in the cells of a honeycomb.* **3** *n* a very small unit of living matter. All living things are made of cells. The human body has blood cells, nerve cells, skin cells, etc. **4** *n* a small battery.

cell phone a phone without any wires attached to it that you can carry around with you. A cell phone works by sending radio signals. **Cellular phone** is the full name.

cel·lar (sel′ər) *n* an underground storage room.

cel·lo·phane (sel′ə fān′) *n* a clear plastic packaging material. CDs, etc. are wrapped in cellophane.

cel·lu·lose (sel′yə lōs′) *n* the woody part of plants, used to make paper, plastics, etc.

cel·lu·loid (sel′yə loid′) *n* a stiff, transparent plastic used for photographic film.

Cel·si·us (sel′sē əs) *adj* the name of a scale for measuring temperature. On this scale water freezes at 0 degrees and boils at 100 degrees.

WORD HISTORY . . . . Celsius

This scale was named after Anders **Celsius** (1701-1744), a Swedish astronomer, who invented it.
It is sometimes referred to as the **centigrade** scale, from the Latin *centum* "a hundred" + *gradus* "degree."

---

ce·ment (sə ment′) *n* a fine, grey powder made by burning clay and limestone. It becomes hard when mixed with water. Sand or gravel is added to the mixture to make concrete.

cem·e·ter·y (sem′ə ter′ē) *n* a place for burying the dead; graveyard. *pl* **cem·e·ter·ies.**

cen·sor (sen′sər) *v* remove unacceptable parts: *Two scenes in the movie had been censored.* **–cen′sor·ship,** *n.*

cen·sure (sen′shər) *v* criticize: *His father censured him for being late.* **cen·sured, cen·sur·ing.**

cen·sus *n* an official count of the people of a country or district.

cent (sent) *n* a coin of Canada and many other countries: *There are 100 cents in one dollar.* Symbol: ¢

cen·ten·ni·al (sen ten′yəl) *n* a hundredth anniversary: *Canada celebrated its centennial in 1967.*

centi– *an SI prefix meaning* hundredth. A centimetre is one hundredth of a metre. The prefix **centi-** can be used with other units too, such as *gram* or *litre.*

cen·ti·pede *n* a small wormlike animal with a long, flat body and many pairs of legs.

cen·tre (sen′tər) **1** *n* the middle point or part: *the centre of a circle, the centre of a room.* **2** *n* a main point: *Toronto is a centre of trade.* **Center** is another spelling. **cen·tred, cen·tring.**

cen·tral **1** *adj* having to do with the centre or main part: *The sun is central in the solar system. What is the central idea in your story?* **–cen′tral·ly,** *adv.*

cen·tu·ry (sen′chə rē) *n* a period of 100 years, especially from one "round" hundred to the next: *From 1800 to 1900, or from 1824 to 1924, is a century. pl* **cen·tu·ries.**

USING WORDS . . . . century

The name of a century is almost always one more than the number of its hundred: 1867 is in the 19th century, 1967 is in the 20th century, and so on.

But what about, for example, the year 1900? Is it the first year of the 20th century, or the last year of the 19th? People have agreed that it should be the last year of the 19th century.

So, what date is the beginning of the 21st century?

Yes, that's right, if December 31, 2000 is the last day of the 20th century, then January 1, 2001 is the first day of the 21st century.

---

ce·ram·ic (sə ram′ik) **1** *adj* having to do with pottery: *a ceramic vase, ceramic tiles.* **2** *pl.n* **ceramics,** the art of making pottery: *We're learning ceramics in art class.*

ce·re·al (sē′rē əl) **1** *n* any grass that produces a grain used as food: *Wheat, rice, corn, oats, and barley are cereals.* **2** *n* food made from the grain, especially breakfast food: *Granola is my favourite cereal.*

cer·e·mo·ny (ser′ə mō′nē) *n* a set of acts to be done on special occasions such as weddings, funerals, graduations, etc.: *A rabbi performed the marriage ceremony. pl* **cer·e·mo·nies.**

cer·tain (sər′tən) **1** *adj* sure: *It is certain that 3 and 2 do not add up to 6.* **2** *adj* definite but not named: *Certain plants will not grow in Canada.* –**cer′tain·ly,** *adv,* –**cer′tain·ty,** *n,* *pl* **cer′tain·ties.**

cer·tif·i·cate (sər tif′ə kit) *n* a written statement that may be used as proof: *a birth certificate.*

CFCs chemicals that have been used to cool refrigerators and to make the mixture inside spray cans shoot out through the tiny opening. Scientists believe that when CFCs escape as gases, they destroy the ozone layer in the earth's atmosphere that helps protect us from harmful rays of the sun. The full name for CFCs is **chlorofluorocarbons** (klôr′ə flôr′ə kär′bəns).

chain (chān) **1** *n* a series of links joined together: *The anchor was attached to a heavy steel chain. We decorated the room with coloured paper chains.* **2** *n* any series of things linked together: *a mountain chain, a chain of events, a restaurant chain.*

chain store one of a group of stores owned and operated by a single company.

chair (cher) *n* a single seat with a back and, sometimes, arms.

chair·per·son *n* the person in charge of a meeting, committee, council, etc. **Chairperson, chairman,** and **chairwoman** are sometimes shortened to **chair.**

A ski chalet

cha·let (sha lā′) *n* a house in the countryside or forest: *They rent a ski chalet in Mont Tremblant during the winter.*

chalk (chok) **1** *n* a soft, white or grey limestone, made up mostly of very tiny bits of sea shell. **2** *n* a material like this used to make sticks for writing on a chalkboard. –**chalk′y,** *adj.*

chalk·board *n* a board with a smooth, hard surface for writing or drawing on with chalk.

chal·lenge (chal′ənj) **1** *v* invite someone to compete or take risk: *They challenged me to a race.* **2** *n* an invitation to compete or take a risk: *A mountain climber sees Mount Logan as a challenge.* **chal·lenged, chal·leng·ing.** –**chal′leng·er,** *n,* –**chal′leng·ing,** *adj.*

An African chameleon— about 20 cm long with the tail

cha·me·le·on (kə mē′lē ən) *n* a lizard that can change the colour of its skin to match its surroundings.

cham·pi·on (cham′pē ən) *n* the winner of a major contest or tournament: *an Olympic champion.* –**cham′pi·on·ship,** *n.*

chance (chans) **1** *n* a possibility: *a chance to make some money. There is a good chance that the sick child will get well.* **2** *n* fate; luck: *We didn't plan to meet; it happened by chance.* **3** *n* risk: *He took a chance when he swam across the Ottawa River.* **chanced, chanc·ing.**

stand a chance, have even the least possibility: *We don't stand a chance of winning without Lauren.*

chan·de·lier (shan′də lēr′) *n* a light fixture that hangs from a ceiling and has branches for individual lights.

change (chānj) **1** *v* make different; become different: *She changed the rules when we complained. He has changed a lot since last term.* **2** *n* the result of this: *There has been a change in plans.* **3** *v* switch: *to change clothes, to change seats, to change direction.* **4** *n* the money you get back when you give more than a thing costs: *If the bread is $1.50 and you pay with a toonie, you'll get 50¢ change.* **changed, chang·ing.** –**change′a·ble,** *adj,* –**change′less,** *adj.*

chan·nel (chan′əl) **1** *n* a passage for water: *The river had cut a channel through the rock.* **2** *n* a TV or radio station. **3** *n* a path on the Internet to information designed to appeal to a particular group of people. The Discover Channel for example, is for people who like science. **chan·nelled** or **chan·neled, chan·nel·ling** or **chan·nel·ing.**

chant (chant) **1** *n* a song where several words are sung to one note: *We have a tape of some Cree chants.* **2** *v* say words over and over to a steady beat: *We chanted, "Go, team, go!"* **–chant′er,** *n.*

cha·os (kā′os) *n* very great confusion; complete disorder: *The tornado left chaos behind it.* **–cha·ot′ic** (kā ot′ik), *adj.*

chap·ter (chap′tər) **1** *n* a main division of a book. **2** *n* a local branch of an organization, which holds its own meetings.

char (chär) *v* burn until black. **charred, char·ring.**

char·coal *n* a form of carbon produced from wood by a special burning process. It is black and can be used for drawing with as well as for fuel and in filters.

char·ac·ter (ker′ik tər) **1** *n* moral nature: *She is a woman of good character, honest and courageous.* **2** *n* a person in a movie, play, or story. **3** *n* any symbol used in writing, including letters, numerals, punctuation marks, math symbols, etc.

charge (chärj) **1** *v* ask as a price: *They charge $2 for eggs.* **2** *v* treat as a debt to be settled later; pay for with a **charge card** or a **charge account**: *Please charge this to my account.* **3** *v* or *n* rush forward, especially to attack: *The angry grizzly bear charged* (*v*). *The captain led the charge against the enemy* (*n*). **4** *v* accuse: *The officer charged me with speeding.* **5** *v* give or get a supply of electrical energy: *to charge a battery.* **6** *n* thrill or amusement: *He gets a real charge out of learning new skateboarding stunts.* **charged, charg·ing.**

in charge, in the position of responsibility: *The parents left a babysitter in charge. Who's in charge of intramural sports?*

char·i·ty (char′ə tē *or* cher′ə tē) **1** *n* gifts or work to help people in need. **2** *n* a group that does work or collects gifts for people in any kind

of need: *She gives money to the United Way and other charities.* *pl* **char·i·ties.**

charm (chärm) **1** *n* the quality that makes a person or thing delightful: *We were impressed by the dancer's grace and charm.* **2** *n* anything supposed to bring good luck. **–charm′ing,** *adj.*

chart (chärt) **1** *n* information arranged in a table, graph, diagram, etc. **2** *n* a sailor's map showing the coastlines, sailing routes, and dangerous places of an ocean.

char·ter (chär′tər) **1** *n* a document granting certain rights: *All Canadian banks must have charters from the federal government.* **2** *v* hire a bus, plane, etc. for private use.

chase (chās) **1** *v* follow or run after in order to catch: *The cat chased the mouse.* **2** *n* the act of going after in order to catch: *The thieves were caught after a long chase down the Trans-Canada Highway.* **3** *v* drive away; shoo: *to chase away flies.* **chased, chas·ing.**

chasm (kaz′əm) *n* a deep opening in the earth.

chat (chat) **1** *n* easy, familiar talk: *They had a nice chat about their holiday in Charlottetown.* **2** *v* talk in an easy, familiar way: *We sat chatting by the fire after supper.* **3** *n* have a discussion by computer. You type what you want to say while logged on to a special **chat line. chat·ted, chat·ting.**

A château in France

châ·teau (sha tō′) *n* a castle or a large country house in France, or a house built in the same style. **Chateau** is another spelling. *pl* **châ·teaux** or **cha·teaux** (sha tōz′).

chat·ter (chat′ər) **1** *v* talk fast and foolishly or make meaningless noise. **2** *n* rapid, foolish talk that goes on and on, or a sound like this. **3** *v* rattle together: *Cold weather makes your teeth chatter.* —**chat′ter·er,** *n.*

chat·ter·box *n* a person who talks on and on about nothing important.

chauf·feur (shō fər′ *or* shō′fər) *n* a person who drives a car for someone rich or famous: *A chauffeur drives the Prime Minister to all events.*

cheap (chēp) **1** *adj or adv* with a low price, or low prices: *cheap clothing, a cheap grocery store* (*adj*). *We sold the car cheap to get rid of it* (*adv*). **2** *adj* not worth very much: *cheap novels, cheap jewellery.* **3** *adv* stingy; not generous: *They were too cheap to give even a small tip to the waiter.* —**cheap′en,** *v,* —**cheap′ly,** *adv,* —**cheap′ness,** *n.*

cheat (chēt) **1** *v* trick someone; do something unfair or dishonest: *You have cheated me out of ten cents change.* **2** *n* a person who is not honest or fair and tries to trick others.

check (chek) **1** *v* see if something is right: *Check your answers before handing in your paper.* **2** *n* the act of doing this: *Run a spell check on this computer file before printing it.* **3** *n* Often, **check mark,** a mark like this [√] to show that something has been looked at and is OK. **4** *n* the bill in a restaurant. **5** *v* stop or hold back: *She started to say something rude, but checked herself just in time.* **6** *n* something that stops or holds back: *a speed check, a hockey check.* **7** *n* a pattern of little squares: *a sports shirt in a blue check.* —**checked,** *adj,* —**check′er,** *n.*

check·up *n* a careful check by a doctor, dentist, car mechanic, etc. to see that everything is OK.

check in, 1 arrive and register at a hotel, etc. **2** go to an airline counter to hand over your baggage and get your boarding pass.

check off, mark something on a list to show that it has been taken care of or is correct.

check on or **check up on,** find out about in order to see if there is some problem: *The police were checking up on her.*

check out, 1 leave a hotel or motel, etc. and pay your bill: *We checked out of the hotel at noon.* **2** in a store, take your purchases to the cashier and pay for them: *It took a long time to check out.*

✽ **chee·cha·ko** (chē chok′ō) *n* a newcomer: *It took the cheechako many months to learn the ways of the Yukon.*

cheek (chēk) **1** *n* either side of the face below the eye. **2** *n* disrespectful talk or behaviour: *That's enough of your cheek!* —**cheek′i·ly,** *adv,* —**cheek′y,** *adj.*

cheer (chēr) **1** *n* a shout of encouragement or praise: *Give three cheers for the birthday girl!* **2** *v* give shouts of encouragement or praise: *Everyone cheered our team.* —**cheer′ful,** *adj,* —**cheer′i·ly,** *adv,* —**cheer′less,** *adj,* —**cheer′y,** *adj.*

cheer up, make or become happier: *Cheer up, perhaps we'll win the next game.*

cheese (chēz) *n* a solid food made from the curds of milk.

A cheetah— about a metre tall

chee·tah (chē′tə) *n* a long-legged animal of the cat family, thought to be the fastest mammal on earth. It has a small head, long tail, and a reddish yellow coat with black spots: *Cheetahs are found in Africa and Asia.*

chef (shef) *n* a skilled cook, especially in a restaurant.

chem·i·cal (kem′ə kəl) **1** *n* a substance made or used in a laboratory: *Plastics, drugs, and insecticides are chemicals.* **2** *adj* having to do with any of these substances: *chemical preservatives, chemical pollution, the chemical industry.*

chem·is·try *n* the science that studies the simple substances (elements) that everything in the world is made of. —**chem′ist,** *n.*

cheque (chek) *n* a small form you can fill out and sign and give instead of cash. It tells the bank to take money from your account and pay it to the person or company you have named: *She pays her bills by cheque.*

chest (chest) **1** *n* the upper front part of the body, containing the ribs, lungs, heart, etc. **2** *n* a large box with a hinged lid: *a linen chest, a tool chest.*

✽ **ches·ter·field** (ches′tər fēld′) *n* a long, covered seat with a back and arms; a sofa.

chest·nut (ches′nut) **1** *n* a sweet nut with a prickly outer shell. **2** *adj* deep reddish brown: *chestnut hair.* **3** *n* a horse of this colour.

chew (chū) *v* crush or grind with the teeth: *Some meat is hard to chew.*

chewing gum candy meant to be chewed without swallowing. It is sticky and stretchy.

chew·y *adj* not crunchy: *a chewy caramel candy.*

chick·en (chik′ən) **1** *n* a hen or rooster, especially a young one. **2** *n* the meat of a chicken, used as food. **3** *adj Slang.* cowardly; timid: *My friends said I was too chicken to jump off the tree branch.*

chick *n* a baby chicken or other bird.

chicken pox a very contagious disease that gives you a fever and a rash. Most children get it once.

chief (chēf) **1** *n* the top leader: *a police chief.* The chief of a First Nations band is elected by the people and speaks for them in dealings with the government. **2** *adj* most important; main: *the chief reason.* –**chief′ly,** *adv.*

child (chīld) **1** *n* a young boy or girl, especially one up to the early teens. **2** *n* a son or daughter: *The Ricos have three grown-up children.* *pl* **chil·dren.** –**child′hood,** *n.*

child·ish 1 *adj* acting like a very young child when in fact you are older and should know better: *How childish to make such a fuss over a little thing like that!* **2** *adj* normal for a child: *childish trust.* A more usual word for this meaning is **childlike.** –**child′ish·ly,** *adv,* –**child′ish·ness,** *n.*

USING WORDS . childish/childlike

Both **childish** and **childlike** mean "like a child."

Usually, **childish** stresses the not-yet-grown-up side of being a child, so it is not a compliment when used to describe an adult: *Childish people can sulk if they don't get their own way.*

But **childlike** stresses that a child has the good qualities of being honest and trusting, so it can be a compliment when used to describe an adult: *The woman has a childlike belief that the people in her family don't tell lies.*

---

chil·i (chil′ē) **1** *n* the spicy dried pod of a kind of red pepper, used for seasoning. **2** *n* short for **chili con carne** (chil′ē kən kár′nē), hamburger cooked with chilies or chili powder, kidney beans, and tomatoes. *pl* **chil·ies.**

chill (chil) **1** *n* unpleasant coldness: *There was a sharp chill in the air.* **2** *n* make cold: *We chilled the pop in the fridge.* **3** *n* a sudden coldness of the body with shivering: *She was very sick with chills and fever.* –**chill′y,** *adj.*

chime (chīm) **1** *pl.n* **chimes,** a set of bells tuned to the musical scale. **2** *v* the musical sound of bells or a sound like it: *We heard the chime of the clock every hour.* **chimed, chim·ing.**

chim·ney (chim′nē) *n* an upright tubelike structure that lets in a draft for a fireplace and carries the smoke out through the roof. *pl* **chim·neys.**

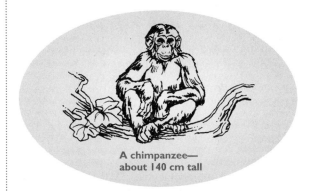

A chimpanzee—
about 140 cm tall

chim·pan·zee (chim′pan zē′ *or* chim pan′zē) *n* an intelligent ape of Africa. The name is often shortened informally to **chimp.**

chin (chin) *n* the bottom of the face at the front.

chi·na (chī′nə) *n* a fine, delicate white pottery made of clay baked by a special process, first used in China. **Porcelain** is another name for it.

chink (chingk) *n* a narrow opening; crack: *The arrow entered a chink in the knight's armour.*

❀ **chi·nook** (shi nùk′) *n* a warm winter wind that blows from the west across the Rocky Mountains into Alberta. When a chinook blows, the temperature can rise 15°C in an hour.

chip (chip) **1** *n* a small, thin piece cut or broken off: *wood chips, dried banana chips.* **2** *n* a place where a small piece has broken off: *One of the new plates has a chip on the edge.* **3** *v* cut or break off in small pieces: *He chipped off the old paint.* **4** *n* in electronics, a small, flat piece of silicon with many tiny electric circuits on it. Chips are used a lot in computers, often to add memory. **chipped, chip·ping.**

chip in, *Informal.* give a share: *If we all chipped in, we'd have enough money for pizza.*

chip·munk (chip′mungk) *n* a small, striped North American ground squirrel.

chis·el (chiz′əl) *n* a tool with a steel cutting edge at the end of a strong blade: *Chisels are used for shaping wood, stone, or metal.*

chiv·al·ry (shiv′əl rē) *n* the rules and customs of knights in the Middle Ages. **chiv′al·rous**, *adj*, **chiv′al·rous·ly**, *adv*.

chlor·ine (klȯr ēn′) *n* a chemical element often added to things to bleach or disinfect them. City tap water and paper pulp are usually **chlorinated**. At normal temperatures chlorine is a greenish yellow, bad-smelling, poisonous gas. –**chlor′in·ate′**, *v*.

chlor·o·phyl (klȯr′ə fil′) *n* the green colouring matter of plants. It changes carbon dioxide, water, and sunlight into food for the plant. Another spelling is **chlorophyll.**

choc·o·late (chok′lit) *n* a dark brown substance used as a food or flavouring and made by roasting and grinding cacao seeds.

choice (chois) **1** *n* the act of choosing: *Be careful in your choice of friends.* **2** *n* the person or thing chosen: *This story was the judges' choice.* **3** *n* a variety to choose from: *a wide choice of vegetables in the market.* **choic·er, choic·est.**

choir (kwīr) *n* an organized group of singers: *a school choir.*

choke (chōk) **1** *v* make or be unable to breathe because the windpipe is being blocked: *The smoke almost choked the firefighters. He choked when some food stuck in his throat.* **2** *v* clog; plug: *Sand is choking the river.* **choked, chok·ing.**
choke up, be or cause to be about to cry: *I choked up when she got to the sad part of her story.*

cho·les·ter·ol (kə les′tə rol′) *n* a chemical fatty substance made by the body and found in foods such as milk and meat. Scientists believe that some forms of it may cause heart disease: *Her doctor advised her to cut down on cholesterol.*

choose (chūz) *v* pick out from different possibilities: *Choose the cake you like best.* **chose, cho·sen, choos·ing.**

choos·y *Informal. adj* hard to please: *She's very choosy when renting a video.*

chop (chop) **1** *v* cut by hitting with something sharp: *to chop wood with an axe.* **2** *v* cut into small pieces: *to chop up cabbage.* **chopped, chop·ping.**

Chopsticks

chop·sticks (chop′stiks′) *pl.n* a pair of light, thin sticks used together in one hand, something like tongs, for picking up food.

chord (kȯrd) *n* three or more notes of music sounded at the same time in harmony.

chore (chȯr) **1** *n* a minor task, especially one that must be done daily: *Feeding the chickens is one of the chores on a farm.* **2** *n* a task that is tiresome: *I found the work quite a chore.*

chor·us (kȯr′əs) **1** *n* a group of singers, sometimes together with dancers. **2** *n* the part of a song that is repeated after each verse.

Christ (krīst) *n* Jesus of Nazareth, regarded by Christians as the Son of God.

Chris·ti·an·i·ty (kris′chē an′ə tē) *n* the religion that accepts Jesus of Nazareth as the Son of God. –**Chris′tian** (kris′chən), *adj or n*.

Christ·mas (kris′məs) *n* the yearly celebration of the birth of Christ. In most Christian churches, Christmas is on December 25.

chron·o·log·i·cal (kron′ə loj′ə kəl) *adj* arranged according to the order in which things happened: *The teacher asked them to put together a chronological list of the events.*

chub·by (chub′ē) *adj* round and plump: *chubby cheeks.* **chub·bi·er, chub·bi·est.**

chuck (chuk) **1** *v* throw; toss: *He chucked his boots in a corner.* **2** *n* *Informal.* in the West, food.
chuck·wag·on *n* in the West, a wagon that carries food and cooking equipment for cowhands, harvest hands, etc. The **chuckwagon race** is a traditional event at rodeos and stampedes in Western Canada.

chuck·le (chuk′əl) **1** *v* laugh quietly: *Mom chuckled as she watched us trying to give the dog a bath.* **2** *n* a soft laugh. **chuck·led, chuck·ling.**

chum (chum) *Informal. n* a friend. –**chum′my**, *adj*.

chunk (chungk) *n* a thick piece or lump: *a chunk of wood, bread, etc.* –**chunk′y**, *adj*.

church (chərch) *n* a building for public Christian worship.

churn (chərn) **1** *n* a machine for turning cream into butter by beating and shaking. **2** *v* seem to move as if beaten and shaken: *The water churns in the Lachine Rapids.*

chute (shūt) *n* a sloping trough for dropping or sliding things down to a lower level. There are chutes for carrying mail, dirty clothes, garbage, etc. A toboggan slide is also called a chute.

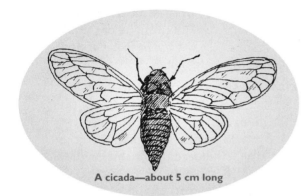

A cicada—about 5 cm long

ci·ca·da (sə kā′də) *n* a large insect with transparent wings. The male cicada makes a buzzing sound in hot, dry weather.

cinch (sinch) **1** *n* a strong belt for fastening a saddle on a horse. **2** *n Informal.* something easy: *Making brownies is a cinch.*

cin·e·ma (sin′ə mə) *n* a movie theatre.

cin·na·mon (sin′ə mən) *n* a spice made of the inner bark of a tree that grows in the East Indies. It is light reddish brown.

cin·quain (sing′ kān) *n* a poem or a verse of poetry that has five lines.

ci·pher (sī′fər) *n* secret writing; code: *The club members sent secret notes in cipher.*

cir·cle (sər′kəl) **1** *n* an exactly round shape. Every point on the curved line of a circle is the same distance from the centre. **2** *v* move around in a circle: *The airplane circled the airport before it landed.* **3** *v* draw a circle around: *Circle the answer you think is correct.* **4** *n* a group of people held together by the same interests: *the family circle, a circle of friends.* **5** in aboriginal culture, a symbol for the way that nature, culture, the community, the Creator, and the individual are all related and touch one another. **cir·cled, cir·cling.** –**cir′cu·lar,** *adj.*

cir·cum·fer·ence (sər kum′fə rəns) *n* the distance around a circle or anything round.

cir·cuit (sər′kit) **1** *n* movement in a circle around something: *It takes a year for the earth to make its circuit of the sun.* **2** *n* the complete path followed by an electric current. A **circuit board** in a computer has various electronic parts mounted on it, for an electric current to pass through. A **circuit breaker** is a switch that automatically breaks the circuit when the current is too strong.

cir·cu·late (sər′kyə lāt′) *v* go or send around; pass from person to person or place to place: *to circulate a rumour. Blood circulates in our veins.* **cir·cu·lat·ed, cir·cu·lat·ing.** –**cir·cu·la′tion,** *n.*

cir·cum·flex (sər′kəm fleks′) *n* a mark (ˆ) used over a vowel in certain languages to show how it is pronounced. There is a circumflex in the French word *hôtel.*

cir·cum·stance (sər′kəm stans′) *n* one of a set of events that influence something: *The place, the weather, and other circumstances made the picnic a great success.*

cir·cus (sər′kəs) *n* a travelling company of acrobats, clowns, jugglers, etc. who put on shows for the public: *The circus is in town.*

cit·a·del (sit′ə dəl) *n* a fortress, especially one in a city: *Halifax has a famous citadel.*

cit·i·zen (sit′ə zən) *n* a member of a state or nation, with certain rights and duties. A person can be a citizen of a country by birth, or become one by going through certain procedures. –**cit′i·zen·ship,** *n.*

cit·y (sit′ē) **1** *n* a large town: *Montréal is one of the largest cities in Canada.* **2** *n* the people living in a city: *The whole city celebrated when the Blue Jays won the World Series.* pl **cit·ies.**

civ·i·li·za·tion (siv′ə lī zā′shən) **1** *n* a people with a well-developed social system and a culture that includes arts and sciences: *The Selkirk First Nation found the remains of a prehistoric civilization in the Yukon.* **2** *n Informal.* all the conveniences of modern life: *After a month of camping, it was good to get back to civilization.*

claim (klām) **1** *v* say that something belongs to you: *Does anyone claim this pencil?* **2** *n* a right to expect something: *She has a claim on us because she gave us a place to live.* **3** *v* declare as a fact, with or without proof: *He claims he can run faster than his older brother.*

stake your claim, choose and claim an area of land, living space, etc.

Hard-shell clams are found in salt water. The shells were used as money, called *wampum*, by some First Nation peoples.

clam (klam) *n* a shellfish with a soft body and a hinged double shell, living in sand along the seashore or at the edges of lakes and rivers. Some clams are good to eat.
clam up, *Informal.* stop talking all of a sudden: *He had been chatting happily, but clammed up as soon as I mentioned the accident.*

clam·my (klam′ē) *adj* cold and damp: *The walls of the cave were clammy.* **clam·mi·er, clam·mi·est.**

clam·our (klam′ər) **1** *n* a loud noise, especially of voices. **2** *v* make a loud noise, especially to complain or ask for something: *The children were clamouring for a picnic.* Another spelling is **clamour.**

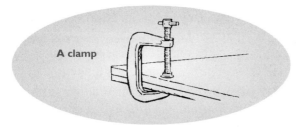

A clamp

clamp (klamp) *n* a device for holding things tightly together: *She used a clamp to hold the joint until the glue dried.*
clamp down on, forbid or punish strictly: *The police are clamping down on cyclists who ride without helmets.*

clap (klap) **1** *n* a sudden, sharp, loud noise, such as a single burst of thunder or the sound of the hands struck together. **2** *v* hit the palms of your hands together: *The audience clapped loudly when the Vancouver Canucks scored a goal.*
clapped, clap·ping.

clash (klash) **1** *n* a loud, harsh sound like metal striking metal. **2** *n* a strong disagreement: *a clash of opinion.* **3** *v* go badly together: *Your tie clashes with your shirt.*

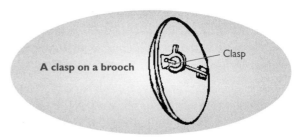

A clasp on a brooch — Clasp

clasp (klasp) **1** *n* a fastener with a hook of some kind: *This suede belt has a gold clasp.* **2** *v* hold tightly with the hand or the arms: *Rahel clasped her new puppy in her arms. He clasped a coin in his hand.*

class (klas) **1** *n* a group of students taught together. **2** *n* any group of people or things thought of together because they are the same in some way. In science, mammals are a class of animals; they all feed their babies with milk.
class·mate *n* a member of the same class in school. **class·room** *n* a room in which classes are held.

clas·sic (klas′ik) **1** *n* a book or artistic work of the highest rank or quality: *Robert Munsch's* The Paper Bag Princess *is a Canadian classic.* **2** *adj* very typical: *a classic example of good handwriting.*
clas·si·cal *adj* recognized over time as being of high artistic excellence: *She likes classical music.*

clas·si·fy (klas′ə fī′) *v* put in groups or classes; group in some way. In the post office, mail is classified according to where it is going.
Classified ads in a newspaper are arranged according to what they are offering or asking for.
clas·si·fied, clas·si·fy·ing. —**class′i·fi·ca′tion,** *n.*

clat·ter (klat′ər) **1** *n* a loud rattling noise: *the clatter of dishes.* **2** *v* move with a loud rattling noise: *The wagon clattered over the stones.*

clause (kloz) *n* a group of words containing a subject and a verb. The sentence *He arrived before we left* has two clauses: *He arrived* is a **main clause** that could stand alone as a sentence and *before we left* is a **subordinate clause** that adds information.

Grammar ✓*Check* .. clause/phrase

A **clause** is a group of words that has a subject and a verb: *when the dog barked.*

A **phrase** is a group of words that does not have a subject and a verb: *with the barking dog.*

claw (klo) **1** *n* a sharp, hooked nail on the toe of a bird or animal: *The chicken scratched the earth with its claws.* **2** *v* scratch, tear, or pull with claws or fingernails: *The kitten was clawing the screen door.*

clay (klā) *n* a sticky kind of earth that can be easily shaped when wet and hardens when dried or baked. Bricks and dishes are made from various kinds of clay.

clean (klēn) **1** *adj* not dirty at all: *clean clothes, clean air.* **2** *adj* make clean: *to clean a room.* **3** *adv* completely; totally: *I clean forgot about the invitation.* –**clean′ly,** *adv,* –**clean′ness,** *n.*

clean·li·ness (klen′lē nis) *n* cleanness as a habit: *Personal cleanliness was very important to him.*

clear (klēr) **1** *adj* not cloudy, misty, or hazy: *a clear morning.* **2** *adj* easy to see through; transparent: *clear glass.* **3** *adj* easily heard, seen, or understood: *a clear voice, a clear outline, a clear explanation. It is clear that it is going to rain.* **4** *adj* make or become clear: *Clear your desk. The sky cleared.* **5** *v* give or get permission for: *I can probably go, but I have to clear it with my parents first.* **6** *v* make as total profit: *We cleared $40 at our bake sale.* –**clear′ly,** *adv.*

clear-cut 1 *adj* clear and distinct; not vague: *a clear-cut image, clear-cut ideas.* **2** *v* cut down all the trees in an area. **clear-cut, clear-cutting.** –**clear′cut′ting,** *n.* **clear·ing** *n* an open space of cleared land in a forest.

clear out, 1 make clear by throwing out or emptying: *to clear out a cupboard.* **2** *Informal.* go away; leave: *We cleared out as soon as the show was over.*

clear up, make or become clear: *The weather will clear up soon. Clear up this mess. Your explanation has cleared up everything.*

clev·er (klev′ər) *adj* bright; quick to learn and good at coming up with solutions, ideas, plans, tricks, etc.: *The clever student solved the difficult puzzle.* –**clev′er·ly,** *adv,* –**clev′er·ness,** *n.*

cli·ché (klē shā′) *n* a word, phrase, or idea that has been used too much and has lost most of its power: *She tried her best to write without clichés. pl* **cli·chés.**

cliff (klif) *n* a steep, high wall of rock or earth: *Great white cliffs line the Gaspé Peninsula.*

cli·mate (klī′mit) *n* the kind of weather patterns a place usually has.

cli·max (klī′maks) *n* the highest point of interest; the most exciting part: *Shooting the rapids of the Nahanni River was the climax of our canoe trip.*

climb (klīm) **1** *v* go up, especially step by step: *to climb a hill, to climb a ladder. The price of food has climbed during the past year.* **2** *n* the act of going up: *Our climb up.* **3** *v* go in any direction with the help of the hands: *to climb down a rope. She climbed under the fence.*

cling (kling) *v* hold tightly: *The child clung to his father. They cling to their hope of a happier future. A vine clings to the wall.* **clung, cling·ing.** –**cling′y,** *adj.*

clin·ic (klin′ik) **1** *n* a place where people can get medical treatment: *They have the latest equipment in the eye clinic.* **2** *n* a special session held to deal with certain problems: *a foot care clinic, a soccer clinic.*

The most famous builder of clipper ships was a Canadian, Donald McKay.

clip (klip) **1** *v* cut or cut out with shears, scissors, or clippers: *to clip your nails. I'm going to clip this recipe and save it.* **2** *n* a short portion from a movie or video: *a film clip.* **3** *n* a fast speed: *We rode through the village at quite a clip.* **4** *n* a fastener that works by squeezing, such as a paperclip. **clipped, clip·ping.**

clip art pictures or designs stored in a computer program or on a compact disc that can be copied and used: *She found an excellent picture of a dinosaur in the clip art.* **clip·board** *n* a small board with a strong spring clip for holding papers. **clip·per 1** Often, **clippers,** *pl.n* a tool for cutting: *hair clippers, a nail clipper.* **2** *n* a sailing ship built for speed: *Clippers from Nova Scotia used to sail all over the world.* **clip·ping** *n* a piece cut out of a newspaper, magazine, etc.

cloak (klōk) *n* a loose outer garment usually without sleeves.

clock (klok) *n* an instrument for measuring and showing time, made to be hung on a wall or set on a desk, etc. but not for wearing on the body.
around the clock, all day and all night.

clock·wise (klok′wīz′) *adv or adj* in the direction in which the hands of a clock move: *Turn the lid clockwise to tighten it (adv).* The opposite direction is **counter-clockwise.**

clock·work (klok′wərk′) *n* the machinery of a clock, or any machinery that works the same way. Wind-up toys are run by clockwork.
like clockwork, very smoothly and regularly: *The launching of the rocket went off like clockwork.*

clog (klog) *v* block or become blocked by filling up; plug up: *Leaves clogged the drain.* **clogged, clog·ging.**

clone (klōn) **1** *v* to copy a plant or animal in every detail by taking a cell from it and developing it in a laboratory: *Everyone was amazed when scientists were able to clone a sheep.* **2** *n* a person or thing that is, or seems to be, an exact copy of another: *In the science fiction story, the girl makes her clone do all her work. The TV show was so successful that many clones of it appeared.* **cloned, clon·ing.**

close (klōz *for 1 and 2,* klōs *for 3-6*) **1** *v* shut: *The sleepy child's eyes are closing.* **2** *v* finish; end: *Our school play closes tomorrow.* **closed, clos·ing.**
3 *adj* near: *close to home.* **4** *adj* nearly equal: *The race was a close contest.* **5** *adj* stifling; stuffy: *With the windows shut, the room was hot and close.* **6** *adj* stingy: *Scrooge was close with his money.* **clos·er, clos·est.** –**close′ly,** *adv,* –**close′ness,** *n.*
closed-cap·tioned (klōzd′ kap′shənd) *adj* broadcast on television with captions underneath the pictures so that people who are deaf can follow the words. –**closed captioning.**
close-up (klōs′up′) *n* a picture taken at close range: *That's a good close-up of the flowers.*

clos·et (kloz′it) *n* a small room or large cupboard for storing things: *Hang your coat in the closet.*

cloth (kloth) *n* material made from wool, silk, linen, cotton, or other fibre: *Cloth is used to make clothes, curtains, sheets, etc.*

clothe (klōŦH) *v* put clothes on; dress. **clothed** or **clad, cloth·ing.**

clothes (klōz *or* klōŦHz) *pl.n* the things that people wear; shirts, dresses, pants, etc. **Clothing** is another word for it.

cloud (kloud) **1** *n* a white or grey mass in the sky, made up of very tiny drops of water or ice particles: *A cloud hid the sun and rain began to fall.* **2** *n* anything thought of as bringing darkness or dimness: *a cloud of gloom, a cloud of dust.* **3** *v* darken or dim: *The sky clouded over. Her face clouded with anger.* –**cloud′less,** *adj,* –**cloud′y,** *adj.*

clout (klout) **1** *v* hit hard: *The bully clouted me on the head.* **2** *n Informal.* power and influence: *He has no clout, because nobody respects him.*

clown (kloun) **1** *n* a person in a costume who makes people laugh with a show full of tricks and jokes: *The clowns in the parade were very funny.* **2** *v* act like a clown; act silly.

club (klub) **1** *n* a heavy stick of wood, thick at one end, used as a weapon. **2** *n* a special stick used in some games to hit a ball: *golf clubs.* **3** *v* beat or hit with a club. **4** *n* a group of people joined together for some special purpose: *a tennis club.* **clubbed, club·bing.**
club together, unite for some special purpose: *We clubbed together to collect items for recycling.*

clue (klū) *n* something that helps to solve a mystery or problem: *The police could find no clues to help them solve the crime.*

clump (klump) *n* a group set very close together: *a clump of trees.*

clum·sy (klum′zē) *adj* always bumping into things, dropping things, etc. **clum·si·er, clum·si·est.** –**clum′si·ly,** *adv.*

clus·ter (klus′tər) **1** *n* a number of things of the same kind grouped close together: *a cluster of grapes, a little cluster of houses.* **2** *v* be in a bunch; gather in a group: *The students clustered around their teacher.*

clutch (kluch) *v* grasp tightly: *The frightened boy clutched his big sister's hand.*

clut·ter (klut′ər) **1** *n* too many things taking up space. **2** *v* fill or cover with things: *His desk was cluttered with books and papers.*

cm *symbol for* centimetre or centimetres.

co– *a prefix meaning* with; together. *Co-operate* means "work together."

coach (kōch) **1** *n* a bus that travels between cities. **2** *n* a passenger car of a railway train. **3** *n* in the old days, a large, closed horse-drawn carriage with seats inside and, often, on top, driven by a **coachman. 4** *n* a person who trains others: *a football coach, a music coach.* **5** *v* train or teach: *His tutor coached him in math.*

coal (kōl) *n* a black mineral formed in the earth from partly decayed plants that have been under great pressure for a long time: *Coal is mined for use as a fuel.*

coarse (kòrs) **1** *adj* made up of fairly large bits. Coarse gravel has bigger stones than fine gravel. **2** *adj* rough; not delicate, elegant, or fine: *coarse food, coarse language.* **coars·er, coars·est. –coars'en,** *v,* **–coarse'ly,** *adv,* **–coarse'ness,** *n.*

coast (kōst) **1** *n* the seashore: *Many ships were wrecked along the coast of the Bruce Peninsula.* **2** *v* move along without using effort or power: *to coast downhill on a bike or snowboard.* **coast·line** *n* the outline of a coast: *the rugged coastline of Newfoundland.*

coat (kōt) **1** *n* a piece of clothing with sleeves, worn over other clothes. **2** *n* the fur or hair of an animal. **3** *n* Sometimes, **coating,** a thin layer: *a coat of paint.* **4** *v* cover with a thin layer: *This pill is coated with sugar.*

coax (kōks) *v* persuade by soft words and gentle ways: *She coaxed the shy newcomer to join the game.*

cob (kob) *n* the central part of an ear of corn, that the kernels grow on.

co·balt (kō'bolt) *n* a silver-white metal used in making steel, paint, etc.

cob·ble (kob'əl) *v* repair shoes. **cob·bled, cob·bling. –cob'bler,** *n.*

co·bra (kō'brə) *n* a very poisonous snake of tropical Asia and Africa. An excited cobra can flatten its neck so that its head looks like a hood.

cob·web (kob'web') *n* an old spider's web that has trapped a lot of dust.

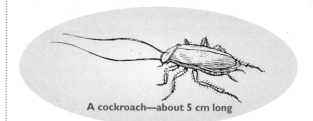
A cockroach—about 5 cm long

cock (kok) **1** *n* a rooster; a male chicken or the male of other birds. **2** *n* a small pile of hay, rounded on top.

cock·pit *n* the place where the pilot sits in an aircraft. **cock·roach** (kok'rōch') *n* an insect with long feelers and a long, flat, shiny body.

co·co·nut (kō'kə nut') *n* the large, round, brown, hard-shelled seed of a tree called the **coconut palm.** Coconuts have a thick white lining inside and a white liquid in the centre called **coconut milk.** Both are good to eat.

co·coon (kə kün') *n* a silky covering that protects a young insect while it is changing into an adult.

cod (kod) *n* a food fish of the cold parts of the northern Atlantic Ocean. *pl* **cod** or **cods.**

code (kōd) **1** *n* any system of symbols to stand for information. Ordinary writing is a well-known code, but a code can also be secret writing, or hand signals, or beeps like the **Morse code.** A computer program is also a code. **2** *n* any collection of laws or rules: *the criminal code, a moral code.* **cod·ed, cod·ing.**

cof·fee (kof'ē) *n* a dark-brown drink or flavouring made from the roasted and ground beans of a tall shrub that grows on mountainsides in the tropics.

coil (koil) **1** *v* wind around and around to form a curl: *The sailor coiled the rope so it would not take up much space. The garter snake coiled around a branch.* **2** *n* a series of such curls: *The coil of hose was hung on the wall.* **3** *n* one or two wires.

coin (koin) *n* a piece of metal stamped by a government for use as money. Loonies are coins. **–coin'age,** *n.*

co·in·ci·dence (kō in'sə dəns) *n* the chance happening of two or more things together that seems remarkable: *My cousin was born on the same day as I was. Isn't that a coincidence?*

cold (kōld) **1** *adj* a lot less warm than your body: *Snow and ice are cold.* **2** *adj* not warm or hot enough: *This coffee is cold. My feet are cold.* **3** *n* coldness; chilly weather; low temperature: *the cold of winter.* **4** *n* a common sickness that causes a stuffy or runny nose and, sometimes, a cough or a sore throat. –**cold′ness,** *n.*

cold-blood·ed *adj* having blood that is about the same temperature as the air or water around the animal: *Cold-blooded animals such as turtles must hibernate to survive the Canadian winter.*

catch cold, become sick with a cold.

have or **get cold feet,** be nervous or afraid.

in cold blood, without feeling sorry at all.

leave someone cold, be completely uninteresting.

out cold, unconscious.

col·lage (kə làzh′) *n* a picture or design made by pasting different items on a background.

col·lapse (kə laps′) *v* break down suddenly: *The old Muskoka chair collapsed when my uncle sat on it.* **col·lapsed, col·laps·ing.**

col·lar (kol′ər) **1** *n* the part of a coat, a dress, or a shirt that fits around the neck. **2** *n* a band around a pet's neck.

col·lect (kə lekt′) **1** *v* gather together: *to collect money for charity. The teacher collected our homework.* **2** *v* gather as a hobby: *Aaron collects stamps and coins.* –**col·lec′tor,** *n.* –**col·lec′tion,** *n.*

Grammar ✓Check . collective noun

- A collective noun refers to a group of people or things, but is singular in form: *The basketball team was chosen early in September. This bunch of flowers smells beautiful.*
- There are many special collective nouns that go with certain groups of animals: *a gaggle of geese, a troop of monkeys, a pride of lions.* Can you think of any others?
  (A good thesaurus will have a list.)

col·lege (kol′ij) *n* a school you can go to after high school.

❧ **col·le·giate** (kə lē′jit) *n* a high school.

col·lide (kə līd′) *v* run into each other; crash: *The lacrosse players collided on the field.* **col·lid·ed, col·lid·ing.** –**col·li′sion** (kə lizh′ən), *n.*

co·logne (kə lōn′) *n* a sweet-smelling liquid like perfume, but with a much weaker scent.

co·lon (kō′lən) *n* a punctuation mark (:) used after a sentence or heading to show that an explanation, example, list, long quotation, etc. follows. *Example: I have been in three countries: Canada, the United States, and Pakistan.*

Grammar ✓Check . . . . . colon

You often see a **colon** just before a list:
Party decorations: Elen, Jacques, Strother.
Please bring the following: snacks, a soft drink, two balloons, and a pair of socks.

col·o·ny (kol′ə nē) **1** *n* a territory ruled by a powerful country far away which has **colonized** it, or taken it by force and sent people to live there: *During the 1800s, England added to its colonies in Africa and Asia.* **2** *n* a group of people who are sent or who decide to go to live there from the conquering country, and the towns and farms that they make. These people are also called **colonists.** **3** *n* a number of people of one country, faith, or occupation living as a group: *There are several Doukhobour colonies in Saskatchewan.* **4** *n* a group of animals or plants of one kind, living or growing together: *We found two colonies of ants under the steps.* *pl* **col·o·nies.**

col·our (kul′ər) **1** *n* red, yellow, blue, or any combination of them: *The colour you get from mixing yellow and blue is green.* **2** *v* give colour to; put colour on: *Colour the sky blue.* **3** *n* an interesting quality: *Add details to the story to give it some colour.*
–**col′our·ful** or **col′or·ful,** *adj,*
–**col′our·less** or **col′or·less,** *adj.*
people of colour, people with brown or black skin.
with flying colours, with great success: *You all passed the test with flying colours.*

USING WORDS . . . . . colour

Colour is the spelling used by most Canadians, but in many places the spelling **color** is preferred.

This also happens with other words, for example: **favour** and **favor, honour** and **honor, labour** and **labor, odour** and **odor.**

co·los·sal (kə los′əl) *adj* huge; gigantic; enormous: *a colossal explosion, a colossal mistake.*

col·umn (kol′əm) **1** *n* a slender, upright structure; pillar. **2** *n* anything narrow and tall or long like a column: *A column of smoke rose from the fire. I added up the column of figures. The children lined up in two columns at the bus stop.* **3** *n* a narrow division of a page reading from top to bottom, kept separate by lines or blank spaces: *This page has two columns.* **4** *n* a piece of writing on a certain subject or by a certain writer, that appears regularly in a newspaper or magazine: *She writes a sports column for the Calgary Herald.*

The comb of a rooster

A comb for hair

comb (kōm) **1** *n* a narrow, short piece of plastic, wood, metal, etc. with teeth, used to tidy the hair or hold it in place. **2** *v* search thoroughly: *We combed the neighbourhood for our lost dog.* **3** *n* the thick, red, fleshy piece on the head of chickens and some other birds: *A rooster has a larger comb than a hen has.*

com·bat (kom′bat) **1** *v* fight against: *The Ojibwa used plants to combat disease.* **2** *n* fighting; battle: *The soldier was wounded in combat.* **com·bat·ted** or **com·bat·ed, com·bat·ting** or **com·bat·ing.**

com·bine (kəm bīn′ *for 1,* kom′bīn *for 2*) **1** *v* join together: *The two classes combined to lead the assembly.* **2** *n* a machine used in harvesting. **com·bined, com·bin·ing.**
com·bi·na·tion (kom′bə nā′shən) **1** *n* the action or result of combining things: *The combination of flour and water makes paste.* **2** *n* a series of numbers you follow to open a certain kind of lock: *He forgot the combination to his bicycle lock.*

com·bust (kəm bust′) *adj* catch on fire and burn: *Oily rags may combust if left lying around.* **–com·bus′ti·ble,** *adj,* **–com·bus′tion,** *n.*

come (kum) **1** *v* move toward the person speaking: *Come over here.* **2** *v* arrive: *The train comes at noon.* **came, come, com·ing.**
come about, happen: *The crash came about by accident.*
come across, meet or find by chance: *He came across a dollar in the street.*
come along, improve; progress: *She is coming along well after her operation.*
come from, be born in or live in: *That boy comes from a rich family. I come from Alberta.*
come out with, say: *His little brother comes out with the funniest things!*
come up, be mentioned: *The question is sure to come up in class.*
come up with, produce, especially as a solution to a problem: *She came up with the right answer.*

com·e·dy (kom′ə dē) *n* a funny movie, play, or show with a happy ending. *pl* **com·e·dies.**
co·me·di·an (kə mē′dē ən) *n* a person who makes people laugh, especially one who does this for a living. **com·ic** (kom′ik) **1** *adj* having to do with comedy: *A clown is a comic actor.* **2** *n* a comedian. **3** *n* a cartoon drawing. A series of them is a **comic strip,** and a whole booklet of them is a **comic book.** A newspaper may have a page or section of them, called the **comics.** **–com′i·cal,** *adj.*

com·et (kom′it) *n* a bright body in space that has a starlike centre and a usually cloudy tail.

com·fort (kum′fərt) **1** *v* lessen someone's sadness: *His kind words comforted the sobbing child.* **2** *n* freedom from hardship: *to have enough money to live in comfort.*
com·fort·a·ble 1 *adj* relaxed: *The warm fire made him feel comfortable after a cold day outdoors.* **2** *adj* that lets you feel relaxed: *a comfortable chair.* **–com′fort·a·bly,** *adv.*

com·ma (kom′ə) *n* a punctuation mark (,), usually used where a pause would be made in saying a sentence out loud.

com·mand (kə mand′) **1** *v* order: *The officer commanded the man to stop.* **2** *n* an order: *He obeyed the officer's command. Key in the command to copy this file onto your computer, please.* **3** *v* be the boss of: *Who commands this ship?* **4** *n* control: *to take command. The captain is in command.* **5** *n* the ability to use well: *She has a good command of the English language.* **6** *v* deserve and get: *Her firm manner commands respect.* **–com·mand′ing,** *adj.*

com·mem·o·rate (kə mem′ə rāt′) v honour the memory of: *This stamp commemorates the first transatlantic radio message received at St. John's, in 1901.* **com·mem·o·rat·ed, com·mem·o·rat·ing.** –**com·mem′o·ra′tion,** n.

com·ment (kom′ent) 1 n a note: *The teacher had written helpful comments on my homework.* 2 v make a note: *Everyone commented on Roberta Bondar's successful space mission.*

com·men·ta·tor n a person who talks about the news, sports, etc. on radio or television: *a sports commentator.*

com·merce (kom′ərs) n trade; business; buying and selling in large amounts.

com·mer·cial (kə mər′shəl) 1 adj having to do with buying and selling: *a commercial TV station.* 2 n an advertisement on radio or TV: *The movie was interrupted by many commercials.*

com·mit (kə mit′) 1 v do (usually something wrong): *A person who steals commits a crime.* 2 v **commit yourself**, make a firm statement: *When I asked if she agreed, she refused to commit herself, and only said "Maybe."* 3 v devote: *a large sum of money has been committed to this project.* –**com·mit·ted, com·mit·ting.** –**com·mit′ment,** n.

com·mit·tee n a group of people chosen to do some special thing: *The student council appointed a committee of four members to plan the banquet.*

com·mon (kom′ən) 1 adj shared by all: *common knowledge, a common effort.* 2 adj ordinary: *a common weed. Snow is common in most of Canada.* 3 n **Commons**, short for the **House of Commons**, the group of elected people who make laws in the government. –**com′mon·ly,** adv.

common denominator a number that is a multiple of all the denominators of a group of fractions. A common denominator of 1/2, 2/3, and 3/4 is 12 because these three fractions can also be expressed as 6/12, 8/12, and 9/12.

common multiple a number that can be divided by two or more other numbers without a remainder: 12 is a common multiple of 2, 3, 4, and 6; they all go into 12 with no remainder.

in common, shared: *You and I have many interests in common.*

common sense (kom′ən sens′) good sense in everyday situations: *Vijay loved to dream, but he also had a lot of common sense.*

com·mon·wealth (kom′ən welth′) n **the Commonwealth**, short for **the Commonwealth of Nations**, a large group of countries that have been under British rule. Many, like Canada, are now independent.

com·mo·tion (kə mō′shən) n noise or disturbance: *His voice could hardly be heard above the commotion.*

com·mu·ni·cate (kə myū′nə kāt′) v share ideas or information: *He and his cousin communicate by e-mail.* **com·mu·ni·cat·ed, com·mu·ni·cat·ing.**

com·mu·ni·ca·tion n the act of sharing ideas or information: *Computers have made communication easier.*

com·mu·ni·ty (kə myū′nə tē) 1 n any neighbourhood: *This lake provides water for six communities.* 2 n a group of people living together or sharing a certain interest: *a community of monks. The arts community includes all artists.* 3 n a group of animals and plants sharing an environment. pl **com·mu·ni·ties.**

com·mute (kə myūt′) v travel every day from your home in one community to your job in another: *She commutes to work by train every day.* **com·mut·ed, com·mut·ing.** –**com·mut′er,** n.

com·pact (kom′pakt or kəm pakt′) adj neatly fitting a lot into a small space: *a compact kitchen.* **compact disc** a small round plate with sounds, pictures, or words digitally stored on it in very tiny pits. A laser beam inside a **compact disc player** or computer finds the information on the disc and changes it back into pictures or sounds. *Abbreviation:* CD

com·pa·ny (kum′pə nē) 1 n a business. 2 n companionship: *The dog provided the man with company during the long winters.* 3 n guests or visitors: *Let's clean up–company's coming!* pl **com·pa·nies.**

com·pan·ion (kəm pan′yən) n a person who goes around with another: *Her twin sister was her closest companion.* –**com·pan′ion·ship′,** n.

com·pan·ion·a·ble adj nice to be with.

keep someone company, go or stay with someone so he or she won't feel lonely.

WORD HISTORY ...... companion

From the Latin *com* "together" + *panis* "bread" a **companion** was a person you shared a meal with.

com·pare (kəm per′) *v* find out or point out how things are alike and how they are different: *Compare the jackets for quality and price before choosing.* **com·pared, com·par·ing.** –**com·par′i·son,** *n.*

com·pa·ra·ble *adj* able to be compared: *A fire is comparable with the sun; both give light and heat.*

com·par·a·tive *n* the second degree of comparison of adjectives and adverbs: *"Taller" is the comparative of "tall." "More quickly" is the comparative of "quickly."* ►See the *Grammar and Usage Mini-Guide.* –**com·par′a·tive·ly,** *adv.*

com·part·ment (kəm pàrt′mənt) *n* a separate section of anything: *That toolbox has several compartments for holding different things.*

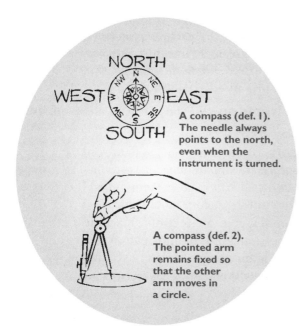

A compass (def. 1). The needle always points to the north, even when the instrument is turned.

A compass (def. 2). The pointed arm remains fixed so that the other arm moves in a circle.

com·pass (kum′pəs) **1** *n* an instrument for showing directions, with a magnetized needle that points to the North Magnetic Pole, which is near the North Pole. **2** *n* an instrument for drawing circles and for measuring.

com·pas·sion (kəm pash′ən) *n* a feeling of wanting to help a person who is suffering: *The doctor was full of compassion for the badly burned child.* –**com·pas′sion·ate,** *adj.*

com·pat·i·ble (kəm pat′ə bəl) **1** *adj* going well together: *My two cats are always fighting; they are just not compatible.* **2** *adj* able to be used with a certain system, such as a computer system, without special changes: *This computer game is compatible with both Macintosh and IBM.*

com·pete (kəm pēt′) *v* try to do better than someone else: *The two girls competed with each other in every subject.* **com·pet·ed, com·pet·ing.** –**com′pe·ti′tion** (kom′pə tish′ən), *n,* –**com·pet′i·tive** (kəm pet′ə tiv), *adj,* –**com·pet′i·tor,** *n.*

com·plain (kəm plān′) *v* say that something is wrong: *to complain about the food, to complain to the police.* –**com·plaint′,** *n.*

com·ple·ment (kom′plə mənt) **1** *n* a thing that makes something complete **2** *v* make something complete. –**com′ple·men′ta·ry,** *adj.*

com·plete (kəm plēt′) **1** *adj* with all the parts: *a complete set of tools.* **2** *v* supply whatever part is missing: *She completed her collection of Dennis Lee's books by buying* Alligator Pie. **3** *adj* finish: *Have you completed your homework?* **com·plet·ed, com·plet·ing.** –**com·plete·ly,** *adv,* –**com·plete′ness,** *n,* –**com·ple′tion,** *n.*

comp·lex (kom′pleks *or* kom pleks′) **1** *adj* made up of a number of parts. A **complex sentence** has more than one clause. **2** *adj* hard to understand: *The directions for assembling the swing set were so complex that we couldn't follow them.* –**com·plex′i·ty,** *n.*

com·plex·ion (kəm plek′shən) *n* the colour and quality of the skin, especially of the face.

com·pli·cat·ed (kom′plə kā′tid) *adj* hard to understand because of too many details: *This game is hard to learn because the rules are so complicated.* –**com′pli·cate′,** *v,* –**com′pli·ca′tion,** *n.*

com·pli·ment (kom′plə mənt *for 1,* kom′plə ment′ *for 2*) **1** *n* something good said about a person. **2** *v* praise; say nice things about: *We complimented him on the good job he had done on the newsletter.* –**com′pli·men′ta·ry,** *adj.*

CONFUSABLES .. compliment

compliment means "praise": *She complimented me on my choice of shoes.*

complement means "complete": *The shoes perfectly complemented the rest of the outfit.*

You can remember the difference by thinking: compl**i**ment has an **i** inside, like pra**i**se. compl**e**ment has an **e** inside, like compl**e**te.

com·po·nent (kəm pō′nənt) *n* one of the parts that something is made up of: *The monitor is an important component of a computer system.*

com·pose (kəm pōz′) *v* make up: *to compose a song or a story. Canada is composed of ten provinces and two territories.*

com·pos·er *n* a person who composes, especially a writer of music. **com·pos·ite** (kom′pə zit *or* kəm poz′it) *adj* made up of various parts: *The photographer made a composite picture by putting together parts of several others.*

composite number a number that has more than two factors: *8 is a composite number with four factors: 1, 2, 4, and 8. The number 5 is not composite; its only factors are 1 and 5.*

com·po·si·tion *n* something composed, such as a piece of music, writing, etc.

com·post (kom′pōst) **1** *n* a mixture of leaves and other parts of plants that decays and is added to soil to make it healthier: *Suzy added some banana peels to the compost heap.* **2** *v* to make compost out of plant material: *We compost all our garden waste.*

Red clover

A compound leaf

com·pound (kom′pound) *adj* having more than one part. A clover leaf is a **compound leaf**. "Spacecraft" is a **compound word**. A **compound sentence** is actually two sentences joined by a conjunction.

compound eye the kind of eye most insects have. It is made up of many separate little eyes, each forming a part of the whole image the insect sees.

Grammar ✓Check . compound sentence

Too many simple sentences can be boring: *Sean was very happy. The sun was shining. He was on his way to meet his best friend. They had decided to tune up their bikes. Then they would go for a ride.*

These simple sentences could be rewritten as a compound sentence:
Sean was very happy because the sun was shining and he was on his way to meet his best friend; they had decided to tune up their bikes, then go for a ride.

com·pre·hend (kom′pri hend′) *v* understand: *If you can use a word correctly, you comprehend it.* **–com′pre·hen′sion,** *n.*

com·pre·hen·sive *adj* that deals with everything or nearly everything: *a comprehensive test.*

com·press (kəm pres′) *v* squeeze together into less space or less time: *Air that has been compressed has a great deal of force when suddenly released.*

com·prise (kəm prīz′) *v* include: *Our school council comprises six students and one teacher.* **com·prised, com·pris·ing.**

com·pro·mise (kom′prə mīz′) **1** *v* settle a quarrel by agreeing that each side will go along with part of what the other one wants: *I wanted to invite twenty friends to my party, but my parents wanted only four, so we compromised and had ten.* **2** *n* an agreement like this: *They both wanted the apple; their compromise was to share it.* **com·pro·mised, com·pro·mis·ing.**

com·pul·so·ry (kəm pul′sə rē) *adj* required: *In Ontario, wearing seat belts is compulsory.*

com·pute (kəm pyūt′) *v* figure out by arithmetic: *It took some time to compute the cost of our trip to Prince Albert.* **com·put·ed, com·put·ing. –com′pu·ta′tion,** *n.*

com·put·er *n* an electronic machine that can process all kinds of information at very high speeds and store it for later use. It runs by a set of instructions called a program.

con·cave (kon kāv′ *or* kon′kāv) *adj* curved like the inside of a bowl. The opposite is **convex.**

con·ceal (kən sēl′) *v* hide: *She concealed the ball behind her back.* **–con·ceal′ment,** *n.*

con·cede (kən sēd′) *v* admit; allow: *He conceded that our idea was better. She conceded us the right to walk across her land.* **con·ced·ed, con·ced·ing.**

con·ceit (kən sēt′) *n* too much pride in yourself: *In his conceit, the track star thought that no one could outrun him.* **–con·ceit′ed,** *adj.*

con·ceive (kən sēv′) *v* imagine; think up: *Sir Sanford Fleming conceived the method of Standard Time, dividing the world into 24 time zones.* **con·ceived, con·ceiv·ing.**

con·ceiv·a·ble *adj* imaginable: *We should take every conceivable precaution against fire.*

con·cen·trate (kon′sən trāt′) **1** *v* bring or come together to one place: *A magnifying glass concentrates the rays of light on a single spot. The population of Canada is concentrated in the southern regions.* **2** *v* pay close attention: *He concentrated on his reading so that he would understand the story.* **3** *v* make stronger, especially by boiling off some of the water. **con·cen·trat·ed, con·cen·trat·ing.** –**con′cen·tra′tion,** *n.*

con·cept (kon′sept) *n* a thought; a general idea: *Equality is a basic concept of democracy.*

con·cern (kən sərn′) **1** *n* or *v* worry: *The father's concern over his sick child kept him awake all night* (n). *I didn't want to concern you with the details of the accident* (v). **2** *v* have to do with: *This letter concerns only me.* **con·cerned 1** *adj* involved; affected: *All those concerned in the school play must attend the dress rehearsal.* **2** *adj* worried: *We are quite concerned about his poor health.* **con·cern·ing** *prep* about: *The police officer asked many questions concerning the accident.*

con·cert (kon′sərt) *n* a performance by one or more musicians or singers.

**A pink conch
of the Caribbean**

conch (kongk *or* konch) *n* a shellfish with a large, spiral shell.

con·cise (kən sīs′) *adj* saying a lot in few words: *He gave a concise report of the meeting.*

con·clude (kən klūd′) **1** *v* finish: *She concluded her speech with a funny story.* **2** *v* figure out: *From the clues we found, we concluded that the thief must have left in a hurry.* **con·clud·ed, con·clud·ing.** –**con·clu′sion,** *n.*
jump or **leap to conclusions,** decide something is true without looking at all the facts.

con·crete (kon′krēt *for 1* , kon′krēt *or* kon krēt′ *for 2*) **1** *adj* a mixture of cement, water, and sand or gravel that hardens as it dries. Concrete is used for building. **2** *adj* existing as a real object, not just an idea: *A painting is concrete; its beauty is abstract.*

concrete poem (kon′krēt pō′əm) a poem arranged in the form of a picture.

con·cus·sion (kən kush′ən) *n* an injury to the brain from a blow: *She suffered a severe concussion in the accident.*

con·demn (kən dem′) **1** *v* say that a person or act is very bad or wrong: *We condemn cruelty and cruel people.* **2** *v* cause to suffer punishment: *The thief was condemned to prison.* **3** *v* declare not safe for use: *This bridge has been condemned.*

con·dense (kən dens′) **1** *v* change from a gas to liquid by cooling. If steam touches cold surfaces, it condenses into water droplets called **condensation**. **2** *v* reduce by getting rid of something: *Milk is condensed before it is canned. A long story can sometimes be condensed into a few sentences.* **con·densed, con·dens·ing.**

con·di·tion (kən dish′ən) **1** *n* the state a person or thing is in; good shape or bad shape: *The condition of his health kept him from doing heavy work.* **2** *n* something that another thing depends on: *You can go, but only on the condition that an adult goes along.*

con·do·min·i·um (kon′də min′ē əm) *n* an apartment or townhouse owned rather than rented by the people living in it. **Condominium** is often shortened to **condo**.
pl. **condos** or **condoes**.

con·dor (kon′dòr) *n* a large bird of prey with no feathers on its head and neck.

con·duct (kon′dukt *for 1,* kən dukt′ *for 2,3*) **1** *n* behaviour: *Their rude conduct was inexcusable.* **2** *v* carry out; do: *We are conducting some experiments with baking soda.* **3** *v* direct; lead: *to conduct an orchestra. Mr. Vanier conducted us through the museum.*

cone (kōn) **1** *n* a solid object that has a flat, round base and narrows evenly to a point at the other end. **2** *n* anything shaped like a cone: *an ice-cream cone, the cone of a volcano.* **3** *n* the part that carries seeds on evergreen trees like pine, spruce, etc.

con·i·cal (kon′ə kəl) *adj* cone-shaped.

con·fed·er·a·tion (kən fed′ə rā′shən) **1** *n* the act of joining together in an alliance: *a plan for the confederation of the colonies.* **2** ❦ *n* **Confederation,** the union of Ontario, Québec, Nova Scotia, and New Brunswick in 1867: *Six other provinces have joined Confederation since 1867–Manitoba, British Columbia, Prince Edward Island, Alberta, Saskatchewan, and Newfoundland.*

con·fer (kən fər′) *v* talk something over together: *The student and his teacher conferred about his marks.* **con·ferred, con·fer·ring.**

con·fer·ence (kon′fə rəns) *n* a meeting to discuss a particular subject. It can be for a few minutes, or last for several days.

con·fess (kən fes′) *v* admit: *He confessed to eating all the cake.* **–con·fes′sion,** *n.*

con·fide (kən fīd′) *v* tell as a secret: *He confided his troubles to his brother.* **con·fid·ed, con·fid·ing. –con′fi·dence,** *n.*

con·fi·den·tial (kon′fə den′shəl) *adj* to be treated as a secret: *The detective locked the confidential report in a filing cabinet.*

con·fi·dence (kon′fə dəns) *n* firm belief or trust: *She went at her work with confidence.* **–con′fi·dent,** *adj.*

con·fis·cate (kon′fə skāt′) *v* take away something that a person is not allowed to have: *The customs officer confiscated the smuggled cigarettes.* **con·fis·cat·ed, con·fis·cat·ing.**

con·flict (kon′flikt) *n* a clash or disagreement: *A conflict arose over what colour to paint our kitchen. I have a conflict in my schedule; piano and swimming are on the same night.*

con·front (kən frunt′) *v* face, especially boldly or in some kind of conflict: *to confront a difficult problem, to confront a bully.* **–con′fron·ta′tion** (kon′frən tā′shən), *n.*

con·fuse (kən fyūz′) *v* mix up: *So many people talking to me at once confused me.* **con·fused, con·fus·ing. –con·fu′sion,** *n.*

con·grat·u·late (kən grach′ə lāt′) *v* say how glad you are: *I congratulated my friend on her success.* **con·grat·u·lat·ed, con·grat·u·lat·ing. –con·grat′u·la′tions,** *n,* **–con·grat′u·la·to′·ry,** *adj.*

con·i·fer (kon′ə fər) *n* a cone-bearing tree. Conifers are usually evergreens with needles. **–co·nif′er·ous** (kə nif′ə rəs), *adj.*

con·junc·tion (kən jungk′shən) *n* in grammar, a type of word used to connect clauses, phrases, or words. In the sentence *They ate their sandwiches and apples but they were too tired to jog or swim,* the words *and, but,* and *or* are conjunctions.

Grammar ✓ *Check* **. . . conjunction**

Some useful conjunctions are: *after, although, and, as, because, before, but, if, or, since, so, than, that, though, unless, until, when, whenever, where, wherever, while, yet.*

con·nect (kə nekt′) *v* join or link: *to connect pipes. This cable connects the keyboard to the computer. We usually connect spring with sunshine and flowers.* **–con·nec′tion,** *n.*

con·quer (kong′kər) *v* overcome or defeat: *to conquer an enemy, to conquer a bad habit.* **–con′quer·or,** *n.*

con·quest (kon′kwest *or* kong′kwest) the act of conquering or the thing conquered: *the conquest of a country. Her latest conquest is the Olympic gold medal in figure skating.*

con·science (kon′shəns) *n* a sense of right and wrong: *The boy's conscience prompted him to return the book he had stolen.*

con·sci·en·tious (kon′shē en′shəs) **1** *adj* careful to do what your conscience tells you is right; wanting to do your best. **2** *adj* done carefully and seriously: *conscientious work.* **–con′sci·en′tious·ly,** *adv.*

con·scious (kon′shəs) **1** *adj* knowing; realizing; aware: *She was not conscious of my presence in the room.* **2** *adj* awake; able to feel: *When he became conscious, he asked what had happened.* **–con′scious·ly,** *adv,* **–con′scious·ness,** *n.*

con·sec·u·tive (kən sek′yə tiv) *adj* following one right after another: *Monday, Tuesday, and Wednesday are consecutive days. The numbers 1, 3, 5, 7, and 9 are consecutive odd numbers.* **–con·sec′u·tive·ly,** *adv.*

con·sent (kən sent′) *v* agree; give permission: *My mother has consented to the birthday sleepover.*

con·se·quence (kon′sə kwens′) *n* result: *The consequence of her fall was a broken leg.* **suffer the consequences,** accept what happens because of your action: *If you do your work carelessly, you'll have to suffer the consequences.*

con·serve (kən sərv′) *v* manage something carefully so that it will not be wasted: *We should conserve our natural resources.* **con·served, con·serv·ing.**

con·ser·va·tion *n* the protection of something, especially the environment, so that it will not be wasted. A **conservation area** is land taken care of by government so that people can enjoy it. –**con′ser′va′tion·ist,** *n.* **con·serv·a·tive** *adj* not liking change: *She is adventurous, while her sister is conservative.*

con·sid·er (kən sid′ər) *v* think about in order to decide: *Take time to consider the problem.* –**con·sid′er·a·tion,** *n.*

con·sid·er·a·ble *adj* enough to be worth thinking about: *Five hundred dollars is a considerable sum of money.* –**con·sid′er·a·bly,** *adv.*

con·sid·er·ate *adj* thoughtful of others and their feelings: *A considerate person does not show disrespect.*

con·sole (kən sōl′) *v* comfort. **con·soled, con·sol·ing.**

con·so·la·tion (kon′sə lā′shən) *n* a comforting person, thing, or event. A **consolation prize** is often given to those in a competition who tried hard but did not win.

con·so·nant (kon′sə nənt) *n* a speech sound made by completely or partly blocking the breath with the lips, tongue, or teeth. In English, the consonants are *b, c, d, f, g, h, j, k, l, m, n, p, q, r, s, t, v, w, x, y, z.*

con·spic·u·ous (kən spik′yū əs) *adj* noticeable: *Canada has played a conspicuous part in the work of the United Nations.* –**con·spic′u·ous·ly,** *adv.*

con·spir·a·cy (kən spēr′ə sē) *n* a secret plot with others to do something wrong: *a conspiracy to overthrow the government.* *pl* **con·spir·a·cies.** –**con·spir′a·tor** (kən spēr′ə tər), *n.*

con·stant (kon′stənt) **1** *adj* not changing: *If you keep walking due north, your direction is constant.* **2** *adj* never stopping: *A clock makes a constant ticking sound.* **3** *adj* faithful; loyal. –**con′stant·ly,** *adv.*

con·stel·la·tion (kon′stə lā′shən) *n* a group of stars: *The Big Dipper is the easiest constellation to find.*

con·ster·na·tion (kon′stər nā′shən) *n* paralysing terror: *To their consternation the kayak rushed toward the waterfall.*

con·sti·tu·tion (kon′stə tyū′shən *or* kon′stə tū′shən) **1** *n* a person's physical or mental nature or make-up: *He has a very healthy constitution.* **2** *n* the basic rules and principles that a country, town, or organization is run by. The Canadian Charter of Rights and Freedoms is part of Canada's constitution and was added by the **Constitution Act, 1982.** –**con′sti·tu′tion·al,** *adj.*

A boa constrictor can grow to be over 4 m long.

con·strict (kən strikt′) *v* squeeze: *The collar was too tight and constricted the dog's neck.*

con·stric·tor *n* any snake that kills by squeezing its prey in its coils. Boas and pythons are constrictors.

con·struct (kən strukt′) *v* build: *to construct a bridge. Sentences are constructed of words.* –**con·struc′tion,** *n.*

con·struc·tive *adj* building up so as to improve; helpful: *People appreciate constructive suggestions.*

con·sume (kən sūm′) **1** *v* eat or drink up: *We consumed a whole cake at the birthday party.* **2** *v* use up or spend: *This machine consumes too much electricity.* **con·sumed, con·sum·ing.** –**con·sum′a·ble,** *adj.*

con·sum·er *n* an ordinary person who buys and uses food, clothing, or anything grown or made by producers.

con·tact (kon′takt) *v* get in touch with; touch: *Contact me as soon as you hear any news. Don't let your fingers contact the hot light bulb.*

con·ta·gious (kən tā′jəs) *adj* passed on to others through contact: *Chicken pox is contagious.*

con·tain (kən tān′) *v* hold: *My wallet contains money. Books contain information.*

con·tain·er *n* a box, can, jar, etc. used to hold something in.

con·tam·i·nate (kən tam′ə nāt′) *v* make unclean or impure: *Flies can contaminate food.* **con·tam·i·nat·ed, con·tam·i·nat·ing.** –**con·tam′i·na′tion,** *n.*

con·tempt (kən tempt′) *n* scorn: *He has contempt for tattletales.*

con·tempt·i·ble *adj* deserving scorn: *Cheating her own family was a contemptible thing for her to do.* **con·temp·tu·ous** (kən temp′chū əs) *adj* scornful: *They are contemptuous of anyone who is different from them.*

con·tent (kon′tent *for 1 and 2,* kən tent′ *for 3*) **1** Usually, **contents,** *pl.n* what is contained: *An old chair, a desk, and a bed were the only contents of the room.* **2** *n* the actual ideas in something written or spoken, rather than how the person expressed them: *The content of your report is excellent, but it is rather messy and the spelling needs work.* **3** *v* satisfied: *They were content with just a short holiday.* **Contented** means much the same thing. **–con·tent′ed·ly,** *adv,* **–con·tent′ment,** *n.*

con·test (kon′test) *n* any activity that has winners and losers. A game or race is a contest; school is not a contest.

con·test·ant *n* a person who takes part in a contest. **no contest,** *Slang.* easily: *Our team will win, no contest!*

con·ti·nent (kon′tə nənt) *n* one of the seven great masses of land on the earth, including North America, South America, Europe, Africa, Asia, Australia, and Antarctica. **–con′ti·nent′al,** *adj.*

Continental Divide the great ridge of the Rocky Mountains in North America. **continental shelf** the submerged shelf of land that borders most continents and ends in a steep slope to deep water.

con·tin·ue (kən tin′yū) **1** *v* go on: *We continued playing until supper. The road continues for quite a distance in this direction.* **2** *v* go on again after stopping: *The play will continue after the intermission.* **con·tin·ued, con·tin·u·ing. –con·tin′u·a′tion,** *n.*

con·tin·u·al *adj* repeated many times. **–con·tin′u·al·ly,** *adv.*

con·tin·u·ous *adj* going on without any break. **–con·tin′u·ous·ly,** *adv.*

CONFUSABLES ... continual

continual means "often repeated": *I'm sick of the continual ringing of that phone!*

continuous means "without interruption": *There was continuous rain for the whole weekend.*

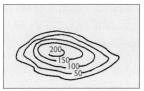 

A contour map of the island shown on the right

con·tour (kon′tūr) *n* the outline of something: *The contour of the Atlantic coast of Canada is very irregular.*

contour map a map showing high and low places on the earth's surface by means of **contour lines.**

con·tract (kən trakt′) *v* shrink or draw together: *Pulling the drawstring contracts the opening of the hood.*

con·trac·tion *n* a shortened form.

Grammar ✓*Check* ... **contraction**

Contractions combine two words, leaving out one or more letters. An apostrophe shows where letters are missing:
can't is a contraction of can*not*
she's is a contraction of she *is* or she *has*
it's is a contraction of it *is*

Notice that **it's** is not possessive:
Look at the tiger. **It's** *licking* **its** *paw.*

---

con·tra·dict (kon′trə dikt′) *v* say the opposite of: *She contradicts everything I say.* **–con′tra·dic′tion,** *n,* **–con′tra·dic′to·ry,** *adj.*

con·trap·tion (kən trap′shən) *n* gadget: *They invented a crazy contraption for removing the shells from boiled eggs.*

con·trast (kon′trast *for 1,* kən trast′ *for 2*) **1** *n* a great and obvious difference: *the contrast between black and white.* **2** *v* compare so as to show differences: *In our science class we contrasted flies and bees.*

con·trib·ute (kən trib′yūt) *v* give money or help: *Everyone contributed suggestions for the class trip.* **con·trib·ut·ed, con·trib·ut·ing. –con′tri·bu′tion,** *n,* **–con·trib′u·tor,** *n.*

con·trol (kən trōl′) **1** *n* power over something: *He has no control over my decision. The rebels are in control of the capital.* **2** *v* have power over: *A ship's captain controls the ship and its crew.* **con·trolled, con·trol·ling.**

con·tro·ver·sy (kon′trə vər′sē) *n* an argument, especially a public one involving many people: *The building of the new highway was delayed by months of controversy about it.* *pl* **con·tro·ver·sies.**

con·tro·ver·sial (kon′trə vər′shəl) *adj* tending to arouse argument.

con·va·lesce (kon′və les′) *v* gradually get better after illness: *Mary will have to convalesce for three weeks after her operation.* **con·va·lesced, con·va·lesc·ing. –con′va·les′cence,** *n,* **–con′va·les′cent,** *adj or n.*

con·vec·tion (kən vek′shən) *n* the transfer of heat from one place to another by the movement of heated particles of a gas or liquid. A forced-air furnace system heats a room by convection.

con·ven·ient (kən vēn′yənt) *adj* easy to do or use: *a convenient storage closet, a convenient plan, a convenient time or place.* **–con·ven′ient·ly,** *adv.* **con·ven·ience** *n* anything handy or easy to use: *Frozen vegetables are a great convenience during the winter.*

con·verse (kən vərs′) *v* talk with someone informally: *We conversed at the table between bites of pizza.* **con·versed, con·vers·ing.** **con·ver·sa·tion** (kon′vər sā′shən) *n* friendly talk.

con·vert (kən vərt′ *for 1,* kon′vərt *for 2*) *v* change; turn: *These machines convert pulp into paper. One last effort converted defeat into victory.* **–con·ver′sion,** *n.*

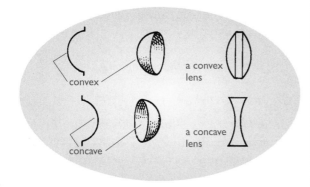

convex

a convex lens

concave

a concave lens

con·vex (kon veks′ *or* kon′veks) *adj* curved like the outside of a ball. The opposite is **concave**.

con·vict (kən vikt′ *for 1,* kon′vikt *for 2*) **1** *v* prove or declare to be guilty: *The evidence convicted the guilty person.* **2** *n* a person serving a prison sentence for some crime.

con·vince (kən vins′) *v* make a person agree to something: *Your encouragement has convinced me that I can do it.* **con·vinced, con·vinc·ing. –con·vinc′ing,** *adj,* **–con·vinc′ing·ly,** *adv.*

con·vulse (kən vuls′) **1** *v* shake or twist violently: *An earthquake convulsed the island. Rage convulsed his face.* **2** *v* throw into fits of laughter: *The comedian's jokes convulsed the audience.* **con·vulsed, con·vuls·ing. –con·vul′sion,** *n.*

cook (kùk) **1** *v* prepare food using heat: *We cooked our sausages over an open fire.* **2** *n* a person who prepares food. **–cook′er·y,** *n.* **cook·ie** *n* a small, sweet, more or less flat cake, usually crisp or crunchy.

WORD HISTORY .... **cookie**

The word **cookie** comes from the Dutch *koekje,* meaning "little cake."

---

cool (kūl) **1** *adj* a bit cold: *We sat in the shade where it was cool.* **2** *adj* not excited or nervous. **3** *adj Slang.* stylish or excellent. **4** *v* make or become cool: *We cooled the pop in the stream.*

co–op·er·ate (kō op′ə rāt′) *v* work together: *The children co-operated in keeping the playroom neat.* **co–op·er·at·ed, co–op·er·at·ing. –co–op′er·a′tion,** *n.* **co–op·er·a·tive** (kō op′ə rə tiv) **1** *adj* willing to work together with others: *The work got done very quickly because everyone was so co-operative.* **2** *adj* Usually shortened to **co–op** (kō′op), a business owned and run by all the people who regularly use it, so that they all share in the costs and profits.

co–or·di·nate (kō ȯr′də nit *for 1 and 2,* kō ȯr′də nāt′ *for 3*) **1** Usually, **co–ordinates,** *pl.n,* things that match or form a set, such as matching pants and top. **2** Usually, **coordinates,** *pl.n,* the two numbers that tell where a point is on any kind of grid or graph, such as lines of latitude and longitude. **3** *v* make different parts work together smoothly: *to co-ordinate your arms and legs in swimming, to co-ordinate the efforts of a team.* **co–or·di·nat·ed, co–or·di·nat·ing. –co·or′di·na′tion,** *n.*

cope (kōp) *v* manage in a difficult situation: *Is she strong enough to cope with the extra work?* **coped, cop·ing.**

cop·y (kop′ē) **1** *n* anything made to be just like another: *We printed 400 copies of the newsletter.* *pl* **cop·ies. 2** *v* make or do the same as: *The artist copied the style of Emily Carr. Adam copies his big brother's way of talking.* **cop·ied, cop·y·ing.** **–cop′i·er,** *n.*

cord (kȯrd) **1** *n* a thick, strong string; a very thin rope. **2** *n* a wire used to plug in an electrical appliance. **–cord′less,** *adj.*

cor·du·roy (kȯr′də roi′) *n* or *adj* thick cloth with a ridged pattern.

❧ **corduroy road** *n* a road made of logs laid crosswise, often across low, wet land. The logs are like the ridges on corduroy.

core (kȯr) *n* the central part of anything. The core of an apple contains the seeds. The earth's core is made of molten iron and is about 6760 m across. **cored, cor·ing.**

A ripe ear of corn, shown in its husk

corn (kȯrn) *n* yellowish kernels that grow in rows along a thick, woody core called a **cob** on a tall grass plant. **Sweet corn** is cooked and eaten as a vegetable; **field corn** is not as sweet and juicy and is used to feed farm animals.

corn·y *Slang. adj* too ordinary or simple: *corny jokes.*

cor·ner (kȯr′nər) **1** *n* the place where two lines or surfaces meet: *the corner of a room, the corner of Main St. and Queen St.* **2** *v* drive around corners: *Cornering on a motorbike is tricky.* **3** *v* force into a corner or into a tough spot: *The lawyer cornered her with a direct question. I finally cornered our dog and got the leash on him.*

cor·ner·stone 1 *n* a block of stone placed at the corner of a building to hold two walls together. **2** *n* the most important part of something because everything else depends on it: *The teacher said that practice was the cornerstone to becoming a good musician.*

corpse (kȯrps) *n* the dead body of a human being.

cor·ral (kə ral′) **1** *n* a fenced area for horses, cattle, etc. **2** *v* surround and keep from escaping: *My friends corralled me in the hall and tried to make me sign up for the school play.* **cor·ralled, cor·ral·ling.**

cor·rect (kə rekt′) **1** *adj* right; proper: *the correct answer, correct manners.* **2** *v* fix the mistakes in: *Correct any errors before you hand in your paper.* **–cor·rec′tion,** *n,* **–cor·rect′ly,** *adv.*

cor·re·spond (kȯr′ə spond′) **1** *v* agree or match: *The arms of a human being correspond to the wings of a bird.* **2** exchange letters: *They rarely saw each other but they corresponded for many years.* **–cor′re·spond′ence,** *n.*

cor·ri·dor (kȯr′ə dȯr) *n* a long hallway with rooms opening off from it: *My mother's office is at the end of the corridor.*

cor·rode (kə rōd′) *v* eat away gradually; rust: *The car body is beginning to corrode.* **cor·rod·ed, cor·rod·ing. –cor·ro′sion,** *n,* **–cor·ro′sive** (kə rō′siv), *adj.*

cos·mic (koz′mik) **1** *adj* having to do with the whole universe: *Cosmic forces produce stars and meteors.* **2** *adj* huge; vast.

cost (kost) **1** *n* the price: *The cost of this toy was $18.* **2** carry a price of: *This toy costs $18.* **cost, cost·ing. –cost′ly,** *adj.*

at all costs or **at any cost,** no matter what must be done: *They had to catch the next boat at all costs, or lose their last chance to escape.*

cos·tume (kos′chūm *or* kos′tyūm) **1** *n* dress belonging to another time or place, or to a character, for acting or pretending: *In our play the actors wore medieval costumes.* **2** *n* a style of dress: *Everyone wore the national costume of their home country.*

co·sy (kō′zē) *adj* having a warm, comfortable feeling: *This is a cosy little apartment!* Another spelling is **cozy. co·si·er** or **co·zi·er, co·si·est** or **co·zi·est. –co′si·ly** or **co′zi·ly,** *adv,* **–co′si·ness** or **co′zi·ness,** *n.*

cot·tage (kot′ij) *n* a small house used for holidaying.

cot·ton (kot′ən) **1** *n* cloth made from the soft, white fluff around the seeds of a plant that grows in warm places. **2** *n* Usually, **cotton wool,** this fluff spun into soft balls. **–cot′ton·y,** *adj.*

couch (kouch) *n* a sofa or chesterfield.

A cougar—
about 183 cm long
excluding the tail

cou·gar (kū′gər) *n* a large, usually sand-coloured wildcat found in many parts of North and South America; mountain lion: *In Canada, cougars are found mainly in Alberta and British Columbia.*

cough (kof) **1** *v* clear your throat by forcing air suddenly with a short, harsh noise. **2** *n* the act or sound of coughing.

could (kūd) *v* the past tense of **can.**

couldn't could not.

❦ **cou·lee** (kū′lē) *n* a deep ravine or gulch, especially on the Prairies. The water flowing in a coulee usually dries up in summer.

coun·cil (koun′səl) *n* a group of leaders called together to give advice and help make decisions about something: *the student council, an arts council, the council of Six Nations.*
coun·cil·lor or **coun·ci·lor** **1** *n* an elected member of the council of a town, village, etc. **2** *n* in Prince Edward Island, a member of the Legislative Assembly elected by the property owners.

coun·sel (koun′səl) **1** *n* advice: *A wise person gives good counsel.* **2** *v* give advice to; advise: *She counsels high school students.* **coun·selled** or **coun·seled, coun·sel·ling** or **coun·sel·ing.**
coun·sel·lor or **coun·sel·or** **1** *n* a person who gives advice: *a guidance counsellor.* **2** *n* a person who supervises at a summer camp.

CONFUSABLES .... counsel

counsel means "advice" or "advise":
Elders give counsel to younger people.
The confused person was counselled by her friend.

council means "a group of advisers":
the town council.

---

count (kount) **1** *v* name numbers in order: *The child can count to ten.* **2** *v* find out exactly how many there are: *He counted the pups to make sure they were all there.* **3** *n* the act or result of doing this: *Let's do a careful count of the votes.*

count·down or **count-down** *n* the minutes and seconds leading up to an event, especially the last ten seconds as they are called out. **count·less** *adj* too many to count: *the countless stars.*

count in, *Informal.* include: *Count me in for the party!*

count on, depend on: *Can I count on you to help? Count on spending at least an hour on this job.*

count·er (koun′tər) **1** *n* a long, flat surface for working. **2** *n* a small, round, flat disk often used to keep score in card games.

coun·terclock·wise (koun′tər klok′wīz′) *adj* or *adv* in the direction opposite to the way the hands of a clock move.

coun·ter·feit (koun′tər fit) *adj* fake: *This $20 bill is counterfeit.*

coun·try (kun′trē) **1** *n* nation; the land belonging to a nation: *the country of Canada. We crossed the border into the United States.* **2** *n* the open land away from towns and cities; farmland: *He likes the country better than the city.* *pl* **coun·tries.**

coun·ty (koun′tē) *n* a division of a country, province, or state. The government of a county may look after schools, certain roads, fire departments, nursing homes, etc. The county form of municipal government is used in Nova Scotia, New Brunswick, Québec, Ontario, and Alberta. *pl* **coun·ties.**

cou·ple (kup′əl) *n* two people or two things that go together; a pair. A husband and wife are a couple; so are the partners in a dance.

cou·plet (kup′lit) *n* two lines of poetry that rhyme and have the same rhythm. *Example:* And then my heart with pleasure fills, And dances with the daffodils.

cou·pon (kū′pon) *n* a slip of paper that lets you get something free or for less money than the usual price.

cour·age (kər′ij) *n* the strength of mind to control fear in the face of danger. **–cou·ra′geous** (kə rāj′əs), *adj.*

🍁 **cou·reur de bois** (kū rər′də bwo′) in history, a French or Métis fur trader or woodsman in the North or Northwest. Radisson and Groseilliers were coureurs de bois. *pl* **cou·reurs de bois** (kū rər′də bwo′).

cour·i·er (kər′ē ər) *n* a person or company that delivers letters and packages, especially when extra speed or careful handling is required: *They sent the urgent package by courier.*

course (kòrs) **1** *n* a series of classes or lessons in some subject at a college, university, or other school: *My cousin is taking a computer course at community college this summer.* **2** *n* a part of a meal served at one time: *The first course of a meal is often soup or salad.* **3** *n* an area marked out for a game or sport: *a golf course, a race course.* **4** *n* a route: *Our course was straight to the north.*
of course, as anyone would expect: *Of course it will rain on the weekend. Of course I'll do it.*

court (kòrt) **1** *n* a place marked off for a game: *a tennis court, a handball court.* **2** *n* a place where trials are held: *The prisoner was brought to court for trial.* **3** *n* a king, queen, or other ruler, his or her family, followers, etc., and the place where they live and work.

court·yard *n* a space enclosed by walls, in or near a large building: *Two big buses stood in the courtyard of the hotel.*

cour·te·sy (kər′tə sē) *n* politeness.
–**cour′te·ous,** *adj.*
by courtesy of or **through the courtesy of,** **1** with the permission of: *The poem is included in that book by courtesy of the author.* **2** as a gift of: *Refreshments are provided in the lounge, by courtesy of the airline.*

cous·in (kuz′ən) *n* the son or daughter of a person's uncle or aunt. **First cousins** have the same grandparents; **second cousins** have the same great-grandparents; and so on for third and fourth cousins.

cove (kōv) *n* a small, sheltered bay.

cov·er (kuv′ər) **1** *n* anything that protects or hides: *Put covers on your school books.* **2** *v* put a cover on: *He covered the sleeping child with his coat. Snow covered the ground.* **3** *v* go through or over: *We covered 400 km on the first day of our trip. This test covers the last unit in math.* –**cov′er·ing,** *n.*

cow (kou) **1** *n* the adult female of cattle. Milk comes from cows. **2** *n* the female of other large adult mammals such as the buffalo, moose, whale, elephant, walrus, or seal.

cowhand *n* a person who looks after cattle on a ranch; a cowboy or cowgirl. **cow·hide** *n* the hide of a cow, made into leather. 🍁 **cow·punch·er** *n Informal.* a cowboy or cowgirl.

cow·ard (kou′ərd) *n* a person who lacks the courage to face danger.
–**cow′ard·ice** (kou′ər dis), *n,* –**cow′ard·ly,** *adj.*
cow·er *v* crouch in fear or shame: *The frightened dog whimpered and cowered under the table.*

🍁 **Cow·i·chan sweater** (kou′i chən) a heavy sweater with a design knitted into the front and back, especially one made by the Cowichans, First Nations people of the Fraser River Valley in British Columbia.

coy (koi) *adj* shy, or pretending to be.
–**coy′ly,** *adv.*

A pair of coyotes—about 45 cm high at the shoulder

coy·ote (kī ō′tē, kī′ōt, *or* kī′ūt) *n* a North American wild animal related to the dog. It is most common on the prairies, has yellowish grey fur, and is noted for the way it howls at night. *pl* **coy·otes** or **coy·ote.**

crab (krab) **1** *n* a shellfish with eight legs, two claws, and a wide, flat shell. Many crabs are good to eat. **2** *v Informal.* be always complaining or finding fault: *Stop crabbing about the food.* **crabbed, crab·bing.** –**crab′by,** *adj.*

crack (krak) **1** *n* a split: *There is a crack in this cup.* **2** *v* break without separating into parts: *You have cracked the window.* **3** a sudden, sharp noise: *the crack of a whip.* **4** *n* expert: *a crack shot.*
crack a joke, tell a joke or say something funny.
crack down on, start to punish strictly: *The police are cracking down on speeders.*
crack up, 1 *Informal.* send or go into fits of laughter: *I crack up every time I hear that joke. This TV show always cracks her up.* **2** *Informal.* have a nervous breakdown.

A cradle-board

cra·dle (krā′dəl) *n* a baby's little bed, usually on rockers or swinging on a frame. **cra·dled, cra·dling.**

❦ **cra·dle-board** *n* a framework of wood, leather, and cloth that First Nations mothers used to use for carrying their babies on their backs.

craft (kraft) *n* artistic skill: *Carpentry is a craft. These totem poles show the craft of the First Nations peoples who carved them.*

cram (kram) *v* pack tightly; stuff: *She crammed all her clothes into the bag.* **crammed, cram·ming.**

cramp (kramp) **1** *v* a sudden pain in the abdomen or the muscles: *The swimmer was seized with a cramp.* **2** *v* limit: *His work was cramped by the very short time he could spend on it.*

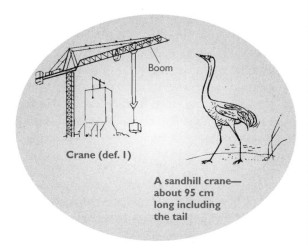

Crane (def. I)

Boom

A sandhill crane— about 95 cm long including the tail

crane (krān) **1** *n* a large machine with a long, swinging arm, for moving very heavy things. **2** *n* a large grey or white wading bird with long legs and neck and quite a long bill. The **sandhill crane** is common in Canada. **3** *v* stretch your neck as a crane does: *She craned her neck to see over the crowd.* **craned, cran·ing.**

crash (krash) **1** *n* a sudden, loud noise like many dishes breaking. **2** *v* make such a noise: *The thunder crashed. The dishes crashed to the floor. The car crashed through the gates.* **3** *n* an accident where a vehicle slams into something: *a plane crash. No one was injured in the car crash.* **4** *v* break down suddenly: *My computer crashed again in the middle of a game.* **5** *Informal.* sleep after being awake for a long time.

crash a party, *Informal.* go to a party without being invited.

cra·ter (krā′tər) **1** *n* the opening at the top of a volcano. **2** *n* a big bowl-shaped hole in the surface of the earth, moon, or other planet.

crave (krāv) *v* long for: *A starving person craves food.* **craved, crav·ing. –crav′ing,** *n.*

crawl (krol) **1** *v* move as a worm or bug does. **2** *v* move on hands and knees: *Babies crawl.* **3** *v* move slowly: *The traffic crawled on the icy roads.* **4** *v* feel creepy: *My skin crawled at the eerie sounds.* **5** *n* a fast way of swimming, using overarm strokes and a continuous kicking motion.

cray·on (krā′on *or* krā′ən) *n* a stick or pencil of coloured wax, oil pastel, chalk, or charcoal for drawing or colouring.

craze (krāz) *n* a short-lived, extreme enthusiasm for one thing: *Every year he has a new craze; this year it's model ships.*

cra·zy 1 *adj* out of one's mind. **2** *adj Informal.* very enthusiastic: *crazy about cats.* **–cra′zi·ly,** *adv,* **–cra′zi·ness,** *n.*

creak (krēk) *v* squeak loudly: *Door hinges creak when they need oiling.* **–creak′y,** *adj.*

cream (krēm) **1** *n* the yellowish part of milk that contains the fat. **2** *n* a smooth, rich mixture like cream: *ice cream, face cream.* **3** *n* **the cream,** the best part of anything: *the cream of the crop.* **–cream′y,** *adj.*

crease (krēs) **1** *n* a fold or wrinkle, or the line left by it: *Pants are pressed with creases down the front.* **2** ❦ *n* in hockey and lacrosse, a small rectangular area marked off in front of a goal.

cre·ate (krē āt′) *v* make, especially something original. **cre·at·ed, cre·at·ing. –cre·a′tion,** *n,* **–cre·a′tive,** *adj.*

crea·ture (krē′chər) *n* any living animal.

cred·it (kred′it) **1** *n* belief; faith or trust: *I don't put much credit in that story.* **2** *n* praise; honour: *The person who does the work should get the credit.* **3** *n* the privilege of borrowing money: *He had no trouble getting credit for his purchase.* **4** *n* the amount of money in an account: *She had a credit of $5000 in her savings account.*

cred·i·ble *adj* believable. **cred·it·a·ble** *adj* bringing praise or honour. **credit card** an identification card that gives a person the right to buy things on credit. **cred·u·lous** *adj* too ready to believe.

give someone credit for, say or believe that someone has some good quality or has done some good thing: *Give her credit for some intelligence and let her try the job herself.*

CONFUSABLES ... credible

credible means "believable": *She spoke so calmly that we all thought her explanation was quite credible.*

creditable means "bringing praise": *Your good work lately has earned you a creditable report.*

credulous means "too ready to believe": *He told his little brother there was a monster under the bed, and the credulous little boy ran away.*

---

creep (krēp) **1** *v* crawl. **2** *v* move slowly and unnoticeably: *The hunter crept silently through the woods.* **3** *n* *Informal.* a nasty or scary character. **4** *n* **the creeps**, *Informal.* an eerie or scary feeling: *That old house gives me the creeps.* **crept, creep·ing.**

creep·y *adj* eerie or scary.

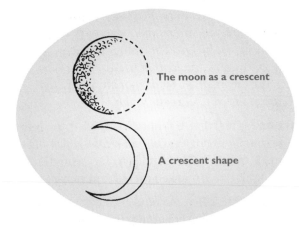

The moon as a crescent

A crescent shape

cres·cent (kres′ənt) *n* the shape of the moon in its first or last quarter. ►See **wane.**

crest (krest) **1** *n* a tuft of feathers, or a growth of skin, on the head of a bird or animal. **2** *n* the symbol or logo of a team, school, or other organization, often worn on a jacket or sweater. **3** *n* the top of a hill or wave. –**crest′ed,** *adj.*

crest·fall·en *adj* very disappointed.

cre·vasse (krə vas′) *n* a deep, often wide crack in the ice of a glacier.

crev·ice (krev′is) *n* a narrow crack: *Tiny ferns grew in crevices in the stone wall.*

crew (krū) *n* a group of people working together, such as the sailors on a ship.

crib (krib) **1** *n* a baby's small bed. **2** *n* a bin for grain on a farm.

crime (krīm) *n* a deed that is against the law: *Stealing is a crime.*

crim·i·nal (krim′ə nəl) *n* a person who has committed a crime.

cringe (krinj) *v* shrink from danger or pain: *The dog cringed at the sound of thunder.* **cringed, cring·ing.**

crip·ple (krip′əl) *v* damage; weaken: *The ship was crippled by the storm.* **crip·pled, crip·pling.**

USING WORDS .... cripple

A creature that is lame or unable to move in its usual way can be called **crippled**: *The crippled deer could not escape from the dogs.*

It is rude to use the word **cripple** about a person. Instead, use **person with a disability.**

---

cri·sis (krī′sis) *n* a time of emergency: *This was a real crisis–the flood had reached our front door! pl* **cri·ses** (krī′sēz).

crisp (krisp) **1** *adj* firm but snapping easily: *Potato chips are crisp.* **2** *adj* fresh; sharp and clear: *The air was cool and crisp.* **3** *adj* clear, firm, and to the point in speaking: *a crisp manner.*

criss·cross (kris′kros′) *adj* or *adv* with crossed lines: *Plaids have a crisscross pattern (adj). He laid the sticks crisscross in the fireplace (adv).*

cri·te·ri·on (krī tē′rē ən) *n* a rule for making a judgment about something: *Entries to the art contest will be judged on the criterion of originality. pl* **cri·te·ri·a.**

crit·ic (krit′ik) **1** *n* an expert who makes thoughtful judgments, often as his or her job: *a film critic, a restaurant critic.* **2** *n* a person who criticizes or finds fault: *She was such a constant critic that the other girls did not like her.* –**crit′i·cism,** *n.*

crit·i·cal 1 *adj* quick to criticize others: *A critical person is hard to work with.* **2** *adj* most important: *Timing is critical in gymnastics.* **3** *adj* urgent or dangerous: *in critical condition, in critical need.* **crit·i·cize** *v* blame; find fault with: *Do not criticize him until you know all the facts.*

A North American crocodile can grow to be about 4 m long.

croc·o·dile (krok′ə dīl′) *n* a large reptile, closely related to the alligator, but faster moving and with a narrower snout. Crocodiles live mainly in the rivers and marshes of the warm parts of Africa, Asia, Australia, and America.

cro·ny (krō′nē) *n* a very close friend; chum. *pl* **cro·nies.**

crook (krŭk) **1** *n* a person who cheats people; a swindler. **2** *n* the curved or bent part of anything: *the crook of a hockey stick.* –**crook·ed,** *adj.*

crop (krop) **1** *n* plants of one kind, grown in order to be used, especially as food: *Wheat is the main crop of Western Canada.* **2** *v* cut until short: *The horse's tail was cropped. The sheep had cropped the grass.* **cropped, crop·ping. crop up,** happen unexpectedly: *All sorts of difficulties cropped up.*

cross (kros) **1** *n* any thing, design, or mark shaped like a + or an x: *I've made a little cross where you have to sign your name.* **2** *v* draw a line through or across: *Cross my name off your list.* **3** *v* put, go, or lie across something or across each other: *to cross your arms, to cross a bridge.* **4** *n* the result of mixing breeds of animals or plants: *A mule is a cross between a horse and a donkey.* **Crossbreed** is another form. **5** *adj* angry or grumpy.

❧ **cross-check** *v* in hockey or lacrosse, check a player illegally by holding your stick in both hands and pushing it in front of his or her face or body. **cross-coun·try** *adj* across fields or open country instead of on a road or track: *a cross-country race.* **cross reference** an instruction in one part of a book, index, etc. to look in another part for more information.

cross section (kros′ sek′shən) **1** the act of cutting anything across, like slicing a tomato. **2** the surface that such a cut makes or would make: *The picture shows a cross section of a log.* **3** a sample; a small number of people or things chosen to stand for a whole group: *They interviewed a cross section of the community.*

cross·word a puzzle with sets of blank squares to be filled in with letters to form words. Some letters belong to two words that cross each other.

cross your mind, come into your mind: *Telling a lie never crossed her mind.*

crow (krō) **1** *n* a big black bird with a harsh cry. **2** *v* celebrate with boastful pride: *They crowed about their victory for weeks.*

as the crow flies, in a straight line.

crowd (kroud) **1** *n* a large number of people, animals, or things together: *A crowd gathered to hear the street musician.* **2** *v* gather, move, or squeeze close together in large numbers: *to crowd around the door.*

crown (kroun) **1** *n* a head covering of precious metal and jewels, worn by a ruler. **2** *n* the top; the highest part: *the crown of a hat, the crown of a mountain.*

❧ **Crown corporation** (kroun′ kȯr pə rā′shən) owned and run by the government of Canada or of one of the provinces to serve the public. Air Canada, the CBC, and the St. Lawrence Seaway Authority are Crown corporations. **crown land** in some Commonwealth countries, land that is owned by the government: *Some crown lands in Canada are set aside as provincial and national parks.*

cru·cial (krū′shəl) *adj* very important: *Proper eating habits are crucial to good health.*

crude (krūd) *adj* before being prepared for use; rough: *crude oil, a crude shelter made out of a box, crude manners.* **crud·er, crud·est.**

cru·el (krū′əl) *adj* eager to hurt others; unkind; causing suffering: *a cruel master. a cruel war, a cruel disease.* –**cru′el·ty,** *n.*

cruise (krūz) **1** *v* sail, drive, or walk around from place to place: *to cruise along the coast in a yacht. Police cars cruised the streets.* **2** *n* a trip from place to place: *We went for a cruise on the Great Lakes last summer.* **cruised, cruis·ing.**

crumb (krum) *n* a very small piece broken from bread, cake, etc.: *You left crumbs all over the floor!*

crum·ble (krum′bəl) *v* break up or fall apart into small pieces or crumbs: *The cookie crumbled when I picked it up. The old wall was crumbling away at the edges.* **crum·bled, crum·bling.** –**crum′bly,** *adj.*

crum·ple (krum′pəl) *v* crush: *She crumpled the letter into a ball. Her shirt was crumpled from sleeping in it.* **crum·pled, crum·pling.**

crunch (krunch) **1** *v* crush or chew noisily: *He crunched the celery.* **2** *n* the act or sound of crunching. **3** *v* make this sound: *The hard snow crunched under our feet.* –**crunch′y,** *adj.*

crush (krush) **1** *v* press so hard as to break: *The horse's hooves crushed the flowers.* **2** *v* thoroughly defeat or discourage: *The enemy was crushed. He was crushed by her refusal to marry him.* **3** *n* a mass of people crowded close together: *There was a terrific crush at the football game.*

crust (krust) *n* the hard outside layer of anything. Bread and pies have a crust. So does the earth. Snow sometimes forms a crust thick enough to walk on. –**crust′y,** *adj.*

cry (krī) **1** *v* shed tears of sadness or pain, often with a noise. **2** *v* shout or call out loudly: *He cried, "Help!"* **3** *n* a loud call; a shout: *We heard the drowning man's cry for help.* **4** *n* a call or noise made by an animal: *a gull's cry, the cry of a wolf.* **cried, cry·ing.** *pl* **cries.**

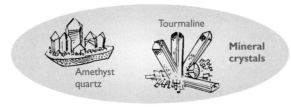

Amethyst quartz   Tourmaline   **Mineral crystals**

crys·tal (kris′təl) **1** *n* a clear, transparent mineral that looks like ice. It is a kind of quartz. **2** *n* clear glass of very fine quality: *wine glasses of crystal.* **3** *n* one of the regularly shaped pieces that make up many solid substances: *crystals of snow, sugar crystals.* –**crys′tal·line** (kris′tə lin′ or kris′tə lēn), *adj.*

crys·tal·lize (kris′tə līz′) *v* form into crystals: *Water crystallizes to form snow.* **crys·tal·lized, crys·tal·liz·ing.**

cub (kub) *n* a young bear, fox, wolf, lion, etc.

cube (kyūb) **1** *n* a solid with six square faces or sides, all equal. **2** *n* the product when a number is used three times as a factor. The cube of 5 is 125; that is, $5 \times 5 \times 5 = 125$.

cu·bic 1 *adj* shaped like a cube. **2** *adj* having length, width, and thickness. A cubic metre is the volume of a cube whose edges are each one metre long.

cu·cum·ber (kyū′kum bər) *n* a long, fleshy green vegetable eaten raw, often in salad, or used to make pickles. It grows on a vine.
cool as a cucumber, calm and relaxed.

cud (kud) *n* food that has been brought up into the mouth from the first and second stomachs of cattle, deer, camels, and similar animals, to be chewed before being swallowed again.

cud·dle (kud′əl) *v* hold close and lovingly: *She cuddled the kittens in her lap.* **cud·dled, cud·dling.**

cue (kyū) **1** *n* a hint or signal to do or say something: *When she says "Why, Charlie?" that's your cue to come on stage.* **2** *n* a long stick used for hitting the ball in billiards or pool.

WORD HISTORY . . . . cue

Both meanings of the word **cue** came from the French word *queue*, meaning "a tail." The pool cue is tail-shaped. The cue for an actor comes at the tail end of another actor's speech.

---

cuff (kuf) **1** *n* a separate piece or a turned-up fold at the end of a sleeve or a pant leg. **2** *v* hit with a paw or with the back of the hand.
off the cuff, without preparation: *I can't answer that off the cuff.*

cul·prit (kul′prit) *n* the guilty person: *Have they found the culprit who did the graffiti?*

cul·ti·vate (kul′tə vāt′) *v* prepare and use land to raise plants: *to cultivate the soil.* **cul·ti·vat·ed, cul·ti·vat·ing.** –**cul′ti·va′tion,** *n.*

cul·ture (kul′chər) *n* way of life; the customs, values, traditions, and beliefs of a nation or people at a certain time: *the culture of the ancient Vikings. Respect for differences is part of Canadian culture.* –**cul′tur·al,** *adj.*

cum·ber·some (kum′bər səm) *adj* hard to manage; clumsy: *long, cumbersome sentences.*

cu·mu·la·tive (kyū′myə lə tiv) *adj* built up from many things added together over time: *The cumulative effect of so many little annoyances finally made him lose his temper.*

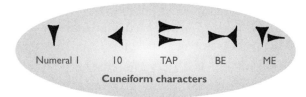
Numeral I   10   TAP   BE   ME
Cuneiform characters

cu·ne·i·form (kyū′ nē ə fòrm′) *n* an ancient writing system using wedge-shaped characters cut in clay or carved on stone.

cun·ning (kun′ing) *adj* crafty; clever; sly: *a cunning spy.*

cup (kup) **1** *n* a small container to drink from, usually with a handle on the side. **2** *n* an ornamental cup given to the winner of a contest; trophy. **–cup′ful′,** *n.*

cup·board (kub′ərd) *n* a closet or cabinet with shelves.

curb (kərb) **1** *n* a raised border of concrete or stone along the edge of a street. **2** *v* hold in check: *We must curb our spending if we want to save enough for a trip.*

cure (kyūr) **1** *v* make well again: *The sick child was soon cured.* **2** *n* something that gets rid of disease or any other problem: *a cure for sore eyes, a cure for laziness.* **3** *v* preserve meat by drying, smoking, or salting it. **cured, cur·ing.** **–cur′a·ble,** *adj.*

cu·ri·ous (kyū′rē əs) **1** *adj* eager to know: *Small children are very curious and ask many questions.* **2** *adj* strange; odd; unusual: *a curious old book.* **–cu′ri·os′i·ty,** *n.*

curl (kərl) **1** *v* twist into rings or coils: *My mother has to curl her hair, but mine curls naturally.* **2** *v* play the game of curling. **–curl′y,** *adj.*

cur·rant (kər′ənt) *n* a small, sour, red or black berry, used for jam, wine, etc. It grows on a bush.

cur·ren·cy (kər′ən sē) *n* the money of a particular country: *Canadian currency cannot be used in Mexico.* pl **cur·ren·cies.**
▶See Appendix.

cur·rent (kər′ənt) **1** *n* a flow or stream that has some force: *ocean currents, a current of air.* **2** *n* the flow of electricity through a wire, etc. **3** *adj* up to date; of the present time: *current fashions, the current month.*

cur·ric·u·lum (kə rik′yə ləm) *n* what is taught in the different subjects or courses at a school, college, or university. *pl.* **cur·ric·u·lums** or **cur·ric·u·la. –cur·ric′u·lar,** *adj.*

curse (kərs) **1** *v* ask a god or other powerful spirit to bring trouble to: *He cursed his enemy solemnly.* **2** *n* the special words said when doing this. **3** *v* swear; use bad language. **cursed, curs·ing.**

cur·sor (kər′sər) *n* a mark on a computer screen, showing where the next character will be placed.

curt (kərt) *adj* short and rude; abrupt: *Her curt answer made him angry.* **–curt′ly,** *adv.* **–curt′ness,** *n.*

cur·tain (kər′tən) **1** *n* a hanging screen that separates the stage of a theatre from the part where the audience is. **2** *n* anything that covers or hides: *a curtain of fog, bedroom curtains.*

curve (kərv) **1** *v* bend into a line with no straight part. **2** *n* something with a rounded or bending shape: *a curve in the road.* **3** *n* in baseball, a ball thrown with a spin so that it swerves in flight. **curved, curv·ing.**
throw someone a curve, confuse a person with something unexpected.

cush·ion (kush′ən) *n* a pillow or pad used to sit, lie, or kneel on.

cus·tom (kus′təm) *n* the usual way of doing things: *He found it hard to adjust to the customs of his new country.* **–cus′tom·ar′i·ly,** *adv,* **–cus′tom·ar·y,** *adj.*

USING WORDS .... custom

The words **custom** and **habit** have similar meanings, but they are used in different situations.

A **custom** is a way of doing things that a person, or a group of people, always follows: *It is a custom among many people to eat turkey at Thanksgiving.*

A **habit** is something a person does without thinking: *Brushing your teeth becomes a habit.*

cus·tom·er (kus′tə mər) **1** *n* a person who buys. **2** *n Informal.* a person: *a rough customer.*

cut (kut) **1** *v* open or shape with something sharp: *to cut a loaf of bread, to cut a hole in a box.* **2** *v* make lower or shorter: *Our ice time was cut by 15 minutes.* **3** *n* the act of cutting, or its result: *a cut in pay, a cut across the field. Make two little cuts in the cardboard. I'll put a bandage on that cut.* **cut, cut·ting.**

cut·ting 1 *n* a small shoot cut from a plant to grow a new plant. **2** *n* an article cut from a newspaper. **3** *adj* sharp; painful; stinging: *a cutting remark, a cutting wind.*

cut both ways, have advantages and disadvantages.

cut corners, try to save time, money, effort, etc. by not doing something thoroughly.

cut it, be good enough: *I'm sorry, but your excuse just doesn't cut it.*

cut it out, *Informal.* stop.

cut off, 1 stop the supply of: *They cut off our hydro.* **2** go right in front of another car when driving, causing the other driver to slam on the brake.

cut short, cause to end suddenly.

cut up, 1 cut into small pieces. **2** *Informal.* show off or clown around.

cute (kyūt) *Informal.* **1** *adj* good-looking, sweet, and lovable: *a cute baby.* **2** *adj* clever in an annoying way. **cut·er, cut·est.**

cut·ler·y (kut′lə rē) *n* knives, forks, and spoons for table use.

cy·ber·space (sī′bər spās′) *n* computer networks, especially the Internet, thought of as a "place" where information, sounds, pictures, etc. exist apart from any particular computer. Cyberspace is not an actual place.

cy·cle (sī′kəl) **1** *n* any action that keeps repeating itself in the same order, like the seasons of the year. **2** *n* a complete set or series: *She went through a whole cycle of auditions to get the part.*

cy·clone (sī′klōn) *n* a severe windstorm caused when winds move in a spiral. Hurricanes and typhoons are cyclones.

cyl·in·der (sil′ən dər) *n* a hollow or solid body shaped like a can.
–**cy·lin′dri·cal** (sə lin′drə kəl), *adj.*

d or **D** (dē) *n* the fourth letter of the English alphabet, or the speech sound that it stands for. The sound of *d* is heard in *day* and *hard*. *pl* **d's** or **D's.**

dab (dab) **1** *v* put something on, or wipe it off, with quick, light touches: *I dabbed some lotion on the burn.* **2** *n* a small blob: *dabs of butter, a dab of paint.* **dabbed, dab·bing.**

dab·ble *v* do only as a hobby: *to dabble at painting, to dabble in politics.*

Daffodils

daf·fo·dil (daf'ə dil') *n* a plant with yellow or white flowers that bloom in spring.

dai·ly (dā'lē) **1** *adj* happening once a day: *a daily visit, a daily newspaper.* **2** *adv* every day: *Her strength is increasing daily.*

dain·ty (dān'tē) *adj* small, delicate, and pretty: *The violet is a dainty spring flower.* **dain·ti·er, dain·ti·est. –dain'ti·ly,** *adv.*

dair·y (der'ē) *adj* having to do with milk, butter, cheese, etc.: *dairy products. A dairy farmer raises milk cows.*

Ox-eye daisies

dai·sy (dā'zē) *n* a plant that has flowers with a yellow centre and many white or pink raylike petals. *pl* **dai·sies.**

A dam and hydro-electric power plant

dam (dam) **1** *n* a wall built to hold back the water of a stream, creek, river, etc. **2** *v* hold back by building a dam: *Beavers had dammed the stream.* **dammed, dam·ming.**

dam·age (dam'ij) **1** *n* injury: *The accident did very little damage to the car.* **2** *v* break or hurt: *I damaged my thumb when I hit it with the hammer.* **dam·aged, dam·ag·ing.**

damp (damp) *adj* slightly wet; moist: *This house is damp in rainy weather.* **–damp'ness.**

damp·en 1 *v* make moist or slightly wet: *I dampened the cloth to wipe the table.* **2** *v* cast a gloom over; depress; discourage: *The bad news dampened our spirits.*

dance (dans) **1** *v* move in time with music: *They can dance very well.* **2** *n* a party where people dance. **danced, danc·ing. –danc'er,** *n.*

dan·de·lion (dan'dē lī'ən) *n* a very common weed with deeply notched leaves and bright yellow flowers that look like pompoms.

dan·ger (dān'jər) *n* anything that may cause harm: *A mountain climber's life is full of danger. Hidden rocks are a danger to ships.* **–dan'ger·ous,** *adj.*

in danger of, likely to have something happen: *The old bridge is in danger of collapsing.*

dank (dangk) *adj* damp and musty: *The cave was dark, dank, and chilly.*

dare (der) **1** *v* be bold enough to do or face something risky: *I wouldn't dare dive from the high board. The explorer dared the perils of the Barren Ground.* **2** *v* or *n* challenge: *I dare you to jump* (*v*). *I took his dare and jumped* (*n*). **dared, dar·ing.**

dare·dev·il *n* a very reckless person, one who is ready to dare almost anything or anyone.

dar·ing *adj* bold; fearless.

dark (dàrk) **1** *adj* without much light: *It turned out to be a dark, cloudy day.* **2** *adj* close to black in colour: *dark eyes.* **–dark'en,** *v,* **–dark'ly,** *adv,* **–dark'ness,** *n.*

in the dark, without information: *They left me in the dark about their plans.*

dash (dash) **1** *v* rush: *They dashed by in a hurry.* **2** *n* a short race: *the 50-m dash.* **3** *n* a mark (–) used in writing to show a break in thought or to stand for missing letters or words. **4** *n* a small amount: *Put in just a dash of pepper.*

da·ta (dā′tə *or* dat′ə) *n* information: *She is gathering data on A.Y. Jackson for her essay on Canadian painting.*

da·ta·base (dā′tə bās′ *or* dat′ə bās′) *n* a large amount of information stored in a computer program that lets you arrange it in different ways and easily find what you want. **Data base** is another spelling.

USING WORDS . . . . . . data

In general everyday English, the word **data** is usually treated as a singular noun: *The data we collected is in this notebook.*

In formal English, the word **data** is treated as plural: *Analyse the data that have been collected.*

---

date (dāt) **1** *n* the day, month, or year when something happens: *The date of Confederation was July 1, 1867. There is a date stamped on every piece of Canadian money.* **2** *n* an appointment for a certain time. **3** *n* a boyfriend or girlfriend that you go out with: *Who is your date for the school dance?* **4** *n* the sweet fruit of a kind of palm tree.
out of date, out of style; old-fashioned: *That dress looks out of date.* **Dated** means the same thing.
up to date, modern; in style.

Grammar ✓*Check* **. . . . . date**

A date can be written in different ways.

- You put a comma between the day, the day of the month, and the year: My brother was born on Monday, February 2, 1998.
- You put a comma between the day of the month and the year: My sister was born on April 4, 1999.
- You don't put a comma in dates like June 2000 or 30 June 2002.
- When you write a date using just numbers, the correct Canadian style is Year-Month-Day. So 30 June 1999 would be written 99-06-30.
- Dates that show on computers are often done in the U.S. style, as Month/Day/Year. So 30 June 2001 would show as 06/30/01.

---

daub (dob) *n* a smear or sticky blob of something: *daubs of paint.*

daugh·ter (dot′ər) *n* a girl or woman in relation to either or both of her parents.

daugh·ter-in-law *n* the wife of a person's son.

daunt (dont) *v* frighten; discourage: *Danger did not daunt the journalist.*

daunt·less *adj* brave: *She is a dauntless firefighter.*

daw·dle (dod′əl) *v* waste time: *Don't dawdle over your work.* **daw·dled, daw·dling.**

dawn (don) **1** *n* the beginning of day. **2** *n* the beginning: *before the dawn of history.*
dawn on someone, finally become clear to a person: *It dawned on me that we weren't even talking about the same thing.*

day (dā) **1** *n* the time of light between sunrise and sunset: *Owls sleep during the day.* **Daytime** means the same thing. **2** *n* the 24 hours that the earth takes to turn on its axis.

day·dream *v* think for a long time about things that are nice but not practical: *He spent a whole hour just daydreaming.* **daylight-saving time** time that is one hour ahead of standard time, giving more daylight in summer evenings. Clocks are set ahead one hour in the spring and back one hour in the fall. One o'clock daylight-saving time is twelve o'clock standard time.

call it a day, *Informal.* stop work: *I'm tired; let's call it a day.*

daze (dāz) **1** *v* confuse: *The child was dazed by the sudden noise and bright lights.* **2** *n* a confused state of mind: *He was wandering around in a daze after the accident.* **dazed, daz·ing.**

The headlights of a car can dazzle your eyes.

daz·zle (daz′əl) **1** *v* hurt the eyes with too bright a light: *To look straight at the sun dazzles the eyes.* **2** *n* a painful brightness: *the dazzle of car headlights.* **daz·zled, daz·zling.**

dead (ded) **1** *adj* not alive: *The flowers in my garden are dead.* **2** *adj* without force, feeling, activity, etc.: *This old battery is dead. Without Mr. Malik the school seemed kind of dead.* **3** *adj* complete or completely: *dead silence, dead wrong.*

dead·en *v* lessen the force or sharpness of: *Some medicines are given to deaden pain.*

dead·line (ded′līn′) *n* a time limit: *If the project isn't ready before the deadline, we'll be in trouble.*

dead·ly **1** *adj* causing death: *a deadly disease, deadly poison.* **2** *adj* lasting till death: *deadly enemies, a deadly hatred.* **3** *adv* extremely: *a deadly serious decision.*

dead to the world, fast asleep.

deaf (def) *adj* not able to hear. **–deaf′en,** *v,* **–deaf′ness,** *n.*

deal (dēl) **1** *v* carry on business; buy and sell: *This store deals in toys and games.* **2** *n* *Informal.* a bargain: *We got a good deal on a used computer game.* **3** *v* give out: *In card games, one player deals the cards to the others.* **dealt, deal·ing.** **–deal′er,** *n,* **–deal′er·ship,** *n.*

a great deal, a lot: *A great deal of her money is spent on CDs.*

dear (dēr) **1** *adj* much loved: *His sister is very dear to him.* **2** *n* a darling: *"Come here, my dear,"* she said. **3** *adj* expensive: *Fresh fruit is dear in winter.* **4** *interj* an exclamation of surprise, trouble, etc.: *Oh, dear! I spilled it!* **–dear′ly,** *adv.*

death (deth) *n* the ending of life.

death·ly **1** *adv* or *adj* like death or likely to cause death: *deathly dangerous* (adv), *a deathly paleness* (adj). **2** *adj* or *adv* extreme; extremely: *a deathly boredom* (adj), *so deathly hot* (adv).

at death's door, about to die.

de·bate (di bāt′) **1** *v* argue or discuss both sides: *We debated whether to go or stay.* **2** *n* a discussion of reasons for and against: *There was a debate about who should be captain.* **de·bat·ed, de·bat·ing.**

debit card (deb′it kärd′) a plastic card that lets you pay for things by directly subtracting the amount from your bank account when you slide it through a card reader in a store: *Mom used a debit card to buy the videos.*

de·bris (də brē′) *n* scattered bits; ruins: *The street was covered with debris from the explosion.*

debt (det) *n* something owed to another: *He used his allowance to pay his debt to Luisa.*

de·bug (dē bug′) *v* find and remove mistakes, especially in a computer program. **de·bugged, de·bug·ging.**

deca– *an SI prefix meaning* ten; 10. A *decagram* is ten grams. The prefix **deca-** can also be used with other metric units, such as *metre* or *litre. Symbol*: da

dec·ade (dek′ād) *n* a period of ten years.

de·cath·lon (di kath′lon) *n* an athletic competition with ten running, jumping, and throwing events.

WORD HISTORY · · · · · · · · **decathlon**

The prefix *deca* means "ten" in Latin. So a **dec**athlon is made up of ten events. A **bi**athlon has two events.
How many events are in a **pent**athlon?

---

de·cay (di kā′) **1** *v* become rotten: *The fallen apples began to decay.* **2** *n* a rotting condition: *The decay in the tree trunk had not proceeded very far.* **–dec′a·dent,** (dek′ədənt), *adj.*

de·ceive (di sēv′) *v* trick or mislead: *They got in trouble for trying to deceive their parents.* **de·ceived, de·ceiv·ing.** **–de·ceit′,** *n,* **–de·ceit′ful,** *adj.*

de·cent (dē′sənt) **1** *adj* proper and right: *a decent burial. The decent thing to do is apologize.* **2** *adj* not vulgar or obscene: *decent language.* **3** *adj* honest, good, sincere, etc.: *They are decent people.* **4** *adj* fairly good: *I get decent marks at school.* **–de′cen·cy,** *n.*

Decibels	Sounds
1	faintest sound heard
10	whisper
30	quiet conversation
50	quiet radio
70	telephone ringing
90	heavy traffic
110	rock band
130	jet takeoff

deci– *an SI prefix meaning* one-tenth. A *decimetre* is one-tenth of a metre. The prefix **deci-** can also be used with other metric units, such as *gram* or *litre. Symbol*: d

dec·i·bel (des′ə bel′) *n* a unit for measuring the loudness of a sound.

dec·i·mal (des′ə məl) *adj* having to do with the number 10: *The metric system is a decimal system of measurement.* **decimal fraction** any number with a dot, or decimal point, between the ones and tenths: *Examples:* 9.5, 4.0.

de·cide (di sīd′) *v* make a choice; make up your mind: *He decided to be a doctor.* **de·cid·ed, de·cid·ing. –de·cid′ed,** *adj,* **–de·ci′sion,** *n.*

CONFUSABLES .... decided

decided means "definite": *Her height gave her a decided advantage in basketball.*

decisive means "firm": *a decisive victory, a decisive manner*

---

de·cid·u·ous (di sij′ū əs) *adj* shedding leaves at a certain time each year: *Maples are deciduous trees, but pines are evergreen.*

deck (dek) **1** *n* the floor on a ship or a platform like this: *a sun deck.* **2** *n* a pack of playing cards.

de·clare (di kler′) *v* announce publicly: *Parliament has declared a national holiday.* **de·clared, de·clar·ing. –dec′la·ra′tion,** *n.*

de·cline (di klīn′) **1** *v* refuse politely: *They invited her to the party, but she declined to go.* **2** *v* get lower, weaker, or worse: *With too little food, his strength had begun to decline.* **de·clined, de·clin·ing.**

dec·o·rate (dek′ə rāt′) **1** *v* add things to make beautiful: *We decorated the windows with coloured lights.* **2** *v* paint or paper a room. **dec·o·rat·ed, dec·o·rat·ing. –dec′o·ra′tion,** *n,* **–dec′o·ra·tive** (dek′ə rə tiv), *adj.*

de·crease (di krēs′ *for 1,* dē′krēs *for 2*) **1** *v* make or become less: *to decrease prices.* **2** *n* a lessening: *When clouds covered the sun, there was a decrease in temperature.* **de·creased, de·creas·ing.**

de·crep·it (di krep′it) *adj* weak, worn out, or falling apart because of age: *Our old car was getting pretty decrepit.*

ded·i·cate (ded′ə kāt′) **1** *v* give over to some person or purpose: *The statue was dedicated to Canadian veterans.* **2** *v* address a book to someone: *She dedicated her first novel to a teacher who had encouraged her to write.* **ded·i·cat·ed, ded·i·cat·ing.**

deed (dēd) *n* an action, especially a remarkable one: *a brave deed, evil deeds.*

deep (dēp) **1** *adj* or *adv* going far down, far back, or far in: *a deep well, a deep forest (adj).*

Dig deep (adv). **2** *adj* low: *a deep voice.* **3** *adj* strong; intense: *deep feelings, a deep sleep.* **–deep′en,** *v,* **–deep′ly,** *adv.*

deep down, in your heart: *He acts happy, but deep down he is sad.*

White-tailed deer— about 1 m high at the shoulder

deer (dēr) *n* a wild, swift, animal with long, slender legs and small split hooves. The male has antlers. The elk, caribou, moose, reindeer, and white-tailed deer are all different kinds of deer. *pl* **deer.**

default (di folt′) *n* something that happens automatically unless you do something to change it: *On the computer, saving files to the c: directory was the default.*

win by default, win a game or contest because an opponent did not play: *Our soccer team won by default.*

de·feat (di fēt′) **1** *v* beat: *to defeat another team in basketball.* **2** *n* the act of defeating or of being defeated: *a crushing defeat.*

de·fect (dē′fekt) *n* a flaw or fault: *This jacket was cheap because of a slight defect in one sleeve.* **–de·fec′tive** (di fek′tiv), *adj.*

de·fend (di fend′) *v* guard from attack or harm; protect. **–de·fend′er,** *n,* **–de·fen′si·ble,** *adj.*

de·fence (di fens′ *for 1,* dē′fens *for 2*) **1** *n* anything that defends: *The walls around Fort Henry were a defence against attack.* **2** *n* in games, the group of players defending a goal: *Our hockey team has a good defence.* **Defense** is another spelling. **–de·fence′less,** *adj.*

de·fer (di fėr′) *v* put off; postpone: *The test was deferred because so many students were sick.* **de·ferred, de·fer·ring. –de·fer′ment,** *n.*

de·fi·ant (di fī′ənt) *adj* openly refusing to obey: *The angry prisoners shouted a defiant answer to the guard.* —**de·fi′ance,** *n.*

de·fine (di fīn′) *v* explain the meaning of: *A dictionary defines words.* **de·fined, de·fin·ing.** —**def′i·ni′tion,** *n.*

def·i·nite (def′ə nit) **1** *adj* clear and firm; positive: *a definite answer. Is it definite that we are going?* **2** *adj* exactly defined: *a definite area, a definite number of players.* —**def′i·nite·ly,** *adv.* **definite article** the word **the.**

de·flate (di flāt′) *v* let the air or gas out of something: *Vlad deflated the balloon.* **de·flat·ed, de·flat·ing.**

de·flect (di flekt′) *v* turn aside: *The ball hit a tree and was deflected into the lake.*

de·fy (di fī′) **1** *v* refuse to obey: *If you defy the law, you must take the consequences.* **2** *v* dare: *The Arctic explorers defied the extreme cold in order to reach their goal.* **de·fied, de·fy·ing.** —**de·fi′ant,** *adj.*

de·gree (di grē′) **1** *n* the amount: *Her interest depends on the degree of risk–the riskier, the better!* **2** *n* a unit for measuring temperature: *The boiling point of water is 100°C. Symbol:* ° **3** *n* a unit for measuring an angle or an arc of a circle: *A right angle measures 90°. Symbol:* ° **4** *n* a title given to a student by a university or college for successfully completing a course of studies.

de·hy·drate (dē hī′drāt) *v* lose or take away water: *Milk can be dehydrated to form a powder. We get thirsty in hot weather because our bodies dehydrate when we sweat.* **de·hy·drat·ed, de·hy·drat·ing.** —**de′hy·dra′tion,** *n.*

de·ject·ed (di jek′tid) *adj* sad; discouraged: *The defeated runner wore a dejected frown.* —**de·ject′ed·ly,** *adv.*

❋ **deke** (dēk) *Slang.* in hockey: *v* draw a player out of position by faking a play. **deked, dek·ing.**

WORD HISTORY . . . . deke

Deke is short for *decoy.* Deking in hockey is similar to what a decoy does to other animals: it tricks them into going to the wrong place at the wrong time!

de·lay (di lā′) **1** *v* put off till later: *They had to delay the party for a week.* **2** *v* be late or make

late because of a stop on the way: *The accident delayed the train for two hours.* **3** *n* a stopping or waiting: *They could afford no further delay.*

del·e·gate (del′ə git *for 1,* del′ə gāt′ *for 2*) **1** *n* a person chosen to act for a group; a representative: *Canada sent a delegate to the conference on the environment.* **2** *v* choose a person to act for others: *The class delegated Chet to buy the flowers.* **del·e·gat·ed, del·e·gat·ing. del·e·ga·tion** *n* a group of representatives.

de·lete (di lēt′) *v* erase: *He deleted the last sentence from his story. Do not delete any of the files on the hard drive of Dad's computer.* **de·let·ed, de·let·ing.** —**de·le′tion,** *n.*

deli (del′ē) *n* a place where different kinds of cheese, cold cooked meats, and salads are sold. **Delicatessen** (del′ə kə tes′ən) is the full name for it. *pl* **del·is.**

de·lib·er·ate (di lib′ə rit) **1** *adj* done on purpose: *That excuse was a deliberate lie.* **2** *adj* slow, careful, and firm: *The fashion show model walked with deliberate steps.* —**de·lib′er·ate·ly,** *adv.*

del·i·cate (del′ə kit) **1** *adj* gentle; graceful; mild; soft: *delicate movements, delicate colours, delicate fragrance.* **2** *adj* easily hurt or broken; not tough: *A spider's web is very delicate.* **3** *adj* finely tuned; sensitive: *delicate instruments.*

de·li·cious (di lish′əs) *adj* very pleasing or satisfying: *a delicious cake, the delicious warmth of the fire.* —**de·li′cious·ly,** *adv.*

de·light (di līt′) **1** *n* great pleasure; joy: *She took great delight in trying new things.* **2** *v* please greatly: *The music delighted the audience.* —**de·light′ed,** *adj,* —**de·light′ful,** *adv.*

de·liv·er (di liv′ər) **1** *v* carry something to the proper place: *Moina delivers newspapers every morning.* **2** *v* give: *to deliver a speech.* —**de·liv′er·er,** *n,* —**de·liv′er·y,** *n.*

del·ta (del′tə) *n* a deposit of earth and sand at the mouth of a river. It is usually shaped like a triangle. Part of Vancouver is on the delta of the Fraser River.

WORD HISTORY . . . . delta

This is the Greek name for the letter D, which in the Greek alphabet is shaped like a triangle.

de·luxe (də luks′) *adj* of top quality; with all the best features. Another form is **de luxe**.

de·mand (di mand′) **1** *v* ask for firmly and expect to get: *My sister demanded an equal share of the candy.* **2** *n* a request that cannot be ignored: *Mother has many demands on her time.* **in demand**, wanted or needed: *Computer skills are very much in demand.*

de·moc·ra·cy (di mok′rə sē) **1** *n* a system of government where the people choose their own leaders, and where all citizens have equal rights. **2** *n* a country that has such a system: *Canada is a democracy.* *pl* **de·moc·ra·cies.** **–dem′o·crat′ic** (dem′ə krat′ik), *adj*.

de·mol·ish (di mol′ish) *v* destroy: *The attackers demolished the fortress. One counterexample demolishes a whole theory.* **–dem′o·li′tion** (dem′ə lish′ən), *n*.

dem·on·strate (dem′ən strāt′) *v* show by actions or speech: *Can you demonstrate that hot air rises?* **dem·on·strat·ed, dem·on·strat·ing.** **–dem′on·stra′tion**, *n*.

den (den) **1** *n* a wild animal's home. **2** *n* a room, usually small, for doing quiet things.

de·nom·i·na·tor (di nom′ə nā′tər) *n* the number below the line in a fraction, which tells how many parts the whole has been divided into: *In the fraction 3/4, 4 is the denominator, and 3 is the numerator.*

dense (dens) **1** *adj* closely packed together: *a dense forest, a dense fog, dense population.* **2** *adj* slow to understand. **dens·er, dens·est.** **den·si·ty 1** *n* the fact of being closely packed together: *The density of the West Coast forest made it hard to see very far ahead.* **2** *n* the amount of matter in a unit of volume: *Lead has greater density than wood, because a cubic metre of lead has more mass than a cubic metre of wood.*

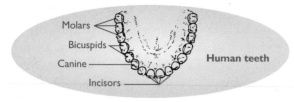

Human teeth

Molars
Bicuspids
Canine
Incisors

den·tist (den′tist) *n* a person who is qualified to take care of people's teeth. **–den′tist·ry**, *n*. **den·tal** *adj* having to do with the teeth: *Proper dental care is important for healthy teeth.*

de·ny (di nī′) **1** *v* say that something is not real or true: *The city officials deny that there is a flu epidemic.* **2** *v* refuse: *Our request was denied.* **de·nied, de·ny·ing.** **–de·ni′al**, *n*.

de·part (di pȧrt′) *v* leave: *The train departs at 6:15 p.m.* **–de·par′ture** (di pȧr′chər), *n*.

de·part·ment (di pȧrt′mənt) *n* a separate part of a whole; section. A **department store** sells many different things arranged in separate sections of the store. *Abbreviation:* dept.

de·pend (di pend′) **1** *v* be a result of; be influenced by: *The success of our sports day depends partly on the weather.* **2** *v* rely: *You can depend on this piece of advice.* **de·pend·a·ble** *adj* reliable. **–de·pend′a·bil′i·ty**, *n*.

de·port (di pȯrt′) *v* send a person out of the country, usually back to the country he or she came from. The action is called **deportation**.

de·pos·it (di poz′it) **1** *v* put something somewhere and leave it there: *She deposited her books on the table.* **2** *n* the material left somewhere by natural means: *a deposit of sand and mud at a river mouth.* **3** *n* money put into an account: *a deposit of $50.* **4** *n* a payment of part of the price of something. You pay a deposit if you rent something, in case you ruin it or fail to return it. You also pay a deposit on an item if you want a store to set it aside for you.

de·press (di pres′) **1** *v* make sad or gloomy: *Rainy weather always depresses me.* **2** *v* press down: *to depress a key on a keyboard.* **–de·pressed′**, *adj*, **–de·pres′sing**, *adj*. **de·pres·sion 1** *n* low spirits: *Finding a good friend cured the boy's depression.* **2** *n* a low place; hollow: *Water filled the depressions in the ground.* **3** *n* a time when the economy is extremely weak, with high unemployment. **The (Great) Depression** took place in the 1930s.

de·prive (di prīv′) *v* take away from: *The barking dog deprived us of sleep.* **de·prived, de·priv·ing.** **–dep′ri·va′tion** (dep′rə vā′shən), *n*.

depth (depth) *n* the distance from the surface to the bottom, or from front to back: *the depth of a hole, the depth of a lake. The depth of our playground is 90 m.* **out of your depth, 1** in water so deep that you cannot touch the bottom. **2** facing something you cannot understand or cope with.

de·rive (di rīv′) **1** *v* get: *She derives much pleasure from her books. The English word "enter" is derived from the French word "entrer."* **2** *v* make new words by adding suffixes or prefixes. From *kind* we can derive *kinder, kindness,* and *unkind* by adding *-er, -ness,* and *un-*. **de·rived, de·riv·ing. –der′i·va′tion** (der′ə vā′shən), *n.*

de·rog·a·to·ry (di rog′ə tô′rē) *adj* putting down others: *No derogatory remarks will be tolerated in this classroom.*

de·scend (di send′) *v* go or come down: *They slowly descended the stairs.* **–de·scent′,** *n.*
de·scend·ant *n* a person born of a certain family or group: *She is a descendant of German settlers.*
be descended from, have as ancestors; be the child, grandchild, great-grandchild, etc. of: *He is descended from Scottish settlers in Nova Scotia.*

de·scribe (di skrīb′) *v* tell what something is like. **de·scribed, de·scrib·ing. –de·scrip′tion** (di scrip′shən), *n,* **–de·scrip′tive,** *adj.*

Part of the Sahara Desert

des·ert (dez′ərt *for 1,* di zərt′ *for 2*) **1** *n* a region with very little water and not much plant or animal life: *The Sahara Desert is a great, sandy region in northern Africa.* **2** *v* go away and leave: *The dog was deserted by its owner.* **–de·sert′er,** *n,* **–de·ser′tion,** *n.*

de·serve (di zərv′) *v* have a right to: *This well-researched project deserves a high mark.* **de·served, de·serv·ing.**

de·sign (di zīn′) **1** *n* a drawing used as a pattern for making something: *a design for a machine, a dress design.* **2** *n* a pattern: *a wallpaper design in green and brown.* **3** *v* plan out: *to design a dress, to design a tree fort.* **–de·sign′er,** *n.*
des·ig·nate (dez′ig nāt′) **1** *v* show: *Red lines on this map of Manitoba designate main roads.* **2** *v* name: *Tiiu was designated team captain.*
by design, on purpose.

de·sire (di zīr′) **1** *v* wish for: *A miser desires money more than anything else.* **2** *n* something wished for: *His greatest desire was to become a writer.* **de·sired, de·sir·ing.**
de·sir·a·ble *adj* worth having: *My parents don't consider snakes to be desirable pets.* **–de·sir′a·bil′i·ty,** *n.*

desk (desk) *n* a piece of furniture on which to write, draw, use a computer, etc. It usually has drawers.
desk·top 1 *adj* so small that it can be used on a desk: *desktop computer, desktop printer.* **2** *n* on a computer, the screen that comes up showing that it is ready to be used.

des·o·late (des′ə lit *or* dez′ə lit) *adj* empty or lifeless: *desolate land, a desolate house.* **–des′o·la′tion,** *n.*

de·spair (di sper′) *n* a hopeless feeling: *Despair filled them as they felt the boat sinking.*
des·per·ate (des′pə rit) **1** *adj* almost hopeless: *She would have to be desperate before she asked for help.* **2** *adj* reckless because there is no hope: *a desperate criminal.* **3** *adj* wanting very badly: *After a week of being cooped up in the cabin, he was desperate to go outside.* **–des′per·a′tion,** *n.*

de·spise (di spīz′) *v* look down on: *Most people despise a traitor.* **de·spised, de·spis·ing.**
des·pic·a·ble (di spik′ə bəl) *adj* disgusting: *Taking away the baby's toy was despicable.* **–des·pic′a·bly,** *adv.*

de·spite (di spīt′) *prep* in spite of: *The children went for a walk despite the rain.*

A delicious dessert

des·sert (di zərt′) *n* a sweet course served at the end of a meal: *Pie, cake, puddings, and ice cream are common desserts.*

des·ti·na·tion (des′tə nā′shən) *n* where a person or thing is going: *The traveller's destination was Rimouski.*

des·ti·ny (des′tə nē) *n* what happens, or will happen, to a person or thing in the end: *It was her destiny to become a Canadian hero.*

des·ti·tute (des′tə tyūt′ *or* des′tə tūt′) *adj* without necessities such as food, clothing, shelter: *A destitute family needs help.*

de·stroy (di stroi′) *v* wreck or ruin: *Some pets destroy furniture.* **–de·struc′tion** (di struk′shən), *n*, **–de·struc′tive,** *adj.*

de·tach (di tach′) *v* unfasten; separate: *She detached a charm from her bracelet.*

de·tail (dē′tāl *or* di tāl′) *n* a small or particular thing or fact: *All the details of getting ready for the birthday party were left to the children.*
go into detail, describe or discuss each small part: *Don't go into detail–we don't have time.*
in detail, part by part: *She described the inside of the airplane in detail.*

de·tain (di tān′) *v* hold back: *I was detained by the heavy snowstorm.*

de·ten·tion (di ten′shən) *n* the act of keeping someone from leaving: *The students' behaviour resulted in a detention at recess.*

de·tect (di tekt′) *v* discover; notice: *Could you detect any strange smell in the room? He was detected stealing cookies.* **–de·tect′a·ble,** *adj.*

de·tec·tive *n* a person who works for the police force or some other employer to find out things that others are trying to keep secret.

de·ter (di tər′) *v* discourage; hinder. **de·terred, de·ter·ring.**

de·te·ri·o·rate (di tē′rē ə rāt′) *v* go bad or get worse: *Machinery will deteriorate if it is not given good care.* **de·te·ri·o·rat·ed, de·te·ri·o·rat·ing.** **–de·te′ri·o·ra′tion,** *n.*

de·ter·mine (di tər′mən) **1** *v* make up one's mind very firmly: *She determined to become the best scout in her troop.* **2** *v* find out for sure: *A diver was hired to determine the position of the sunken wreck along the Newfoundland coast.* **de·ter·mined, de·ter·min·ing.** **–de·ter′mi·na′tion,** *n.*
de·ter·mined *adj* having a mind firmly made up: *a determined look on her face.*

de·test (di test′) *v* hate: *I detest cockroaches.* **–de·test′a·ble,** *adj.*

de·tour (dē′tūr) *n* a roundabout way instead of the usual direct way.

de·vel·op (di vel′əp) **1** *v* grow and mature: *Plants develop from seeds.* **2** *v* come up with: *They've developed their own secret language.* **3** *v* build new houses, tourist attractions, dams, etc. in some area: *They have developed the old downtown.* **4** *v* treat a photographic plate or film with chemicals so that the picture shows: *I took the film in to be developed.* **–de·vel′op·ment,** *n.*

de·vice (di vīs′) *n* a tool: *A can opener is a device for opening cans.*

de·vise (di vīz′) *v* think up; come up with; invent: *The boys are trying to devise some scheme for earning the money for their trip to Kamloops.*

CONFUSABLES ..... device

device is a noun: *A can opener is a useful device.*
devise is a verb: *She devised a really complicated plan to avoid doing her work.*

dev·il (dev′əl) **1** *n* any evil spirit. **2** *n* a person who is wicked, reckless, mischievous, etc. **–dev′il·ish,** *adj.*

de·vote (di vōt′) *v* set apart or give up for a particular purpose: *She devoted all her spare time to sports. The museum devotes two floors to First Nations exhibits.* **de·vot·ed, de·vot·ing.**
de·vo·tion *n* a deep, steady love: *the devotion of a father to his child.* **–de·vot′ed,** *adj.*

de·vour (di vour′) *v* eat something up quickly and completely: *The wolves devoured the caribou. He devours four books a week.*

dew (dyū *or* dū) *n* moisture from the air that collects in small drops of water (**dew drops**) on cool surfaces during the night. **–dew′y,** *adj.*

di·ag·nose (dī′əg nōs′) *v* figure out what the problem is: *The doctor diagnosed the child's disease as measles.* When you have figured it out, you have made a **diagnosis. di·ag·nosed, di·ag·nos·ing.**

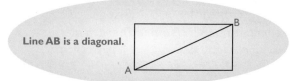
Line AB is a diagonal.

di·ag·o·nal (dī ag′ə nəl) **1** *n* a straight line joining any two corners that are not next to each other in a figure with four or more sides. **2** *adj* slanting, like a diagonal: *a diagonal stripe in a candy cane.* **–di·ag′o·nal·ly,** *adv.*

di·a·gram (dī′ə gram′) *n* a drawing meant to explain something.

di·al (dī′əl) **1** *n* a circle with amounts marked around the edge and a pointer that moves around it to show a measurement. The face of a clock is a dial. **2** *v* enter a phone number to make a call: *She dialled her mother's office.* **di·alled** or **di·aled, di·al·ling** or **di·al·ing.**

di·a·logue (dī′ə log′) **1** *n* a conversation: *They had a long dialogue about their summer plans in Muskoka.* **2** *n* all the talking in a story, play, movie, etc.: *That book has a good plot and realistic dialogue.*

Grammar ✓Check .... dialogue

You can report what people say: Jacko said that he wanted ice cream. You can also give a direct quotation: Jacko said, "I want ice cream."

Dialogue is the actual words that people say. Put dialogue in quotation marks.

Start a new paragraph when a different person is speaking. Sometimes you don't have to tell which person is speaking, because the kind of language used makes it clear.

> Jacko said, "I want ice cream. You said if I was good I could, after supper."
>
> "That's right, I did say that," Mary replied. "You may choose any flavour you like."
>
> "Chocolate! Chocolate! I like chocolate!"
>
> "All right, chocolate it is."

Who spoke last?

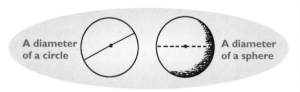

A diameter of a circle   A diameter of a sphere

di·am·e·ter (dī am′ə tər) *n* a straight line through the centre of a circle or sphere from one side to the other.

dia·mond (dī′mənd) **1** *n* a clear precious stone. Diamond is the hardest substance known. **2** *n* a figure shaped like this: ◊ **3** *n* the part of a baseball field inside the four lines that connect the bases.

di·a·per (dī′pər) *n* a pad of material used as underpants for a baby.

di·a·ry (dī′ə rē) *n* a book for writing down what happens or what you think and feel each day. *pl* **di·a·ries.**

dice (dīs) *pl.n* small cubes with a different number (often shown by spots) on each side. The singular is **die**. Dice are used in games.

dic·tate (dik′tāt *or* dik tāt′) **1** *v* say something out loud for someone else to write or key in: *The teacher dictated the spelling list.* **2** *v* tell others what to do: *No one is going to dictate to me.* **dic·tat·ed, dic·tat·ing. –dic·ta′tion,** *n.*

dic·ta·tor (dik′tā tər *or* dik tā′tər) *n* a ruler who has total power over the people. **–dic·ta′tor·ship′,** *n.*

dic·tion (dik′shən) *n* a style of speaking.

dic·tion·ar·y *n* a book that lists words in alphabetical order and gives the meaning, spelling, and often the pronunciation.

did (did) *v* the past tense of **do.** **didn't** did not.

die (dī) **1** *v* stop living. **2** *v* get weaker or stop: *The motor sputtered and died.* **died, dy·ing. be dying,** *Informal.* want very much: *I'm just dying to hear your news.*

di·et (dī′ət) **1** *n* the usual food and drink of a person or animal: *The diet of the giraffe is young leaves and shoots.* **2** *n* any special choice of foods eaten to get well, stay healthy, lose or gain weight, etc.: *The doctor ordered a diet of liquids for the sick child.* **3** *v* eat special food, especially to lose weight: *He can't eat sweets because he's dieting.* **di·et·ed, di·et·ing.**

dif·fer (dif′ər) *v* be not the same; disagree: *My answers differed from hers. They differed about how they should spend the money.*

dif·fer·ence (dif′ rəns) **1** *n* the fact of being unlike one another: *There is a difference between juice and pop.* **2** *n* what is left after subtracting one number from another: *The difference between 6 and 15 is 9.* **3** *n* a disagreement: *They sat down for a talk to try to settle their differences.*

dif·fer·ent *adj* not alike; not the same; unusual. **–dif′fer·ent·ly,** *adv.*

dif·fi·cult (dif′ə kult′) **1** *adj* hard to do or understand: *The heavy rock was difficult to move. Spelling is difficult for me.* **2** *adj* hard to get along with: *Don't be difficult–try to co-operate.* **–dif′fi·cul′ty,** *n.*

dig (dig) *v* make a hole in the ground: *to dig a hole or a tunnel.* **dug, dig·ging.**

dig in your heels, be stubborn about something.

di·gest (dī jest′) **1** *v* change food to liquid in the stomach and intestines, taking the useful parts into the blood as nourishment and getting rid of the rest. **2** *v* think over something until you understand it clearly: *It often takes a long time to digest new ideas.* **–di·ges′tion,** *n.*

dig·it (dij′it) **1** *n* any of the numerals 0, 1, 2, 3, 4, 5, 6, 7, 8, 9: *The number 472 has three digits.* **2** *n* a finger or toe.

dig·it·al *adj* giving or storing information in the form of numerals. A digital clock shows the time by numerals alone rather than by hands moving over a dial.

> **WORD HISTORY .... digit**
>
> **Digit** means "finger" in Latin. It was first used in English to mean "a numeral below ten," because people counted these on their fingers.
>
> The Latin word *digit* came from *dicitus* meaning "pointer," from which we get the English word "indicate."

dig·ni·ty (dig′nə tē) *n* a manner that commands respect.

dig·ni·fied *adj* commanding respect; rather serious and formal: *The chief of the First Nations band has a dignified manner.*

di·lap·i·dat·ed (di lap′ə dā′tid) *adj* old and falling to pieces: *When all the dilapidated houses are cleared away, we can build new homes.*

di·late (dī lāt′) *v* make or become wider, especially an opening: *The pupil of the eye dilates when the light gets dim.* **di·lat·ed, di·lat·ing.**

di·lem·ma (di lem′ə) *n* a situation where the only choices seem to be bad ones: *What a dilemma! I have to miss either the trip out West with my cousins, or my last chance at playing in the soccer finals.*

di·lute (dī lūt′) *v* make weaker or thinner by adding liquid, usually water. **di·lut·ed, di·lut·ing.**

dim (dim) **1** *adj* not bright: *dim light.* **2** *adj* not clear: *dim eyesight.* **dim·mer, dim·mest.** **3** *v* make or become dim: *This switch dims the dining room lights.* **dimmed, dim·ming.** **–dim′ly,** *adv,* **–dim′mer,** *n,* **–dim′ness,** *n.*

dime (dīm) *n* a coin worth ten cents.

di·men·sion (di men′shən) *n* the measurement of length, width, or thickness: *The dimensions of my room are 4.2 m by 3.1 m.*

di·min·ish (di min′ish) *v* make or become smaller or less: *The tiger population has diminished over the years because of hunting.*

din (din) *n* a loud, confused, long-lasting noise.

dine (dīn) *v* eat dinner. **dined, din·ing.**

din·er (dī′nər) **1** *n* a person who is eating dinner. **2** *n* a railway car where meals are served. **3** *n* a restaurant, usually not very fancy.

din·ner (din′ər) *n* the main meal of the day. The time that you eat it is called **dinnertime.**

din·ghy (ding′ē) *n* a small boat. *pl* **din·ghies.**

din·gy (din′jē) *adj* dim, dull, and dirty-looking: *dingy old curtains.* **din·gi·er, din·gi·est.**

Dinosaur: a brontosaurus—
about 22 m long

di·no·saur (dī′nə sȯr′) *n* an extinct creature that may have been a reptile. Some dinosaurs were bigger than elephants; others were smaller than cats; some even flew.

dip (dip) **1** *v* put or go quickly into and then out of a liquid: *She dipped her foot into the cool water of Georgian Bay.* **2** *n* a sudden small drop: *a dip in prices, a dip in the road.* **dipped, dip·ping.**

diph·thong (dif′thong′ *or* dip′thong′) *n* a vowel sound made up of two vowels run together and pronounced in one syllable, such as *oi* in *noise* or *ou* in *out.*

di·plo·ma (di plō′mə) *n* a paper given by a school or college, which says that a person has completed certain studies and has graduated.

di·plo·ma·cy (də plō′mə sē) *n* the business of keeping friendly relations between different countries.

dip·lo·mat *n* a person involved in handling the relations between his or her own country and other countries. **–dip′lo·mat′ic**, *adj*.

di·rect (də rekt′ *or* dī rekt′) **1** *v* guide: *The teacher directs the work of the class.* **2** *v* order: *The crossing guard directed us to stop.* **3** *v* show the way: *Can you direct me to the library?* **4** *v* aim: *The firefighter directed the hose at the flames.* **5** *adj* or *adv* without a break or turn; straight: *A bee makes a direct flight home to the hive (adj). The airplane goes to St. John's direct (adv).* **6** *adj* honest; clear and plain: *a direct answer.* **–di·rect′ly**, *adv*.

di·rec·tion (də rek′shən *or* dī rek′shən) **1** *n* the way that something points, faces, or travels: *"What direction are we driving–north or south?"* **2** *n* telling what to do, how to do, where to go, etc.: *Can you give me directions to the lake?* **3** *n* guidance: *The school is under the direction of the principal.* **4** *n* an order or command. **direct object** a noun, a pronoun, or a phrase with a noun in it that completes the meaning of a verb by telling who or what received the action. *Example: the puck in She hit the puck into the net.*

di·rec·tor (də rek′tər *or* dī rek′tər) *n* a manager; a person who directs, especially the leader of an organization or someone who directs a play or movie. **di·rec·to·ry** (də rek′tə rē *or* dī rek′tə rē) *n* a list of names, phone numbers, and addresses.

dirt (dərt) **1** *n* mud, dust, or earth: *a shovel full of dirt.* **2** *n* a stain, smudge, or other mark that is not wanted. **3** *n Slang.* information; news; bad rumours.

dirt·y 1 *adj* not clean: *Children playing in the mud get dirty.* **2** *adj* hurtful; not nice: *a dirty trick, a dirty joke.*

dis– a *prefix meaning* the opposite or the reverse. *Disadvantage* is the opposite of *advantage*.

USING WORDS . . . . dis

The prefix **dis-** means "the opposite of" or "the reverse of." For example, *disappear* is the opposite of *appear*, and *disconnect* is the reverse of *connect*.

---

dis·a·ble (di sā′bəl) **1** *v* do something to a thing to stop it from working: *to disable an alarm.*

2 *v* **disabled,** having a disability: *Many disabled athletes participate in the Special Olympics.* **dis·a·bled, dis·a·bling.**

dis·a·bil·i·ty (dis′ə bil′ə tē) *n* a lack of the usual ability in some area: *She has a learning disability.*

dis·ad·van·tage (dis′əd van′tij) *n* anything that makes it harder to succeed: *His shyness was a disadvantage in making new friends.* **–dis′ad·van′taged**, *adj*.

dis·a·gree (dis′ə grē′) **1** *v* have different opinions: *Doctors sometimes disagree about treatment.* **2** *v* have a bad effect: *Some foods disagree with him.* **dis·a·greed, dis·a·gree·ing. –dis′a·gree′ment**, *n*.

dis·a·gree·a·ble *adj* not pleasant: *a disagreeable person, a disagreeable task.*

dis·ap·point (dis′ə point′) *v* make a person sad by not turning out as expected: *The news that Grandma could not come disappointed the whole family.* **–dis′ap·point′ment**, *n*.

dis·as·ter (də zas′tər) *n* an event that causes much suffering: *floods, fires, wars, and other disasters.* **–dis·as′trous**, *adj*.

dis·card (dis kàrd′) *v* throw away.

dis·ci·pline (dis′ə plin) **1** *v* teach good behaviour: *to discipline a dog.* **2** *n* self-control: *Her calm reaction to their insults showed real discipline.* **dis·ci·plined, dis·ci·plin·ing.**

dis·count (dis′kount) *n* the amount taken off a price: *The store offers a ten percent discount for seniors on Thursdays.*

dis·cour·age (dis kər′ij) **1** *v* take away someone's hopes: *Don't let your failures discourage you.* **2** *v* advise against something: *My parents discourage us from eating sugary snacks.* **dis·cour·aged, dis·cour·ag·ing. –dis·cour′age·ment**, *n*.

dis·cov·er (di skuv′ər) *v* find out; see or learn about something for the first time: *On one of our hikes in Fundy National Park we discovered a cave.* **–dis·cov′er·er**, *n*, **–dis·cov′er·y**, *n*.

dis·crim·i·nate (di skrim′ə nāt′) **1** *v* notice the small but important differences: *Can you discriminate between real and artificial diamonds?* **2** *v* treat people differently when their differences don't matter: *Employers should not discriminate against any nationality when hiring.* **dis·crim·i·nat·ed, dis·crim·i·nat·ing. –dis·crim′i·na′tion**, *n*.

dis·cuss (di skus′) *v* talk over the various sides of a question: *The class discussed several problems.* **–dis·cus′sion,** *n.*

dis·ease (də zēz′) *n* sickness; illness: *Disease kills some plants each year. Chicken pox is an infectious disease.* **–dis·eased′,** *adj.*

dis·grace (dis grās′) **1** *n* shame; a loss of respect or honour: *There is no disgrace in losing.* **2** *v* bring shame upon: *He disgraced his family by his behaviour.* **3** *n* something to be ashamed of: *Their unfriendly attitude to the new neighbours was a disgrace.* **dis·graced, dis·grac·ing.** **–dis·grace′ful,** *adj.*

dis·guise (dis gīz′) **1** *v* make a person look like someone else: *She disguised herself as a much older woman, using a wig, make-up, and different clothes.* **2** *n* the clothes or actions used for this: *Her disguise also included glasses and a hat.* **dis·guised, dis·guis·ing.**

dis·gust (dis gust′) **1** *n* sickening dislike: *Their cruelty to the animals filled us with disgust.* **2** *v* cause sickening dislike in: *The smell of the garbage dump disgusted them.* **–dis·gust′ing,** *adj.*

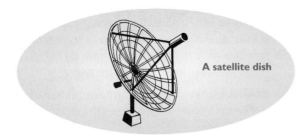

A satellite dish

dish (dish) **1** *n* a small bowl: *a dish of ice cream.* **2 dishes,** *pl.n* anything to serve food in, such as plates, bowls, cups, and saucers. **3** *n* food prepared a certain way: *Lasagna is my favourite dish.* **4** *n* a radio or TV antenna that is shaped like a huge bowl and receives signals from communications satellites in space. It is also called a **dish antenna** or **satellite dish**.
dish out, give out, especially words or actions: *to dish out compliments.*

dis·in·fect (dis′in fekt′) *v* kill the germs in or on: *A doctor's instruments are disinfected before they are used.* **–dis′in·fect′ant,** *n.*

dis·in·te·grate (di sin′tə grāt′) *v* break apart completely into small bits: *The explosion completely disintegrated the building.* **dis·in·te·grat·ed, dis·in·te·grat·ing.**

The hard disk is inside the computer.

The floppy disk goes here.

A computer

disk (disk) **1** *n* any flat, thin round object. **2** *n* a thin, small, magnetic plate used for storing computer data. There are two main types: the **floppy disk** and the **hard disk**. Any part of a computer that can read data from a disk is called a **disk drive**.

disk·ette (di skett′) *n* a thin, round, bendable magnetic plate for storing computer data, protected by a hard, plastic case that can't be removed. A diskette is put into a computer and taken out again every time it is used. **Floppy disk** is another name for it.

dis·like (dis līk′) **1** *n* a feeling of not liking; a feeling against: *Dad has a dislike for the neighbour's dog.* **2** *v* have this feeling against; not like: *She dislikes studying and would rather play football.* **dis·liked, dis·lik·ing.**

dis·mal (diz′məl) *adj* dreary and gloomy: *Cold, rainy days are dismal.*

dis·may (dis mā′) **1** *n* a feeling of very heavy spirits from fear or great disappointment: *The family stared in dismay at the burned remains of their house.* **2** *v* fill with this feeling: *The thought that she might never see her friend again dismayed her.*

dis·miss (dis mis′) *v* send away; let go: *The teacher dismissed the class at noon. They dismissed the cook because his cooking was awful.* **–dis·miss′al,** *n.*

dis·pel (di spel′) *v* drive away and scatter: *The captain's cheerful laugh dispelled their fears.* **dis·pelled, dis·pel·ling.**

dis·pense (dis pens′) *v* give out, whether for money or as a gift: *a machine that dispenses candy. The aid workers dispensed food and clothing to the homeless refugees. A pharmacist dispenses medicines.* **dis·pensed, dis·pens·ing.**

dis·perse (di spərs′) *v* scatter; go or send off in different directions: *The crowd dispersed when the curling match was over.* **dis·persed, dis·pers·ing.**

rock

water

This rock displaces 150 mL of water.

dis·place (dis plās′) **1** *v* take the place of: *Computers have displaced the typewriter.* **2** *v* put out of place: *When we dropped a rock into the beaker, it displaced 150 mL of water—the water level rose from 300 mL to 450 mL.* **dis·placed, dis·plac·ing.** –**dis·place′ment,** *n*.

dis·play (dis plā′) **1** *v* or *n* show: *He displayed his knowledge by answering all our questions* (*v*). *A tantrum is a display of bad temper* (*n*). **2** *n* something specially set up for people to look at: *Grade 4 had two displays of student drawings.*

dis·please (dis plēz′) *v* make angry or unhappy. **dis·pleased, dis·pleas·ing.** –**dis·pleas′ure,** *n*.

dis·pos·a·ble (dis pō′zə bəl) *adj* designed to be thrown away after use: *disposable paper cups.* **dispose of,** get rid of: *Dispose of that junk.*

dis·prove (dis prūv′) *v* prove false. **dis·proved, dis·prov·ing.**

dis·pute (dis pyūt′) **1** *v* argue or fight over. **2** *n* an argument or fight. **dis·put·ed, dis·put·ing.**

dis·qual·i·fy (dis kwol′ə fī′) *v* keep someone from doing something because he or she does not meet certain requirements: *The runner was disqualified from the race after she made three false starts.* **dis·qual·i·fied, dis·qual·i·fy·ing.**

dis·re·gard (dis′ri gàrd′) *v* pay no attention to; take no notice of.

dis·sat·is·fied (dis sat′is fīd′) *adj* unhappy; not content. –**dis·sat′is·fac′tion,** *n*.

dis·sect (di sekt′ *or* dī sekt′) *v* cut up an animal or plant in order to study it. –**dis·sec′tion,** *n*.

dis·solve (di zolv′) **1** *v* mix completely with a liquid: *Sugar dissolves in water.* **2** *v* fade away: *My fears dissolved when I saw her smile.* **dis·solved, dis·solv·ing.**

dis·tance (dis′təns) **1** *n* the space in between: *The distance from the farm to the town is 5 km.* **2** *n* a long way: *The campground is quite a distance from the highway.*

dis·tant *adj* not close: *stories from the distant past. We could see the distant mountains from the top of the tower.*

dis·tinct (di stingkt′) **1** *adj* separate: *two distinct sounds.* **2** *adj* different: *Mice are distinct from rats.* **3** *adj* clear: *Your speech should be distinct so everyone will understand it.* –**dis·tinct′ly,** *adv*.

dis·tinc·tion **1** *n* the act of making a difference: *She treated all alike, without distinction.* **2** *n* a difference: *What is the distinction between ducks and geese?* **3** *n* excellence: *an achievement of great distinction.* –**dis·tinc′tive,** *adj*.

dis·tin·guish (di sting′gwish) **1** *v* tell apart: *Can you distinguish real leather from fake leather?* **2** *v* see or hear clearly: *It was too dark for her to distinguish the outline of the house.* **3** *v* be a special feature of: *What distinguishes the elephant is its trunk.* **4** *v* win honour for: *Lester B. Pearson distinguished himself by winning a Nobel Peace Prize.*

dis·tin·guished **1** *adj* famous; well-known: *a distinguished artist.* **2** *adj* excellent; outstanding: *She received a medal for distinguished conduct.*

dis·tract (di strakt′) *v* draw the attention away: *Noise distracts me from my studying.* –**dis·tract′ed,** *adj,* –**dis·trac′tion,** *n*.

dis·tress (di stres′) **1** *n* great pain, sorrow, or anxiety: *The loss of her dog caused her great distress.* **2** *v* cause pain, anxiety, or sorrow to: *The idea of moving to another town distressed him.*

dis·trib·ute (di strib′yūt) *v* give out: *She distributed the cookies among all the children.* **dis·trib·ut·ed, dis·trib·ut·ing.** –**dis′tri·bu′tion** (dis′trə byū′shən), *n*.

dis·trict (dis′trikt) *n* a part of a larger area: *Northern Ontario is an important mining district in Canada. They lived in a quiet district of Port Alberni.*

D
d

dis·trust (dis trust′) **1** *v* put no trust in: *I didn't tell him the secret because I distrusted him.* **2** *n* lack of trust; suspicion: *She looked sideways at the stranger with distrust.*

dis·turb (di stərb′) **1** *v* destroy the peace of: *Heavy truck traffic disturbed the neighbourhood all day long.* **2** *v* mess up: *Someone has disturbed my shell collection.* **3** *v* make uneasy: *She was disturbed by the news of his illness.* **–dis·turb′ance,** *n,* **–dis·turbed,** *adj.*

A diver in a deep-sea diving suit

dive (dīv) **1** *v* jump headfirst into the water. A pool often has a bouncy **diving board** for this purpose. **2** *v* go down fast: *The airplane dived suddenly.* **dived** or **dove, dived, div·ing. –div′er,** *n.*

USING WORDS......dived

Dived and **dove** are both used for the past tense of *dive,* although dived is used more in formal English.

---

di·vide (di vīd′) **1** *v* separate into parts: *The Fontaine River divides and forms two streams.* **2** *v* in mathematics, show a number as separated into equal parts by a smaller number: *When you divide 8 by 2, the result is two equal parts of 4.* Symbol: ÷ **3** *v* share: *The children divided the pizza.* **4** *n* a ridge of land separating the regions drained by two different river systems. The Rocky Mountains are called the **Great Divide. di·vid·ed, di·vid·ing.**

di·vi·sion (di vizh′ən) **1** *n* the process of showing how many times one number is contained by another: *10 ÷ 2 = 5 is a simple division.* **2** *n* one of the parts into which a thing is divided: *a division of the animal kingdom, the primary division of a school.*

di·vis·i·ble (di viz′ə bəl) *adj* capable of being divided with no remainder: *12 is divisible by 4.*

di·vorce (di vôrs′) *n* the legal ending of a marriage. **di·vorced, di·vorc·ing.**

Di·wa·li (di va′lē) *n* a religious festival that Hindus celebrate in mid-November as their New Year. At Diwali lamps are lit, special meals are made, and gifts are exchanged. **Divali** is another spelling.

diz·zy (diz′ē) *adj* feeling like your head is spinning: *Sometimes when I get up suddenly, I feel dizzy.* **diz·zi·er, diz·zi·est. –diz′zi·ly,** *adv,* **–diz′zi·ness,** *n.*

do (dū) **1** *v* carry out; perform; finish: *She did her work. The portrait is done.* **2** *v* behave: *You did wisely in returning the money that you found.* **3** *v* get along: *How are they doing in their new school?* **4** *v* be good enough: *He said any kind of paper would do.* **5** *v* go: *We did 600 km today. This dirt bike can do 70 km/h.* **does, did, done, do·ing. –do′a·ble,** *adj.*

Do is also used in certain types of sentences as an auxiliary verb: **1** in asking questions: *Do you like milk?* **2** to emphasize a verb: *I do want to go. Do hurry, please.* **3** to stand for another verb already used: *My dog goes everywhere I do.* **4** in statements that contain **not**: *I do not tell lies.*

Docks with a ship loading

dock (dok) *n* a platform built on the shore, where boats can come alongside.

doc·tor (dok′tər) *n* a person having a licence to practise medicine: *a medical doctor.*

doc·u·ment (dok′yə mənt) **1** *n* something written that gives information, especially something official: *Show these documents to the principal.* **2** *n* a computer file made with an ordinary piece of writing software. **3** *n* give or keep a record of something: *Our summer trip is documented in this big photo album.*

doc·u·men·ta·ry *n* a movie, a radio or TV program, or a book that presents facts in an artistic way. If it adds some fiction for greater interest, it is called a **docudrama** (dok′yə drä′mə).

dodge (doj) **1** *v* move quickly to one side: *I dodged the ball as it came flying toward my head.* **2** *v* get away from or avoid by some trick: *She has dodged her chores again.* **dodged, dodg·ing.**

doe (dō) *n* the female of deer, antelope, rabbit, hare, and most other animals whose male is called a buck.

do·jo (dō′jō) *n* a school or hall where martial arts are taught: *After school Wendy went to the dojo for her karate lesson.* pl **do·jos.**

dol·drums (dol′drəmz) **1** *pl.n* certain parts of the ocean near the equator where the wind is very light or constantly shifting. Sailing ships caught in the doldrums were often unable to move for days. **2** *pl.n* a gloomy feeling; low spirits: *The whole family was in the doldrums because of the rainy weather.*

dol·lar (dol′ər) *n* the unit of money in Canada and some other countries. In Canada, it is sometimes called a **loonie.** *Symbol:* $

WORD HISTORY . . . . dollar

The track of the word **dollar** goes like this. It came into English through German *daler,* from an earlier German word *thaler.* This word *thaler* is short for *Joachimsthaler,* a kind of silver coin. *Joachimsthal,* meaning "Joachim's valley" is the place in Germany where the silver for this coin was found.

---

dol·phin (dol′fən) *n* a sea mammal related to the whale and porpoise, having a snout shaped like a beak. Dolphins are very intelligent.

dome (dōm) *n* a large, rounded roof. ❧ **dome fastener** a small fastener made up of two parts, one with a small, round bump in the centre that snaps into a hole in the other part.

do·mes·tic (də mes′tik) **1** *adj* having to do with the home or family: *domestic chores, a domestic scene.* **2** *adj* having to do with your own country; not foreign: *domestic news. Canadians eat a lot of domestic cheese.*
do·mes·ti·cate *v* tame an animal or plant: *The dog was one of the first animals to be domesticated.*

dom·i·nate (dom′ə nāt′) *v* control or rule: *Dandelions will dominate over grass if they are not kept out.* **dom·i·nat·ed, dom·i·nat·ing.** **–dom′i·na′tion,** *n.*
dom·i·nant *adj* main controlling: *Hockey is Canada's dominant sport in winter.* **Dominion** *n* a former name of some independent countries in the Commonwealth of Nations: *The Dominion of Canada was established on July 1, 1867.*

do·nate (dō nāt′ *or* dō′nāt) *v* give; contribute: *Our parents donated money and books to the school library.* **do·nat·ed, do·nat·ing. –do·na′tion,** *n.*
do·nor (dō′nər) *n* a person who donates.

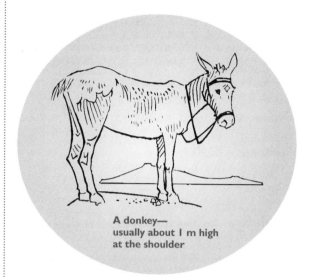

A donkey— usually about 1 m high at the shoulder

don·key (dong′kē) *n* an animal related to the horse, but smaller. pl **don·keys.**

doo·dle (dū′dəl) *v* make drawings or marks of any kind while thinking of something else: *He doodled while he was talking on the telephone.* **doo·dled, doo·dling.**

doom (dūm) **1** *n* a terrible fate; ruin; death: *The soldiers marched to their doom.* **2** *v* **doomed,** headed for something bad: *Her plan seemed doomed to failure because everything had gone wrong from the beginning.*

door (dôr) **1** *n* an opening in a wall for going in and out: *I saw him just as he came through the door.* **Doorway** is another word for this. **2** *n* a flat piece of wood, metal, or glass, for closing an opening.
out of doors, outside.
show someone the door, send someone away; tell someone to leave.

do·ry (dôr′ē) *n* a rowboat with a narrow, flat bottom and high sides: *Dories are often used for ocean fishing.* pl **do·ries.**

DOS (dos) a set of basic instructions that tells a computer system how to make its parts work together. Its full name is **disk operating system.**

dose (dōs) *n* an amount of medicine to be taken at one time. The **dosage** is the size of this amount and how often you are to take it.

dot (dot) **1** *n* a small round mark: *There is a dot over each "i" in this line.* **2** *v* mark with a dot or dots. **dot·ted, dot·ting.**

on the dot, exactly at the time mentioned: *The meeting is at five o'clock and you must be there on the dot.*

dou·ble (dub′əl) **1** *adj* twice as much: *The waiter was given double pay for working on Sunday.* **2** *v* make or become twice as much or twice as many: *He doubled the amount of each ingredient to make more cookies.* **3** *v* fold over: *I doubled my slice of bread to make a sandwich.* **dou·bled, dou·bling. –doub′ly,** *adv.*

dou·ble-cross *v Informal.* cheat or play a nasty trick on: *When my friend didn't show up, I realized I had been double-crossed.*

double back, turn back suddenly the other way: *The fox doubled back on its track and escaped the dogs.*

doubt (dout) **1** *v* not believe; not be sure: *The captain doubted that the damaged ship would reach land.* **2** *n* an unsure feeling: *We had doubts about which road to take.* **–doubt′ful,** *adj.*

dough (dō) **1** *n* the uncooked mixture of flour, milk, fat, and other things that bread, biscuits, pies, etc. are made of. **2** *n Slang.* money.

dough·nut *n* a ring or roll of sweetened dough cooked in deep fat.

Douk·ho·bours (dū′kə bòrz′) *pl.n* a Christian sect that started in Russia about 200 years ago. Several thousand Doukhobours left Russia in 1898 and settled in Western Canada. **Doukhobors** is another spelling.

down (doun) **1** *adv* to or at a lower place or a lower amount: *They ran down from the top of the hill. His fever is down to 38°C now.* **2** *prep* along, especially to a lower place: *to ride down a hill, sail down a river, or walk down a street.* **3** *n Informal.* a period of bad luck or unhappiness: *Her life is full of ups and downs.* **4** *adv* swallow: *He downed the juice in one gulp.* **5** *adv* not working: *Our computer is down.* **6** *n* a chance to move a football forward. In Canadian football, a team is allowed three downs in which to move the ball forward ten yards (about 9 m). **7** *n* soft, fine feathers or hair: *the down on a duck.*

down·load *v* move data or programs from one computer or network to another: *Mom downloaded some games for us from the Internet.*

down·pour *n* a heavy rainfall.

down·stairs 1 *n* the lower floor of a building: *We rented the downstairs of the house.* **2** *adv* down the stairs to a lower floor: *He fell downstairs.*

down·stream *adv* in the direction of the current of a stream or river: *It is easy to swim or row downstream.*

down·town *adj* or *adv* to or in the main business section of a town: *a downtown store* (adj). *She goes downtown to her office* (adv).

come down with, get sick with.

down and out, going through very bad times.

down on, *Informal.* against; attacking: *He's down on anybody who doesn't like sports.*

down with! get rid of! We don't want!

doze (dōz) *v* sleep lightly; nap: *We found the cat dozing in the armchair.* **dozed, doz·ing.**

doz·en (duz′ən) *n* 12; a group of 12. *pl* **doz·ens** or (after a number) **doz·en.**

Dr. or **Dr** abbreviation for: **1** Doctor: *Dr. M. H. Smith.* **2** Drive: *220 Rideau Dr., Ottawa.*

draft (draft) **1** *n* a current of air. **2** *n* a rough sketch or piece of writing: *He made three different drafts of his speech before he had it in final form.* **–draft′y,** *adj.*

Grammar ✓*Check* ..... **draft**

You should make several draft versions of a piece of writing, until it is exactly what you want.

- Make your first draft have all the ideas that you want to include. Don't worry about things like checking spelling yet.
- In your next draft, check that all the information you have is correct, and organize your ideas so that they flow from one to the next. (You may need to make another draft here.)
- In the next draft, check and fix any errors in grammar, punctuation, or spelling.
- Your final version should be clean. Make sure you give it a title, and write your name on it.

---

drag (drag) **1** *v* pull or be pulled along the ground: *A team of horses dragged the big log out of the forest. Her long skirt was dragging in the dust of the street.* **2** *v* go too slowly: *Time drags when you have nothing to do.* **dragged, drag·ging.**

A dragon

drag·on (drag′ən) *n* in stories, a fierce fire-breathing creature like a huge lizard with wings and claws.

drain (drān) **1** *v* let liquid flow off or out of: *to drain a cup, to drain a swamp for farmland.* **2** *n* the process of draining or something that drains: *a cellar drain.*

dra·ma (dram′ə *or* drä′mə) **1** *n* a play, especially a serious one. **2** *n* the art of writing and putting on plays: *He wants to study drama.* **dra·mat·ic 1** *adj* having to do with plays or acting. **2** *adj* full of action, suspense, or feeling: *There was a dramatic pause and then the lion leaped.* –**dra·mat′i·cal·ly,** *adv.* **dram·a·tize** (dram′ə tīz′ *or* drä′mə tīz′) **1** *v* make into a play: *The class dramatized a Mi'kmaq legend.* **2** *v* make exciting: *She had a way of dramatizing the stories she told the children.* –**dram′a·ti·za′tion,** *n.*

drape (drāp) **1** *v* hang with cloth falling loosely in folds: *He draped the blanket over a chair.* **2 drapes,** *pl.n* long, heavy curtains that are made to hang in folds. Another word for these is **draperies**; the cloth used for them is **drapery** fabric. **draped, drap·ing.**

dras·tic (dras′tik) *adj* extreme; extraordinary: *drastic changes. The police took drastic measures to put a stop to drunk driving.*

draw (dro) **1** *v* make a picture with pen, pencil, crayon, etc.: *Draw a circle. He draws very well.* **2** *v* attract: *A parade always draws crowds.* **3** *v* move: *I saw him draw back in fear. The car drew near.* **4** *v* pull: *The horses draw the wagon. She drew the rope tight.* **5** *v* get or take: *to draw water from a well, to draw money from the bank.* **6** *n* in certain games, an equal score for both sides. **7** *n* a lottery: *Dean won a bicycle in a draw.* **drew, drawn, draw·ing.**

draw·back *n* a bad point about something: *Our trip was interesting, but the cold weather was a drawback.* **draw·er** *n* a box with handles that slides in and out of a dresser, desk, etc.: *She kept her shirts in the dresser drawer.*

draw·ing 1 *n* a picture or design done with pen, pencil, crayon, etc. **2** *n* the making of pictures: *Drawing is taught in art classes.*

back to the drawing board, back to the beginning.

draw a blank, try to do something, especially remember or guess, and fail completely.

draw the line, set the limit: *Joking is fine, but we draw the line at putting others down.*

draw out, 1 make or become long: *Don't draw the story out so much.* **2** persuade to talk: *We asked the new boy about his old school to draw him out.*

draw up, 1 write out: *to draw up a list.* **2** stop: *The taxi drew up at the entrance of the hotel.*

dread (dred) **1** *v* look ahead to something with fear or dislike: *He dreaded the long drive home to Grande Prairie.* **2** *n* great fear: *She hated the cold and lived in dread of winter.*

dread·ful *adj* causing dread; terrible; fearful. –**dread′ful·ly,** *adv.*

A dream catcher

dream (drēm) **1** *n* something you imagine while you are asleep. **2** *n* something you hope or wish for: *The boy had dreams of being an astronaut.* **dreamed** or **dreamt** (dremt), **dream·ing.** –**dream′er,** *n.*

dream catch·er *n* among some First Nations people, a round frame with a knotted web of strings or leather strips across it, often decorated with beads and feathers. According to tradition, only good dreams can pass through the web. Bad dreams get caught and disappear with the night.

drear·y (drē′rē) *adj* dull; depressing; gloomy. **drear·i·er, drear·i·est.**

dredge (drej) **1** *n* a machine with a scoop, or a whole series of scoops, for digging out the bottom of a harbour or channel. **2** *v* a sort of large net, used for gathering oysters, etc. from the bottom of a river or the sea.

dregs (dregz) *pl.n* the solid bits of matter that settle to the bottom of a liquid such as coffee.

drench (drench) *v* wet thoroughly; soak: *We were drenched by heavy rain.*

dress (dres) **1** *n* a piece of clothing worn by women and girls. **2** *n* clothing: *He was wearing rather casual dress for a wedding.* **3** *v* put clothes on. **4** *v* put medicine, bandages, etc. on a wound or sore: *The nurse dressed the wound every day.* **dressed, dress·ing.**

dress·er *n* a piece of furniture with drawers for clothes and, usually, a mirror. **dress·ing 1** *n* a sauce for salad. **2** *n* a mixture of bread crumbs, spices, etc. used to stuff chickens and turkeys before cooking. **Stuffing** is another word for this. **3** *n* the medicine, bandage, etc. put on a wound or sore.

dress rehearsal (dres′ ri hər′səl) the final practice of a play, with the actors wearing their costumes.

dress up, put on your best clothes, or a costume.

drib·ble (drib′əl) **1** *v* flow or let flow in small amounts; trickle: *The water dribbled from the bottle.* **2** *v* move a ball along by bouncing it or giving it short kicks. **drib·bled, drib·bling.**

dried (drīd) *v* the past tense of **dry.**

drift (drift) **1** *v* be carried along by currents of air or water: *A raft drifts if it is not steered.* **2** *v* snow, sand, etc. heaped up by the wind: *After the heavy snow there were deep drifts in the yard.*

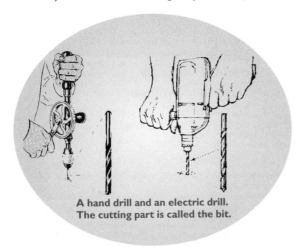

A hand drill and an electric drill.
The cutting part is called the bit.

drill (dril) **1** *n* a tool or machine for making holes in wood, metal, etc. **2** *v* make a hole with a drill. **3** *v* teach by making someone do a thing over and over: *The teacher drilled the class in arithmetic.* **4** *n* the process of doing a thing over and over to learn it: *The gym teacher gave us plenty of drills in soccer skills.*

drink (dringk) **1** *v* swallow something liquid: *The children drink milk for breakfast.* **2** *n* liquid swallowed to make you less thirsty. **drank, drunk, drink·ing.**

drip (drip) **1** *v* fall or let fall in drops: *Rain drips from an umbrella.* **2** *n* the falling of a liquid in drops. **dripped, drip·ping.**

drive (drīv) **1** *v* operate or be in a car, truck, etc.: *to drive a motorboat. We drove to Manitoba.* **2** *n* a trip in a car or other vehicle: *the long drive to Grandpa's.* **3** *v* make go: *He drove the cow out of the barn.* **4** *n* a special campaign to raise money, get new members, etc.: *Our school had a drive to get money for charity.* **drove, driv·en, driv·ing. –driv′er,** *n.*

drive·way *n* a private road leading from the street to a house or garage.

driz·zle (driz′əl) **1** *v* rain gently, in very small drops like mist. **2** *n* light rain that is like mist. **driz·zled, driz·zling.**

drone (drōn) **1** *n* a male bee. Drones do no work in the hive. **2** *n* a lazy person. **3** *n* a low hum: *We could hear the drone of the plane's engines.* **4** *v* talk or say in a boring voice: *to drone on and on about nothing.* **droned, dron·ing.**

drool (drül) *v* let spit run from the mouth.

droop (drüp) *v* hang down; bend down: *These flowers are starting to droop; put them in water.*

drop (drop) **1** *v* fall or let fall: *The package dropped into a puddle. The temperature is dropping. She dropped the bag.* **2** *n* a fall or the length of a fall: *a drop in prices, a drop of 10 m.* **3** *n* a small, round blob of liquid, usually one that falls: *a drop of rain, a drop of blood.* **4** *v* stop doing, using, etc.: *Let's drop this argument.* **dropped, drop·ping.**

drop off, 1 go to sleep: *He dropped off in his armchair.* **2** let passengers out of a car, bus, etc.: *Drop me off right here.*

drop out, quit: *She had to drop out of the race when she twisted her ankle.*

drought (drout) *n* a long period with no rain.

drown (droun) **1** *v* die or kill under water or some other liquid because there is no air to breathe: *The man almost drowned when his boat overturned on Buffalo Lake.* **2** *v* be so loud as to keep something else from being heard: *The boat's whistle drowned out the girl's voice.*

drowse (drouz) *v* be half asleep: *She drowsed, but did not quite fall asleep.* **drowsed, drows·ing. drowsier, drowsiest. –drow′sily,** *adv,* **–drow′siness,** *n,* **–drow′sy,** *adj.*

drug (drug) *n* a non-food substance that changes your body's functions when you take it. Some drugs are used as medicine. It is dangerous to abuse drugs.

drunk (drungk) *adj* overcome by alcoholic liquor: *He was so drunk he could not stand up.*

dry (drī) **1** *adj* not wet: *dry leaves, a dry climate.* **dri·er, dri·est. 2** *v* make or become dry: *We were drying dishes.* **dried, dry·ing. –dry′ly,** *adv,* **–dry′ness,** *n.*

dry-clean *v* clean clothes, fabrics, etc. by chemicals instead of water. **–dry cleaner,** *n,* **–dry cleaning,** *n.*

dry·er *n* a machine that uses heat or blowing air to dry things: *a clothes dryer, a hair dryer.*

du·al (dyū′əl *or* dū′əl) *adj* having two parts; double: *This piece of software has a dual purpose: learning and fun.*

**A mallard duck—
about 60 cm long
including the tail**

duck (duk) **1** *n* a water bird that has webbed feet. **2** *v* go or push out of sight for a short time, especially under water: *They ducked him in the pool.* **3** *v* lower the head to escape being hit or seen: *She ducked to avoid a low branch.*

duct (dukt) *n* a tube for carrying liquid or air: *Warm air from the furnace is blown through ducts to all the rooms in this house. Tears flow from tear ducts in your upper eyelids.*

due (dyū *or* dū) **1** *adj* that is expected: *The monthly car payment is due today. Respect is due to older people. The train from Saskatoon is due at noon.* **2** *adv* straight: *due west.*
due to, caused by: *The accident was due to his careless use of the scissors.*
in due time, after a certain amount of time.

du·el (dyū′əl *or* dū′əl) *n* a formal fight to settle a quarrel. **du·elled** *or* **du·eled, du·el·ling** *or* **du·el·ing.**

du·et (dyū et′ *or* dū et′) *n* a piece of music for two voices or instruments.

dug·out (dug′out′) **1** *n* a canoe made by hollowing out a large log. **2** *n* a small shelter at the side of a baseball field, used by players not on the field.

dull (dul) **1** *adj* not sharp: *a dull knife, a dull pain, dull eyes, a dull colour, a dull day.*
2 *adj* slow to understand: *a dull mind.*
3 *adj* boring: *a dull book, a dull visit.* **4** *v* make or become dull: *Cutting that carpet dulled the scissors.* **–dull′ness,** *n,* **–dul′ly,** *adv.*

dumb (dum) **1** *adj* not speaking, or not able to speak: *dumb with fright.* **2** *adj Informal.* stupid. **–dumb′ly,** *adv.*

dum·found *or* **dumbfound** *v* amaze to the point of being unable to speak.

dum·my (dum′ē) **1** *n* a figure of a person, used for store window displays, for putting in a car that is being crash-tested, etc. **2** *adj* made to look like the real thing; pretend: *dummy swords.*
pl **dum·mies.**

dump (dump) **1** *v* empty out; throw down: *The truck dumped the gravel on the sidewalk. Don't just dump your books on the floor.* **2** *n* a place where people throw garbage.
down in the dumps, feeling gloomy or sad: *He was down in the dumps because his bike was broken.*

dune (dyūn *or* dūn) *n* a mound of loose sand heaped up by the wind.

dung (dung) *n* the solid waste of animals; manure: *Dung is used as fertilizer.*

dun·geon (dun′jən) *n* a strong underground room in a castle, to keep prisoners in.

dunk (dungk) **1** *v* dip something into a liquid: *to dunk doughnuts in coffee.* **2** *v Informal.* push somebody into water. **3** *v* in basketball, score by jumping up and dropping the ball through the hoop.

du·o (dyū′ō *or* dū′o) *n* a pair; two people who do something together: *In the last part of the movie the fearless duo broke out of jail.* *pl* **du·os.**

dupe (dyūp *or* dūp) **1** *v* deceive; trick: *The stranger tried to dupe us into going with him.*
2 *n* a person who is easily deceived or tricked. **duped, dup·ing.**

❧ **duplex** (dyū′pleks *or* dū′pleks) *n* a building with two dwellings in it, either side by side or one above the other.

du·pli·cate (dyū′plə kit *or* dū′plə kit *for 1,* dyū′plə kāt′ *or* dū′plə kāt′ *for 2*) **1** *adj* exactly alike: *We have duplicate keys for the front door.* **2** *v* make an exact copy of; repeat exactly. **du·pli·cat·ed, du·pli·cat·ing.** —**du′pli·ca′tion,** *n.*

du·ra·tion (dyə rā′shən *or* də rā′shən) *n* the time that something lasts: *The other team was scoreless for the duration of the game.*

du·ra·ble (dyū′rə bəl *or* dū′rə bəl) *adj* lasting a long time; tough; strong: *durable plastic, durable clothing.* **dur·ing** (dyū′ring *or* dū′ring) *prep* while something is going on: *Come to see us sometime during the holidays.*

Dur·ga Pu·ja (dūr′gə pū′jə) *n* an important Hindu festival in honour of Durga, the goddess of power. Another name for this festival is **Navaratri.**

Durum wheat

durum (dyù′rəm *or* dù′rəm) *n* a hard wheat grown a lot in Western Canada. The flour in pasta is made from it.

dusk (dusk) *n* the time just before dark: *At dusk, the lights started going on in the houses.*

dust (dust) **1** *n* fine, dry dirt; any fine powder: *Dust lay thick on the shelf. The ashes in the fireplace had turned to dust.* **2** *v* brush or wipe the dust from: *My job is dusting the furniture.* **3** *v* sprinkle with fine powder: *Dad dusted the cake with icing sugar.* —**dust′y,** *adj.*

bite the dust, *Slang.* **1** fall dead or wounded: *A shot rang out and one of the outlaws bit the dust.* **2** end: *Another soccer season bites the dust.*

du·ty (dyū′tē *or* dū′tē) **1** *n* the thing that a person is supposed to do: *It is your duty to obey the law.* **2** *n* a tax on articles brought into a country. In a **duty-free** shop you can buy goods without paying this tax on them. *pl* **du·ties. du·ti·ful** (dyū′tə fəl *or* dū′tə fəl) *adj* obedient. **off duty,** not working. **on duty,** working.

duvet (dū vā′ *or* dyū vā′) *n* a bedcover stuffed with soft material, often feathers.

DVD a disk similar to a CD-ROM but able to hold a much greater amount of information, such as a whole movie. The full name is **digital video disk.**

dwarf (dwôrf) **1** *n* a person, animal, or plant much smaller than the usual size for its kind. **2** *n* in fairy tales, a member of a short race of people, often with magic powers. *pl* **dwarfs** or **dwarves** (dwôrvz).

dwell (dwel) *v* an old or poetic word for have your home: *The princess dwelt in a beautiful castle.* **dwelt** or **dwelled, dwell·ing.**

dwell·ing *n* a formal or poetic word for a home: *a two-family dwelling.*

dwell on, think, speak, or write about for a long time.

dwin·dle (dwin′dəl) *v* become smaller and smaller or less and less: *During the sale, the supply of toys and games dwindled rapidly.* **dwin·dled, dwin·dling.**

dye (dī) **1** *n* a substance used to colour cloth, hair, etc. **2** *v* colour by treating with such a substance: *I dyed the T-shirt blue.* **dyed, dye·ing.**

dy·nam·ic (dī nam′ik) *adj* active; energetic: *The teacher has a dynamic way of talking.*

dy·na·mite (dī′nə mīt′) *n* a powerful explosive often used to blow up rocks.

dy·nas·ty (dī′nəs tē *or* din′əs tē) *n* a series of rulers who belong to the same family. *pl* **dy·nas·ties.**

dys·lex·i·a (dis lek′sē ə) *n* a disorder that makes it hard for people to read or write because they have trouble recognizing differences in the shapes of letters. —**dys·lex′ic,** *adj.*

e or **E** (ē) *n* the fifth letter of the English alphabet, or any sound that it stands for. The sound of *e* in *wet* is different from the sound of *e* in *equal*. *pl* **e's** or **E's**.

each (ēch) **1** *adj* or *pron* every one of a group thought of one by one: *Each boy has a crayon* (*adj*). *Each of the girls has a book* (*pron*). **2** *adv* for one: *These pencils cost ten cents each.*
each other, each one to the other one: *"The sisters helped each other" means "Each of the two sisters helped the other one."*

ea·ger (ē'gər) *adj* wanting very much: *The Ottawa Rough Riders were eager for victory.* —**ea'ger·ly,** *adv,* —**ea'ger·ness,** *n.*

A bald eagle— about 88 cm long including the tail

ea·gle (ē'gəl) *n* a large bird with a hooked beak, sharp claws, and good eyesight. Eagles nest in high places.
eagle feather *n* among some First Nations, a feather of an eagle, which gives the person holding it the right to speak in a group. For certain other First Nations, a different object is used for this because the eagle feather is sacred and can be held only by certain individuals.

ear (ēr) **1** *n* the part of the body that people and animals hear with. **2** *n* the part of certain plants that contains the grains: *The grains of corn, wheat, barley, and rye are formed on ears.*
ear·drum *n* the thin skin that stretches across the middle ear and vibrates when sound waves strike it. **ear·mark** *v* set aside for some special purpose: *Half the profit from the concert was earmarked to buy new band instruments.*

ear·phone *n* a small loudspeaker worn over or in the ear for listening to a radio, hearing aid, etc.
ear·ring *n* a piece of jewellery for the ear.
be all ears, be eager to hear something.
go in one ear and out the other, not really get through to the person hearing it: *She gets lots of advice, but it just goes in one ear and out the other.*
play by ear, play music without reading it.
play it by ear, decide what to do as you go along.

ear·ly (ər'lē) **1** *adj* or *adv* near the beginning: *the early years* (*adj*). **2** *adj* or *adv* before the expected time: *Please come early to help set up* (*adv*). **ear·li·er, ear·li·est.**

earn (ərn) **1** *v* get in return for work: *She earns $8 an hour.* **2** *v* deserve and get: *Your honest answer has earned our respect.*

ear·nest (ər'nist) *adj* serious and firm: *an earnest campaigner for children's rights.* —**ear'nest·ly,** *adv* —**ear'nest·ness,** *n.*
in earnest, serious or seriously: *We could see she was in earnest about the project. We had felt a few drops, but now it began to rain in earnest.*

earth (ərth) **1** *n* the planet we live on, the third from the sun. ▶See Appendix. When used as a name, this word is capitalized: *We know that Earth is round. China is on the other side of the earth from Canada.* **2** *n* dirt; soil: *The earth in this garden is good for growing vegetables.*
earth·quake *n* a movement of the earth's crust. Earthquakes start far below the surface and are sometimes violent.
down to earth, practical.

ease (ēz) **1** *n* comfort: *She lived a life of ease, with lots of free time and plenty of money.* **2** *v* make less; lighten: *Some medicines ease pain.* **3** *v* move slowly and carefully: *He eased the big box through the door.* **eased, eas·ing.**
eas·i·ly 1 *adv* without pain or difficulty: *He solved the puzzle easily.* **2** *adv* by far; without question: *She is easily the best player on the field.*
eas·y 1 *adj* not hard to do: *an easy job.* **2** *adj* free from worry: *an easy life.*
eas·y·go·ing *adj* tending not to worry: *She's such an easygoing person that she never gets angry.*
at ease, comfortable.
ease up or **off,** lessen; lighten: *The rain is beginning to ease up.*
with ease, without having to try hard: *She learned to read with ease.*

E e

ea·sel (ē′zəl) *n* a stand for supporting a painting, chalkboard, etc.

east (ēst) **1** *n* the direction of the sunrise. **2** *adv* or *adj* to or from the east: *They travelled east for two days* (adv). *There was a strong east wind across Reindeer Lake* (adj). —**east′er·ly,** *adj,* —**east′ern,** *adj.*

east·ward *adv* or *adj* toward the east; east: *He walked eastward* (adv). *The orchard is on the eastward slope of the hill* (adj). **Eastwards** is another form for the adverb.

❦ **back East** or **down East,** in or toward any place in the eastern part of Canada.

Easter (ēs′tər) *n* a Christian festival celebrating Christ's rising from the dead, held in March or April.

eat (ēt) **1** *v* chew and swallow: *Cows eat grass and grain.* **2** *v* have a meal: *We ate at the Hussains' place last night.* **3** *v* destroy: *The acid has eaten through the metal.* **ate, eat·en, eat·ing.** —**eat′er,** *n.*

eaves·drop (ēvz′drop′) *v* listen in on a private conversation. **eaves·dropped, eaves·drop·ping.** —**eaves′drop′per,** *n.*

WORD HISTORY . . . . eavesdrop

Eavesdrop comes from the Old English word *efesdrype,* meaning "the place where the water drips from the eaves." If you wanted to hear what was going on inside a house, somewhere just under the eaves of a house would have been a good place to stand!

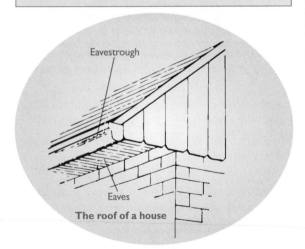

Eavestrough

Eaves

The roof of a house

eaves·trough (ēvz′trof′) *n* a gutter placed under the edge or **eaves** of a roof to catch rain water and carry it away.

ebb (eb) **1** *n* a flowing of the tide away from the shore. **2** *n* a lessening or weakening; a low point: *Their confidence was at its lowest ebb.*

ec·cen·tric (ek sen′trik) **1** *adj* out of the ordinary: *Singing on a public bus is eccentric.* **2** *n* a person who behaves oddly.

ech·o (ek′ō) *n* the repeating of a sound when it is bounced back from a surface. *pl* **ech·oes.**

e·clipse (ē klips′) *n* a darkening of the sun or the moon. An eclipse of the sun happens when the moon passes between the earth and the sun. An eclipse of the moon happens when the earth passes between the sun and the moon, leaving the moon in shadow.

e·col·o·gy (ē kol′ə jē) *n* the study of the relationship of living things to their surroundings and to each other. —**e′co·log′i·cal** *adj,* —**e·col′o·gist,** *n.*

e·con·o·my (i kon′ə mē) *n* management of money and resources to avoid waste.
e·co·nom·i·cal (ek′ə nom′ə kəl *or* ē′kə nom′ə kəl) *adj* avoiding waste; using less money or fewer supplies: *Walking is an economical way of travelling short distances.*
e·con·o·mize *v* use or spend as little as possible.

e·co·sys·tem (ē′kō sis′təm) *n* all the animals and plants in one area, together with their surroundings and the ways they all live with each other.

ec·sta·sy (ek′stə sē) *n* very great joy. —**ec·stat′ic** (ek stat′ik), *adj.*

edge (ej) **1** *n* the place where something ends: *the edge of the paper, the edge of the table.* **2** *n* the thin side that cuts: *The knife had a very sharp edge.* **3** *v* move sideways or little by little: *He edged his chair nearer to the table.* **4** *v* win a narrow victory over: *The Calgary Flames edged the visitors 3–2.* **edged, edg·ing.**
get a word in edgeways, get a chance to say something when others are talking.
on edge, nervous; tense: *Everyone was on edge during the storm.* Another word for this is **edgy.**
take the edge off, lessen the sharpness of: *A cup of herbal tea took the edge off her headache.*

ed·i·ble (ed′ə bəl) *adj* fit to eat: *Not all mushrooms are edible.*

ed·it (ed′it) *v* improve the style, correct errors, check facts, etc. in something: *Edit your report at least once before handing it in.* **–ed′i·tor,** *n.*

e·di·tion *n* the set of all the copies of a book, newspaper, etc. printed exactly alike and at the same time: *The first edition of* The Vancouver Sun *was printed in 1912.*

Grammar ✓ Check . . . . . edit

Use these editing tips to liven up your writing:

• **Vary sentence lengths.** Make some sentences short, and others long.

• **Use active verbs.** Say *The dog bit the man.* instead of *The man was bitten by the dog.*

• **Don't overuse the verb "to be."** Change *The weather is sunny...* to *The sunny weather...*

ed·u·cate (ej′ə kāt′) *v* teach or train, especially in a school or with formal lessons: *She was educated at the University of Regina.* **ed·u·cat·ed, ed·u·cat·ing. –ed′u·ca′tion,** *n,* **–ed′u·ca′tion·al,** *adj,* **–ed′u·ca′tor,** *n.*

eel (ēl) *n* a fish shaped like a snake.

ee·rie (ē′rē) *adj* strange in a scary way; creepy or spooky: *an eerie scream.* **ee·ri·er, ee·ri·est. –ee′ri·ly,** *adv.*

ef·fect (i fekt′) **1** *n* a result: *One of the effects of Hurricane Hazel was widespread power failure.* **2** *n* the way something seems: *The way he has painted these racehorses creates an effect of action and speed.* **3 effects,** *pl.n* belongings: *They lost all their personal effects in the fire.*

ef·fec·tive *adj* able to cause the desired result: *These new drugs are very effective.*

CONFUSABLES . . . . . effect

effect means "result": *It had no effect on me.*
affect means "influence": *Did that affect you?*

ef·fer·ves·cent (ef′ər ves′ənt) *adj* fizzy; giving off bubbles of gas, like pop.

ef·fi·cient (i fish′ənt) *adj* able to get a job done well without wasting time, energy, etc.: *If we were better organized, we could be more efficient.* **–ef·fi′cien·cy,** *n.*

ef·fort (ef′ərt) **1** *n* the use of energy to do something: *Climbing a steep hill takes a lot of effort.* **2** *n* a hard try; a strong attempt: *The loser was congratulated for his fine effort.* **–ef′fort·less,** *adj.*

e.g. *abbreviation for* for example: *I love many different flavours of ice cream, e.g., vanilla, chocolate, and strawberry.*

egg (eg) *n* a round or oval body laid by female birds, reptiles, and fish. Young hatch from them.

egg roll a small, narrow pastry filled with chopped vegetables and often pieces of meat and then deep-fried: *We started our dinner at the Lucky Dragon with an order of egg rolls.*

egg on, urge by teasing, making dares, etc.: *Other boys egged him on to fight.*

have egg on your face, be embarrassed.

Eid·ul Ad·ha (ā′dul ȧd hä′) *n* a Muslim festival in honour of the prophet Abraham's sacrifice long ago. It takes place in April.

eight (āt) ►See Appendix.

ei·ther (ē′ᴛʜər *or* ī′ᴛʜər) *adj* or *pron* one or the other of two: *She can write with either hand* (adj). *Choose either of the twins as your partner* (pron).

e·ject (i jekt′) *v* push out; cause to come out: *Push this button to eject the disk from the computer.*

e·lab·o·rate (i lab′ə rit *for 1,* i lab′ə rāt′ *for 2*) **1** *adj* very fancy and complicated: *The bride wore an elaborate gown.* **2** *v* give more details: *Could you elaborate on your suggestion to give us a clearer idea?* **e·lab·o·rat·ed, e·lab·o·rat·ing.**

e·lapse (i laps′) *v* pass; slip by: *Many hours elapsed while the boy slept.* **e·lapsed, e·laps·ing.**

e·las·tic (i las′tik) *adj* stretchy; able to return to a certain shape after being pulled or pressed out of that shape. Toy balloons, sponges, and steel springs are elastic.

e·lat·ed (i lā′tid) *adj* joyful. **–e·la′tion,** *n.*

el·bow (el′bō) *n* the joint between the upper arm and forearm.

eld·er (el′dər) **1** *adj* older: *my elder brother.* **2** *n* an older person: *The children showed respect for their elders.* **3** *n* one of the leaders in a community, chosen for his or her wisdom and experience. Some churches have elders. So do many First Nations communities.

eld·er·ly *adj* getting old. **eld·est** *adj* oldest.

e·lect (i lekt′) **1** *v* choose a person by voting: *The club elected a new president.* **2** *v* choose: *Francesca elected to spend the week with her grandparents rather than go to summer camp in Port Perry.* **–e·lec′tion,** *n.*

e·lec·tric (i lek′trik) **1** *adj* having to do with electricity: *electric power, an electric current.* **Electrical** is another form for this meaning. **2** *adj* run or operated by electricity: *an electric train, an electric guitar.* **3** *adj* very exciting; thrilling: *The dancer gave an electric performance.*

e·lec·tri·cian (i lek′ trish′ən) *n* a person who installs or fixes electric wiring and things that run by electricity. **e·lec·tric·i·ty** (i lek′tris′ə tē) *n* a form of energy. With it we can produce light, heat, motion, sound, pictures, etc.: *Lightning is caused by a discharge of electricity between clouds.*

e·lec·tri·fy 1 *v* give an electric charge or current to. **2** *v* excite; thrill: *The final race electrified everyone in the stadium.*

e·lec·tron·ics *n* the science that deals with electrons in motion: *Radar, radio, television, computers, etc. are based on the principles of electronics.* −**e·lec′tron′ic,** *adj.*

el·e·gant (el′ə gənt) *adj* showing good taste: *elegant furnishings, elegant manners.*

el·e·ment (el′ə mənt) **1** *n* one of the simple substances making up the whole physical universe. An element cannot be broken down into other different substances. Gold, oxygen, carbon, and tin are elements. Water is not an element, since it can be broken down into oxygen and hydrogen. **2 the elements,** *pl.n* the weather; rain, wind, snow, UV rays, etc.: *We keep our bikes in the shed to protect them from the elements.*

el·e·men·ta·ry *adj* simple; basic: *We learned addition and subtraction in elementary arithmetic.* **elementary school** in Canada, a school that goes up to grade five, six, or eight and usually includes kindergarten.

An African elephant—about 3.5 m high at the shoulder

el·e·phant (el′ə fənt) *n* a huge, strong animal of Africa and Asia with thick grey skin and a long flexible snout called a trunk.

el·e·vate (el′ə vāt′) *v* raise; lift up: *The Prime Minister spoke from an elevated platform.* **el·e·vat·ed, el·e·vat·ing.**

el·e·va·tion 1 *n* the height above sea level: *The elevation of Calgary is 1045 m.* **2** *n* a drawing of the front, back, or side of a structure.

el·e·va·tor 1 *n* a box like a small room that can carry people or things up and down in a building. **2** *n* a tall building for storing grain: *Elevators are a familiar sight on the Prairies.*

e·lev·en (i lev′ən) ▶See Appendix.

elf (elf) *n* in stories, a tiny being with magic powers who likes to play tricks. *pl* **elves.**

e·lim·i·nate (i lim′ə nāt′) **1** *v* get rid of: *The new air filter eliminates dust.* **2** *v* put out of a competition by defeating: *Our team was eliminated in the first round of hockey playoffs.* **e·lim·i·nat·ed, e·lim·i·nat·ing.** −**e·lim′i·na′tion,** *n.*

else (els) **1** *adj* different or differently: *That shirt is dirty–put on something else. How else can he act?* **2** *adj* more: *Is there anything else we need besides milk and bread?*

else·where *adv* in or to some other place; somewhere else.

or else, *Informal.* or suffer for it: *You'd better return my bike, or else.*

e—mail (ē′māl′) *n* a system of sending messages by computer. E-mail can be sent over telephone lines or within a computer network. Its full name is **electronic mail.**

em·bar·rass (em ber′əs) *v* make uncomfortable, nervous, or ashamed: *She embarrassed me by pointing out my mistake in front of everyone.* −**em·bar′rass·ment,** *n.*

em·bas·sy (em′bə sē) *n* the official home and office of an ambassador and his or her staff in a foreign country: *Canada has an embassy in Paris.* *pl* **em·bas·sies.**

em·blem (em′bləm) *n* a symbol: *The beaver and the maple leaf are both emblems of Canada.*

em·brace (em brās′) *v* or *n* hug: *The two friends embraced (v). She gave me a warm embrace (n).* **em·braced, em·brac·ing.**

em·broi·der (em broi′dər) **1** *v* decorate cloth with a design or pattern of stitches. **2** *v* add imaginary details to: *He didn't exactly tell lies, but he did embroider his stories.* −**em·broi′der·y,** *n.*

em·bry·o (em'brē ō') **1** *n* an animal before birth or hatching: *A chicken within an egg is an embryo.* **2** *n* an undeveloped plant within a seed. *pl* **em·bry·os.**

e·merge (i mərj') *v* come out after being covered: *The sun emerged from behind a cloud.* **e·merged, e·merg·ing. –e·mer'gence,** *n.*

e·mer·gen·cy (i mər'jən sē) *n* a serious or dangerous situation that comes up suddenly and needs quick action: *He keeps a first-aid kit in his car for emergencies.* *pl* **e·mer·gen·cies.**

em·i·grate (em'ə grāt') *v* leave your own country to settle in another. A person who does this is an **emigrant**: *Many people emigrate from countries where there is war.* **em·i·grat·ed, em·i·grat·ing. –em'i·gra'tion,** *n.*

CONFUSABLES ... emigrate

emigrate means "leave": *My family emigrated from Greece to Canada in 1960.*

immigrate means "go": *My family immigrated to Canada from Greece in 1960.*

e·mit (i mit') *v* send out; give off: *A volcano emits smoke. The lion emitted a roar of rage.* **e·mit·ted, e·mit·ting. –e·miss'ion,** *n.*

e·mo·tion (i mō'shən) *n* a feeling, such as love, anger, sadness, or excitement. **–e·mo'tion·al,** *adj,* **–e·mo'tion·less,** *adj.*

e·mo·ti·con (i mō'tə kon') *n* a tiny picture that computer users make from letters and punctuation as a way to show an emotion. For example, :-), a sideways smiling face, means that the person typing it has been joking.

em·pha·sis (em'fə sis) **1** *n* stress; importance: *That school puts emphasis on arithmetic and reading.* **2** *n* the special force of voice put on particular syllables or words when speaking: *In the word ecological, the emphasis is on the third syllable.* *pl* **em·pha·ses** (em'fə sēz').

em·pha·size (em'fə sīz') *v* call people's attention to give special importance to: *The police officer emphasized the need to follow bike safety rules.*

em·pire (em'pīr) **1** *n* a group of countries under one ruler or government: *the British Empire.* **2** *n* any country whose ruler is called an emperor or empress: *the Japanese Empire.* **3** *n* a very large business controlled by one person or group: *a fast-food empire.*

em·ploy (em ploi') **1** *v* give work and pay to: *The hotel employs a cook.* The person or company that gives the work is the **employer**; the person who is paid to do the work is the **employee**. **2** *v* use: *He employed every argument he could think of to persuade us.* **–em·ploy'ment,** *n.*

emp·ty (emp'tē) **1** *adj* with nothing in it: *The birds had gone and their nest was empty.* **emp·ti·er, emp·ti·est. 2** *v* take out all that is in a thing: *Empty the sand out of the bucket.* **3** *v* flow out: *The Niagara River empties into Lake Ontario.* **emp·tied, emp·ty·ing. –emp'ti·ness,** *n.*

en·a·ble (en ā'bəl) *v* make a person or thing able to do something: *This medicine will enable him to get a good night's sleep in spite of his bad cold.* **en·a·bled, en·a·bling.**

e·nam·el (i nam'əl) **1** *n* a glasslike substance melted and then cooled to make a smooth, shiny, hard coating on metal, pottery, etc. **2** *n* a paint or varnish that forms a smooth, glossy surface when dry. **3** *n* the outer layer of a tooth. **e·nam·elled** or **e·nam·eled, e·nam·el·ling** or **e·nam·el·ing.**

en·chant (en chant') **1** *v* use magic on; put under a spell: *The witch had enchanted the princess.* **2** *v* delight: *The little children were enchanted by the puppet play.* **–en·chant'ing,** *adj,* **–en·chant'ment,** *n.*

en·close (en klōz') **1** *v* shut in on all sides: *Many forts are enclosed by stone walls or wooden fences.* **2** *v* put in along with something else: *A cheque was enclosed with the letter.* **en·closed, en·clos·ing. –en·clo'sure,** *n.*

en·core (ong'kȯr *or* on'kȯr) *n* a last extra performance by a musician or other entertainer.

en·coun·ter (en koun'tər) **1** *v* meet unexpectedly: *We encountered an old friend in the store.* **2** *n* a meeting or coming face to face: *a chance encounter, an encounter with the neighbourhood bully.*

en·cour·age (en kər'ij) *v* give help or support to: *The cheers of the crowd encouraged her. High prices for grain encourage farming.* **en·cour·aged, en·cour·ag·ing. –en·cour'age·ment,** *n.*

en·cy·clo·pe·di·a (en sī'klə pē'dē ə) *n* a book or set of books giving information arranged alphabetically on all kinds of subjects. **Encyclopaedia** is another spelling.

end (end) **1** *n* the last part: *Tell us the end of the story.* **Ending** is another word for this. **2** *n* the place where something stops: *Those birch trees mark the end of their property.* **3** *v* bring or come to an end: *Let us end this fight.* —**end′less**, *adj,* —**end′less·ly**, *adv.*

❦ **end of steel** the end of a railway, especially going north.

at loose ends, not settled or not really knowing what to do next.

end to end, with the end of one object set next to the end of another: *The dominoes were arranged end to end on the table.*

end up, finish; turn out a certain way: *He'll end up at the top of his class. It ended up that no one could come.*

go off the deep end, do something extreme.

no end, *Informal.* very much: *That dog causes no end of trouble.*

on end, 1 upright in position: *It is not easy to stand a pencil on end.* **2** one after another: *It snowed for days on end.*

put an end to, stop.

en·dan·ger (en dān′jər) **1** *v* cause danger to: *Drunk drivers endanger lives.* **2** *v* put a species of animal or plant in danger of becoming extinct. The whooping crane is an **endangered species**. ▶See Appendix. —**en·dan′ger·ment**, *n.*

en·deav·our (en dev′ər) *v* or *n* try; attempt: *She endeavoured to make us feel at home* (*v*). *He finally succeeded in his endeavour to persuade his parents* (*n*). Another spelling is **endeavor**.

en·dure (en dyūr′ *or* en dūr′) **1** *v* last; keep on without weakening: *The Pyramids have endured for thousands of years.* **2** *v* go through; suffer: *Canadian pioneers endured many hardships.* **en·dured, en·dur·ing.** —**en·dur′ance**, *n.*

en·e·my (en′ə mē) *n* a person or group that hates and fights against another: *He decided to forgive the enemy who had hurt him.* pl **en·e·mies.**

en·er·gy (en′ər jē) **1** *n* the active strength or force needed to do things: *Digging the garden took all my energy.* **2** *n* the power to move, or to move other objects. Heat is a form of energy. pl **en·er·gies.** —**en′er·get′ic** (en′ər get′ik), *adj,* —**en′er·get′i·cal·ly**, *adv.*

en·er·gize (en′ər jīz′) *v* give energy to a person or thing: *The coach's encouraging pep talk energized the gymnastics team.*

en·gage (en gāj′) **1** *v* keep busy: *The girls were engaged in building a tree fort.* **2** *v* **engaged**, committed to getting married. **en·gaged, en·gag·ing.** —**en·gage′ment**, *n.*

en·gine (en′jən) **1** *n* a machine that makes something else, especially a vehicle, move; a motor. **2** *n* the car of a train that contains the motor.

en·gi·neer 1 *n* a person who takes care of or runs engines: *The driver of a locomotive is an engineer.* **2** *n* a person who uses science to design roads and bridges, buildings, dams, machines, medicines, and many other kinds of useful things. This work is called **engineering**.

en·joy (en joi′) *v* have or use with joy; like; take pleasure in: *We enjoyed our trip to Prince Edward Island.* —**en·joy′a·ble**, *adj,* —**en·joy′ment**, *n.*

en·large (en lärj′) *v* make or become larger: *to enlarge a photograph, to enlarge a house.* **en·larged, en·larg·ing.** —**en·large′ment**, *n.* **enlarge on,** talk or write more about: *You said your trip was fun–could you enlarge on that?*

en·list (en list′) *v* get the help of; get someone to join: *The teacher enlisted several of us to set up tables in the gym. The cross-country team is enlisting new members.*

Tyrannosaurus rex has been extinct for over 200 million years

e·nor·mous (i nôr′məs) *adj* huge: *an enormous appetite. Long ago there were enormous dinosaurs on the earth.*

e·nough (i nuf′) *adj, pron,* or *adv* as many or as much as needed: *Are there enough seats for all* (*adj*)? *Has he had enough to eat* (*pron*)? *You have studied enough* (*adv*).

en·rol (en rōl′) *v* register; sign up: *The principal enrolled ten new students this term. She enrolled in a fitness program.* **Enroll** is another spelling. **en·rolled, en·rol·ling. –en·rol′ment** or **en·roll′ment,** *n.*

en route (on rūt′) on the way: *We shall stop at Gander en route from St. John's to Corner Brook.*

en·ter (en′tər) **1** *v* go or come in: *Open the door and let them enter. He entered the house.* **2** *v* become a part or member of: *He entered the piano competition. Parents enter their children in school.* **3** *v* put an item in a book, list, computer file, etc.: *Enter the e-mail address and press* Return. **entrant** *n* a person who enters a contest.

en·try (en′trē) **1** *n* the act of entering. **2** *n* a way to get in. **3** *n* a word on a list, an article in an encyclopedia, a piece of data keyed into a computer file, etc.: *This dictionary entry has four definitions.* **4** *n* something that is entered in a contest: *Anil's picture was the winning entry in the art contest.*

en·ter·tain (en′tər tān′) **1** *v* be fun for; hold someone's interest in an enjoyable way: *The funny story entertained the children.* **2** *v* have as a guest or guests: *He entertained ten people to dinner.* **–en·ter·tain′er,** *n,* **–en·ter·tain′ing,** *adj,* **–en·ter·tain′ment,** *n.*

en·thu·si·asm (en thū′zē az′əm) *n* lively enjoyment: *The band played* O Canada! *with great enthusiasm.* **–en·thu·si·as′tic,** *adj,* **–en·thu·si·as′ti·cal·ly,** *adv.*

en·thu·si·ast *n* a person who is filled with lively interest in something; a fan: *a hockey enthusiast.*

en·tire (en tīr′) *adj* whole; complete; having all the parts: *The entire house was repainted, inside and out.* **–en·tire′ly,** *adv.*

en·ti·tle (en tī′təl) **1** *v* give someone the right to have or do a particular thing: *The one who guesses the answer is entitled to ask the next question.* **2** *v* give as a title; name: *The author entitled her book* Underground to Canada. **en·ti·tled, en·ti·tling.**

en·trails (en′trālz) *pl.n* the inner parts of the body of a human being or animal: *Before stuffing the Thanksgiving turkey, he removed the entrails.*

en·trance (en′trəns *for 1 and 2,* en trans′ *for 3*) **1** *n* the act or the right of entering: *The actor's entrance was greeted with applause. This ticket gives you entrance to the fair.* **2** *n* a way to get in. **3** *v* delight: *The girl was entranced by the beautiful music.* **en·tranced, en·tranc·ing.**

en·tre·pre·neur (on′trə prə nər′) *n* someone who has business ideas and is ready to risk his or her own money by starting up a business: *Duncan was a real entrepreneur; in grade two he bought and sold baseball cards and made quite a profit.*

e·nu·mer·ate (i nyū′mə rāt′ *or* i nū′mə rāt′) **1** *v* name one by one: *The sign enumerates all the pool safety rules.* **2** ✤ *v* put a person's name on the official list of voters: *My 18-year-old sister has been enumerated for the first time.* **e·nu·mer·at·ed, e·nu·mer·at·ing.**

en·vel·op (en vel′əp) *v* wrap, cover, or hide: *Fog enveloped Rocky Harbour.* **en·vel·oped, en·vel·op·ing.**

en·ve·lope (en′və lōp′ *or* on′və lōp′) *n* a folded paper cover for mailing a letter.

en·vi·ron·ment (en vī′ərn mənt) **1** *n* all the surrounding things that affect the growth of living things: *A child needs a safe, loving environment to grow up in.* **2** *n* the earth, air, and water as the home of living things: *A polluted environment can harm wildlife.* Something that is **environment-friendly** does no harm to the environment. **–en·vi′ron·men′tal,** *adj.*

en·vi·ron·men·tal·ist *n* a person who values the environment: *A group of environmentalists asked the government to set this area aside for parkland.*

en·vy (en′vē) **1** *n* a strong feeling of wishing you had what someone else has, and being unhappy or angry that you don't: *I was filled with envy when I saw her new bicycle.* **2** *v* feel envy toward someone or because of something: *He envied his sister's ability to ski.* pl **en·vies. en·vied, en·vy·ing. –en′vi·a·ble,** *adj,* **–en′vi·ous,** *adj.*

e·on (ē′on) *n* a very long time; many thousands of years: *According to the theory of evolution, eons passed before life existed on Earth.*

ep·ic (ep′ik) **1** *n* a long, serious poem or story about heroic adventures and noble deeds: *Homer's poem* The Odyssey *is an epic.* **2** *adj* like an epic; worth writing an epic about: *Flying over the Atlantic for the first time was an epic deed.*

ep·i·dem·ic (ep′ə dem′ik) *n* a disease that spreads quickly: *All the schools in the city were closed during the epidemic of measles.*

ep·i·sode (ep′ə sōd′) **1** *n* a single happening in real life or in a story: *The summer I spent on the farm was an important episode in my life.* **2** *n* one complete show in a TV series or a chapter in a continuing story: *We have that episode of Degrassi Junior High on videotape.*

e·pis·tle (i pis′əl) *n* a fancy word for letter: *When I printed out her e-mail, it turned out to be a three-page epistle.*

ep·i·taph (ep′ə taf′) *n* a short statement on a tombstone in memory of the person buried there.

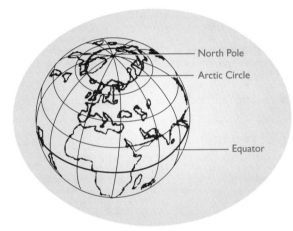

North Pole
Arctic Circle
Equator

e·qual (ē′kwəl) **1** *adj* the same in amount, size, value, or importance: *Give each child an equal amount of ice cream.* **2** *v* be the same as (in amount, size, etc.): *Two times three equals six.* The symbol for this, =, is called an **equal sign**. **e·qualled** or **e·qualed**, **e·qual·ling** or **e·qual·ing**. —**e·qual′i·ty** (i kwol′ə tē), *n*, —**e′qual·ize′**, *v*, —**e′qual·ly**, *adv*.

e·quate (i kwāt′) *n* say that two things are equal: *Don't equate doing your best with showing off.* An **equation** (i kwā′zhən) is a mathematical statement that two quantities are equal. *Example:* 4 + 5 = 9. **e·qua·tor** *n* an imaginary circle around the middle of the earth, halfway between the North Pole and the South Pole: *Canada is north of the equator.* —**eq′ua·to′ri·al** (ek′wə tôr′ē əl), *adj*.

e·qui·nox (ē′kwə noks′) *n* either of the two times in the year when day and night are of equal length all over the earth. At those times the sun is directly over the equator: *There is an equinox about March 21 and another about September 22.*

e·quip (i kwip′) *v* provide with what is needed. **e·quipped**, **e·quip·ping**.

e·quip·ment *n* what a person has or needs in order to do something: *Each player buys his or her own hockey equipment.*

–er *a suffix meaning:* **1** a person or thing that does some action. An *admirer* is a person who *admires* somebody or something. A *burner* is something that *burns* fuel. **2** a native or inhabitant of. A *Newfoundlander* is a person born in or living in *Newfoundland*. A *villager* is a person who lives in a *village*.

USING WORDS .... -er/-est

Usually you can add **-er** ("more") and **-est** ("most") to adjectives and adverbs that have only one syllable: *sweeter, fastest.*

With two or more syllables, you usually use **more** and **most**: *more beautiful, most quickly.*

---

e·ra (er′ə *or* ē′rə) *n* an age in history or geology: *We live in an era of space travel. Dinosaurs lived during the Mesozoic Era.*

e·rad·i·cate (i rad′ə kāt′) *v* destroy or get rid of completely: *Yellow fever has been eradicated in some countries.* **e·rad·i·cat·ed**, **e·rad·i·cat·ing**.

e·rase (i rās′) *v* wipe out: *He erased the wrong answer and wrote in the right one. I accidentally erased the whole hard drive of my computer.* **e·rased**, **e·ras·ing**. —**e·ras′er**, *n*.

e·rect (i rekt′) **1** *adj* standing straight up: *When a dog's ears are erect, it is a sign that it is alert.* **2** *v* build: *That building was erected 40 years ago.* —**e·rec′tion**, *n*.

e·rode (i rōd′) *v* eat away; wear away: *Water erodes soil and rock.* **e·rod·ed**, **e·rod·ing**. —**e·ro′sion**, *n*.

err (er *or* ər) *v* make a mistake: *Everyone errs at some time or other.* —**er′ror**, *n*.

er·rat·ic *adj* first running or acting in one way, then in another way: *an erratic clock. His erratic manner puzzled many people.*

er·rand (er′ənd) *n* a trip to do something: *He has gone on an errand to the store.*

e·rupt (i rupt′) **1** *v* burst forth: *The volcano erupted and lava and ashes poured out.* **2** *v* break out in a rash: *Your skin erupts when you have chicken pox.* —**e·rup′tion**, *n*.

es·ca·late (es′kə lāt′) *v* grow bigger, higher, more serious, etc.: *escalating prices.* **es·ca·lat·ed**, **es·ca·lat·ing**.

es·ca·la·tor *n* a moving stairway.

es·cape (ə skāp′) **1** *v* get free: *The convict escaped from prison.* **2** *n* an act of escaping: *There was no escape from the trap.* An **escape artist** is a person who entertains an audience by escaping from chains, from a trap, etc. **Escape velocity** is the speed needed to escape the gravitational pull of a planet. **es·caped, es·cap·ing.**

es·cort (es′kȯrt *for 1,* i skȯrt′ *for 2*) **1** *n* a person or group going along with someone as a guard or to show honour: *The royal party was provided with an escort of Mounties.* **2** *v* go with as an escort: *Sergei escorted Cathy to the movies.*

ESL *abbreviation for* English as a second language. ESL is taught to people who already speak another language but do not know English.

es·pe·cial·ly (i spesh′ ə lē) **1** *adv* most of all: *I like science, especially astronomy.* **2** *adv* more than usual: *This was an especially busy week.*

CONFUSABLES ... especially

especially means "particularly":
The weather was especially cold last December.

specially means "for one purpose":
Many movies are specially made for television.

---

es·say (es′ā) *n* an organized piece of writing telling what you have found out and what you think about a certain subject.

es·sen·tial (i sen′shəl) *adj* absolutely necessary: *Good food and enough rest are essential to good health.* —**es·sen′tial·ly,** *adv.*

es·tab·lish (i stab′lish) **1** *v* set up: *An organization has been established to protect wildlife.* **2** *v* cause to be accepted: *to establish a custom, to establish a fact.* —**es·tab′lish·ment,** *n.*

es·tate (i stāt) **1** *n* all that a person owns: *When the rich man died, he left an estate of two million dollars.* **2** *n* a piece of land, especially a large one, belonging to a person: *They have a beautiful country estate in Nanaimo with a big house and a swimming pool.*

es·ti·mate (es′tə mit *for 1,* es′tə māt′ *for 2*) **1** *n* a judgment of an amount in round figures: *He didn't know the exact length of the fish, but his estimate was 40 cm.* **2** *v* form a judgment in round figures: *She estimated the value of the used bike to be $50.* **es·ti·mat·ed, es·ti·mat·ing.** —**es′ti·ma′tion,** *n.*

es·tu·ar·y (es′chū er′ē) *n* the wide mouth of a river where it flows into the sea and is affected by the tide: *The estuary of the St. Lawrence River is over 320 km long.* *pl* **es·tu·ar·ies.**

etc. *abbreviation for* **et cetera,** a Latin expression meaning "and other things."

e·ter·ni·ty (i tėr′nə tē) *n* all the past and all the future.

e·ter·nal *adj* having no beginning or ending, and never changing.

eth·nic (eth′nik) *adj* having to do with any group of people united by their customs, language, and the part of the world they are originally from. There are many different ethnic groups in Canada.

eu·phe·mism (yū′fə miz′əm) *n* a "nicer" word used instead of one that people think is harsh: *"Pass away" is a common euphemism for "die."*

e·vac·u·ate (i vak′yū āt′) *v* remove people from a dangerous place: *Firefighters evacuated the people from Winnipeg during the floods.* **e·vac·u·at·ed, e·vac·u·at·ing.** —**e·vac′u·a′tion,** *n.*

e·val·u·ate (i val′yū āt′) *v* decide how good something is, how much it is worth, etc.: *The judges will evaluate the performance of each skater.* **e·val·u·at·ed, e·val·u·at·ing.** —**e·val′u·a′tion,** *n.*

e·vap·o·rate (i vap′ə rāt′) **1** *v* turn from a liquid into a gas. When water dries up or turns to steam, it is evaporating. It becomes part of the air. **2** *v* remove water from a substance by boiling. Sap is evaporated to make maple syrup. **e·vap·o·rat·ed, e·vap·o·rat·ing.** —**e·vap′o·ra′tion,** *n.*

eve (ēv) **1** *n* the evening or day before some holiday or special day: *New Year's Eve.* **2** *n* the time just before: *on the eve of an election.*

e·ven (ē′vən) **1** *adj* level; flat; smooth: *Set up your tent on even ground.* **2** *adj* staying about the same; steady: *an even speed, an even temper.* **3** *v* make even: *to even the score.* —**e′ven·ly,** *adv,* —**e′ven·ness,** *n.*

even number a number that can be divided by 2 with no remainder: *The even numbers are 2, 4, etc.*

break even, get back as much as you have lost: *I bought six packets of lemonade crystals but hardly sold enough lemonade to break even.*

get even, hurt someone back after he or she has hurt you.

**E
e**

eve·ning (ēv′ning) *n* the last part of day and early part of night.

e·vent (i vent′) **1** *n* anything that happens, especially something important: *everyday events. The opening of the new library in Swift Current was certainly an event.* **2** *n* a contest in a sports program: *The long jump was the last event.*

e·ven·tu·al (i ven′chū əl) *adj* coming in the end: *After several failures, her eventual success was a pleasant surprise.* —**e·ven′tu·al·ly,** *adv.*

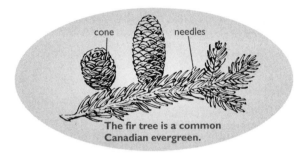

cone   needles

**The fir tree is a common
Canadian evergreen.**

ev·er (ev′ər) *adv* at any time: *Is she ever here?*
ev·er·green *adj* having green leaves or needles throughout the year. **eve·ry** (ev′rē) *adj* each one of all that there are: *Read every word on the page.*
eve·ry·bod·y *pron* every person.
eve·ry·day *adj* ordinary.
eve·ry·one *pron* each person.
eve·ry·thing *pron* all things.
eve·ry·where (ev′rē wer′) *adv* in or to every place.
every other, skipping one each time: *If you write on every other line, you can get only half as much on a page.*

ev·i·dence (ev′ə dəns) *n* facts showing that something is probably true: *The jam on his face was evidence that he had been in the kitchen.*
ev·i·dent *adj* easy to see or figure out.

e·vil (ē′vəl) **1** *adj* very bad; wrong; doing great harm: *an evil murderer, evil acts.* **2** *n* a very bad thing: *racism and other evils.* —**e′vil·ly,** *adv.*

e·volve (i volv′) *v* change or develop gradually. **e·volved, e·volv·ing.**
ev·o·lu·tion (ev′ə lū′shən *or* ē′və lū′shən) *n* a gradual development: *The museum display showed the evolution of airplanes from the first experiments by the Wright brothers up until the present.*

ex– *a prefix meaning:* **1** out or away, as in *exit, export.* **2** that was, but is no longer, as in *ex-member.*

ex·act (eg zakt′) *adj* true or correct: *an exact description, the exact amount.* —**ex·act′ly,** *adv.*

ex·ag·ger·ate (eg zaj′ə rāt′) *v* make something out to be more than it really is: *You were exaggerating when you said there were a million cats in the backyard.* **ex·ag·ger·at·ed, ex·ag·ger·at·ing.** —**ex·ag′ger·a′tion,** *n.*

ex·am·ine (eg zam′ən) **1** *v* look at closely and carefully: *The mechanic examined the car engine.* **2** *v* test the knowledge or ability of: *The lawyer examined the witness by asking many questions.* **ex·am·ined, ex·am·in·ing.** —**ex·am′i·na′tion,** *n.*

ex·am·ple (eg zam′pəl) **1** *n* one thing given to show what the others are like: *Vancouver is an example of a busy city. The exercise in the math textbook was accompanied by two examples.* **2** *n* something to imitate: *Parents should try to be a good example to their children.*

ex·ca·vate (ek′skə vāt′) **1** *v* remove dirt, sand, rock, etc. to make a hole or tunnel, usually with a large digging machine called an **excavator:** *to excavate a site for the foundation of a new building. Big machines excavated the dirt and loaded it into trucks.* **2** *v* uncover by digging: *They excavated the banks of Old Crow River and discovered the Bluefish Caves.* **ex·ca·vat·ed, ex·ca·vat·ing.** —**ex′ca·va′tion,** *n.*

ex·ceed *v* go beyond; be more than: *The motorist was fined for exceeding the speed limit.*

ex·cel (ek sel′) *v* be or do better than others; do very well: *She excels in sports. Our class excels in music.* **ex·celled, ex·cel·ling.** —**ex′cel·lence,** *n.* —**ex′cel·lent,** *adj.*

ex·cept (ek sept′) *prep* leaving out: *He comes every day except Wednesday.* Another word for this is **excepting.**

ex·cep·tion **1** *n* something left out: *She liked the songs on the tape, with two exceptions.* **2** *n* anything that is different from the usual way: *He usually comes on time, but today is an exception.* **ex·cep·tion·al** *adj* unusual; out of the ordinary. —**ex·cep′tion·al·ly,** *adv.*

CONFUSABLES .... except

except means "other than":
Everyone smiled, except me.

accept means "receive":
Will you accept this prize?

ex·cerpt (eg′zərpt) *n* a passage taken from a book, speech, etc.: *The article included excerpts from the author's diary.*

ex·cess (ek ses′ *or* ek′ses) *n* the part that is too much: *Pour off the excess.*

ex·ces·sive *adj* going beyond reasonable limits: *She thought being grounded for a week was excessive punishment.* –**ex·ces′sive·ly,** *adv.*

ex·change (eks chānj′) *v* trade for something else: *I'm going to take this shirt back and exchange it for a bigger one.* **ex·changed, ex·chang·ing.**

ex·cite (ek sīt′) *v* stir up strong feelings in: *His new snowboard excited envy among the other boys.* **ex·cit·ed, ex·cit·ing.** –**ex·cit′a·ble,** *adj,* –**ex·cite′ment,** *n.*

ex·claim (ek sklām′) *v* speak suddenly and with strong feeling: *"Here you are at last!" exclaimed his mother.*

ex·cla·ma·tion *n* something said suddenly. Exclamations may be interjections such as *Ouch!* or full sentences such as *What a surprise!* In writing, they always end with an **exclamation mark:** !

ex·clude (ek sklūd′) *v* leave out; keep out: *Children over the age of ten are excluded from the playplace.* **ex·clud·ed, ex·clud·ing.** –**ex·clu′sion,** *n.*

ex·clud·ing *prep* except for: *All of the neighbours, excluding those away on holidays, will be at the Canada Day picnic.* **ex·clu·sive** *adj* not shared with others: *The drummer gave an exclusive interview to Maclean's magazine.*

ex·cur·sion (ek skər′zhən) *n* a pleasure trip; an outing.

ex·cuse (ek skyūz′ *for 1 and 2,* ek skyūs′ *for 3*) **1** *v* give reasons for an action that are supposed to make it all right: *She excused her own faults by blaming others.* **2** *n* a reason given for an action: *He had many excuses for coming late.* **3** *v* let off: *You are excused from washing the dishes today.* **ex·cused, ex·cus·ing.**

excuse me, I'm sorry; something you say out of politeness after burping, sneezing, accidentally stepping on someone's toes, etc., or in order to interrupt someone.

ex·e·cute (ek′sə kyūt′) *v* do or perform: *Elvis Stojko executed each figure skating move with graceful ease.* **ex·e·cut·ed, ex·e·cut·ing.**

ex·ec·u·tive *n* a person who makes decisions and then sees that they get carried out: *The president of a business is an executive.*

ex·empt (eg zempt′) **1** *v* let out of doing: *She was exempted from the test because she had been away from school for most of that unit.* **2** *adj* free from some duty: *School property is exempt from all taxes.*

ex·er·cise (ek′sər sīz′) **1** *n* activity to train and strengthen the body or mind: *Listening is good exercise for your mind.* **2** *v* do or cause to do such activity: *A person should exercise daily.* **3** *n* something specially designed to give practice or training: *Do the multiplication exercise on the worksheet.* **ex·er·cised, ex·er·cis·ing.**

ex·ert (eg zərt′) *v* use: *We exerted all our strength and moved the large rock.* –**ex·er′tion,** *n.* **exert yourself,** make an effort: *We had to exert ourselves to get there on time.*

ex·hale (eks hāl′) *v* breathe out. **ex·haled, ex·hal·ing.**

ex·haust (eg zost′) **1** *v* tire out: *The climb up the hill exhausted us.* **2** *v* use up completely: *to exhaust the food supply, to exhaust your strength.* **3** *n* the used steam, gases, etc. that escape from an engine: *The exhaust from an automobile engine is very poisonous.* –**ex·haust′ed,** *adj,* –**ex·haus′tion** (eg zos′chən), *n.*

ex·hib·it (eg zib′it) *n* something to show to the public: *I especially like the dinosaur exhibit at the Tyrrell Museum.*

ex·hi·bi·tion (ek′sə bish′ən) **1** *n* a large public display: *an exhibition of student art in the mall.* **2** *n* a big fair with displays of farm animals, flowers, computers, things from around the world, etc., along with shows, rides, games, and other fun things. The **Canadian National Exhibition** happens every August in Toronto.

ex·hil·a·rate (eg zil′ə rāt′) *v* fill with energy or excitement. **ex·hil·a·rat·ed, ex·hil·a·rat·ing.** –**ex·hil′a·ra′tion,** *n.*

ex·ile (eg′zīl *or* ek′sīl) **1** *v* force a person to leave his or her own country: *The traitor was exiled from his country for life.* **2** *n* a person forced to leave his or her own country. **ex·iled, ex·il·ing.**

ex·ist (eg zist′) *v* be or live: *The world has existed a long time. A person cannot exist without air.* –**ex·ist′ence,** *n.*

ex·it (eg′zit *or* ek′sit) **1** *n* a way out: *The theatre had six exits.* **2** *v* go out: *Please exit by this door.*

ex·or·bi·tant (eg zȯr′bə tənt) *adj* much too high: *Eight dollars is an exorbitant price to pay for a dozen eggs.*

A red flamingo—about 150 cm high when standing. Flamingos are tropical birds.

ex·ot·ic (eg zot′ik) **1** *adj* not native to a country: *Flamingos are exotic birds in Canada.* **2** *adj* unusual in a fascinating way: *exotic tales of adventures in far-off places.*

ex·pand (ek spand′) **1** *v* make or become bigger: *The balloon expanded as it was filled with air.* **2** *v* write or talk in more detail: *Could you expand on that idea a little?* **–ex·pan′sion,** *n.*
ex·panse *n* a wide, unbroken area or surface: *The Pacific Ocean is a vast expanse of water.*

ex·pect (ek spekt′) *v* think that something is likely or right: *We expect snow in winter. I expect she'll be late again. A restaurant is expected to be clean.* **–ex′pec·ta′tion,** *n.*

ex·pe·di·tion (ek′spə dish′ən) *n* a trip for a special purpose.

ex·pel (ek spel′) **1** *v* force to leave: *The violent student was expelled from school.* **2** *v* push out: *When you burp you expel air from the stomach.* **ex·pelled, ex·pel·ling. –ex·pul′sion,** *n.*

ex·pend (ek spend′) *v* spend; use up: *A lot of time and energy has been expended on this project.* **–ex·pen′di·ture** (ek spen′də chər), *n.*
ex·pense *n* the cost: *The expense of a new computer is too great for our family to afford right now.* **ex·pen·sive** *adj* costing a lot.

ex·pe·ri·ence (ek spē′rē əns) **1** *n* what happens to a person: *We had many wonderful experiences on our trip to Fort McMurray.* **2** *n* practice: *Do you have any experience in this kind of work?* **ex·pe·ri·enced, ex·pe·ri·enc·ing. –ex·pe′ri·enced,** *adj.*

ex·per·i·ment (ek sper′ə ment′ *for 1,* ek sper′ə mənt *for 2*) **1** *v* try something in order to find out what happens: *I experimented with paint to get the colour I wanted.* **2** *n* a trial or test to find out something: *Scientists test theories by experiment.* **–ex·per′i·men′tal,** *adj.*

ex·pert (ek′spərt) *n* a person who has a great deal of skill or knowledge in some special area.

ex·per·tise (ek′spər tēz′) *n* special skill or knowledge: *The school is looking for a grade two teacher with expertise in music.*

WORD HISTORY . . . . experiment

The word **experiment** comes from the Latin word *experiri*, meaning "to try out." The same Latin root is in the word **experience**. You can get experience by experimenting, and you may become an **expert**!

---

ex·pire (ek spīr′) **1** *v* run out; become worthless after a certain time limit called the **expiry date**: *This coupon expires in two weeks, so use it soon.* **2** *v* die. **ex·pired, ex·pir·ing.**

ex·plain (ek splān′) *v* tell why and how: *The teacher explained percent to us.* **–ex′pla·na′tion,** *n.*

ex·plode (ek splōd′) *v* blow up with a loud noise; blow apart into pieces: *Many roads on the Canadian Shield were built by exploding the rock with dynamite.* **ex·plod·ed, ex·plod·ing. –ex·plo′sion,** *n,* **–ex·plo′sive,** *adj or n.*

ex·plore (ek splȯr′) *v* go through a place in order to find out what is there: *Champlain explored the Ottawa River and Georgian Bay and made maps of the area.* **ex·plored, ex·plor·ing. –ex′plo·ra′tion,** *n,* **–ex·plor′er,** *n.*

ex·port (ek′spȯrt, *also* ek spȯrt′ *for 1*) **1** *v* sell things to another country: *Canada exports millions of tonnes of wheat each year.* **2** *n* something sent to another country for sale: *Oranges are an important export of Florida.*

ex·pose (ek spōz′) *v* uncover: *The bandage came off, leaving the wound exposed.* **ex·posed, ex·pos·ing. –ex·po′sure,** *n.*

ex·press (ek spres′) **1** *v* put into words: *You can express your ideas clearly.* **2** *v* show by look, voice, or action: *A smile expresses joy.* **3** *adj* fast and direct; with no stops along the way: *an express train.*

ex·pres·sion 1 *n* a look on a person's face that shows a feeling: *A grin is a happy expression.* **2** *n* a word or group of words used as a unit: *Chill out is a slang expression.*

ex·tend (ek stend′) *v* stretch in time, space, or direction: *to extend a visit, to extend a line. The beach along Grand Bend extended for several kilometres in each direction.*

ex·ten·sion 1 *n* addition: *A new extension was built onto the old school.* **2** *n* an extra telephone added to the same line as the main one.

ex·ten·sive *adj* far-reaching: *extensive changes, an extensive park.* **ex·tent** *n* the size, length, amount, or degree of something; how far a thing reaches: *The news was broadcast through the whole extent of the country. The extent of a judge's power is limited by law.*

extended family, parents and children plus grandparents, aunts, uncles, cousins, etc.

ex·te·ri·or (ek stē′rē ər) *n* the outside: *I saw only the exterior of the house, not the interior.*

ex·ter·nal (ek stər′nəl) *adj* outer; outside: *Don't swallow this stuff; it says,* for external use only. *–***ex·ter′nal·ly,** *adv.*

ex·ter·mi·nate (ek stər′mə nāt′) *v* destroy completely: *This poison will exterminate rats.* **ex·ter·mi·nat·ed, ex·ter·mi·nat·ing.** *–***ex·ter′mi·na′tion,** *n,* *–***ex·ter′mi·na′tor,** *n.*

ex·tin·guish (ek sting′gwish) *v* put out a flame, a light, etc.: *Water extinguished the fire.*

ex·tinct (ek stingkt′) **1** *adj* a once-living thing that no longer exists: *The dinosaur is an extinct animal.* **2** *adj* no longer active: *an extinct volcano.* *–***ex·tinc′tion,** *n.*

ex·tra (ek′strə) *adj* beyond what is usual, expected, or needed: *extra pay, extra clothes. Do you have an extra pencil?*

ex·tra·cur·ric·u·lar (ek′strə kə rik′yə lər) *adj* outside school or outside actual schoolwork: *The photography club was Alissa's favourite extra-curricular activity.*

ex·traor·di·nar·y (ek strȯr′də ner′ē) *adj* very unusual: *Two and a half metres is an extraordinary height for a person.* *–***ex·traor′di·nar′i·ly,** *adv.*

ex·tra·ter·res·tri·al (ek′strə tə res′trē əl) *n* an alien; a being from beyond the earth.

ex·trav·a·gant (ek strav′ə gənt) *adj* spending or costing more than is sensible: *an extravagant person. They spent a whole day's pay on an extravagant dinner.* *–***ex·trav′a·gance,** *n.*

ex·tract (ek strakt′ *for 1,* ek′strakt *for 2*) **1** *v* take out: *to extract iron from the earth, to extract a tooth.* **2** *n* something taken out: *I read several extracts from the book.* *–***ex·trac′tion,** *n.*

ex·treme (ek strēm′) *adj* going too far: *extreme poverty, extreme wealth. The temperatures in the desert are extreme.* *–***ex·treme′ly,** *adv.*

ex·trem·i·ty (ek strem′ə tē) **1** *n* the farthest point: *Windsor is at the southern extremity of Canada.* **2 extremities,** *pl.n* the hands and feet. **3** *n* an extreme action: *They were forced to the extremity of eating shoe leather to stay alive.*

ex·u·ber·ant (eg zū′bə rənt) *adj* full of joyful excitement. *–***ex·u′ber·ance,** *n.*

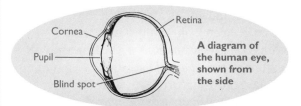

A diagram of the human eye, shown from the side

eye (ī) **1** *n* either of the two parts of the body that humans and animals see by. **2** *n* something like an eye in some way: *the eye of a needle, the eye of a potato.* **3** *v* look at: *The children eyed the stranger curiously.* **eyed, ey·ing** or **eye·ing.**

eye·piece *n* the lens or lenses in a telescope, microscope, etc. that the user looks through.

eye·wit·ness *n* a person who actually sees some act or happening.

catch someone's eye, attract someone's attention: *The bright red scarf caught my eye.*

see eye to eye, agree; be in agreement: *My sister and I don't usually see eye to eye when choosing TV programs.*

with your eyes shut, very easily.

f or **F** (ef) *n* the sixth letter of the English alphabet, or any speech sound that it stands for. The sound of *f* in *chief* is different from the sound of *f* in *of*. *pl* **f's** or **F's.**

fa·ble (fā′bəl) *n* a story that is made up to teach a lesson. Fables are often about animals who can talk, such as *The Hare and the Tortoise.*

fab·u·lous (fab′yə ləs) *adj* imaginary; unreal: *The centaur is a fabulous creature.*

fab·ric (fab′rik) *n* cloth.

face (fās) **1** *n* the front part of the head. The eyes, nose, and mouth are parts of the face. **2** *n* in geometry, one of the flat surfaces of a solid: *A cube has six faces.* **3** *n* the front side of anything: *I turned one of the cards face upward.* **4** *v* have the front turned toward: *The house faces the street. One dancer faced the other.* **faced, fac·ing.**
face off, in hockey, lacrosse, etc., start play by dropping or placing the puck, ball, etc. between the sticks of two players facing each other: *The referee faced off the puck at centre ice.* This act is called the **face-off.**
face up to, meet bravely: *to face up to an enemy.*
lose face, have your pride hurt.

fa·cil·i·ty (fə sil′ə tē) **1** Usually, **facilities,** *pl.n* the suitable space, equipment, etc., that make an activity possible: *The school has excellent lab facilities.* **2** *n* the ability to do something well: *The girl ran and dodged with such facility that no one could catch her.*

fact (fakt) *n* something known to be true or to have happened: *The War of 1812 is a historical fact.* –**fac′tu·al** (fak′chū əl), *adj.*
in fact, really: *She said she could do it when in fact she couldn't.*

fac·tor (fak′tər) **1** *n* one part of a situation: *Good soil is a factor in successful farming; enough rain is another.* **2** *n* any of the numbers or expressions that can be multiplied together to get another number: *2 and 5 are factors of 10.*

fac·to·ry (fak′tə rē) *n* a place where things are made or manufactured: *There are a number of car factories in Ontario.* *pl* **fac·to·ries.**

> **WORD HISTORY . . . . factory**
>
> **Factory** used to have another meaning in Canada, "trading post." That's because a trader was a factor. There are place names in Canada that still show this old meaning, like Moose Factory in Ontario.

fad (fad) *n* a very popular fashion or craze.

fade (fād) **1** *v* lose or cause to lose colour: *Sunlight will fade the colours in some fabrics.* **2** *v* get weaker and weaker: *The sound faded after the train went by.* **fad·ed, fad·ing.**

Fahr·en·heit (fer′ən hīt′) *adj* measured by the Fahrenheit temperature scale. On this scale, water freezes at 32°F (0°C) and boils at 212°F (100°C). It is not metric.

fail (fāl) **1** *v* not manage to do what you try to do: *He tried hard to win the race, but failed.* **2** *v* get a mark that is too low to pass: *She failed the spelling quiz.* –**fail′ure** (fāl′yər), *n.*

faint (fānt) **1** *adj* not clear; so weak that you can hardly tell what it is: *a faint cry, a faint idea, faint colours.* **2** *v* fall unconscious.

fair (fer) **1** *adj* treating everyone with the same rules: *A judge must be fair.* **2** *adj* not very good but not bad: *There is a fair crop of wheat this year.* **3** *adj* light-coloured: *She had fair hair and skin.* **4** *adj* clear and sunny: *The weather in Edmundston will be fair today.* **5** *n* show of things for sale. Often there are rides, games, food, and entertainment: *Mr. Gibson's bull won first prize at the Brantford fair. We tried out some new games at the computer fair.* The outdoor space where a fair is held is a **fairground.** Many Canadian communities have a **fall fair** every September. –**fair′ly,** *adv,* –**fair′ness,** *n.*
fair enough, an expression of agreement; OK.

fair·y (fer′ē) *n* in stories, a tiny magical being, usually with wings, who can help or harm people. A **fairy tale** is a story with fairies or other magical beings in it like witches, elves, ogres, etc. *pl* **fair·ies.**

faith (fāth) **1** *n* belief; trust: *We have faith in our friends.* **2** *n* religion: *People of many different faiths live in Canada.*
faith·ful *adj* that can be trusted: *a faithful friend, a faithful servant.* **Faithless** is the opposite.
in bad faith, dishonestly.
in good faith, honestly.

fake (fāk) **1** *adj* not the real thing: *This is fake leather.* **2** *v* make or do something that seems real but isn't: *He faked a bad cough so he could go home.* **faked, fak·ing.** –**fak′er,** *n.*

fall (fol) **1** *v* drop down from a higher place: *Leaves fall from the trees.* **2** *v* trip and go down: *The first time I went skating at Nathan Phillips Square, I kept falling.* **3** *n* the season of the year between summer and winter; autumn. **4** *n* happen: *My birthday falls on Monday this year.* **5** *n* the act of falling: *a nasty fall on the steps, a fall in temperature.* **6** *n* the amount of something that falls, or how far it falls: *a fall of 3 m from the balcony. They had a heavy fall of snow in Paulatuk last night.* **fell, fall·en, fall·ing.**
fall behind, be unable to keep up.
fall out, stop being friends.
fall through, fail: *His plan fell through.*

false (fols) **1** *adj* not true; not correct: *The witness gave a false statement.* **2** *adj* not real; artificial or pretended: *As part of her disguise she spoke with a false accent.* **fals·er, fals·est.** –**false′ness,** *n.*

fame (fām) *n* the condition of being well-known: *Marc Garneau achieved fame as the first Canadian in space.* –**fa′mous,** *adj.*

fam·i·ly (fam′ə lē) **1** *n* a group of people who are related. **2** *n* a group of related animals or plants or things: *Lions, tigers, and leopards belong to the cat family.* pl **fam·i·lies.**
fa·mil·iar (fə mil′yər) **1** *adj* known to everyone; everyday: *A knife is a familiar tool.* **2** *adj* knowing a person or thing well: *Mary is familiar with the rules.* –**fa·mil′iar′i·ty** (fə mil′yer′ə tē), *n,* –**fa·mil′iar·ize′,** *v.*

fam·ine (fam′ən) *n* an extreme lack of food, with people starving: *Canada sends wheat and other food to countries where there is famine.*
fam·ished (fam′isht) *adj* very hungry; starving.

fan (fan) **1** *n* a thing for moving air in order to cool something. A fan can be something flat you wave or a machine. **2** *n* short for **fanatic,** a person who is extremely interested in a particular thing or person: *He's a baseball fan and has many books about games and players. She's a big fan of Kurt Browning.* **Fan mail** is mail received from fans.

fan·cy (fan′sē) **1** *adj* with a lot of details or extra things: *fancy clothes. We don't need such a fancy computer system.* **2** *n* a liking: *They took a great fancy to each other and became close friends.* **fan·ci·er, fan·ci·est.**
fancy dress, costumes worn to a party.
fancy yourself, think too highly of yourself: *That girl really fancies herself.*

The fangs of a rattlesnake

fang (fang) **1** *n* a long, sharp tooth of some meat-eating animals such as wolves. **2** *n* a snake's tooth that injects poison.

fan·ta·sy (fan′tə sē) **1** *n* a daydream. **2** *n* a story about things that could never be real: Alice in Wonderland *is a fantasy.* pl **fan·ta·sies.**
fan·ta·size *v* daydream. **fan·tas·tic 1** *adj Informal.* unbelievably good: *That was a fantastic meal.* **2** *adj* impossible; unreal: *The idea that a house can float in the air is fantastic.* –**fan·tas′ti·cal·ly,** *adv.*

far (fàr) *adv* or *adj* a long way away in time or space: *to look far into the future, a journey to a far country.* **far·ther, far·thest.**
far·a·way 1 *adj* distant; far away: *faraway countries.* **2** *adj* dreamy: *A faraway look in his eyes showed that he was thinking of something else.*
far-fetched *adj* hard to believe. **far·ther** *adj* or *adv* a longer way away: *Three kilometres is farther than two (adj). We walked farther than we meant (adv).* The matching word meaning "most far" is **farthest.**
by far, easily: *She was by far the better swimmer.*
so far so good, things have been fine up till now.

fare (fer) **1** *n* the money that a person pays to ride in a train, car, bus, etc. **2** *n* food: *home-cooked fare.*

fare·well (fer'wel') *n* or *interj* good luck; goodbye.

farm (fȧrm) **1** *n* the land, water, and buildings that someone uses to raise crops or animals. **2** *v* use land to raise crops or animals either to eat or to sell: *Her parents farm for a living in Moose Jaw.* –**farm'er,** *n,* –**farm'ing,** *n.*

fas·ci·nate (fas'ə nāt') *v* catch and hold the attention: *Grandpa's stories of life at sea fascinated the children.* **fas·ci·nat·ed, fas·ci·nat·ing.** –**fas'ci·na'tion,** *n.*

fash·ion (fash'ən) **1** *n* the current popular style in clothes, cars, music, etc.: *They always have to follow the latest fashion.* **2** *v* make: *He fashioned a whistle out of a piece of wood.* –**fash'ion·a·ble,** *adj.*

fast (fast) **1** *adj* or *adv* quick: *a fast runner (adj). Airplanes go fast (adj or adv).* **2** *adj* or *adv* firm: *Tina and Myra are fast friends (adj). He held fast to the rope so he would not fall (adv).* **3** *v* go without food for a while: *Followers of that religion fast on certain days.* **4** *n* the act or fact of going without food: *The fast lasted all through Ramadan.*

fas·ten (fas'ən) *v* attach in some way: *to fasten a dress, to fasten a door. The necklace fastens with a little clip. They tried to fasten the blame on me.* –**fas'ten·er** or **fas'ten·ing,** *n.*

fast asleep, completely asleep.

pull a fast one, play a trick.

fat (fat) **1** *n* a white or yellow oily substance formed in the bodies of animals and also in some seeds. **2** *adj* big around: *a fat little piglet.* **fat·ter, fat·test.** –**fat'ness,** *n,* –**fat'ten,** *v,* –**fat'ty,** *adj.*

fa·tal (fā'təl) *adj* causing death: *fatal accidents.* –**fa·tal'i·ty,** *n,* –**fa'tal·ly,** *adv.*

fate (fāt) *n* what happens to a particular person, group, etc., especially when thought of as being beyond human control: *In every race it was her fate to be second.*

fa·ther (fo 'тнər) *n* a male parent. –**fa'ther·ly,** *adj.*

fa·ther-in-law *n* the father of a person's husband or wife. *pl* **fathers-in-law.**

fa·tigue (fə tēg') **1** *n* tiredness. **2** *v* make tired. **fa·tigued, fa·ti·guing.**

This faucet mixes hot and cold water.

fau·cet (fos'it) *n* a tap for turning a flow of liquid on or off.

fault (folt) **1** *n* something that is not as it should be: *A fault in the brake made it difficult to stop the bike.* **2** *n* a cause for blame: *It was your fault that the rabbit escaped; you left the cage open!* –**fault'less,** *adj,* –**fault'y,** *adj.*

fa·vour (fā'vər) **1** *n* an act of kindness: *Will you do me a favour?* **2** *v* treat better than others: *He thought the teacher favoured his twin brother.* Another spelling is **favor.**

fa·vour·ite or **fa·vor·ite** *adj* most liked: *What is your favourite colour?*

in favour of, on the side of: *The referee's decision was in favour of the Calgary Flames.*

fax (faks) **1** *n* a written or printed message or picture that is sent or received by a special machine over a telephone line. **Fax** is short for **facsimile. 2** *v* send a message using a fax machine.

fear (fēr) **1** *n* a feeling that something bad is going to happen: *His fear made his heart pound as he crossed the high, narrow bridge over the Niagara River.* **2** *v* be afraid: *Our cat fears the big dog next door.* –**fear'less,** *adj.*

fear·ful 1 *adj* full of fear: *fearful of the dark.* **2** *adj* causing fear; terrible: *The great fire was a fearful sight.* **fear·some** *adj* causing fear; frightening: *The tornado that hit Barrie was a fearsome sight.*

feast (fēst) *n* a big, rich meal: *We went to the wedding feast.*

feat (fēt) *n* a great achievement: *Landing on the moon was a remarkable feat.*

feath·er (feтн'ər) *n* one of the soft, light, thin coverings on a bird's body. –**feath'ered,** *adj,* –**feath'er·y,** *adj.*

fea·ture (fē′chər) **1** *n* a part of the face. The eyes, nose, mouth, chin, and forehead are features: *She has very big features.* **2** *n* a special part or quality: *An outstanding feature of British Columbia is the Selkirk Mountain Range.* **3** *v* offer as something good or special: *The store was featuring radios in its fall sale.* **fea·tured, fea·tur·ing.**

fed·er·al (fed′ə rəl) *adj* having to do with the central government of Canada, or of any other country made up of provinces or states that have their own separate governments but are joined together under one big one. The **Federal Government** sits in Ottawa.

fed·er·a·tion (fed′ə rā′shən) *n* a group of provinces, states, or nations joined together by agreement: *Canada was formed as a federation.*

fee (fē) *n* a charge: *Dentists charge a fee for fixing teeth.*

WORD HISTORY . . . . fee

Fee comes from an Old Germanic word *feoh,* meaning "cattle." The same word meant "money." Long ago, people would pay for things with cattle.

---

fee·ble (fē′bəl) *adj* very weak. **fee·bler, fee·blest. –fee′ble·ness,** *n,* **–fee′bly,** *adv.*

feed (fēd) **1** *v* give food to: *We feed babies since they cannot feed themselves.* **2** *n* food for animals: *Give the chickens their feed.* **fed, feed·ing. feed·back** *n* opinions about whether something was good or bad: *Before the contest, Mona tried her speech out on her family so she could get their feedback.*

feel (fēl) **1** *v* touch something or notice something touching you: *Feel this piece of cloth. I felt the cool breeze.* **2** *v* experience inside yourself: *They feel pity. I feel angry.* **3** *v* think: *If you feel you need more time to decide, just say so.* **felt, feel·ing.**

feel·ing 1 *n* the sense of touch: *After the needle there was no feeling on the right side of my mouth.* **2** *n* emotion: *a feeling of sadness.* **3 feelings,** *pl.n,* the inward part of a person that may be hurt by words, by being left out or laughed at, etc.: *Respect people's feelings.*

fell (fel) *v* cut down or knock down: *Loggers will fell the trees around Babine Lake.*

fel·low (fel′ō) **1** *n* a name given in a friendly way to male people or animals: *That dog is a nice old fellow.* **2** *adj* sharing the same activities, feelings, conditions, etc.: *fellow citizens, fellow classmates.* **–fel′low·ship,** *n.*

fe·male (fē′māl) **1** *adj* having to do with the sex that gives birth to young or produces eggs. Mares, cows, and hens are female animals. Girls and women are also female. **2** *n* a person or an animal belonging to this sex: *There are ten females on the school staff.*

fem·i·nine (fem′ə nin) *adj* having to do with women or girls or things that are supposed to be typical of them: *Sylvia hates wearing feminine clothes like dresses and skirts, but Monique likes them.* **fem·i·nist** *n* someone who believes that women should have the same rights and chances to do things as men have. **–fem′i·nism′,** *n.*

fence (fens) **1** *n* something put around a yard, garden, etc. to show where it ends: *Most fences are made of wood, wire, or metal.* **2** *v* compete in the sport of **fencing,** fighting with long, thin swords called **foils,** that have no sharp point. **fenced, fenc·ing. –fenc′er,** *n.*

fern (fərn) *n* a kind of plant that has roots, stems, and leaflike fronds, but no flowers.

fe·ro·cious (fə rō′shəs) *adj* fierce; savage: *a ferocious wolverine.* **–fe·roc′i·ty** (fə ros′ə tē), *n.*

Fer·ris wheel (fer′is wēl′ *or* fer′is hwēl′) a large, round framework of steel with swinging seats that hang from its rim. Ferris wheels are found at amusement parks and fairs.

fer·ry (fer′ē) **1** *n* a boat that carries people and goods back and forth across a river or other stretch of water. It's also called a **ferryboat. 2** *v* go or carry on a boat that goes back and forth: *Hundreds of visitors are ferried to Vancouver Island every day in summertime.* pl **fer·ries. fer·ried, fer·ry·ing.**

fer·tile (fər′tīl *or* fər′təl) **1** *adj* good for growing plants: *Sand is not very fertile.* **2** *adj* able to have babies or produce fruit. **–fer·til′i·ty** (fər til′ə tē), *n.*

fer·ti·lize (fər′tə līz′) **1** *v* make soil richer by adding manure or some other fertilizer. **2** *v* cause an egg or seed to start growing into a new animal or plant by joining male and female cells. **–fer′ti·li·za′tion,** *n.* **fer·ti·liz·er** *n* any substance that makes soil richer in plant foods.

fes·tive (fes′tiv) *adj* full of a spirit of celebration: *festive decorations.*

fes·ti·val 1 *n* a celebration, often in memory of some great happening: *Passover is an important Jewish festival.* **2** *n* a day, week, or season of arts events, sometimes with competition among the performers: *a drama festival, a choir festival.*

fes·tiv·i·ty (fes tiv′ə tē) *n* something done to celebrate: *The wedding festivities lasted all day.*

fetch (fech) *v* go and get; bring: *Please fetch me my glasses.*

fe·tus (fē′təs) *n* a baby human, animal, or bird just before birth or hatching.

feud (fyūd) *n* a long and bitter quarrel.

fe·ver (fē′vər) **1** *n* a body temperature that is greater than usual: *A sick person usually has a fever.* **2** *n* any sickness that heats the body: *scarlet fever.* –**fe′ver·ish,** *adj.*

few (fyū) *adj, n,* or *pron* not many; a small number: *There are few children who read before they are five (adj). She was one of the lucky few who survived (n). Many people try this, but few succeed (pron).*

few and far between, rare.

quite a few, many.

CONFUSABLES .....**fewer**

fewer means "not so many," and usually refers to countable things: *There are fewer raccoons in our neighbourhood than there were last year.*

less means "not so much": *There is less damage from raccoons than there was last year.*

---

fi·an·cé, fi·an·cée (fē ȧn′sā *or* fē′ȧn sā′) *n* the man (fiancé) or woman (fiancée) that someone is engaged to marry.

fib (fib) *n Informal.* a lie that someone thinks is small and unimportant.

fi·bre (fī′bər) **1** *n* one of the threadlike parts or strands that make up certain substances: *Hemp fibres can be spun into rope.* **2** *n* a tough part of grains, fruits, and vegetables that is not digested but helps other foods move through the digestive system.

fic·tion (fik′shən) *n* stories telling mainly of imaginary happenings to imaginary people: *Short stories and novels are fiction.* –**fic′tion·al,** *adj.*

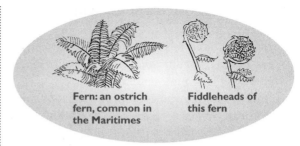

Fern: an ostrich fern, common in the Maritimes   Fiddleheads of this fern

fid·dle (fid′əl) **1** *v* make little movements: *The girl fiddled with her buttons as she waited.* **2** *n Informal.* violin. **3** *v Informal.* play on a violin. **fid·dled, fid·dling.** –**fid′dler,** *n.*

fid·dle·head *n* the young, curled-up tops of certain ferns, eaten as a delicacy: *Fiddleheads are found in Nova Scotia and New Brunswick.*

fidg·et (fij′it) *v* move restlessly: *My little brother fidgets if he has to sit still a long time.* –**fidg′et·y,** *adj.*

field (fēld) **1** *n* an open stretch of land used for crops or for pasture: *a wheat field.* **2** *n* a piece of land used for some special purpose: *a playing field, a landing field for aircraft.* **3** *v* in baseball, stop a batted ball and throw it in. The player who does this is a **fielder.**

fiend (fēnd) **1** *n* a devil; an evil spirit. **2** *n* a very wicked or cruel person. –**fiend′ish,** *adj.*

fierce (fērs) *adj* savage and wild: *a fierce lion, fierce anger.* **fierc·er, fierc·est.** –**fierce′ly,** *adv,* –**fierce′ness,** *n.*

fifth (fifth) ►See Appendix.

fight (fīt) **1** *n* a violent struggle: *One punch can lead to a fight.* **2** *n* a quarrel; angry argument. **3** *v* take part in any kind of fight: *Soldiers fight.* **fought, fight·ing.**

fig·ure (fig′ər *or* fig′yər) **1** *n* a symbol for a number. The symbols 1, 2, 3, etc. are called figures. **2 figure out,** *v* think out; understand; find out by thinking: *I finally figured out what she meant.* **3** *n* a shape: *I could see the figure of a woman against the window.* **4** *n* a diagram: *Fix the bell on the handlebar as shown in Figure B.*

figure skating the art of performing graceful movements on ice skates, usually to music. –**fig′ure-skate′,** *v,* –**fig′ure-skat′er,** *n.*

figure of speech, an expression using words out of their normal meaning or in unusual combinations to add beauty or force: *"He is a tiger on the playing field" is a figure of speech.*

file (fīl) **1** *n* a set of papers kept in order, often in a folder in the drawer of a **filing cabinet**: *The doctor has a file on each of her patients.* **2** *v* store papers or other information in order. **3** *n* a document stored in a computer under a certain name: *Don't delete the file* Mars.doc–*that's my project!* **4** *n* a row of persons or things one behind another: *a file of cars waiting at the lights.* **5** *n* a long tool with many small ridges on it. It is used to smooth rough edges by rubbing. **6** *v* smooth with a file. **filed, fil·ing.**

fill (fil) **1** *v* make or become full: *Fill this bottle with water. The bath filled with water.* **2** *n* something that fills. Earth or rock used to make uneven land level is called fill. **3** *v* supply what is needed for: *The pharmacist filled the doctor's prescription.* **–fill'ing,** *n.*
fill in, 1 take somebody's place who can't be there: *Mr. Vos is filling in for our usual teacher.* **2** tell someone what has been going on: *I was away all last week; fill me in on what happened.*
fill out, 1 write down information asked for on a form: *to fill out a questionnaire.* **2** become rounder and bigger; swell.

film (film) **1** *n* a roll of thin material covered with a special coating and used to take photographs: *He bought two rolls of film for the camera.* **2** *n* a movie. **3** *n* a very thin layer: *a film of dust.*

fil·ter (fil'tər) **1** *n* a device for cleaning liquids or air by screening out dirt or other unwanted stuff. **2** *v* put through a filter: *We filter this water for drinking.*

filth (filth) *n* disgusting dirt: *Filth clogged the drain from the sink.* **–filth'y,** *adj.*

fi·nal (fī'nəl) *adj* at the end; closing; last: *the final chapter of a book, a final decision.*
–fi·nal'i·ty (fə nal'ə tē), *n,* **–fi'nal·ly,** *adv.*
fi·na·le (fə nal'ē *or* fə nä'lē) *n* the last part of a piece of music or a play. **fi·nal·ize** (fī'nə līz') *v* making something final: *We haven't finalized our summer plans yet.*

fi·nance (fī'nans *or* fə nans') **1** *n* money matters: *The Ministry of Finance is in charge of setting taxes and government spending.* **2** *v* pay for: *She financed her daughter's way through university.* **3** **finances,** *pl.n* money; funds.
fi·nanced, fi·nanc·ing.
–fi·nan'cial (fə nan'shəl), *adj.*

find (fīnd) *v* notice or discover something: *She finally found the lost mitten.* **found, finding.**
–find'er, *n.*

fine (fīn) **1** *adj* very small or thin: *Thread is finer than rope. Sand is finer than gravel.* **2** *adj* excellent: *Everybody praised her fine work as baseball coach.* **3** *adj* clear and sunny: *fine weather.* **4** *n* a sum of money paid as a punishment. **fin·er, fin·est. –fine'ly,** *adv.*
fin·er·y *n* fancy clothes, jewellery, etc.

fin·ger (fing'gər) **1** *n* one of the five end parts of the hand, especially the four besides the thumb. **2** *v* touch with the fingers: *to finger the keyboard of a piano.*
fin·ger·print *n* a mark left by a finger.

fin·ish (fin'ish) *v* bring or come to an end: *to finish a meal. The hockey game did not finish until midnight.*

fiord (fyòrd) *n* a long, narrow inlet bordered by steep cliffs: *Norway has many fiords.* **Fjord** is another spelling.

fire (fīr) **1** *n* the flame, heat, and light caused by something burning: *Fire destroys many hectares of forest each summer in Canada.* **2** *v* stir up; excite: *Stories of adventure fire the imagination.* **3** *v* shoot a gun or other weapon: *The hunter fired four times at the fleeing deer.* **4** *v* Informal. dismiss from a job. **–fier'y,** *adj.*
fire·arm *n* any gun that a person can carry.
fire·break *n* a strip of land with the trees cut down or the soil dug and turned over to keep a forest fire or a prairie fire from spreading.
fire·crack·er *n* a paper roll containing gunpowder and a fuse. Firecrackers explode with a loud noise. **fire engine** a truck for fighting fires. **Fire truck** is another name for it. **fire extinguisher** (fīr' ek sting'gwish ər) a container filled with chemicals that can be sprayed on a fire to put it out. **fire·fight·er** *n* a person whose job is to fight fires. ❦ **fire hall** a building where firefighting equipment is kept or where a fire department has its offices. It is also called a **fire station. fire·proof** *adj* that will not burn easily: *A building made entirely of steel and concrete is fireproof.* **fire·works** *pl.n* firecrackers, skyrockets, and other things that explode and make a loud noise or a beautiful display in the night sky.
play with fire, meddle with something dangerous.

Ff

firm (fərm) **1** *adj* hard: *a firm apple, firm ground.* **2** *adj* determined: *a firm voice.* **3** *n* two or more people in business together: *She works for a law firm in Neepawa.*

first (fərst) **1** *adj* or *adv* before all others; 1st: *He is first in his class* (*adj*). *She finished first* (*adv*). ▶See Appendix. **2** *adv* for the first time: *When I first met her, she was a child.*

first aid the emergency treatment given to an injured person before a doctor comes. **first class** the highest class or best quality; the best seats, cabins, etc. on a ship, plane, or train. –**first′-class′,** *adj.* **first-hand** *adj* or *adv* direct from the original source: *first-hand information* (*adj*), *to hear something first-hand* (*adv*). ❦ **First Nations** communities made up of people whose ancestors first lived in Canada long before the Europeans arrived. **Native people, aboriginal people,** and **Indians** are other names for these people. ▶See Appendix. **first person 1** in grammar, the category that includes *I, we,* and all their related forms. *Me, us, mine,* and *ours* are pronouns of the first person; *am* and *are* are the forms of the verb *be* that go with the first person. **2** a way of telling a story that makes it seem as if the author is one of the characters. A story told in the first person uses *I* and *me.*

at first, in the beginning: *At first, he did not like school.* **first thing,** right away: *I'll do it first thing tomorrow morning.*

not know the first thing about, know nothing about: *He doesn't know the first thing about riding a horse.*

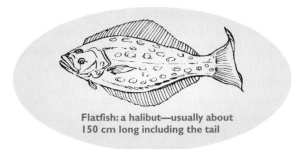

Flatfish: a halibut—usually about 150 cm long including the tail

fish (fish) **1** *n* a cold-blooded animal with fins that lives in the water. Fish have gills instead of lungs for breathing. **2** *v* try to catch fish: *They have been away fishing in Lake Rousseau all day.* *pl* **fish** or **fish·es.**

fish·er *n* a person, animal, or bird that catches fish. **fish·er·man** *n* a person who fishes, especially one who makes a living by doing so.

fish·y 1 *adj* like a fish, especially in smell or taste. **2** *adj Informal.* suspicious; questionable; unlikely: *Their story sounds fishy.*

> ### USING WORDS ...... fish
>
> The plural of **fish** is usually fish, except when speaking of different kinds of fish: *She had a string of eight fish. Most of the catch is made up of three fishes—salmon, trout, and mackerel.*

fist (fist) *n* the hand, closed tightly: *He shook his fist at me.* A **fistfight** is a fight using the fists to punch.

fit (fit) **1** *v* be or make the proper shape and size: *The last piece of the puzzle didn't fit.* **2** *adj* healthy and strong: *You must exercise and eat well to stay fit.* **3** *n* a sudden, sharp attack of sickness or of strong feeling: *a fit of coughing, a fit of anger.* **fit** or **fit·ted, fit·ting, fit·ter, fit·test.** –**fit′ness,** *n.*

by fits and starts, starting, stopping, and starting again, on and on.

five (fīv) ▶See Appendix.

fix (fiks) **1** *v* mend or repair: *to fix a watch.* **2** *v* attach: *to fix the blame on someone. There was a sign fixed to the gate.* **3** *Informal. n* a bad situation: *The boy who cried wolf got himself into a bad fix.* –**fixed,** *adj.*

fix·ture (fiks′chər) *n* something put in place to stay: *Toilet and sink are bathroom fixtures.*

fizz (fiz) **1** *v* bubble up with a hissing sound. **2** *n* a hissing sound; bubbling: *the fizz of soda water.* –**fizz′y,** *adj.*

fiz·zle *v* hiss weakly and then die out: *The firecracker fizzled instead of exploding with a bang.* **fiz·zled, fiz·zling.**

flab (flab) *adj* flesh that has too much fat and not enough muscle. –**flab′by,** *adj.*

flab·ber·gast (flab′ər gast′) *v* amaze and surprise: *I was flabbergasted that no one told me about the party.*

flag (flag) *n* a piece of cloth that shows the sign of a country, a province, etc.: *The Canadian flag has a red maple leaf on a white and red background.* **flag·pole** *n* the pole that a flag is flown from. **Flagstaff** is another word for it.

flair (fler) *n* a natural talent: *a flair for making rhymes, a flair for bargains.*

flake (flāk) **1** *n* a small, flat, thin piece that breaks or falls apart easily: *a flake of snow, flakes of rust, corn flakes.* **2** *n* a frame used in fishing communities for drying fish; fish flake. **3** *n Informal.* a slightly weird person. **flake out,** *Slang.* become so tired that you can't go on.

flame (flām) **1** *n* a tongue of fire, usually bright yellow or orange, caused when gas or vapour is burning. **2** *n* a condition of burning with flames: *to burst into flame.* **3** *n* something, such as love or anger, that suggests flame. A sweetheart is a flame; so is an angry e-mail message. **–flame′proof′,** *adj.*

flam·boy·ant (flam boi′ənt) *adj* very bright and showy, almost too much so: *flamboyant colours.*

flam·ma·ble *adj* easily set on fire.

USING WORDS ... flammable

Flammable and **inflammable** mean the same thing. In science and industry, and on warning labels, they take care to use the word **flammable**, so that there will be no possible confusion.

The opposite is **non-flammable**.

---

flap (flap) **1** *v* move something, especially wings, quickly up and down: *The Canada goose flapped its wings but could not rise from the ground.* **2** *n* a piece fastened at one edge only: *a flap over the top of a pocket.* **flapped, flap·ping.**

flare (fler) **1** *v* flame up suddenly: *The campfire flared when the grease spilled on it.* **2** *n* a stick of something burnable that can be lit as a signal: *The officers put flares around the smashed car.* **flared, flar·ing. –flare′-up′,** *n.*

flash (flash) **1** *n* a sudden, short burst of anything: *a flash of lightning, a flash of temper.* **2** *v* come and go very suddenly: *A bird flashed by our noses.* This can also be used as an adjective: *a flash flood, a flash fire.* **3** *v* give out a sudden light: *The light on the radio tower flashes every four seconds.*

flash·back *n* a scene in a book, play, or movie that shows something that happened earlier in the story. **flash·light** *n* an electric light for carrying in your hand. **flash·y** *adj* bright and showy so as to attract attention: *flashy clothes, a flashy billboard.*

flat (flat) **1** *adj* smooth and level; even: *flat pavement. A tabletop is flat.* **2** *n* an apartment or set of rooms on one floor of a house. **flat·ter, flat·test. –flat′ness,** *n,* **–flat′ten,** *v.*

flat·ter (flat′ər) *v* try to please by praise, often not true. **–flat′ter·er,** *n,* **–flat′ter·y,** *n.*

fla·vour (flā′vər) **1** *n* the taste of something: *This gum has a minty flavour.* **2** *v* make more interesting: *We use spices to flavour food. He flavoured his story with funny details.* Another spelling is **flavor. –fla′vour·ing** or **–fla′vor·ing,** *n.*

flaw (flo) *n* a slight fault: *a flaw in a glass. His bad temper is the only flaw in his character.* **–flaw′less,** *adj.*

flea (flē) *n* a small jumping insect without wings: *Fleas feed on blood.*

flea market a market selling cheap or odd items, used goods, antiques, etc.

fleck (flek) *n* or *v* spot: *Freckles are brown flecks on the skin* (*n*). *My eyes are flecked with brown* (*v*).

flee (flē) *v* run away. **fled, flee·ing.**

fleece (flēs) *n* the fluffy wool that covers a sheep. **–fleec′y,** *adj.*

fleet (flēt) *n* a group of boats, planes, cars, etc.: *a fleet of fishing boats. A fleet of trucks carried the emergency supplies to Peterborough.*

flesh (flesh) **1** *n* in a human or animal body, the softer substance that covers the bones and is covered by skin. It is made up mostly of muscles and fat. **2** *n* the soft part of fruits and vegetables or the part that can be eaten: *The McIntosh apple has crisp, white flesh.* **–flesh′y,** *adj.* **in the flesh,** actually present: *There stood Leilani in the flesh.*

flex (fleks) *v* bend: *He slowly flexed his stiff arm.* **flex·i·ble** *adj* bending easily: *Leather, rubber, and wire are flexible materials.* **–flex′i·bil′i·ty,** *n.*

flick (flik) *n* a sudden, light stroke or jerk: *The secret to skipping stones is in the flick of the wrist.* **flick·er 1** *v* move very quickly back and forth: *The rattlesnake's tongue flickered in and out.* **2** *n* a light or a movement like this: *the flicker of a candle, the flicker of an eyelash.*

flight (flīt) **1** *n* the act of flying: *the flight of a bird through the air.* **2** *n* a trip in an aircraft. **3** *n* a group of things flying through the air together: *a flight of geese.* **4** *n* a set of stairs. **–flight′less,** *adj.*

flim·sy (flim′zē) *adj* not solid enough: *The flimsy wrapping paper kept tearing. What a flimsy excuse for not getting your work done!* **flim·si·er, flim·si·est.**

flinch (flinch) *v* pull back quickly: *The toddler flinched when he touched the hot radiator.*

fling (fling) **1** *v* throw forcefully or roughly: *The angry woman flung her gloves on the floor.* **2** *n* a fun time: *We took our cousin out for one last fling before she went back home.* **flung, fling·ing.**

flip (flip) **1** *v* toss lightly with a quick movement of the wrist or fingers: *The girl flipped her eraser into the air.* **2** *v* turn over quickly: *I flipped the pages of the magazine. He flipped the eggs before serving them.* **flipped, flip·ping.**
flip·pant *adj* not serious when you should be: *a flippant answer.*
flip a coin, settle something by tossing a coin in the air and seeing which side is up when it lands.
flip out or **flip your lid,** lose control of yourself.

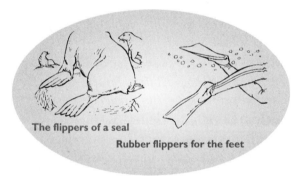
The flippers of a seal
Rubber flippers for the feet

flip·per (flip′ər) **1** *n* a broad, flat fin especially adapted for swimming. Seals and walruses have flippers. **2** *n* a piece of rubber or plastic that fits onto the foot and has a broad, flat part sticking out past the toe, worn for extra power when swimming under water: *A pair of flippers is part of every skindiver's equipment.*

flirt (flərt) **1** *v* play at being in love with someone. **2** *v* turn something over in your mind, but not seriously: *He flirted with the idea of taking riding lessons.* **–flir·ta′tion,** *n,* **–flir·ta′tious,** *adj.*

flit (flit) *v* fly or go lightly and quickly: *A moth flitted by. Many thoughts flitted through his mind as he lay in the sun.* **flit·ted, flit·ting.**

float (flōt) **1** *v* be held up by air, water, or other liquid: *A cork floats but a stone sinks.* **2** *n* anything that stays up in water, such as a buoy.

flock (flok) *n* animals of one kind that feed and move around in a group, especially sheep or birds: *a flock of sparrows.*

floe (flō) *n* a large mass of floating ice.

flood (flud) **1** *n* a huge amount of water, especially when it flows over or into a place that is usually dry: *a flood in the basement. Heavy rains caused a flood in the low areas around the Red River.* **2** *v* cover or fill with water: *The attendants flood the rink before every hockey game.* **3** *n* a huge amount of anything: *a flood of words.*
flood·light *n* a lamp that gives a broad beam of bright light.

floor (flȯr) **1** *n* the flat surface at the bottom of anything: *the floor of a room, the ocean floor, the floor of a pool.* **2** *n* a storey of a building: *We live on the fourth floor.*

flop (flop) **1** *v* fall or move heavily or loosely: *He flopped down into a chair.* **2** *v* Informal. fail completely: *Our clever plan flopped.* **3** *n* Informal. a complete failure: *The new play was a flop.* **flopped, flop·ping.**
flop·py *adj* Informal. very droopy or bendy: *She bought a sun hat with a big floppy brim.*
floppy disk a small, thin magnetic platter used for storing computer data. **Diskette** is another name for it.

flo·ra (flȯ′rə) *n* all the plants of a particular region: *Arctic flora.*
flo·ral *adj* having to do with flowers: *floral decorations.* **flo·rist** *n* the owner of a store that sells flowers.

floun·der (floun′dər) *v* struggle awkwardly; stumble around: *People and horses were floundering in the deep snow beside the road.*

flour (flour) *n* the fine powder you get by grinding grain, especially wheat.

flow (flō) **1** *v* run like water: *Blood flowed from his nose.* **2** *v* move smoothly: *The words flowed from his mouth.*
go with the flow, relax and let things happen.

flow·er (flou′ər) *n* a blossom; the part of a plant that produces the seed. **–flow′er·ing,** *adj.*
flow·er·y *adj* full of fancy words and phrases: *a flowery speech.*

flu (flū) *n* influenza.

flue (flū) *n* a tube, pipe, etc. to let smoke or hot air escape.

flu·ent (flū′ənt) *adj* smooth, fast, and confident in speech or writing: *Long practice enabled them to speak fluent French.* –**flu′en·cy,** *n.*

fluff (fluf) *n* a mass of very soft, light material: *After its bath and a rub with the towel, the puppy looked like a ball of fluff.* –**fluff′y,** *adj.*

flu·id (flū′id) *n* any liquid or gas; something that will flow: *Water, mercury, air, and oxygen are fluids.*

flur·ry (flər′ē) **1** *n* a light fall of snow. **2** *n* a sudden gust of wind: *The flurry lifted off his hat and carried it away.* **3** *n* a sudden burst of excited action or feeling: *a flurry of alarm.* *pl* **flur·ries.**

flush (flush) **1** *v* clean out with a sudden rush of water: *to flush a toilet.* **2** *v* go pink in the face: *The girl flushed when they laughed at her.*

flus·ter (flus′tər) *v* make nervous or embarrassed: *He was a little flustered by all the attention.*

flut·ter (flut′ər) **1** *v* move quickly and lightly: *to flutter your eyelashes. The leaf fluttered to the ground.* **2** *n* a state of excitement: *The surprise announcement caused a flutter in the crowd.*

fly (flī) **1** *n* a flying insect with two wings: *Houseflies, black flies, and horseflies are a great nuisance.* *pl* **flies. 2** *v* move or make move through the air: *Birds fly. We heard a plane fly over. Our flag flies every day. She loves to fly a kite.* **flew, flown, flying.**
fly·er or **fli·er 1** *n* a person or thing that flies, such as a bird, an airplane pilot or passenger, a very fast train, etc. **2** *n* a sheet of paper or brochure with advertising on it. **flying saucer** an alien spaceship that is round and almost flat, according to some people who say they have seen one. Another name for it is **UFO,** which means **U**nidentified **F**lying **O**bject.
fly off the handle, lose your temper.

foal (fōl) *n* a young horse or donkey.

foam (fōm) **1** *n* a mass of very small bubbles. **2** *n* a spongy material made from plastic, rubber, etc. –**foam′y,** *adj.*

fo·cus (fō′kəs) **1** *v* adjust a lens, the eye, etc. so that it brings rays of light together to give a clear image: *A near-sighted person cannot focus well on faraway objects. Turn the little knob to focus the binoculars.* **2** *n* something that everyone is paying attention to: *The new baby was the focus of attention.* *pl* **fo·cus·es. 3** *v* concentrate: *He focussed his mind on the lesson.* **fo·cus·ses** or **fo·cus·es, fo·cussed** or **fo·cused, fo·cuss·ing** or **fo·cus·ing.**

foe (fō) *n* enemy.

fog (fog) *n* a cloud of fine drops of water; thick mist. –**fog′gy,** *adj.*

foil (foil) **1** *n* metal that has been made into a very thin sheet: *aluminum foil.* **2** *v* prevent a person's plans from being carried out: *The hero foiled the villain.*

fold (fōld) **1** *v* bend over on itself: *He folded the letter and put it in an envelope.* **2** *n* a layer of something folded, or the line where it has been folded: *He hid the money between the folds of his blanket. The old map is falling apart at the folds.* **3** *v* close up or quit because of failure: *Their typewriter repair business has folded.*
fold·er 1 *n* a holder for papers, made of cardboard folded once. **2** *n* a grouping of computer files together under one title.

fo·li·age (fō′lē ij) *n* the leaves of a plant.

folk (fōk) **1** *n* people: *city folk, country folk. The Vikings were traditionally a seafaring folk.* **2 folks,** *n Informal.* relatives, especially parents: *How are your folks?* **3** *adj* traditional: *folk medicine, folk tales, folk dances, folk music.*

fol·low (fol′ō) **1** *v* be after or as a result of: *Night follows day. Follow the leader. Your headache follows directly from a lack of sleep.* **2** *v* understand: *He found the explanation hard to follow.*

fond (fond) *adj* loving; affectionate: *a fond look.* –**fond′ly,** *adv,* –**fond′ness,** *n.*
be fond of, like: *My uncle is fond of dogs.*

food (fūd) *n* anything that plants, animals, or people take in to keep them alive and make them grow.
food bank a place where people with little or no money can get food for free. **food chain** a group of animals and plants connected by their eating habits so that each one uses another one for food. For example, people eat cattle, cattle eat grass, and grass consumes nutrients from the soil. **food web** all the groups of plants and animals that live together and have eating habits that depend on each other. A food web is made up of many food chains.

fool (fūl) **1** *n* a person without sense.
2 *v* trick: *Ha ha, I fooled you! There's no quiz after all!* –**fool'ish,** *adj.*

fool·proof *adj* so safe or simple that even a fool can use it: *a foolproof device, a foolproof plan.*

foot (fut) **1** *n* the end part of a leg.
2 *n* the bottom or end: *the foot of a hill, the foot of a page.*
3 *n* a non-metric measure of length equal to about 30 cm. *pl* **feet.**

foot·hill *n* one of the low hills at the base of a mountain range: *We went for a long walk in the foothills of the Monashee Mountains.*

foot·note *n* a note or explanation at the bottom of a page, about something on that page.

foot·step *n* a person's step, or the sound of it. *We heard footsteps in the hall.*

put your best foot forward, try to make a good impression.

put your foot down, act firmly.

put your foot in it, *Informal.* make a mess of something.

put your foot in your mouth, say something that gets you in trouble.

for·bid (fər bid') *v* not allow: *The teacher forbids chewing gum in class. His sister forbade him to play with her toys.*
for·bade (fər bad'), **for·bid·den, for·bid·ding.**

for·bid·ding *adj* looking rather scary: *The coast of Newfoundland is rocky and forbidding.*

force (fòrs) **1** *n* power or strength: *The force of the wind broke the power pole.* **2** *v* make a person do something: *Pressing with their hands on his shoulders, they forced him to sit down.* **3** *n* a group of people who work together: *the police force.* **4** *n* in science, any cause that changes, moves, or stops something: *the force of gravity, magnetic force.* **forced, forc·ing.**

force·ful *adj* powerful: *He is a quiet but forceful speaker.*

fore– *a prefix meaning:* **1** front, as in *forehead.*
2 before; beforehand, as in *foresee.*

fore·bod·ing (fòr bō'ding) *n* a feeling that something bad is going to happen: *As the storm grew worse, the pioneers were filled with foreboding.*

fore·cast (fòr'kast') *v* tell what is coming: *Cooler weather is forecast for tomorrow.*

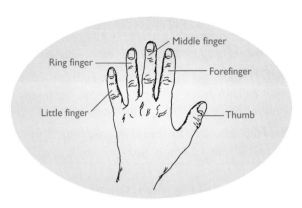

fore·fin·ger (fòr'fing'gər) *n* the finger next to your thumb.

fore·ground (fòr'ground') *n* the part of a picture or scene nearest to the person looking at it: *The cottage is in the foreground and the Coast Mountains are in the background.*

fore·head (fòr'hed') *n* the part of your face above your eyes.

for·eign (fòr'ən) *adj* having to do with or coming from countries other than your own: *foreign countries, a foreign ship, foreign money.* A visitor from another country is a **foreigner.**

fore·noon (fòr'nūn') *n* the time between early morning and noon.

for·est (fòr'ist) *n* a large area of land covered with trees. –**for'est·ed,** *adj.*

for·est·ry *n* planting and taking care of forests. –**for'est·er,** *n.*

for·ev·er (fə rev' ər) *adv* without ever ending: *She doesn't believe the earth will last forever.*

forge (fòrj) **1** *v* make or write something false or counterfeit: *to forge someone else's signature, to forge a passport.* **2** *v* heat metal to a high temperature and then shape it while it is soft: *The blacksmith forged the bar of iron into a big strong hook.* **3** *v* make; build or form: *They forged a strong and lasting friendship.* **4** *v* move forward slowly but steadily: *One runner forged ahead of the others and won the race.* **forged, forg·ing.**

for·ge·ry *n* a fake meant to deceive people: *The painting was a forgery.*

for·get (fər get') **1** *v* not remember: *I couldn't phone her because I had forgotten her last name.*
2 *v* leave behind without meaning to: *I'll have to go back–I forgot my lunch.* **for·got, for·got·ten, for·get·ting.** –**for·get'ful,** *adj.*

for·give (fər giv′) *v* give up being angry or wanting revenge: *Please forgive my rude behaviour.* **for·gave, for·giv·en, for·giv·ing.** –**for·give′ness,** *n.*

fork (fȯrk) **1** *n* an eating tool with a handle and two or more long, pointed prongs. **2** *n* a tool shaped like this but bigger, for digging, lifting hay, etc.; pitchfork. **3** *n* the part of a tree, road, etc. where it divides into two parts: *When you come to the fork in the road, go left.*

form (fȯrm) **1** *n* or *v* shape: *The form of a tree appeared out of the fog* (n). *The cook formed the dough into loaves* (v). **2** *v* come to be: *Water forms ice when it freezes.* **3** *v* set up: *We formed a club.* **4** *n* a kind; sort: *Heat and light are two forms of energy.* **5** *n* a printed paper with blank spaces to be filled in: *To get a licence, you must fill out a form.* –**for·ma′tion,** *n.*

for·mal 1 *adj* stiff and proper; not relaxed: *a formal introduction, a formal suit.* **2** *adj* done in the official way: *A written contract is a formal agreement to do something.* **3** *n* a party that people wear formal clothes to. –**for′mal·ly,** *adv.*

for·mat (fȯr′mat) *n* the way in which something is presented or arranged: *book format, tape format, DOS format.*

for·mer (fȯr′mər) **1** *adj* earlier; past: *former times. He is a former student of this school.* **2 the former,** *n* the first of two: *When Rani is offered ice cream or pie, she always chooses the former.* –**for′mer·ly,** *adv.*

for·mi·da·ble (fȯr′mə də bəl) *adj* taking a lot of courage and effort: *a formidable task, a formidable enemy.*

for·mu·la (fȯr′myə lə) **1** *n* a recipe; prescription: *a formula for making soap.* **2** *n* a mixture for feeding a baby.

fort (fȯrt) **1** *n* a strong building for defence against an enemy. **2** ❧ *n* in the early days of Canada, a trading post of the Hudson's Bay Company: *Winnipeg is built on the site of Fort Garry, an old Hudson's Bay Company post.*

for·ti·fy (fȯr′tə fī′) **1** *v* build forts, walls, etc.: *Many old towns such as Halifax and Saint John were fortified with thick stone walls.* **2** *v* make stronger or more effective: *Breakfast cereal is often fortified with vitamins.* –**for′ti·fi·ca′tion,** *n.*

for·tress *n* a large, strong, and well-protected fort; a fortified place.

forth (fȯrth) *adv* forward; onward: *From that day forth he lived alone. The sun came forth from behind the clouds.*

forth·right *adj* outspoken; straightforward; direct: *She was very forthright in her criticism.*

and so forth, and so on: *We ate cake, candy, nuts, and so forth.*

back and forth, first one way and then the other.

for·tune (fȯr′chən) **1** *n* a lot of money. **2** *n* luck.

for·tu·nate *adj* lucky. –**for′tu·nate·ly,** *adv.*

for·ward (fȯr′wərd) **1** *adv* Often, **forwards,** onward: *She strode bravely forward into the darkness.* **2** *adv* to the front: *to come forward.* **3** *n* in certain games, a player whose position is in the front line.

fos·sil (fos′əl) *n* the remains of animals or plants that lived very long ago, preserved in rocks. Fossil footprints of dinosaurs have been discovered in Alberta.

> **WORD HISTORY** .... **fossil**
>
> **Fossil** comes from the Latin word *fossilis,* meaning "dug up."

fos·ter (fos′tər) *v* help something to grow: *to foster good work habits, to foster a child.*

foul (foul) **1** *adj* very dirty or disgusting: *foul water, a foul smell.* **2** *adj* unfair; against the rules: *foul play.* **Foul play** can also mean dishonest or criminal behaviour. **3** *adj* in baseball, falling outside the **foul lines,** the lines that join first and third base to home plate: *to hit a foul ball.*

foul up, make a mess of.

found (found) *v* set up; establish: *Québec City was founded by Champlain in 1608.* –**found′er,** *n.*

foun·da·tion (foun dā′shən) **1** *n* the bottom of a building: *The foundation of the house was entirely underground.* **2** *n* the act of founding: *The foundation of King's College, Nova Scotia, took place in 1788.*

foun·tain (foun′tən) *n* a stream of water rising into the air, either naturally from the earth or through a pipe.

four (fȯr) ▶See Appendix.

fowl (foul) **1** *n* any bird: *a water fowl.* **2** *n* a large bird raised for its meat and eggs: *Chickens, ducks, geese, etc. are fowls.* pl **fowls** or **fowl.**

F
f

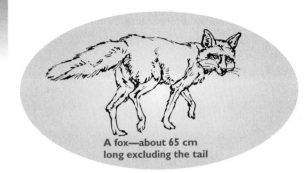

A fox—about 65 cm
long excluding the tail

fox (foks) *n* a wild animal that looks like a small dog.

foy·er (foi′ā) *n* an entrance hall.

frac·tion (frak′shən) **1** *n* a part of a whole number: *1/2 and 0.5 are fractions.* **2** *n* a very small amount: *Turn it up just a fraction.*

frac·ture *v* or *n* break or crack: *The boy fell from a tree and fractured his arm* (*v*). *The X ray showed where the fracture was* (*n*). **frac·tured, frac·tur·ing.**

frag·ile (fraj′īl or fraj′əl) *adj* easily broken: *Be careful; that thin glass is fragile.*

frag·ment (frag′mənt) *n* a broken part: *fragments of a broken clay pot.*

fra·grant (frā′grənt) *adj* sweet-smelling, like perfume or flowers –**fra′grance,** *n.*

frail (frāl) *adj* weak: *My grandmother has become quite frail since her illness.*

frame (frām) **1** *n* a supporting structure: *the frame of a house.* **Framework** is another word for it. **2** *n* the solid border that holds a thing placed into it: *a window frame, a picture frame, glasses frames.* **3** *v* try to make someone appear guilty: *The real criminal tried to frame someone else.* **framed, fram·ing.**

❦ **Fran·co·phone** or **fran·co·phone** (frangk′ə fōn′) *n* a person whose first or main language is French, living in a bilingual or multilingual country, especially Canada.

frank (frangk) *adj* not hiding what is in your mind: *To be very frank, I find that music boring.* –**frank′ly,** *adv,* –**frank′ness,** *n.*

fran·tic (fran′tik) *adj* wild; so excited that you are out of control: *The mother was frantic when her child went missing.* –**fran′ti·cal·ly,** *adv.*

fraud (frod) **1** *n* cheating: *A person who passes counterfeit money is guilty of fraud.* **2** *n* a phony person or thing. –**fraud′u·lent** (frod′jə lənt), *adj.*

freak (frēk) **1** *n* something very strange: *A green leaf growing in the middle of a rose would be called a freak of nature.* **2** *n Slang.* someone extremely enthusiastic about a certain thing: *a health freak, a hockey freak.* **3** *n Slang.* Often, **freak out**, react in an extreme way: *He freaked when I told him our family was moving.* –**freak′ish,** *adj,* –**freak′y,** *adj.*

freck·le (frek′əl) *n* a small, light-brown spot on the skin.

free (frē) **1** *adj* loose: *The hens were allowed to run free in the yard.* **2** *adj* not under the control of anything: *free speech, free nations.* **3** *adj* with no cost: *These tickets are free.* **4** **free of** or **free from,** *adj* without: *free from fear, air free of dust.* This meaning often occurs in compound words like *sugar-free, hassle-free.* **fre·er, fre·est.** **5** *v* make free: *They had trouble freeing the boat from the weeds.* **freed, free·ing.** –**free′dom,** *n,* –**free′ly,** *adv.*

free·hand *adj* done by hand without using instruments, measurements, etc.: *freehand drawing.* **free verse** poetry that does not have a fixed rhythm or rhyme scheme. **free·way** *n* a high-speed highway.

free and easy, relaxed.

freeze (frēz) **1** *v* turn into ice: *Water freezes at 0°C.* **2** *v* cool something so that all the water in it turns to ice: *In the Far North the ground is permanently frozen.* **3** *v* be or feel very cold: *The campers in the tent will freeze in this weather.* **4** *v* use a drug to make a part of the body numb: *The dentist froze the patient's gums before filling the tooth.* **5** *v* become motionless: *The mouse froze as the snake moved toward it.* **froze, fro·zen, freez·ing.**

freez·er *n* a refrigerator cabinet for storing food at a temperature below freezing.

❦ **freeze-up** *n* the time of year when the rivers and lakes freeze over; the start of winter.

freight (frāt) *n* the goods that a ship or a train carries.

freight car a railway car for carrying freight. **freight·er** *n* a ship or aircraft that carries mainly freight.

fren·zy (fren′zē) *n* a state of being nearly crazy with pain, grief, excitement, anger, etc.: *The spectators were in a frenzy after the Edmonton Oilers finally scored.* –**fren′zied,** *adj.*

fre·quen·cy (frē′kwən sē) *n* how often something happens: *The flashes of light came with a frequency of three per minute.*

fre·quent (frē′kwənt *for 1*, fri kwent′ *for 2*) **1** *adj* happening often: *Storms are frequent in March.* **2** *v* go to often: *Frogs frequent ponds and marshes.* —**fre′quent·ly**, *adv.*

fresh (fresh) **1** *adj* just made or received: *fresh bread, fresh news.* **2** *adj* not frozen, canned, or pickled: *fresh vegetables.* **3** *adj* not salty: *There is fresh water in the Great Lakes.* **4** *adj* clean: *a fresh shirt, fresh air.* —**fresh′ly**, *adv*, —**fresh′ness**, *n.*

fric·tion (frik′shən) *n* a rubbing of one thing against another. The greater the friction the slower or more difficult the motion becomes: *Oil reduces friction in engines.*

fridge (frij) *n Informal.* refrigerator.

friend (frend) *n* a person who knows and likes you. —**friend′less,** *adj*, —**friend·ly,** *adj*, —**friend′ship,** *n.*

fries (frīz) *pl.n* strips of potato cooked in deep fat till they are crisp on the outside. **French fries** is the full name.

fright (frīt) *n* sudden great fear.

fright·en *v* make afraid. **fright·ful** *adj* terrible or very big: *a frightful thunderstorm, a frightful mess.*

frill (fril) **1** *n* a fancy, bunchy strip of cloth on a piece of clothing, curtain, etc. **2** *n* something extra that is nice but useless: *It was a plain house with few frills.* —**frill′y,** *adj.*

frisk (frisk) **1** *v* jump around playfully: *Our lively puppy frisks all over the house.* **2** *v Informal.* search a person for hidden weapons, stolen goods, etc. by running a hand quickly over his or her clothes. —**frisk′y,** *adj.*

A leopard frog—head and body about 7 cm long

frog (frog) *n* a small, leaping amphibious animal with webbed feet that lives in or near water.

frol·ic (frol′ik) *v* play around joyfully: *The children frolicked with the kitten.* **frol·icked, frol·ick·ing.** —**frol′ic·some,** *adj.*

front (frunt) **1** *n* the side or end that faces forward; the first part: *The picture is near the front of the book.* **2** *n* a fake surface or appearance hiding what is underneath: *to put a stone front on a wooden house. He turned out to be really nasty—that friendly welcome was just a front.* **3** *n* the surface where two different air masses meet: *The weather report says there is a cold front approaching from the northwest.*

fron·tier (fron tēr′ *or* frun tēr′) **1** *n* the edge of settled country, where the wild or unknown part begins: *Life can be rough on the frontier.* **2** *n* the border between two countries.

frost (frost) **1** *n* a condition of freezing; temperatures below 0°C: *The plants were killed by a heavy frost.* **2** *n* moisture from the air that has frozen on a solid surface, often looking like feathery crystals of ice: *frost on the grass, frost on the windows.* —**frost′y,** *adj.*

frost·bite *n* the freezing of some part of the body, such as the toes. —**frost′bit′ten,** *adj.*

froth (froth) *n* a mass of very small bubbles: *If you shake a can of pop, it turns to froth.*

frown (froun) **1** *n* draw your eyebrows together, showing anger or deep thought: *He frowned with annoyance.* **2** *v* the act of frowning: *She answered him with a frown.*

fruit (frūt) **1** *n* the product of a tree, bush, shrub, or vine that is sweet and good to eat. Apples, bananas, and grapes are fruits. **2** *n* in science, the part of a plant that contains the seeds. Tomatoes, acorns, and grains of wheat are also fruits. —**fruit′y,** *adj.*

fry (frī) *v* cook in hot fat, in a deep or shallow pan: *She is frying potatoes.* **fried, fry·ing.**

fudge (fuj) *n* a soft candy made of sugar, milk, butter, and a flavouring such as chocolate or caramel.

fu·el (fyū′əl) *n* something burned to keep a fire going or provide power, such as wood, gas, or oil. **fu·elled** or **fu·eled, fu·el·ling** or **fu·el·ing.**

fu·gi·tive (fyū′jə tiv) *n* a person who is running away: *The prisoner escaped and became a fugitive.*

–ful *a suffix meaning:* **1** full of; showing. *Cheerful* means full of *cheer*. *Careful* means showing *care*. **2** the amount that fills. A *cupful* means the amount that will fill a *cup*.

full (fùl) **1** *adj* that can hold no more: *a full cup*. **2** *adv* directly: *The ball hit him full in the face*. **–ful′ly,** *adv*.

full moon the moon seen as a whole circle.

full blast, as loud, as fast, as hot, etc. as possible; with all the power available. **Full steam** has a similar meaning.

WORD HISTORY . . . . full blast

This is originally a term used about heavy industrial furnaces. A strong draft, or **blast**, of air is blown in through the bottom of the furnace to make the fire burn very hot, so it could melt metal. A furnace that was burning as hot as it could, with the strongest draft, was said to be at **full blast**.

---

fum·ble (fum′bəl) **1** *v* feel around clumsily: *He fumbled in the darkness for the doorknob.* **2** *v* handle or do awkwardly: *The first baseman fumbled the ball, and two runs were scored. I fumbled my speech.* **fum·bled, fum·bling.**

fume (fyūm) **1** **fumes,** *pl.n* gas or smoke, especially if harmful or strong-smelling: *The strong fumes of the acid nearly choked him.* **2** *v* complain angrily: *He fumed about the slowness of the traffic.* **fumed, fum·ing.**

fu·mi·gate *v* spray with poisonous fumes in order to kill bugs.

fun (fun) *n* playfulness; games, jokes, laughter, etc.; a good time: *They had a lot of fun at the Labour Day picnic.*

make fun of, laugh at.

func·tion (fungk′shən) **1** *n* what something does or is meant to do: *The function of the stomach is to digest food.* **2** *v* work: *This old refrigerator does not function very well.* **3** *n* a formal gathering: *The mayor gets invited to a lot of public functions; today she was at the opening ceremony for a new library in Summerside.*

fund (fund) **1** *n* a sum of money set aside for a particular purpose: *Our school has a fund to buy books with.* **2** *v* supply the money for: *The provincial government is funding this tree-planting project.* Raising money is called **fund-raising.**

fu·ner·al (fyū′nə rəl) *n* the ceremonies held to honour a person who has just died, often including a religious service.

Fungi growing on a tree

fun·gus (fung′gəs) *n* a plant that has no flowers or leaves: *Mushrooms, toadstools, moulds, and mildews are fungi.* pl **fun·gi** (fung′gī or fung′gē, fun′jī or fun′jē) or **fun·gus·es.**

A funnel used in pouring

fun·nel (fun′əl) *n* a cone-shaped container with a tube at the bottom, used for pouring something through a small opening: *He used a funnel to pour the salt into the shaker.* **fun·nelled** or **fun·neled, fun·nel·ling** or **fun·nel·ing.**

fun·ny (fun′ē) **1** *adj* making you laugh: *a funny clown, a funny story.* **2** *adj Informal.* strange; peculiar; odd: *funny behaviour.* **fun·ni·er, fun·ni·est.**

fur (fər) *n* the soft covering of hair on the skin of many animals. **–fur′ry,** *adj*.

fur·nace (fər′nis) *n* large metal box or cylinder with a fire in it to provide heat.

fur·nish (fər′nish) **1** *v* supply: *to furnish a school with sports equipment. The sun furnishes heat and light.* **2** *v* put furniture in: *to furnish a bedroom.*

fur·ni·ture (fər′nə chər) *n* chairs, tables, beds, desks, cabinets, and other large movable objects used in homes and offices.

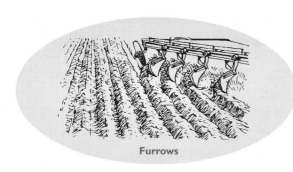
Furrows

fur·row (fėr′ō) *n* the long, narrow track dug in the soil by a plough.

fur·ther (fėr′ŦHėr) **1** *adj* or *adv* a greater distance away: *It was too dark to go further* (*adv*). **2** *adj* or *adv* more: *Do you need further help* (*adj*)? *We will discuss the matter further tomorrow* (*adv*).

fur·thest *adj* or *adv* at or to the greatest distance in space or time: *Cut down the furthest tree in the first row* (*adj*). *Of all the family, Grandfather could remember furthest into the past* (*adv*).

fur·tive (fėr′tiv) *adj* sneaky: *He made a furtive attempt to read his sister's letter.* **–fur′tive·ly,** *adv.*

fu·ry (fyū′rē) **1** *n* a wild fit of anger; rage. **2** *n* violence; extreme force or energy: *the fury of a hurricane.* **–fu′ri·ous,** *adj.*

fuse (fyūz) *n* a separate piece in an electric circuit, specially designed to melt and break if the current becomes dangerously strong.

blow a fuse, 1 cause a fuse to melt and break an electric circuit. **2** lose your temper; get very angry.

fuss (fus) **1** *n* a lot of bother about something unimportant: *There was a great deal of fuss about the lost dime.* **2** *v* make a fuss: *Stop fussing about the time; we're only a minute late!*

fuss·y *adj* hard to please: *She is very fussy about what she eats.*

fu·ture (fyū′chėr) *n* the time to come: *You cannot change the past, but you can do better in the future.*

future tense a verb form that expresses action in the future. In English it uses the auxiliary verbs **will** and **shall**. *Example: I will see you next week.*

fuzz (fuz) *n* light hairs that feel like short, soft fur: *Some caterpillars are covered with fuzz.*

fuzz·y 1 *adj* covered with fuzz or like fuzz: *a fuzzy teddy bear, fuzzy hair.* **2** *adj* not clear: *a fuzzy outline, a fuzzy idea.*

F
f

Gg

g or **G** (jē) *n* the seventh letter of the English alphabet, or any speech sound that it stands for. The sound of *g* in *get* is different from the sound of *g* in *giant*. *pl* **g's** or **G's.**

gab (gab) *Informal. n* or *v* chat; talk. **gabbed, gab·bing. –gab′by,** *adj.*

gab·ble *n* or *v* chatter with no sense: *to gabble on foolishly* (*v*), *such meaningless gabble* (*n*).

Green Gables, the farm house near Cavendish, P.E.I. that is featured in *Anne of Green Gables*, by L.M. Montgomery

ga·ble (gā′bəl) *n* the end of a peaked roof, with the triangular piece of wall that it covers.

gadg·et (gaj′it) *n* a small machine or tool, especially one that seems not necessary.

gag (gag) **1** *n* something put in or over a person's mouth to keep him or her from talking. **2** *v* stop up someone's mouth in this way: *The bandits tied the security guard's arms and gagged him.* **3** *v* choke: *The strong, horrible smell made me gag.* **4** *n Informal.* a joke. **gagged, gag·ging.**

gain (gān) **1** *v* get or win: *to gain someone's trust.* **2** *v* end up with more than you started with: *I have gained five kilos this year.* **3** *n* something gained: *a gain in speed, a gain of ten percent.* **–gain′ful,** *adj.*

gain on, catch up to: *The Canadian speed skater is gaining on the American.*

gal·ax·y (gal′ək sē) *n* a very large number of stars forming one system: *The Milky Way is the galaxy that contains the earth, our sun, and the other planets in our solar system.* *pl* **gal·ax·ies.**

gale (gāl) *n* a very strong wind.

gal·ler·y (gal′ə rē) *n* a building or room where paintings, sculptures, and other works of art are shown: *an art gallery.* *pl* **gal·ler·ies.**

gal·lon (gal′ən) *n* a non-metric measure for liquids, about the same as 4.5 L.

gal·lop (gal′əp) *n* the fastest run of a horse or other four-footed animal. In a gallop, all four feet are off the ground together at each leap.

ga·losh (gə losh′) *n* Usually, **galoshes,** *pl* a rubber boot worn over the shoe in wet or snowy weather.

gam·ble (gam′bəl) **1** *v* play games of chance where you win or lose money. **2** *v* take a chance: *We hiked the extra 4 km to Mila's house, gambling on her being home.* **3** *n* a risky action: *His attempt to cross Niagara Falls on a rope was a gamble.* **gam·bled, gam·bling. –gam′bler,** *n.*

game (gām) **1** *n* something done for fun: *a game of catch, an action figure game.* **2** *n* an activity with certain rules, where there are winners and losers: *Our team did their best to win the baseball game.* **3** *n* animals and birds that are hunted. A **game warden** enforces the hunting and fishing laws in an area. **4** *adj* brave: *Are you game enough to swim across Nipisquit River?* **gam·er, gam·est.**

gang (gang) **1** *n* a group of people involved in crime together: *a gang of thieves.* **2** *n* a group of people going around together or working together as a unit: *a gang of tourists. Two gangs of workers were mending the basketball courts.*

gang·ster *n* a member of a gang of criminals.

gang up on, go together as a group against someone else: *Let's gang up on that bully.*

gap (gap) **1** *n* a broken place; opening: *a gap in a fence or wall.* **2** *n* a wide difference in opinion, lifestyle, etc.: *the generation gap.*

gape (gāp) **1** *v* open wide: *A deep hole in the earth gaped before us.* **2** *v* stare with mouth open: *The children gaped when they saw the huge birthday cake.*

ga·rage (gə ràzh′ *or* gə raj′) **1** *n* a place for keeping cars. **2** *n* a place where cars are fixed.

garage sale a sale of used household items, usually held in a private garage or driveway.

gar·bage (gàr′bij) **1** *n* waste: *The garbage in Orillia is collected weekly.* **2** *n Informal.* anything worthless: *This TV show is pure garbage.*

gar·ble (gàr′bəl) *v* to say or write something in a mixed-up way: *Sal garbled the report of our class meeting.* **gar·bled, gar·bling.**

gar·gle (gàr′gəl) *v* move liquid around in your throat: *He treated his sore throat by gargling with salt water.* **gar·gled, gar·gling.**

Gargoyles on the Peace Tower of the Houses of Parliament, Ottawa

gar·goyle (gàr′goil) *n* an ugly stone figure decorating the outside of a building, especially on older buildings.

gar·ish (ger′ish) *adj* so bright that it is ugly or hurts the eyes: *garish neon signs, the garish light of an unshaded bulb.*

gar·lic (gàr′lik) *n* a plant related to the onion. It grows a strong-smelling bulb that is made up of small sections called cloves. **–gar′lick·y,** *adj.*

gar·ment (gàr′mənt) *n* any piece of clothing.

gas (gas) **1** *n* any substance that is not a solid or a liquid but is like air in form. **2** *n* any mixture of gases that can be burned. Gas is used in some stoves and furnaces. **3** *n Informal.* short for **gasoline,** the poisonous liquid used as a fuel for cars, planes, tractors, etc. It comes from petroleum, and you buy it at a **gas station.** *pl* **gas·es. –gas′e·ous,** *adj.*
gas up, fill the tank of a motor vehicle with gasoline: *Be sure to gas up before going on a trip.*
step on the gas, 1 push down the accelerator, or **gas pedal,** in a motor vehicle to make it go faster. **2** hurry.

gash (gash) *n* a long, deep cut.

gasp (gasp) *n* a sudden, short breath taken in through the mouth: *After her hard run, her breath came in gasps.*

gate (gāt) *n* a door in a fence or outside wall: *Close the gate so the dog can't get out.*

gate·way 1 *n* an opening in a wall or fence with a gate across it. **2** *n* a way in or out: *Winnipeg is known as the "Gateway to the West."*

gath·er (gaᴛн′ər) **1** *v* collect: *She gathered her books and papers and left for school. A crowd gathered at the scene of the accident.* **2** *v* figure out: *I gathered from his tone of voice that he was very upset.*

gath·er·ing *n* a meeting: *A gathering of friends welcomed the family's newly adopted son.*

gauge (gāj) *n* an instrument for measuring and showing how much: *Every car has a fuel gauge.*

gaunt (gont) *adj* very thin and bony.

gawk (gok) **1** *v Informal.* stare rudely or stupidly: *The tourist stood gawking at the strange sights.* **2** *n* an awkward person; clumsy fool. **–gawk′y,** *adj.*

gaze (gāz) *v* look long and steadily: *For hours the dog sat gazing at the fire.* **gazed, gaz·ing.**

gear (gēr) **1** *n* a wheel with teeth that fit into teeth on another wheel. Gears turn other gears by their teeth as part of a machine.
2 *n* equipment needed for some purpose: *Justin took his fishing gear on the trip to Lobster Lake.*
gear up, 1 shift to a higher gear. **2** get ready to start something: *Saskatoon is gearing up for the fall fair.* **Gear down** means the opposite.
in gear, 1 connected to the motor. **2** working; active: *Her brain is always in gear.* **Out of gear** means the opposite.

gel (jel) *n* a very thick liquid. One kind of perfumed gel is used instead of soap in baths and showers, and another kind is used to style hair. Other gels have other uses.

gem (jem) *n* a precious stone that has been cut and polished; jewel. Diamonds are gems.

gen·der (jen′dər) **1** *n* the fact of being male or female. **2** *n* in many languages, the grouping of nouns into classes such as masculine, feminine, neuter. In English, the marking of gender has mostly disappeared except in pronouns (*he, she, it*), but in French every noun is masculine or feminine. This sense of gender does not necessarily have anything to do with male or female sex.

gene (jēn) *n* in a plant or animal cell, a tiny part that determines what the plant or animal will be like and how it will develop. Genes inherited from your parents determine the colour of your hair, your body shape, and so on.

ge·net·ics (jə net′iks) *n* the study of how the genes in living things pass on characteristics from one generation to another.

gen·er·al (jen′ə rəl) **1** *adj* having to do with all the people or things in a certain group. A **general election** involves all voters. A **general store** sells all kinds of things. **2** *adj* not detailed; rough: *a general idea; a general description.* **3** *n* the highest officer in an army. **4** *adj* chief: *The Attorney General is the chief law officer of Canada.* –**gen′er·al·ly,** *adv.*

gen·er·al·ize 1 *v* say something that is supposed to be true about all the people or things in a certain group: *When Kate said "Kids like to eat," she was generalizing.* **2** *v* talk vaguely, without giving details. –**gen′er·al·i·za′tion,** *n.*

gen·er·ate (jen′ə rāt′) *v* make or produce: *Boiling water generates steam. The steam can generate electricity by turning an electric generator.* **gen·er·at·ed, gen·er·at·ing.** –**gen′er·a′tor,** *n.*

gen·er·a·tion *n* the people or animals born in the same period: *Your parents belong to one generation; you belong to the next generation.*

ge·ner·ic *adj* having to do with something that belongs to a group, rather than something that is special. A generic pair of jeans is an ordinary pair with no special designer name.

gen·er·ous (jen′ə rəs) *adj* glad to share with others: *a generous boy.* –**gen′er·os′i·ty,** *n.*

gen·ius (jēn′əs) *n* a person who is extremely brilliant or talented. *pl* **ge·ni·us·es.**

gen·tle (jen′təl) *adj* light; kind; polite: *a gentle tap, a gentle breeze, a gentle slope, a gentle heart, gentle manners.* **gen·tler, gen·tlest.** –**gen′tle·ness,** *n,* –**gent′ly,** *adv.*

gen·tle·man *n* a man who is polite and considerate of others.

gen·u·ine (jen′yū ən) *adj* real; true: *genuine leather, a genuine diamond, genuine sorrow.*

ge·nus (jēn′yəs) *n* one of the groups into which scientists classify living things. A genus is smaller than a family and larger than a species.

In the two-word scientific name of a plant or animal, the first word is the genus. *Example: Homo* in *Homo sapiens. pl* **gen·er·a** (jen′ə rə).

ge·og·ra·phy (jē og′rə fē) *n* the study of the earth's surface, climate, continents, countries, peoples, industries, and products. –**ge′o·graph′i·cal** (jē′ə graf′ə kəl), *adj.*

WORD HISTORY .... geography

The word **geography** comes from the Greek words *ge* "earth" + *graphein* "describe." Similarly, **geology** is the science of the earth's crust. The word **geometry** originally referred to measuring the earth and its natural features, like mountains. Later, geometry came to mean the complete study of shapes and solids, not just their measurement.

---

ge·ol·o·gy (jē ol′ə jē) *n* the science that deals with the earth's crust, the rocks and minerals that make up its different layers, and their history. –**ge′o·log′i·cal** (jē′ə loj′ə kəl), *adj.*

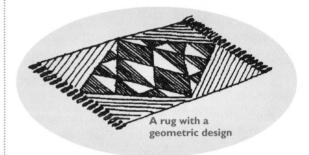
A rug with a geometric design

ge·om·e·try (jē om′ə trē) *n* the part of mathematics that measures and compares lines, angles, surfaces, and solids. –**ge′o·met′ric** (jē′ə met′rik) or **ge′o·met′ri·cal,** *adj.*

ger·bil (jər′bəl) *n* a small animal closely related to the mouse and rat, with long hind legs. Gerbils are often kept as pets.

germ (jərm) **1** *n* a very tiny living thing that causes disease. Bacteria and viruses are germs. Germs are too small to be seen without a microscope. **2** *n* a seed or bud.

ger·mi·nate *v* begin to grow: *In the spring, seeds germinate in the warm soil.* –**ger′mi·na′tion,** *n.*

ges·ture (jes′chər) **1** *n* a movement of the hands or any part of the body, used to show an idea or a feeling: *She shook her fist and made other angry gestures at us.* **2** *v* make gestures. **ges·tured, ges·tur·ing.**

get (get) **1** *v* come to have: *I got a new hockey stick yesterday.* **2** *v* go and bring back: *Get my glasses, please.* **3** *v* become: *It is getting colder.* **4** *v* cause to be, to happen, or to do: *I can't get the door open. She got her hair cut. Try to get him to come.* **5** *v* arrive: *I got to Whitehorse early last night.* **6** *v* understand: *I don't get it.* **got, got** or **got·ten, get·ting.**

get along, be on good terms: *He doesn't get along with his classmates.*

get around to, find time for: *I want to read that book but I never seem to get around to it.*

get away with, do something and not get punished: *He thought he could get away with being late, but he was caught.*

get back at, hurt someone who has hurt you. **Get even with** means the same.

get down to, start: *It's time to get down to work.*

get on, be on good terms: *My sister and I don't get on.*

get out, become known: *It didn't take long for the secret to get out.*

get over, recover from: *Michael was a long time getting over the measles.*

get through, communicate: *No one can get through to her when she's angry.*

get to, 1 annoy; upset: *Don't let it get to you.* **2** make an impression on: *What really got to me was how kind they all were.*

USING WORDS ...... got

The words **got** and **gotten** can both be used as past participles of the verb **get**: *I wish had gotten the card in time for her birthday. I've got her present wrapped.*

Sometimes, you should try to use different wording instead of **got**. For example: *I wish she had gotten the card in time for her birthday. I've wrapped her present.*

---

gey·ser (gī′zər) *n* a spring that sends up fountains or jets of hot water and steam every now and then.

Gham·bar (gum′bȧr) *n* any of the six yearly festivals of the Zoroastrian religion which celebrate different parts of creation, such as earth, water, plants, and so on. Each Ghambar lasts about five or six days.

ghast·ly (gast′lē) *adj* horrible. **ghast·li·er, ghast·li·est.**

gher·kin (gėr′kən) *n* a small, prickly kind of cucumber often used for pickles.

ghet·to (get′ō) *n* a part of a city where people live who share some characteristic, such as being poor or speaking a certain language. *pl* **ghet·tos.**

ghost (gōst) *n* the spirit of a dead person. A ghost is supposed to live in another world and appear to living people as a pale, shadowy form. –**ghost′ly,** *adj.*

ghost town a town that has been deserted by all the people who used to live there: *When the gold rush was over, Richfield became a ghost town.*

gi·ant (jī′ənt) **1** *n* a huge person. Giants are imaginary. **2** *adj* huge: *a giant potato.*

gi·gan·tic (jī gan′tik) *adj* huge; enormous: *a gigantic dinosaur.*

gib·ber·ish (jib′ər ish) *n* something said or written that is so mixed up you can't make sense of it.

gid·dy (gid′ē) *adj* dizzy: *It makes me giddy to go on a roller coaster.* **gid·di·er, gid·di·est.**

gift (gift) **1** *n* something given: *a birthday gift.* **2** *n* a natural talent: *a gift for painting.*

gift·ed *adj* having special ability: *The class president is a gifted leader and was easily elected.*

giga– *an SI prefix meaning* one billion; 1 000 000 000. A *gigametre* is one billion metres.

gig·a·byte (gig′ə bīt *or* jig′ə bīt) one billion bytes of computer memory.

gig·gle (gig′əl) **1** *v* laugh in a silly or nervous way. **2** *n* a silly or nervous laugh. **gig·gled, gig·gling.** –**gig′gly,** *adj.*

gill (gil) *n* one of the breathing organs of some animals that live under water: *Fish, tadpoles, and crabs have gills.*

gim·mick (gim′ik) *n* a trick or clever idea that attracts attention: *The team's latest gimmick was to include a set of miniature plastic players with every season ticket it sold.*

gin·ger (jin′jər) *n* the root of a tropical Asian plant. It is used as a spice, either fresh or dried and powdered. **Ginger ale** is a soft drink, **gingerbread** is a sort of cake or thick cookie, and a **gingersnap** is a thin, crisp cookie.

gi·raffe (jə raf′) *n* a large African animal with a very long neck and legs and a spotted skin: *Giraffes are the tallest living animals.*

gird·er (gėr′dər) *n* a main supporting beam: *Steel girders are often used to make the framework of bridges and tall buildings.*

girl (gərl) *n* a female child. –**girl′hood′**, *n*, –**girl′ish**, *adj.*

girth (gərth) *n* the measure around anything: *the girth of a tree.*

gist (jist) *n* the main idea: *The gist of the argument was clear.*

give (giv) **1** *v* let someone have, especially as a present: *Jeff likes to give baseball cards to his friends.* **2** *v* hand over: *Give me that pencil.* **3** *v* make a sound or movement: *She gave a loud shout.* **4** *v* move, stretch, break, or bend when force is applied: *The lock gave when we pushed hard against the door.* **gave, giv·en, giv·ing.** –**giv′er**, *n.*
giv·en *adj* stated: *You must finish the test in a given time.* **given name** a person's first name: *Mordecai is the given name of Mordecai Richler.* **give away,** let something be known: *His face gave away his true feelings. Don't give away our secret!* **give in,** let someone have his or her way in the end: *They kept asking their mother until she gave in.* **give or take,** approximately, within a certain amount: *It's six o'clock, give or take a few minutes.* **give up,** stop doing or trying: *to give up smoking. He tried hard to learn tennis but he finally gave up.*

giz·mo (giz′mō) *n* any small thing you can't remember the name of.

gla·cier (glā′shər) *n* a very large mass of ice formed on land from snow. Glaciers move very slowly, often down mountainsides or along valleys. –**gla′cial**, *adj.*

glad (glad) **1** *adj* happy; joyful: *I'm glad you could come to our school play.* **2** *adj* very willing: *I'd be glad to help.* **glad·der, glad·dest.** –**glad′den**, *v*, –**glad′ly**, *adv*, –**glad′ness**, *n.*

glam·our (glam′ər) *n* charm: *the glamour of being a movie star.* Another spelling is **glamor**. –**glam′or·ize**, *v*, –**glam′or·ous**, *adj.*

glance (glans) **1** *v* look quickly: *I glanced at the clock.* **2** *n* a quick look. **glanced, glanc·ing.**

gland (gland) *n* an animal or plant organ that makes and gives out some substance: *There are sweat glands in your skin. A cow has glands that make milk. Glands in flowers produce perfume.*

glare (gler) **1** *n* a strong light that hurts your eyes: *The glare from the snow blinded us.* **2** *v* stare fiercely and with anger: *She glared at her disobedient son.* **glared, glar·ing.**

🍁 **glare ice** ice that has a smooth, glossy surface.
glar·ing (gler′ing) *adj* bad and very obvious: *The writer made a glaring spelling mistake.*

glass (glas) **1** *n* a substance that can usually be seen through and breaks easily. **2** *n* a small container to drink out of, made of glass or other material. **3 glasses,** *pl.n* eyeglasses; a pair of lenses in a frame, worn over the eyes to help them see properly. –**glass′ful′**, *n*, –**glass′y**, *adj.*

gleam (glēm) **1** *n* a flash of light: *We saw the gleam of headlights through the rain.* **2** *v* shine.

glee (glē) *n* merriment: *The children laughed with glee.* –**glee′ful**, *adj.*

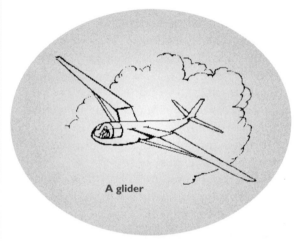

A glider

glide (glīd) **1** *v* move along smoothly, evenly, and easily: *The canoe glided through the still water of Lake Rossignol.* **2** *n* a smooth, even, easy movement. **glid·ed, glid·ing.**
glid·er *n* an airplane with long wings and no engine. Rising air currents keep it up.

glim·mer (glim′ər) *n* a faint, unsteady light.
glimpse (glimps) **1** *n* a very quick view: *I got a glimpse of Alexandra Falls as our plane flew over.* **2** *v* get a quick view of.

glint (glint) *n* or *v* gleam or flash: *the glint of a sword blade* (*n*). *The cat's eyes glinted in the light* (*v*).

glis·ten (glis′ən) *v* sparkle; shine with tiny points of reflected light: *The moonlight glistened on the snow.*

glitch (glich) a small problem that gets in the way of doing something well: *There were a few glitches at the start of our project.*

glit·ter (glit′ər) *v* sparkle; shine with a bright light reflected off something hard and smooth: *The jewel glittered in the sunlight.*

gloat (glōt) *v* gaze at or think about with a feeling of triumph or satisfaction: *Don't gloat over the other team's mistakes.*

globe (glōb) **1** *n* anything that is round like a ball. **2** *n* the earth; world.

glob·al *adj* worldwide: *Global drought would cause a great famine.* **glob·ule** *n* a very small ball: *Globules of sweat stood out on the sprinter's forehead.* This word is often shortened to **glob.**

gloom (glüm) **1** *n* dim light: *He could hardly see in the gloom.* **2** *n* dark thoughts; sadness: *She sat there, lost in gloom.* –**gloom'y,** *adj.*

Gloo·scap (glü'skap) *n* a trickster who appears often in the myths of certain First Nations such as the Micmacs.

glo·ry (glôr'ē) **1** *n* great praise and honour: *Sir Frederick Banting's discovery of insulin brought him glory.* **2** *n* beauty and greatness: *We were amazed by the glory of the northern lights.* *pl* **glo·ries.** –**glo'ri·fy,** *v,* –**glo'ri·ous,** *adj.*

gloss (glos) *n* a smooth, shiny surface: *This enamel paint will give the wood trim a high gloss.* –**gloss'y,** *adj.*

glos·sa·ry (glos'ə rē) *n* a list of unusual or difficult words with explanations. *pl* **glos·sa·ries.**

> **Grammar** ✓*Check* . . . . **glossary**
>
> Giving a **glossary** is a way of explaining special or technical words without interrupting the flow of a piece of writing. Look in a math or science textbook for an example of a glossary.

glove (gluv) *n* a covering for the hand with separate places for each of the four fingers and the thumb.

glow (glō) **1** *n* the shine from something that is red-hot or white-hot: *The glow from the burning coals gave a little light to the room.* **2** *v* shine softly or with heat: *A jack-o'-lantern glowed in the window.*

glu·cose (glü'kōs) *n* a form of natural sugar found in fruit and other substances.

glue (glü) **1** *n* a liquid used to stick things together. It hardens when dry. **2** *v* stick with glue. **glued, glu·ing.** –**glue'y,** *adj.*

glum (glum) *adj* gloomy; downhearted: *a glum look.* **glum·mer, glum·mest.**

glut·ton (glut'ən) *n* a greedy person; a person who eats too much. –**glut'ton·y,** *n.*

gnash (nash) *v* strike or grind the teeth together: *The ogres gnashed their teeth in rage.*

gnat (nat) *n* a small, annoying fly.

gnaw (no) *v* wear away by biting: *A mouse has gnawed right through the oatmeal box.*

gnome (nōm) *n* in folk tales, a dwarf that lives in the earth and guards treasure.

go (gō) **1** *v* move, especially from one place to another: *James went to Labrador. The wheels go around.* **2** *v* leave: *Don't go yet.* **3** *v* work; run: *How do you make this thing go?* **4** *v* turn out; have a certain result: *How did the game go?* **5** *v* belong, match, or fit: *Those socks don't go with your pants. Where does this piece go?* **went, gone, go·ing.**

from the word "go," from the very beginning.

go all out, make the greatest possible effort: *They went all out to make Gina's birthday a happy one.*

go for it, *Informal.* give it your best effort.

go into, discuss: *Let's not go into that now.*

go it alone, act by yourself.

go through with, carry out to the end: *She disliked the job so much that she refused to go through with it.*

on the go, *Informal.* being worked on: *I already have two projects on the go.*

to go, to take out from a restaurant: *a hamburger to go.*

goal (gōl) **1** *n* in certain games, the space between two posts that you aim a puck or ball into. **2** *n* the action of scoring in this way, or the points earned by doing it: *to score a goal. There were two goals by Gretzky.* **3** *n* something you are aiming for or working toward: *His goal was to be a dancer.*

goal·ie *n* the player who guards the goal to keep the other team from scoring. A more formal word is **goalkeeper** or **goaltender.**

goat (gōt) *n* an animal with horns that curve backward. Goats are related to sheep but are stronger, less timid, and more active.

get someone's goat, *Informal.* make a person angry or annoyed.

gob·ble (gob'əl) **1** *v* eat fast and greedily. **2** *n* the noise a turkey makes. A male turkey is called a **gobbler. gob·bled, gob·bling.**

gob·lin (gob′lən) *n* in stories, a mischievous, ugly creature.

god (god) *n* a being that is worshipped; a being that people believe is greater and more powerful than any human. –**god′like′**, *adj.*

god·dess *n* a female god.

gog·gles (gog′əlz) *pl.n* a pair of large, close-fitting spectacles for protecting the eyes: *She wore safety goggles while she was welding.*

gold (gōld) **1** *n* a heavy, soft, yellow precious metal. **2** *n* a bright, beautiful, or precious thing or material: *Wheat is prairie gold.* Oil is often called **black gold.** –**gold′en**, *adj.*

❧ **gold·eye** *n* a freshwater fish found in rivers and lakes from Ontario to the Northwest Territories. **gold·fish** *n* a small golden-orange fish kept in garden pools or indoor aquariums.

golf (golf) *n* an outdoor game played by hitting a **golfball** with different clubs. –**golf′er**, *n.*

gon·do·la (gon′də lə) **1** *n* a long, narrow boat with a high peak at each end, used on the canals of Venice. The person operating it is a **gondolier** (gon′də lēr′). **2** *n* a sort of box that hangs under a hot air balloon. **3** ❧ *n* a broadcasting booth near the roof of a hockey arena.

gong (gong) *n* a piece of metal shaped like a disk or saucer, which makes a loud noise when you hit it.

good (gůd) **1** *adj* doing what is right: *a good boy, good deeds.* **2** *adj* well done: *a good piece of work.* **3** *adj* suitable: *Fresh air is good for the body.* **4** *adj* enjoyable: *Have a good time.* **5** *adj* skilled: *a good skater, good at math.* **bet·ter, best.** –**good′ness**, *n.*

Grammar ✓*Check* . . . . . **good**

Need a good way to remember how to use the words **good** and **well** correctly? Try this.

- The word **good** is an adjective, so it always has a noun to describe: *a good way.*
- The word **well** is an adverb, so it always has a verb to describe: *You write well.*

So, using **good** and **well** correctly is *a good way to write well!*

---

good·bye or **good-bye** (gůd′bī′) *n* farewell; what people say when they leave.

good-for-noth·ing *adj* worthless; useless.

good-look·ing *adj* handsome; attractive.

goods *pl.n* things that can be owned, bought, or sold: *Mr. Taylor left all his goods to his children.*

good·y *n Informal.* something very good to eat: *There were lots of goodies at the party.*

as good as, almost: *The day is as good as over.*

for good, forever; finally; permanently: *They have left Canada for good.*

Canada geese—
about 85 cm long
including the tail

goose (gūs) *n* a domestic or wild water bird larger than a duck. A male goose is a **gander.** A young goose is a **gosling.** *pl* **geese.**

go·pher (gō′fər) *n* a small furry animal of the prairies that lives mostly underground.

gorge (gòrj) **1** *n* a deep, narrow valley. **2** *v* eat too much at once: *They gorged themselves on pizza.* **gorged, gorg·ing.**

gor·geous *adj* very beautiful.

go·ril·la (gə ril′ə) *n* the largest and most powerful ape.

gor·y (gò′rē) *adj* bloody; full of bloodshed. **gor·i·er, gor·i·est.**

gos·sip (gos′ip) *n or v* talk about other people and their personal lives: *Gossip is often hurtful and untrue (n).* *They gossiped on the phone for hours (v).* **gos·siped, gos·sip·ing.** –**gos′sip·y**, *adj.*

gouge (gouj) **1** *n* a deep scratch: *There was a long gouge in the desktop.* **2** *v* charge an unfairly high price: *They gouged us $40 for a plate of spaghetti.* **gouged, goug·ing.**

gourd (gūrd *or* gòrd) *n* the squashlike fruit of a vine. Its hard, dried shell is used as a container in some cultures.

gov·ern (guv′ərn) *v* rule; control; manage: *Govern your temper. The premier and his or her cabinet govern the province.* –**gov′ern·ment**, *n,* –**gov′er·nor**, *n.*

Governor General in Canada, the representative of the Queen or King.

gown (goun) **1** *n* a woman's long dress. **2** *n* a loose outer garment worn as a symbol of someone's position: *Students graduating from university wear gowns.*

grab (grab) *v* take quickly and roughly: *The dog grabbed the meat and ran.* **grabbed, grab·bing.**

grace (grās) **1** *n* beauty of movement: *He skated with great skill and grace.* **2** *n* an extra allowance of time: *The library gave him two days' grace to return the book.* **graced, grac·ing.**
grace·ful *adj* beautiful, elegant, or tasteful: *a graceful birch tree, a graceful dance.*
–grace′ful·ly, *adv.* **gra·cious** (grā′shəs) *adj* very polite and thoughtful; generous: *a gracious host, a gracious offer.*

grade (grād) **1** *n* one of the divisions of a school program: *Most children enter grade one when they are six.* **2** *n* a number or letter that shows how well a student has done: *Her grade in Music is B.* **3** *v* give a grade to; mark: *The teacher graded the papers. Eggs are graded by size.* **4** *n* the slope of a hill: *The car had trouble getting up the steep grade.* **grad·ed, grad·ing. –grad′er,** *n.*
grad·u·al (graj′ū əl) *adj* changing little by little: *a gradual increase in sound, a gradual slope.*
–grad′u·al·ly, *adv.* **grad·u·ate 1** *v* finish school and receive a diploma: *Marya graduated from Simon Fraser University last year.* The ceremony where this happens is called a **graduation. 2** *n* a person who has graduated. **3** *v* mark out in equal spaces: *My ruler is graduated in centimetres.* **grad·u·at·ed, grad·u·at·ing.**

graf·fi·ti (grə fē′tē) *n* words and pictures that are written, drawn, or sprayed on a wall or other surface and are meant to be rude, funny, or clever: *One wall was covered with graffiti.*

grain (grān) **1** *n* a plant like wheat, oats, or corn. The seeds of these plants are used as food and may be stored in a tall building called a **grain elevator. 2** *n* a tiny hard bit of something like sand, sugar, or salt: *A few grains of sugar lay on the table.* **–grain′y,** *adj.*

gram (gram) *n* a metric unit of mass. There are one thousand grams in a kilogram. *Symbol:* g

gram·mar (gram′ər) *n* the correct use of words according to the rules of a language: *Good grammar is important in formal writing.*
–gram·mat′i·cal, *adj.* ▶See the *Grammar and Usage Mini-Guide.*

gran·a·ry (gran′ə rē *or* grā′nə rē) *n* a place or building where grain is stored. *pl* **gran·a·ries.**

grand (grand) **1** *adj* big and impressive: *grand mountains, a very grand palace.* **2** *adj* great and noble: *grand deeds.*
Grand Banks a shallow part, or shoal, of the ocean lying southeast of Newfoundland: *The Grand Banks are famous as a fishing ground.*
grand·child *n* the child of a person's son or daughter; a **granddaughter** or **grandson.** *pl* **grand·chil·dren.**
gran·deur (gran′jər *or* grand′yər) *n* greatness: *The grandeur of Niagara Falls is famous.*
grand·fa·ther *n* the father of a person's father or mother. Some people call their grandfathers **grandad, grandpa,** or **grampa.**
grand·moth·er *n* the mother of a person's mother or father. Some people call their grandmothers **grandma, gramma,** or **granny.**
grand·par·ent *n* a grandfather or grandmother.
gra·no·la (grə nō′lə) *n* a cereal made from mixed grains, nuts, and seeds.

grant (grant) *v* say yes to: *to grant three wishes.*

grape (grāp) *n* a small, round fruit that grows in bunches on a vine. Grapes can be red, purple, dark blue, or pale green and are eaten fresh or dried and made into raisins.
grape·fruit *n* a large, pale yellow, juicy, sour fruit, related to oranges and lemons.

graph (graf) *n* a chart or diagram that uses lines, bars, sections of a circle, or rows of little pictures to stand for different amounts: *This graph shows how your height has changed each year.*
graph·ic 1 *adj* using words to make a clear image: *The reporter from the* Brantford Expositor *gave a graphic account of the fire.* **2** *adj* having to do with drawing, painting, design, etc.: *Milos is studying the graphic arts.* **3 graphics,** *n* printed pictures, graphs, and other things that are not words: *This computer game has great graphics.*

WORD HISTORY .... **graph**

Graph comes from the Greek *graphein,* meaning "draw" or "write." You can see this same word in **cardiograph** (heartbeat writing), **calligraphy** (beautiful writing), **geography** (writing about the earth), **photograph** (drawing done by light), **telegraph** (far writing).

grasp (grasp) **1** *v* take hold of tightly with your hand: *He grasped the railing to keep from falling.* **2** *v* understand: *to grasp the meaning of the word.* **grasp·ing** *adj* greedy.

grass (gras) *n* any plant that has jointed stems and long, narrow leaves: *Wheat, corn, oats, rice, and sugar cane are grasses. Horses, cows, and sheep eat grass.* –**grass′y**, *adj.*

grass·land *n* land that is mainly covered with grass and has few trees on it. Prairies are grasslands.

grate (grāt) **1** *n* a framework of iron bars for building a fire. **2** *v* rub against a rough surface: *to grate cheese.* **grat·ed, grat·ing.** –**grat′er**, *n.*

grate·ful (grāt′fəl) *adj* thankful; full of deep appreciation: *They were grateful for our help.* –**grate′ful·ly**, *adv*, –**grat′i·tude**, *n.*

grave (grāv) **1** *n* a place to bury a dead body. **2** *adj* serious: *grave danger, a grave decision.* **grav·er, grav·est.** –**grave′ly**, *adv.* **grave·yard** *n* a cemetery.

grav·el (grav′əl) **1** *n* small pieces of rock. Gravel is often used for roads and driveways. **2** *v* lay or cover with gravel. **grav·elled** or **grav·eled, grav·el·ling** or **grav·el·ing.**

grav·i·ty (grav′ə tē) **1** *n* the natural force that causes objects to move or tend to move toward the centre of the earth, moon, planet, etc. **2** *n* the natural force that makes heavenly bodies tend to move toward or around each other. **3** *n* heaviness; weight. **Zero gravity** means weightlessness. **4** *n* seriousness: *She soon realized the gravity of the situation.* *pl* **grav·i·ties.**

gra·vy (grā′vē) *n* a sauce made from the juices that come out of meat or vegetables in cooking.

graze (grāz) **1** *v* feed on growing grass: *Cattle were grazing in the field.* **2** *v* scrape: *The snowball grazed the top of the fence. I fell and grazed my knee.* **grazed, graz·ing.**

grease (grēs) **1** *n* animal fat that has been melted: *bacon grease.* **2** *n* any thick, slippery substance. **3** *v* put grease on: *to grease an engine. Grease the pan before putting in the dough.* **greased, greas·ing.** –**greas′y**, *adj.*

great (grāt) **1** *adj* big: *a great house, a great crowd.* **2** *adj* important: *a great singer, a great event, a great picture.* **3** *adj Informal.* very good: *This is great soup!* –**great′ly**, *adv*, –**great′ness**, *n.*

Great Divide in Canada, the high ridge of land extending northwest along the Rocky Mountains, from which rivers flow west to the Pacific Ocean or east and north to Hudson Bay and the Arctic Ocean. It is also called the **Continental Divide**.

great-grand·child *n* the son or daughter of a person's grandchild. **great-grand·par·ent** *n* the father or mother of a grandparent. **Great Lakes** the five large bodies of fresh water that are included in the St. Lawrence Seaway; Lakes Superior, Michigan, Huron, Erie, and Ontario.

greed (grēd) *n* a desire to get more, or to get a lot in a hurry. –**greed′i·ly**, *adv*, –**greed′y**, *adj.*

green (grēn) **1** *n* the colour of the leaves of most growing plants in summer. **2** *adj* not ripe: *These cherries are still green.* **3** *adj* not experienced. **4** *adj* not harming the environment: *green products, a green company.* –**green′ish**, *adj.*

green·horn *n Informal.* a person without experience. **green·house** *n* a building with a glass roof and glass sides, kept warm for growing plants. It is also called a **hothouse.**

greenhouse effect the gradual warming of the air around the earth, mostly because of the water vapour and gases caused by pollution. This warming changes the weather patterns.

greet (grēt) *v* say or do something when you meet a person: *Mom greeted me with a kiss.*

greet·ing 1 *n* a welcome. **2 greetings**, *pl.n* friendly wishes on a special occasion: *birthday greetings.*

grey (grā) **1** *n* or *adj* any shade that is a mix of black and white. **2** *adj* dark; gloomy: *a grey day.* **3** *v* make or become grey: *greying hair.* –**grey′ish**, *adj.*

grey jay another name for the **Canada jay**, a North American bird with black and grey feathers.

grid (grid) *n* a system of lines or bars crisscrossing at right angles. The lines of latitude and longitude form a grid. So do the main streets of some cities.

grief (grēf) *n* very great sadness, usually because of losing someone or something very precious: *Emilio sobbed with grief when his puppy died.* –**grieve**, *v.*

grill (gril) *n* a framework of metal bars for barbecuing food on.

grim (grim) *adj* stern and harsh: *grim, stormy weather, a grim expression.* **grim·mer, grim·mest.**

gri·mace (grim′is) *n* a twisting of the face in fear, pain, or disgust: *a grimace caused by pain.*

grime (grīm) *n* dirt rubbed deeply in: *the grime on a coal miner's hands.* –**grim′y,** *adj.*

grin (grin) **1** *v* smile broadly. **2** *n* a broad smile. **grinned, grin·ning.**
grin and bear it, suffer without complaining.

grind (grīnd) **1** *v* crush into bits: *That mill grinds coffee beans.* **2** *v* rub harshly together: *to grind your teeth.* **3** *n Informal.* long, hard, dull work: *To some of us, gardening is a grind.* **ground, grinding.** –**grind′er,** *n.*

grip (grip) **1** *n* a firm hold. **2** *v* hold tightly: *The dog gripped the stick in its teeth.* **gripped, grip·ping.**

gripe (grīp) *v Informal.* complain: *They're always griping about something.* **griped, grip·ing.**

gris·ly (griz′lē) *adj* frightful; horrible: *a grisly accident.* **gris·li·er, gris·li·est.**

grit (grit) **1** *n* very fine bits of sand: *There was grit in the spinach.* **2** *n* toughness and courage: *The firefighter showed lots of grit.* **grit·ted, grit·ting.** –**grit′ty,** *adj.*

griz·zly (griz′lē) *n* short for **grizzly bear,** a large, fierce brown bear of western North America. *pl* **griz·zlies.**

groan (grōn) **1** *n* a sound made to express grief, pain, or disapproval: *We heard the groans of the wounded soldiers.* **2** *v* give a groan.

gro·cer·y (grō′sə rē) **1** **groceries,** *pl.n* food and household supplies bought in a store. **2** *adj* having to do with food and household supplies: *our grocery bill, a grocery store.* *pl* **gro·cer·ies.**

grog·gy (grog′ē) *adj* wobbly on your feet and unable to think clearly: *After the operation he awoke still groggy from the anesthetic.*

groom (grūm) **1** *n* short for **bridegroom,** a man about to get married or just married. **2** *v* take care of your personal appearance or of an animal's appearance: *Our dog hates to have his fur groomed.* **3** *n* a person who feeds and takes care of horses.

groove (grūv) *n* a line that has been cut evenly into a surface: *These cupboard doors open and close by sliding in a groove at the top and bottom.*

grope (grōp) *v* feel around with your hands: *He groped for a flashlight when the lights went out.* **groped, grop·ing.**

gross (grōs) **1** *adj* disgusting; vulgar: *Her manners are gross.* **2** *adj* very bad and very obvious: *gross misconduct.* **3** *n* twelve dozen; 144. *pl* **gross.**

gro·tesque (grō tesk′) *adj* so weird or unnatural that it is ugly or even a bit frightening: *The book was full of pictures of grotesque imaginary creatures.*

grouch (grouch) *Informal.* **1** *v* a sulky, crabby person: *Why must you be such a grouch?* **2** *n* be sulky or crabby; complain. –**grouch′y,** *adj.*

A groundhog—
about 50 cm long
excluding the tail

ground (ground) **1** *n* the solid surface of the earth: *Snow covered the ground.* **2** *n* any piece of land used for some purpose: *The Yukon was their favourite hunting ground.* **3** *v* prevent an activity: *The planes were grounded by the fog. I was grounded for a month after I stayed out too late.*
ground·hog *n* a small North American burrowing animal that hibernates; woodchuck. On **Groundhog Day,** February 2, the groundhog is supposed to come out of its hole to see if the sun is shining. If the sun is shining, the groundhog sees its shadow and returns to its hole for six more weeks of winter.
get off the ground, make a successful start.
stand your ground, keep your position; refuse to give in or back down.

group (grūp) **1** *n* a number of people or things together: *A group of children were playing tag.* **2** *v* form into a group or into groups: *to group books by subject. On playday, younger students were grouped with older ones for each team.*

grouse (grous) *Informal.* **1** *v* grumble; complain. **2** *n* complaint. **3** *n* a person who complains; grumbler. **groused, grous·ing.**

G **g**

grow (grō) **1** *v* get bigger: *Her business has grown fast.* **2** *v* live: *Few trees grow in the desert.* **3** *v* plant and care for: *We grow wheat in many parts of Canada.* **4** *v* get naturally as a part of itself: *If this lizard loses its tail it can grow a new one.* **5** *v* become: *It grew cold.* **grew, grown, grow·ing.** –**growth,** *n.*
grow on someone, become more and more likable or comfortable for someone: *I didn't like the cat at first, but it started to grow on me.*

growl (groul) *n* low rumbling like the sound that a dog makes in its throat as a warning.

grub (grub) **1** *n* a smooth, thick, wormlike larva of an insect, especially of a beetle. **2** *n Slang.* food.

grudge (gruj) *n* an angry feeling held against someone for a long time: *George carried a grudge against me because I won the game.*
grudg·ing·ly *adv* unwillingly.

gru·el·ling (grü′ə ling) *adj* very tiring; long and difficult: *a gruelling cross-country race.*

grue·some (grü′səm) *adj* causing fear or horror; horrible; frightful: *a gruesome sight.*

grum·ble (grum′bəl) *v* complain in a cranky way. **grum·bled, grum·bling.**

grump (grump) *n* a bad-tempered, crabby person. –**grump′y,** *adj.*

grun·gy (grun′jē) *adj* disgustingly dirty or messy: *grungy clothes.*

grunt (grunt) *n* the low, rough sound that a pig makes, or a sound like it.

guar·an·tee (ger′ən tē′) **1** *n* a promise to replace or repair something, or give the customer's money back, if the thing is not satisfactory. **2** *v* make this kind of promise. **guar·an·teed, guar·an·tee·ing.**

guard (gàrd) **1** *v* watch over: *The dog guards the house.* **2** *v* keep from escaping: *The soldiers guarded the prisoners day and night.* **3** *n* a person or group that guards.
guard·i·an 1 *n* someone who takes care of a person or thing. **2** *n* a person chosen by law to take care of someone who is young or who cannot take care of himself or herself: *After the boy's parents died, his aunt became his guardian.*
off guard, unready: *The pitcher was off guard when the ball was hit to him.*

guess (ges) **1** *v* have or give an opinion of something without being sure: *She guessed at the height of the tree.* **2** *n* an opinion: *My guess is that it will rain tomorrow.* **3** *v* think; believe; suppose: *I guess it's OK.*

guest (gest) *n* a visitor.

guide (gīd) **1** *v* show the way; lead: *The trapper guided the hunters.* **2** *n* a person or thing that shows the way: *Mountain climbers sometimes hire guides. Your feelings can be a poor guide for making decisions.* **guid·ed, guid·ing.** –**guid′ance,** *n.*
guide·line *n* a rule about the best way to do something: *When we started the job nobody gave us any guidelines.*

guile (gīl) *n* dishonesty; sly tricks. –**guile′less,** *adj.*

guilt (gilt) *n* the fact, state, or feeling of having done wrong: *The evidence proved his guilt. When she saw the result of her careless act, she was overwhelmed with guilt.* –**guilt′less,** *n,* –**guilt′y,** *adj.*

guinea pig (gin′ē pig′) **1** a small, short-eared, short-tailed animal kept as a pet and for scientific experiments. It is native to South America. **2** any person or thing used for an experiment or for testing something: *The school used our class as guinea pigs to test the new timetable.*

Spanish guitar

Electric guitar

gui·tar (gə tàr′) *n* a musical instrument that usually has six strings, played with the fingers or with a pick. A **bass guitar** has four strings. –**gui·tar′ist,** *n.*

gulf (gulf) *n* a large bay; part of an ocean or sea reaching far into the land: *The Gulf of St. Lawrence lies at the mouth of the St. Lawrence River, on the east coast of Canada.*

gulp (gulp) **1** *v* swallow quickly or greedily: *Don't gulp your milk.* **2** *n* a big, fast, or hard swallow.

gum (gum) **1** *n* a sticky juice of certain trees and plants. Gum is used to make glue, drugs, candy, and other things. **2** *n* a substance made of this, with sweetening and flavour, for chewing. It is also called **chewing gum. 3** Often, **gums,** *pl.n,* the flesh around the teeth.

gun (gun) **1** *n* a weapon with a metal tube for shooting bullets, shot, or cannonballs; a cannon, rifle, or pistol: *Cannons, rifles, and pistols are commonly called guns.* **2** *n* a hand-held device shaped like a gun, for applying something: *a glue gun. He used a spray gun to paint the car.*
gun·fire *n* the shooting of a gun or guns.
gun·pow·der *n* a powder that explodes with force when touched with fire or hammered. Gunpowder is used in cartridges, blasting, and fireworks.
gun the engine, accelerate.
jump the gun, start too early.

gur·dwa·ra (gŭr dwä′rə) *n* a Sikh place of worship. A gurdwara usually has a yellow flag with the symbol of Sikhism on it, a circle with two swords crossed under the bottom and one sword standing upright in the middle. This symbol is called the **Khanda** (kun′də).

gur·gle (gər′gəl) *v* make the sound of bubbling, flowing water: *The stream gurgled over the stones.* **gur·gled, gur·gling.**

gu·ru (gū′rū *or* gŭr′ū) **1** *n* a Hindu teacher. **2** *n* anyone that people trust to lead them or to give them expert advice: *a fitness guru.*
Guru Granth Sa·hib (gū′rū grunt′ sə hēb′) *n* the holy book of the Sikh religion, containing the teachings of the ten Sikh gurus or prophets. It is also called the **Adi Granth.**

gush (gush) **1** *v* pour or flow out in a sudden rush: *Water gushed from the broken pipe.* **2** *v* speak or write with a rush of enthusiasm.

gust (gust) *n* a sudden, strong blast of wind. –**gust′y,** *adj.*

gut (gut) **1 guts,** *pl.n Slang.* **a** intestines. **b** courage. **2** *n Slang.* the stomach or belly. **3** *v* remove or destroy the insides of: *They gutted the fish. The building was gutted by fire.* **gut·ted, gut·ting.** –**gut′less,** *adj,* –**gut′sy,** *adj.*

gut·ter (gut′ər) **1** *n* a ditch along the side of a street or road to carry off water; the low part of a street beside the sidewalk. **2** *n* eavestrough; a trough along the edge of a roof to carry away water.

guy (gī) *Slang.* **1** *n* a man or boy: *Most of the guys wore suits to the graduation.* **2** *n* a person.

guz·zle (guz′əl) *v* drink greedily; drink too much. **guz·zled, guz·zling.**

gym (jim) **1** *n* short for **gymnasium** (jim nā′zē əm), a building or large room equipped for indoor sports or exercise. **2** *n* physical education as a school subject: *Ms. Khan teaches us gym.*
gym·nas·tics *n* exercises for developing strength, flexibility, and balance.

WORD HISTORY . . . . gymnastics

Gymnastics comes from the Greek word *gymnos,* meaning "naked." In earlier times in Greece, physical exercises were for males only. The gymnasium was usually an outdoor area, covered in sand. The custom was to train naked.

Gyp·sy (jip′sē) *n* a person belonging to a wandering race of dark-skinned, dark-eyed people who came from India in the 1400s and 1500s. Their language is called **Romany.** *pl* **Gyp·sies.**

WORD HISTORY . . . . Gypsy

Gypsy was made from the word Egyptian. When the gypsies first went to England in the 1500s, they were thought to come from Egypt.

---

gy·rate (jī′rāt) *v* move in a circle or spiral; whirl; rotate: *A top gyrates.* **gy·rat·ed, gy·rat·ing.**

h or **H** (āch) *n* the eighth letter of the English alphabet, or the speech sound that it stands for. We hear the sound of *h* in *home* but not in *hour*. *pl* **h's** or **H's**.

h *symbol for* hour or hours.

ha (hȧ *or* ha) **1** *interj* a word shouted in surprise or triumph: *"Ha! We have won!" shouted the team.* **2** *interj* in writing, a way of indicating laughter: *"Ha! ha! ha!" laughed the boys.*

hab·it (hab′it) *n* a person's usual way of acting: *It is her habit to check her spelling before handing in her homework.* –**ha·bit′u·al** (hə bich′ū əl), *adj*.

hab·i·tat (hab′ə tat′) *n* the place where an animal or plant naturally lives or grows: *The arctic coast is the habitat of polar bears.*

✤ **hab·it·ant** (hab′ə tont′ *or* ab ē tȧn′) *n* a French-Canadian farmer, especially in earlier times.

hack (hak) **1** *v* cut roughly: *She hacked the crate apart with an old axe.* **2** give short, dry coughs: *Steve hacked all night.* **3** *Slang. v* handle; put up with: *I can hack anything for one day.* **4** *v* fool around on the computer using programming knowledge gained by experience.

hag·gard (hag′ərd) *adj* looking worn out from pain, tiredness, worry, hunger, etc.: *The haggard faces of the rescued sailors showed how much they had suffered after their ship sank.*

hai·ku (hī′kū) *n* a Japanese poem that has three lines. The first and last lines have five syllables, and the second line has seven.

hail (hāl) *n* tiny balls of ice that come down from the clouds: *Hail fell with such violence that it broke windows.* An individual piece of hail is a **hailstone**.

hair (her) **1** *n* a fine, threadlike growth from the skin. **2** *n* a mass of such growths, especially on a person's head: *Sara's hair is getting long.* –**hair′less**, *adj*, –**hair′y**, *adj*.

hair·dress·er *n* a person who cuts and styles people's hair. A **hairstylist** is the same thing.

hair·rais·ing *Informal. adj* so scary that it makes you feel as if your hair were standing on end: *a hair-raising story.*

split hairs, make a big deal out of differences that are too small to matter.

hajj (haj) *n* a journey to Mecca, the holy city of Islam, which all Muslims should make. **Haj** is another spelling.

ha·lal (ha lal′) *adj* permitted under Islamic religious law: *halal meat.* The opposite is **haram**.

half (haf) **1** *n* or *adj* one of two equal parts of something: *A half of 4 is 2. Two halves make a whole* (*n*). *A half litre is 500 mL* (*adj*). **2** *adv* partly: *half cooked, half asleep. pl* **halves**.

half brother a brother related through one parent only. **half-heart·ed** *adj* with little enthusiasm or interest; not serious: *a half-hearted attempt.* **half sister** a sister related through one parent only.

half·way *adj* or *adv* at or to half the total distance or time: *the halfway mark* (*adj*). *The rope reached only halfway to the boat* (*adv*). *Halfway through the concert Corbin lost his voice* (*adv*).

halve (hav) *v* divide into two equal parts or shares: *The two girls agreed to halve the pizza.*

half past, 30 minutes past the hour. *Half past six means 6:30.*

hall (hol) **1** *n* a narrow part in a building, with rooms opening off it: *The bathroom was at the end of a long hall.* **Hallway** is another word for this meaning. **2** *n* a large room for holding meetings, banquets, etc.: *Our town needs a bigger hall for wedding receptions.* **3** *n* a large public building serving some special purpose: *The Hockey Hall of Fame. The offices of the mayor and city councillors are in the city hall.*

Hal·low·een or **Hal·low·e'en** (hal′ə wēn′) *n* the evening of October 31, celebrated by dressing up in costumes.

WORD HISTORY .... Halloween

Halloween is short for *All Hallow Even.* The even (or evening) of October 31 is the evening before All Saint's Day (November 1). On this day, Christians honoured all the saints who had died: *hallow* is an old word for "saint."

ha·lo (hā′lō) **1** *n* in pictures, a golden circle of light shown over the head of a holy person or an angel. **2** *n* a ring of light around a shining body such as the sun or moon. *pl* **ha·los** or **ha·loes.**

halt (holt) *v* or *n* stop: *The joggers halted for a short rest (v). All work came to a halt (n).*

ham (ham) **1** *n* salted and smoked meat from the upper part of a pig's hind leg. **2** *n Informal.* an actor who performs in an exaggerated style, or someone who likes to clown in front of a camera.

ham·burg·er (ham′bər′gər) *n* ground beef shaped into a flat patty and fried or broiled, especially when served in a split bun. This word is sometimes shortened to **burger.**

ham·mer (ham′ər) *n* a tool with a heavy metal part set across the top of a long handle. It is used to drive nails and to beat metal into shape.

ham·per (ham′pər) **1** *v* get in the way of: *The cast on my arm hampered my efforts at getting dressed.* **2** *n* a large container, usually with a cover: *a picnic hamper, a clothes hamper.*

ham·ster (ham′stər) *n* a small, short-tailed animal of the rat family with large pouches in its cheeks, which it uses for carrying food. Hamsters can be kept as pets.

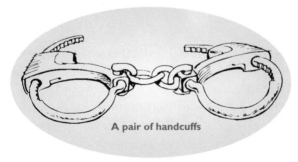

A pair of handcuffs

hand (hand) **1** *n* the end part of the arm below the wrist, including the fingers and thumb. **2** *n* anything like a hand: *The hands of a clock show the time.* **3** *n* a hired worker: *a farm hand, a factory hand.* **4** *v* give with the hand; pass: *Please hand me a spoon.*

hand·bag *n* a woman's purse, used to hold money, keys, and so on. **hand·book** *n* a small book of rules or instructions. **hand·cuff** *n* one of a pair of two steel bracelets joined by a chain that are fastened around the wrists of a prisoner. **hand·ful 1** *n* as much as the hand can hold: *a handful of candy.* **2** *n* a small number or

quantity: *Only a handful of students entered the talent contest.* **han·dle 1** *n* a part of a thing used to hold it or control it with your hand. A mug, a hairbrush, and a pair of pliers all have handles. **2** *v* touch, feel, or use with the hand: *Don't handle that until you buy it.* **han·dle·bars** *pl.n* the part of a bicycle, motorcycle, etc. that the rider holds to steer. **hand·made** *adj* made by hand, not machinery. **hand·shake** *n* the clasping and shaking of each other's hands by two people as a sign of friendship when meeting or parting, or to seal an agreement. **hand·some** (han′səm) *adj* good-looking: *a handsome baby boy.* **hand·writ·ing** *n* writing done by hand. **hand·y 1** *adj* easy to get at: *Keep these instructions handy.* **2** *adj* useful: *a handy tool.* **3** *adj* skilful with the hands: *She is handy with tools.*

give someone a hand, 1 help someone. **2** clap for someone.

hand down, pass along to someone younger: *Brandon's old clothes were handed down to his younger brother.*

hand in, give something to a person in charge: *Hand in your project now.*

hand out, give out: *The storekeeper handed out free flags on Canada Day.*

hand over, give up: *When Vito asked for his book, I handed it over.*

have your hands full, have as much to do as you can manage.

lend a hand, help.

on the one hand, on the other hand, considering each side of the question: *On the one hand, it's a great bike; on the other hand, I can't afford to buy it.*

hang (hang) *v* fasten or be fastened to swing freely: *The swing hangs from a tree.* **hung, hang·ing. hang·ar** (hang′ər) *n* a building for storing and working on aircraft. **hang·er** *n* anything used for hanging something up: *a coat hanger.*

get the hang of, *Informal.* learn how to do: *It took me a while to get the hang of walking on stilts.*

hang around, spend time, or spend time with: *He just hangs around the house all day. She hangs around with Judy a lot.*

hang back, hesitate.

hang in, keep going when things are tough: *He was tired, but hung in till the job was done.*

hang in there, often said to encourage someone.

hang on, 1 hold tight. **2** wait: *Hang on, I'm not quite ready.*

hang up, end a phone call.

Ha·nuk·kah (hȧ′nə kə) *n* an eight-day Jewish festival that falls in December, celebrating the defeat of the Greeks who had forbidden Jewish law and ritual in the land of Israel. **Chanukah** is another spelling.

hap·pen (hap′ən) *v* take place: *Nothing interesting happens here. Accidents will happen.* –**hap′pen·ing,** *n.*

hap·haz·ard (hap′haz′ərd) *adj* not organized: *If you do your homework in such a haphazard way, it will take longer.*

hap·py (hap′ē) *adj* feeling or showing pleasure: *a happy smile.* **hap·pi·er, hap·pi·est.** –**hap′pi·ly,** *adv,* –**hap′pi·ness,** *n.*

hap·py-go-luck·y *adj* taking things easily; trusting to luck.

har·ass (har′əs *or* hə ras′) *v* keep attacking someone in small ways; bug: *Stop harassing me about my height.*

har·bour (hȧr′bər) *n* a place of shelter for boats and ships near the shore: *Many yachts are in the harbour.* **Harbor** is another spelling.

hard (hȧrd) **1** *adj* not soft: *Rocks are hard.* **2** *adj* difficult: *a hard test, a hard person to get along with.* **3** *adv* with a lot of force: *Try hard to lift this log* (adv). **4** *adj* causing much pain, trouble, worry, etc.: *a hard winter.* –**hard′en,** *v,* –**hard′ness,** *n.*

hard copy anything printed out from a computer on to paper: *It's easier to find mistakes when you read your hard copy rather than the screen.* **hard disk** a round, flat metal plate used inside a computer to store large amounts of data and programs. A **hard drive** is the place inside the computer that holds and reads the hard disk. You cannot take the hard disk out of the computer. **hard·ly 1** *adv* only just: *We hardly had time to eat breakfast.* **2** *adv* not really: *She may have exaggerated, but it is hardly fair to call her a liar.* **hard·ship** *n* something hard to bear; a hard condition of living: *Hunger, cold, and sickness were among the hardships of pioneer life in Canada.* **hard·ware 1** *n* articles made from metal, used to build and repair things: *Locks, hinges, nails, screws, utensils, and tools are hardware.* **2** *n* the mechanical or electronic parts of a computer system but not the programs that run the system. **har·dy** *adj* tough: *Cold weather does not kill hardy plants.*

hard up, *Informal.* needing money or anything very badly: *He is always hard up the day before he is paid.*

harm (hȧrm) **1** *v* or *n* hurt; damage: *The skydiver was not harmed in the accident* (v). *The ice storm did a lot of harm to the trees in our neighbourhood* (n). **2** *n* wrong: *What harm is there in borrowing a friend's bicycle?* –**harm′ful,** *adj,* –**harm′less,** *adj.*

har·mo·ny (hȧr′mə nē) **1** *n* a beautiful arrangement of different colours, musical, sounds, shapes, etc., so that they go well together. **2** *n* agreement of feelings, ideas, or actions: *There was perfect harmony between the two brothers.* –**har·mo′ni·ous** (hȧr mō′nē əs), *adj,* –**har′mo·nize′,** *v.*

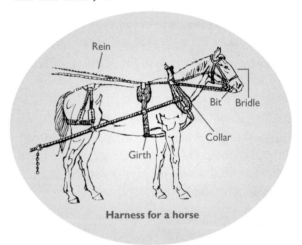

Harness for a horse

Labels: Rein, Bit, Bridle, Collar, Girth

har·ness (hȧr′nis) **1** *n* leather fittings for a horse or other animal, which connect it to a buggy, sled, or plough or which are used in riding. **2** *n* an arrangement of straps to fasten or hold: *a parachute harness, a climber's harness.*

harsh (hȧrsh) *adj* rough: *a harsh voice, a harsh climate.*

har·vest (hȧr′vist) **1** *v* cut or pick ripe grain and other crops: *to harvest wheat.* **2** *n* the action or the time of doing this. The full moon of late September is called the **harvest moon. 3** *n* the crop that is picked and gathered: *The apple harvest in the Okanagan Valley was good this year.* –**har′vest·er,** *n.*

hash (hash) **1** *n* a mixture of cooked meat, potatoes, etc. **2** *v* discuss thoroughly: *They spent hours hashing out their problems.* **3** *n* a mixture or muddle.

make a hash of, make a mess of.

has·sle (has′əl) *Informal.* **1** *n* trouble or bother: *Moving is just one big hassle.* **2** *v* give someone a hard time: *The movie star was being hassled by reporters.* **has·sled, has·sling.**

haste (hāst) *n* rush: *All his haste was of no use; he ended up in a traffic jam.* **–has′ten,** *v,* **has′ty,** *adj.*

hat (hat) *n* a covering for the head, especially one with a brim.

hat trick three goals scored in a single game by the same player.

hatch (hach) *v* break out as a live baby animal from the egg: *Three chicks hatched today.*

hate (hāt) **1** *v* have very strong feelings against: *Sydney hates people who are cruel to animals.* **2** *n* strong feelings against a person or thing: *hearts full of hate.* **hat·ed, hat·ing.** **–hate′ful,** *adj,* **–ha′tred,** *n.*

haugh·ty (hot′ē) *adj* conceited and snobby. **haugh·ti·er, haugh·ti·est. –haugh′ti·ly,** *adv.*

haul (hol) **1** *v* pull something heavy: *The logs were hauled to the mill by horses.* **2** *n* distance: *It is a long haul from Thunder Bay to Charlottetown.*

haunt (hont) *v* stay or keep appearing in a place as a ghost or other spiritual force: *People say ghosts haunt that old house.* **–haunt′ed,** *adj.*

have (hav) **1** *v* hold, own, take, eat, or experience: *I have a book in my hand. She has a big house. Let's have lunch and a rest. I'm having a good time.* **2** *v* become the father or mother of: *She had a baby yesterday.* **3** *v* **Have** is also used with past participles, such as *asked, been, broken, done,* or *called,* to express completed action: *They have eaten. She had gone before. I have called her.* **has, had, hav·ing.**

have to (haf′ tə), must: *We have to go now because it is very late.*

I've had it, I am so annoyed or disappointed that I can't take it any more.

hay (hā) *n* grass or another green plant that is cut and dried as food for cattle and horses.

hay fever an allergy with symptoms like those of a cold. It is set off by the pollen of some plants.

haz·ard (haz′ərd) *n* a risk; danger: *The life of an explorer is full of hazards.* **–haz′ard·ous,** *adj.*

haze (hāz) **1** *n* a small amount of mist or smoke in the air: *A thin haze hung over the distant hills of Grasslands National Park.* **2** *n* vagueness or confusion. **–ha′zy,** *adj.*

head (hed) **1** *n* the top part of the human body, where the face and the brain are, or the same part on an animal. **2** *n* the top, front, or rounded end of anything: *the head of a pin, the head of a line of cars, a head of cabbage.* **3** *n* the chief person; leader. **4** *v* move or lead toward: *We headed for home.* **–head′less,** *adj.*

head·ache (hed′āk′) *n* a pain in the head.

head·dress *n* a decorative covering for the head.

head·light *n* a bright light at the front of a vehicle, used to show the way ahead.

head·line *n* the title of an article in a newspaper or a magazine.

head·phone *n* an earphone on a band worn over the head, used for listening to a radio, computer, tape player, etc.

head·quar·ters *pl.* or *sing.n* the main office: *The headquarters of the company is in London, Ontario.*

head start an advantage that lets someone get ahead: *The younger boy was given a head start.*

head·strong *adj* foolishly determined to have your own way.

head·way *n* forward motion or progress: *We could make no headway against the strong wind.*

go to someone's head, make a person silly or conceited: *All that attention has gone to his head.*

head on, with the head or front first: *The car crashed head on into the wall.*

heads up, be careful; watch out: *Heads up! Their next batter is very good!*

lose your head, get too excited.

make head or tail of, understand any of.

heal (hēl) *v* make or become healthy again: *His cut finger healed in a few days.*

health (helth) *n* wellness; freedom from any kind of sickness or damage.

heap (hēp) *n* a pile; a bunch of things thrown or lying together: *a heap of stones, a garbage heap.*

hear (hēr) **1** *v* receive sounds through the ear: *Our old dog still hears very well.* **2** *v* get news: *Have you heard from your brother in St. John's?* **heard** (hərd), **hear·ing. –hear′er,** *n.*

hear·say *n* information you get from other people's talk; gossip.

CONFUSABLES ..... hear

hear means "listen to": *Did you hear me?*
here means "at this place": *I am here. I've been here for hours.*

heart (hårt) **1** *n* the muscular organ in animals that pumps the blood through the body. **2** *n* the centre of human feelings: *Her heart was filled with pride when her daughter won the medal.* **3** *n* courage; spirit: *The losing team showed plenty of heart.* **4** *n* the middle or centre. **5** *n* the main or central part: *the heart of the city.* **6** *n* a figure shaped like this: ♥
heart attack a sudden failure of the heart to beat normally. **Heart failure** means the same thing.
heart·break *n* very deep sadness or grief. **Heartache** is the same thing.
–**heart′break′ing,** *adj,* –**heart′bro′ken** or **bro′ken-heart′ed,** *adj.* **heart·less** *adj* cruel.
heart·y *adj* enthusiastic: *a hearty laugh, hearty wishes for a happy birthday.* –**heart′i·ly,** *adv.*
at heart, in your deepest thoughts or feelings: *He is kind at heart, though he seems unfriendly.*
break someone's heart, cause someone to feel great sadness or grief.
by heart, from memory.
have a heart, be kind.
have your heart in the right place, have good intentions.
heart of gold, a very kind nature.
set your heart on, be eager and determined to have or do.
with all your heart, really meaning it.

heat (hēt) **1** *n* the condition of being hot: *the heat of a fire, the heat of summer.* **2** *v* make hot: *The fire heats the cottage.* **3** *n* excitement: *In the heat of the moment he said things he was sorry for later.* A **heated** argument is a rather fierce one. –**heat′er,** *n.*

heave (hēv) *v* lift, throw, or pull with great effort: *They heaved on the rope.* **heaved, heav·ing.**

heav·en (hev′ən) *n* in some religions, the place where God lives.

heav·y (hev′ē) **1** *adj* hard to lift: *a heavy log, heavy bricks.* **2** *adj* large: *a heavy rain, a heavy meal.* **3** *adj* serious: *a heavy discussion, heavy reading.* **4** *adj* sad or gloomy: *a heavy heart, a heavy atmosphere.* **heav·i·er, heav·i·est.** –**heav′i·ly,** *adv,* –**heav′i·ness,** *n.*

hec·tare (hek′ter *or* hek′tår) *n* a metric unit used to measure land area. It is equal to ten thousand square metres. *Symbol:* ha

hec·tic (hek′tik) *adj* very busy, fast-paced, or wild: *Mrs. Conway leads a hectic life.*

hecto– *an SI prefix meaning* one hundred; 100. A **hectometre** is one hundred metres. *Symbol:* h

hedge (hej) *n* a thick row of bushes or small trees planted as a fence.

heed (hēd) **1** *v* give careful attention to: *Heed what I say.* **2** *n* careful attention; notice: *They paid no heed to the rain, and just kept on walking.* –**heed′less,** *adj.*

heel (hēl) **1** *n* the back part of a person's foot, below the ankle, or the part of a sock or shoe that covers it. **2** *n* *Informal.* a very mean and cowardly person.
cool your heels, wait.
drag your heels, act slowly or try to avoid doing something.
kick up your heels, have fun.
take to your heels, run away.

height (hīt) **1** *n* the tallness of anyone or anything; the distance from top to bottom: *My father's height is 187 cm.* **2** *n* a high point; peak: *the height of rush hour.* –**height′en,** *v.*

heir (er) *n* a person who has the right to somebody's property after the owner dies.
heir·loom *n* an article handed down from generation to generation: *This clock is a family heirloom.*

Rotor

A helicopter

hel·i·cop·ter (hel′ə kop′tər) *n* an aircraft that can fly up, down and sideways, and can hover.

hell (hel) *n* in some religions, the home of the Devil. –**hell′ish,** *adj.*

hel·lo (hə lō′) *interj* or *n* a word used to greet people, and sometimes to express surprise or impatience. *pl* **hel·los.**

Helmets worn by a knight, a football player, and an astronaut

hel·met (hel′mit) *n* a hard covering to protect the head.

help (help) **1** *v* do something to make a situation easier: *Help me with my homework, please. This medicine should help your sore throat.* **2** *n* an action, a person, or a thing that does this: *Do you need some help with your homework?* **3** *v* avoid; keep from: *He cannot help falling asleep.* **4** *v* give food to: *Help your aunt to tea and cookies.* One serving of food is called a **helping.** –**help′er,** *n,* –**help′ful,** *adj.*
help·less *adj* not able to help or protect yourself: *A little baby is helpless.* –**help′less·ness,** *n.*
help yourself, take what you wish: *Help yourself to a drink while you wait.*

hem (hem) **1** *n* a neat edge on a garment, made by folding over the cloth and sewing it down. **2** *v* fold over and sew down the edge of: *He hemmed his new pants.* **hemmed, hem·ming.**
hem in, surround on all sides: *hemmed in by trees.*

hem·i·sphere (hem′əs fēr′) **1** *n* half of a sphere or globe. **2** *n* half of the earth's surface. North and South America are in the **western hemisphere;** Europe, Asia, and Africa are in the **eastern hemisphere.** All the countries north of the equator are in the **northern hemisphere;** the countries south of the equator are in the **southern hemisphere.**

hen (hen) **1** *n* a female chicken. **2** *n* the female of some other birds: *a hen sparrow.*

herb (hərb *or* ərb) *n* a plant whose leaves and stems are used for medicine, seasoning, or food: *Sage, mint, and basil are herbs.*
herb·i·vore (hərb′ə vôr′) *n* an animal that eats only plants. –**her·biv′o·rous** (hər biv′ə rəs), *adj.*

herd (hərd) *n* a number of animals together: *a herd of cows, a herd of elephants.*

here (hēr) *n or adv* this place; in, at, or to this place: *Where do we go from here (n)? Bring those things here (adv).*

her·it·age (her′ə tij) *n* the values and traditions handed on to a person from his or her ancestors: *Freedom of speech is part of Canada's heritage.*

he·ro (hē′rō) **1** *n* a person who is greatly admired for his or her courage, leadership, strength, skill, and so on. **2** *n* the most important character in a story, play, or movie. *pl* **he·roes.** –**he·ro′ic,** *adj.*
her·o·ine (her′ō in) *n* a hero who is a woman or girl. **her·o·ism** (her′ō iz′əm) *n* great courage.

hes·i·tate (hez′ə tāt′) *v* hold back, usually because you are not sure: *Louis hesitated before asking the question.* **hes·i·tat·ed, hes·i·tat·ing.** –**hes′i·ta′tion,** *n.* –**hes′i·tant,** *adj.*

hi·ber·nate (hī′bər nāt′) *v* spend the winter in sleep, as some snakes, bats, groundhogs, bears, and other wild animals do. **hi·ber·nat·ed, hi·ber·nat·ing.** –**hi′ber·na′tion,** *n.*

hic·cup (hik′up) *n* an interruption in regular breathing that makes a sound like a click. **Hiccough** is another spelling of this word.

hide (hīd) **1** *v* put or keep out of sight: *Hide it in this little hole behind the bricks.* **2** *n* an animal's skin, either raw or made into leather. **hid, hid·den** or **hid, hid·ing.**

hid·e·ous (hid′ē əs) *adj* ugly; frightful; horrible: *a hideous monster, hideous crimes.* –**hid′e·ous·ly,** *adv.*

high (hī) **1** *adj* far above the ground: *a high mountain, an airplane high in the air.* **2** *adj* greater, stronger, or better than average: *a high price, a high wind. Sir Wilfrid Laurier was a person of high character.* –**high′ly,** *adv.*
high·light 1 *n* the most interesting part: *The highlight of our trip was the drive along the Cabot Trail.* **2** *v* make stand out: *The new calculator was highlighted in the store catalogue.* **3** *n* a streak or patch of extra brightness or colour in something.* **high·rise** *n* a tall building with many storeys: *They live on the 23rd floor of a highrise in downtown Ottawa.* ❦ **high·stick·ing** *n* in hockey, the act of checking a player with your stick carried above the level of your shoulder. **high-strung** *adj* easily excited or upset. **high·way** *n* a main road or route.
high spirits, happy excitement.
high time, the time just before it is too late: *It was high time that Josh began to study.*
search high and low, look everywhere for something.

hi·jack (hī′jak′) *v* stop a vehicle in order to steal it or its cargo, or to force the driver to go to a certain place: *The plane was hijacked.* **–hi′jack′er,** *n.*

hike (hīk) *n* a long walk, especially one for pleasure. **hiked, hik·ing.**

hi·lar·i·ous (hə ler′ē əs) *adj* very funny.

hill (hil) *n* a raised part of the earth's surface, smaller than a mountain. **–hill′y,** *adj.*

hin·der (hin′dər) *v* hold back or get in the way of: *Deep mud hindered travel. Don't hinder me from my work.* **–hin′drance,** *n.*

Hin·du·ism (hin′dū iz′əm) *n* the main religion of India, based on the worship of one God who takes many forms. A follower of Hinduism is a **Hindu.**

hinge (hinj) *n* the joint that a door, lid, etc. is attached by so that it can move back and forth. **hinged, hing·ing.**

hint (hint) **1** *n* a slight sign; tip: *A small black cloud gave a hint of the coming storm.* **2** *v* give a slight sign; suggest in an indirect way: *They hinted that they wanted their guests to leave by saying, "Do you often stay up this late?"*

hip·po·pot·a·mus (hip′ə pot′ə məs) *n* a huge, thick-skinned, plant-eating, hairless animal that lives in and around rivers in tropical Africa. Its name is often shortened to **hippo.** *pl* **hip·po·pot·a·mus·es** or **hip·po·pot·a·mi** (hip′ə pot′ə mī).

hire (hīr) **1** *v* agree to pay someone to do a job: *We hired a teenager to cut the lawn while we were on vacation.* **2** *v* rent something, especially together with someone's services, such as a vehicle with a driver. **hired, hir·ing.**

hiss (his) **1** *v* make a sound like the *s* in *see*: *The snake hissed as we approached.* **2** *n* such a sound.

his·to·ry (his′tə rē) *n* everything that has happened in the past: *We don't know the whole history of the earth.* A **historian** studies history. **his·tor·ic** (his tòr′ik) *adj* famous or important in history: *July 1, 1867, was a historic day for Canada.* **his·tor·i·cal** (his tòr′ə kəl) *adj* based on actual history: *It is a historical fact, not legend, that John Cabot sailed to Canada in 1497.* **make history,** do something that will always be remembered.

hit (hit) **1** *v* come against with some force: *Anna hit the ball with a bat.* **2** *n* a blow; stroke. **3** *n* a popular success. **hit, hit·ting.** **–hit′ter,** *n.* **hit it off,** *Informal.* agree or get along well with someone: *Gary hit it off well with Teo right away.*

hitch (hich) **1** *v* attach with a hook, ring, rope, or other fastener: *The farmer hitched the hay wagon to the tractor.* **2** *n* a part used to connect two things together, such as a car and trailer. **3** *n* something that goes wrong: *A hitch in their plans made them miss the train to Moncton.*

HIV a virus that keeps a person's body from fighting infections, causing the disease called AIDS. HIV stands for **human immunovirus.**

hive (hīv) **1** *n* a colony of bees, or its home. **2** *n* a busy, crowded place: *On Saturdays the mall is a hive of activity.*

hoard (hòrd) **1** *v* save carefully and store up: *The squirrel hoarded nuts for the winter.* **2** *n* the things stored: *Bilbo saw the dragon's hoard of jewels.*

hoarse (hòrs) *adj* talking with a rough, croaking voice: *All that shouting has made him hoarse.* **hoars·er, hoars·est.** **–hoarse′ness,** *n.*

hoax (hōks) *n* a made-up story meant to trick people: *The reported discovery of buried treasure in the Northwest Territories was a hoax.*

hob·by (hob′ē) *n* something a person likes to do in his or her spare time. *pl* **hob·bies.**

ho·bo (hō′bō) *n* a homeless person who travels from town to town, taking whatever work or help can be found. *pl* **ho·bos** or **ho·boes.**

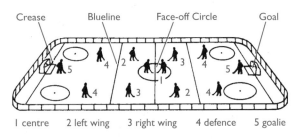

A hockey rink and the players

hock·ey (hok′ē) **1** *n* a game played on ice by two teams of six players wearing skates and carrying hooked sticks. Each team tries to shoot a black rubber disk, the puck, into the opposing team's goal. The full name is **ice hockey. 2** *n* any similar game, such as **road hockey, floor hockey,** and **field hockey.**

hog (hog) **1** *n* a pig, especially a full-grown pig raised for food. **2** *n* a selfish, greedy person. **3** *v Slang.* take more than your share of: *Don't hog the ice cream.* **hogged, hog·ging.**

hoist (hoist) *v* raise or lift, often with ropes and pulleys: *to hoist a flag, to hoist sails, to hoist blocks of stone in building.*

hold (hōld) **1** *v* keep, often in your hands or arms: *Hold my watch while I play this game.* **2** *v* keep in some place or position: *This clamp holds the paper steady while I draw.* **3** *v* contain: *This jar holds 300 mL of water.* **4** *v* have: *Shall we hold a meeting of the club?* **5** *n* the space below a ship's deck where cargo is kept. **held, hold·ing.** –**hold′er,** *n.*

hold·up 1 *n* the act of stopping by force and robbing. **2** *n* delay: *The fog caused a holdup in air travel over Calgary International Airport.*
hold off, delay doing something.
hold on, 1 not give up. **2** wait.
hold out, 1 last: *The water supply will not hold out much longer.* **2** not give in: *I managed to hold out against all their persuasion.* A **holdout** is someone who resists after everyone else has given in.
hold up, continue; last; endure: *Jacob held up well under all that pressure.*
hold your breath, 1 stop breathing on purpose. **2** wait for something to happen.

hole (hōl) **1** *n* a gap; an opening that goes right through something: *a hole in a pocket, a hole in a board.* **2** *n* a hollow place in the ground: *a hole in the road. She hit the golfball into the hole.* **3** *n* a difficult situation. –**hol′ey,** *adj.*
hole up, 1 of animals, go into a hole: *Bears hole up during winter.* **2** *Slang.* go into hiding for a time: *The gangsters holed up in an old cabin.*
in the hole, in debt.
shoot holes in, argue successfully against something. You can also **pick holes in** something.

CONFUSABLES ..... hole

hole means "empty space":
There's a hole in my sock.

whole means "entire":
I ate the whole box of cookies.

Ho·li (hō′lē) *n* a Hindu spring festival dedicated to Krishna, one of the most famous forms of the Hindu God.

hol·i·day (hol′ə dā′) **1** *n* a day when schools and most places of work and business are closed to celebrate something: *July 1st is a holiday for all Canadians.* **2** Often, **holidays,** *pl.n* vacation; the time spent away from work or school: *Nina always goes to camp during the summer holidays.*

hol·low (hol′ō) **1** *adj* with empty space inside; not solid: *a hollow log, a hollow chocolate egg.* **2** *n* a bowl-shaped or sunken place: *a hollow in the driveway.*

A branch of holly

hol·ly (hol′ē) *n* a tree or shrub with shiny, sharp-pointed evergreen leaves and bright-red berries, used especially as Christmas decorations. *pl* **hol·lies.**

ho·lo·gram (hol′ə gram′ *or* hō′lə gram′) a kind of photograph made with a laser. It changes colour and shape when you look at it from different angles.

ho·ly (hō′lē) *adj* having to do with God or religion. **ho·li·er, ho·li·est.**

home (hōm) **1** *n* the place where a person, family, or animal lives: *Her home is at 25 South Street. The owl made its home in our barn.* **2** *n* a place where a person or thing comes from, belongs, or is found: *The Canadian tundra is the home of the musk-ox.* –**home′less,** *adj.*
home·land *n* the country that is one's home; one's native land. **home·made** *adj* made at home: *homemade bread.* **home·mak·er** *n* a person who manages a home. **home plate** in baseball, the base you stand beside to bat the ball. **home run** in baseball, a run scored on a hit that lets the batter run round all the bases without stopping. It is also called a **homer.**
home·sick *adj* sad and longing for home. –**home′sick′ness,** *n.* **home·stead** (hōm′sted′) **1** *n* a farm with its buildings. **2** *n* in Western Canada, public land granted to a settler by the federal government. –**home′stead′er,** *n.*
home·work *n* schoolwork to be done outside of class time.

hom·o·nym (hom′ə nim′) *n* a homophone or a homograph. Some homonyms are both, like *mail* meaning *"letters"* and *mail* meaning *"armour."*

Grammar ✓*Check* . . . **homonym**

Homonyms are words that have the same form, but have different meanings. For example, *a bank* can mean "a heap of something," like snow. But it can also mean "a shallow place in water," or "a place that deals with money," or "one side of a river," or "a group of something," like electric switches.

Sometimes, homonyms will sound the same, but have different spellings, like *tale* and *tail*. Words like these are called **homophones**.

Sometimes, homonyms will look the same, but sound different, like *lead* meaning "go in front" and *lead* meaning "a metal." Words like these are called **homographs**.

---

hon·est (on′ist) *adj* truthful; not lying or stealing: *He was an honest man.* **–hon′est·ly,** *adv,* **–hon′es·ty,** *n.*

hon·ey (hun′ē) *n* a sweet liquid that bees make. **hon·ey·moon** *n* the holiday spent together by a newly married couple.

honk (hongk) **1** *n* the sound made by a goose or a car horn. **2** *v* make or cause to make this sound: *to honk a horn.* **Honker** is a nickname for the Canada goose.

hon·our (on′ər) **1** *n* the respect given to someone who is loved and admired. **2** *v* show this kind of respect to: *We honour our country's dead soldiers on Remembrance Day.* **3 honours,** *pl.n* a special mention or grade given to a student for having done outstanding work. **4 Honour,** *n* a title of respect for a judge, mayor, etc.: *"Yes, Your Honour." Her Honour will make a short speech.* Another spelling is **honor.** **hon·our·a·ble** or **hon·or·able 1** *adj* having, showing, or bringing honour: *an honourable achievement. It was not honourable for you to cheat.* **2 Honourable,** *adj* a title given to certain officials of the government in Canada. **–hon′our·a·bly** or **hon′or·a·bly,** *adv.*

hood (hùd) **1** *n* a soft covering for the head and neck, either separate or as part of a coat or top: *My raincoat has a hood.* **2** *n* anything shaped or used like a hood, such as the covering over the engine of a car. **–hood′ed,** *adj.*

hood·lum (hūd′ləm) *n Informal.* a rough, rowdy, sometimes violent or destructive person, often a gang member. This word is sometimes shortened to **hood.**

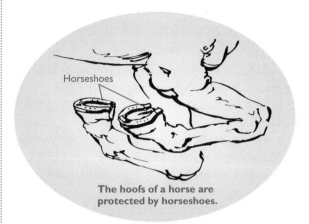

Horseshoes

The hoofs of a horse are protected by horseshoes.

hoof (hūf *or* hùf) *n* the foot of a horse, cow, deer, and some other animals, especially the hard covering on the bottom, made of something like horn. **Hoofbeats** are the sound made by the hoofs on the ground when the animal runs. *pl* **hoofs** or **hooves.**

hook (hùk) *n* a piece of metal, wood, or other stiff material, curved or sharply bent, for catching or holding something: *a fish-hook, a clothes hook.* **by hook or by crook,** in any way at all, including trickery if necessary. **hooked on, 1** addicted to: *hooked on drugs.* **2** an enthusiastic fan of: *Nicola was instantly hooked on the idea of visiting Winnipeg.* **off the hook,** set free from a responsibility: *You're off the hook, we found out it was Austin's fault.*

hool·i·gan (hū′li gan) *n* a noisy person who likes to fight or cause damage.

hoop (hūp) *n* any large ring. A **hoop earring** is plain, large, and ring-shaped.

hoot (hūt) **1** *n* the sound that an owl makes. **2** *v* make this sound or one like it, especially in laughter or disapproval: *She hooted at my ridiculous mistake. The crowd hooted angrily at the mayor's remarks.* **not give a hoot,** not care at all: *I don't give a hoot what he says.*

hop (hop) *v* move by jumping on one foot, both feet, or all feet at once: *Maya hopped back to get her other boot, which was stuck in the snow. The bird hopped around on the lawn.* **hopped, hop·ping.**

hope (hōp) **1** *n* a feeling that something good could happen: *Her promise to help gave me hope that we could finish the job on time.* **2** *v* wish and expect: *I hope to do well in school this year.* **hoped, hop·ing.** –**hope′ful,** *adj,* –**hope′less,** *adj.*
hope·ful·ly 1 *adv* in a hopeful manner: *Hearing a car in the driveway, the child ran hopefully to the door.* **2** *adv Informal.* I hope; we hope: *Hopefully, the weather will improve.*

horde (hȯrd) *n* a large crowd or swarm: *hordes of grasshoppers.*

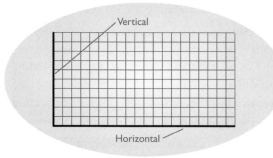

ho·ri·zon (hə rī′zən) *n* the line where the earth and sky seem to meet.
hor·i·zon·tal (hȯr′ə zon′təl) *adj* flat; level; stretching sideways, like a floor, and not up and down like a wall.

horn (hȯrn) **1** *n* a hard growth, usually curved and pointed, on the heads of cattle, sheep, goats, and some other animals. **2** *n* a musical instrument played by blowing. **3** *n* a device sounded as a warning signal: *a car horn, a bicycle horn, a foghorn.*
blow your own horn, brag about yourself.

hor·ror (hȯr′ər) **1** *n* shock, fear, and disgust. **2** *n* a very strong dislike: *Some people have a horror of snakes and spiders.*
hor·ri·ble *adj* causing horror; frightful; shocking: *a horrible crime, a horrible disease.* **Horrific** (hȯr if′ik) means about the same. –**hor′ri·bly,** *adv.* **hor·rid** *adj* nasty or awful. **Horrendous** (hə ren′dəs) means about the same. **hor·ri·fy** *v* fill with horror.

horse (hȯrs) *n* a large, strong, four-legged animal with solid hoofs and a mane and tail of long, coarse hair.
horse·back *adv* on the back of a horse: *to ride horseback.* **horse·shoe** *n* a U-shaped metal plate nailed to a horse's hoof to protect it.
hold your horses, wait; be patient.
horse around, *Slang.* fool around.

hose (hōz) **1** *n* a flexible tube for carrying any liquid a short distance: *a watering hose for the lawn, the hose of a gas pump.* **2** *pl.n* an old-fashioned word for stockings or socks. Another similar word is **hosiery** (hō′zhər ē).

hos·pi·tal (hos′pi təl) *n* a place where sick or injured people may be treated and cared for.
hos·pi·ta·ble (hə spit′ə bəl) *adj* giving a warm welcome to guests or strangers: *a hospitable family.* –**hos′pi·ta·bly,** *adv,* –**hos′pi tal′i·ty,** *n.*

host (hōst) **1** *n* a person who has guests or visitors. **2** *n* a person who leads or runs a talk show, game show, or talent show. **3** *n* an animal or plant that a parasite lives in or on.
hos·tage *n* a person taken and held by an enemy as a way of forcing someone to do something.
hos·tel 1 *n* a cheap place for homeless people or travellers to spend the night and get meals. **2** *n* a home for young people who need special help. **host·ess** *n* a host who is a woman.

hos·tile (hos′tīl *or* hos′təl) *adj* of or like an enemy; unfriendly: *a hostile army. They were very hostile to our suggestion.* –**hos·til′i·ty,** *n.*

hot (hot) **1** *adj* having, feeling, or giving a lot of heat: *a hot fire, the hot sun. The long race made the cyclists hot.* **2** *adj* having a sharp, burning taste: *Pepper and mustard are hot.* **3** *adj* full of strong, excited feeling: *a hot temper, hot with rage.* **4** *adj* very popular and exciting: *a hot new rock band.* **5** *adj* new; fresh: *a hot scent, a hot trail.* **hot·ter, hot·test.** –**hot′ly,** *adv.*
hot cake a pancake. **hot dog** a wiener inside a long bun. **hot·house** *n* a heated building with walls and roof of glass for growing plants in.
hotline *n* a special phone line that people can call to get information or talk about something.
go or **sell like hot cakes,** be sold quickly: *The candy we made for the fall fair sold like hot cakes.*
hot air, talk that sounds important and meaningful but isn't.
hot under the collar, very angry.
in hot water, in trouble.

ho·tel (hō tel′) *n* a place where travellers can get private rooms and restaurant meals for pay.

hound (hound) **1** *n* a dog, especially one used for hunting. Most hounds have large, drooping ears and short hair. **2** *v* keep on chasing or pestering: *She hounded me until I finally gave her the book.*

hour (our) *n* a period of sixty minutes: *Twenty-four hours make a day. Symbol:* h
hour·ly *adv* or *adj* every hour: *Give two doses of the medicine hourly (adv). There are hourly news reports on this radio station (adj).*

house (hous) **1** *n* a building for people to live in. **2** *n* an assembly for making laws: *In Canada's parliament, the House of Commons is the Lower House; the Senate is the Upper House.* **3** *n* an audience: *The pop singer sang to a large house.* **4** *n* in curling, the goal or target. *pl* **hous·es** (hou′ziz). –**house′ful′,** *adj.*
house·bro·ken *adj* of a pet, such as a cat or dog, trained not to make a mess indoors. **House of Assembly** the law-making body of the province of Newfoundland. **House of Commons** in Canada, the body of elected representatives who meet in Ottawa to make laws and debate questions of government. ▶See Appendix.
house·work *n* the work to be done in a home, such as washing, ironing, cleaning, and cooking.
on the house, paid for by the owner of the business; free: *After visiting the candy factory, we were each given a box of chocolates on the house.*

A ruby-throated hummingbird— about 10 cm long including the tail—hovers over a flower.

hov·er (huv′ər *or* hov′ər) **1** *v* stay in one place in the air: *The hummingbird hovered in front of the flower.* **2** *v* stay nearby, waiting or watching: *The dogs hovered around the table at mealtime.*

how (hou) **1** *adv* or *conj* in what way; by what means: *How can it be done (adv)? Tell me how it happened (conj).* **2** *adv* to what degree or amount: *How tall are you? I don't know how long it will take.* **3** *adv* or *conj* in what state or condition: *How is your health (adv)? Let's see how she is (conj).* **4** *adv* why: *How is it you are late?*
how·ev·er 1 *adv* in spite of that: *We were very late for dinner; however, there was plenty left for us.* **2** *adv* no matter how: *I'll come however busy I am.*
how come, *Informal.* why: *How come you didn't call me?*

howl (houl) **1** *v* give a long, loud, mournful cry: *Our dog sometimes howls at night. The winter winds howled around our cabin.* **2** *n* a long, loud, mournful cry: *the howl of a wolf.* **3** *v* or *n* yell; shout: *It was so funny that we howled with laughter (v). We heard a howl of pain (n).*

hub (hub) **1** *n* the central part of a wheel, often covered with a **hubcap. 2** *n* a centre of interest or activity: *The mall is the hub of our small town.*

hub·bub (hub′ub) *n* a loud, confused noise; an uproar: *There was a hubbub when the crowd was told to move.* **Hullabaloo** means the same.

hud·dle (hud′əl) **1** *v* to crowd close: *The sheep huddled in a corner of the pen.* **2** *v* crouch or curl up: *The cat huddled on the cushion.* **hud·dled, hud·dling.**
go into a huddle, in football, gather as a team to plan the next play, decide on signals, and so on.

hue (hyū) *n* a colour: *all the hues of the rainbow.*

huff (huf) *n* a fit of anger or sulkiness. –**huff′i·ly,** *adv,* –**huff′y,** *adj.*

hug (hug) **1** *v* put the arms around and hold close: *Andrea hugged her new puppy.* **2** *n* a tight clasp with the arms: *Give me a hug.* **3** *v* keep close to: *The boat hugged the shore of Glace Bay.* **hugged, hug·ging.**

huge (hyūj) *adj* extremely big: *a huge sum of money. An elephant is a huge animal.* **hug·er, hug·est.** –**huge′ly,** *adv.*

hull (hul) **1** *n* the main body of a ship or seaplane. **2** *n* the outer covering of a seed.

hum (hum) **1** *v* make a smooth, low sound like a bee or an electric motor: *The printer hums busily.* **2** *v* sing with closed lips: *She was humming a tune.* **hummed, hum·ming.**

hu·man (hyū′mən) **1** *adj* being a person: *Men, women, and children are human beings.* **2** *adj* Usually, **human being,** a person. A being that is not a human, but resembles one, is a **humanoid. 3** *n* having to do with all people: *Selfishness is a human weakness.* –**hu′man·ly,** *adv.*
hu·mane (hyū mān′) *adj* kind; not cruel. –**hu·mane′ly,** *adv.* **hu·man·i·ty** (hyū man′ə tē) **1** *n* people; all human beings: *Recent advances in medicine have helped humanity.* **Humankind** means about the same. **2** *n* humane treatment; kindness: *Treat animals with humanity.*

hum·ble (hum′bəl) *adj* not thinking too highly of yourself: *Maya is a fantastic guitarist but is so humble about it–she never brags.* **hum·bler, hum·blest.** –**hum′bly,** *adv.*

hum·drum (hum′drum′) *adj* without variety; boring; dull: *a humdrum movie.*

hu·mid (hyū′mid) *adj* moist; damp: *The air is very humid near the sea.* –**hu·mid′i·fi·er,** *n,* –**hu·mid′i·fy,** *v,* –**hu·mid′i·ty,** *n.*

❀ **hu·mi·dex** (hyū′mə deks′) *n* a scale that measures how the heat and moisture in the air is likely to feel to our bodies. If the humidex is 36°C, it means that it feels like 36°C, even if the temperature is less than that.

hu·mil·i·ate (hyū mil′ē āt′) *v* make totally embarrassed and ashamed: *Marc was humiliated when his parents scolded him in front of the guests.* **hu·mil·i·at·ed, hu·mil·i·at·ing.** –**hu·mil′i·a′tion,** *n.*

hu·mour (hyū′mər) **1** *n* a funny quality: *The speech was full of humour and made everybody laugh.* **2** *v* give in to someone's wishes just to keep him or her happy: *Try to humour your little brother; he's not feeling well.* **3** *n* a state of mind; a mood or temper: *She awoke in a good humour.* –**hu′mor·ist,** *n,* –**hu′mor·ous,** *adj.* **Humor** is another spelling.

sense of humour or **humor,** the ability to see the funny side of things.

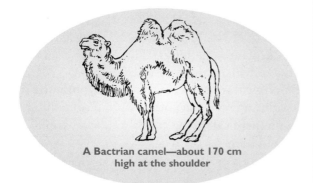

A Bactrian camel—about 170 cm
high at the shoulder

hump (hump) *n* a rounded shape that sticks out: *Some camels have two humps on their backs.*

hu·mus (hyū′məs) *n* a dark-brown or black soil formed from dead leaves and other decayed plant parts. It is very rich in nutrients for plants.

hunch (hunch) *n Informal.* a feeling or suspicion that cannot be explained: *I had a hunch they would show up today.*

hun·dred (hun′drəd) ▶See Appendix.

hun·ger (hung′gər) **1** *n* a desire or need for food: *After two days without food, the caged lion roared with hunger.* **2** *n* a strong desire for something: *a hunger for books.* –**hun′gri·ly,** *adv,* –**hun′gry,** *adj.*

go on a hunger strike, refuse to eat until someone does what you want.

hunk (hungk) *n Informal.* a big lump, piece, or slice: *a hunk of cheese.*

hunt (hunt) **1** *v* go after wild animals to catch or kill them for food or as a sport: *to hunt deer.* **2** *v* search; look for something for a long time: *to hunt for a lost book.* –**hunt′er,** *n.*

hur·dle (hər′dəl) **1** *n* in a race, a barrier for people or horses to jump over. **2** *n* a problem.

hurl (hərl) *v* throw with force: *to hurl a book across the room, to hurl insults at someone.*

hur·rah (hə rä′) *interj* or *n* a shout of joy or approval: *"Hurrah!" they shouted as Hamilton Collegiate scored again* (*interj*). *Give a hurrah for the hero* (*n*). **Hurray** (hə rā′) is another form of the word.

hur·ri·cane (hər′ə kān′) *n* a tropical storm with a violent wind and, usually, very heavy rain: *The wind in a hurricane blows over 120 km/h.*

hur·ry (hər′ē) *v* move or do something faster than usual: *to hurry supper, to hurry a sick child to the doctor. If you hurry, your work may be too sloppy.* **hur·ried, hur·ry·ing.** –**hur′ried,** *adj,* –**hur′ried·ly,** *adv.*

in a hurry, trying to move fast: *I can't wait, I'm in a hurry!*

hurt (hərt) **1** *v* cause pain to a person, animal, or thing; wound; injure: *The stone hurt his foot badly.* **2** *v* suffer pain; feel pain: *My hand hurts.* **3** *v* or *n* damage or harm: *Will it hurt this hat if it gets wet* (*v*)? *Not being chosen for the play was a hurt to her pride* (*n*). **hurt, hurt·ing.** –**hurt′ful,** *adj.*

hus·band (huz′bənd) *n* the man that a woman is married to.

hush (hush) **1** *v* make or become silent or quiet: *The wind has hushed.* **2** *n* a stopping of noise; silence; quiet. –**hushed,** *adj.*

hush up, 1 be quiet. **2** keep secret: *The whole incident was hushed up.*

husk (husk) **1** *n* the dry outer covering of certain seeds or fruits: *to peel the husk off an ear of corn.* **2** *v* remove the husk from: *Husk the corn.*

husk·y (hus′kē) **1** *adj* dry in the throat: *A cold sometimes causes a husky cough.* **2** *adj* big and strong: *a husky young man.* **3** *n* a strong dog, used in the North for pulling sleds. **husk·i·er, husk·i·est.** *pl* **husk·ies** or **Husk·ies.** –**husk′i·ness,** *n.*

hus·tle (hus′əl) *v* hurry: *Mom hustled the boys off to soccer practice. We'll have to hustle to get there by 5:00.* **hus·tled, hus·tling.**

hut (hut) *n* a small, roughly made house: *a village of mud huts.*

hy·brid (hī′brid) *n* the offspring of two animals or plants of different kinds: *Most garden roses are hybrids.* Hybrids are produced to combine the best qualities of different kinds of plant or animal.

hy·drant (hī′drənt) *n* a short, wide, capped pipe that comes up from below ground near the street. It is connected to the main water pipes below and has a place to attach a hose so the water can be used to put out fires.

WORD HISTORY .... **hydrant**

Words beginning with **hydr** all have to do with water. These words come from the Greek word *hydor*, meaning "water."

🍁 **hy·dro** (hī′drō) *n* electric power that comes from flowing or falling water: *Niagara Falls provides hydro for many factories. The hydro was off for two hours during the storm.* The full name is **hydro-electricity** and the adjective is **hydro-electric.**

hy·dro·plane (hī′drə plān′) **1** *n* a motorboat that skims along on top of the water. **2** *v* to skim along on top of water. **3** *n* an aircraft that can take off and land on water; seaplane. **hy·dro·planed, hy·dro·plan·ing.**

hy·e·na (hī ē′nə) *n* a wild, wolflike animal of Africa and Asia: *Hyenas have a cry that sounds like laughter.*

hy·giene (hī′jēn) *n* the rules of health, especially for avoiding disease by keeping clean. –**hy·gien′ic** (hī jē′nik *or* hī jen′ik), *adj,* –**hy·gien′ist** (hī jēn′ist *or* hī jen′ist), *n.*

hymn (him) *n* a song of praise.

hype (hīp) *n* *Informal.* a lot of exaggerated advertising to say how good something is: *There is a lot of hype for this new movie.*

hy·phen (hī′fən) *n* a mark (-) used to join the parts of some compound words, or to divide a word at the end of a line of printing or writing. To **hyphenate** a word is to write it with a hyphen. ▶See the *Grammar and Usage Mini-Guide.*

hyp·no·tize (hip′nə tīz′) *v* put into a state somewhat like sleep, called **hypnosis** (hip nō′sis). A hypnotized person cannot think or make decisions in the normal way, and carries out the suggestions of the person who has hypnotized him or her. **hyp·no·tized, hyp·no·tiz·ing.** –**hyp·not′ic** (hip not′ik), *adj,* –**hyp′no·tism,** *n,* –**hyp′no·tist,** *n.*

hyp·o·crite (hip′ə krit′) *n* a person who pretends to be more concerned about doing right than he or she really is. –**hy′poc′ri·sy** (hi pok′rəsē), *n,* –**hyp′o·crit′i·cal,** *adj.*

hy·po·der·mic (hī′pə dər′mik) *n* or *adj* having to do with injection under the skin: *I get my allergy shots with a hypodermic (n). The doctor used a hypodermic needle (adj).*

hy·poth·e·sis (hī poth′ə sis) *n* an idea that may explain something but has not yet been proven, which can be tested by doing experiments or gathering data. To **hypothesize** is to come up with a hypothesis about something. **hy·po·thet·i·cal** (hī pə thet′ə kəl) *n* possible, but not known to be true.

hys·ter·i·cal (hi ster′ə kəl) *adj* excited and unable to stop laughing, screaming, or crying: *hysterical with grief, hysterical fans at a concert.* This condition is called **hysteria** (hi stēr′ēə *or* hi ster′ē ə). –**hys·ter′i·cal·ly,** *adv.*
go into hysterics, become hysterical.

i or **I** (ī) *n* the ninth letter of the English alphabet, or any speech sound that it stands for. The sound of *i* in *bit* is different from the sound of *i* in *bite. pl* **i's** or **I's.**

ice (īs) **1** *n* water made solid by cold. **2** *v* cover with icing: *to ice a cake.* **3** *v* in hockey, shoot a puck from your own end zone past the red line at the other end of the rink. **iced, ic·ing.**

ice age a time when much of the earth was covered with glaciers. The name of the most recent one, which ended around 8000 B.C., is usually capitalized: *the Ice Age.* **ice·berg** *n* a large mass of ice floating in the sea: *About 90 percent of an iceberg is below the surface of the water.*

ice·cap *n* a very large mass of ice and snow that covers a mountaintop or polar region throughout the year: *the polar icecaps.* **ice cream** a frozen dessert made of cream, sweetened and flavoured. **ice field** a huge sheet of ice covering some land or floating in the sea. **ice storm** a storm with freezing rain that covers everything with a thin layer of ice. **ice time 1** in hockey, the amount of time a player gets on the ice during a game. **2** time given to a person or group to use the ice at a rink. **i·ci·cle** (ī'sə kəl) *n* a pointed, hanging stick of ice formed by the freezing of dripping water. **ic·ing** *n* a sweet, creamy mixture used to cover cakes, cookies, and so on. Another name for it is **frosting. i·cy 1** *adj* very cold: *an icy blast of wind.* **2** *adj* covered with ice: *icy roads.* **3** *adj* very unfriendly: *He gave her an icy stare.* –**i'ci·ly,** *adv.*

break the ice, get people feeling relaxed with each other: *The birthday party started with a few games to break the ice.*

ice over, become covered with ice.

on thin ice, in a dangerous position.

i·con (ī'kon) **1** *n* a small sign or picture on a computer screen. **2** *n* an image; a statue or picture. –**i·con'ic,** *adj.*

i·de·a (ī dē'ə) *n* thought in your mind: *I had an idea for making the job a lot easier.*

i·de·al 1 *n* a perfect model to be followed: *Her mother is her ideal.* **2** *adj* perfect; the best you could wish for: *The flat wooded areas of Terra Nova National Park were ideal for camping.* –**i·de'al·ly,** *adv.*

i·den·ti·fy (ī den'tə fī') **1** *v* recognize: *Can you identify each of these shapes?* **2** *v* make the same; treat as the same: *The good ruler identified his people's welfare with his own.* **i·den·ti·fied, i·den·ti·fy·ing.**

i·den·ti·cal *adj* exactly alike: *The two new loonies were identical.*

i·den·ti·fi·ca·tion (ī den'tə fə kā'shən) *n* something used to identify a person or thing: *Callan showed her student card as identification.*

i·den·ti·ty 1 *n* who or what someone or something is: *The robber revealed his identity by removing his mask.* **2** *n* exact likeness: *The identity of the two bank robberies led the police to think that the same person committed them. pl* **i·den·ti·ties.**

id·i·om (id'ē əm) *n* a phrase or expression whose meaning cannot be understood from the ordinary meanings of its individual words: *"How do you do?" and "catch a cold" are English idioms.* –**id'i·o·mat'ic** (id'ēə mat'ik), *adj.*

Grammar ✓ *Check* . . . . . **idiom**	
Idioms that contain prepositions can cause trouble. Here are some to watch out for.	
DON'T SAY	SAY
different than	*different from*
try and	*try to*
be sure and	*be sure to*
off of	*off*

id·i·ot (id'ē ət) *n* a very stupid or foolish person. –**id'i·ot'ic** (id'ē ot'ik), *adj,* –**id'i·o·cy** (id'ēəsē), *n.*

i·dle (ī'dəl) **1** *adj* doing nothing; not busy or working: *idle machines, the idle hours of a holiday.* **2** *adj* lazy: *an idle good-for-nothing.* **i·dler, i·dlest. 3** *v* run slowly without being in gear: *The bus idled for ten minutes while the driver waited for the students.* **i·dled, i·dling.** –**i'dle·ness,** *n,* –**i'dler,** *n,* –**i'dly,** *adv.*

i·dol (ī′dəl) **1** *n* an object worshipped as a god. The worship of idols is called **idolatry** (ī dol′ə trē). **2** *n* a person or thing that is loved or admired very much: *The baby girl was the idol of her family.* –**i′dol·ize′**, *v.*

if (if) **1** *conj* supposing that: *If it rains, we'll stay at home.* **2** *conj* whether: *I wonder if he called.*

ig·loo (ig′lū) *n* an Inuit house, especially one shaped like a dome and built of blocks of hard snow. *pl* **ig·loos.**

ig·nite (ig nīt′) *v* start burning: *Gasoline ignites easily.* **ig·nit·ed, ig·nit·ing.**

ig·ni·tion (ig nish′ən) *n* in a gasoline engine, the system that starts the engine.

ig·nore (ig nôr′) *v* pay no attention to: *We ignored their insults.* **ig·nored, ig·nor·ing.**

ig·no·rant (ig′nə rənt) **1** *adj* knowing little or nothing: *I had never been out of Fredericton and felt very ignorant when I first arrived at the ranch.* **2** *adj* not knowing a particular thing: *Trevor was ignorant of the fact that his house had burned down.* –**ig′no·rance**, *n.*

I'll (īl) I will.

ill (il) **1** *adj* sick; not well. **2** *adj* bad: *ill luck.* **worse, worst.** –**ill′ness**, *n.*
ill at ease, uncomfortable.

il·le·gal (i lē′gəl) *adj* against the law. –**il·le′gal·ly**, *adv.*

il·leg·i·ble (i lej′ə bəl) *adj* very hard or impossible to read: *The ink had faded so that many words were illegible.*

il·lit·er·ate (i lit′ə rit) *adj* unable to read or write.

il·lu·mi·nate (i lū′mə nāt′) *v* light up; make bright: *The Calgary Saddledome was illuminated by hundreds of lights.* **il·lu·mi·nat·ed, il·lu·mi·nat·ing.** –**il·lu′mi·na′tion**, *n.*

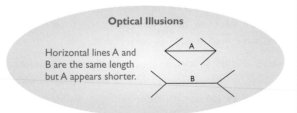

Optical Illusions

Horizontal lines A and B are the same length but A appears shorter.

il·lu·sion (i lū′zhən) **1** *n* something that is not what it seems to be: *On some nights the moon looks twice as big as usual, but it's only an illusion.* **2** *n* a false idea or belief: *Many people have the illusion that money brings happiness.*

il·lus·trate (il′ə strāt′) **1** *v* provide with pictures, diagrams, maps, etc. that explain or decorate: *This book is well illustrated.* **2** *v* make clear or explain by stories, examples, comparisons, etc.: *The way that a pump works was used to illustrate how the heart sends blood around the body.* **il·lus·trat·ed, il·lus·trat·ing.** –**il′lus·tra′tion**, *n*, –**il′lus·tra′tor**, *n.*

im– *a prefix often meaning* not. It is a form of the suffix **in-** used before the letters *b, m,* and *p,* as in *imbalance, immoral, impatient.*

I'm (īm) I am.

im·age (im′ij) **1** *n* an exact reflection or likeness: *You will see your image in this mirror. She is the image of her mother.* **2** *n* a picture or statue: *images on a TV screen.* **3** *n* a picture in the mind: *I have a clear image of what I want.* **4** *n* the way a person is seen by other people: *Lars thinks it will ruin his image if he wears galoshes.*

i·mag·i·nar·y (i maj′ə ner′ē) *adj* existing only in the imagination; not real: *The equator is an imaginary line around the earth halfway between the North and South Poles.* **i·mag·i·na·tion** *n* the ability to form pictures in your mind or to think up new ideas: *The child's imagination filled the woods with strange animals and fairies.*
i·mag·i·na·tive *adj* having or showing a good imagination: *an imaginative child, an imaginative story.* **i·mag·ine 1** *v* see in your mind: *Maria likes to imagine life as a great actor.* **2** *v* suppose; guess: *I imagine he's already left by now.* –**i·mag′i·na·ble**, *adj.*

i·mam (i màm′) *n* a Muslim leader of prayer.

im·i·tate (im′ə tāt′) *v* try to be like: *Cameron imitates his older brother.* **im·i·tat·ed, im·i·tat·ing.** –**im′i·ta′tion**, *n* or *adj.*

im·me·di·ate (i mē′dē it) *adj* coming at once, without delay: *Please send an immediate reply.* –**im·me′di·ate·ly**, *adv.*

im·mense (i mens′) *adj* huge: *An ocean is an immense body of water.* –**im·mense′ly**, *adv.*

im·merse (i mərs′) *v* put completely under water or other liquid: *Do not immerse this electric frying pan when washing it.* **im·mersed, im·mers·ing.** –**im·mer′sion**, *n.*

im·mi·grate (im′ə grāt′) *v* come into a country or region to live: *My parents immigrated to Canada in 1990.* A person who immigrates is called an **immigrant. im·mi·grat·ed, im·mi·grat·ing.** –**im′mi·gra′tion,** *n.*

CONFUSABLES .. immigrate

immigrate means "go": *My family immigrated to Canada from India in 1960.*

emigrate means "leave": *My family emigrated from India to Canada in 1960.*

im·mor·tal (i mȯr′təl) *adj* living forever or remembered forever: *the immortal Shakespeare.* –**im′mor·tal′i·ty** (im′ȯr tal′ə tē), *n.*

im·mune (i myūn′) *adj* protected from disease, poison, etc.: *Some people are immune to poison ivy; they can touch it without getting a rash.* Your **immune system** is the way your body fights disease. –**im·mu′ni·ty,** *n,* –**im′mu·ni·za′tion,** *n,* –**im′mu·nize′,** *v.*

im·pact (im′pakt) **1** *n* a hitting of one thing against another; collision: *The impact of the stone against the window shattered the glass.* **2** *n* an effect or influence: *Computers have had a strong impact on our lives.*

im·pair (im per′) **1** *v* weaken: *Poor food will impair your health.* **2** *v* **impaired,** affected by drinking alcohol: *impaired driving.*

im·par·tial (im pȧr′shəl) *adj* not favouring one side more than another: *A judge should be impartial.* –**im·par′tial·ly,** *adv.*

im·pe·ri·al (im pē′rē əl) **1** *adj* having to do with an empire or its ruler. **2** *adj* belonging to the old British standard of measures: *The imperial gallon is 20% bigger than the U.S. gallon.*

im·per·son·al (im pər′sə nəl) *adj* without thoughts and feelings: *Some people don't like to bank by machine because it is so impersonal.* **impersonal pronoun** any of the words *it, one, they,* or *you* when used to refer to a person or thing not named or identified. *Examples: It is humid in Victoria today. You should eat lots of fruits and vegetables.*

im·per·son·ate (im pər′sə nāt′) *v* imitate the voice, appearance, and manners of, especially in order to fool others: *The comedian impersonated a pop singer.* **im·per·son·at·ed, im·per·son·at·ing.**

im·per·ti·nent (im pər′tə nənt) *adj* cheeky; rude. –**im·per′ti·nence,** *n.*

im·pet·u·ous (im pech′ū əs) *adj* acting hastily, without thinking: *As soon as she heard the story, the impetuous Claudia fired off a very angry e-mail to her cousin, which she later regretted.* –**im·pet′u·ous·ly,** *adv.*

im·ply (im plī′) *v* mean something without saying it outright: *She gave a big smile to imply that she agreed with me.* **im·plied, im·ply·ing.** –**im′pli·ca′tion** (im′plə kā′shən), *n.*

im·port (im pȯrt′ *for 1,* im′pȯrt *for 2*) **1** *v* bring in from a foreign country for sale or use: *Canada imports sugar from Cuba.* **2** *n* something brought in from another country: *Rubber is a useful import.* –**im′por·ta′tion,** *n.*

im·por·tant (im pȯr′tənt) **1** *adj* worth paying attention to: *important decisions, an important occasion.* **2** *adj* famous or powerful: *The Prime Minister is an important person in Canada.* –**im·por′tance,** *n,* –**im·por′tant·ly,** *adv.*

im·pos·tor (im pos′tər) *n* a person who adopts a false name or character to trick others.

im·press (im pres′) *v* fill with admiration or respect: *Her generosity and courage really impressed me.* –**im·pres′sive,** *adj.*

im·pres·sion **1** *n* an effect produced on a person: *The fable of* The Tortoise and the Hare *seemed to make an impression on the class.* **2** *n* an idea or notion: *I have a vague impression that I locked my bicycle.* **3** *n* a mark made by pressing or stamping: *A dog had left the impression of its paws in the wet concrete.*

im·promp·tu (im promp′tū) *adj or adv* without thought or preparation beforehand: *an impromptu speech (adj). The pianist played a few songs impromptu (adv).*

im·prove (im prūv′) *v* make or become better: *You could improve this house by painting the walls.* **im·proved, im·prov·ing.** –**im·prove′ment,** *n.*

im·pro·vise (im′prə vīz′) **1** *v* perform something, such as a song or skit, making it up as you go along: *Quentin improvised a new verse for the school song at the football game.* **2** *v* make something with whatever happens to be around: *The girls improvised a tent out of two blankets and some long sticks.* **im·pro·vised, im·pro·vis·ing.** –**im′pro·vi·sa′tion,** *n.*

im·pu·dent (im′pyə dənt) *adj* rude and disrespectful: *The impudent boy made a face at the bus driver.* –**im′pu·dence,** *n,* –**im′pu·dent·ly,** *adv.*

im·pulse (im′puls) *n* a sudden desire to do something, without thinking about why: *On an impulse Claude decided to throw out all his hockey cards.* –**im·pul′sive,** *adj,* –**im·pul′sive·ly,** *adv.*

in (in) **In** is used with many different meanings, but its main meaning has to do with place or time: *Your snack is in the fridge; I will be back in an hour* (prep). *Bring the dog in* (adv).
in for, sure to get: *We are in for a storm.*
in on something, taking part; included or involved: *Are you in on the surprise party for Evan?*
ins and outs, the many different parts or details: *The coach knows the ins and outs of the game better than the players.*

in– *a prefix meaning* not, the opposite of, the absence of. *Incorrect* means "not *correct.*" *Inattention* means the opposite of *attention.*

in·au·gu·rate (i nog′yə rāt′) *v* mark the official opening of something: *The new stadium was inaugurated with a parade and ball game.* **in·au·gu·rat·ed, in·au·gu·rat·ing.** –**in·au′gu·ra′tion,** *n.*

in·born (in′bȯrn′) *adj* born in a person; natural: *an inborn sense of rhythm.*

in·cense (in′sens) *n* a substance that gives off a sweet-smelling smoke when burned.

in·ces·sant (in ses′ənt) *adj* never stopping; continual: *The roar of Niagara Falls is incessant.* –**in·ces′sant·ly,** *adv.*

inch (inch) *n* a non-metric measure of length, equal to about 2.5 cm.

in·ci·dent (in′sə dənt) *n* a happening; event, especially a minor one.

in·ci·den·tal (in′sə den′təl) *adj* happening by chance: *an incidental meeting of old friends on the street.* **in·ci·den·tal·ly** *adv* as a small thing along with something else: *She mentioned incidentally that she had seen Tony at the library.*

in·cin·er·ate (in sin′ə rāt′) *n* burn to ashes. An **incinerator** is a sort of furnace for burning garbage.

in·ci·sion (in sizh′ən) *n* a cut made in something: *The doctor made a small incision to remove the splinter from her foot.*

A person pushing a wheelbarrow up an incline

in·cline (in klīn′) *v* to slope: *The skateboard ramp inclines slightly.* An **inclined plane** is the scientific name for a ramp. **in·clined, in·clin·ing. be inclined,** have a desire, tendency, or interest: *I am inclined to agree with you. That child is inclined to be lazy.*

in·clude (in klūd′) **1** *v* put with others in a group: *They included the new student in all their games.* **2** *v* contain: *Canada's population includes people of many different cultural backgrounds.* **in·clud·ed, in·clud·ing.** –**in·clu′sion,** *n.*
in·clu·sive (in klū′siv) *adj* including: *"Read pages 10 to 20 inclusive"* means begin at page 10 and read through to the very end of page 20.

in·come (in′kum) *n* money that comes in from work, business, renting property, etc.: *Her yearly income is $40 000.*

in·crease (in krēs′ *for 1,* in′krēs *for 2*) **1** *v* make or become more or greater: *The number of students has increased every year.* **2** *n* a gain in size, numbers, etc.: *There was a great increase in my height last year.* **in·creased, in·creas·ing. in·creas·ing·ly** *adv* more and more: *As we continued to travel south, the weather became increasingly warm.*

in·cred·i·ble (in kred′ə bəl) *adj* hard to believe: *It's incredible that anyone could swim across Lake Ontario.* –**in·cred′i·bly,** *adv.*

in·cred·u·lous (in krej′ə ləs) *adj* unbelieving: *Dad listened to our story with an incredulous smile.* –**in·cred′u·lous·ly,** *adv.*

in·cu·bate (ing′kyə bāt′) *v* keep eggs, bacteria, etc. warm so that they will hatch or grow. An **incubator** is a machine with a box that can be kept at a set temperature; there are different kinds for hatching eggs and growing bacteria. Another kind is used in hospitals for babies born too early. **in·cu·bat·ed, in·cu·bat·ing.**

in·deed (in dēd′) **1** *adv* in fact: *She is hungry; indeed, she is almost starving.* **2** *interj* an expression of surprise: *Indeed! I never would have thought it.*

in·def·i·nite (in def′ə nit) **1** *adj* not exact: *"Maybe" is a very indefinite answer. "Anybody" and "something" are examples of* **indefinite pronouns**. **2** *adj* not limited: *We have an indefinite time to finish this work.* –**in·def′i·nite·ly,** *adv.*

indefinite article either of the articles **a** and **an.**

in·dent (in dent′) **1** *v* make or form notches or jags in an edge: *an indented coastline.* **2** *v* begin a line of writing farther from the margin than other lines. The first line of a paragraph is often indented. –**in′den·ta′tion,** *n.*

in·de·pend·ent (in′di pen′dənt) **1** *adj* not needing, wanting, or getting help from others: *Bears teach their cubs to be independent by showing them how to hunt for food.* **2** *adj* not influenced, ruled, or controlled by others: *Canada is an independent nation.* –**in′de·pen′dence,** *n,* –**in′de·pend′ent·ly,** *adv.*

in·dex (in′deks) *n* a list of what is in a book, telling on what pages to find certain names, topics, etc. It is usually at the end of the book. *pl* **in·dex·es** or **in·di·ces.**

index finger the finger next to the thumb; forefinger.

in·di·cate *v* point out; show: *The arrow on the sign indicates the way to Port Hope. A clock indicates the time.* –**in′di·ca′tion,** *n,* –**in′di·ca′tor,** *n.*

Indian (in′dē ən) **1** *n* a person whose homeland is India. **2** *adj* having to do with India or its people: *the Indian flag.* **3** *n* a somewhat old name for a person whose ancestors lived south of the Arctic in North or South America before the Europeans came.

USING WORDS . . . . . Indian

The name **Indian** came from a mistake that Christopher Columbus made. When he landed in America, he thought he had reached India, and so he called the people Indians.

Some people still use this name, and you can see it in the names of things like Indian corn. Generally it is better to use **First Nations**, **aboriginal people**, or **Native people**. Better still, use the exact name of the group (for example, Cree, Nisga'a) if you know it. See the map of Canada in the Appendix.

---

in·dif·fer·ent (in dif′ə rənt) *adj* not caring one way or the other: *Rose enjoyed the trip, but Gareth was indifferent.* –**in·dif′fer·ence,** *n,* –**in·dif′fer·ent·ly,** *adv.*

Musk-ox—about 150 cm high at the shoulder. Musk-ox are indigenous to Canada.

in·dig·e·nous (in dij′ə nəs) *adj* native; originally living or growing in a particular country, region, soil, climate, etc.: *The Inuit are an indigenous people of North America.*

in·dig·nant (in dig′nənt) *adj* angry at something unfair or mean: *We were indignant at the nasty rumours, which were totally untrue.* –**in·dig′nant·ly,** *adv,* –**in′dig·na′tion,** *n.*

in·di·vid·u·al (in′də vij′ū əl) **1** *n* a single person, animal, or thing: *She is a very talented individual. We saw a herd of giraffes containing 30 individuals.* **2** *adj* for one only: *A bench is for several people; chairs are individual seats.* **3** *adj* belonging to one person or thing: *Each person has an individual style of handwriting.* –**in′di·vid′u·al′i·ty,** *n,* –**in′di·vid′u·al·ly,** *adv.*

in·door (in′dòr′) **1** *adj* done, found, or used inside a building: *indoor skating, an indoor rink.* **2 indoors,** *adv* inside a building: *Let's eat our lunch indoors.*

in·dulge (in dulj′) *v* give in to the wishes of: *I indulged myself by sleeping in till noon.* **in·dulged, in·dulg·ing.** –**in·dul′gence,** *n,* –**in·dul′gent,** *adj.*

in·dus·try (in′dəs trē) **1** *n* any branch of business or manufacturing: *the auto industry.* **2** *n* hard work: *Through industry and determination the pioneer built up a successful farm in Manitoba.* *pl* **in·dus·tries.** –**in·dus′tri·al,** *adj.* **in·dus·tri·al·ize** *v* to develop a lot of large industries in a place. –**in·dus′tri·al·i·za′tion,** *n.* **in·dus·tri·ous** *adj* working hard and steadily: *The honey bee is a most industrious insect.*

in·ev·i·ta·ble (in ev'ə tə bəl) *adj* sure to happen: *Mistakes are the inevitable result of carelessness.* –**in·ev'i·ta·bly,** *adv.*

in·fa·mous (in'fə məs) *adj* having a very bad reputation: *an infamous traitor.*

in·fant (in'fənt) *n* a very young baby. –**in'fan·cy,** *n,* –**in'fan·tile',** *adj.*

in·fect (in fekt') **1** *v* cause disease: *Dirt infects an open cut.* **2** *v* influence by spreading from one to another: *A computer virus has infected this disk.*

in·fec·tion 1 *n* the entry of germs or viruses: *The cut was cleaned and bandaged to prevent infection.* **2** *n* a disease caused by germs or viruses: *Measles is an infection that spreads from one person to another.* –**in·fec'tious,** *adj.*

in·fer (in fər') *v* form an opinion by drawing your own conclusions: *From her big smile I inferred that she agreed with me.* **in·ferred, in·fer·ring.**

in·fe·ri·or (in fē'rē ər) **1** *adj* not very good: *an inferior grade of maple syrup.* **2** *adj* lower in quality than another thing or person: *This cloth is inferior to real silk.* **3** *n* a person of lower rank: *She was a good leader and respected her inferiors.* –**in·fe'ri·or'i·ty,** *n.*

in·field (in'fēld') **1** *n* the part of a baseball field inside the base lines. **2** *n* the first, second, and third base players and shortstop of a baseball team: *That team has a good infield.* –**in'field'er,** *n.*

in·fi·nite (in'fə nit) *adj* without limits; endless: *the infinite extent of space. Training our dog took infinite patience.* –**in'fi·nite·ly,** *adv,* –**in·fin'i·ty,** *n.*
in·fin·i·tive (in fin'ə tiv) *n* the basic form of a verb, that names an action but does not show who did it or when it was done. Infinitives are used with *to* or together with another verb. *Example: sing* in *It is fun to sing* or *She can sing.*

in·firm (in fərm') *adj* weak; in poor health. –**in·firm'i·ty,** *n.*
in·fir·ma·ry *n* a place where sick or injured people are cared for in a school, camp, etc.

in·flame (in flām') **1** *v* excite very much: *The leader's stirring speech inflamed the crowd.* **2** *v* make or become hot, red, sore, or swollen: *The smoke had inflamed the firefighter's eyes.* **in·flamed, in·flam·ing.** –**in'flam·ma'tion,** *n.*

in·flam·ma·ble (in flam'ə bəl) *adj* easily set on fire: *Paper and gasoline are inflammable.*

in·flate (in flāt') **1** *v* fill with air or gas: *to inflate a balloon.* **2** *v* increase prices beyond a normal amount. **in·flat·ed, in·flat·ing.** –**in·fla'tion,** *n.*

in·flu·ence (in'flü əns) **1** *n* the power to affect someone or something without using force: *Because she's an expert she has a lot of influence. Mountains and oceans have an important influence on climate.* **2** *n* a person or thing that has such power: *Hon-Wah was a good influence in our class.* **3** *v* have an effect on: *The moon influences the tides.* **in·flu·enced, in·flu·enc·ing.** –**in'flu·en'tial** (in'flü en'shəl), *adj.*

in·flu·en·za (in'flü en'zə) *n* an infectious disease resembling a very bad cold with fever, aches, and often stomach upset. This name is usually shortened to **flu.**

in·form (in fôrm') *v* tell; let someone know: *Report cards inform parents about a child's progress at school.*

in·for·ma·tion (in'fər mā'shən) *n* knowledge; facts; news: *A dictionary gives information about words.* Something that gives information is **informative** (in fôr'mə tiv). **information highway** the entire system of computers, telephones, and electronic links all over the world that move words, numbers, and images from one place to another.

in·fu·ri·ate (in fyu'rē āt') *v* make very angry: *The man was infuriated when the passing cyclist splashed him with mud.* **in·fu·ri·at·ed, in·fu·ri·at·ing.**

in·ge·ni·ous (in jēn' yəs) *adj* clever; showing creative imagination: *Using her belt and a key ring, the ingenious girl managed to pull the kite out of the tree.* –**in·gen'ious·ly,** *adv,* –**in'ge·nu'i·ty** (in'jə nyü'ə tē), *n.*

in·gen·u·ous (in jen'yü əs) *adj* open and honest, and trusting everyone else to be the same way: *It never occurred to the ingenuous child that anyone would try to cheat.* –**in·gen'u·ous·ly,** *adv,* –**in·gen'u·ous·ness,** *n.*

in·gre·di·ent (in grē'dē ənt) *n* one of the parts of a mixture: *Flour is one of the ingredients of bread.*

in·hab·it (in hab'it) *v* live in: *Fish inhabit the Great Lakes.* –**in·hab'i·tant,** *n.*

in·hale (in hāl′) *v* breathe in. An **inhalator** (in′hə lā′tər) is a device used for breathing in medicine. **in·haled, in·hal·ing.**

in·her·it (in her′it) *v* get as a gift from another person after he or she dies: *Mrs. Chan's nephew inherited the farm after she died.* –**in·her′it·ance,** *n.*

in·hu·man (in hyū′mən) *adj* without ordinary human kindness; cruel: *inhuman acts of torture.* –**in′hu·man′i·ty,** *n.*

i·ni·tial (i nish′əl) **1** *adj* coming at the beginning; first: *John's initial effort at skating was a failure.* **2** *n* the first letter of a word: *The initials P.E.I. stand for Prince Edward Island.*

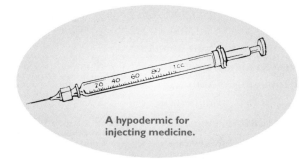
A hypodermic for injecting medicine.

in·ject (in jekt′) *v* give medicine by needle, through the skin: *The doctor injected her with painkiller.* –**in·jec′tion,** *n.*

in·jure (in′jər) *v* hurt: *She injured her ankle while skiing.* **in·jured, in·jur·ing.** –**in′ju·ry,** *n.*

ink (ingk) *n* the black or coloured liquid in a pen or printer: *Do you always write with green ink?* –**ink′y,** *adj.*

in·land (in′land′ *or* in′lənd) *adj* or *adv* away from the coast or the border; toward the inner part of a country: *an inland town (adj). The source of the river is 300 km inland (adv).*

in·let (in′let′ *or* in′lət) *n* a narrow strip of water running from a larger body of water into the land: *Port Alberni is located on a deep inlet of Vancouver Island.*

in·line skates (in′līn′ skāts′) roller skates that have four wheels in a single row, one behind the other. –**inline skating.**

inn (in) *n* especially in earlier times, a place where travellers and others could get a room to sleep in and meals. An inn was smaller and more homelike than most modern hotels, and was run by an **innkeeper.**

in·ner (in′ər) **1** *adj* farther in; inside: *an inner office.* **2** *adj* private; secret: *She kept her inner thoughts to herself.*

in·ning (in′ing) *n* a division of a baseball game giving each team a turn at bat. Unless a tie must be broken, there are nine innings in a game.

in·no·cent (in′ə sənt) **1** *adj* doing no wrong; not guilty: *The accused man was found innocent of the crime.* **2** *adj* not knowing about evil, and so not expecting it: *innocent trust.* **3** *adj* doing or meaning no harm: *an innocent prank.* –**in′no·cence,** *n,* –**in′no·cent·ly,** *adv.*

in·no·va·tion (in′ə vā′shən) *n* a change in the way things are done: *The new principal made many innovations.* –**in′no·vate′,** *v,* –**in′no·va′tive,** *adj.*

in·put (in′pùt′) **1** *n* suggestions, comments, or additional information from interested people: *We need everyone's input to plan our trip to Nova Scotia.* **2** *v* feed information into a computer. **in·put, in·put·ting.**

in·quest (in′kwest) *n* a legal inquiry to find out the cause of a sudden death.

in·quire (in kwīr′) *v* ask for information. **in·quired, in·quir·ing.** –**in·quir′y** (in kwĭ′rē *or* in′kwə rē), *n.*

in·quis·i·tive (in kwiz′ə tiv) **1** *adj* curious; asking many questions: *Children are usually inquisitive.* **2** *adj* nosy: *being spied on by inquisitive neighbours.*

in·scribe (in skrīb′) *v* write or engrave on: *The school ring was inscribed with her name.* **in·scribed, in·scrib·ing.** –**in·scrip′tion,** *n.*

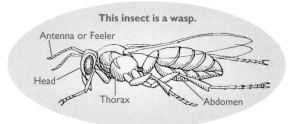
This insect is a wasp.
Antenna or Feeler
Head
Thorax
Abdomen

in·sect (in′sekt) *n* a small animal whose body is divided into three parts and has no backbone. Insects have three pairs of legs and usually one or two pairs of wings. Flies, mosquitoes, gnats, wasps, and bees are insects.

in·sec·ti·cide (in sek′tə sīd′) *n* a substance for killing insects.

in·se·cure (in′si kyūr′) **1** *adj* lacking confidence: *Marcel felt quite insecure among all the older kids at camp.* **2** *adj* not safe or dependable: *an insecure position.* –**in′se·cu′ri·ty,** *n.*

in·sert (in sərt′) *v* put in; set in: *to insert a key into a lock, to insert a word into a sentence.* –**in·ser′tion,** *n.*

in·side (in′sīd′) *n, adj, adv,* or *prep* **Inside** has to do with the inner part or surface of something: *The inside of the box was lined with coloured paper* (n). *I hope we can get an inside seat at the game* (adj). *I guarded the opening to the cave while Jo went inside* (adv). *The nut is inside the shell* (prep).
an inside job, something, usually a crime, done to an organization by an **insider,** one of its own members.
inside information, information that only those inside a certain group know. Similarly, an **inside joke** is a private joke.
inside out, 1 so that the part that should be inside is showing on the outside: *He turned his pockets inside out.* **2** completely: *I know this lesson inside out.*

in·sist (in sist′) *v* do, demand, or say something and refuse to back down: *He insists on biking to school in every kind of weather.* –**in·sist′ence,** *n,* –**in·sist′ent,** *adj.*

in·so·lent (in′sə lənt) *adj* extremely disrespectful or rude. –**in′so·lence,** *n,* –**in′so·lent·ly,** *adv.*

in·sol·u·ble (in sol′yə bəl) **1** *adj* unable to dissolve in a liquid. **2** *adj* impossible to solve: *an insoluble problem.*

in·spect (in spekt′) *v* look over carefully: *A dentist inspects my teeth twice a year.* –**in·spec′tion,** *n.*
in·spec·tor *n* an official whose job is to inspect: *The public health inspector visits all restaurants.*

in·spire (in spīr′) *v* give someone an idea, a feeling, or a reason to do something: *Abby's experience of rafting on the Firth River inspired her to write a story.* **in·spired, in·spir·ing.** –**in′spi·ra′tion,** *n.*

in·stall (in stol′) *v* put equipment into a building, car, or other place and make it ready for use: *to install a dishwasher.* –**in′stal·la′tion,** *n.*

in·stal·ment (in stol′mənt) **1** *n* a part of a sum of money to be paid at stated times: *She has to pay the $100 in ten monthly instalments of $10.* **2** *n* one part of a series: Chatelaine *had a serial story in six instalments.* Another spelling is **installment.**

in·stance (in′stəns) **1** *n* a person or thing that can be used as an example: *That rude question was an instance of bad manners.* **2** *n* case; situation: *In this instance Derrick decided it was best not to go along.*
for instance, as an example: *Her many hobbies include, for instance, skating and stamp collecting.*

in·stant (in′stənt) **1** *n* a moment: *He paused for an instant.* **2** *adj* immediate: *The medicine gave instant relief from pain.* **3** *adj* made quickly using a mix or kit: *instant pudding, instant potatoes.* –**in′stant·ly,** *adv.*
in·stan·ta·ne·ous (in′stən tā′nē əs) *adj* happening or done in an instant: *A flash of lightning is instantaneous.*

in·stead (in sted′) *adv* in place of someone or something else; rather than this or that: *Emma stayed home, and her sister went riding instead.*
instead of, rather than; in place of: *Instead of studying, she read a story.*

in·stinct (in′stingkt) *n* a natural ability that causes animals to behave in a certain way without having to learn it; for instance, it is by instinct that birds fly south for the winter. –**in·stinc′tive,** *adj.*

in·sti·tu·tion (in′stə tyū′shən *or* in′stə tū′shən) **1** *n* an organization set up to serve the public in some way, such as a church, hospital, or prison. An institution carries on its work in a building. **2** *n* an established law or custom: *Summer camp at Algonquin Park is an institution in our family.*

in·struct (in strukt′) **1** *v* teach. Something that teaches you a lot is **instructive. 2** *v* tell; give orders: *The owners of the house instructed their agent to sell it.*
in·struc·tion 1 *n* teaching or lessons: *to give instruction in music.* **2 instructions,** *pl.n* orders: *Their instructions were to pick him up at seven o'clock.* **3 instructions,** *pl.n* an explanation of how to do or use something: *The kit comes with instructions for building the model dinosaur.*
in·struc·tor *n* teacher.

in·stru·ment (in'strə mənt) **1** *n* something used to make music, such as a trumpet, guitar, or piano. **2** *n* a tool or machine: *a dentist's instruments. A thermometer is an instrument for measuring temperature.*

in·sult (in sult' *for 1*, in'sult *for 2*) **1** *v* treat very rudely or disrespectfully: *The protestors insulted the flag by throwing mud on it.* **2** *n* remark or action that shows a complete lack of respect; a put-down: *To be called a dope is an insult.*

in·tact (in takt') *adj* not damaged or injured and with no part missing: *The money was returned intact by the boy who found it.*

in·te·grate (in'tə grāt') *v* bring separate units or parts together into a whole: *The two schools were integrated to cut costs. Knowing English helps newcomers to integrate more quickly into Canadian society.* **in·te·grat·ed, in·te·grat·ing.** –**in'te·gra'tion,** *n.*

in·tel·li·gence (in tel'ə jəns) *n* the ability to learn and think: *A dog has more intelligence than a worm.*

in·tel·li·gent *adj* able to learn and think well; quick to understand. –**in·tel'li·gent·ly,** *adv.*

in·tel·li·gi·ble *adj* able to be understood; clear: *My baby brother babbles a lot but hasn't said any intelligible words yet.*

in·tend (in tend') *v* plan: *We intend to return to Regina soon. I didn't intend to hurt your feelings.*

in·tent 1 *adj* paying complete attention: *intent on a task.* **2** *adj* determined: *I was intent on winning.* –**in·tent'ly,** *adv.*

in·ten·tion *n* a plan: *Lucas had no intention of hurting her feelings.*

in·ten·tion·al *adj* done or made on purpose: *That fire was no accident–it was intentional.* –**in·ten'tion·al·ly,** *adv.*

in·tense (in tens') *adj* very great: *A bad burn causes intense pain.* –**in·tense'ly,** *adv.*

inter– *a prefix meaning* one with the other, or between, as in *international, interchange.*

in·ter·act (in'tər akt') **1** *v* have an effect on each other: *The oxygen in the air interacts with the metal to cause rust.* **2** *v* communicate directly with a computer program to make things happen. An **interactive** computer program may ask you a question that you have to answer before the program will continue. –**in'ter·ac'tion,** *n.*

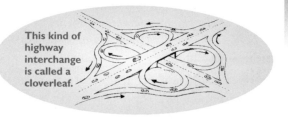

This kind of highway interchange is called a cloverleaf.

in·ter·change (in'tər chānj' *for 1*, in'tər chānj' *for 2*) **1** *v* switch; exchange: *The two girls interchanged hats.* **in·ter·changed, in·ter·chang·ing.** **2** *n* a place where you can get on or off a highway by using a ramp.

in·ter·change·a·ble (in'tər chān'jə bəl) *adj* that can be used in place of each other: *These two bicycles have many interchangeable parts.*

in·ter·com (in'tər kom') *n* a radio or telephone system that makes it possible to speak to everyone in different parts of a building.

in·ter·est (in'trist *or* in'tə rest') **1** *n* a feeling of wanting to know, see, do, or have: *an interest in music.* **2** *v* catch the attention of: *A good story interests us.*

in·ter·est·ed (in'tris tid *or* in'tə res'təd) *adj* feeling or showing interest.

in·ter·est·ing (in'tris ting *or* in'tə res'ting) *adj* holding someone's attention: *Stories about travel are interesting.*

in someone's interest, to someone's advantage: *It is in everyone's interest to protect the environment.*

in the interest of, for the sake of: *In the interest of safety, wear a bicycle helmet.*

USING WORDS ... interested

The adjective **interested** has two opposites.

uninterested means "not interested": *He was uninterested in watching the game.*

disinterested means "neutral and fair": *A disinterested onlooker agreed to referee the game.*

---

in·ter·fere (in'tər fēr') **1** *v* clash or conflict: *I can change my plan if it interferes with your holiday.* **2** *v* get involved in other people's business. **in·ter·fered, in·ter·fer·ing.**

in·ter·fer·ence 1 *n* the act of interfering: *Her interference spoiled our game.* **2** *n* in radio or television, the interruption of the signal causing poor sound or picture quality. **3** *n* in football, hockey, and other sports, the act of blocking an opposing player in a way not allowed by the rules.

in·ter·im (in'tə rim) **1** *n* meantime; the time between: *The plane couldn't leave till the blizzard stopped, so they slept in the interim.* **2** *adj* for the meantime; temporary: *an interim report.*

in·te·ri·or (in tē'rē ər) **1** *adj* or *n* inside: *an interior surface* (*adj*). *The interior of the house was beautifully decorated* (*n*). **2** *n* the land away from the coast: *The interior of Victoria Island is thinly populated.*

in·ter·ject (in'tər jekt') *v* throw in between other remarks: *Every now and then the speaker interjected a joke or story to keep us interested.*

in·ter·jec·tion 1 *n* an exclamation of surprise, pain, joy, or other feeling. Some common interjections are *Wow! Ouch!* and *Hurrah!* **2** *n* a remark thrown in.

in·ter·lock (in'tər lok') *v* fit tightly together; lock together: *the interlocking pieces of a jigsaw.*

in·ter·me·di·ate (in'tər mē'dē it) *adj* in between: *The language school offers beginning, intermediate, and advanced courses in French. Grey is intermediate between black and white.*

in·ter·mis·sion (in'tər mish'ən) *n* a break, especially in a show: *The band played from 7:00 to 10:00 with a short intermission at 8:30.*

in·ter·mit·tent *adj* continually stopping and starting again: *The intermittent noise of the streetcars kept him awake.* **–in'ter·mit'tent·ly,** *adv.*

in·ter·nal (in tər'nəl) *adj* inner; on the inside: *internal injuries, the internal parts of a machine.* **–in·ter'nal·ly,** *adv.*

in·ter·na·tion·al (in'tər nash'ə nəl) *adj* between or among nations; involving more than one nation: *All countries are governed by international law.* **–in'ter·na'tion·al·ly,** *adv.*

Internet (in'tər net') *n* a huge computer network that links many smaller networks around the world. You can send and receive e-mail, find information, and shop or do banking on the Internet. Its name is often shortened to **the Net.**

in·ter·plan·e·tar·y (in'tər plan'ə ter'ē) *adj* between the planets: *interplanetary travel.*

in·ter·pret (in tər'prit) **1** *v* translate a speaker's words into another language. **2** *v* explain the meaning of: *to interpret a coded message.* **–in·ter'pre·ta'tion,** *n,* **–in·ter'pret·er,** *n.*

in·ter·ro·gate (in ter'ə gāt') *v* ask someone a lot of detailed questions: *The lawyer took two hours to interrogate the witness.* **in·ter·ro·gat·ed, in·ter·ro·gat·ing. –in·ter'ro·ga'tion,** *n.*

in·ter·rog·a·tive (in'tə rog'ə tiv) *adj* or *n* asking a question. An **interrogative sentence** is a question. *Who, why, when, where,* and *what* are **interrogative words** or **interrogatives.**

> **Grammar** ✓*Check* . **interrogatives**
>
> The interrogatives **who, why, when, where,** and **what** are called **the five W's.** Reporters often think of questions using the five W's to make sure they have included all the important information they need in their news stories.

in·ter·rupt (in'tə rupt') **1** *v* break in on something going on and cause it to stop: *A fire drill interrupted the lesson.* **2** *v* begin talking when someone else is talking: *It is not polite to interrupt.* **–in'ter·rup'tion,** *n.*

in·ter·sect (in'tər sekt') *v* cross: *Portage and Main are two streets that intersect in Winnipeg.* An **intersection** is a place where two things cross, especially two streets.

in·ter·stel·lar (in'tər stel'ər) *adj* among or between the stars: *We dream of interstellar travel.*

in·ter·val (in'tər vəl) *n* the time or space between: *There is an interval of one hour between trains. There are trees at intervals of 10 m.*

in·ter·view (in'tər vyū') **1** *n* a meeting or conversation to talk over something special or get information: *My father had an interview with the teacher about my work.* **2** *v* meet and talk with, especially to obtain information: *The employer interviewed six students for the job before hiring any of them.*

in·ti·mate (in'tə mit) **1** *adj* very familiar and close: *an intimate friend.* **2** *adj* personal: *an intimate conversation.* **–in'ti·ma·cy,** *n,* **–in'ti·mate·ly,** *adv.*

in·tim·i·date (in tim'ə dāt') *v* make afraid or nervous; influence by fear: *They used threats to intimidate us. We were intimidated into silence.* **in·tim·i·dat·ed, in·tim·i·dat·ing. –in·tim'i·da'tion,** *n.*

in·trep·id (in trep'id) *adj* fearless; very brave: *The intrepid Canadian explorers were not deterred by wild animals or freezing weather.*

in·trigue (in trēg′) **1** *n* secret plotting: *The mystery novel was filled with intrigue.* **2** *v* stir up someone's curiosity: *The book's unusual title intrigued me so I borrowed it from the library.* **in·trigued, in·tri·guing.**

in·tro·duce (in′trə dyūs′ *or* in′trə dūs′) **1** *v* tell others who someone is: *The principal introduced the speaker to us.* **2** *v* begin; start: *He introduced his speech with a joke.* **in·tro·duced, in·tro·duc·ing.** **–in′tro·duc′to·ry** (in′trə duk′tə rē), *adj.*

in·tro·duc·tion (in′trə duk′shən) **1** *n* the act of introducing: *We were waiting for an introduction to her visitor.* **2** *n* a beginning section that leads up to the main part: *This book has a ten-page introduction by the editor.*

in·trude (in trūd′) *v* come in where you aren't expected: *Do not intrude on the privacy of your neighbours.* **in·trud·ed, in·trud·ing.** **–in·trud′er,** *n,* **–in·tru′sion,** *n.*

in·tu·i·tion (in′tyū ish′ən *or* in′tū ish′ən) *n* a way of knowing or understanding things directly without being able to explain why.

❧ **I·nu·it** (in′ū it *or* in′yū it) **1** *pl.n* an aboriginal people living mainly in the arctic regions of Canada and on the northwestern coasts of Alaska. They are the original inhabitants of the Arctic. The Inuit speak two main languages, **Inuktitut** (i nŭk′tə tŭt′) and **Inupiat** (i nū′pē at′). **2** *adj* having to do with these people: *Inuit traditions, Inuit art.* *sing* **I·nuk** (in′ŭk).

> ### USING WORDS ..... Inuit
>
> In Canada, the word **Inuit,** which means "the people," should be used instead of **Eskimo.** The word **Eskimo** comes from an old Algonquian word meaning "eaters of raw flesh," and is not used by the Inuit.

in·vade (in vād′) *v* enter with force or as an enemy: *Soldiers invaded the country to conquer it.* **in·vad·ed, in·vad·ing.** **–in·vad′er,** *n,* **–in·va′sion,** *n.*

in·va·lid (in′və lid) *n* person who is weak because of sickness or injury. An invalid cannot get around and do things.

in·val·u·a·ble (in val′yə bəl) *adj* more valuable than anyone can say: *Good health is an invaluable possession.*

Armand Bombardier invented the snowmobile when he was only fifteen years old.

in·vent (in vent′) **1** *v* think up something new. **2** *v* make up; think up: *to invent an excuse.* **–in·ven′tion,** *n,* **–in·ven′tive,** *adj,* **–in·ven′tor,** *n.*

in·vert (in vərt′) **1** *v* turn upside down: *He inverted the glass and the water ran out.* **2** *v* switch the order or position of: *If you invert I can, you have can I.* **–in·ver′sion,** *n.*

in·ves·ti·gate (in ves′tə gāt′) *v* look into something carefully to find out about it: *Detectives investigate crimes. Scientists investigate nature.* **in·ves·ti·gat·ed, in·ves·ti·gat·ing.** **–in·ves′ti·ga′tion,** *n,* **–in·ves′ti·ga′tor,** *n.*

in·vite (in vīt′) *v* ask someone politely to come to some place or to do something: *Joel invited his friends to the Canada Day picnic.* **in·vit·ed, in·vit·ing.** **–in′vi·ta′tion,** *n.*

in·volve (in volv′) **1** *v* have as a necessary condition: *Babysitting involves a lot of responsibility.* **2** *v* bring into a situation: *Don't involve me in your argument!* **3** *v* take up the attention of: *Isabella was completely involved in her puzzle.* **4 involved,** *adj* complicated. **in·volved, in·volv·ing.** **–in·volve′ment,** *n.*

in·ward (in′wərd) *adv or adj* toward the inside: *a passage leading inward* (*adv*). *the inward parts of the body* (*adj*). **Inwards** is another form you can use for the adverb.

i·ron (ī′ərn) **1** *n* a useful metal, from which tools and many other things are made: *Steel is made from iron.* **2** *n* an electrical appliance with a flat surface that is heated and used to smooth clothing. It used to be made of this metal. **3** *v* smooth with an iron: *My brother irons his own shirts.*

ir·reg·u·lar (i reg′yə lər) **1** *adj* not even: *irregular breathing. Newfoundland has a very irregular coastline.* **2** *adj* not following a pattern: *irregular behaviour, irregular mail delivery, an irregular verb form.* –**ir·reg′u·lar′i·ty**, *n.*

ir·rel·e·vant (i rel′ə vənt) *adj* off the topic: *He interrupted the discussion several times with irrelevant remarks about the weather.*

ir·re·sist·i·ble (ēr′i zis′tə bəl) *adj* that cannot be resisted: *an irresistible desire to laugh. That chocolate cake looks irresistible.*

ir·re·spon·si·ble (ēr′i spon′sə bəl) *adj* not thinking or caring about the consequences of your actions: *It was irresponsible to leave the broken glass on the sidewalk.* –**ir′re·spon′si·bil′i·ty**, *n,* –**ir·re·spon′si·bly**, *adv.*

ir·ri·gate (ēr′ə gāt′) *v* bring water to an area of land using ditches, pipes, sprinklers, etc.: *Farmers in Saskatchewan irrigate dry land to make crops grow better.* **ir·ri·gat·ed, ir·ri·gat·ing.** –**ir′ri·ga′tion**, *n.*

ir·ri·tate (ēr′ə tāt′) **1** *v* make impatient or angry; bug: *The boy's foolish questions irritated his mother. Flies irritate horses.* A person who is easily irritated is **irritable**. **2** *v* make unnaturally sensitive or sore: *Some soaps irritate the skin.* **ir·ri·tat·ed, ir·ri·tat·ing.** –**ir′ri·ta′tion**, *n.*

–ish *a suffix meaning:* **1** sort of or sort of like. *Greenish* means *"sort of green." Fallish* means *"sort of like fall."* **2** having to do with a particular people or their language: *Polish, Scottish.*

Is·lam (is làm′) the religion of Muslims, based on the Qu'ran, the holy book that contains God's message to the prophet Muhammad. –**Is·lam′ic**, *adj.*

is·land (ī′lənd) *n* a body of land smaller than a continent and completely surrounded by water. A person who lives on an island is an **islander**.

i·so·late (ī′sə lāt′) *v* separate from others or from each other; keep alone: *The prison guards isolated the prisoner who had attacked his cellmate.* **i·so·lat·ed, i·so·lat·ing.** –**i′so·la′tion**, *n.*

is·sue (ish′yū) **1** *n* one publishing of a magazine or newspaper: *Did you read the March issue of* Owl *magazine?* **2** *n* something that is being discussed or that needs to be settled: *We would like to make a trip to Saskatchewan this summer, but cost is an issue.* **is·sued, is·su·ing.**

make an issue of, treat something as a problem: *Do you have to make an issue of every little thing?*

i·tal·ic (i tal′ik) **1** *adj* describing type whose letters slant to the right: *These words are in italic type.* **2 italics,** *pl.n* type whose letters slant to the right: *Put the title in italics.* When you put something in italics, you **italicize** it.

itch (ich) **1** *n* a ticklish, prickling feeling in your skin that makes you want to scratch. **2** *v* have or cause this feeling: *Mosquito bites itch. My finger itches.* **3** *n* a restless, eager desire: *Amanda always had an itch to get out and explore.* **4** *v* have such a desire: *He was itching to find out their secret.* –**itch′y**, *adj.*

i·tem (ī′təm) **1** *n* an individual thing or article: *The list had twelve items on it.* **2** *n* a piece of news: *There were several interesting items in today's* Edmonton Journal.

its (its) *adj* the possessive form of **it**; belonging to it: *The cat chased its tail.*

it's (its) **1** it is: *It's my turn.* **2** it has: *It's been a beautiful day.*

CONFUSABLES .... its/it's

its means "belonging to it": *The dog ate its food.*
it's means "it is": *It's almost four o'clock.*

it·self (it self′) *pron* a form used instead of **it** when referring back to the subject of the sentence: *The horse tripped and hurt itself. The dog saw itself in the mirror.*

I've (īv) I have.

i·vo·ry (ī′və rē) **1** *n* the hard, white substance that the tusks of elephant and walrus are made of. **2** *n* or *adj* creamy white.

j or **J** (jā) *n* the tenth letter of the English alphabet, or the sound that it stands for. *pl* **j's** or **J's.**

jab (jab) *v* stick something pointed into: *Joss jabbed his fork into the potato.* **jabbed, jab·bing.**

jab·ber (jab′ər) *v* talk very fast or foolishly.

jack (jak) **1** *n* a device for raising heavy things a short distance. It may be used to raise one end of a car in order to change a tire. **2** *n* a place to plug something in, especially a phone.
jack-knife 1 *n* a large, strong pocketknife. **2** *v* fold or double up like a jack-knife: *The car and its trailer jack-knifed on the icy Trans-Canada highway.* **3** *n* a dive that you perform by bending to touch your toes in the air and then straightening out again before hitting the water.
jack-o'-lan·tern *n* a pumpkin hollowed out and cut to look like a face, lit up by a candle inside and used as a Halloween decoration. **jack pine** a pine tree of North America. Jack pine cones usually stay tightly closed. They release their seeds only when there is high heat, such as in a forest fire. **jack·pot** *n* a large pool of prize money that keeps increasing until someone wins it. **jack-rab·bit** *n* a large hare of North America, with long ears and long back legs.
hit the jackpot, have a stroke of very good luck; have great success.
jack up, *Informal.* raise prices, wages, etc.: *Stores jacked up many prices this month.*

jack·et (jak′it) **1** *n* a short coat. **2** *n* an outer covering: *a book jacket.*

jag·ged (jag′id) *adj* with sharp points sticking out; unevenly cut or torn: *We cut our bare feet on the jagged rocks along the Newfoundland coast.*

jag·uar (jag′wȧr) *n* a large wild cat that has yellowish brown fur with black spots. Jaguars live in the jungles of Central and South America.

jail (jāl) *n* a place where people are kept locked up while waiting to be tried in court or as punishment for a minor offence.

Jain (jīn) *n* a follower of the teachings and practices of **Mahavira** (mȧ′hə vē′rə), who lived in the 500s B.C., around the same time as Buddha. Jains believe in reincarnation and lead a very simple lifestyle. Because they are against any form of violence against any living creature, they are vegetarian. **–Jain′ism,** *n.*

ja·lop·y (jə lop′ē) *n Informal.* an old car in bad shape. *pl* **ja·lop·ies.**

jam (jam) **1** *n* fruit boiled with sugar until it forms a thick, sweet mixture: *raspberry jam.* **2** *v* push or squeeze: *They jammed us all into one bus.* **3** *v* block up by crowding: *Powell River was jammed with logs.* **Jam-packed** means "completely filled up." **4** *v* stick: *The window has jammed.* **jammed, jamming. 5** *n Informal.* a difficulty: *What a jam! I lost my key and it was pouring rain.* **–jam′my,** *adj.*

jan·gle (jang′gəl) *v* make a loud, clanging noise: *The pots and pans jangled in the kitchen. The camp counsellor jangled a bell.* **jan·gled, jan·gling.**

jar (jȧr) *n* a deep container made of glass or clay with a wide mouth and usually a lid: *a jar of jam, a cookie jar.*

jar·gon (jȧr′gən) **1** *n* language that fails to communicate because it is full of long or fancy words, and very complicated sentences. **2** *n* the technical words of a special group or profession: *medical jargon.*

Grammar ✓*Check* . . . . . **jargon**

Remember to use words your audience will understand. If you are explaining a computer game to someone who had never played, for example, you should avoid **jargon** such as "warping," or "jump block." Either find simple English words to replace them, or explain what they mean.

---

jaunt (jont) *n* a short trip, especially for fun.
jaun·ty *adj* carefree and light: *The happy child walks with a jaunty step.* **–jaun′ti·ly,** *adv.*

jave·lin (jav′lin) *n* a light spear. The **javelin throw** is a track-and-field event won by the person who throws the javelin the farthest.

jaw (jo) **1** Also, **jawbone,** *n* either of two skull bones that hold your teeth.
2 jaws, *pl.n* anything that grips, swallows, or forms an opening like a mouth: *the jaw of a canyon, the jaws of a pair of pliers.*

jay (jā) *n* a bird found in North America and Europe, related to the crow. Two kinds found in Canada are the **Canada jay** and the **bluejay.**.
jay·walk *v Informal.* walk across a street without paying attention to traffic. –**jay'walk'er,** *n.*

jazz (jaz) **1** *n* a light-hearted style of music with a strong, fast, changeable rhythm.
2 jazz up, *v* make fancier or more interesting. –**jazz'y,** *adj.*

jeal·ous (jel'əs) **1** *adj* afraid that someone you love may prefer someone else: *When my sister sees Dad holding the new baby, she gets jealous.*
2 *adj* envious: *Jim is jealous of your good grades.* –**jeal'ous·ly,** *adv,* –**jeal'ous·y,** *n.*

jeans (jēnz) *pl.n* casual pants made of a strong cotton cloth called denim.

jeer (jēr) *v* make fun of in a very rude or unkind way: *Do not jeer at the mistakes or misfortunes of others.*

Je·ho·vah's Wit·ness·es (jə hō'vəz wit'nis iz) Jehovah's Witnesses believe that the religious faith of an individual is more important than the rules of governments, and that the world will soon be judged and renewed by God. Jehovah is one of the names of God in the Bible.

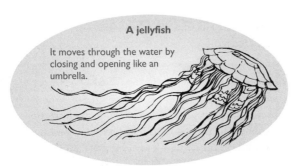

A jellyfish

It moves through the water by closing and opening like an umbrella.

jell (jel) *v* become definite: *Once we wrote them down our ideas began to jell.*
jel·ly *n* a food that is liquid when hot but rather firm when cold. *pl* **jel·lies. jel·ly·bean** or **jelly bean** *n* a small, bean-shaped candy.
jel·ly·fish *n* a boneless sea animal with a saucer-shaped body that looks like it is made of jelly. Most jellyfish have long, trailing tentacles with stinging hairs on them.

jerk (jərk) **1** *n* a sudden, sharp pull or twist: *Doug gave the cord a jerk to start the gas lawn mower.* **2** *v* pull or twist sharply and suddenly. –**jerk'y,** *adj.*

jerk·y (jər'kē) *n* strips of spiced, salted dried beef.

jest (jest) *n* a rather formal word for "joke."
jest·er *n* in the Middle Ages, an entertainer hired to do tricks and make jokes.
in jest, in fun; not seriously: *His words were spoken in jest.*

Je·sus (jē'zəs) *n* Jesus Christ, the central figure of the Christian religion.

jet (jet) **1** *n* a stream of gas or liquid shot with force from a small opening: *The fountains in Vancouver's Robson Square send up jets of water.*
2 *v* shoot out in a stream: *Water jetted from the broken pipe.* **jet·ted, jet·ting. 3** *n* an airplane driven by engines that work by forcing out a powerful stream of air and gas.
jet lag a feeling of tiredness or confusion after travelling by plane to a different time zone.
jet·ty *n* a long pier or dock.

Jew (jū) **1** *n* a person descended from the people of ancient Israel. **2** *n* a person whose religion is Judaism. –**Jew'ish,** *adj.*

jew·el (jū'əl) *n* a precious stone: *diamonds, rubies, and other jewels.*
jew·el·ler·y (jū'əl rē) *n* jewels and ornaments set with gems: *Louise keeps her jewellery in a box.*

jibe (jīb) *v Informal.* be in harmony; agree: *There were no problems in forming the band, because they found that their ideas jibed very well.* **Jive** is another form of this word. **jibed, jib·ing.**

jif·fy (jif'ē) *n Informal.* a very short time; moment: *I'll be there in a jiffy.* *pl* **jif·fies.**

jig (jig) **1** *n* a lively dance or the music for it.
2 *n* a fishing lure made of one or more hooks with pieces of bright metal attached. You jerk it up or down or pull it through the water. **3** *v* fish with a jig. **jigged, jig·ging.**
jig·gle *v* shake or jerk slightly: *Please don't jiggle the desk when I'm trying to write.*
jig·saw 1 *n* short for **jigsaw puzzle,** a picture cut into irregular pieces that can be fitted together again. **2** *n* a saw with a narrow blade, used to make these puzzles because it can cut curves or irregular lines.

jin·gle (jing′gəl) **1** *n* a sound like little bells ringing or of coins striking together. **2** *n* a short song with catchy words and rhythm, used in a radio or TV commercial.

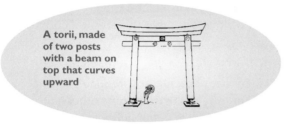
A torii, made of two posts with a beam on top that curves upward

jin·ja (jin′jə) *n* a Shinto shrine. Most jinjas have a special entrance gate called a **torii** (tȯr′ ē ē′).

jinx (jingks) *n Slang.* a person or thing that is believed to bring bad luck: *He must be a jinx; we've lost every game since he joined the team.*

jit·ters (jit′ərz) *pl.n Slang.* great nervousness: *I've got the jitters about my piano recital tomorrow.* —**jit′ter·y,** *adj.*

job (job) **1** *n* anything a person has to do: *It's my job to walk the dog.* **2** *n* work done for pay; employment: *His sister is hunting for a job.* **3** *n* a piece of work done: *They did a lousy job painting the boat.* —**job′less,** *adj.*

jog (jog) **1** *v* run at a slow, steady rate: *My mother goes jogging every day in Stanley Park.* **2** *n* shake or bump: *She jogged his elbow to get his attention.* **jogged, jog·ging.** —**jog′ger,** *n.* **jog someone's memory,** give someone a little reminder.

join (join) **1** *v* bring or come together: *Confederation Bridge joins Prince Edward Island to the mainland.* **2** *v* become a member of: *He joined the chess club.*

joint 1 *n* the place where two parts are joined together, especially two bones that let you bend part of your body. Knees and elbows are joints. **2** *adj* involved in something together: *By our joint efforts we succeeded.* **3** *n Slang.* a place, especially a cheap restaurant. —**joint′ly,** *adv.*

joke (jōk) **1** *n* something said or done to make somebody laugh. **2** *v* say or do funny things; try to make people laugh. **3** *n* a person or thing that is laughed at. **joked, jok·ing.**
joc·u·lar (jok′yə lər) *adj* funny; joking: *a jocular mood.* **jok·er 1** *n* a person who jokes a lot. **2** *n Slang.* any person who has made you angry: *Who does that joker think he is?*

jol·ly (jol′ē) *adj* very cheerful; full of fun. **jol·li·er, jol·li·est.**
get your jollies, *Slang.* get pleasure or excitement, especially in a foolish or mean way.

jolt (jōlt) *n or v* jerk; shake: *The bad news gave me quite a jolt* (n). *The wagon jolted us when it went over the rocks* (v).

jos·tle (jos′əl) *v* shove, push, or crowd against: *We were jostled by the impatient crowd at the entrance to the stadium.* **jos·tled, jos·tling.**

jot (jot) **1** *v* write briefly or quickly: *The waiter jotted down the order.* **2** *n* a little bit; very small amount: *I don't care a jot.* **jot·ted, jot·ting.**

jour·nal (jər′nəl) **1** *n* a daily record of what happens, or of a person's thoughts and feelings. **2** *n* a newspaper or magazine.
jour·nal·ism *n* the work of finding out news and reporting it to the public, either in a newspaper or magazine or on radio or TV. —**jour′nal·ist,** *n.*

jour·ney (jər′nē) **1** *n* a trip, especially a fairly long one: *a journey across Canada.* **2** *v* travel; take a trip: *We journeyed to the Yukon.* *pl* **jour·neys. jour·neyed, jour·ney·ing.**

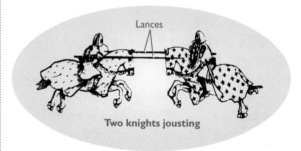
Lances
Two knights jousting

joust (joust *or* just) **1** *n* a contest between two knights on horseback, armed with lances. They would charge at each other and each would try to knock the other off his horse. **2** *v* take part in one of those contests.

jo·vi·al (jō′vē əl) *adj* good-natured and full of fun: *Santa Claus is pictured as a jovial old fellow.*

joy (joi) **1** *n* a strong feeling of happiness. **2** *n* something that causes gladness or happiness: *The new baby was a joy to his parents.* —**joy′ful,** *adj,* —**joy′ous,** *adj.*
joy ride *Informal.* a ride in a car for fun, especially when a car is driven recklessly or without the owner's permission.
joystick *n* a lever that you use to control the movement of something on a computer screen.

Ju·da·ism (jū′dā iz′əm) *n* the religion of the Jews, based on the teachings of Moses and the prophets as found in the Torah and Jewish bible.

judge (juj) **1** *n* a government official whose job is to hear and decide cases in a law court. **2** *n* a person chosen to settle a dispute or to decide who wins a contest. **3** *v* do the work of a judge; settle or decide something: *to judge a criminal case, to judge an art contest.* **judged, judg·ing. 4** *n* any person who tries to form an opinion of how good a thing is: *a good judge of dogs, a poor judge of poetry.*

judg·ment or **judge·ment** (juj′mənt) **1** *n* an opinion or estimate: *In my judgment this song is better than the other one.* **2** *n* the ability to form wise opinions; good sense: *She has good judgment when it comes to spending money.*

jug (jug) *n* a container for holding liquids. A jug usually has a handle and a spout.

jug·gle (jug′əl) *v* keep several objects moving in the air at the same time: *I can juggle three oranges at once.* **jug·gled, jug·gling. –jug′gler,** *n.*

juice (jūs) *n* the flavourful liquid in fruits, vegetables, and meats: *the juice of a lemon, meat juices.* **–juic′y,** *adj.*

jum·ble (jum′bəl) **1** *v* mix up: *She jumbled up everything in the drawer while hunting for her gloves.* **2** *n* a confused mess: *A jumble of shoes lay at the front door.* **jum·bled, jum·bling.**

jum·bo (jum′bō) *adj* very big: *a jumbo ice-cream cone.* A **jumbo jet** carries several hundred passengers. *pl* **jum·bos.**

jump (jump) **1** *v* spring up from the ground: *Terry jumped off the diving board.* **2** *v* give a sudden jerk in surprise or fear: *I jumped when I heard the bang.* If you are nervous and easily startled, you are **jumpy. 3** *n* the act or fact of jumping: *a jump in prices. She crossed the room in two jumps.* **4** *v* attack with a rush: *The robbers jumped the storekeeper.*

jump·suit *n* an outfit that combines a shirt and pants all in one piece.

jump at, accept eagerly: *to jump at a chance.*

jump on, *Informal.* criticize harshly. To **jump all over someone** means the same.

jump the gun, start too soon.

jump to conclusions, make a judgment without enough facts.

junc·tion (jungk′shən) *n* an action or place of joining or meeting: *the junction of two rivers.* A **railway junction** is a place where railway lines meet or cross.

jun·gle (jung′gəl) *n* land thickly covered with bushes, vines, and trees in a tropical climate; rain forest.

jun·ior (jūn′yər) **1** *adj* having to do with younger people: *a junior tennis tournament.* **2** *adj* of lower rank than some others: *the junior partner in a firm, a junior officer in the army.* **be someone's junior,** be younger than someone: *My sister is two years my junior.*

junk (jungk) *n* worthless stuff. **Junk food** is food that has little value for your body. **Junk mail** is advertising and other things delivered to your house that you don't want to read. **–junk′y,** *adj.*

ju·ry (jū′rē) *n* a group of people, called **jurors,** chosen to listen to a case in a court of law and give a decision based on the evidence. *pl* **ju·ries.**

just (just) **1** *adj* holding to what is right; honest and fair: *a just reward, a just decision, a just ruler.* **2** *adv* exactly: *That is just a metre.* **3** *adv* very close; immediately: *a picture just above the fireplace. She arrived just after lunch.* **4** *adv* a very short time ago: *Santos just left.* **5** *adv* barely: *I just made it.* **6** *adv* only; merely: *just an ordinary person.* **7** *adv* Informal. positively: *The weather is just glorious.* **just now,** a very short time ago: *I saw him just now.*

jus·tice (jus′tis) *n* just treatment: *Judges should have a sense of justice.*

justice of the peace, an official with some of the same powers as a judge.

jut (jut) *v* stick out: *A ledge is jutting out from the side of the cliff. A pier juts out from the shore into the lake.* **jut·ted, jut·ting.**

ju·ve·nile (jū′və nīl′ *or* jū′və nəl) **1** *adj* immature: *juvenile behaviour.* **2** *n* a young person. **3** *adj* having to do with children and young people: *a juvenile court.*

Kk

A kayak has an opening for one person, or sometimes two people.

k or **K** (kā) *n* the eleventh letter of the English alphabet, or the sound that it stands for. The sound of *k* in *kayak* is the same as the sound of *c* in *cat*. *pl* **k's** or **K's**.

ka·lei·do·scope (kə lī′də skōp′) *n* a tube with an eyepiece at one end, and bits of coloured glass and two or more mirrors inside. As you look inside and turn the tube the mirrors reflect changing coloured patterns.

ka·mi (kȧ′mē) *pl.n* the gods of Shintoism and their powers. A **kamidana** (kȧ′mē dȧ′nə) is a simple shrine inside a home, for daily worship.

🍁 **ka·mik** (ka′mik) *n* a soft, high, waterproof boot traditionally made of sealskin or caribou hide, worn in the Arctic. **Kamik** is the Inuktitut word; **mukluk** is the Yupik word for it.

The female kangaroo has a pouch to carry its young.

kan·ga·roo (kang′gə rū′) *n* an animal of Australia and New Guinea with small forelegs and very strong hind legs, which give it great leaping power. *pl* **kan·ga·roos** or **kan·ga·roo.**

ka·ra·te (kə rȧ′tē) *n* a Japanese method of self-defence without weapons, using different kinds of hand or foot strokes.

kar·a (kȧr′ə) *n* the steel bracelet worn by all baptized Sikhs.

kar·ma (kȧr′mə) *n* in the Buddhist and Hindu religions, all of a person's actions, good and bad, which determine how he or she will be reborn.

kay·ak (kī′ak) **1** *n* an Inuit boat made of skins stretched over a light frame of wood or bone. The Inuktitut spelling is **qajaaq**. **2** *n* a similar craft made of other material. **–kay′ak·er,** *n,* **–kay′ak·ing,** *n.*

keen (kēn) **1** *adj* sharp: *a keen blade, a keen wind, a keen sense of smell.* **2** *adj Informal.* enthusiastic: *a keen player.* **–keen′ly,** *adv,* **–keen′ness,** *n.*
keen on, enthusiastic about: *They're not keen on camping.*

keep (kēp) **1** *v* have or hold for a long time or forever: *You may keep this book.* **2** *v* have and take care of: *My grandparents keep chickens.* **3** *v* prevent: *Keep the books from falling.* **4** *v* stay or continue: *to keep awake, to keep working,* **5** *v* be faithful to: *to keep a promise, to keep the rules.* **6** *n* the strongest part of a fortress or castle.
kept, keep·ing.
for keeps, 1 with the agreement that the winner may keep the winnings: *to play for keeps.* **2** *Informal.* forever.
keep on, go on; continue: *The girls kept on swimming across Horse Lake in spite of the rain.*
keep to yourself, 1 not do much with other people. **2** not tell to other people: *She kept the news to herself.*
keep up, 1 continue: *They kept up their attack until dawn.* **2** keep in good condition: *It was hard to keep up the appearance of the old boat.* **3** stay close or alongside and not fall behind: *I had to run to keep up with the bike.*

kelp (kelp) *n* a large, tough, brown seaweed.

ken·nel (ken′əl) **1** *n* a house for a dog or dogs. **2** Often, **kennels,** *pl.n* a place where dogs may be left and cared for while their owners are away.

ker·nel (kėr′nəl) **1** *n* the softer part inside the hard shell of a nut or inside the stone of a fruit. **2** *n* a grain or seed of a plant such as wheat.

ker·o·sene (ker′ə sēn′) *n* a thin oil made from petroleum, used as a fuel. It was invented by a Canadian, Abraham Gesner, in 1853.

ketch·up (kech′əp) *n* a sauce used with hot dogs, French fries, and so on, made of tomatoes, onions, salt, sugar, and spices.

ket·tle (ket′əl) **1** *n* a container with a handle and a spout, for heating water. **2** *n* any large metal container for boiling liquids.

key (kē) **1** *n* a small, specially shaped piece of metal that opens and closes a lock. **2** *n* the answer to a puzzle or problem: *the key to a secret code.* **3** *adj* very important: *the key industries of Canada.* **4** *n* a chart explaining the symbols or abbreviations used in a dictionary, map, or diagram: *There is a pronunciation key at the beginning of this dictionary.* **5** *n* one of a set of small parts pressed down by the fingers in playing a piano or operating a computer or other machine: *Don't hit the keys so hard.* **6** *n* a scale or set of related notes in music based on a particular note: *a song written in the key of B flat.* **7** *v* enter information in a computer using a keyboard: *Sunil keyed in the numbers.* **keyed, key·ing.**
key·board *n* the set of keys on a piano, synthesizer, or computer. –**key′board′ing,** *n.*
key·hole *n* an opening in a lock for fitting a key into. **key·stone** *n* the middle stone at the top of an arch, holding the other stones in place.
key up, 1 make very excited: *The kids are so keyed up they can't sit still.* **2** raise someone's courage or nerve: *She keyed herself up to ask for a raise.*

kick (kik) **1** *v* hit with the foot: *Kick the ball.* **2** *n* a blow with the foot: *The horse's kick knocked the pail over.* **3** *n Slang.* thrill; excitement: *He gets a kick out of skiing fast.*
kick in, 1 *Informal.* start operating or having an effect: *It takes the medicine a while to kick in.* **2** *Informal.* give a share: *If we all kick in $3 we can buy her a gift.*
kick off, 1 put a football into play with a kick. **2** begin: *The new TV show kicks off this fall.* The noun form is **kickoff.**
kick out, *Informal.* send out in a humiliating or disgraceful way: *She was kicked out of the game.*

kid (kid) **1** *n* a young goat, or the leather made from its skin. **2** *n Informal.* child. **3** *v Slang.* tease playfully; talk in a joking way: *He's only kidding.* **kid·ded, kid·ding.**

kid·nap *v* take a person by force and keep as a prisoner: *The banker's son was kidnapped and held for ransom.* **kid·napped** or **kid·naped, kid·nap·ping** or **kid·nap·ing.** –**kid′nap′per** or **kid′nap′er,** *n.*
no kidding, seriously.

kill (kil) **1** *v* cause to die: *The Halifax explosion of 1917 killed 1600 people.* **2** *n* the animal killed in a hunt: *All the lions shared the kill.* **3** *v* put an end to; get rid of: *to kill odours, to kill rumours.* **4** *v* use up: *We killed an hour at the zoo.* **5** *v Informal.* overcome with pain, disgust, or laughter: *My sore foot is killing me. His jokes kill me.* –**kill′er,** *n.*
killer whale a black and white whale that hunts and eats fish, seals, and other whales. It is also called an **orca.**

kilo– *an SI prefix meaning* thousand. One kilowatt is a thousand watts. The prefix *kilo-* can be used with almost any SI unit, such as *gram, metre,* or *litre. Symbol:* k
kil·o·byte (kil′ ə bīt′) *n* about a thousand bytes (actually 1024) of computer memory. *Symbol:* KB

A traditional Japanese kimono

ki·mo·no (kə mō′nə) *n* a loose outer garment held in place by an **obi,** a wide belt or sash. Kimonos are worn by men and women in Japan. *pl* **ki·mo·nos.**

kin (kin) **1** *n* family or relatives: *All our kin came to the family reunion.* **Kinsfolk** and **kindred** are more poetic words. **2** *adj* related: *My cousins are kin to me.* –**kins′man,** *n,* –**kin′ship,** *n,* –**kins′wo′man,** *n.*
next of kin, a person's closest living relative or relatives: *My parents are my next of kin.*

kind (kīnd) **1** *adj* friendly, caring, and helpful; doing good to others: *The kind girl offered her sweater to the shivering little boy.* **Kind-hearted** means the same. –**kind'ness**, *n.* **2** *n* sort; variety: *Kevin likes most kinds of candy. A viper is a kind of snake.*

kind·ly (kīnd'lē) **1** *adj* good-hearted and friendly: *kindly faces, kindly people.* **2** *adv* in a kind or friendly way: *Treat your pets kindly.* –**kind'li·ness**, *n.*

kind of, *Informal.* nearly; almost; somewhat; rather: *The room was kind of dark.*

of a kind, of the same sort: *The brothers were two of a kind–easy-going and intelligent.*

take kindly to, like or accept: *He does not take kindly to criticism.*

USING WORDS . . . . . kind of

You can usually find a better choice than **kind of** to mean "somewhat." Try using *a bit, rather, quite, slightly, almost, nearly, not quite,* or *barely.*

---

kin·der·gar·ten (kin'dər gär'tən) **1** *n* the year of school that comes before grade one. **2** *n* a school for young children; a nursery school.

kin·dle (kin'dəl) *v* start burning: *Light a match to kindle the bonfire.* **Kindling** is small pieces of wood for starting a fire. **kin·dled, kin·dling.**

king (king) **1** *n* the male ruler of a nation who is not elected but who inherits his position: *Richard the Lion-Hearted was a king of England.* **2** *n* a person, animal, or thing that ranks highest in a certain group: *The lion is called the king of beasts. Costa was the king of skateboarders.* –**king'ly**, *adj,* –**king'ship'**, *n.*

king·dom 1 *n* a country that is governed by a king or a queen. **2** *n* one of the three divisions of the natural world. They are the animal kingdom, the plant kingdom, and the mineral kingdom. **king-size** *adj Informal.* very large for its kind: *a king-size bed, a king-size sandwich.*

kink (kingk) **1** *n* a twist or curl in thread, rope, hair, etc. **2** *n* pain or stiffness in a muscle.

kiosk (kē'osk) *n* a small building, usually with one or more sides open, or a stand or booth inside a building. A kiosk may be used for a bank machine, information booth, etc.

kir·pan (kēr'pun) *n* a dagger or short sword worn by all baptized Sikhs.

kiss (kis) **1** *n or v* touch with the lips as a sign of love, greeting, or respect: *a goodbye kiss* (*n*). *He kissed the baby's cheek* (*v*).

kit (kit) **1** *n* a set of supplies and equipment needed for a certain job or purpose: *a first-aid kit, a sewing kit.* **2** *n* a set of parts you can put together to make something: *a radio kit.*

kitch·en (kich'ən) *n* a room where food is cooked or prepared. A small one is a **kitchenette.**

kite (kīt) *n* a light frame covered with paper, cloth, or plastic and flown in the air on the end of a long string.

kit·ten (kit'ən) *n* a young cat. **Kitty** is an informal word.

knack (nak) *n* a special skill: *That clown has a knack for making kids laugh.*

Grammar ✓Check . . . . . . silent k

Words that begin with the letters **kn-** are easy to misspell because the **k** is usually silent. Remind yourself how to spell them by saying the silent **k** in your head as you write or read them: *k-night; k-nead, k-nee.*

---

knead (nēd) **1** *v* mix or soften by pressing and stretching, usually with the hands: *to knead bread dough, to knead clay before shaping it.* **2** *v* massage: *The trainer kneaded the muscles of the runner.*

knee (nē) **1** *n* the joint between your thigh and the lower leg. The bone covering the front of the joint is the **kneecap. 2** *v* strike with the knee: *Jim kneed his karate opponent in the thigh.* **kneed, knee·ing.**

kneel (nēl) *v* go down or stay on your knees: *She knelt to pick up a loonie.* **knelt** or **kneeled, kneel·ing.**

knife (nīf) *n* a tool that has a thin, flat, metal blade fastened in a handle, for cutting or spreading. *pl* **knives** (nīvz).

knight (nīt) **1** *n* in the Middle Ages, a high-ranking man who fought for a king or lord and promised to act honourably. Knights wore armour and rode horses. **2** *n* in modern times, a man raised to an honourable rank because of great achievement or service: *A knight has the title* Sir *before his name.* –**knight'hood**, *n,* –**knight'ly**, *adj.*

K k

knit (nit) **1** *v* make by looping yarn or thread together in interlocking stitches with long needles or by machine: *She is knitting a sweater.* **2** *v* grow together: *A broken bone knits as it heals.* **knit·ted** or **knit, knit·ting.**
knit your brows, frown.

knob (nob) **1** *n* the round handle on a door or drawer. **2** *n* a round control on a radio or other machine, that you work by turning it. **3** *n* any rounded lump. –**knob′by,** *adj.*

knock (nok) **1** *v* hit or bump against sharply: *She knocked her head on the cupboard door.* **2** *v* make a noise by hitting with the knuckles: *I knocked on the door.* **3** *v* make a rattling or banging noise: *That engine knocks.*
knock around, *Informal.* **1** wander from place to place. **2** hit repeatedly; treat roughly.
knock off, *Informal.* **1** take off; deduct: *They knocked ten dollars off the price of the computer program.* **2** stop: *Hey, knock off the fighting! The workers knock off at noon for lunch.*
knock out, hit so hard as to make the person unconscious.
knock yourself out, try your hardest: *I knocked myself out to get this fixed in time.*

knot (not) **1** *n* a fastening made by tying together pieces of rope, string, etc.: *She showed me how to make a slip knot.* **2** *v* a tangle: *There's a knot in my shoelace.* **3** *v* a knot or knots in something: *to knot a thread. My hair was all knotted.* **4** *n* the place where a branch has grown out, which shows in a board as a small, dark, hard, oval part. When it falls out it leaves a **knothole.** **5** *n* a non-metric measure of speed used by ships and airplanes, equal to one nautical mile per hour (1852 m/h). *This ship's usual speed is about 18 knots.* **knot·ted, knot·ting.** –**knot′ty,** *adj.*

know (nō) **1** *v* be aware; realize: *I didn't know you were living in Alberta.* **2** *v* have true information, understanding, or skill: *to know your lesson, to know how to look. We know that 2 plus 2 equals 4.* **3** *v* be familiar with: *I know her very well, but I've never met her sister.* **4** *v* tell apart from others: *You will know him by his bright red scarf.* **knew, known, know·ing.**
know-how *n* the knowledge needed to do something: *Betta has a lot of know-how when it comes to camping.*

knowl·edge *n* what someone knows: *Her knowledge of whales is extensive.*
be in the know, have knowledge not shared by everyone.

knuck·le (nuk′əl) *n* a joint in a finger.
knuckle down, *Informal.* work hard.
knuckle under, submit; give in: *He refused to knuckle under to his enemies.*

A koala with its young. Adult koalas are about 60 cm long.

ko·a·la (kōä′lə) *n* a grey, furry animal of Australia that carries its young in a pouch, and lives in trees. Koalas look a bit like teddy bears.

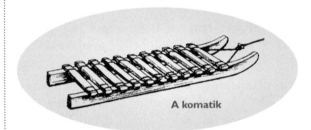
A komatik

kom·a·tik (kom′ə tik′) *n* a large wooden dogsled used in the North, made of closely spaced crossbars lashed to two broad runners. It sometimes has a raised bar at the back for a standing rider to hold on to.

ko·sher (kō′shər) *adj* fit to eat according to Jewish religious law: *kosher meat.*

WORD HISTORY . . . . kosher
Kosher comes from the Hebrew word *kasher*, meaning "proper."

kung fu (kung′fū′) *n* an ancient Chinese art of fighting using hands and feet.

Kwan·zaa (kwän′zə) *n* a festival held by some black people in North America to celebrate their culture. It runs from December 6 to January 1.

l or **L** (el) *n* the twelfth letter of the English alphabet, or the sound that it stands for. You hear the sound of *l* at the beginning and end of *lull.* *pl* **l's** or **L's.**

la·bel (lā′bəl) **1** *n* a slip of paper or other material attached to something to show what or whose it is, or where it is to go: *The label on the pop bottle lists the ingredients.* **2** *v* put or write a label on: *The bottle is labelled* Poison. **la·belled** or **la·beled, la·bel·ling** or **la·bel·ing.**

la·bour (lā′bər) **1** *n* hard work: *He was well paid for his labour.* **2** *v* work hard: *She laboured all day in the factory.* **Labor** is another spelling. A **labourer** does physical work for a living.

lab·o·ra·to·ry (lab′rə tô′rē *or* lə bôr′ə tôr′ē) **1** *n* Often shortened to **lab,** a place where scientific work is done: *a chemical laboratory.* **2** *n* a place where students work on practical skills, often independently: *a language lab, a computer lab.* **Labour Day** or **Labor Day** the first Monday in September, a holiday in honour of workers. **la·bo·ri·ous** (lə bôr′ē əs) *adj* taking a lot of hard work: *Climbing a mountain is laborious.* –**la·bo′ri·ous·ly,** *adv.*

lace (lās) **1** *n* a string or leather strip for pulling parts by tying together: *These shoes need new laces.* **2** *v* fasten with laces: *Lace up your skates.* **3** *n* see-through cloth made of threads woven together in a fancy pattern. **laced, lac·ing.**

lack (lak) **1** *v* be without: *Some guinea pigs lack tails.* **2** *n* the fact of being without: *Lack of food had made him thin and weak.*

❧ **la·crosse** (lə kros′) *n* a game invented by the Algonquian peoples. It is played by two teams of ten players each, using a rubber ball and stick with a net on one end.

lad·der (lad′ər) *n* a set of steps, or **rungs,** fastened into two long sidepieces, used for climbing up or down.

la·dle (lā′dəl) *n* a large, deep spoon with a long handle, for dipping out liquids.

la·dy (lā′dē) **1** *n* a woman of high or noble rank. **2** *n* a woman who is polite and considerate of others. *pl* **la·dies.**

> **USING WORDS . . . . . . lady**
>
> In formal English, **lady** is used to mean "a woman of high social position." When **lady** is used in everyday speech to refer to any woman (*lady cab driver, the lady at the store*), many people think **woman** is a better word to use.

la·dy·bug (lā′dē bug′) *n* a small beetle with a rounded back, usually red or orange with black spots. Ladybugs eat harmful insects.

lag (lag) *v* fall behind: *The child lagged because he was tired.* **lagged, lag·ging.**

la·goon (lə gün′) *n* a shallow pond of fresh or salt water connected with a lake or sea but partly separated from it by ridges of sand, or coral.

lair (ler) *n* the den of a wild animal.

lake (lāk) *n* a large body of fresh water usually completely surrounded by land except where rivers come in and go out. Canada has millions of lakes.

go jump in the lake, *Slang.* take your silly ideas elsewhere.

lamb (lam) *n* a young sheep.

lame (lām) **1** *adj* not able to walk properly for a while because of a hurt leg or foot. **2** *adj* not very good: *a lame excuse.* **lam·er, lam·est.**

lamp (lamp) *n* something that gives light. It can usually be moved around: *a desk lamp.*

land (land) **1** *n* the solid part of the earth's surface: *We stood on dry land.* A **landholder** may own or rent land. **2** *n* a country region: *Canada is a large land.* **3** *v* come or bring to land from the air or water: *The ship landed at the pier. The pilot landed the airplane in a field on Manitoulin Island. The car landed in the ditch.*

land·ing 1 *n* the act of coming to land from the air or water: *The landing was smoother than the take-off.* **2** *n* a platform between flights of stairs. **3** *n* a dock or pier for unloading ship's cargo or passengers.

land·mark (land′märk′) **1** *n* something familiar or easily seen that lets you figure out where you are: *The lighthouse at Peggy's Cove is a famous landmark.* **2** *n* an event of great importance: *The invention of the printing press is a landmark in the history of communication.*

land·scape (land′skāp′) **1** *n* a wide view of an area of land: *The low, tree-covered hills make a beautiful landscape in fall.* **2** *n* a piece of art showing such a view.

land·slide (land′slīd′) *n* the sliding down of a mass of soil or rock on a steep slope.

lane (lān) *n* a narrow path or anything like this: *Swimmers in a race must keep to their own lanes.*

lan·gar (lung′gàr) *n* a kitchen in a Sikh temple serving free food to anyone who wishes. Eating together is an important part of Sikh religion.

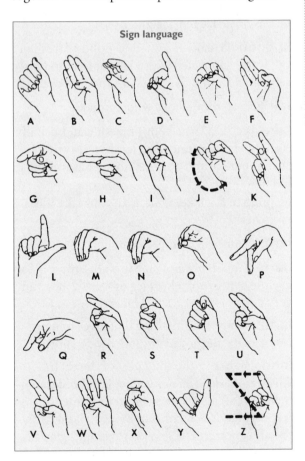

Sign language

lan·guage (lang′gwij) **1** *n* human speech, spoken or written: *We can explain our feelings through language.* **2** *n* the speech used by a nation or people group: *the French language, the Ojibwa language.* **3** **Sign language** uses a system of hand signs instead of speech.

lap (lap) **1** *n* the front part of a person sitting down, from the waist to the knees: *My cat likes to sleep on my lap.* **2** *n* one time around a track: *Who won the first lap of the race?* **3** *v* drink by lifting up with the tongue: *Cats and dogs lap water.* **4** *v* move or beat gently with a light splashing sound: *Little waves lapped against the boat.* **lapped, lap·ping.**

lap·top (lap′top′) *n* a small portable computer that can run on batteries and fits on your lap.

in the lap of luxury, surrounded by luxuries.

large (làrj) *adj* big: *Large crowds come to see our lacrosse team play.* **larg·er, larg·est.**

large·ly *adv* mostly: *Northern Ontario consists largely of forests.*

at large, free: *Is the escaped prisoner still at large?*

❧ **lar·ri·gan** (ler′ə gən) *n* an oiled leather moccasin.

lar·va (làr′və) *n* the wormlike form of an insect after it is an egg: *A caterpillar is the larva of a butterfly or moth.* *pl* **lar·vae** (làr′vē).

la·ser (lā′zər) *n* a device that produces a very narrow beam of light. In a **laser printer**, a laser beam gives the paper an electric charge that is the exact shape of the letter or other image. This makes the printer's ink stick to the paper in that shape.

lash (lash) **1** *n* or *v* whip: *The leather lash snapped in the air* (*n*). *Do not lash the horses* (*v*). **2** *n* one of the hairs on the edge of your eyelid; eyelash. **3** *v* tie or fasten with a rope or cord: *The pioneers lashed logs together to make a raft.*

las·so (lə sū′) **1** *n* a long rope with a loop at the end, used for catching horses and cattle. *pl* **las·sos** or **las·soes.** **2** *v* catch with a lasso. **las·soed, las·so·ing.**

last (last) **1** *adj* at the end; after all others: *the last page of a book.* **2** *adj* the one just before this: *last week, last year.* **3** *v* go on: *The festival lasted three days.* **4** *v* be used without wearing out or running out: *How long will our money last?* —**last′ing,** *adj,* —**last′ly,** *adv.*

at last, finally: *So you have come home at last.*

have the last word, be the last to speak in an argument; say something that the other person cannot answer.

see or **hear the last of,** be finished with.

the last straw, the thing that finally makes someone lose his or her patience.

late (lāt) **1** *adj* or *adv* after the usual or proper time: *We had a late supper* (adj). *She worked late* (adv). **2** *adv* or *adj* near the end: *It rained late in the evening* (adv). *We came home from Europe in late August* (adj). **3** *adj* recently dead: *The late John Candy was a great actor.* **lat·er, lat·est** or **last.** –**late′ness,** *n.*

late·ly *adv* a little while ago; recently: *Samir has not been looking well lately.* **lat·ter** (lat′ər) **1** *adj* toward the end: *the latter part of the week.* **2** **the latter,** *n* the second of two things: *Mice and rats are similar, but the latter are bigger.*

Lat·in (lat′ən) *n* the language of the ancient Romans.

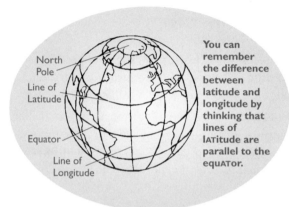

North Pole
Line of Latitude
Equator
Line of Longitude

You can remember the difference between latitude and longitude by thinking that lines of lATitude are parallel to the equATor.

lat·i·tude (lat′ə tyūd′ *or* lat′ə tūd′) *n* the distance north or south of the equator, measured in degrees. On maps, lines of latitude are horizontal, and lines of longitude are vertical.

laugh (laf) **1** *v* make the sounds and movements that show you think something is funny: *We all laughed at the joke.* **2** *n* the act or sound of laughing: *a loud laugh.* –**laugh′a·ble,** *adj,* –**laugh′ter,** *n.* **have the last laugh,** win or turn out to be right when everyone expected the opposite.

launch (lonch) **1** *v* put a boat into the water. **2** *v* send up in the air: *to launch a rocket or missile.* Rockets are launched from a **launching pad. 3** *n* the act of launching something: *We watched the space launch on television.*

laun·dry (lon′drē) **1** *n* clothes, sheets, and so on to be washed. **2** *n* a place where clothes and so on are washed and ironed. *pl* **laun·dries.** –**laun′der,** *v.*

lav·a (lav′ə *or* lä′və) *n* hot melted rock flowing from a volcano.

lav·ish (lav′ish) *adj* bigger, fancier, more expensive, etc. than necessary: *a lavish helping of pudding, a lavish wedding.*

law (lo) *n* a rule made by a government. –**law′ful,** *adj,* –**law′less,** *adj.*

law·yer *n* a person whose work is to give advice or to speak for others in a law court.

law and order, the peaceful environment resulting from people's obedience to law.

lay down the law, insist that things will be done a certain way.

lawn (lon) *n* land covered with grass kept cut, especially near a house. A **lawn mower** is a machine with moving blades for cutting grass.

lax (laks) *adj* not strict; careless: *Don't let yourself become lax about doing your homework.* –**lax′ness** or **lax′i·ty,** *n.*

lay (lā) **1** *v* place flat; put down: *to lay a carpet. Lay your books on the table.* **2** *v* produce eggs: *Birds, fish, and reptiles lay eggs.* **laid, lay·ing.**

lay down, declare: *The principal laid down the rules for using the computer lab.*

lay in, get and store up for the future: *The settlers laid in enough supplies for their winter in the Yukon.*

lay into, *Slang.* scold: *My parents laid into me for not doing my work.*

lay off, *Informal.* stop hassling: *Let's lay off her and give her another chance.*

CONFUSABLES ...... lay

lay means "put": *Lay your book on the desk.*

lie means "recline": *Lie down on the bed.*

Remember, the past tense of **lay** is **laid**, and the past tense of **lie** is **lay.**

lay·er (lā′ər) *n* one thickness, level, or coating: *another layer of clothing, layers of rock, a thin layer of ice.*

la·zy (lā′zē) **1** *adj* not willing to work or be active: *She was too lazy to get up and turn off the TV.* **Lazybones** is a nickname for a lazy person. **la·zi·er, la·zi·est.** –**la′zi·ly,** *adv,* –**la′zi·ness,** *n.*

LCD *abbreviation for:* **1** liquid crystal display, the type of electronic screen on a calculator, telephone, laptop computer, or digital watch. **2** lowest common denominator, the lowest number that can be evenly divided by all the denominators, a set of fractions.

lead (lēd *for 1-4,* led *for 5, 6*) **1** *v* show the way by going in front of: *Richard led the horses to water.* **2** *v* be chief of: *A general leads an army.* **3** *v* be first in a group: *Lisa leads the rest of the class in spelling.* **led, lead·ing.**
4 *n* the main part in a play or movie.
5 *n* a soft, heavy, bluish-grey metal.
6 *n* the very long, thin piece in the middle of a pencil.
–**lead′er,** *n,* –**lead′er·ship′,** *n.*
it's your lead (lēd), it's your turn to go first.

leaf (lēf) **1** *n* one of the thin, usually flat, parts of a green plant that grow along its stems.
2 *n* a sheet of paper: *Each side of the leaf of a book is a page.* pl **leaves.** –**leaf′less,** *adj,* –**leaf′y,** *adj.*
leaf·let *n* a small booklet; a flyer: *advertising leaflets.*
turn over a new leaf, make a new start, trying to do or be better in the future: *I promised to turn over a new leaf in the New Year.*

league (lēg) **1** *n* a group of teams that play a schedule of games against each other: *the National Hockey League.* **2** *n* a group of people or organizations joined together to help each other. **3** *n* an old non-metric measure of distance equal to almost 5 km.

leak (lēk) **1** *n* a hole or crack that lets something in or out: *a leak in a boat, a leak in a tire.* **2** *v* go in or out in this way: *The air leaked out of the balloon.* –**leak′age,** *n,* –**leak′y,** *adj.*

lean (lēn) **1** *v* stand slanting, not upright; bend: *The tower of Pisa leans. My teacher leaned over to check my work.* **2** *v* rest in a sloping or slanting position: *Lean the ladder against the wall.*
3 *adj* with very little fat: *a lean piece of meat.*
leaned or **leant** (lent), **lean·ing.**
lean-to *n* a small building built on to the side of a larger, higher building.

leap (lēp) *v* or *n* jump, especially high or far: *This frog can leap very high* (*v*). *She crossed the huge puddle in one leap* (*n*). *A sudden breeze made the flames leap up* (*v*). **leaped** or **leapt** (lept), **leap·ing.**
leap year a year with 366 days, the extra day being February 29. A year is a leap year if its number can be divided exactly by four, except years at the end of a century, which must be exactly divisible by 400. So 1980 and 2000 are leap years, but 1990 and 1900 are not.

learn (lərn) **1** *v* gain knowledge or skill: *He learned that salt is a mineral. We are learning about Canada's history. How did you learn to play the piano?* **2** *v* memorize: *I have to learn this part for the school play in two weeks.*
learned, learn·ing. –**learn′er,** *n,* –**learn′ing,** *n.*

CONFUSABLES .... learn

learn means "understand":
I want to learn how to swim.
teach means "instruct":
Can you teach me how to swim?

lease (lēs) **1** *n* a written agreement to rent something: *to sign a lease for a car.* **2** *v* to rent: *We have leased an apartment for one year.*
leased, leas·ing.

leash (lēsh) *n* a strap or chain for holding or leading an animal: *You should always keep your dog on a leash when there is traffic nearby.*

least (lēst) **1** *adj* smaller than all others in size, amount, or importance: *Of all our dogs, this one eats the least food.* **2** *adv* less than all others: *She liked that book least of all.* **3** *n* the smallest amount; the smallest thing: *The least you can do is to thank him.*
at least, 1 at the lowest estimate: *The temperature was at least 35°C.* **2** still; if nothing else; in any case: *Joshua was late, but at least he came.*

leath·er (leтн′ər) *n* a material made from the skins of animals: *Jackie's new gloves are made of leather.* –**leath′er·y,** *adj.*

leave (lēv) **1** *v* go away: *We leave tonight for Charlottetown. Please leave the room.* **2** *v* stop belonging to or taking part in: *to leave your job. The lead singer has left the band.* **3** *v* let stay in a certain place or condition: *We left the window open. I left a book on the table.* **4** *v* not do, use, take, etc.: *Leave a bit for me! I will leave my homework till tomorrow.* **5** *n* consent; permission: *They gave us leave to go.* **6** a time that someone spent away from work with special permission: *maternity leave.*
left, leav·ing.
leave off, stop: *Continue reading the story from where I left off.*
leave out, not say, do, or put in: *Josie left out two words when she read the sentence.*
take leave of, say goodbye to.

lec·ture (lek′chər) **1** *n* a planned talk on a certain subject in front of an audience. **2** *n* a long scolding: *My parents give me a lecture when I come home late.* **lec·tured, lec·tur·ing.**

LED *abbreviation for* light-emitting diode, a small electrical device that gives off red or green light, usually to show whether a machine is on or off.

ledge (lej) *n* a narrow shelf: *a window ledge, a ledge of rock.*

leech (lēch) *n* a sort of worm that sucks the blood of animals.

leek (lēk) *n* a vegetable related to the onion. It is larger, tube-shaped, and milder in flavour.

left (left) one of two sides of any person or thing. The opposite is **right**. The numeral 9 is on the left side of a clock. In cars sold in Canada, the driver sits on the left.
left-hand·ed *adj* using the left hand more easily and readily than the right: *Cindy is left-handed.*

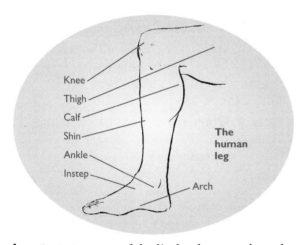

Knee
Thigh
Calf
Shin
Ankle
Instep
The human leg
Arch

leg (leg) **1** *n* one of the limbs that people and animals stand and walk on: *Dogs have four legs and human beings have two.* **2** *n* anything shaped or used like a leg: *a table leg.*
on your last legs, about to break down: *I feel as if I am on my last legs, but a swim will revive me.*
pull someone's leg, *Informal.* fool someone: *We didn't really see a UFO — I was just pulling your leg.*
leg·gings (leg′ingz) **1** *pl.n* tight, stretchy pants. **2** *pl.n* extra outer coverings for the legs, especially ones for wearing outside in cold weather.

le·gal (lē′gəl) **1** *adj* having to do with law or lawyers: *legal knowledge, legal advice.*
2 *adj* following the law; allowed by: *Hunting is legal only during certain seasons.* **–le′gal·ize′,** *v.*

leg·end (lej′ənd) **1** *n* a story coming down from the past that is partly based on fact: *the legend of Robin Hood.* **2** *n* on a map or chart, a list of the symbols used and what they mean. **–leg′end·ar′y,** *adj.*

leg·i·ble (lej′ə bəl) *adj* clear and easy to read: *Make sure your handwriting is legible.*

leg·is·late (lej′i slāt′) *v* make laws: *Parliament legislates for Canada.* A law is a piece of **legislation. leg·is·lat·ed, leg·is·lat·ing. –leg′is·la′tive,** *adj,* **–leg′is·la′tor,** *n.*
Legislative Assembly in Canada, the group of representatives elected to the legislature of a province or territory. **leg·is·la·ture** *n* a group of people who make laws.
le·git·i·mate (lə jit′ə mit) *adj* right or acceptable according to some rule: *a legitimate excuse.* **–le·git′i·ma·cy,** *n.*

lei·sure (lezh′ər *or* lē′zhər) *n* free time; time to relax.

lem·on (lem′ən) **1** *n* a sour-tasting, light yellow fruit. You can make a drink with it called **lemonade. 2** *n Slang.* something, especially a car, that gives a lot of trouble.

lend (lend) *v* let someone have for a while: *Will you lend me your bike for an hour? Banks lend money to people.* **lent, lend·ing. –lend′er,** *n.*
lend a hand, help: *He lent a hand with the dishes.*

length (length) **1** *n* how long a thing is from end to end: *the length of your arm, eight centimetres in length.* **2** *n* how long something lasts or goes on: *the length of a visit, a speech, or a book.* **–length′en,** *v.*
length·wise *adj* or *adv* in the direction of the length: *a lengthwise cut* (adj). *She folded the cloth lengthwise* (adv).

len·ient (lēn′yənt) *adj* mild or merciful; not strict: *a lenient judge, a lenient punishment.* **–len′ien·cy,** *n,* **–len′ient·ly,** *adv.*

lens (lenz) *n* a piece of glass or plastic that bends the rays of light passing through it. The lenses in a telescope make things look larger or nearer. *pl* **lens·es.**

leop·ard (lep′ərd) *n* a large animal of the cat family native to Africa and Asia, usually with dull yellowish fur spotted with black. A **panther** is the same animal only it is all black.

le·o·tard (lē′ə tård′) **1** *n* a stretchy, one-piece, close-fitting garment worn by dancers, acrobats, and so on. **2 leotards,** *pl.n* tights.

less (les) **1** *adj* or *adv* not as much: *of less importance. Five is less than seven (adj). She is less interested now (adv).* **2** *n* a smaller amount or quantity: *Put less on each plate.* **3** *prep* minus: *a year less two days.* –**less′er,** *adj.*

less·en *v* make or become less: *Take this to lessen the pain.*

more or less, about; approximately: *The cost is $50, more or less.*

USING WORDS ... less/fewer

Use **less** to talk about things that can't be counted, and **fewer** to talk about things that can: *We have fewer students than the other school because we have less space.*

–less *a suffix meaning* without, as in *homeless, hopeless.*

les·son (les′ən) **1** *n* something learned or taught at one time: *I didn't understand the science lesson today.* **2** *n* a meeting with a teacher to study a special subject: *a piano lesson, karate lessons.*

let (let) **1** *v* allow; permit: *Let the dog have a bone.* **2** *v* allow to come or go: *Let the cat in.* **3 Let** is used in giving suggestions: *Let's go fishing on Lake Simcoe.* **let, let·ting.**

let down, disappoint: *Don't let us down today; we're counting on you to help us.* A **letdown** is something disappointing.

let go, 1 allow to go free. **2** stop holding: *Grab the rope and don't let go!*

let off, 1 allow to go free with little or no punishment: *The culprit was let off with a warning.* **2** fire; explode: *to let off a firecracker.*

let off steam, express feelings of anger or tension: *He let off steam by shouting.*

let someone in on something, share a secret with someone, especially a secret place.

le·thal (lē′thəl) *adj* able to cause death: *a lethal weapon.*

let·ter (let′ər) **1** *n* a written message: *Astrid sent me a letter about her trip to Victoria.* A **letter carrier** is a person who delivers mail for the post office. **2** *n* a symbol of an alphabet: *There are 26 letters in the English alphabet.*

to the letter, very exactly: *I carried out your order to the letter.*

let·tuce (let′is) *n* a garden plant with large, crisp, green leaves that are used in salads or in sandwiches.

lev·el (lev′əl) **1** *adj* completely flat and even: *a level floor.* **2** *adj* of equal height; even: *The table is level with the edge of the window.* **3** *n* height: *The flood rose to a level of ten metres.* **4** *n* a grade, standard, or rank: *She reached a high level of skill.*

on the level, *Informal.* straightforward; honest.

le·ver (lē′vər *or* lev′ər) **1** *n* a bar for raising or moving something, supported at some point called a **fulcrum.** When you press on one end, a load at the other end is lifted. A crowbar and a seesaw are both levers. **2** *n* a control stick on a machine: *the gearshift lever of a car.*

li·a·ble (lī′ə bəl) **1** *adj* likely; unpleasantly likely: *Glass is liable to break. You are liable to slip on ice.* **2** *adj* responsible according to the law: *Canada Post is not liable for damage to a parcel sent by mail unless the parcel is insured.*

li·ar (lī′ər) *n* a person who tells lies.

lib·er·ty (lib′ər tē) *n* freedom: *The prisoner yearned for liberty.* *pl* **lib·er·ties.**

lib·er·ate *v* set free. –**lib′er·a′tion,** *n,* –**lib′er·a′tor,** *n.*

li·brar·y (lī′brer′ē) **1** *n* a room or building where a collection of books, magazines, videos, CD-ROMs, or other material is kept for people to use or borrow. A **librarian** takes care of the collection. **2** *n* any collection of books: *My aunt has a library of history books in her living room.* *pl* **lib·rar·ies.**

lice (līs) *n* plural of **louse,** a small insect that lives in the skin or hair of people or animals, and causes itching.

li·cence (lī′səns) **1** *n* permission to do something, given by law: *Mr. Taylor has a licence to drive a car.* **2** *n* the paper, card, etc. showing such permission: *The barber hung his licence on the wall.*

li·cense *v* give a licence to: *to license a new driver.*

CONFUSABLES .... licence

licence is the noun:
He has a driver's licence.

license is the verb:
He is licensed to drive.

li·chen (lī′kən) *n* a non-flowering plant that looks like moss, hair, or scaly leaves growing in patches on rocks, trees, and other hard surfaces.

lick (lik) **1** *v* pass the tongue over: *to lick a stamp.* **2** *n* a stroke of the tongue over something: *He gave the ice-cream cone a big lick.* **3** *v Informal.* defeat or overcome: *So far we've licked every problem without help.*

lic·o·rice (lik′ə rish) *n* the sweet-tasting, dried root of a European plant. A black substance obtained from this root is used in medicine and candy.

lid (lid) **1** *n* a movable cover; top: *the lid of a jar.* **2** *n* eyelid.

lie (lī) **1** *n* something that is not true, said in order to fool or trick someone: *Saying his friend stole it was a lie.* **2** *v* tell a lie: *She finally admitted she was lying.* **lied, ly·ing. 3** *v* put or keep your body in a flat position on a surface: *to lie down on the grass, to lie in bed.* **4** *v* rest on a surface: *The book was lying on the table.* **lay, lain, ly·ing.**

lieu·ten·ant (lef ten′ənt *or* lū ten′ənt) *n* a person who acts for someone in authority: *He was one of the club leader's lieutenants.* **lieu·ten·ant-gov·er·nor** *n* the official head of a provincial government.

life (līf) **1** *n* the state of being alive. People, animals, and plants have life; they can grow and reproduce. Rocks and minerals do not. **Life sciences** are the sciences that deal with living things. **2** *n* the time of being alive: *Prime Minister John Diefenbaker enjoyed a long life.* **3** *n* a person: *Five lives were lost in the fire.* **4** *n* a way of living: *a dull life.* **5** *n* spirit; vigour: *Put more life into your singing.* pl **lives** (līvz). **–life′less,** *adj,* **–life′like′,** *adj.*
life·boat *n* a strong boat carried on a ship, for use in case the ship has to be abandoned.
life cycle all the different stages of growth that a plant or animal goes through from birth to death. Egg and tadpole are two stages in the life cycle of a frog. **life·guard** *n* a person trained in lifesaving, whose job is to guard the safety of swimmers. **life preserver** a wide belt, jacket, doughnut-shaped tube, etc. designed to keep a person afloat in the water until rescued. One shaped like a garment with armholes is a **life jacket. life·saving** *n* the practice of saving people's lives, especially by preventing drowning.

life-size *adj* as big as the real person, animal, etc.: *a life-size statue.*
life·style *n* the way a person lives: *an active lifestyle, a simple lifestyle.* **life·time** the time of being alive: *Grandfather has seen many changes during his lifetime.*
as large (or **big**) **as life, 1** as big as the real person or thing. **2** in person.
for dear life, as hard as you would to save your life: *She held on for dear life.*

lift (lift) **1** *v* raise up higher or into the air; pick up: *My father gently lifted the baby from her crib.* **2** *n* the act of lifting: *Do 50 leg lifts.* **3** *n* a machine that lifts people or things: *a ski lift.*
lift·off *n* the firing or launching of a rocket: *The liftoff took place at noon yesterday.*
give someone a lift, 1 help someone lift something heavy: *Could you give me a lift with this box?* **2** give someone a ride: *Mrs. Rae gave us a lift to school.*

light (līt) **1** *n* that which makes it possible to see; the opposite of darkness: *The sun gives light to the earth.* **2** *n* anything that gives light, such as a lamp or a candle. **3** *adj* having light; bright: *It stays light longer on summer evenings.* **4** *adj* pale in colour: *light hair, light blue.* **5** *v* set fire to; start burning: *Let's light the candles.* **light·ed** or **lit, light·ing. 6** *adj* having little mass for its size: *Feathers are light.* **–light′en,** *v,* **–light′er,** *n,* **–light·ly,** *adv,* **–light′ness,** *n.*
light-head·ed 1 *adj* dizzy: *He felt light-headed from hunger.* **2** *adj* silly: *not serious enough.*
light-heart·ed *adj* carefree; cheerful; happy.
light·house *n* a tower with a bright light that shines far over the water. Lighthouses are usually located at dangerous places to warn and guide ships. **light·ning** *n* a flash of light in the sky caused by static electricity between clouds. What we call thunder is the sound that lightning makes during a storm.
light-year *n* the distance that light travels in one year; almost ten million million (10 000 000 000 000) kilometres. The nearest star is more than four light-years away.
bring to light, cause to be known: *Many facts were brought to light in court.*
in the light of, when you think of: *In the light of all these facts, what they did was right.*
make light of, treat as not important.
shed light on, make clear; explain.

like (līk) **1** *prep* much the same as; similar to: *Angela looks like her sister.* **2** *v* enjoy: *My cat likes milk.* **3** *v* have a friendly feeling for: *The children liked their new teacher.* **4** *v* want; wish: *I'd like more time to finish this. Come whenever you like.* **liked, lik·ing. –lik′a·ble,** *adj,* **–lik′ing,** *n.*
like·ness 1 *n* the fact of being alike: *The boy's likeness to his father was striking.* **2** *n* a picture, sculpture, or other image: *The great artist painted a likeness of the Prime Minister.* **like·wise** *adv* the same; in the same way; also: *Whatever I do, I expect you to do likewise.*
like crazy, very much, very hard, very fast, etc.: *We worked like crazy.* Another expression is **like anything.**
the likes of, anyone or anything like: *This place is too fancy for the likes of you and me.*

–like *a suffix meaning:* like; similar to, as in *wolflike, childlike.*

like·ly (līk′lē) **1** *adj* probable; to be expected: *A likely result of this heavy rain is a flood. It is likely to snow today.* **2** *adv* probably: *I shall very likely be at home all day.* **like·li·er, like·li·est. –like′li·hood′,** *n.*

limb (lim) **1** *n* a leg, arm, or wing. **2** *n* a large branch: *They sawed the dead limb off the tree.*
out on a limb, in a risky situation.

lim·er·ick (lim′ə rik′) *n* a kind of humorous poem with five lines. The first two lines rhyme with the last, and the third and fourth lines rhyme with each other. *Example:*
There was a young lady named Lyn
Who was so exceedingly thin
That when she was made
To drink lemonade
She slid down the straw and fell in.

lim·it (lim′it) **1** *n* where something ends or must end: *the limit of a person's vision. I have reached the limit of my patience.* A **speed limit** is the highest speed allowed. **2 limits,** *pl.n* boundary: *the limits of Metropolitan Toronto.* **3** *v* set a limit to: *We will limit the cost to $10.* **–lim′i·ta′tion,** *n,* **–lim′it·ed,** *adj,* **–lim′it·less,** *adj.*

lim·ou·sine (lim′ə zēn′ *or* lim′ə zēn′) *n* a big, luxurious car, especially one driven by a paid driver. It sometimes has a pane of glass separating the passenger seats from the driver's seat. This word is often shortened to **limo.**

limp (limp) **1** *v* walk with difficulty because of a hurt leg or foot: *After falling down the stairs, he limped for several days.* **2** *n* this kind of difficulty in walking: *She walked with a limp.* **3** *adj* not stiff or firm; or droop: *The lettuce had lost its crispness and was quite limp.* **–limp′ly,** *adv,* **–limp′ness,** *n.*

line (līn) **1** *n* a long, narrow mark: *Draw two lines here.* **2** *n* a number of people or things one after another: *a line of cars.* **3** *n* a row of words on a page: *a poem of 12 lines.* **4** *n* a rope or wire, especially for a purpose: *a fishing line, a telephone line.* **5** *v* cover the inside of something with a layer of material: *to line a jacket. The box was lined with velvet.* **lined, lin·ing. –lin′ing,** *n.*
draw the line, set a limit: *Where do you draw the line between borrowing and stealing?*
hold the line, stay on the phone and wait.
line up, form a line: *People lined up to buy tickets.* A line formed by people waiting is a **line-up.**
out of line, not suitable or proper: *Her last remark was out of line.*
read between the lines, find a hidden meaning in something.
toe the line, do as you are expected.

lin·ger (ling′gər) *v* stay on; go slowly, as if not wanting to leave: *Daylight lingers long in summer. Bridget lingered after the others left.*

link (lingk) **1** *n* one ring or loop of a chain. **2** *v* join or connect: *They linked arms.* **3** *n* anything that joins or makes a connection.
link·ing verb a verb that expresses no action itself, but links the subject of a sentence to a word or phrase that describes it. For example, the verb *is* in *She is sad.*
▶See the *Grammar and Usage Mini-Guide.*

A lion and lioness— about 80 cm at the shoulder

li·on (lī′ən) *n* a large, strong, wild cat, with a dull-yellow coat, found in Africa and southern Asia. The male lion has a brown mane of hair. A female is called a **lioness.**
the lion's share, the biggest or best part.

lip (lip) *n* either one of the two soft, pinkish, movable edges of your mouth.

lip-sync (lip′singk′) silently move your lips as a song is played, so that you seem to be the singer.

button your lip, be quiet.

keep a stiff upper lip, be brave.

liq·uid (lik′wid) *n* a substance that is not a solid or a gas; a substance that flows like water.

liq·ue·fy (lik′wə fī′) *v* change into a liquid; make or become liquid: *The ice liquefied when left out in the hot sun.*

liq·uor (lik′ər) *n* a strong alcoholic drink made by distilling, such as brandy, whisky, or rum.

lisp (lisp) **1** *v* use a sound of *th* instead of the sound of *s* or *z* in speaking; for example, "thoup" for "soup." **2** *n* the act of speaking in this way: *He speaks with a lisp.*

list (list) **1** *n* a set of names, numbers, words, or phrases written one after the other: *a shopping list.* **2** *v* make a list of: *The winners' names are listed in the* Chatham Daily News.

lis·ten (lis′ən) *v* try to hear; pay attention to a sound: *She listened for the sound of a car. I like to listen to music.* –**lis′ten·er,** *n.*

lit·er·ate (lit′ə rit) **1** *adj* able to read and write. **2** *n* knowing at least the basics about something: *Are you computer literate?* –**lit′er·a·cy,** *n.*

lit·er·a·ture (lit′ə rə chər) **1** *n* written works, such as novels, plays, and poetry, that are admired because of their excellent style or thought: *Jean Little is a famous name in Canadian children's literature.* Anything to do with literature is **literary.** **2** *n* printed information; brochures.

lit·er·al *adj* using words in their normal or basic meaning; actual. When you say *He flew down the stairs,* you do not mean *fly* in the literal sense of the word. –**lit′er·al·ly,** *adv.*

li·tre (lē′tər) *n* a unit for measuring the volume of liquids. *Symbol:* L

lit·ter (lit′ər) **1** *n* bits of garbage scattered around: *Don't leave litter on the playground.* **2** *v* leave bits of garbage and other things lying around: *You have littered the room with candy wrappers.* **3** *n* the young animals born at the same time from one mother: *a litter of puppies.*

lit·tle (lit′əl) **1** *adj* not big or long; small or short: *A grain of sand is little. Wait a little while.* **2** *adj* small in amount or importance: *little food, a little problem.* **3** *n* a small amount; a short time or distance: *to move up a little.* **less** or **less·er, least;** or **lit·tler, lit·tlest.**

little by little, gradually.

make little of, treat as unimportant.

live (liv *for 1 and 2,* līv *for 3-5*) **1** *v* have life; be or stay alive: *All people have an equal right to live.* **2** *v* have your home: *My aunt lives in Nanaimo.* **lived, liv·ing. 3** *adj* having life; living: *a live animal.* **4** *adj* carrying an electric current: *a live wire.* **5** *adj* in radio or television, as something is happening, not from a tape or film: *a live interview with Karen Kain.*

live·ly (līv′lē) *adj* full of life, energy, and spirit: *A good night's sleep made us all lively again.* **live·li·er, live·li·est.** –**live′li·ness,** *n.*

live·stock (līv′stok′) *n* farm animals, such as cows, horses, sheep, and pigs.

liv·ing (liv′ing) **1** *adj* having life; alive: *a living plant.* **2** *n* a way of supporting yourself: *She earned her living as a plumber.*

live down, cause others to forget or overlook a past mistake because of your good behaviour: *He is determined to live down that disgrace.*

live it up, *Informal.* enjoy lots of pleasures.

live up to, act according to; do what is expected: *The car has not lived up to its description.*

live with, be satisfied with.

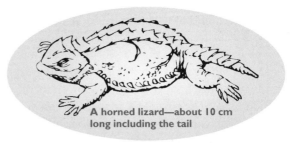

A horned lizard—about 10 cm long including the tail

liz·ard (liz′ərd) *n* a reptile with a long body, long tail, movable eyelids, and usually four legs.

lla·ma (lä′mə *or* lam′ə) *n* a woolly South American animal like a camel, but smaller and without a hump. *pl* **lla·mas** or **lla·ma.**

load (lōd) **1** *n* anything being carried: *She had a load of books in her knapsack.* **2** *v* put something on or in a carrier of some kind: *to load a van with camping gear. The workers are loading grain into the ships.* **3 loads,** *pl.n Informal.* a large amount: *We have loads of food.* **4** *v* put something needed into a machine: *to load film into a camera.*

loaf (lōf) **1** *n* bread that is shaped and baked as one piece. **2** *n* anything shaped like this: *a meat loaf.* **3** *v* spend time doing nothing: *I can loaf all day Saturday.* *pl* **loaves.**

loan (lōn) **1** *n* anything that someone lends or borrows, especially money: *Henri asked his brother for a loan.* **2** *v* lend: *Ursel loaned me her pen.* **3** *n* the act of lending: *She asked for the loan of his pen.*

loathe (lōᴛʜ) *v* hate: *I loathe ketchup.* Something you hate is **loathsome. loathed, loath·ing.**

lob·by (lob′ē) *n* a large entrance hall or waiting area: *a hotel lobby, a theatre lobby.* *pl* **lob·bies.**

❀**lob·stick** (lob′stik′) *n* in the North, a spruce or pine tree trimmed of all but the top branches. Travellers often used lobsticks as landmarks.

lo·cate (lō kāt′ *or* lō kāt′) **1** *v* set up in a place: *Early settlers located where there was water.* **2** *v* find: *Locate Regina on the map.* **lo·cat·ed, lo·cat·ing.**

lo·cal *adj* having to do with just a certain limited place: *local news.* **–lo′cal·ly,** *adv.*

lo·ca·tion *n* position; place: *The cottage was in a sheltered location on Lake Huron.*

on location, at a place outside the movie or TV studio: *All the outdoor scenes were shot on location.*

lock (lok) **1** *n* a device for fastening a door, lid, suitcase, etc. so that it cannot be opened without a key. **2** *v* fasten with a lock: *to lock a door, to lock up jewels in a safe.* **3** *n* a section of a canal closed off with gates so that the level of the water inside it can be changed. **4** *v* join, fit, snap, or hold in place: *The pieces lock securely together.* **5** *n* a curl of hair. **Locks** is another word for "hair." **lock·er** *n* a little metal closet or cupboard that can be locked.

lock, stock, and barrel, completely.

lo·co·mo·tive (lō′kə mō′tiv) *n* a railway engine.

lodge (loj) **1** *n* a building with places to sleep, that is part of a tourist resort, hunting camp, etc.: *They run a ski lodge up the mountains, near Banff.* **2** *n* a traditional First Nations dwelling. **3** *n* the home of a beaver or otter.

loft (loft) *n* an open storage space under a roof. In a barn, it is used for hay; other lofts may be turned into studios or small apartments. **loft·y** *adj* very high: *lofty mountains.*

log (log) **1** *n* a length of wood just as it comes from the tree. **2** *v* cut down trees, and get them out of the forest. **logged, log·ging. –log′ger,** *n,* **–log′ging,** *n.* **3** *n* the daily record of a ship's voyage, or any other record to keep track of events. A log is often kept in a **logbook.**

log in, sign a book to show that you have arrived. You **log out** when you leave.

log on, start a session at a computer by keying in a password or other identification. You **log off** by shutting the computer down correctly.

log·ic (loj′ik) *n* sound, careful, clear reasoning. **–log′i·cal,** *adj,* **–log′i·cal·ly,** *adv.*

lo·go (lō′gō) *n* a special symbol used by a company as a trademark, or in advertising.

loi·ter (loi′tər) *v* hang around in a place: *Tina loitered on the corner, waiting for her friends.*

lol·li·pop (lol′ē pop′) *n* a piece of hard candy on the end of a small stick; sucker.

lone·ly (lōn′lē) **1** *adj* feeling sad because you are alone: *Luke was lonely while his brother was away.* **2** *adj* without many people around: *a lonely road.* **Lonesome** is another word for either meaning. **lone·li·er, lone·li·est. –lone′li·ness,** *n.* **lone** *adj* alone; single: *a lone pine tree.* A **loner** is someone who spends most of the time alone.

long (long) **1** *adj* from one end to the other; from beginning to end: *My table is one metre long. The movie is two hours long.* **2** *adj* measuring far from end to end, or taking a lot of time: *a long driveway, a long story.* **long·er** (long′gər), **long·est** (long′gist). **3** *v* have a very strong desire: *He longed for his mother.* Such a desire is a **longing. –long′ing·ly,** *adv.*

a long face, a sad expression.

in the long run, over a long period of time; eventually: *The new computer system will work out well in the long run.*

A Huron longhouse

long·house (long'hous') *n* a large house that some First Nations people used to live in, big enough for a group of related families. Nowadays, longhouses are used for community meetings. **Big house** is another name for it.

lon·gi·tude (long'gə tyūd' *or* lon'jə tyūd') *n* a distance east or west on the earth's surface, measured from the imaginary line running north and south through Greenwich in England. The distance is measured in degrees. ►See **latitude**.

look (lùk) **1** *v* try to see something; pay attention with your eyes: *Look at the pictures.* **2** *v* search: *I looked all over for my mitts.* **3** *n* a glance: *Tom took a quick look at* Chickadee *magazine.* **4** *v* seem; appear: *She looks pale.* **5 looks,** *pl.n* personal appearance: *Alexei has his father's good looks.*
look·out 1 *n* a place to keep watch from: *From the lookout, she could see the smoke 20 km away in Huntsville.* **2** *n* a person or group whose job is to watch for something. **3** *n* job; responsibility: *Don't expect me to clean up; that's your lookout.*
look after, take care of: *He looked after his brother.*
look down on, think of as not very important.
look forward to, expect with pleasure: *We look forward to seeing you.*
look into, try to find out about.
look out, be careful; watch out: *Look out for cars as you cross the street.*
look over, examine; inspect: *The police officer looked over his driver's licence.*
look up, 1 find in a book: *She looked up the word in the dictionary.* **2** *Informal.* call on; visit: *Look me up when you come to town.* **3** improve: *Things are looking up.*
look up to, respect; admire.

loom (lūm) *v* appear as a large, threatening shape: *A large iceberg loomed through the fog on Baffin Bay.*

loon (lūn) *n* a large, mostly black-and-white diving bird that nests in northern lands and has a loud, wild cry.
❧ **loon·ie** (lū'nē) *n* the Canadian one-dollar coin. It has a picture of a loon on one side.

loon·y (lū'nē) *adj Informal.* crazy or very foolish: *What a loony idea!* **loon·i·er, loon·i·est.**

loop (lūp) *n* the curved shape of a string, ribbon, etc. that crosses over itself or bends back on itself.
throw someone for a loop, *Informal.* surprise and confuse someone.

loose (lūs) **1** *adj* not firmly set or fastened: *a loose tooth, a loose thread.* **2** *adj* not tight: *loose clothing.* **3** *adj* not attached together or packaged: *loose papers.* **4** *adj* not shut in or tied up: *The dogs are loose.* **loos·er, loos·est.** –**loose'ly,** *adv,* –**loos'en,** *v.*

CONFUSABLES ..... loose

loose means "not tight": *My tooth is loose.*
lose means "misplace": *Don't lose your key.*

---

loot (lūt) **1** *n* stolen goods: *The burglars tried to sell their loot.* **2** *v* rob, especially in war or during a riot: *Hooligans looted the jewellery store.* **3** *n Informal.* goodies from a party or collected at Halloween. –**loot'er,** *n.*

lop·sid·ed (lop'sī'did) *adj* larger or heavier on one side than the other; unevenly balanced. –**lop'sid'ed·ly,** *adv,* –**lop'sid'ed·ness,** *n.*

lore (lôr) *n* learning; knowledge.

lose (lūz) **1** *v* not have any longer because it has been taken away from you by an accident, a death, punishment, or in any other way: *to lose a grandparent, to lose a privilege. They lost all their furniture in the fire.* **2** *v* be unable to find: *to lose your way, to lose a book.* **3** *v* fail to win: *Our team lost the game.* **4** *v* fail to keep: *to lose your balance. I lost interest.* **lost, los·ing.** –**los'er,** *n.*

loss (los) *n* the person, thing, or amount lost: *The fire was finally put out, but her house was a complete loss.*
at a loss, puzzled; not sure what to do or say: *Sanford was at a loss for words.*

lot (lot) **1** Often, **lots,** *pl.n Informal.* a great many; a great deal: *You have lots of time. I have a lot of marbles.* **2** *n* a piece of ground: *His house is between two empty lots.* **3** *n* a number of people or things considered as a group; a collection: *This lot of oranges is not as good as the last.*

lo·tion (lō′shən) *n* a liquid medicine or a beauty product that you put on your skin.

lot·ter·y (lot′ə rē) *n* a game where you can win a prize of money. In a lottery a large number of tickets are sold, but only some of them win prizes. *pl* **lot·ter·ies.**

loud (loud) *adj* not quiet or soft; with a powerful sound: *a loud voice. A balloon bursts with a loud bang* (*adj*). —**loud′ly,** *adv,* —**loud′ness,** *n.*

lounge (lounj) **1** *v* stand, sit, or lie in a relaxed, lazy way: *He lounged in an old chair.* **2** *n* a comfortable room where people can sit and relax: *a hotel lounge.* **lounged, loung·ing.**

lous·y (lou′zē) *adj Informal.* bad; miserable: *I don't like that restaurant because the food is lousy.* **lous·i·er, lous·i·est.**

love (luv) **1** *v* care very much for: *She loves her mother. I love Canada.* **2** *n* the deep feeling you have toward someone or something thought of in this way: *love for your family, love for a sweetheart.* **3** *v* like very much; take great pleasure in: *He loves music. Most kids love ice cream.* **loved, lov·ing.** —**lov′a·ble,** *adj,* —**lov′er,** *n,* —**lov′ing,** *adj.*

love·ly **1** *adj* beautiful in looks or character: *a lovely sunset. She is one of the loveliest girls we know.* **2** *adj Informal.* very nice: *We had a lovely holiday in the Maritimes.* **love·li·er, love·li·est.**
fall in love, begin to love.
in love, feeling love.

low (lō) **1** *adj* not high or tall: *a low bridge, a low shelf, a low jump. That was a low trick.* **2** *adj* less than usual: *a low temperature, low pay.* **3** *adj* not loud: *a low whisper.*

low·er **1** *v* let down, take down, or come down: *We lower the Canadian flag at night. The level of the lake has lowered.* **2** *v* lessen: *to lower the volume of the radio.* **3** *adj* or *adv* less; farther down: *My marks were lower last year than this* (*adj*). *The boat sank lower in the water* (*adv*).

lower case letters that are not capitals. The letters *a* and *b* are lower case, while *A* and *B* are not. Capitals are called **upper case.**

lie low, *Informal.* stay hidden: *The robbers will lie low for a time.*

low in something, having little of something: *These crackers are low in fat.*

low tide, the time when the ocean is lowest on the shore.

loy·al (loi′əl) *adj* true and faithful to someone or something: *a loyal friend.* —**loy′al·ly,** *adv,* —**loy′al·ty,** *n.*

luck (luk) **1** *n* whatever seems to happen or come to a person by accident; chance: *Luck was against the losers, even though they played better on the whole.* **2** *n* good fortune: *Lots of luck to you.* —**luck′i·ly,** *adv,* —**luck′less,** *adj,* —**luck′y,** *adj.*
down on your luck, *Informal.* having bad luck.
in luck, having good luck; lucky: *I'm in luck; I found a toonie.* **Out of luck** is the opposite.
luck out, *Informal.* be very lucky: *She lucked out and won $100.*
push your luck, *Informal.* take needless risks when things are going well.
try your luck, see what you can do or get: *Try your luck with this game.*

lug (lug) *v* pull along or carry with effort: *We lugged the heavy bags of groceries all the way home.* **lugged, lug·ging.**

lug·gage *n* suitcases and so on used by a traveller to carry his or her things; baggage.

luke·warm (lūk′wôrm′) **1** *adj* neither hot nor cold; slightly warm or cool. **2** *adj* showing little enthusiasm; half-hearted: *a lukewarm reaction.*

lull (lul) **1** *v* make or become calm or quiet: *to lull a baby to sleep. The wind lulled.* **2** *n* a period of calmness or quietness: *We ran home during a lull in the storm.*

lul·la·by (lul′ə bī′) *n* a song to lull a baby to sleep.

lum·ber (lum′bər) *n* wood cut into boards or beams. A **lumberjack** cuts down trees and gets logs to the mills and a **lumberyard** is an outdoor area for storing lumber.

lump (lump) **1** *n* a solid mass of no particular shape: *a lump of coal.* **2** *n* a swelling; a bump: *There is a lump on my head where I bumped it.* —**lump′y,** *adj.*

lu·nar (lū′nər) *adj* having to do with the moon: *a lunar eclipse.* A **lunar month** is the time for the moon to go around the earth, about 29.5 days.

lunch (lunch) **1** *n* a light meal, usually around noon. A **luncheon** (lun′chən) is a fancy or formal lunch. **2** *v* eat such a meal: *We lunched outside under a tree.*

lung (lung) *n* either one of the pair of breathing organs found in the chest of humans and other air-breathing animals.

lunge (lunj) **1** *v* move or throw yourself suddenly forward: *The dog lunged at the stranger.* **2** *n* this kind of movement; a rush or thrust: *The catcher made a lunge toward the ball.* **lunged, lung·ing.**

lure (lūr) **1** *v* attract; tempt: *Bees are lured by the scent of flowers. They lured the rat into the trap with a piece of cheese.* **2** *n* attraction: *Many people feel the lure of the sea.* **3** *n* anything used on purpose to attract or tempt, especially an object made to look like a fly or worm to attract fish. **lured, lur·ing.**

lurk (lərk) *v* wait quietly and out of sight: *A tiger was lurking in the jungle outside the village.*

lus·cious (lush′əs) *adj* delicious; rich or juicy and full of flavour: *a luscious peach.*

lush (lush) *adj* full of thick, healthy growth: *lush grass, lush fields.*

lux·u·ry (luk′shə rē) *n* any of the comforts and beauties of life beyond what are really necessary: *We can't afford luxuries like banana splits and movies all the time.* pl **lux·u·ries.**

lux·u·ri·ant (lug zhū′rē ənt) *adj* growing in a vigorous and healthy way; thick and lush: *In spring the grass on our lawn is luxuriant.*

lux·u·ri·ous (lug zhū′rē əs) *adj* very comfortable and beautiful: *Some houses are very luxurious.*

USING WORDS ....luxuriant

Luxuriant and **luxurious** are related words with very different meanings.

Luxuriant means "growing thick and lush."
Luxurious means "giving luxury." You can remember the difference by looking at the word endings: *a luxuriant plant; a luxurious house.*

–ly *a suffix meaning* in a certain way or manner. *Cheerfully* means in a *cheerful* way. Many adverbs are made by adding *-ly* to an adjective.

A Canada lynx—
about 80 cm long

lynx (lingks) *n* a kind of wildcat found in North America, Europe, and Asia, with a short tail, pointed ears with long tufts of hair on them, and large paws. The two kinds of lynx found in North America are the **Canada lynx** and the **bobcat.** *pl* **lynx·es** or **lynx.**

m or **M** (em) *n* the thirteenth letter of the English alphabet or the sound that it stands for. The sound is the sound of *m* in *humming*. *pl* **m's** or **M's.**

ma·chine (mə shēn′) **1** *n* an arrangement of fixed and moving parts for doing work, each part having some special job to do: *The blade of a lawn mower is the part of the machine that cuts the grass.* **2** *n* a device for applying force or changing direction: *A lever is a simple machine.*

ma·chin·er·y 1 *n* machines: *There is a lot of machinery in a car factory.* **2** *n* the parts or works of a machine: *This clear plastic watch lets you see the machinery inside.*

mad (mad) **1** *adj* out of your mind; insane. **2** *adj Informal.* very angry: *The insult made Dan mad.* —**mad′den,** *v,* —**mad′ly,** *adv,* —**mad′ness,** *n.*

like mad, *Informal.* furiously; very hard or fast: *I ran like mad to catch the bus.*

mag·a·zine (mag′ə zēn′ *or* mag′ə zēn′) *n* a publication issued regularly, containing stories, pictures, etc.: *Canadian Geographic is a magazine that is published six times a year.*

The maggot on the left becomes the adult fly on the right.

mag·got (mag′ət) *n* a fly in the earliest, legless stage, just after leaving the egg. Maggots often live in rotting food.

mag·ic (maj′ik) **1** *n* in stories, the art of using charms and tricks to make unnatural things happen: *The fairy's magic changed the brothers into swans.* **2** *n* the skill of producing puzzling effects by tricks or juggling: *The magician pulled flags from his ear by magic.* —**mag′i·cal,** *adj,* —**ma·gi′cian,** *n.*

mag·net (mag′nit) *n* a stone or piece of metal that attracts iron or steel to it.

mag·net·ic (mag net′ik) *adj* with the properties of a magnet: *the magnetic needle of a compass.*

mag·nif·i·cent (mag nif′ə sənt) **1** *adj* richly decorated: *a magnificent palace.* **2** *adj* extraordinarily fine: *a magnificent view of the Rockies.* —**mag·nif′i·cent·ly,** *adv.*

mag·ni·fy (mag′nə fī′) *v* cause to look larger than the real size: *A microscope magnifies small things so that they can be seen and studied.* **mag·ni·fied, mag·ni·fy·ing.**

mag·ni·fi·ca·tion (mag′nə fə kā′shən) **1** *n* the power to magnify: *The magnification of this microscope is fifty times, so it makes objects appear fifty times larger.* **2** *n* a magnified copy: *This picture is a magnification of a fly's eye.*

magnifying glass a lens or combination of lenses that makes things look larger.

maid (mād) **1** *n* an old or poetic word for a young, unmarried woman; a girl. **Maiden** is another word for this. **2** *n* a woman servant: *a kitchen maid.*

mail (māl) **1** *n* letters, cards, parcels, etc. sent by post. **2** *v* send by mail: *Bill mailed the birthday card yesterday.*

mail·box 1 *n* a public box from which mail is collected. **2** *n* a private box to which mail is delivered. **mail carrier** *n* a person whose work is carrying and delivering mail; letter carrier.

main (mān) **1** *adj* most important; largest: *the main dish at dinner, the main street of a town.* **2** *adj* a large pipe for water, gas, etc.: *When the water main broke, University Avenue was flooded.*

main·land (mān′land′ *or* mān′lənd) *n* the main part of a continent or land mass; land that is not a small island or peninsula.

main·land·er (mān′lan′dər *or* mān′lən dər) *n* a person who lives on the mainland.

main·ly *adv* for the most part; chiefly: *Aldo is interested mainly in sports but he also likes reading mystery stories.*

main·tain (mān tān′) **1** *v* keep; carry on: *You must maintain your balance when riding a bicycle.* **2** *v* keep in good repair: *Maintain your bicycle and it will last longer.* **3** *v* declare to be true: *Donna maintained that she was innocent.*

main·te·nance (mān′tə nəns) *n* keeping in good repair: *The airline spends a lot of money for the maintenance of its airplanes.*

maize (māz) *n* corn.

maj·es·ty (maj′is tē) **1** *n* a stately appearance; dignity; nobility: *We were impressed by the majesty of the First Nations powwow.* **2 Majesty,** *n* a title used in speaking to or of a king, queen, emperor, empress, etc.: *Your Majesty, His Majesty, Her Majesty.*
ma·jes·tic *adj* grand; noble. –**ma·jes′ti·cal·ly,** *adv.*

ma·jor (mā′jər) **1** *adj* larger; more important: *The major part of a baby's life is spent in sleeping.* **2** *adj* very serious or important: *a major disaster.*

ma·jor·i·ty (mə jòr′ə tē) **1** *n* the larger part; more than half: *A majority of students passed the test.* **2** *n* the number by which the votes on one side are more than those on the other: *Since Amarjit had 18 votes and Bruce had 12, Amarjit had a majority of 6.* pl **ma·jor·i·ties.**

make (māk) **1** *v* bring into being; build; create: *to make a Halloween costume, to make cookies.* **2** *n* a kind; a brand: *What make of car is this?* **3** *v* cause; bring about: *to make a noise, to make trouble.* **4** *v* cause to; force to: *Julie made me go.* **5** *v* get ready for use; arrange; prepare: *to make the beds, to make supper.* **6** *v* Informal. get on; get a place on: *Kristin made the volleyball team.*
made, mak·ing.
make believe, pretend: *The girl liked to make believe she was a movie star.*
make up, 1 invent: *to make up a story.* **2** become friends again after a quarrel. **3** put paint, powder, or other cosmetics on your face. **4** decide: *Make up your mind.*

male (māl) **1** *n* a man, boy, or male animal: *All fathers are males.* **2** *adj* of or having to do with men or boys: *Male voices are usually lower than female voices.*

mal·ice (mal′is) *n* a wish to hurt or make suffer: *Sasha spoke frankly but without malice.*
ma·li·cious *adj* wishing to hurt; spiteful: *I think that story is malicious gossip.*

mall (mol) *n* a large covered area with many stores. **Shopping mall** is another name for this.

mal·let (mal′it) *n* a hammer with a head of wood, rubber, or other fairly soft material.

mam·mal (mam′əl) *n* a warm-blooded animal with a backbone; the female produces milk for feeding her young. Human beings, cattle, dogs, cats, and whales are all mammals.

mam·moth (mam′əth) **1** *n* a large kind of elephant, now extinct, with hairy skin and long, curved tusks. **2** *adj* huge; gigantic: *Digging the St. Lawrence Seaway was a mammoth undertaking.*

man (man) *n* an adult male human being. *pl* **men** (men). Many people think that using *man* and words like *mankind* and *man-made* is offensive when talking about the human race.
man·kind *n* the human race.
man-made *adj* not natural; artificial: *a man-made lake, man-made material.*

USING WORDS...... man

Although **man** used to mean "all people," its meaning has changed over time. Nowadays, when you want to talk about all people, use words like *the human race, humanity, human beings,* or *people.*

man·age (man′ij) **1** *v* control; handle: *My aunt and uncle manage a small grocery store.* **2** *v* be able to do something: *I managed to finish the jigsaw puzzle, with some help from my big brother.* **man·aged, man·ag·ing.**
–**man′age·ment,** *n,* –**man·ag·er,** *n.*

mane (mān) *n* the long, heavy hair growing on the neck of a horse, a lion, etc.

ma·ni·a (mā′nē ə) *n* an unusual fondness; a craze: *Bronte has a mania for reading science fiction.*
ma·ni·ac *n* a person who behaves in a wild or irresponsible way: *That cyclist is a maniac.*

man·i·cure (man′ə kyūr′) *n* treatment of hands and fingernails, especially shaping and polishing nails: *Her mother had a manicure at the beauty salon.*

❁ **man·i·tou** (man′ə tū′) *n* in the traditional religion of First Nations people, a spirit seen as the Creator, a force in nature, or the spirit living in all creation.

M
m

man·ner (man′ər) **1** *n* the way something happens or is done: *Alain used his crutches in a careful manner.* **2** *n* a person's way of acting or behaving; a style: *The clown dresses in a strange manner.* **3** **manners,** *pl.n* ways of behaving toward others: *bad manners, good manners.*

man·tra (mun′trə) *n* in Hinduism and Buddhism, a verse from the holy writings, spoken over and over again in prayer.

man·u·al (man′yū əl) **1** *adj* of, or using the hands: *manual work.* **2** *adj* operated by hand, not automatically: *Our car has a manual transmission.* **3** *n* a book that helps its readers to understand or use something: *The manual that came with our computer is very hard to understand.*

man·u·fac·ture (man′yə fak′chər) *v* to make by machine: *A big factory manufactures things by using machines and dividing the work among many people.* **man·u·fac·tured, man·u·fac·tur·ing.**

ma·nure (mə nyūr′ *or* mə nūr′) *n* a substance, especially animal waste, put on or in the soil as fertilizer: *The dirt from a stable is an environment-friendly kind of manure.*

man·u·script (man′yə skript′) *n* an unpublished book or paper written by hand or on a word processor.

man·y (men′ē) *adj* a great number of: *Many Canadians live in cities.* **more, most.**
a good many, a fairly large number; a lot.

map (map) *n* a flat drawing of the earth's surface or of part of it, usually showing countries, towns, rivers, seas, mountains, etc.

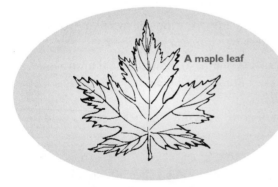

A maple leaf

ma·ple (mā′pəl) *n* a tree such as the sugar maple or the Manitoba maple, used for its hard wood or for the production of maple syrup.
maple leaf a leaf of the maple tree, used as a popular Canadian emblem: *"The Maple Leaf Forever" was written in 1867 by Alexander Muir.*

maple sugar sugar made from the sap of the sugar maple. **maple syrup** syrup made from the sap of the sugar maple.

mar·a·thon (mar′ə thon′ *or* mer′ə thon′) **1** *n* in sports, a foot race of 42.195 km. **2** *n* a long race or contest: *a marathon swim.*

mar·ble (mår′bəl) **1** *n* a hard stone that can take a beautiful polish. **2** *n* **marbles,** a game played with small balls made of marble, glass, etc.

march (mårch) **1** *v* to walk as soldiers do, with steps of the same length. **2** *n* the act of marching: *The students' march was a great success and earned hundreds of dollars for the Canadian Cancer Society.*

mare (mer) *n* a female horse, donkey, etc.

mar·ga·rine (mår′jə rin) *n* a substitute for butter, usually made from vegetable oils.

mar·gin (mår′jən) *n* the blank space around the writing or printing on a page: *Do not write in the margin of your test.*

ma·rine (mə rēn′) *adj* of the sea: *Seals and whales are marine animals.*

ma·ri·na *n* a place along a waterfront where boats may be tied. **mar·i·ner** *n* a sailor.

mar·i·time (mar′ə tīm′ *or* mer′ə tīm′) *adj* on or near the sea: *St. John's is a maritime city.*
Maritime Provinces New Brunswick, Nova Scotia, and Prince Edward Island. Another name is **the Maritimes. Mar·i·tim·er** *n* a person born in or living in the Maritime Provinces.

USING WORDS : Maritime Provinces

The **Maritime Provinces** or **Maritimes** do not include the province of Newfoundland and Labrador. The four **Atlantic Provinces** are: New Brunswick, Nova Scotia, Prince Edward Island, and Newfoundland and Labrador.

---

mark (mårk) **1** *n* a trace left by some object on another. A line, dot, spot, stain, or scar is a mark. **2** *v* make a mark on: *Be careful not to mark the desk.* **3** *n* a guide or sign: *the starting mark in a race, a question mark.* **4** *v* show by means of a sign: *Mark the capital city of each province and territory on this map of Canada.* **5** *n* a letter or number to show how well one has done: *My mark in language arts was B.* **6** *v* give scores to: *The teacher marked our project.*

mar·ket (mär′kit) **1** *n* a meeting for the purpose of buying and selling: *There is a farmer's market in St. John's every Saturday.* **2** *v* sell: *The farmer cannot market all of her wheat.*
in the market for, be a possible buyer of: *Carlos is in the market for a new bike.*

ma·roon (mə rün′) **1** *v* put a person on a desert island or in a deserted place: *Pirates used to maroon people on desert islands.* **2** *v* leave in a lonely, helpless position: *During the storm we were marooned in a cabin far from town.*

mar·ry (mar′ē *or* mer′ē) *v* take as husband or wife. **mar·ried, mar·ry·ing. –mar′ried,** *adj.*
mar·riage (mar′ij *or* mer′ij) **1** *n* living together as husband and wife. **2** *n* a wedding.

marsh (märsh) *n* an area of wet, muddy land sometimes partly covered with water. Its plant life is mainly grasses. **–marsh′y,** *adj.*

marsh·mal·low (märsh′mal′ō *or* märsh′mel′ō) *n* a soft, usually white, spongy candy, covered with powdered sugar.

mar·tial (mär′shəl) *adj* of or suitable for war or fighting: *martial music.* **Martial arts** is a sport in which you use all of your body in fighting. **Judo, karate,** and **tae kwon do** are martial arts.

mar·vel (mär′vəl) **1** *n* something amazing: *Computers are a marvel for organizing and storing information.* **2** *v* be filled with wonder: *Purna marvelled at the runner's speed.* **mar·velled** or **mar·veled, mar·vel·ling** or **mar·vel·ing.**
mar·vel·lous 1 *adj* causing wonder; extraordinary: *Young children like stories of marvellous events, such as those in the tale of Aladdin and his lamp.* **2** *adj Informal.* excellent; splendid. **Marvelous** is another spelling.

mas·cot (mas′kot) *n* something or someone supposed to bring good luck: *The swim team kept the stuffed fish as a mascot.*

mas·cu·line (mas′kyə lin) *adj* having to do with men or boys or things that are supposed to be typical of them: *masculine clothing, a masculine voice.*

mash (mash) *v* crush to a soft mass: *I'll mash the potatoes.*

mas·jid (mus′jid) *n* the Arabic word for a mosque, a Muslim place of worship.

mask (mask) **1** *n* a covering for the face, worn for disguise, for protection, or in fun: *a Halloween mask. The burglar wore a mask.* **2** *v* hide or disguise: *A smile masked Paulette's disappointment.*

mas·quer·ade (mas′kə rād′) **1** *n* a party or dance at which masks and costumes are worn. **2** *v* disguise yourself: *The king masqueraded as a beggar to find out if his people really liked him.*

mass (mas) **1** *n* a lump: *a mass of pizza dough.* **2** *n* a large quantity together: *a mass of flowers.* **3** *n* the quantity of matter anything contains: *The mass of a piece of ice does not change when you melt it.* **4 the masses,** *pl.n* the general population: *Most television programs are entertainment for the masses.*

mas·sive *adj* big and heavy. **mass media** the various modern means of communication that reach a large audience. Television, radio, movies, the Internet, newspapers, and magazines are examples of mass media.

mas·sa·cre (mas′ə kər) **1** *n* a killing of many people or animals. **2** *v* kill many people or animals. **mas·sa·cred, mas·sa·cring.**

mas·sage (mə säzh′) **1** *n* a rubbing of muscles and joints to make them work better and to increase the circulation of the blood. **2** *v* give a massage to. **mas·saged, mas·sag·ing.**

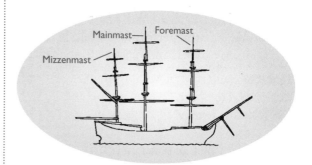

Mainmast— Foremast
Mizzenmast—

mast (mast) *n* any tall, upright pole: *a flag mast, a tall TV mast, a ship's mast.*

mas·ter (mas′tər) **1** *n* a person who rules or commands people, animals, or things: *My sister's ambition is to become the master of a cruise ship.* **2** *n* an expert.
mas·ter·piece *n* an excellent piece of work.

mat (mat) **1** *n* a piece of some thick material used to protect something: *a table mat, a gymnastics mat, a bathmat.* **2** *n* anything growing thickly packed or tangled together: *a mat of weeds, a mat of hair.* **3** *v* tangle together in a mat: *The swimmer's wet hair was matted.* **mat·ted, mat·ting.**

match (mach) **1** *n* a person or thing equal to another or much like another: *I can't get dressed until I find the match to this sock.* **2** *v* look alike; go well together: *These sheets match the wallpaper in my room.* **3** *n* a short, thin piece of wood tipped with a mixture that takes fire when rubbed on a rough or special surface. **4** *n* a game or contest: *a tennis match.*

match·less *adj* so great or wonderful that it cannot be equalled.

mate (māt) **1** *n* one of a pair: *Where is the mate to this glove?* **2** *n* either of a pair (male and female) of animals or birds: *One bird watched the nest while its mate went for food.* **3** *v* be together as a pair to produce young: *Birds mate in the spring.* **mat·ed, mat·ing.**

ma·te·ri·al (mə tē′rē əl) *n* what is used to make or do something: *dress material, building materials. Rick Hansen's Man in Motion tour made good material for a book.*

math·e·mat·ics (math′ə mat′iks) *n* the study of number, measurement, and space. Arithmetic and geometry are parts of mathematics. –**math·e·mat′i·cal,** *adj,* –**math′e·mat′i·cal·ly,** *adv,* –**math′e·ma·ti′cian** (math′ə mə tish′ən), *n.*

mat·i·née (mat′ə nā′ *or* mat′ə nā′) *n* a dramatic or musical performance held in the afternoon. **Matinee** is another way to spell this.

mat·ter (mat′ər) **1** *n* what things are made of: *Matter takes up space.* **2** *v* be important: *It doesn't matter to me if I have to sit in the back seat of the car.*
as a matter of fact, in truth; in reality.
no matter, regardless of: *Ian wants a bicycle, no matter what it costs.*
What is the matter? What is wrong?

mat·tress (mat′ris) *n* a thick pad made of cotton, foam rubber, or other material, used on a bed: *Many mattresses have springs inside.*

ma·ture (mə chūr′ *or* mə tyūr′) **1** *adj* ripe or full-grown: *He is tall for his age, but that doesn't mean he is mature.* **2** *v* ripen; come to full growth: *These apples are maturing fast.* **ma·tured, ma·tur·ing.** –**ma·tu′ri·ty,** *n.*

max·i·mum (mak′sə məm) *adj* greatest possible: *The maximum score on this test is 100.* *pl* **max·i·mums** *or* **max·i·ma** (mak′sə mə).

may (mā) an auxiliary (helping) verb used: **1** *v* to ask for or give permission: *You may go now. May I have an apple?* **2** *v* to show that something is possible: *It may rain tomorrow. I may go skiing if the weather is good.* *past tense* might.

may·be (mā′bē) *adv* possibly or perhaps.

CONFUSABLES ..... may

maybe means "perhaps":
Maybe I should give him a call.
may be means "could be":
He may be in trouble.

may·or (mā′ər) *n* the person at the head of the government of a city, town, or village.

maze (māz) *n* a network through which it is hard to find your way: *The shores of the French River are a maze of channels and bays.*

me (mē) *pron* the objective form of the pronoun *I: She said, "Give the dog to me. I like it and it likes me."*

mead·ow (med′ō) *n* a piece of grassy land, especially used for growing hay.

meal (mēl) **1** *n* breakfast, lunch, dinner, or supper. **2** *n* grain ground up: *corn meal.*

mean (mēn) **1** *v* refer to: *The word "meat" means animal flesh used for food.* **2** *v* have in mind: *Do you think they mean to go with us?* **3** *adj* unkind: *It is mean to spread gossip.* **4** *adj* stingy or selfish: *A miser is mean about money.* **5** *adj* average: *The mean temperature for July in Yarmouth is 16°C.* **6** *n* **means,** the method by which something is made to happen: *Airplanes are a fast means of travel.* **meant, mean·ing.**
mean·ing *n* what is meant: *The meaning of that sentence is clear.* **mean·ing·ful** *adj* full of meaning: *a meaningful look.*
by any means, in any possible way.
by no means, certainly not: *This jacket is by no means warm.*

mean·time (mēn′tīm′) *n* the time between: *The play starts on Friday; in the meantime we will keep rehearsing.*

mean·while (mēn′hwīl′ *or* mēn′wīl′) *adv* at the same time, especially in a different place: *I'll make the salad; meanwhile, you can set the table.*

mea·sles (mē′zəlz) *n* an infectious disease that causes a fever and a rash of small, red spots.

meas·ure (mezh′ər) **1** *v* find out the size, amount, length, width, height, depth, etc. of anything, by using some kind of tool: *When we measured the room, we found that it was 6 m long, 4.5 m wide, and 2.2 m high. We measured the capacity of the pail by finding out how many litres of water it would hold.* **2** *v* be of a certain size: *We use paper that measures 21 cm by 28 cm.* **3** *n* a bar of music. **meas·ured, meas·ur·ing.**

meas·ure·ment *n* the size found by measuring: *The measurements of the garden are 16 m by 15 m.*

measure up, meet a certain standard: *The party did not measure up to what she expected.*

meat (mēt) *n* animal flesh used for food: *Fish and chicken are usually not called meat.*

Mec·ca (mek′ə) *n* the holy city of Islam in Saudi Arabia. Muslims face toward Mecca for daily prayers and have a duty to make at least one pilgrimage to Mecca.

me·chan·ic (mə kan′ik) *n* a person skilled with tools, especially one who makes or repairs machinery: *an automobile mechanic.*

me·chan·i·cal **1** *adj* having to do with machinery: *a mechanical engineer.* **2** *adj* like a machine; without expression: *Her dancing is very mechanical.* **–me·chan′i·cal·ly,** *adv.*

mech·a·nism *n* a machine or its working parts: *Something must be wrong with the starter mechanism of our lawn mower.*

med·al (med′əl) *n* a small piece of metal with a design, given as an honour: *The firefighter won a medal for bravery. Patti won the gold medal for doing the best artwork in the school.*

med·dle (med′əl) *v* interfere in other people's things or affairs: *Don't meddle with my bike.* **med·dled, med·dling. –med′dler,** *n,* **–med′dle·some,** *adj.*

me·di·a (mē′dē ə) *pl.n* kinds of communication: *Newspapers, television, radio, magazines, and billboards are all important media for advertising.*

med·i·cine (med′ə sən) **1** *n* any substance, such as a drug, used to cure disease or improve health. **Medication** is another word for this. **–me·dic′i·nal,** *adj.* **2** *n* the science of curing disease or improving health: *Ingrid decided to study medicine.* **–med′i·cal,** (med′ə kəl) *adj.*

medicine lodge a building used for healing ceremonies by some aboriginal peoples. Among some First Nations of the Pacific coast, it is a place for ceremonies meant to cleanse the person's body, mind, and soul using steam. This is also called a **sweat lodge.**

medicine man or **medicine woman** among North American aboriginal peoples, a person who uses herbs, songs, ceremonies, and traditional wisdom to heal or teach other people or to influence events. **Shaman** is another word for this person.

In medieval times, a rich lord might be entertained by a poet-musician, called a troubadour.

me·di·e·val (mē′dē ē′vəl *or* med′ē ē′vəl) *adj* belonging to the Middle Ages, the period from about A.D. 500 to about A.D. 1450: *medieval customs, a medieval castle.* **Mediaeval** is another way to spell this.

me·di·um (mē′dē əm) **1** *adj* in a middle position or condition: *Eggs can be cooked hard, soft, or medium. A medium height for a man is 170 cm.* **2** *n* a way: *Radio is a medium of communication.* *pl* **me·di·a** (mē′dē ə).

meet (mēt) **1** *v* come face to face with something or someone: *I met the bully as he came around the corner.* **2** *v* keep an appointment with: *Meet me for lunch at one o'clock.* **3** *v* receive and welcome on arrival: *We're going to the airport to meet my aunt.* **4** *n* a sports competition: *a swim meet.* **met, meeting. –meet′ing,** *n.*

mega– **1** *a prefix meaning* great; large, as in *megaproject.* **2** *an SI prefix meaning* million: *A megavolt is one million volts. Symbol:* M

meg·a·byte (meg′ə bīt′) *n* a million bytes. *Symbol:* MB

mel·low (mel′ō) **1** *adj* ripe, sweet, and juicy: *a mellow apple*. **2** *adj* soft and rich: *a violin with a mellow sound*. **3** *adj* softened and made gentle by age and experience.

mel·o·dy (mel′ə dē) *n* sweet music; any sweet sound. *pl* **mel·o·dies.** –**me·lo′di·ous,** *adj*.

mel·on (mel′ən) *n* a large, juicy fruit that grows on a vine, such as a watermelon.

melt (melt) **1** *v* change from solid to liquid by heating: *Ice becomes water when it melts.* **2** *v* dissolve: *Sugar melts in water.* **3** *v* soften: *The sight of the hungry puppy melted his heart.*

mem·ber (mem′bər) *n* part of a group: *Every member of the family came to our cottage in Keswick this summer.*

mem·ber·ship *n* the members: *The whole membership of the chess club was present.*

Member of Parliament in Canada, a title given to each of the representatives elected to the Federal Parliament in Ottawa. *Abbreviation:* MP ►See Appendix.

mem·o (mem′ō) *n* a note written as a reminder, or short report, or to give instructions. The full form is **memorandum.**

mem·o·ry (mem′ə rē) **1** *n* the ability to remember: *She has a better memory than her sister has.* **2** *n* a person, thing, or event that is remembered: *Chelsea enjoys her memories of summer camp at Lake Scugog.* **3** *n* the part of a computer that stores data. *pl* **mem·o·ries.**
mem·o·rize *v* learn by heart: *We have all memorized the alphabet.*

men·ace (men′is) **1** *n* a threat: *In dry weather forest fires are a great menace.* **2** *v* threaten: *Floods menaced the valley towns with destruction.*
men·aced, men·ac·ing.

mend (mend) *v* repair: *to mend a road, to mend a broken doll, to mend torn clothing.*
on the mend, getting better.

Men·non·ite (men′ə nīt′) *n* a member of a Christian group that has a simple lifestyle and refuses to go to war. The first Mennonites in Canada came from the U.S. to avoid the American Revolution. The first Mennonites in Western Canada came from Russia much later, during the Communist era.

me·nor·ah (mə nòr′ə) *n* the eight-branched candleholder used on Hanukkah.

–ment *a suffix meaning:* **1** the act of. *Enjoyment* means the act of *enjoying*. **2** the state of being. *Amazement* means the state of being *amazed*. **3** the result of. *Pavement* means the result of *paving*.

men·tal (men′təl) **1** *adj* of the mind: *a mental test, mental health.* **2** *adj* done in the mind without being spoken or written down: *mental arithmetic.* –**men′tal·ly,** *adv.*

men·tion (men′shən) *v* speak about: *Do not mention the surprise party to Martina.*

men·u (men′yū) **1** *n* a list of the food served at a restaurant. **2** *n* in computer programs, a list of choices that allows you to pick a topic.

mer·chant (mər′chənt) *n* a person who buys and sells articles for profit.

mer·chan·dise (mər′chən dīs′ *or* mər′chən dīz′) *n* goods for sale.

mer·cy (mər′sē) *n* more kindness than being fair requires: *The judge showed mercy to the young offender. pl* **mer·cies.** –**mer′ci·ful,** *adj,* –**mer′ci·less,** *adj.*

mere (mēr) *adj* only: *The cut was a mere scratch.* Superlative **mer·est.** –**mere′ly,** *adv.*

mer·it (mer′it) **1** *n* worth: *All dance competitors will get a mark according to the merit of their performance.* **2** *v* deserve: *The guitarist's performance merits praise.*

mer·maid (mər′mād) *n* an imaginary sea creature. A mermaid was said to have the head and chest of a woman, but the body of a fish from the waist down.

Most merry-go-rounds play music as they turn.

mer·ry (mer′ē) *adj* full of fun: *a merry laugh.* **mer·ri·er, mer·ri·est.** –**mer′ri·ly,** *adv,* –**mer′ri·ment,** *n.*

mer·ry-go-round *n* a set of animal figures and seats on a platform that is driven round by machinery and that people ride for fun.

mess (mes) **1** *n* a dirty or untidy group of things; a dirty or untidy condition: *Her bedroom was a mess.* **2** *v* spoil: *He messed up his book by scribbling on the pages. A sore ankle messed up her chances of winning the race.* **3** *n* an unpleasant situation: *Losing their luggage made a mess of their vacation.* –**mess′y,** *adj.*

mes·sage (mes′ij) *n* information sent from one person to another: *a message of welcome.*

mes·sen·ger (mes′ən jər) *n* a person who carries a message or goes on an errand.

met·al (met′əl) *n* a substance that is usually shiny and can be made into wire, or hammered into sheets. Gold, silver, copper, iron, lead, tin, and aluminum are metals.

me·tal·lic (mə tal′ik) *adj* made of, or like, metal: *metallic paint, a metallic sound.*

met·a·phor (met′ə fər *or* met′ə fôr′) *n* a figure of speech in which a word or phrase that ordinarily means one thing is used to describe another thing. *Examples: a blanket of snow, arrows of flame, a heart of stone.*

USING WORDS . metaphor/simile

Metaphors and **similes** are two ways to make comparisons.

A **metaphor** talks about one thing as if it were another: *Arrows of flame shot into the air.*

A **simile** compares two things, using like or as: *Flames shot into the air like arrows.*

---

me·te·or (mē′tē ər) *n* a mass of rock that comes toward the earth from space at great speed. Meteors become so hot from flying through the air that they usually burn up in the atmosphere.

me·te·or·ite *n* a mass of rock that has fallen to the earth from outer space; a fallen meteor.

me·te·or·ol·o·gy (mē′tē ə rol′ə jē) *n* the science of the atmosphere and weather. Weather forecasting is a part of meteorology. –**me′te·or·ol′o·gist,** *n.*

me·ter (mē′tər) *n* a device that measures: *a parking meter, a water meter.*

meth·od (meth′əd) *n* a way of doing something: *Roasting is one method of cooking meat.*

me·thod·i·cal (mə thod′ə kəl) *adj* done according to a method; organized: *The pilot made a methodical check of the instruments.*

Mé·tis (mā tēs′ *or* mā tē′) *n* a person descended from Europeans and First Nations people who established themselves in the Red, Assiniboine, and Saskatchewan river valleys during the 1800s. **Metis** is another way to spell this. *pl* **Mé·tis.**

me·tre (mē′tər) *n* a unit for measuring length. A door is about two metres high. *Symbol:* m

met·ric system a decimal system of measurement, or one that counts by tens. It is based on the **metre** for length, the **kilogram** for mass, and the **litre** for volume.

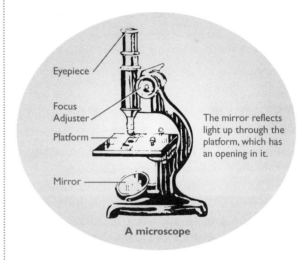

Eyepiece

Focus Adjuster

Platform

Mirror

The mirror reflects light up through the platform, which has an opening in it.

A microscope

micro– **1** *a prefix meaning* very small, as in *microscope.* **2** *a prefix meaning* one millionth: *A microsecond is one one-millionth of a second.*

mi·crochip *n* used in computers, a tiny piece of material that contains a whole set of electronic parts. **mi·cro·phone** *n* a device that can be used with a loudspeaker to make the sound louder.

mi·cro·scope *n* an instrument with lenses for making small objects look larger so that one can see small things clearly. **mi·cro·scop·ic** (mī′krə skop′ik) *adj* tiny: *microscopic germs.*

mi·cro·wave oven an oven using microwaves to cook food. The waves heat the food by vibrating it.

mid– *a prefix meaning* middle. **mid·day** *n* the middle of the day; noon. **mid·dle 1** *adj* halfway between; in the centre: *the middle desk in the row.* **2** *n* the centre: *the middle of the road.* **mid·night** *n* twelve o'clock at night; the middle of the night.

mid·way 1 *adv* or *adj* halfway: *situated midway between the two towns* (adv), *a midway point on the chart* (adj). **2** *n* at a fair or exhibition, the place for games, rides, and other amusements.

in the midst of, in the middle of.

M m

midg·et (mij′it) *adj* much smaller than the usual size: *midget golf.*

might (mīt) *n* great power; strength: *Run with all your might.* —**might′i·ly,** *adv,* —**might′y,** *adj.*

mi·grate (mī′grāt *or* mī grāt′) *v* move from one place to another: *Pioneers from Ontario migrated to Western Canada. Many birds migrate to warmer regions in the winter.* **mi·grat·ed, mi·grat·ing.**
mi·grant (mī′grənt) **1** *adj* migrating; roving: *Many migrant workers are hired to pick fruit in the Okanagan Valley.* **2** *n* a person, animal, bird, or plant that migrates. —**mi·gra′tion,** *n.*

mild (mīld) **1** *adj* gentle: *mild manners.* **2** *adj* not harsh or severe: *a mild winter.* **3** *adj* not sharp or strong in taste: *mild cheese.*

mile (mīl) *n* a measure of distance on land equal to about 1.6 km.

mil·i·tar·y (mil′ə ter′ē) *adj* having to do with soldiers or war: *military training.*

milk (milk) **1** *n* the white liquid produced by female mammals as food for their young, especially from cows. **2** *v* draw milk from: *The farmer used to milk 20 cows a day.* —**milk′y,** *adj.*
milk shake a drink consisting of milk, flavouring, and often ice cream, shaken until frothy. **milk·weed** *n* a weed whose stem contains a white juice that looks like milk.
Milky Way a broad band of faint light that stretches across the sky at night. It is made up of countless stars, too far away to be seen separately without a telescope. The earth, sun, and all the planets around the sun are part of the Milky Way galaxy.

An old-fashioned mill (def. 2)

mill (mil) **1** *n* a machine for grinding: *A flour mill grinds wheat into flour. A coffee mill grinds coffee beans.* **2** *n* a building containing a machine for grinding grain. **3** *n* a building where manufacturing is done: *A paper mill makes paper from wood pulp.*

mil·len·ni·um (mi len′ē əm) *n* a period of 1000 years, or the time when a new period of 1000 years begins: *People have decided that the year 2000 starts a new millennium.* *pl* **mil·len·ni·ums** *or* **mil·len·ni·a.**

milli– *a prefix meaning* thousandth. *Symbol:* m
mil·li·gram *n* one thousandth of a gram. *Symbol:* mg
mil·li·li·tre *n* one thousandth of a litre. *Symbol:* mL
mil·li·metre *n* one thousandth of a metre. *Symbol:* mm

mil·lion (mil′yən) **1** *n or adj* one thousand thousand (1 000 000). ▶See Appendix. **2** *n or adj* a very large number: *He claims to have millions of dollars (n). She can always think of a million reasons for not helping with the dishes (adj).*
mil·lion·aire (mil′yə ner′) *n* a person who has a million or more dollars.

mime (mīm) **1** *n* a form of drama that uses gestures but no words. **2** *v* communicate in this way: *The Inuit boy mimed his story of the seal hunt.* **mimed, mim·ing.**

mim·ic (mim′ik) **1** *v* make fun of by imitating. **2** *v* copy closely; imitate: *A parrot can mimic a person's voice.* **3** *n* a person or thing that imitates. **mim·icked, mim·ick·ing.**

mind (mīnd) **1** *n* the part of a person that thinks and feels emotion. **2** *v* take care of: *Please mind the baby.* **3** *v* feel badly about; object to: *Some people don't mind cold weather.*
bear in mind, remember. **Keep in mind** means the same thing.
make up your mind, decide: *I made up my mind to study harder and get better grades.*

mine (mīn) **1** *n* a large hole dug in the earth in order to get out valuable minerals: *a coal mine, a gold mine.* **2** *n* a bomb under the surface of water or buried in the ground.
min·er *n* a person who works in a mine: *a coal miner.* —**min′ing,** *n.*

min·er·al (min′ə rəl) *n* a substance obtained by digging in the earth: *Coal is a mineral.*

min·gle (ming′gəl) **1** *v* combine; blend: *The Fraser and Thompson rivers join and mingle their waters near Lytton.* **2** *v* mix with other people: *Colin is very shy and does not mingle much with the children at school.* **min·gled, min·gling.**

mini– *a prefix meaning* small for its kind: *miniskirt, minivan.*

min·i·a·ture (min′ ə chər) *adj* tiny: *Rowena had miniature furniture for her doll's house.*

min·i·mum *adj* least possible: *Twenty-five is the minimum needed to pass this test.* *pl* **min·i·mums** or **min·i·ma** (min′ə mə).

min·is·ter (min′is tər) **1** *n* a person in charge of a government department: *the Minister of Finance.* **2** *n* an official who performs the ceremonies in a church.

mi·nor (mī′nər) **1** *adj* smaller; less important: *minor details, minor errors.* **2** *n* a person who is legally not an adult.

mi·nor·i·ty **1** *n* the smaller part; less than half: *The minority must often accept what the majority decides to do.* **2** *n* a group within a country, province, etc. that differs in race, religion, or national origin from the larger part of the population.

mint (mint) **1** *n* a sweet-smelling plant used for flavouring. **2** *n* a place where money is manufactured. **3** *n Informal.* a large amount: *She made a mint at the garage sale.*

mi·nus (mī′nəs) *prep* less; decreased by; subtracting: *12 minus 3 leaves 9. Symbol:* –

min·ute (min′it *for 1-3,* mī nyūt′ *or* mī nūt′ *for 4*) **1** *n* one of the 60 equal periods of time that make up an hour; 60 seconds: *Symbol:* min **2** *n* a short time: *I'll be there in a minute.* **3 minutes,** *pl.n* an official account of what happened at a meeting. **4** *adj* tiny: *a minute speck of dust.*

mir·a·cle (mir′ə kəl) *n* something marvellous; a wonder: *It would be a miracle if the sun did not rise. It was a miracle you weren't hurt in that accident.* –**mi·rac′u·lous,** *adj.*

mi·rage (mə ràzh′) *n* a misleading appearance in which some distant object seems close and, often, upside down. In a mirage, the actual object is reflected by layers of air of different temperatures like you find over a hot desert.

mir·ror (mir′ər) *n* a glass surface that reflects light.

mis– *a prefix meaning* bad, wrong, badly, or wrongly, as in *misdeed, misconduct, misbehave, misjudge.*

mis·cel·la·ne·ous (mis′ə lā′nē əs) *adj* not all of one kind: *Judy had a miscellaneous collection of stones, butterflies, marbles, and many other things.*

mis·chief (mis′chif) **1** *n* behaviour that causes trouble, often without meaning it: *A child's mischief with matches may cause a serious fire.* **2** *n* merry teasing: *Her eyes were full of mischief.* –**mis′chie·vous,** *adj.*

mi·ser (mī′zər) *n* a person who loves money and hates to spend it. –**mis′er·ly,** *adj.*

mis·er·y (miz′ə rē) **1** *n* an unhappy state of mind: *Think of the misery of having no home or friends.* **2** *n* poor conditions: *Some very poor people live in misery, without enough food.* –**mis′er·a·ble,** *adj,* –**mis′er·a·bly,** *adv.*

mis·guid·ed (mis gī′did) *adj* trying to be helpful but making things worse: *Our misguided attempt to rescue the kitten made it climb even higher up the tree.*

mis·lead (mis lēd′) *v* send someone in the wrong direction or make them believe in something that is not true: *His cheerfulness misled us into believing that everything was all right.* **mis·led, mis·lead·ing.**

mis·place (mis plās′) *v* put something in a place and then forget where it is; lose: *I have misplaced the key.* **mis·placed, mis·plac·ing.**

miss (mis) **1** *v* fail to hit, catch, or score: *He tried twice, but both throws missed.* **2** *n* a failure to hit, catch, or score: *to make more misses than hits.* **3** *v* fail to find, or meet: *I set out to meet my father, but in the dark I missed him.* **4** *v* feel sad in the absence of: *He missed his mother when she went to Saint John.* **5** *n* **Miss,** a title sometimes put before the name of a girl or an unmarried woman: *Miss Baratty.*

miss·ing **1** *adj* out of its usual place: *One of the books was missing.* **2** *adj* absent: *Four students were missing from class today.*

mis·sile (mis′īl *or* mis′əl) **1** *n* an object that is thrown, such as a stone. **2** *n* a self-propelled rocket containing explosives: *Missiles can be launched from land, air, or water.*

mis·sion (mish′ən) *n* sending or being sent on some special work: *a rescue mission.*

mis·spell (mis spel′) *v* spell wrongly. **mis·spelled** or **mis·spelt, mis·spell·ing.**

mist (mist) *n* a cloud of very fine drops of water in the air; fog. –**mist′y,** *adj.*

mis·take (mi stāk′) **1** *n* an error; misunderstanding: *I used your towel by mistake.* **2** *v* take to be some other person or thing; confuse with: *I mistook that stick for a snake.* **mis·took, mis·tak·en, mis·tak·ing.**

mis·tak·en *adj* having made a mistake: *A mistaken person should admit being wrong.* –**mis·tak′en·ly,** *adv.*

Mis·ter (mis′tər) *n* a title put before a man's name. It is usually written **Mr.:** *Mr. Antartis was our teacher last year.*

mit·ten (mit′ən) *n* a kind of glove, covering the four fingers together and the thumb separately. This is often shortened to **mitt.**

mix (miks) **1** *v* stir well together: *We mix butter, sugar, milk, and flour for a cake.* **2** *n* an already-mixed preparation: *a cake mix.* **3** *v* make friends easily: *She found it difficult to mix with the other students at her new school.*

mixed number a number made up of a whole number and a fraction, such as $1\frac{1}{2}$.

mix·ture *n* something that has been mixed; a product of mixing: *Orange is a mixture of yellow and red.*

mix up, 1 confuse: *I was so mixed up that I lost my way.* **2** involve: *He was mixed up in a scheme to steal a car.*

moan (mōn) **1** *n* a long, low sound of suffering. **2** *v* make moans. **3** *v* complain: *Jason was always moaning about his bad luck.*

moat (mōt) *n* a deep, wide ditch dug around a castle or town as a protection against enemies. Moats were usually kept filled with water.

mob (mob) **1** *n* a lawless crowd, easily moved to act without thinking. **2** *v* crowd around: *The eager children mobbed the ice-cream wagon.*

mo·bile (mō′bīl *or* mō′bəl) **1** *adj* easily movable: *a mobile home, a mobile phone. The tongue is mobile.* **2** *n* a decoration that moves in a breeze: *The children used heavy paper and string to make a mobile of birds in flight.*

Moccasins are often decorated with beads.

moc·ca·sin (mok′ə sən) *n* a style of shoe with the sides and sole made from one piece of leather. Moccasins were the traditional footwear of many North American aboriginal peoples.

mock (mok) **1** *v* make fun of, usually by imitating. **2** *adj* an imitation; fake: *mock chicken loaf, a mock battle.* –**mock′er·y,** *n.*

mod·el (mod′əl) **1** *n* a small-scale copy: *a model of a ship.* **2** *v* make: *Model a bird's nest in clay.* **3** *n* a particular style or design of a thing: *Some car makers produce a new model every year.* **4** *n* a thing or person to be imitated: *The boy wrote so well that the teacher used his story as a model for the class.* **6** *n* a person who poses for artists, photographers, etc. **7** *n* a person employed to help sell clothing by wearing it for customers to see. **mod·elled** or **mod·eled, mod·el·ling** or **mod·el·ing.**

mo·dem (mō′dəm) *n* an electronic device that uses a telephone or cable line to send pictures and words from one computer to another.

mod·er·ate (mod′ə rit) *adj* not extreme: *moderate expenses, a moderate climate.*

mod·ern (mod′ərn) *adj* of the present time: *The CD-ROM is a modern invention.*

mod·est (mod′ist) **1** *adj* not thinking too highly of yourself: *In spite of the honours she received, the scientist remained a modest woman.* **2** *adj* not too great; not asking too much: *a modest request.* –**mod′es·ty,** *n.*

mod·i·fy (mod′ə fī′) **1** *v* change in some way. **2** *v* limit the meaning of: *Adverbs modify verbs and adjectives.* **mod·i·fied, mod·i·fy·ing.**

mod·i·fi·er *n* in grammar, a word that limits the meaning of another word. Adjectives and adverbs are modifiers. In *a very tight coat,* the adjective *tight* is a modifier of *coat,* and the adverb *very* is a modifier of *tight.*

WORD HISTORY . . . . mob

Mob comes from the Latin phrase *mobile vulgus* meaning "unpredictable crowd."

moist (moist) *adj* slightly wet; damp.
–**moist′en,** (moi′sən), *v,* –**moist′ness,** *n,*
–**mois′ture,** (mois′chər), *n.*

A star-nosed mole—
about 13 cm long
without the tail

mole (mōl) **1** *n* a spot on the skin, present
from birth, and usually brown. **2** *n* a small
burrowing animal that lives underground most
of the time.

mol·e·cule (mol′ə kyūl′) *n* the smallest bit
into which a substance can be divided without
chemical change. A molecule is made up of atoms.

mo·lest (mə lest′) *v* meddle with and injure;
interfere with: *It is cruel to molest animals.*

mol·lusc (mol′əsk) *n* an animal with a soft
body that is usually protected by a shell. Snails,
slugs, oysters, and clams are molluscs. **Mollusk**
is another way to spell this.

mo·ment (mō′mənt) *n* a very short space of
time; an instant: *I'll be there in a moment.*

mo·men·tum (mō men′təm) *n* the force with
which something moves. A falling object gains
momentum as it falls.

mon·arch (mon′ərk) *n* a king, queen,
emperor, etc.; a ruler.

mon·ar·chy *n* government by a monarch.

mon·ey (mun′ē) *n* coins and paper notes.

mon·grel (mong′grəl *or* mung′grəl) *n* an
animal or plant of mixed breed, especially a dog.

mon·i·tor (mon′ə tər) **1** a student in school
with special duties, such as helping to keep
order and taking attendance. **2** *v* check and
listen to by using such a device. **3** *n* a screen
that provides a video display of a computer's
output.

mon·key (mung′kē) **1** *n* an animal with a
long tail, and hands and feet adapted for
climbing and grasping.

2 *v Informal.* play; fool; trifle: *Don't monkey
with the computer.* *pl* **mon·keys.**
mon·keyed, mon·key·ing.

mono– *a prefix meaning* one, or single.

mon·o·logue (mon′ə log′) *n* a long speech by
one person. **mon·o·syl·la·ble** *n* a word of one
syllable. *Yes* and *no* are monosyllables.

mon·o·tone *n* sameness of tone, style of writing,
colour, etc.: *Don't read in a monotone; use more
expression.* –**mo·not·o·nous** (mə not′ə nəs), *adj.*

mon·soon (mon sūn′) **1** *n* a seasonal wind in
the Indian Ocean and southern Asia. The
monsoon blows from the southwest from April
to October and from the northeast during the
rest of the year. **2** *n* the rainy season during
which this wind blows from the southwest.

mon·ster (mon′stər) **1** *n* an imaginary
creature of strange appearance: *The story was
about monsters from Mars.* **2** *n* a huge creature
or thing. **3** *n* a person who is evil or cruel.
–**mon·strous,** *adj.*

month (munth) *n* one of the twelve periods of
time into which a year is divided.

month·ly 1 *adj* happening once a month: *a
monthly newsletter.* **2** *adv* every month: *My uncle
phones us monthly from Inuvik.*

mon·u·ment (mon′yə mənt) *n* something set
up to keep a person or an event from being
forgotten. A monument may be a building,
statue, tomb, or poem.

mood (mūd) *n* a state of mind or feeling: *I am
in the mood to play just now; I don't want to study.*

mood·y 1 *adj* likely to have changes of mood:
*Perry's a very moody person, so it's hard to say what
he'll do.* **2** *adj* gloomy or sullen: *The little girl sat
in moody silence.* –**mood′i·ly,** *adv,* –**mood′i·ness,** *n.*

moon (mūn) **1** *n* the heavenly body that
revolves around the earth once in about $29\frac{1}{2}$
days. **2** *n* a satellite of any other planet: *the
moons of Jupiter.*

moon·beam *n* a ray of moonlight. **moon·light** *n*
the light of the moon.

moor (mūr) *v* put a ship or boat in place with
ropes or chains fastened to the shore or to
anchors.

moose (mūs) *n* a very large animal of the deer
family that lives in Canada and the northern
part of the United States. *pl* **moose.**

mop (mop) **1** *n* sponge or cloth fastened at the end of a stick, for cleaning floors, dishes, etc. **2** *v* clean with a mop: *to mop the floor.* **mopped, mop·ping.**

mope (mōp) *v* be dull, silent, and sad. **moped, mop·ing.**

mor·al (mȯr′rəl) **1** *adj* good in character or conduct. **2 morals,** *pl.n* behaviour in matters of right and wrong. **3** *n* the lesson in a story: *The moral of the story was "Look before you leap."*

mo·rale (mə ral′) *n* mental attitude as regards confidence, enthusiasm, etc.: *The morale of the soccer team was low after its defeat.*

CONFUSABLES .....**moral**

moral means "a lesson": *The moral of the story is, "Slow and steady wins the race."*

morale means "mental condition": *The team's morale was high after they won the tournament.*

---

more (mȯr) **1** *adj* greater in amount or number: *more heat. Six is more than five.* **2** *adv* in addition: *Take one step more.* **3** *adj* additional: *This plant needs more sun.* **4** *adv* **More** is used with most adverbs and adjectives when comparing two things or ideas as in *more easily, more truly, more careful.* **more or less,** about; approximately: *The distance from Regina to Calgary is 650 km, more or less.*

morgue (mȯrg) *n* a place to keep dead bodies until they can be identified.

Mor·mon (mȯr′mən) *n* a member of the **Church of Jesus Christ of Latter-Day Saints,** also called the Mormon Church. It was founded by Joseph Smith in the United States in 1830, and is based on the **Book of Mormon.**

morn·ing (mȯr′ning) *n* the early part of the day, ending at noon.

mor·sel (mȯr′səl) *n* a small bite; a mouthful.

mor·tal (mȯr′təl) **1** *adj* sure to die sometime. **2** *n* a human being. **3** *adj* causing death: *a mortal wound, a mortal illness.* —**mor′tal·ly,** *adv.*

mo·sa·ic (mō zā′ik) *n* a picture or design made of small pieces of stone, glass, wood, etc. of different colours, set together: *Mosaics are used in the floors, walls, or ceilings of some fine buildings.*

mosque (mosk) *n* a Muslim place of worship. Another word for this is **masjid** (mus′jid).

mos·qui·to (mə skē′tō) *n* a small insect. The female mosquito can pierce the skin of people and animals and draw blood, causing a sting that itches. *pl* **mos·qui·toes** or **mos·qui·tos.**

moss (mos) *n* very small, soft, green or brown plants that grow close together like a carpet on the ground, on rocks, on trees, etc.

most (mōst) **1** *adj* greatest in amount or number: *I have the most fun on Saturday.* **2** *adj* almost all: *Most people like ice cream.* **3** *adv* **Most** is used with most adverbs and adjectives when comparing more than two things or ideas as in *most easily, most careful.* **most·ly** *adv* almost all; mainly. **at most,** not more than.

mo·tel (mō tel′) *n* a roadside hotel providing rooms for motorists. The word is a short form of *mo*tor *ho*tel.

moth (moth) *n* a winged insect very much like a butterfly, but flying mostly at night.

moth·er (muтн′ər) **1** *n* a female parent. **2** *v* take care of: *She mothers her baby sister.* **3** *adj* belonging to a person because of birth; native: *Canada is my mother country, and English is my mother tongue.* —**moth′er·ly,** *adj.*

moth·er-in-law *n* the mother of a person's husband or wife. *pl* **mothers-in-law.**

mo·tion (mō′shən) *n* movement: *He swayed with the motion of the moving train. Every object is either in motion or at rest.* —**mo′tion·less,** *adj.*

mo·tive (mō′tiv) *n* the thought or feeling that makes you do something: *His motive in weight training was a wish to strengthen his muscles.* **mo·ti·vate** *v* make someone want to do something.

mo·tor (mō′tər) *n* an engine that makes a machine go: *an electric motor, a gasoline motor.* **mo·tor·ist** *n* a person who drives a car.

mot·to (mot′ō) *n* a short sentence giving a rule of conduct: *"Think before you speak"* is a good *motto. pl* **mot·toes** or **mot·tos.**

mould (mōld) **1** *n* a hollow shape in which something is formed: *a jelly mould.* **2** *n* a furry growth of fungus that appears on food when it is left in a warm, damp place. —**mould′y** or **mold·y** (mōl′dē), *adj.* **3** form into shape: *We are moulding clay to make model animals.* **Mold** is another way to spell **mould.**

moult (mōlt) *v* shed feathers, skin, etc. before a new growth. Birds and snakes moult. **Molt** is another way to spell this.

mound (mound) **1** *n* a bank or heap of earth or stones. **2** *n* the slightly elevated ground from which a baseball pitcher pitches.

mount (mount) **1** *v* get up on: *to mount a horse, to mount a platform.* **2** *n* a horse for riding: *The jockey had an excellent mount.* **3** *v* increase: *Excitement mounted as the holidays approached.* **4** *n* a mountain. **Mount** is often used before the names of mountains: *Mount Columbia.*

moun·tain (moun'tən) **1** *n* a very high hill: *the Rocky Mountains.* **2** *n* a huge amount: *a mountain of rubbish. She overcame a mountain of difficulties.*

moun·tain·eer *n* a person who climbs mountains for sport. **moun·tain·ous 1** *adj* covered with mountain ranges: *mountainous country.* **2** *adj* huge: *a mountainous wave.*

mountain range a row of connected mountains; a large group of mountains.

❦ **Mount·ie** or **mount·ie** (moun'tē) *n* *Informal.* a member of the Royal Canadian Mounted Police. *pl* **Mount·ies** or **mount·ies.**

mourn (mȯrn) *v* feel or show sadness: *She mourned over her lost kitten.* **–mourn·ful,** *adj.*

A house mouse—about 10 cm long excluding the tail

mouse (mous) *n* a small rodent, having a pointed snout, large ears, and a long, thin tail. *pl* **mice.**

mouth (mouth) **1** *n* the opening through which a person or animal takes in food. **2** *n* an opening suggesting a mouth: *the mouth of a cave, the mouth of a bottle.* **3** *n* a part of a river, creek, etc. where its waters empty into some other body of water: *The mouth of the Moose River is at James Bay.*

mouth·ful *n* the amount the mouth can easily hold. **mouth-watering** *adj* looking or smelling so good it makes your mouth water: *Klara's mother made us a mouth-watering apple pie.*

mouthwash *n* a liquid that you swirl around in your mouth to kill germs.

down in the mouth, *Informal.* in low spirits; discouraged.

move (mūv) **1** *v* change the position of: *Do not move your hand.* **2** *n* movement: *If you make a move, the dog will bark.* **3** *v* change your home or job: *We move to Fredericton next week.* **4** *n* a player's turn to move: *It is your move now.* **moved, mov·ing. –mov'a·ble** (mū'və bəl), *adj.* **move·ment** *n* the act of moving. **mov·ie** *n* motion picture.

mow (mō) *v* cut down with a machine or a scythe: *to mow grass.* **mowed, mowed** or **mown, mow·ing. –mow'er,** *n.*

Mr. or **Mr** (mis'tər) Mister, a title used in front of a man's name: *Mr. Jackson.*

Mrs. or **Mrs** (mis'iz) a title used in front of a married woman's name: *Mrs. Milano.*

Ms. or **Ms** (miz) a title used in front of the name of a married or unmarried woman or girl: *Ms. Bauer.*

much (much) **1** *adj* in great amount: *much rain, much pleasure, not much money.* **2** *n* a great amount: *Eating too much of this cake will make you sick.* **more, most.**

mu·cus (myū'kəs) *n* a slimy substance that is given off by the lining of your nose and throat: *A cold can make mucus drip out of your nose.*

mud (mud) *n* earth so wet that it is soft and sticky: *Mud covered the bottom of the pond.* **–mud'dy,** *adj.*

mu·ez·zin (myū ez'in *or* mū ez'in) *n* in Islam, a crier who calls the people to prayer at certain hours of the day.

muff (muf) **1** *v* fail to catch and hold a ball when it comes into your hands. **2** *v* handle awkwardly: *My brother muffed his chance to get that job.*

muf·fin (muf'ən) *n* a small, round cake, often containing bran, raisins, fruit, etc.

muf·fle (muf'əl) **1** *v* cover up: *Geneva muffled her throat in a warm scarf.* **2** *v* dull a sound: *The heavy drapes helped muffle the noise of the traffic outside.* **muf·fled, muf·fling.**

muf·fler 1 *n* a scarf worn around the neck for warmth. **2** *n* any device that dulls a sound, especially that of an automobile engine.

mug (mug) **1** *n* a usually large and heavy cup.
2 *v* attack and rob someone.

Mu·ham·mad (mə häʹmad) *n* the prophet of
Islam. Muslims believe that he is God's
messenger. Another spelling is **Mohammed.**

❧ **muk·luk** (mukʹluk) *n* a soft, high,
waterproof boot traditionally made of sealskin
or caribou hide. **Mukluk** is the Yupik word;
kamik is the Inuktitut word for the same thing.

mule (myūl) *n* an animal that is part donkey
and part horse.

mul·lah (mulʹə) *v* speak softly and not clearly,
as a person does when his lips are partly closed.

multi– *a prefix meaning* many.

mul·ti·cul·tur·al (mulʹtē kulʹchə rəl) *adj*
having several different cultures side by side in
the same country, city, etc.

mul·ti·me·di·a (mulʹtē mēʹdē ə) *adj* using a
mixture of sound, pictures, and text, often with
a computer: *a multimedia encyclopedia on a CD,
multimedia software.*

mul·ti·tude (mulʹtə tyūdʹ *or* mulʹtə tūdʹ) *n*
a great many; a crowd: *a multitude of friends.*

mul·ti·ply (mulʹtə plīʹ) **1** *v* take a number a
given number of times. To multiply 6 by 3 means
to take 6 three times, making a total of 18.
Symbol: × –**mul·ti·pli·ca'tion** *n.* **2** *v* increase in
number or amount: *The dangers and difficulties
multiplied as we went higher up Mount Brazeau.*
mul·ti·plied, mul·ti·ply·ing.

mul·ti·ple 1 *n* a number that contains another
number a certain number of times without a
remainder: *Twelve is a multiple of three.*
2 *adj* with many parts: *a multiple-choice test.*

mum·ble (mumʹbəl) *v* speak softly and not
clearly, as a person does when his lips are partly
closed. **mum·bled, mum·bling.**

An Egyptian mummy
and coffin. The body
was treated with
chemicals and
wrapped in linen.

mum·my (mumʹē) *n* a dead body preserved
from rotting by the ancient Egyptian method.
pl **mum·mies.**

mumps (mumps) *n* a disease that causes
swelling of your neck and face and difficulty in
swallowing.

munch (munch) *v* chew noisily: *The horse
munched its oats.*

mu·nic·i·pal (myū nisʹə pəl) *adj* having
something to do with the affairs of a city or
town: *The provincial police assisted the municipal
police.*

mu·nic·i·pal·i·ty (myū nisʹə palʹə tē) *n* a city,
town, county, district, township, or other area
having local self-government.
pl **mu·nic·i·pal·i·ties.**

mu·ral (myūʹrəl) *n* a picture painted on a wall.

mur·der (mərʹdər) **1** *n* the unlawful killing of
a human being. **2** *v* kill a human being on
purpose.

mur·mur (mərʹmər) **1** *n* a softly spoken word
or speech. **2** *v* say in a murmur: *The little girl
murmured her thanks.*

mus·cle (musʹəl) *n* the parts of the bodies of
people and animals that can be tightened or
loosened so as to make the body move.

mus·cu·lar (musʹkyə lər) *adj* having
well-developed muscles; strong: *a muscular arm.*

mu·se·um (myū zēʹəm) *n* the building or
rooms in which a collection of objects
illustrating science, history, art, or other
subjects is kept and displayed.

mush (mush) **1** *n* any soft, thick substance: *The
heavy rain made mush of the dirt road.* **2** *n* a
command to go, given to sled dogs.

mush·y 1 *adj* like mush; pulpy. **2** *adj Informal.*
weakly sentimental: *The children thought the
movie was mushy.*

mush·room (mushʹrūm) *n* a small fungus,
shaped like an umbrella, that grows very fast:
Some mushrooms are poisonous.

mu·sic (myūʹzik) *n* the art of putting sounds
together in beautiful, or interesting ways.

mu·si·cal 1 *adj* having to do with music:
musical instruments. **2** *n* a stage entertainment
or motion picture in which a story is told mainly
through music, singing, and dancing.

–**mu'si·cal·ly,** *adv.* **mu·si·cian** (myū zishʹən) *n*
a person skilled in music, especially one who
earns a living by playing music.

✽ **mus·keg** (mus′keg) *n* an area of bog composed of decaying plant life, especially moss. There are vast regions of muskeg in northern Alberta.

✽ **musk–ox** (musk′oks′) *n* a large arctic animal with a shaggy coat and a musky smell. *pl* **musk-ox** or **musk-ox·en.**

Mus·lim (mus′lim *or* muz′lim) **1** *n* a follower of Islam. **2** *adj* having to do with Islam or its followers.

muss (mus) *Informal.* **1** *v* put into disorder: *Don't muss up my hair.* **2** *n* a mess: *Straighten up your room; it's in a dreadful muss.*

mus·sel (mus′əl) *n* a mollusc with two hinged parts to its shell: *Sea mussels have dark-blue shells and can be eaten.*

must (must) an auxiliary (helping) verb used: **1** *v* to mean that someone is forced or required to do something: *You must be on time for the rehearsal. I must work hard to get on the team.* **2** *v* to indicate that something is probably correct: *It must be time for lunch.*

USING WORDS... must have

Must have, could have, and **may have** (*I must have left my knapsack at school.*) are often mistakenly written as *must of, could of,* or *may of.* Avoid using these incorrect expressions in your writing.

---

mus·tache (mus′tash *or* mə stash′) *n* the hair that grows on a man's upper lip.

mus·tang (mus′tang) *n* a small, wild or half-wild horse of the North American plains.

mus·tard (mus′tərd) *n* a yellow powder or paste used to give food a sharp taste.

mus·ty (mus′tē) *adj* having a stale smell or taste: *a musty room, musty crackers.* **mus·ti·er, mus·ti·est.**

mute (myūt) **1** *adj* silent: *The little boy was mute with embarrassment.* **2** *v* soften or deaden the sound of something: *He muted the TV during the commercial breaks.* **mut·ed, mut·ing.**

mut·ter (mut′ər) **1** *v* speak low and unclearly, with your lips partly closed. **2** *v* grumble.

muz·zle (muz′əl) **1** *n* the nose, mouth, and jaws of a four-footed animal. **2** *n* a cover of straps or wire for putting over an animal's head and mouth to keep it from biting or eating. **3** *n* the open front end of a gun. **muz·zled, muz·zling.**

my (mī) *adj* a possessive form of **I;** of me; belonging to me: *I learned my lesson. My house is just around the next corner.* **My** and **mine** are the possessive forms of **I. My** is always followed by a noun: *This is my hat.* **Mine** stands alone: *This hat is mine.*

my·self (mī self′) **1** *pron* a form used instead of **me** when talking about the subject of the sentence: *I hurt myself. I can do it by myself.* **2** *pron* a form of **I** used to make a statement stronger: *I will go myself. I myself opened the jar.* *pl* **our·selves.**

mys·ter·y (mis′tə rē) **1** *n* something that is not explained or understood: *the mystery of the migration of birds.* **2** *n* a story, play, etc. about a crime: *My sister likes reading mysteries.* *pl* **mys·ter·ies.**

mys·te·ri·ous (mis tē′rē əs) *adj* hard to explain or understand: *The cause of the accident remains mysterious.*

mys·ti·fy (mis′tə fī′) *v* puzzle: *The magician's tricks mystified the audience.* **mys·ti·fied, mys·ti·fy·ing.**

myth (mith) *n* a traditional story about imaginary beings, such as gods, heroes, and monsters. Myths usually explain how natural events or social customs came to be. **–myth′i·cal,** *adj.*

my·thol·o·gy (mi thol′ə jē) *n* a group of myths concerning a particular people or person: *Greek mythology.* *pl* **my·thol·o·gies.**

n or **N** (en) *n* the fourteenth letter of the English alphabet, or the sound that it stands for. You hear the sound of *n* twice in *nine*. *pl* **n's** or **N's.**

nab (nab) *v Informal.* catch; grab: *The police soon nabbed the thief.*

nag (nag) *v* find fault or complain a lot: *My older brother is always nagging at me to walk faster.* **nagged, nag·ging.**

nail (nāl) **1** *n* a small, thin, pointed piece of metal to be hammered through pieces of wood or other material to hold them together. **2** *v* fasten with nails. **3** *n* the thin hard layer at the end of your fingers or toes. **hit the nail on the head,** *Informal.* say or do something just right.

na·ive (nī ēv′) *adj* innocent; inexperienced: *Jessica was so naive she believed the ghost stories her big brother told her.*

na·ked (nā′kid) *adj* with no clothes on: *The boys enjoyed swimming naked in Wolfe Lake.* **–na′ked·ness,** *n.* **naked eye,** the bare eye, not helped by any telescope or microscope: *Germs are too small to be seen with the naked eye.*

name (nām) **1** *n* what a person or thing is called: *Our dog's name is Smokey. The name of our country is Canada.* **2** *v* give a name to: *They named the baby Kalpna.* **3** *v* give the right name for: *Can you name these flowers?* **4** *n* reputation: *Dakota made a name for himself as a trouble maker.* **named, nam·ing.** **name·ly** *adv* that is to say: *Only two students got 100 in the test—namely, Karen and Jan.* **call names,** insult by using bad names.

nap (nap) **1** *n* a short sleep: *Most babies have a nap in the afternoon.* **2** *v* take a short sleep. **napped, nap·ping.**

nap·kin (nap′kin) *n* a piece of cloth or paper used at meals for protecting your clothes or for wiping your lips or fingers; a serviette.

nar·rate (ner′āt or nə r′āt′) *v* tell the story of: *The sailor narrated exciting old stories about the sea.* **nar·rat·ed, nar·rat·ing. –nar·ra′tor,** *n.*

nar·row (ner′ō) **1** *adj* not wide: *It was a narrow path, just wide enough for one person.* **2** *adj* close: *a narrow escape.*

nar·row-mind·ed *adj* not willing to listen to other points of view; prejudiced: *Stephanie is a very narrow-minded person and says all rock music is rubbish.*

the narrows, the narrow part of a river, strait, sound, valley, pass, etc.

Tusk

A narwhal—about 6 m long without the tusk

nar·whal (når′wəl) *n* a small whale living in the Arctic seas. The male has a long tusk.

nas·ty (nas′tē) **1** *adj* disgustingly dirty; filthy: *a nasty room, a nasty smell.* **2** *adj* very unpleasant: *nasty weather, a nasty temper, a nasty person.* **nas·ti·er, nas·ti·est.**

na·tion (nā′shən) **1** *n* the people living in the same country: *The Prime Minister appealed to the nation for support of his plan.* **2** *n* a group of people with the same history and language: *the Iroquois nation.* **–na′tion·al** (nash′ə nəl), *adj.* **na·tion·al·i·ty** *n* the fact of belonging to a nation: *Rod's passport showed that his nationality was Canadian.*

na·tive (nā′tiv) **1** *n* a person born in a certain place or country: *She is a native of Edmonton.* **2** *adj* belonging to a person because of being born in a place: *Canada is my native land. English is my native language.* **Na·tive peo·ple** one of the peoples whose ancestors lived in Canada for a long time before immigrants from other lands arrived. Scientists believe that the ancestors of these peoples first crossed into North America from Asia at the end of the Ice Age and spread out to many parts of North, Central, and South America.

na·ture (nā′chər) **1** *n* the outdoor world of plant and animal life. **2** *n* the abilities a person or animal is born with: *It is the nature of beavers to build dams.*

nat·u·ral (nach′ə rəl) **1** *adj* not artificial: *Wood is a natural product; plastic isn't.* **2** *adj* belonging to the nature a person or animal is born with: *It is natural for babies to cry.*

nat·u·ral·ly (nach′ə rə lē) **1** *adv* in a natural way: *Speak naturally into the microphone; don't shout.* **2** *adv* by nature, without studying: *a naturally musical child.* **3** *adv* of course: *Heather offered me some candy; naturally, I took it.*

nat·u·ral re·source any material found in nature that is used by people: *Minerals, forests, fish, and hydro power are all natural resources.*

naugh·ty (not′ē) *adj* bad; not obedient: *The naughty child pulled his sister's hair.* **naugh·ti·er, naugh·ti·est. –naugh′ti·ness,** *n.*

nau·se·a (noz′ē ə) *n* the feeling that you are going to throw up.

nau·se·at·ing (noz′ē āt′ing) *adj* causing you to feel sick: *I think changing my baby brother's diaper is nauseating.* **nau·se·ous** (noz′e əs *or* nosh′əs) *adj* feeling sick: *The child felt nauseous riding in the car along the bumpy roads.*

nau·ti·cal (not′ə kəl) *adj* having something to do with ships or sailors.

nav·i·gate (nav′ə gāt′) *v* sail, steer, or manage a ship, aircraft, etc. **nav·i·gat·ed, nav·i·gat·ing. –nav′i·ga·tor,** *n.*

nav·i·ga·ble *adj* that ships can travel on: *The St. Lawrence River is deep enough to be navigable.*

Naw Ruz (nov′ rūz) *n* the festival of the New Year in the Bahai and Zoroastrian religions.

near (nēr) **1** *adv* or *adj* close by; not far: *They searched far and near (adv). The convenience store is quite near (adj).* **2** *prep* close to; not far from: *We live near Churchill Falls.* **–near′ness,** *n.*

near·by *adj* or *adv* near; close at hand: *They live in a nearby house (adj). They live nearby (adv).*

near·ly *adv* almost: *It is nearly bedtime.*

neat (nēt) **1** *adj* clean and in order: *a neat desk, a neat room.* **2** *adj* skilful; clever: *a neat trick.* **–neat′ness,** *n.*

nec·es·sar·y (nes′ə ser′ē) *adj* needed; required.

ne·ces·si·ty (nə ses′ə tē) *n* anything that cannot be done without: *Food and water are necessities.*

neck (nek) **1** *n* the part of the body that joins your head to your shoulders. **2** *n* a narrow part like a neck: *a neck of land, the neck of a bottle.*

neck·lace (nek′lis) *n* a string of jewels, gold, silver, beads, etc. worn around your neck as an ornament.

neck and neck, being equal or even in a race or contest: *The two runners ran neck and neck during the sprint.*

risk your neck, put yourself in a dangerous position: *You risk your neck when you don't use your seat belt.*

need (nēd) **1** *v* be unable to do without: *Plants need water.* **2** *v* ought to or ought to have: *I need to go to the dentist. I need new shoes.* **3** *n* anything needed: *In the desert their need was fresh water.*

need·less *adj* not needed; unnecessary: *Cycling without a helmet is a needless risk.* **need·y** *adj* very poor; not having enough to live on.

CONFUSABLES ..... **need**

need means "be in want of":
I need a drink of water.

knead means "press with the hands":
She will knead the dough to make bread.

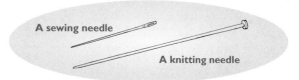

A sewing needle

A knitting needle

nee·dle (nē′dəl) **1** *n* a slender tool with a sharp point at one end and a hole, or eye, at the other to pass a thread through, used in sewing. **Needlework** is sewing or embroidery.
2 *n* anything shaped like a needle: *a knitting needle, a pine needle, a compass needle.*
3 *v* *Informal.* tease: *The children needled their little brother into losing his temper.*
nee·dled, nee·dling.

neg·a·tive (neg′ə tiv) **1** *adj* saying no: *a negative answer.* **2** *adj* not positive or helpful: *My friend's negative comments on my project didn't help me at all.* **3** *adj* showing an absence of the germs, signs, etc. of an illness: *The doctor explained that the test results were negative and that Victoria didn't have measles.* **4** *n* in photography, a piece of film on which the lights and shadows of the object photographed are reversed.

neg·lect (ni glekt′) **1** *v* give too little care or attention to. **2** *n* being neglected: *The cat suffered from neglect.* **3** *v* omit; fail: *Don't neglect to take out the garbage.*

ne·go·ti·ate (ni gō′shē āt′) *v* talk over and arrange terms: *The students negotiated with their teacher for more time to complete their projects.* **ne·go·ti·at·ed, ne·go·ti·at·ing. –ne·go′ti·a′tion,** *n.*

neigh·bour (nā′bər) *n* someone who lives next to you, or nearby. **Neighbor** is another spelling. **neigh·bour·hood** or **neigh·bor·hood** *n* an area where people live: *Ours is a very quiet neighbourhood.*

neither (nē′ᴛнər *or* nī′ᴛнər) **1** *conj, adj,* or *pron* not either; not one or the other: *Neither you nor I will go* (conj). *Neither statement is true* (adj). *Neither of the statements is true* (pron). **2** *conj* nor: *My friends don't smoke cigarettes and neither do I.*

neph·ew (nef′yū) *n* the son of a person's brother or sister; the son of a person's brother-in-law or sister-in-law.

nerve (nərv) **1** *n* a fibre connecting your brain to parts of your body. **2** *n* courage: *The diver lost his nerve and wouldn't go off the high board.* **3** *n* Informal. impudence. **nerv·ous 1** *adj* of the nerves: *The brain is a part of the nervous system of the human body.* **2** *adj* easily excited or upset: *Not getting enough sleep can make you nervous.* **3** *adj* restless or uneasy: *Jean is nervous about staying alone at night.* **–nerv′ous·ness,** *n.* **get on someone's nerves,** *Informal.* annoy or irritate someone.

–ness *a suffix meaning* the quality, state, or condition, as in *blackness* and *carefulness.*

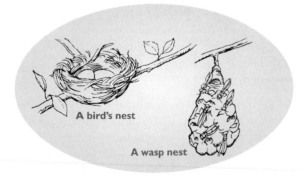

A bird's nest

A wasp nest

nest (nest) *n* something built by birds and other creatures as a place to lay eggs or keep their young. Nests are often made of twigs, straw, and mud: *a robin's nest, a squirrel's nest.*

net (net) *n* a loose fabric made of string, cord, thread, or wire, knotted together leaving holes: *a fish net, a tennis net.*

net·work *n* any system of lines that cross or connect: *a network of vines, a network of highways, a TV network.*

neu·tral (nyū′trəl *or* nū′trəl) *adj* not taking sides in a quarrel, contest, or war: *He's the referee; he must be neutral.*

nev·er (nev′ər) **1** *adv* not ever; at no time: *I have never swum in an ocean.* **2** *adv* not at all: *These skates will never do; they're too tight.* **nev·er·the·less** (nev′ər ᴛнə les′) *adv* in spite of it: *Dianne was very tired; nevertheless, she kept on walking.*

never mind, 1 pay no attention to: *Never mind the noise.* **2** it doesn't matter; forget it.

new (nyū *or* nū) **1** *adj* not existing before: *a new invention, a new idea.* **2** *adj* recently bought: *a new coat, a new car.* **3** *adj* recently arrived: *Our class has a new teacher.* **4** *adj* up-to-date; modern: *a new fashion.*

news (nyūz *or* nūz) *n* information about something that has just happened or will soon happen: *The news that our teacher was leaving made us sad. We listen to the news on the radio every morning, and watch it on television in the evening.*

news·pa·per (nyūs′pā′pər *or* nūs′pā′pər) *n* sheets of paper, usually printed daily with news stories and pictures, advertisements, weather reports, etc.

break the news, make something known; tell something.

CONFUSABLES ..... new

new means "unused" :
Do you like my new shoes?

knew means "understood":
I knew you would say that!

next (nekst) **1** *adj* following at once: *the next train, next week.* **2** *adj* nearest: *My best friend sits at the next desk.* **3** *adv* in the place or time or position that is nearest: *I am going to do my arithmetic problems next.*

next door, in the next home to your home: *Anwar lives next door to us.*

next to, beside: *Who is the girl next to you?*

nib·ble (nib'əl) **1** *v* eat with quick, small bites, as a rabbit or a mouse does. **2** *n* a small bite. **nib·bled, nib·bling.**

nice (nīs) **1** *adj* pleasant; enjoyable: *a nice day, a nice time.* **2** *adj* thoughtful or kind: *The camp counsellor was nice to us.* **nic·er, nic·est.**

nick (nik) *n* a place where a small bit has been cut or broken out: *She dropped a saucer and made a nick in the edge of it.*
in the nick of time, just at the right moment.

nick·el (nik'əl) *n* a five-cent coin.

nick·name (nik'nām') **1** *n* a short form of a proper name: *Rebecca's nickname is "Becky."* **2** *n* a name used instead of a proper name: *Roy's nickname was "Buzz."*

niece (nēs) *n* the daughter of a person's brother or sister; the daughter of a person's brother-in-law or sister-in-law.

night (nīt) *n* the time between evening and morning; the time from sunset to sunrise, when it is dark.
night·ly every night: *Performances are given nightly.* **night·mare** (nīt'mer') **1** *n* a frightening dream. **2** *n* a very unpleasant or frightening experience: *The dust storm was a nightmare.*

nil (nil) *n* nothing.

nim·ble (nim'bəl) *adj* quick-moving: *We watched the nimble monkeys swinging in their cage at the Calgary zoo.* **nim·bler, nim·blest.** –**nim'bly,** *adv.*

nine (nīn) ▶See Appendix.

nip (nip) **1** *v* squeeze tight and suddenly; pinch: *The crab nipped my toe.* **2** *n* a tight squeeze or pinch; a sudden bite. **nipped, nip·ping.**

no (nō) **1** *adv* a word used to deny, refuse, or disagree; the opposite of **yes:** *Will you come with us? No. Can a cow fly? No.* **2** *adv* not in any degree; not at all: *He is no better.* **3** *adj* not any; not at all: *Dogs have no wings. He has no friends.* *pl* **noes.**

no·ble (nō'bəl) **1** *n* a person born into a titled family. A duke is a noble. **2** *adj* great; admirable: *a noble person, a noble deed. Niagara Falls is a noble sight.* **no·bler, no·blest.** –**no'bly,** *adv.*

no·bod·y (nō'bud'ē *or* nō'bə dē) **1** *pron* no one; no person. **2** *n* a person of no importance. *pl* **no·bod·ies.**

nod (nod) **1** *v* bow your head slightly and raise it again quickly. **2** *n* a quick bow of your head: *Our teacher gave us a nod as he passed.* **nod·ded, nod·ding.**

noise (noiz) *n* a loud or harsh sound: *The noise kept me awake.* –**noise'less,** *adj,* –**nois'i·ly,** *adv,* –**nois'y,** *adj.*

nom·i·nate (nom'ə nāt') **1** *v* to suggest as candidate for an office: *A local lawyer was nominated for Member of Parliament.* **2** *v* appoint to duty: *Our class nominated Antonia to represent us on the student council.* **nom·i·nated, nom·i·nat·ing.** –**nom·i·na'tion,** *n.*

non– *a prefix meaning* not, as in *non-breakable.*
non-fiction writing that has to do with facts, not imagination.
non-prof·it *adj* not operated for making a profit. Non-profit organizations, such as the Canadian Wildlife Federation, collect money to pay their expenses but do not try to make any more money than they need.
non-re·new·a·ble *adj* that cannot be replaced. Forests are a renewable resource because they will grow again; oil is a non-renewable resource because once it is used up, it is gone forever.

none (nun) **1** *pron* not any: *We have none of that chocolate cake left.* **2** *pron* not one: *None of these cookies has peanuts in them.*

non·sense (non'sens) *n* foolish talk or action.

noo·dles (nū'dəlz) *pl.n* a pasta made of flour and water, or flour and eggs, made in flat strips.

noon (nūn) *n* 12 o'clock in the daytime; 12 p.m; the middle of the day.

no one *or* **no–one** (nō'wun') *pron* no person; nobody: *No one was hurt in the accident.*

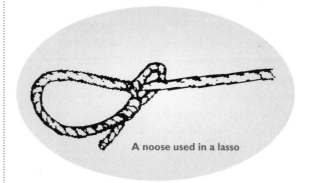

A noose used in a lasso

noose (nūs) *n* a loop with a slip knot that tightens as the string or rope is pulled.

nor (nȯr) **1** *conj* and no: *There was neither river nor stream in that desert.* **2** *conj* and not: *I have not been there, nor am I going.*

Grammar ✓ *Check* .... **nor**

When the subject of a sentence contains **nor** or **or**, the verb agrees with the word closest to it:

Neither my uncles nor my father has any hair.
Neither my father nor his brothers have any hair.

---

nor·mal (nȯr′məl) *adj* usual: *The normal temperature of the human body is 37°C.* –**nor′mal·ly,** *adv.*

north (nȯrth) **1** *n* the direction to which a compass needle points; the direction to the right as you face the setting sun. **2** *adv* or *adj* to or from the north: *Go north for two blocks (adv). There was a cold north wind today (adj).* –**north′er·ly,** *adj,* –**north′ern,** *adj.*
3 the North, *n* in Canada, the northern parts of the provinces from Québec westward and the territory lying north of these provinces.
north·east *n* the direction halfway between north and east. **northern lights** the bands of light that appear in the northern sky at night; another name is aurora borealis. In the southern sky, similar lights are called aurora australis.
North Pole the northern end of the earth's axis.
north·ward *adv* or *adj* toward the north: *She walked northward. (adv) The lake is on the northward side of the hill (adj).* You can also say **northwards** for the adverb.
north·west *n* the direction halfway between north and west.

nose (nōz) *n* the part of your face that stands out just above your mouth. A nose has openings called **nostrils** for breathing and smelling.
nose-dive 1 *n* a swift headfirst dive by an aircraft. **2** *n* a sharp, sudden drop: *The thermometer took a nose-dive during the night.*
nos·ey (nō′zē) *adj* too curious about other people's business: *Don't ask nosey questions.* Another spelling is **nosy.**
look down your nose at, treat with scorn.
pay through your nose, *Informal.* pay a great deal too much.
poke your nose into, *Informal.* pry into; meddle in: *Don't poke your nose into other people's business.*
turn up your nose at, refuse, often in a rude way.

not (not) *adv* a word used to make a negative statement: *Six and two do not add up to ten.*

notch (noch) **1** *n* a V-shaped nick or cut: *to cut notches on a stick to keep count of numbers.*
2 *n* *Informal.* a small amount: *Turn the volume down a few notches; that music is too loud!*

note (nōt) **1** *n* words written down to remind you of something: *Sometimes our teacher asks us to take notes on what we read. I must make a note of that date.* **2** *v* write down as a thing to be remembered: *I noted the time of my appointment.*
3 *n* a very short letter: *a thank-you note.*
4 *n* greatness; fame: *Terry Fox was a person of note.* **5** *v* pay attention to: *Please note what I say.*
6 *n* a single musical sound. **not·ed, not·ing.**
note·book *n* a book in which to write notes of things to be learned or remembered.
not·ed (nō′tid) *adj* well-known; famous: *Glenn Gould was noted as a pianist.*

noth·ing (nuth′ing) **1** *n* not anything: *Nothing arrived by mail.* **2** *n* a person or thing of no importance: *People regard him as a nothing.*
3 *n* zero.

no·tice (nō′tis) **1** *n* attention: *A sudden movement caught the trapper's notice.* **2** *v* see; give attention to: *I noticed that Jen had a new jacket.* **3** *n* a written or printed sign: *We put up notices advertising our school concert.* **no·ticed, no·tic·ing.**
no·tice·a·ble *adj* easily seen or noticed: *Our kitten is very noticeable because its fur is yellow.*
no·ti·fy (nō′tə fī′) *v* let know; give a notice to: *Our teacher notified us that there would be a field trip to Napanee next week.*

no·tion (nō′shən) *n* an opinion; belief: *One common notion is that red hair goes with a quick temper.*

no·to·ri·ous (nō tȯ′rē əs) *adj* well-known because of something bad: *a notorious liar.*

noun (noun) *n* a word that is used to name a person, place, thing, quality, or event. In the sentence *Margot showed great excitement when her brother arrived at the party with a new puppy,* the words *Margot, excitement, brother, party,* and *puppy* are all nouns.

nour·ish (nər′ish) *v* make grow, or keep alive and well, with food; feed: *Milk is all that is needed to nourish a newborn baby.* –**nour′ish·ment,** *n.*

nov·el (nov′əl) **1** *n* a non-fiction story with characters and a plot, long enough to fill one or more books. **2** *adj* strange; new: *The trip in a small plane was a novel experience for me.*

nov·el·ty 1 *n* newness: *After the novelty wore off, Nicole found the video game boring.* **2** *n* a new or unusual thing: *Staying up late was a novelty to the children, and they enjoyed it.*

nov·ice (nov′is) *n* one who is new to a sport, an activity, an occupation, etc.; a beginner: *Novices are likely to make some mistakes.*

now (nou) **1** *adv* at this time: *He is here now.* **2** *n* the present; this time: *by now, until now, from now on.* **3** *adv* then; next: *We have signed the petition and it now goes to the school principal.*

now·a·days *adv* at the present day: *Nowadays most people use computers rather than typewriters.*

just now, only a few moments ago.

now and again, or **now and then,** once in a while.

no·where (nō′wer′ *or* nō′hwer′) *adv* in no place; not anywhere.

noz·zle (noz′əl) *n* a tip put on a hose to let you control the flow of liquid.

nu·cle·us (nyū′klē əs *or* nū′klē əs) **1** *n* a central part or thing around which other parts or things are collected: *The gift of books became the nucleus of our class library.* **2** *n* in science, the central part of an atom. *pl* **nu·cle·i** (nyū′klē ī *or* nū′klē ī) *or* **nu·cle·us·es.**

nuclear energy (nyū′klē ər *or* nū′klē ər en′ər jē) energy that is released from the atomic nuclei of radioactive substances.

nuclear reactor a device for producing nuclear energy. Canada makes a good one, called the **Candu** reactor.

nude (nyüd *or* nüd) *adj* naked.

in the nude, without clothes on: *They went swimming in the nude.*

nudge (nuj) **1** *v* push slightly; jog with the elbow. **2** *n* a slight push or jog: *When my little sister gave me a nudge, I spilled the milk.* **nudged, nudg·ing.**

nui·sance (nyü′səns *or* nü′səns) *n* any thing or person that annoys you: *Flies are a nuisance.*

numb (num) *adj* having lost the power of feeling or moving: *My fingers are numb with cold.*

num·ber (num′bər) **1** *n* a word that tells exactly how many: *Two, thirteen, twenty-one, fifty,* and one hundred are numbers. **2** *n* the sum of a group of things or persons: *The number of students in our class is twenty.* **3** *n* a figure that stands for a number; a numeral: *2, 13, 21, 50, and 100 are numbers.* **4** *v* give a number to: *The pages of my science book are numbered.* **5** *n* a quantity, especially a large quantity: *We saw a number of whales around the Queen Charlotte Islands.*

nu·mer·al (nyū′mə rəl *or* nū′mə rəl) *n* a figure standing for a number. 2, 15, and 100 are Arabic numerals. II, XV, and C are Roman numerals for 2, 15, and 100. ► See Appendix.

nu·mer·a·tor (nyū′mə rā′tər *or* nū′mə rā′tər) *n* the number above the line in a fraction: *In* $\frac{3}{8}$, *3 is the numerator, and 8 is the denominator.*

nu·mer·i·cal (nyū mer′ə kəl *or* nū mer′ə kəl) *adj* having something to do with numbers: *Put the numbers 3, 5, 1, 2, 4 in numerical order and you get 1, 2, 3, 4, 5.*

nu·mer·ous (nyū′mə rəs *or* nū′mə rəs) *adj* very many: *Charlie asked numerous questions before choosing his new computer.*

Nu·na·vut (nùn′ə vùt′) *n* an area in the Northwest Territories that began to govern itself in 1999.

nurse (nərs) **1** *n* a person who takes care of people who are sick, injured, very old, or very young: *Hospitals employ many nurses.* **2** *v* act as a nurse. **nursed, nurs·ing.**

nurs·er·y (nər′sə rē) **1** *n* a room set apart for the use of babies and children. **2** *n* a place where plants are grown for sale. *pl* **nurs·er·ies.**

nursery rhyme a short poem for young children: *"Humpty Dumpty sat on a wall" is the beginning of a famous nursery rhyme.*

nut (nut) **1** *n* a dry fruit or seed with a hard shell. **2** *n* a kind of metal ring that screws on to a bolt to hold the bolt in place.

nut·crack·er *n* a tool for cracking nutshells.

nu·tri·ent (nyū′trē ənt *or* nū′trē ənt) *n* something that nourishes; a nutritious ingredient in food: *Plants extract their nutrients from the soil.*

nu·tri·tion (nyū trish′ən *or* nū trish′ən) *n* food; nourishment: *A balanced diet gives good nutrition.* **–nu·tri′tious,** *adj.*

ny·lon (nī′lon) *n* an extremely strong plastic substance, used to make clothing.

Oo

o or **O** (ō) *n* the fifteenth letter of the English alphabet or the sound that it stands for. The sound of *o* in *hope* is different from the sound of *o* in *hop*. *pl* **o's** or **O's.**

oar (ȯr) *n* a long pole with a broad, flat blade at one end, used for rowing a boat.

o·a·sis (ō ā′sis) *n* a fertile spot in the desert: *Water is always available at an oasis. pl* **o·a·ses** (ō ā′sēz).

oath (ōth) *n* a solemn promise to tell the truth or do what you have said. *pl* **oaths** (ōϮHz *or* ōths).

o·bese (ō bēs′) *adj* so fat that it is unhealthy: *The vet said our dog was obese and should go on a diet.*

o·bey (ō bā′) *v* do what you are told to do: *Trained pets obey their owners.* —**o·be′di·ence** (ō bē′dē əns), *n,* —**o·be′di·ent,** *adj,* —**o·be′di·ent·ly,** *adv.*

A traditional Japanese kimono, worn with an obi

ob·i (ō′bē) *n* a long, broad sash worn around the waist in the traditional outfit of Japanese women and children.

object (ob′jikt *for 1, 2, and 4,* əb jekt′ *for 3*) **1** *n* anything that can be seen or touched: *What is that object in your hand?* **2** *n* something aimed at; purpose: *My object in calling you is to wish you a happy birthday.* **3** *v* be opposed: *I made my suggestion, but Eric objected.*

4 *n* in grammar, the person or thing that is affected by the action of the verb in a sentence, or that follows a preposition. In the sentence *Ethan threw the ball to his brother, ball* is the object of the verb *threw,* and *brother* is the object of the preposition *to.*

ob·jec·tion (əb jek′shən) *n* a reason or argument against something.

ob·jec·tive (əb jek′tiv) *n* something aimed at: *My objective this summer will be to canoe along the Mersey River.*

Grammar ✓*Check* ......**object**

A **direct object** answers the questions "what?" or "whom?" about a verb:
 Sunil gave me (what?) a book.
An **indirect object** comes right after the verb and answers the questions "to whom?" or "for whom?":
 Sunil gave (to whom?) me a book.

---

o·blige (ə blīj′) **1** *v* force: *I am obliged to leave now to catch my bus.* **2** *v* do a favour for: *Oblige me by keeping quiet, please.* **o·bliged, o·blig·ing.**
o·blig·ing *adj* willing to do favours; helpful: *Her obliging good nature makes her very popular.*

ob·lique (ə blēk′) *adj* slanting; not straight up and down; not straight across: *an oblique line.*

ob·long (ob′long) *adj* longer than broad: *A basketball court is oblong.*

ob·nox·ious (əb nok′shəs) *adj* hateful; very disagreeable: *His disgusting table manners made him obnoxious.*

ob·serve (əb zėrv′) **1** *v* notice: *Did you observe anything strange in his behaviour yesterday?* **2** *v* study: *An astronomer observes the stars.* **3** *v* keep; obey: *All hockey players must observe the rules.* **4** *v* celebrate: *to observe Canada Day.* **ob·served, ob·serv·ing.** —**ob·ser′va·tion,** *n,* —**ob·serv′er,** *n.*
ob·serv·ant *adj* quick to notice: *If you are observant you may see how the magician does his tricks.* **ob·serv·a·to·ry** *n* a building with a telescope for observing the stars and planets.

ob·so·lete (ob′sə lēt′) *adj* out-of-date; old-fashioned: *Typewriters are obsolete.*

ob·sta·cle (ob′stə kəl) *n* something that is in the way; a hindrance: *Why does the dog make himself an obstacle by lying in the doorway?*

ob·sti·nate (ob′stə nit) *adj* stubborn: *In spite of her father's warning, the obstinate girl climbed even farther up the tree.* —**ob·sti·na·cy,** *n.*

ob·struct (əb strukt′) *v* be in the way of: *The new highrise obstructs our view of Lake Ontario.* —**ob·struc′tion,** *n.*

ob·tain (əb tān′) *v* get, especially as a result of effort: *We study to obtain knowledge.* —**ob·tain′a·ble,** *adj.*

ob·vi·ous (ob′vē əs) *adj* easily seen or understood: *an obvious mistake.*

oc·ca·sion (ə kā′zhən) **1** *n* a particular time: *We have met on several occasions.* **2** *n* a special event: *My sister's wedding was a great occasion.* **oc·ca·sion·al** *adj* happening once in a while: *The weather has been fine except for an occasional thunderstorm.* —**oc·ca′sion·al·ly,** *adv.*

oc·cu·py (ok′yə pī′) **1** *v* take up; fill: *The building occupies an entire block.* **2** *v* keep busy: *Sports often occupy Shalah after school.* **3** *v* live in: *Our family occupies our apartment.* **oc·cu·pied, oc·cu·py·ing.**

oc·cu·pa·tion (ok′yə pā′shən) *n* business or employment: *Teaching is a teacher's occupation.*

oc·cur (ə kėr′) **1** *v* happen; take place; exist: *The letter "e" occurs in print more often than any other letter.* **2** *v* come to mind: *Has it occurred to you to phone home?* **oc·curred, oc·cur·ring.**

oc·cur·rence (ə kėr′əns) *n* a happening; an event: *an unexpected occurrence.*

o·cean (ō′shən) *n* the body of salt water that covers almost three-quarters of the earth's surface; the sea. It has five main divisions—the Atlantic, Pacific, Indian, Arctic, and Antarctic.

o'clock (ə klok′) according to a time shown on the clock: *It is one o'clock.*

oc·ta·gon (ok′tə gon′) *n* ▶See Appendix.

A common octopus— about 3 m across with the tentacles spread out

oc·to·pus (ok′tə pəs) *n* a sea animal with a soft body and eight arms with suckers on them.

odd (od) **1** *adj* left over; extra: *Here are ten plums for three of you; Matthew may have the odd one.* **2** *adj* being one of a set of which the rest is missing: *There seems to be an odd sock in the wash.* **3** *adj* strange; peculiar: *It is odd that I cannot remember her name, because her face is familiar.*
odd number a number that has a remainder of 1 when divided by 2. Three, five, and seven are odd numbers. **odds** *pl.n* the chance of an event happening, expressed in numbers. The odds of flipping heads (or tails) with a coin are fifty-fifty. **odds and ends,** things left over; odd pieces; scraps; remnants.

o·dom·e·ter (ō dom′ə tər) *n* an instrument for measuring the distance a vehicle travels.

o·dour (ō′dər) *n* a smell or scent: *the odour of roses, the odour of garbage.* It can also be spelled **odor.** —**o′dour·less** or **o′dor·less,** *adj.*

of (uv) **1** *prep* belonging to: *the captain of the ship.* **2** *prep* made from: *a house of bricks.* **3** *prep* that has as a quality: *a look of happiness.* **4** *prep* named: *the city of Sudbury.* **5** *prep* concerning; about: *be fond of.*

off (of) **1** *adv* from the usual position: *The hockey player took off his skates.* **2** *adv* away: *My father drove off in his car.* **3** *prep* from: *She pushed me off the bench.* **4** *adj* not on: *The electricity is off.* **5** *adj* no longer due to take place: *The rugby match was called off.* **6** *adj* wrong: *Your answers are way off.*
off·hand *adv* without thought or preparation: *The carpenter could not tell offhand how much the work would cost.* **off·shore** *adj* off or away from the shore: *an offshore wind, offshore fisheries.*
off·stage *n* the side of a stage, not seen by the audience.
off and on, now and then: *He has lived in Europe off and on for ten years.*

of·fend (ə fend′ *or* ō fend′) *v* hurt the feelings of: *My friend was offended when I laughed at her.*
of·fence (ə fens′ *or* ō fens′ for *1, 2,* ō′fens for *3*) **1** *n* a breaking of the law: *The punishment for that offence is two years in prison.* —**of·fend′er,** *n.*
2 *n* hurting someone's feelings: *No offence was intended.* **3** *n* an attacking force: *Our football team has a good offence.* **of·fen·sive 1** *adj* hurtful: *"Shut up" is an offensive remark.* **2** *adj* having something to do with attack: *offensive play in a football game.*

of·fer (of′ər) **1** *v* hold out to be taken or refused: *to offer advice, to offer help.* **2** *n* the act of offering: *an offer of money for a house, an offer of support.*

of·fice (of′is) **1** *n* the place where the work of a business or profession is done: *The principal's office was on the second floor.* **2** *n* a position, especially in the government: *The MP was appointed to the office of Minister of Defence.*

of·fi·cer 1 *n* a person who holds an office in the government: *a police officer, a health officer.* **2** *n* a person who commands others in the armed forces, such as a captain.

of·fi·cial (ə fish′əl) **1** *n* an officer: *government officials.* **2** *adj* having to do with an office or officers: *Police wear an official uniform.* **3** *adj* having authority: *The basketball tournament was run according to official rules.* —**of·fi′cial·ly,** *adv.*

off·spring (of′spring′) *n* the young of a person, animal, or plant; descendant: *Every one of his offspring had red hair just like his own.*

of·ten (of′ən *or* of′tən) *adv* many times: *It snows often in the Mackenzie Mountains.*

o·gre (ō′gər) *n* in stories, a giant or monster that eats people.

oil (oil) **1** *n* a thick greasy liquid that will float on water. Some oils are used as fuel, and some are used in cooking: *fuel oil, olive oil.* **2** *v* put oil on or in: *I oiled the chain and wheels of my bike.* —**oil′y,** *adj.*

oint·ment (oint′mənt) *n* a substance made from oil or fat, rubbed on the skin to heal or to make it soft.

OK (ō′kā′) *adj Informal.* all right; You can use OK as a noun, verb, adjective, or adverb: *We gave it our OK's (n). I OK'd it (v). It is OK (adj). I feel OK (adv).* It can be written **O.K.** or **okay.**

USING WORDS . . . . . . OK

OK, O.K., and **okay** are all OK in informal speech and writing, but not **O.K.** when you want to sound more formal. Okay?

---

old (ōld) **1** *adj* having existed for a long time: *an old fort. We are old friends.* **2** *adj* of age: *The baby is ten months old.* **3** *adj* not new: *old clothes.* **old·er** or **eld·er, old·est** or **eld·est.**

old-fash·ioned (ōld′fash′ənd) *adj* out-of-date.

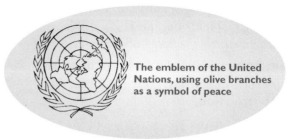

The emblem of the United Nations, using olive branches as a symbol of peace

ol·ive (ol′iv) *n* the fruit of the olive tree. Olives can be eaten raw or squeezed to make **olive oil.** An **olive branch** is often used as a symbol of peace.

O·lym·pic games (ō lim′pik gāmz′) modern athletic contests held every four years in a different country: *Athletes from many nations competed in the Winter Olympics held in Calgary in 1988.*

o·mit (ō mit′) *v* leave out or not do: *He made many mistakes in spelling by omitting letters.* **o·mit·ted, o·mit·ting.** —**o·mis′sion,** *n.*

on (on) **1** *prep* above and supported by: *This book is on the table.* **2** *prep* touching so as to cover: *There's new paint on the ceiling.* **3** *adv* farther: *Go on.* **4** *prep* in the condition of: *on purpose, on sale.* **5** *adj* not off: *The light is on.* **6** *prep* during: *They left on Sunday.* **7** *prep* concerning: *a book on animals.* **8** *prep* among: *I am on the committee.*

on·look·er *n* a person who watches without taking part. **on·shore** *adj* or *adv* toward the shore: *an onshore wind (adj). The wind was blowing onshore (adv).* **on·to** *prep* to a position on: *to get onto a horse.* **on·ward** *adv* or *adj* forward: *The campers hiked onward (adv). An onward movement began (adj).* **Onwards** means the same thing.

and so on, and more of the same.

on and off, at some times and not others.

on and on, without stopping: *The sports announcer talked on and on.*

once (wuns) **1** *adv* one time: *Read it once more.* **2** *adv* at some time in the past: *I once lived in The Pas.*

all at once, 1 suddenly: *All at once the music stopped.* **2** at the same time.

at once, 1 immediately: *You must come home at once.* **2** at the same time: *All three spoke at once.*

once and for all, finally.

once upon a time, long ago.

one (wun) **1** *n* the number 1. ►See Appendix.
2 *adj* a single: *A human being has only one head.*
3 *n* a single thing: *I like all the ones in that box but I like this one best.*

one·self *pron* someone's real or true self: *It's nice to be myself again after my illness.*

one-sid·ed 1 *adj* seeing only one side: *The umpire made several one-sided decisions.*
2 *adj* unequal: *If one team is much better than the other, we get a one-sided game.*

one by one, one after another: *The students walked onto the stage one by one.*

one or two, a few.

on·ion (un′yən) *n* a plant with a root shaped like a bulb, used as a vegetable. Onions have a sharp, strong smell and taste.

on·ly (ōn′lē) **1** *adj* one and no more: *an only child. This is the only way to go.* **2** *adv* just; merely: *He sold only two.* **3** *conj* except that; but: *She would have gone swimming, only it rained.*
if only, I wish: *If only the sun would shine!*
only if, on the condition that: *I'll take you, but only if you promise to be good.*

USING WORDS ......only

Be careful where you put **only** in a sentence. It should go as close as possible to the word it modifies. Look at how the meaning of the following sentence changes when **only** is moved to different positions:
Only he lifts heavy weights with his left hand.
He lifts only heavy weights with his left hand.
He lifts heavy weights with only his left hand.

ooze (üz) **1** *v* leak little by little: *Blood oozed from his scraped knee.* **2** *n* soft mud or slime, especially at the bottom of a lake, etc. **oozed, ooz·ing.**

o·paque (ō pāk′) *adj* not letting any light through: *Wood is opaque; glass isn't.*

o·pen (ō′pən) **1** *adj* not shut: *The open windows let in the fresh air, an open drawer.* **2 the open,** *n* open or clear space: *City people like to get out in the open.* **3** *v* make or become open: *to open a door, open a book. The early settlers opened up the West.* **4** *v* begin: *School opens in September.* **5** *adj* ready to consider new ideas: *Our teacher listens to us and is always open to suggestions.* **–o′pen·ly,** *adv.*

o·pen·ing 1 *n* a gap or hole: *an opening in a wall.* **2** *n* the first part; the beginning: *the opening of the story.* **3** *adj* first; beginning: *the opening game of the hockey series.* **o·pen-mind·ed** *adj* having a mind open to new ideas.

open a person's eyes, make a person see what is really going on.

op·er·ate (op′ə rāt′) **1** *v* run; make something run: *The machinery operates night and day. Do you know how to operate the dishwasher?* **2** *v* in medicine, remove or repair some diseased or injured part of someone's body: *The doctor operated on the injured boy.* **op·er·at·ed, op·er·at·ing.** **–op′er·a′tion,** *n,* **–op′er·a′tor,** *n.*

o·pin·ion (ə pin′yən *or* ō pin′yən) *n* what you think or believe: *In my opinion we should have won that game.*

op·por·tu·ni·ty (op′ər tyū′nə tē *or* op′ər tü′nə tē) *n* a good chance; favourable time or convenient occasion: *I had an opportunity to earn some money picking blueberries. I have had no opportunity to give him your message, because I have not seen him.* *pl* **op·por·tu·ni·ties.**

op·pose (ə pōz′) *v* be against: *Many people opposed the widening of the street.* **op·posed, op·pos·ing.** **–op′po·si′tion,** *n.*

op·po·nent (ə pō′nənt) *n* a person who is on the other side in a fight, game, or argument.

op·po·site (op′ə sit) **1** *adj* as different as can be: *North and south are opposite directions.* **2** *n* a thing as different as can be: *North is the opposite of south.* **3** *prep* directly across from: *There is a bus stop opposite the school.*

opt (opt) *v* choose or decide: *The class opted to have a bake sale to raise money for charity.*

op·tion (op′shən) *n* choice: *My options were to play volleyball or basketball.* **op·tion·al** *adj* allowing a choice: *Music is an optional subject at my sister's school.*

opt out of, decide not to take part in: *She opted out of flying to Moosonee.*

op·ti·mist (op′tə mist) *n* a person who looks on the bright side of things. The opposite is **pessimist.** **–op′ti·mism,** *n,* **–op′ti·mist′ic,** *adj.*

or (ôr) *conj* a word used to show a choice: *Is it true or false? Shall we walk or take the bus?*

–or *a suffix meaning* a person or thing that. *Actor* means a person that *acts. Generator* means a thing that *generates.*

o·ral (ô′rəl) *adj* spoken: *An oral agreement is not enough; give us a written promise.* —**o′ral·ly,** *adv.*

or·ange (ôr′inj) **1** *n* a round, reddish yellow, juicy fruit that is good to eat. **2** *n* the colour made by mixing red and yellow.

or·bit (ôr′bit) *n* the path of a heavenly body, planet, or satellite around another body in space.

or·chard (ôr′chərd) *n* a piece of ground on which fruit trees are grown.

or·ches·tra (ôr′kis trə) *n* a large group of musicians who play on various instruments.

or·deal (ôr dēl′) *n* a difficult experience: *the ordeal of being lost in the snowstorm.*

or·der (ôr′dər) **1** *n* the way one thing follows another: *in order of size, in alphabetical order.* **2** *n* a condition in which everything is in its right place: *to put a room in order.* **3** *n* a command: *The orders of the captain must be obeyed.* **4** *v* tell what to do: *The judge ordered the people in the courtroom to be quiet.* **5** *v* give a request for: *Would you like to order now?*

or·der·ly *adj* regularly arranged: *an orderly row of books.*

in order to, for the purpose of: *He searched his pockets in order to find the key.*

out of order, 1 in the wrong arrangement. **2** not working properly.

to order, according to the buyer's wishes.

ordinal number a number that shows order or position in a series. *First, second, third, fourth* are ordinal numbers. ▶See Appendix.

or·di·nar·y (ôr′də ner′ē) *adj* usual: *Ngoc's ordinary lunch consists of soup, a sandwich, and milk.* —**or′di·nar′i·ly,** *adv.*

out of the ordinary, unusual.

ore (ôr) *n* mineral or rock containing a valuable substance such as metal: *Iron ore is mined and worked to get the iron it contains.*

or·gan (ôr′gən) **1** *n* a musical instrument like a piano. **2** *n* any part of an animal or plant that does a special task. The eyes, stomach, heart, and lungs are organs of the body.

or·gan·ic (ôr gan′ik) *adj* produced by plants or animals: *organic fertilizer.*

or·gan·ize (ôr′gə nīz′) **1** *v* arrange in a system. **2** *v* plan and carry out: *The explorer organized an expedition to Ellesmere Island.* **or·gan·ized, or·gan·iz·ing.** —**or′gan·i·za′tion,** *n.*

or·i·gin (ôr′ə jin) *n* the beginning; the thing from which anything comes: *Nobody remembered the origin of the quarrel. The origin of that story is a Haida legend.* —**o·rig′i·nate′,** *v.*

o·rig·i·nal (ə rij′ə nəl) **1** *adj* earliest: *The computer has been marked down from its original price.* **2** *adj* not done before or copied: *It is hard to think of an original birthday present for Mom.* **3** *n* anything from which something else is copied: *The original of this picture is in a museum in Ottawa.* —**o·rig′i·nal·ly,** *adv.*

o·rig·i·nal·i·ty *n* freshness; novelty: *Our teacher praised my story for its originality.*

or·na·ment (ôr′nə mənt) *n* something to add beauty or decoration.

or·phan (ôr′fən) *n* a child whose parents are dead.

Orthodox Church (ôr′thə doxs′) a group of Christian churches that started up in eastern Europe and western Asia. Their leader is the patriarch of Constantinople.

oth·er (uᴛн′ər) **1** *adj* remaining: *Abraham is here, but the other boys are at school.* **2** *adj* additional or further: *I have some other books you can borrow.* **3** *adj* not the same: *Come some other day.* **4** *pron* some other person or thing: *She helps others.*

oth·er·wise 1 *adv* in other ways: *He is noisy, but otherwise a nice boy.* **2** *conj* or else: *Come at once; otherwise you will be too late.*

every other, every second: *I have swimming lessons every other day.*

the other day, night, etc., recently.

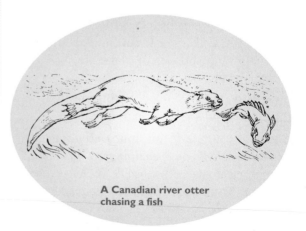

A Canadian river otter
chasing a fish

ot·ter (ot′ər) *n* a fish-eating animal. The otter is a good swimmer and has webbed feet with claws. *pl* **ot·ters** or **ot·ter.**

ouch (ouch) *interj* an exclamation expressing sudden pain.

ought (ot) an auxiliary (helping) verb used: **1** *v* to show duty: *You ought to obey the rules.* **2** *v* to show that something should happen: *The fastest one ought to win the race.*

ounce (ouns) *n* a non-metric unit for measuring mass. One ounce is a bit less than 30 g.

our (our *or* àr) *adj* belonging to us: *We put on our soccer gear.*

ours *pron* the one belonging to us: *That car is ours. Their farm is huge, but ours is small.*

our·selves 1 *pl.pron* a form used instead of **us** when talking about the subject of the sentence: *We cook for ourselves.* **2** *pl.pron* a form of **we** or **us** used to make a statement stronger: *We will do the work ourselves if we have to.* *sing* **myself.**

USING WORDS . . . . our/ours

Our is always followed by a noun:
This is our car.

Ours stands alone:
That car is ours.

—ous *a suffix meaning* full of, as in *joyous.*

out (out) **1** *adv* outside, away: *She went out at noon.* **2** *adj* not burning: *The camp fire is out.* **3** *adj* made known; able to be seen: *The secret is out now. The roses are out.* **4** *adv* plainly: *Speak out so that we can all hear.* **5** *adv* in baseball, not at bat: *We were soon out and the other team was at bat.*

out·er *adj* on the outside; farther out: *The outer door is locked. The outer suburbs of Dartmouth.*

outer space *n* space immediately beyond the atmosphere: *The moon is in outer space.*

out of, 1 without: *He is out of work. We are out of coffee.* **2** from: *It is made out of wood.*

out of hand, out of control: *The excited crowd soon got out of hand.*

pick out, choose.

out— *a prefix meaning* more than or better than, as in *outgrow, outlast, outnumber, outrun.*

out·burst (out'bèrst') *n* a sudden rush: *an outburst of laughter.*

out·come (out'kum') *n* a result: *the outcome of a race.*

out·door (out'dòr') *adj* having to do with being outside: *outdoor games.*

out·doors *adv* out in the open air: *Mom won't let us go outdoors until it stops raining.*

out·field (out'fēld') **1** *n* in baseball, the part of the field beyond the diamond or infield. **2** *n* the three players in the outfield. **–out'field'er,** *n.*

out·fit (out'fit) **1** *n* the clothes and equipment needed for something: *the outfit for a camping trip, a bride's outfit.* **2** *v* provide everything necessary for something: *Dimitri outfitted himself for camp.* **out·fit·ted, out·fit·ting.**

out·go·ing (out'gō'ing) *adj* friendly; sociable: *Rosie is a very outgoing person and enjoys meeting people.*

out·house (out'hous') **1** *n* a building or shed outside the main house. **2** *n* an outside toilet.

out·ing (ou'ting) *n* a short pleasure trip: *On Sunday we went on an outing to Grand Bend.*

out·law (out'lo') **1** *n* criminal. **2** *v* make unlawful: *A group of nations agreed to outlaw hijacking.*

out·let (out'lət) **1** *n* a way out; an opening or exit. **2** *n* a place for inserting an electric plug.

out·line (out'līn') **1** *n* the line that shows the shape of an object: *The outline of Italy looks like a boot.* **2** *n* a brief plan; a rough draft: *Make an outline before trying to write a composition. The teacher gave a brief outline of the work planned for the term.* **3** *v* give a plan of; sketch: *She outlined their trip to Lunenburg.* **out·lined, out·lin·ing.**

out·look (out'lùk') **1** *n* what seems likely to happen: *Because of the black clouds, the outlook for our picnic is not very good.* **2** *n* a way of thinking about things: *He had a cheerful outlook on life.*

out·ly·ing (out'lī'ing) *adj* far from the centre: *the outlying houses in the settlement.*

❀ **out·port** (out'pòrt') *n* a small harbour, especially one of the isolated fishing villages along the coasts of Newfoundland and Labrador.

out·post (out'pōst') *n* a settlement in an outlying place: *an outpost in the North.*

out·put (out'pùt') **1** *n* the amount produced: *the daily output of cars from a factory.* **2** *n* the information produced by a computer. The output can be printed on paper, or stored on a disk.

out·rage (out′rāj′) **1** *n* a very shameful act: *Cruelty to animals is an outrage.* **2** *v* insult; anger: *I was outraged when she called me a liar.* **out·raged, out·rag·ing.**

out·ra·geous (out rā′jəs) *adj* very bad or insulting: *outrageous behaviour.*

out·side (out′sīd′) **1** *n* the surface that faces out: *the outside of a house.* **2** *adv* outdoors: *Run outside and play.* **3** ❧ *n* the settled parts of Canada: *In the North, people refer to the rest of Canada as the outside.*

an outside chance, a very small chance.

at the outside, at the most: *I can do it in a week, at the outside.*

out·sid·er (out′sī′dər) **1** *n* a person not belonging to a particular group, set, company, party, district, etc. **2** ❧ *n* a person who does not live in the North: *The people of Whitehorse call the people of Edmonton outsiders.*

out·skirts (out′skėrts′) *pl.n* the outer parts or edges of a place: *They have a farm on the outskirts of Assiniboia.*

out·stand·ing (out stan′ding) **1** *adj* very much better than others: *She is an outstanding basketball player.* **2** *adj* unpaid: *outstanding debts.*

out·ward (out′wərd) *adv* toward the outside; away: *Emergency exit doors open outward.* **Outwards** means the same thing.

out·wit (out wit′) *v* get the better of; be too clever for: *The fox outwitted the dogs and escaped.* **out·wit·ted, out·wit·ting.**

o·val (ō′vəl) *adj* shaped like an egg.

ov·en (uv′ən) *n* a space in a stove for baking or roasting food.

o·ver (ō′vər) **1** *prep* above: *the sky over our heads.* **2** *prep* across: *to jump over a wall.* **3** *adv* across a distance: *Go over to the store for me.* **4** *adv* on top of, so as to cover: *Put your hands over your ears.* **5** *adv* again: *I will have to do my essay over.* **6** *adv* at an end: *The play is over.* **7** *prep* more than: *It cost over ten dollars.*

over again, once more: *Let's do that over again.*

over and over, again and again: *He keeps telling the same story over and over.*

over– *a prefix meaning* too, too much, or too long, etc., as in *overcrowded, overdo, overheat, overload, oversleep, overweight, overwork.*

Farmers wearing overalls

o·ver·alls (ō′və r olz′) *pl.n* loose trousers worn over clothes to keep them clean. Overalls usually have a part that covers the chest.

o·ver·board (ō′vər bȯrd′) *adv* from a boat into the water: *Don't throw that garbage overboard.*

go overboard, go too far in an effort because of extreme enthusiasm: *Christine went overboard and bought more than she needed.*

o·ver·cast (ō′vər kast′) *adj* cloudy: *The sky was overcast before the storm.* **o·ver·cast, o·ver·cast·ing.**

o·ver·coat (ō′vər kōt′) *n* a coat worn for warmth over regular clothing.

o·ver·come (ō′vər kum′) *v* get over difficulties: *Lorna overcame her fear of heights and climbed the ladder.* **o·ver·came, o·ver·come, o·ver·com·ing.**

o·ver·due (ō′vər dyū′ *or* ō′vər dū′) *adj* late: *The train is overdue.*

o·ver·flow (ō′vər flō′) *v* go over the top or out beyond: *Stop! The milk is overflowing the cup. The crowd overflowed the room and filled the hallway.* **o·ver·flowed, o·ver·flown, o·ver·flow·ing.**

o·ver·grown (ō′vər grōn′) *adj* covered with weeds, etc.: *The wall is overgrown with vines.*

o·ver·head (ō′vər hed′) *adv* over your head; above: *A helicopter flew overhead.*

o·ver·hear (ō′vər hēr′) *v* hear when you are not meant to hear: *They spoke so loudly that I could not help overhearing what they said.* **o·ver·heard, o·ver·hear·ing.**

o·ver·joyed (ō′vər joid′) *adj* very joyful; filled with joy; delighted.

o·ver·lap (ō'vər lap') v place or be placed so that one piece covers part of the next: *Shingles on the roof are laid to overlap each other.* **o·ver·lapped, o·ver·lap·ping.**

o·ver·look (ō'vər lük') **1** v fail to see: *Here are some letters that you overlooked.* **2** v excuse: *I will overlook your bad behaviour this time.* **3** v have a view of from above: *This high window overlooks half of Bonavista.*

o·ver·night (ōvər nīt') **1** adv for one night: *to stay overnight with a friend.* **2** adj lasting one night: *an overnight stop.*

o·ver·pass (ō'vər pas') n a bridge over a road, railway, canal, etc.

o·ver·pow·er (ō'vər pou'ər) v beat; be much greater or stronger than: *He overpowered all his enemies. The wind brought a horrible smell that overpowered me.*

o·ver·seas (ō'vər sēz') adv across the sea; abroad: *to travel overseas.*

o·ver·sight (ō'vər sīt') n a failure to notice or think of something: *Through an oversight, the kitten got no supper last night.*

o·ver·take (ō'vər tāk') v pass: *The blue car overtook our truck.* **o·ver·took, o·ver·tak·en, o·ver·tak·ing.**

o·ver·time (ō'vər tīm') n extra time: *The factory worker was paid extra for overtime. The game went into overtime.*

o·ver·view (ō'vər vyū') n a brief, general survey: *Our teacher gave an overview of the project before she explained all the details.*

o·ver·whelm (ō'vər welm' or ō'vər hwelm') v crush; overcome completely: *She was overwhelmed with grief.*

owe (ō) v be in debt: *Here's the loonie I owe you.* **owed, ow·ing.**

owing to, because of: *Owing to chicken pox, she was absent from school for a week.*

A great grey owl— about 75 cm long including the tail

owl (oul) n a bird with a big head, big eyes set in the front of the head, and a short, hooked beak. Owls hunt mice and small birds at night.

own (ōn) **1** v have; possess: *I own many books.* **2** adj belonging to: *This is my own book. She makes her own clothes.* **–own'er,** n, **–own'er·ship,** n.

on your own, not ruled by someone else; alone.

ox (oks) n a domestic bull used for farm work and for beef. pl **ox·en.**

ox·y·gen (ok'sə jən) n a gas without colour or smell that makes up about one fifth of the air. Animals and plants cannot live without oxygen. Fire will not burn without oxygen.

oys·ter (oi'stər) n a shellfish used a lot as food. It has a rough, irregular shell in two halves. Oysters are found in shallow water along seacoasts. Some kinds of oysters yield pearls.

o·zone (ō'zōn) n a form of oxygen with a sharp smell. The **ozone layer** is a part of the atmosphere that contains a lot of ozone. It protects us from dangerous radiation from the sun.

A pagoda in the Chinese style of architecture

p or **P** (pē) *n* the sixteenth letter of the English alphabet, or the sound that it stands for. We hear the sound of *p* in *spot, pie,* and *skip. pl* **p's** or **P's.**

pace (pās) **1** *n* a step. **2** *v* walk with regular steps: *The polar bear paced up and down his cage.* **3** *n* a speed of walking: *He sets a fast pace in walking.* **paced, pac·ing.**
set the pace, be an example for others to follow.

pack (pak) **1** *n* a bundle of things held together for carrying: *The mountaineer carried a pack on his back.* **2** *v* put together in a bundle: *Pack your books in this box.* **3** *v* crowd closely together: *A hundred people were packed into one small room.* **4** *n* a set: *a pack of thieves, a pack of lies.* **5** *n* a number of animals hunting together: *Wolves hunt in packs; tigers hunt alone.*
pack·age *n* a bundle of things wrapped together: *a package of candies.*

pad (pad) **1** *n* sheets of paper fastened tightly together. **2** *n* the launching platform for a rocket.

pad·dle (pad′əl) **1** *n* a short oar with a broad blade at one end or both ends, used to propel a canoe or a kayak. **2** *v* move a canoe with a paddle: *We paddled across Manitoba Lake.* **pad·dled, pad·dling.**

pad·lock (pad′lok′) *n* a lock that can be put on and removed. A padlock hangs by a curved bar that is passed through a loop.

page (pāj) **1** *n* one side of a sheet of paper. **2** *n* a messenger in the House of Commons, the Senate, or the Legislative Assembly. **3** *v* try to get a message to a person: *You can page someone by calling their special page number and giving your phone number.* **paged, pag·ing.**
pa·ger *n* a small device that is carried around and beeps to tell the person wearing it that there is a phone message.

pa·go·da (pə gō′də) *n* a temple with a roof curving upward from each level: *There are pagodas in India, Japan, and China.*

pail (pāl) *n* a small bucket with a handle going over its top.

pain (pān) *n* a feeling of being hurt: *A cut finger causes pain.* –**pain′less,** *adj,* –**pain′ful,** *adj.*
pains·tak·ing *adj* very careful.
take pains, be careful: *Jasmine took pains to make her writing neat.*

paint (pānt) **1** *n* a coloured liquid used to cover a surface. **2** *v* cover or decorate with paint: *to paint a house.* **3** *v* make a picture with paint. –**paint′er,** *n,* –**paint′ing,** *n.*

pair (per) *n* a set of two: *a pair of shoes.*

CONFUSABLES ..... pair

pair means "two":
A pair of brown eyes were looking at me.
pare means "peel":
Do you know how to pare an apple?
pear is a fruit: *I will have a pear for dessert.*

pal·ace (pal′is) *n* the official home of a king, queen, or some other important person.

pale (pāl) **1** *adj* without much colour. When you have been ill, your face is often pale. This lack of colour is called **pallor.** **2** *adj* not bright: *pale blue.* **pal·er, pal·est.**

pal·ette (pal′it) *n* a thin board used by painters to mix colours.

pal·in·drome (pal′in drōm′) *n* a word, phrase, or sentence that reads the same backward as forward. The word *level* is a palindrome.

palm (pom) **1** *n* the inside of your hand between your wrist and fingers. **2** *n* a tree growing in warm climates, that usually has large featherlike leaves at the top of a tall trunk.

pam·per (pam′pər) *v* spoil: *They pampered the dog with expensive foods.*

pam·phlet (pam′flit) *n* a short booklet, usually with a paper cover: *The doctor's office has lots of pamphlets about health care.*

pan (pan) *n* a dish or pot for cooking. **pan·cake** *n* a thin, flat cake made of batter and fried in a pan.

pan out, turn out or work out: *Kevin's latest scheme panned out well.*

Giant pandas—
about 120 cm long

pan·da (pan′də) *n* a bearlike animal. The giant panda is black and white, and lives in China.

pan·de·mon·i·um (pan′də mō′nē əm) *n* a situation in which there is a lot of noise, excitement, and confusion: *When the concert started there was pandemonium as people jumped up from their seats.*

pane (pān) *n* a single piece of glass in a window or door.

pan·el (pan′əl) **1** *n* a flat piece of something, usually in a door or on a wall: *Dad put wood panels on the basement walls.* **2** *n* a group of people brought together to discuss something.

pang (pang) *n* a sudden, short, sharp pain.

pan·ic (pan′ik) **1** *n* a sudden fear that causes you to lose self-control. **2** *v* feel panic: *The cyclist panicked when his brakes failed.* **pan·icked, pan·ick·ing.**

pan·o·ram·a (pan′ə ram′ə) *n* a wide view: *a panorama of the lake and all its islands.*

pant (pant) **1** *v* breathe hard and quickly: *He is panting because he has been running.* **2** *v* speak with short, quick breaths: *"Help, help, over here," panted Alec.*

pa·per (pā′pər) *n* thin sheets used for writing, wrapping packages, and many other purposes: *This book is made of paper.*

pa·per·back *n* a book with a soft cover made of paper. **pa·pier-mâché** (pā′pər ma shā′) *n* paper soaked in paste and used for modelling. It becomes hard and strong when dry. The name comes from French *papier mâché,* meaning "chewed paper."

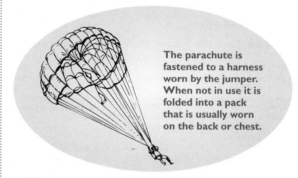

The parachute is fastened to a harness worn by the jumper. When not in use it is folded into a pack that is usually worn on the back or chest.

par·a·chute (per′ə shūt′) *n* a device made to give a slow fall to a person or thing dropping from an aircraft. The top of a parachute looks like an umbrella.

pa·rade (pə rād′) **1** *n* a march for display; a procession: *We loved all the parades that we saw during Klondike Days.* **2** *v* to march in a procession; to walk proudly as if in a parade. **3** *v* make a great show of: *The little girl paraded around in her sister's clothes.*

par·a·dise (par′ə dīs′ *or* per′ə dīs′) *n* heaven; a place of great happiness: *The summer camp at Kawagama was a paradise for her.*

par·a·graph (per′ə graf′) *n* a group of sentences about the same idea. Paragraphs usually begin on a new line, farther from the margin than other lines.

par·al·lel (per′ə lel′) *adj* at the same distance apart everywhere, like the two rails of a railway track.

par·a·lyse (per′ə līz′) *v* make a person lose movement or feeling: *Fear paralysed my mind. His left arm was paralysed.* Another spelling is **paralyze. par·a·lysed, par·a·lys·ing.**
–**pa·ral′y·sis** (pə ral′ə sis), *n.*

par·a·pher·nal·ia (per′ə fər nā′lē ə) *pl.n* belongings or equipment: *My brother leaves his hockey paraphernalia all over the house.*

par·a·site (per′ə sīt′) *n* an animal that lives and feeds on another animal. Lice are parasites on animals.

par·cel (pàr′səl) *n* a package.

parch (pàrch) *v* make thirsty: *The farm workers were parched with the heat.*

par·don (pàr′dən) **1** *n* forgiveness: *I beg your pardon but I'm afraid I am late.* **2** *v* forgive: *Pardon me.*

par·ent (per′ənt) *n* a father or mother. –**pa·ren′tal,** *adj.*

pa·ren·the·sis (pə ren′thə sis) *n* the curved line (or) used to enclose something in a sentence. *pl* **pa·ren·the·ses.**

Grammar ✓ *Check* .. **parentheses**

Use **parentheses** to add comments or explain something within a sentence: *The hamster (we decided to call him Tim) soon became a member of the family.* Remember that the information in parentheses is extra. The sentence should still make sense when you take it away: *The hamster soon became a member of the family.*

---

park (pàrk) **1** *n* a piece of land set apart for public recreation: *Let's have a picnic in the park. Canada has fine national and provincial parks.* **2** *v* leave a vehicle for a time in a certain place: *Park your car here.* A place where many cars can park is called a **parking lot. 3** *v Informal.* put or leave: *Just park your books on the table.*

A style of parka commonly worn in most parts of Canada in the winter

par·ka (pàr′kə) *n* a long, warm jacket with a hood: *Parkas made of fur were first worn by the Inuit people.*

par·lia·ment (pàr′lə mənt) *n* a group of people elected to make laws. In Canada, Parliament includes the House of Commons and the Senate.

par·rot (per′ət) *n* a tropical bird with a hooked bill and, often, brightly coloured feathers. Some parrots can imitate words.

part (pàrt) **1** *n* something less than the whole: *Grant ate part of an apple.* **2** *n* a share: *They had no part in the mischief.* **3** *n* a character in a play; the words spoken by a character: *Anne took the part of Helen Keller in our play.* **4** *v* force apart: *The mounted police parted the crowd.* **5** *v* go apart: *The friends parted in anger.*

par·tial (pàr′shəl) **1** *adj* not complete: *a partial success.* **2** *adj* inclined to favour one side more than another: *Parents should not be partial to any one of their children.* –**par′tial·ly,** *adv.*

partial to, having a liking for: *She is partial to chocolate.*

part·ing 1 *n* going away: *The friends were sad at parting.* **2** *n* a separation: *Her hair is arranged with a side parting.* **part·ly** *adv* not completely: *We are partly to blame.*

part of speech a class of words. The main parts of speech in English are noun, pronoun, adjective, verb, adverb, preposition, conjunction, and interjection.

in good part, in a friendly way: *Chris took the teasing in good part.*

part and parcel, a necessary part: *Practising is part and parcel of learning to play the piano.*

part with, give up.

take part, be a part of; participate in.

par·tic·i·pate (pàr tis·ə pāt′) *v* take part: *The teacher participated in the children's games.* **par·tic·i·pat·ed, par·tic·i·pat·ing.** –**par·tic′i·pant,** *n,* –**par·tic′i·pa′tion,** *n.*

par·ti·ci·ple (pàr′tə sip′əl) *n* in grammar, the **present participle,** which ends in -*ing,* as in *running, talking,* or the **past participle,** which ends in -*ed* for most verbs, as in *talked, closed.* Participles can be used as adjectives, as in *running water, a closed door.* They can also be used with an auxiliary (helping) verb, as in *I am talking, I have talked.*

par·ti·cle (pàr′tə kəl) *n* a very little bit: *I got a particle of dust in my eye.*

par·tic·u·lar (pər tik′yə lər) **1** *adj* apart from others: *I don't just want a bike, I want that particular bike.* **2** *adj* hard to please: *She is very particular; nothing but the best will do.*

par·tic·u·lar·ly *adv* especially: *I am particularly fond of milk chocolate.*

part·ner (pàrt′nər) *n* a person who shares or joins with another: *On our camping trip to Sturgeon Lake, I put up the tent while my partner built a fire. My sister is my tennis partner.* –**part′ner·ship**, *n.*

par·ty (pàr′tē) **1** *n* a gathering of people to have a good time together: *Isabella had a party on her birthday.* **2** *n* a political organization. *pl* **par·ties.**

pass (pas) **1** *v* go by: *The parade passed. We passed the big truck. Time passed quickly.* **2** *v* hand around or over: *Please pass the butter. Pass the ball.* **3** *v* to complete successfully: *We all passed the arithmetic test.* **4** *n* a note, ticket, etc. allowing you to do something: *The reporter needed a pass to enter the building.* **5** *n* a narrow road, path, channel, etc.: *A pass crosses the mountains.* **passed, pass·ing.**

pas·sen·ger *n* a person who travels in a train, bus, boat, airplane, etc.

pass out, 1 give out; distribute. **2** *Informal.* faint; lose consciousness.

pass up, give up: *to pass up a chance to go to the movies.*

pas·sage (pas′ij) **1** *n* a hall or way through a building. **2** *n* part of a piece of writing: *Read this passage carefully.*

pas·sion (pash′ən) *n* very strong feeling: *Love and hate are passions. He has a passion for music.* –**pas′sion·ate**, *adj.*

Pass·o·ver (pas′ō′vər) *n* a Jewish festival celebrating how the Jews were freed from slavery in ancient Egypt. According to the Bible, a destroying angel punished the Egyptians by killing the first-born son in each household, but passed over the homes of the Jews.

pass·port (pas′pòrt′) *n* an official document giving permission to travel in a foreign country, under the protection of your own government.

pass·word (pas′wərd′) *n* a secret word or phrase that identifies a person and allows him or her to pass a guard or use private computer files.

past (past) **1** *adj* gone by: *It's September and summer is past.* **2** *n* time gone by: *Life began far back in the past.* **3** *prep* after: *half past two. It is past noon.* **4** *prep* so as to pass by or beyond: *The bus goes past our house.*

past tense in grammar, a verb tense that shows an action that happened in time gone by. In the sentence *I went to bed early last night,* went is in the past tense.

Grammar ✓*Check* ... **past tense**

To make the **past tense** of most English verbs, add-*ed* to the root word: *aim* becomes *aimed; walk* becomes *walked,* and so on.

Irregular verbs form the past tense in other ways, for example *hold* becomes *held*, and *bring* becomes *brought.* If you are not sure of the past tense of a verb, check the root word in a dictionary.

---

pas·ta (pàs′tə *or* pas′tə) *n* dough made of flour and water, shaped into spaghetti, macaroni, ravioli, noodles, etc.

paste (pāst) **1** *n* a mixture, such as flour and water, that will stick things together. **2** *v* to stick with paste: *to paste a picture in a scrapbook.* **past·ed, past·ing.**

pas·tel (pas tel′) **1** *n* a kind of crayon used in drawing. **2** *adj* soft and pale in colour: *pastel pink, pastel shades.*

pas·try (pās′trē) **1** *n* dough used to make pie crusts, tarts, etc. **2** *n* a pie, tart, etc. of this kind. *pl* **pas·tries.**

pas·ture (pas′chər) *n* a field or grassland on which cattle, sheep, or horses can feed.

pat (pat) **1** *v* strike lightly: *to pat a dog. The baker patted the dough into a flat cake.* **2** *n* a light stroke. **pat·ted, pat·ting.**

patch (pach) **1** *n* a piece of some material put on to mend a hole: *I sewed a patch on my jeans.* **2** *v* mend with a patch. *The workers patched the hole in the road.* **3** *n* a small area: *a patch of red on your skin, a garden patch.*

path (path) *n* a narrow track for walking on: *He laid stone for a garden path.* *pl* **paths.**

pa·thet·ic (pə thet′ik) *adj* pitiful; causing pity: *A lost child is a pathetic sight. She made a pathetic attempt to sing.*

pa·tience (pā′shəns) *n* the ability to accept calmly things that annoy, or that require waiting or effort: *When watching the mouse hole, the cat showed patience.*

pa·tient 1 *adj* having patience. 2 *n* a person who is being treated by a doctor, dentist, etc.

pat·i·o (pat′ē ō) *n* a paved area outside a building: *Many restaurants in Ottawa have patios for eating outside in the summer.* pl **pat·i·os.**

pat·ter (pat′ər) 1 *n* a series of quick taps, or the sound they make: *the patter of raindrops, the patter of bare feet.* 2 *n* quick and easy talk such as that of a salesperson or comedian.

pat·tern (pat′ərn) 1 *n* a design: *the pattern on the wallpaper.* 2 *n* a model: *Follow the easy pattern to make this dress.*

pause (poz) 1 *n* a short stop: *She made a short pause and then went on reading.* 2 *v* stop and wait: *The dog paused when it heard me.* **paused, paus·ing.**

pave (pāv) *v* cover a street, sidewalk, etc. with cement, etc.: *The workers are going to pave the driveway with blacktop.* **paved, pav·ing.**
pave·ment *n* a paved surface.

paw (po) *n* the foot of a four-footed animal with claws. Cats and dogs have paws.

pay (pā) 1 *v* give money for goods, services, or work: *She paid the plumber by cheque.* 2 *n* money given for goods, services, or work: *The waiter gets his pay every Saturday.* 3 *v* give: *to pay attention, to pay a compliment, to pay a visit.* 4 *v* be worth while: *It paid her to be patient.* **paid, pay·ing. –pay′ment,** *n.*
pay back, give the same treatment as received: *I'll pay her back for her help by inviting her to lunch. I'll pay you back for being mean to me!*

A peace pipe

peace (pēs) 1 *n* freedom from war: *We are working for world peace.* 2 *n* quietness: *We enjoy the peace of the wilderness.* **–peace′ful,** *adj.*
peace pipe a pipe smoked by First Nations people as a token of peace.

A peacock and peahen. The male is about 180 cm long including the 120 cm tail.

pea·cock (pē′kok′) *n* a large male bird with beautiful green, blue, and gold feathers. The peacock's tail feathers have spots resembling eyes and can be spread out and held upright like a fan. The female bird is called a **peahen.** pl **pea·cocks** or **pea·cock.**

peak (pēk) 1 *n* the pointed top of a mountain or hill: *the snowy peaks of the Selwyn Mountains.* 2 *n* the highest point: *to reach the peak of your strength.* 3 *n* the front part or the brim of a cap.

pearl (pərl) *n* a rounded, whitish gem that has a soft shine. Pearls are formed inside the shell of some oysters.

peas·ant (pez′ənt) *n* a person, usually very poor, who works on the land, especially a farm worker.

peb·ble (peb′əl) *n* a small stone, usually worn smooth and round by being rolled about by water.

pe·cul·iar (pi kyūl′yər) *adj* strange; odd; unusual: *It is peculiar that Bobby didn't call me, because he promised he would.*

ped·al (ped′əl) 1 *n* a lever worked by your foot. You push a bike's pedals to make it move. Pianos have pedals for changing the loudness of the music. 2 *v* move by pedals: *She pedalled her bicycle slowly up the hill.* **ped·alled** or **ped·aled, ped·al·ling** or **ped·al·ing.**

ped·dle (ped′əl) *v* sell in small quantities, often from a cart: *to peddle hot dogs, to peddle souvenirs.* **ped·dled, ped·dling. –ped′dler,** *n.*

pe·des·tri·an (pə des′trē ən) *n* a person who goes on foot: *Pedestrians have to watch for cars turning corners.*

peek (pēk) 1 *v* look quickly or secretively: *You must not peek while you are counting in games such as hide-and-seek.* 2 *n* a quick secretive look. Another word for these is **peep.**
peep·hole *n* a hole through which you can peek.

peel (pēl) **1** *n* the rind or skin of fruit or vegetables. **2** *v* strip the outer covering from: *to peel an orange, to peel a potato. The paint on the shed is peeling.*

keep your eyes peeled, *Informal.* be on the alert: *Keep your eyes peeled for a good place for a picnic.*

peer (pēr) **1** *n* a person who is an equal: *She got along just as well with older children as she did with her peers.* **2** *v* look closely: *Leeanne peered at the tag to read the price.*

pee·wee (pē′wē) **1** *n* a very small person or thing. **2** *n* in sports, a player aged between 8 and 12.

peg (peg) *n* a pin or small bolt made of wood or metal used in lots of ways: *a tent peg, a clothes peg, a marker peg.* **pegged, peg·ging.**

peg·board *n* a board with evenly spaced holes in which pegs or hooks can be inserted.

take someone down a peg, lower someone's pride.

pel·let (pel′it) *n* a little ball of mud, paper, hail, snow, etc.; a pill.

pelt (pelt) **1** *v* throw things at; pound: *The boys were pelting each other with snowballs. The rain pelted against the cottage windows.* **2** *n* the skin of a fur-bearing animal like a sheep, beaver, fox, wolf, etc.

❦ **pem·mi·can** (pem′i kən) *n* lean meat that has been preserved by being dried, pounded, and mixed with fat.

WORD HISTORY . . . . pemmican

Pemmican comes from Cree *pimii*, meaning "fat," and *-kan*, meaning "prepared."

---

pen (pen) **1** *n* a writing tool that gives a flow of ink, such as a ball-point pen, a fountain pen, or a felt-tip pen. **2** *n* a small enclosure, such as a playpen for a baby or a yard for cows, sheep, pigs, chickens, etc.

pen name a false name used to hide the writer's identity.

pen·al·ty (pen′əl tē) *n* a punishment for breaking a law or rule: *Her penalty for illegal parking was a fine of twenty dollars.* *pl* **pen·al·ties.** –**pe′nal·ize′** (pē′nə līz′), *v.*

pen·cil (pen′səl) *n* a pointed tool for writing or drawing, usually made of wood with a thin piece

of black or coloured material in the centre. **pen·cilled** or **pen·ciled, pen·cil·ling** or **pen·cil·ing.**

Emperor penguins— about 120 cm high

pen·guin (peng′gwin) *n* a black and white sea bird with wings like flippers, which it uses for diving and swimming. Penguins cannot fly. They live in Antarctica.

pen·in·su·la (pə nin′sə lə *or* pə nin′syə lə) *n* a piece of land almost surrounded by water, or extending far out into the water: *Nova Scotia is a large peninsula.*

pen·nant (pen′ənt) **1** *n* a flag, usually long and pointed, used for signalling, as a school banner, etc. **2** *n* a flag or other trophy: *The team from British Columbia won the baseball pennant.*

pen·ny (pen′ē) *n* a cent; a copper coin of Canada and the United States. *pl* **pennies.**

pen·ni·less *adj* without a penny; very poor: *a penniless family.*

pen·ta·gon (pen′tə gon′) *n* ▶See Appendix.

pent·house (pent′hous′) *n* an apartment at the top of a building.

peo·ple (pē′pəl) **1** *n* men, women, boys, and girls; persons. **2** *n* a nation: *the Canadian people.* **3** *n* persons in general; the public.

pep (pep) *Informal.* **1** *n* spirit; energy. **2 pep up,** *v* fill with energy or enthusiasm: *The cheerleaders did their best to pep up the team.* –**pep′py,** *adj.*

pep·per·mint (pep′ər mint′) *n* a herb used as a flavouring in candy and toothpaste.

per (pər) *prep* for each: *a litre of milk per child, one ticket per person.*

per·cent (pər sent′) *n* parts in each hundred. Five percent (5%) is 5 out of each 100. *Symbol:* %

per·cent·age *n* a part or proportion: *A large percentage of books are paperbacks.*

perch (pərch) **1** *n* a branch, or anything else a bird rests on. **2** *v* sit, especially on something high: *She perched on a stool.*

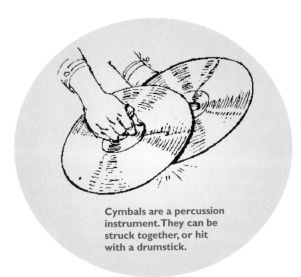

Cymbals are a percussion instrument. They can be struck together, or hit with a drumstick.

per·cus·sion (pər kush′ən) *n* the striking of something against something else: *Caps are exploded by percussion.*

percussion instrument a musical instrument played by striking it, such as a drum or cymbal.

per·fect (pər′fikt) **1** *adj* having no faults; not spoiled at any point: *a perfect score, a perfect apple.* **2** *adj* complete: *a perfect stranger.* –**per·fec′tion**, *n,* –**per′fect·ly**, *adv.*

per·fo·rate (pər′fə rāt′) *v* make a row of holes through: *Sheets of postage stamps are perforated.* **per·fo·rat·ed, per·fo·rat·ing.**
per·fo·ra·tion *n* a series of holes in something: *Juan removed the coupon by tearing along the perforation.*

per·form (pər fôrm′) **1** *v* do or carry out: *The skater performed a triple jump.* **2** *v* act, play, sing, or do tricks in public: *Our class performed a musical play.* –**per·form′ance**, *n,* –**per·form′er**, *n.*

per·fume (pər′fyūm *or* pər fyūm′) **1** *n* a liquid with a sweet smell, especially a liquid applied to your skin. **2** *n* a sweet smell: *We enjoyed the perfume of the flowers.* **per·fumed, per·fum·ing.**

per·haps (pər haps′) *adv* maybe; possibly.

per·il (per′əl) *n* danger: *This bridge is not safe; cross it at your peril.* –**per′il·ous**, *adj.*

pe·rim·e·ter (pə rim′ə tər) *n* the outer edge of a shape or a flat surface: *A fence marks the perimeter of the field.*

pe·ri·od (pēr′yəd) **1** *n* a length of time: *She visited us for a short period.* **2** *n* the dot (.) marking the end of most sentences or showing an abbreviation, as in Mr. or Dec. **3** *n* one of the three twenty-minute parts of a hockey game.
pe·ri·od·i·cal (pē′rē od′ə kəl) *n* a magazine that appears regularly.
pe·ri·od·i·cal·ly (pē′rē od′ik lē) *adv* every now and then: *My aunt from Manitoba visits us periodically.*

per·i·scope (per′ə skōp′) *n* a device that lets people in a submarine get a view of the surface. A periscope is a tube with mirrors that reflect light rays down the tube.

per·ish (per′ish) *v* be destroyed; become spoiled; die: *Buildings perish in flames. Fruit will perish quickly in hot weather. Flowers perish when frost comes.*
per·ish·a·ble *adj* liable to spoil or rot: *Fresh fruit is perishable.*

perk (pərk) *v* raise smartly: *The sparrow perked up his tail.*
perk·y *adj* smart; brisk; cheeky: *a perky squirrel.*
perk up, brighten up; become lively and vigorous: *We all perked up after a good lunch.*

❧ **per·ma·frost** (pər′mə frost′) *n* ground that is permanently frozen: *There is a great deal of permafrost in the Canadian North.*

per·ma·nent (pər′mə nənt) *adj* intended to last for a long time: *a permanent filling in a tooth.* –**per′ma·nence**, *n.*

per·mit (pər mit′ *for 1,* pər′mit *for 2*) **1** *v* let; allow: *I will go with you if my mother permits.* **2** *n* a formal written order allowing you to do something: *a permit to fish, a parking permit.* **per·mit·ted, per·mit·ting.** –**per·mis′si·ble**, *adj,* –**per·mis′sion**, *n.*

per·pet·u·al (pər pech′ū əl) *adj* continuous; never stopping: *the perpetual movement of the ocean.* –**per·pet′u·al·ly**, *adv.*

per·plex (pər pleks′) *v* puzzle; bewilder: *This problem is hard enough to perplex us all. I was perplexed by his sudden unfriendliness.*

per·se·vere (pər′sə vēr′) *v* continue to do something that may be difficult: *They persevered in their search for gold in the Klondike.* **per·se·vered, per·se·ver·ing.**
per·se·ver·ance *n* never giving up what you have set out to do: *By perseverance anyone can do well in school.*

per·sist (pər sist′) *v* refuse to stop or be changed: *She persisted in trying to move the heavy box.* –**per·sist′ence,** *n,* –**per·sist′ent,** *adj.*

per·son (pər′sən) *n* a man, woman, boy, or girl; a human being: *Any person who wishes may come to the meeting.*
per·son·al·i·ty (pər′sə nal′ə tē) **1** *n* the qualities that make one person be different or act differently from another: *A baby two weeks old does not have much personality.* **2** *n* a famous person. *pl* **per·son·al·i·ties.**
in person, with your own presence: *Come in person; do not write or phone.*

per·son·al (pər′sə nəl) **1** *adj* by oneself, not through others; private: *a personal letter, a personal appearance.* **2** *adj* about or against a person: *personal remarks, personal insults.*
per·son·al·ly **1** *adv* in person; not with the help of others: *The hostess personally saw to the comfort of her guests.* **2** *adv* as far as someone is concerned: *Personally, I like apples better than oranges.* **3** *adv* as being meant for one person: *Do not take what he said personally.*
personal pronoun in grammar, a type of pronoun that shows the person speaking, the person spoken to, or the person or thing being spoken about. The personal pronouns are *I, me, we, us, you, he, him, she, her, it, they,* and *them.*

per·son·nel (pər′sə nel′) *n* persons employed in any workplace: *Hospital personnel includes nurses, doctors, cooks, etc.*

per·spire (pər spīr′) *v* sweat. **per·spired, per·spir·ing.** –**per′spi·ra′tion,** *n.*

per·suade (pər swād′) *v* make someone think or do something by talking to them: *I knew I should do my homework, but he persuaded me to play a video game.* **per·suad·ed, per·suad·ing.** –**per·sua′sion,** *n,* –**per·sua′sive,** *adj.*

pes·ky (pes′kē) *adj Informal.* troublesome; annoying: *pesky mosquitoes.*

pe·so (pā′sō) ▶See Appendix.

pes·si·mist (pes′ə mist) *n* a person who sees mostly difficulties and disadvantages. The opposite is **optimist.** –**pes′si·mis′tic,** *adj.*

Grasshoppers are pests to wheat farmers, because these insects can eat up a lot of the crop.

pest (pest) *n* any animal or person that causes trouble, injury, or destruction; a nuisance. Flies, grasshoppers, and mosquitoes are pests: *Insect pests destroyed the apple crop in Tillsonburg.*
pes·ter *v* annoy; trouble: *Flies pester us. Don't pester me with foolish questions.* **pes·ti·cide** *n* any chemical used to destroy plant or animal pests.

pet (pet) **1** *n* an animal treated with affection. **2** *v* stroke or pat: *She is petting the kitten.* **pet·ted, pet·ting.**

pet·al (pet′əl) *n* one of the parts of a flower that usually have a colour other than green: *A rose has many petals.*

pe·ti·tion (pə tish′ən) *n* a request to someone in authority: *Our class signed a petition asking the principal to let the students give the morning announcements.*

phan·tom (fan′təm) *n* a shadowy appearance; a ghost.

phar·ma·cy (fär′mə sē) *n* a drugstore. *pl* **phar·ma·cies.**
phar·ma·cist *n* a person who prepares drugs, medicine, etc.

phase (fāz) *n* one of the stages of development of a person or thing: *a baby in the crawling phase.*

phe·nom·e·non (fə nom′ə non′) *n* something or someone extraordinary: *The northern lights are an interesting phenomenon. pl* **phe·nom·e·na** or **phe·nom·e·nons.**
phe·nom·e·nal *adj* extraordinary: *a phenomenal memory.*

phi·lan·thro·pist (fə lan′thrə pist) *n* a person who gives money for or works for charitable organizations.

pho·bi·a (fō′bē ə) *n* an unreasonable, exaggerated fear of a particular thing or situation: *I have a phobia of snakes.*

pho·ny (fō′nē) *Slang.* **1** *adj* not genuine; fake. **2** *n* a fake; pretender.

pho·to·cop·y (fō′tə kop′ē) *n* a copy made by a machine of something written or drawn: *It costs a few cents to make a photocopy at the library.* The machine that does this is called a **photocopier.** *pl* **pho·to·cop·ies.**

pho·to·graph (fō′tə graf′) **1** *n* a picture made with a camera onto a piece of film. It is often shortened to **photo.** **2** *v* take a photograph of. –**pho·tog′ra·phy,** *n.*

pho·tog·ra·pher (fə tog′rə fər) *n* a person whose business is taking photographs.

phrase (frāz) *n* a group of words used as a part of a clause or sentence. In the sentence *He went to the house,* the words *to the house* make a prepositional phrase because they contain a preposition, *to.*

Grammar ✓*Check* **..... phrases**

Phrases can be used in three main ways:

- as adjectives: In the sentence *The girl with the red hair was running,* the phrase *with the red hair* is an adjective describing *girl.*

- as adverbs: In the sentence *The girl was drawing with a pencil,* the phrase *with a pencil* is an adverb describing *was drawing.*

- to modify a whole sentence: *On second thought, I will stay home.* The phrase *on second thought* modifies the meaning of the sentence *I will stay home.*

---

phys·i·cal (fiz′ə kəl) **1** *adj* of your body: *physical exercise, physical strength.* A **physical** is a checkup of your body by a doctor, who is a **physician.** **2** *adj* made of matter; solid: *a physical object.* –**phys′i·cal·ly,** *adv.*

phy·sique (fə zēk′) *n* the body: *That athlete has a muscular physique.*

phys·ics (fiz′iks) *n* the science that deals with matter and energy. Physics includes the study of force, motion, heat, light, sound, and electricity. **phys·i·cist** *n* a person whose work is physics.

A grand piano

pi·an·o (pē an′ō) *n* a large musical instrument with strings that sound when its black and white keys are pressed. *pl* **pi·an·os.** –**pi·an′ist** (pē an′ist *or* pē′ənist), *n.*

A pickaxe being used to break up hard ground

pick (pik) **1** *v* choose; select: *I picked the winning ticket in the raffle.* **2** *v* pull away with your fingers; gather: *We pick fruit or flowers.* **3** *n* sharp-pointed tool: *Ice is broken into pieces with a pick.* –**pick′er,** *n.*

pick·axe *n* a heavy metal tool that is pointed at one or both ends, used for breaking up dirt, rocks, etc. **pick·pock·et** *n* a person who steals from people's pockets. **pick·up** **1** *n* a picking up: *the daily pickup of mail.* **2** *n* a small, light truck with an open back.

pick on, *Informal.* tease: *The bigger boys picked on the new boy during recess.*

pick up, **1** take up: *The boy picked up a stone. Carolyn picked up the chance to make some money by babysitting.* **2** learn without being taught: *She picks up games easily.* **3** go faster: *pick up speed.*

pick·le (pik′əl) **1** *n* a cucumber or other vegetable preserved in salt water or vinegar. **2** *v* preserve in pickle: *Grandmother pickled beets this year.* **3** *n* *Informal.* trouble; difficulty: *I got in a bad pickle today.* **pick·led, pick·ling.**

pic·nic (pik′nik) **1** *n* a meal eaten outdoors, often on a **picnic table. 2** *v* eat in picnic style. **pic·nicked, pic·nick·ing. –pic′nick·er,** *n.*

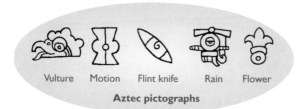

Vulture   Motion   Flint knife   Rain   Flower

Aztec pictographs

pic·ture (pik′chər) **1** *n* a drawing, painting, or photograph: *The yearbook has a good picture of Robin.* **2** *v* form a picture in your mind; imagine: *It is hard to picture life in Canada a hundred years ago.* **pic·tured, pic·tur·ing.**

pic·to·graph (pik′tə graf′) **1** *n* a picture or symbol used to represent a word or idea. **2** *n* a chart with symbols to represent quantities.

pic·to·ri·al (pik tô′rē əl) *adj* having to do with pictures: *A photograph album is a pictorial record.*

pic·tur·esque (pik′chə resk′) **1** *adj* interesting enough to be a picture: *the picturesque old mill in Elora Gorge.* **2** *adj* making a picture for your mind: *picturesque language.*

pie (pī) *n* fruit, meat, etc. put in pastry and baked: *apple pie, chicken pie.*

piece (pēs) **1** *n* one of the parts into which a thing is divided or broken; a bit: *The cup broke in pieces, a piece of bread.* **2** *n* a single work of art: *a piece of music, a piece of poetry.*

a piece of your mind, a scolding: *Glyn's father gave him a piece of his mind for coming late again.*

pier (pēr) *n* a structure built out over water, and used as a walk or a landing place for boats.

pierce (pērs) *v* stab a hole in: *A nail pierced the tire of our car.* **pierced, pierc·ing.**

pierc·ing *adj* penetrating; sharp: *piercing cold, a piercing scream.*

An adult pig—about 200 kg

pig (pig) **1** *n* a farm animal with a long snout with a flat end, a heavy body, and a short thin tail. Pigs are raised for their meat.

2 *n Informal.* a person who is greedy or dirty.

pig·gy·back *n* a carrying or being carried on the back or shoulders: *He gave the child a piggyback across the stream.*

pig-head·ed *adj* stubborn.

pi·geon (pij′ən) *n* a bird with a stout body, a small head, and feathers of various colours.

pi·geon·hole 1 *n* a small place built for a pigeon to nest in. **2** *n* one of a set of boxlike compartments for holding papers.

pile (pīl) **1** *n* many things lying one on top of another: *a pile of wood, a pile of newspapers.* **2** *n* a heap: *a pile of dirt.* **3** *v* make into a pile. **4** *n Informal.* a large amount: *a pile of work, a pile of dishes.*

pil·grim (pil′grəm) *n* a person who goes on a journey to a sacred place: *Many people go as pilgrims to Jerusalem and Mecca.*

pil·grim·age *n* a journey to some sacred place.

pill (pil) *n* medicine made up into a tiny tablet to be swallowed.

pil·lar (pil′ər) *n* a post or column. Pillars are usually made of stone, wood, concrete, or metal to support buildings.

pil·low (pil′ō) *n* a bag or case filled with feathers, or some other soft material, usually to support your head when resting or sleeping.

pi·lot (pī′lət) **1** *n* a person who operates the controls of an aircraft or spacecraft in flight. **2** *n* a person whose business is to steer ships in or out of a harbour.

pim·ple (pim′pəl) *n* a small, inflamed swelling on your skin.

pin (pin) **1** *n* a short, stiff piece of wire with a point at one end, used for fastening things together: *a safety pin.* **2** *n* a badge or brooch with a clasp to fasten it to clothing: *a class pin, a gold pin.* **3** *n* a bottle-shaped piece of wood used in the game of bowling. **4** *v* fasten with a pin. **5** *v* hold fast in one position: *When the tree fell, it pinned his shoulder to the ground.* **pinned, pin·ning.**

pin·point 1 *n* something very small or sharp: *We could see a pinpoint of light through a hole in the blind.* **2** *v* find precisely: *Can you pinpoint your town on the map of Canada?*

pin on, *Informal.* fix blame on: *You can't pin that prank on me, I'm innocent!*

pinch (pinch) **1** *v* squeeze with thumb and forefinger: *Barney pinched his little sister's arm.* **2** *v* get squeezed: *He pinched his finger in the door.* **3** *n* a sharp squeeze that hurts. **4** *n* a small amount: *a pinch of salt.* **5** *v* *Slang.* steal; pilfer: *His father caught him pinching apples.*
pinch-hit *v* in baseball, to bat for another player, especially when a hit is badly needed.
in a pinch, in an emergency.

A pineapple   A branch of pine, with a cone

pine (pīn) *n* an evergreen tree that has cones and needle-shaped leaves.
pine·ap·ple *n* a large, juicy, tropical fruit that looks like a large pine cone.
✾**pin·go** (ping′gō) *n* a cone-shaped hill, usually with ice at its core, found in tundra regions.
pint (pīnt) *n* a non-metric unit of capacity equal to about half a litre.
pi·o·neer (pī′ə nēr′) **1** *n* a person who settles in a region that is not his or her native home and has not been settled before. **2** *v* open up for others: *Astronauts are pioneering space travel.*
pip (pip) *n* the seed of an apple, orange, grape, etc.
pipe (pīp) **1** *n* a tube through which a liquid or gas flows. **2** *n* a tube with a bowl at one end, for smoking tobacco. **3** *n* a musical instrument with a tube into which the player blows. **piped, pip·ing. –pip′er,** *n.*
pipe down, *Slang.* be quiet; shut up.
pi·ra·nha (pə rà′nə) *n* a small freshwater fish of tropical America. Schools of piranha will attack and eat human beings or large animals.
pi·rate (pī′rit) *n* a person who attacks and robs ships at sea. **pi·rat·ed, pi·rat·ing. –pi′ra·cy,** *n.*

pis·til (pis′təl) *n* the seed-bearing part of a flower.
pis·tol (pis′təl) *n* a small, short gun.
pit (pit) **1** *n* a hole dug deep in the earth. **2** *n* the hard seed of a cherry, peach, plum, etc.
pitch (pich) **1** *v* throw; fling; hurl; toss: *She pitched the garbage into the pail.* **2** *v* in baseball, to throw a ball to the person batting. **3** *v* fix firmly in the ground; set up: *to pitch a tent.* **4** *n* the degree of highness or lowness of a sound: *A whistle has a higher pitch than a drum.*
pitch·er 1 *n* the player on a baseball team who pitches the ball to the batter. **2** *n* a container with a lip and a handle: *a juice pitcher.*
pitch·fork *n* a large fork with a long handle for lifting and throwing hay or straw.
pitch in, work hard: *All the neighbours pitched in to get the barn built.*
pit·y (pit′ē) **1** *n* a feeling for the suffering of others. **2** *v* feel pity for: *Mom pitied any child who was hurt. pl* **pit·ies. pit·ied, pit·y·ing. –pit′i·less,** *adj.*
pit·i·a·ble 1 *adj* deserving pity. **2** *adj* deserving scorn: *Her half-hearted apology was pitiable.*
pit·i·ful 1 *adj* causing pity: *The deserted wet puppy was a very pitiful sight.* **2** *adj* deserving scorn: *Driving away after hitting a squirrel is a pitiful act.*
piz·za (pēt′sə) *n* an open pie, usually made of a layer of bread dough covered with a mixture of tomatoes, cheese, olives, etc. and baked.
place (plās) **1** *n* a spot; location: *a good place for a picnic.* **2** *n* someone's home: *We all went to my place after skating.* **3** *n* a rank or position: *We won first place in the contest.* **4** *n* a space for a person: *We took our places at the table.* **5** *v* put in a particular spot: *Place the books on the table.* **placed, plac·ing.**
in place of, instead of: *Use water in place of milk in that recipe.*
take place, happen.
plague (plāg) **1** *n* a very dangerous disease that spreads rapidly and often causes death. **2** *n* a great calamity, misfortune, or evil: *The prairie wheat crop was destroyed by a plague of grasshoppers.* **plagued, pla·guing.**
plaid (plad) *n* a pattern of checks or crisscross stripes.

plain (plān) **1** *adj* clear; easy to understand; easily seen or heard: *The meaning is plain.* **2** *adj* without decoration; not fancy: *a plain dress.* **3** *n* a flat stretch of land; prairie: *the western plains. Cattle wander over the plains of Saskatchewan.*

plan (plan) **1** *n* a way of doing something that has been worked out beforehand: *Our plans to go to New Brunswick were upset by my brother's illness.* **2** *v* make a plan. **3** *n* a drawing to show how a garden, a floor of a house, etc. is arranged. **planned, plan·ning.**

plane (plān) **1** *n* a flat or level surface. **2** *n* an airplane. **3** *n* a tool for smoothing wood. **planed, plan·ing.**

plan·et (plan'it) *n* one of the heavenly bodies that move around the sun in regular paths. ▶See Appendix.

plan·e·tar·i·um (plan'ə ter'ē əm) *n* a place with an apparatus that shows the movements of the sun, moon, planets, and stars by projecting lights on the inside of a dome.

plank (plangk) *n* a long, flat piece of wood.

plank·ton (plangk'tən) *n* the very small animals and plants that float near the surface of oceans and lakes, providing food for other water animals.

plant (plant) **1** *n* any living thing that is not an animal. Trees, bushes, grass, fungi, and seaweed are all plants. **2** *v* put in the ground to grow: *Farmers plant seeds.* **3** *n* the building, machinery, tools, etc. used in a business: *There is an aluminum plant in Kingston.*

plas·tic (plas'tik) *n* a synthetic substance that can be easily shaped. Some of the most common plastics are vinyl, polyester, and nylon.

plastic surgery surgery that changes your appearance: *He had plastic surgery to straighten his broken nose.*

plate (plāt) **1** *n* a dish, usually round, that is almost flat: *Our food is served on plates.* **2** *v* cover with a thin layer of silver, gold, or some other metal: *Those earrings are plated with silver.* **3** *n* a thin, flat piece: *Some dinosaurs had skin made of bony plates.* **4** *n* in baseball, the home base. **plat·ed, plat·ing.**

pla·teau (plə tō') *n* a large, high plain. *pl* **pla·teaus.**

plat·form (plat'fòrm) *n* a raised, level surface: *There is a platform beside the track at the railway station. The hall has a platform for speakers.*

Platypus—about 50 cm long with the tail

plat·y·pus (plat'ə pəs) *n* a small egg-laying water mammal of Australia. It has a snout like a duck's bill, four webbed feet, and a flat tail. *pl* **plat·y·pus·es** or **plat·y·pi** (plat'ə pī').

play (plā) **1** *n* fun; sport; something done to amuse yourself: *The children are happy at play.* **2** *v* have fun; do something in sport; perform: *The kitten plays with its tail. Simon played a joke on his sister.* **3** *n* a story acted on stage: *I'm hoping to get a part in our class play.* **4** *v* act the part of: *Jason played the hero in the story.* **5** *v* make music; produce music on an instrument: *to play a tune, to play a piano.* **play·er 1** *n* a person who plays: *a baseball player, a chess player.* **2** *n* a device that plays: *a CD player.* **play·ful** *adj* fond of playing. **play·ground** *n* a place for outdoor play. **play·off 1** *n* an extra game played to settle a tie. **2** *n* **playoffs,** a series of games to decide a championship. **play·wright** (plā'rīt') *n* a writer of plays. **play into the hands of,** give the advantage to. **play up to,** *Slang.* try to get the favour of; flatter: *to play up to a famous person.*

WORD HISTORY . . . . playwright

In **playwright**, *wright* is not related to *write*, but is an old English word meaning "maker" or "builder." We still use *wright* in this way in words like *millwright, wheelwright,* and *shipwright.*

---

pla·za (plaz'ə *or* plä'zə) **1** *n* a shopping centre. **2** *n* a public square in a city or town.

plea (plē) *n* a request: *The people of the flooded Red River area made a plea for help.*

plead (plēd) *v* ask in a begging way: *I pleaded with my Dad, but he wouldn't let me stay up late.* **plead·ed, plead·ing.**

P
p

please (plēz) **1** *v* give enjoyment to: *Toys please children. Sunshine pleases most people.* **2** *v* wish; think fit: *Do what you please.* **3** *v* **Please,** is used for politeness in asking a person to do something: *Come here, please.* **pleased, pleas·ing.**
pleas·ant (plez′ənt) **1** *adj* giving pleasure. **2** *adj* friendly. **pleas·ure** (plezh′ər) **1** *n* the feeling of being pleased: *The child's pleasure in the gift was good to see.* **2** *n* something that pleases: *It would be a pleasure to visit the Yukon Territory again.*

pledge (plej) **1** *n* a solemn promise: *Mr. Medappa signed a pledge to give money to charity.* **2** *v* to promise solemnly: *Jack and Stavros pledged to be friends forever.* **pledged, pledg·ing.**

plen·ty (plen′tē) *n* a full supply: *You have plenty of time to catch the train to Gananoque.* –**plen′ti·ful,** *adj.*

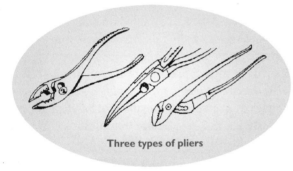
Three types of pliers

pli·ers (plī′ərz) *sing* or *pl.n* a hinged tool for bending or cutting wire, for holding small objects, etc.

plod (plod) *v* walk heavily and slowly: *We plodded up the hill.* **plod·ded, plod·ding.**

plop (plop) **1** *n* a sound like that of a flat stone hitting water without a splash. **2** *v* drop heavily: *The dog plopped itself down on the rug.*

plot (plot) **1** *n* a secret plan, especially to do something wrong: *They formed a plot to steal a car.* **2** *v* to plan secretly with others. **3** *n* the plan or main story of a play, novel, poem, etc.: *I like plots dealing with adventure and mystery.* **4** *n* a small piece of ground: *a garden plot.* **plot·ted, plot·ting.**

plough (plou) **1** *n* a farm device used for cutting the soil and turning it over. **2** *n* a machine for clearing snow, usually called a snowplough. Another spelling is **plow. 3** *v* use a plough: *to plough a field.*

pluck (pluk) **1** *v* pull at: *She plucked the strings of her guitar.* **2** *v* pull the feathers out of: *The farmer was busy plucking chickens.*

plug (plug) **1** *n* something used to stop up a hole: *a bath plug.* **2** *n* a device to make an electrical connection. **3** *v* stop up or fill with a plug. **3** *v* *Informal.* work steadily: *She plugged away at her report.* **plugged, plug·ging.**

plumb·er (plum′ər) *n* a person whose work is putting in and repairing water pipes and fixtures: *When the water pipe froze, we sent for a plumber.*

plump (plump) *adj* rounded out: *A healthy baby has plump cheeks.*

plun·der (plun′dər) **1** *v* rob by force: *The pirates entered the harbour and began to plunder the town.* **2** *n* things stolen: *The pirates buried their plunder in a secret place.*

plunge (plunj) **1** *v* throw or thrust with force into something, especially a liquid: *to plunge one's hand into water, to plunge into a lake.* **2** *n* a sudden rush or jump. **plunged, plung·ing.**

plu·ral (plū′rəl *or* plər′əl) *adj* more than one: *The plural form of* child *is* children.

Grammar ✓ *Check* ...... **plural**

Plural nouns are usually formed by adding *-s* to a singular noun: *house* becomes *houses*; *ray* becomes *rays*; *cat* becomes *cats*.

However, there are many exceptions to this rule. Here are some:

- If the word ends in **s**, **sh**, **ch**, **x**, or **z**, add *-es*: *watches, foxes.*
- If the noun ends in a **consonant plus -y**, change the *-y* to *-i* and add *-es*: *ponies, candies.*

---

plus (plus) **1** *prep* added to: *Three plus two equals five.* **2** *adj* higher than: *His mark was B plus.* **3** *n* the sign (+) meaning that a quantity is to be added. **4** *prep* something extra: *The movie was good, and the free pass was a plus.*

p.m. *abbreviation for* the time from noon to midnight: *Her birthday party lasted till 8 p.m.*

pock·et (pok′it) *n* a small bag sewn into clothing, used for carrying small things.

pod (pod) *n* the shell in which plants like beans and peas grow their seeds.

po·em (pō′əm) *n* a piece of writing in which the words are arranged in lines that have rhythm and often rhyme.

po·et *n* a person who writes poems.

po·et·ic (pō et′ik) *adj* showing imaginative language: *She wrote a poetic description of the sky, calling the clouds big white ships on a blue lake.*

po·et·ry *n* poems.

point (point) **1** *n* a sharp end: *the point of a pencil.* **2** *n* a dot; a punctuation mark. **3** *n* a particular place or time: *She drew a circle around a point on the map of New Brunswick. At that point he lost interest in the game.* **4** *n* the main idea: *I did not get the point of his argument.* **5** *v* aim: *Don't point your finger at me.* **6** *v* show direction: *The sign points north.* **7** *n* a unit of scoring in a game: *Our basketball team needed two points to win the game.*

point of view, an opinion: *Farmers and campers have different points of view about rain.*

beside the point, having nothing to do with the main idea.

point out, call attention to: *Please point out my mistakes.*

Poison ivy has leaves grouped in threes, and white berries.

poi·son (poi′zən) **1** *n* a drug or other substance very dangerous to health and capable of causing death. **2** *v* kill or harm by poison: *He poisoned the heroine of the story.* —**poi′son·ous,** *adj.*

poison ivy a plant that looks like ivy and causes a painful rash on most people if they touch it.

poke (pōk) **1** *v* push against with something pointed: *to poke a person in the ribs, to poke a fire.* **2** *v* push through: *Spencer poked his head in the kitchen window.* **3** *v* Informal. punch: *He threatened to poke his brother in the nose.* **poked, pok·ing.**

poke fun at, tease.

poke your nose into, interfere.

🌿 poke·lo·gan (pōk′lō′gən) *n* a small stagnant backwater in a stream.

A polar bear— about 2.5 m long excluding the tail

po·lar (pō′lər) *adj* having to do with the North or South Pole: *It is very cold in the polar regions.*

polar bear a large, white bear living in the Arctic.

pole (pōl) **1** *n* a long, slender piece of wood, metal, etc.: *a telephone pole, a flagpole, a ski pole.* **2** *n* either end of the earth's axis. The North Pole and the South Pole are opposite each other. **3** *n* either of two parts where opposite forces are strongest. A magnet or a battery has both a positive pole and a negative pole.

po·lice (pə lēs′) *n* the department of government whose duty is to keep law and order.

police officer a member of a police force.

pol·ish (pol′ish) **1** *v* make smooth and shiny: *to polish shoes.* **2** *n* a substance used to give smoothness or shine: *silver polish.*

po·lite (pə līt′) *adj* showing good manners: *The polite boy gave the girl his seat on the bus.* —**po·lite′ness,** *n.*

pol·i·tics (pol′ə tiks′) *sing* or *pl.n* the management of public affairs: *Mackenzie King was engaged in politics for many years.* —**po·lit′i·cal** (pə lit′ə kəl), *adj,* —**pol′i·ti′cian** (pol′ə tish′ən), *n.*

poll (pōl) **1** *n* a collection of votes: *The class had a poll to decide where it would have its picnic.* **2** *v* take or register the votes of.

pol·len (pol′ən) *n* the fine, yellowish powder in flowers.

pol·li·nate *v* carry pollen from flower to flower. **pol·li·nat·ed, pol·li·nat·ing.** —**pol′li·na′tion,** *n.*

pol·lute (pə lūt′) *v* make dirty; defile: *The lake was polluted by waste from the town.* **pol·lut·ed, pol·lut·ing.** —**pol·lu′tion** (pə lū′shən), *n.*

pol·lu·tant *n* a substance that makes the air, water, or soil unhealthy to breathe, drink, or use: *They did some tests and found that the drinking water was full of pollutants.*

pol·y·gon (pol′i gon′) *n* in geometry, a closed figure with three or more angles and straight sides. ▶See Appendix.

pond (pond) *n* a body of still water, smaller than a lake: *a duck pond.*

po·ny (pō′nē) *n* a small horse. *pl* **po·nies.**

pool (pūl) **1** *n* a small pond. **2** *n* a tank of water to swim in. **3** *n* a puddle of any spilled liquid: *a pool of oil under a car.* **4** *n* a game played on a special **pool table.** The players use long sticks to try to drive balls of various colours into pockets at the edges of the table. **5** *v* put things or money together: *My brothers pooled their savings to buy Mom a present.*

poor (pūr) **1** *adj* not having enough money to live on. **2** *adj* not good: *She is in poor health. The soil in our garden is poor, a poor crop, a poor chance.* –**pov′er·ty,** *n.*

pop (pop) **1** *n* a short, quick, explosive sound: *We heard the pop of a cork.* **2** *v* make such a sound. **3** *v* move suddenly or unexpectedly: *Our neighbour popped in for a short visit.* **4** *n* a fizzy soft drink. **5** *an abbreviation for* popular: *pop song.* **popped, pop·ping.**

pop·corn *n* a kind of corn whose kernels burst open and puff out when heated.

pop·si·cle (pop′sə kəl) *n* a fruit-flavoured ice on a small stick.

pop·u·la·tion (pop′yə lā′shən) **1** *n* the people of a city, country, or district. **2** *n* the number of people: *The population of Saskatchewan is about one million.*

pop·u·lar (pop′yə ler) *adj* liked by many people: *He is the most popular boy in the class.* –**pop·u·lar′i·ty** (pop′yə lar′ə tē *or* pop′yə ler′ə tē), *n.*
pop·u·lous *adj* full of people: *Southern Ontario is one of Canada's most populous regions.*

The porch on the front of Alexander Graham Bell's house in Brantford, Ontario

porch (pôrch) *n* a covered entrance to a building: *Our house has a big porch.*

A North American porcupine—about 90 cm long including the tail

por·cu·pine (pôr′kyə pīn′) *n* a large slow-moving rodent with sharp spines on its back and tail.

pore (pôr) **1** *v* study: *He would rather pore over a book than play with friends.* **2** *n* a very tiny opening. Sweat comes through the pores in our skin. **pored, por·ing.**

pork (pôrk) *n* the meat from a pig.

po·rous (pô′rəs) *adj* full of pores. Clay flowerpots are porous.

port (pôrt) **1** *n* a harbour. **2** *n* a town or city with a harbour: *Vancouver is an important Canadian port.* **3** *n* the left side of a ship or aircraft when you face the front. The right side is called **starboard.**

port·a·ble (pôr′tə bəl) **1** *adj* capable of being moved easily: *a portable TV.* **2** *n* a temporary building used as an extra classroom.

por·tage (pôr tàzh′) **1** *n* the act of carrying canoes, boats, food, etc. overland from one stretch of water to another: *We found the last portage the most difficult.* **2** *v* carry canoes, etc. from one stretch of water to another: *We had to portage five times during the trip through Yoho National Park.* **por·taged, por·tag·ing.**

port·fo·li·o (pôrt fō′lē ō′) *n* samples of work by an artist or student: *Miss Riddell and I chose some of my drawings and one story to put in my portfolio.*

por·tion (pôr′shən) *n* a part; helping: *A portion of each school day is set aside for arithmetic. My mother serves large portions of food.*

por·tray (pôr trā′) **1** *v* describe or picture in words: *The book* Black Beauty *portrays the life of a horse.* **2** *v* make a picture of. **3** *v* represent in a play or movie; act.

por·trait (pôr′trit *or* pôr′trāt) *n* a picture of a person, especially of the face.

pose (pōz) **1** *n* a position of the body: *That photo shows her in an attractive pose.* **2** *v* hold a position: *He posed for an hour for his portrait.* **3** *v* pretend: *He posed as a rich man though he wasn't.* **4** *v* put forward: *to pose a question.* **posed, pos·ing.**

po·si·tion (pə zish'ən) **1** *n* a place where a thing or person is: *I didn't like the position of my chair, so I moved it.* **2** *n* a way of being placed: *a comfortable position.* **3** *n* a job: *He has a position in a bank.* **4** *n* the place held by a player on a team: *My position on the hockey team was defence.*

pos·i·tive (poz'ə tiv) **1** *adj* absolutely sure: *We are positive that the earth moves around the sun.* **2** *adj* helpful: *Don't just make a negative criticism; give us some positive suggestions.* –**posi'tive·ly,** *adv.*

Grammar ✓*Check* ..... **positive**

Adjectives and adverbs can be written in three forms:

- **positive** (*strong, strongly*), used for regular descriptions:
  She is a strong swimmer. She swims strongly.

- **comparative** (*stronger, more strongly*), used to compare two things:
  She is the stronger of the two swimmers. She swims more strongly than he does.

- **superlative** (*strongest, most strongly*), used for more than two things:
  She is the strongest of all the swimmers. Of the whole team, she swims most strongly.

---

pos·sess (pə zes') **1** *v* own: *I don't possess a watch.* **2** *v* control; influence strongly: *What possessed you to take such a risk?*

pos·ses·sion *n* something possessed; property: *Please move your possessions out of your locker.*

pos·ses·sive 1 *adj* having a strong desire to own things: *That child has a possessive nature.* **2** *adj* in grammar, having to do with the form of a noun or pronoun that shows that it refers to the owner of something. *My is the possessive form of I in my books. Bird's is the possessive form of bird in a bird's wing.* ▶See Appendix.

Grammar ✓*Check* ... **possessives**

To make a singular noun **possessive**, add *'s*: *A dog's coat should be shiny.* If the noun is plural and already ends in -s, add just an apostrophe ('): *Dogs' teeth can be sharp.*

---

pos·si·ble (pos'ə bəl) **1** *adj* that can be; that can be done; that can happen: *It is now possible to land on the moon.* **2** *adj* that can be true or a fact: *It is possible that he left early.*

pos·si·bil·i·ty (pos'ə bil'ə tē) *n* being possible: *There is a possibility that the bus will be late.*

pos·si·bly 1 *adv* no matter what happens: *I can't possibly go.* **2** *adv* perhaps: *Possibly you are right.*

post (pōst) **1** *n* a length of timber, iron, etc. firmly set up, usually to support something else: *a signpost, a gatepost.* **2** *v* fasten a notice up: *The list of winners will be posted soon.* **3** *n* a trading station. **4** *n* a system for sending letters, packages, etc.: *I shall send it by post.* **5** *v* send by mail: *to post a letter.*

post·age *n* the amount paid to send something by mail. **postal code** ❦ a system of letters and numerals that describes a particular place: *The postal code of Ladysmith, B.C. is V0R 2E0.*

post·card *n* a card for sending a message by mail. Most postcards have a picture on one side.

post office a place where mail is handled and postage stamps are sold.

post– *a prefix meaning* after, as in *postpone.*

post·er (pōs'tər) *n* a large advertisement or notice, often with a picture, put up on a wall.

post·pone (pōst pōn') *v* put off till later: *The ball game was postponed because of rain.* **post·poned, post·pon·ing.**

pos·ture (pos'chər) *n* the position of your body: *Good posture is important to health.*

pot (pot) *n* a deep container: *a cooking pot, a flower pot, a coffee pot.*

po·ta·to (pə tā'tō) *n* a round, hard vegetable with a thin brown skin. *pl* **po·ta·toes.**

potato chip a thin slice of potato, fried or baked until crisp.

po·tion (pō'shən) *n* a drink, especially one that is used as a medicine or poison.

❦ **pot·latch** (pot'lach) *n* a ceremony or celebration of various First Nations peoples of the West Coast, where the host gave gifts to the guests. Among the Haida, the potlatch was a way to mark special events such as the birth, marriage, or death of an important person, the raising of a new building or totem pole, and so on. It included singing, dancing, storytelling, feasting, and speeches as well as gift-giving.

Pottery. The drawing at the left shows a vase being formed by hand on a potter's wheel.

pot·ter·y (pot'ə rē) *n* pots, dishes, vases, etc. made from clay and hardened by heat. *pl* **pot·ter·ies.** –**pot'ter,** *n.*

pouch (pouch) *n* a bag or sack: *a mail carrier's pouch.*

poul·try (pōl'trē) *n* birds raised for their meat or eggs, such as chickens, turkeys, ducks, and geese.

pounce (pouns) *v* come down with a rush onto something: *The cat pounced on the mouse.* **pounced, pounc·ing.**

pound (pound) **1** *n* a non-metric unit for mass, equal to about half a kilogram. **2** *n* an enclosed place in which to keep stray animals. **3** *v* hit hard again and again; beat hard: *He pounded the door with his fist. After a hard run your heart pounds.* **4** *v* crush to powder: *to pound cement into dust.*

pour (pȯr) **1** *v* cause to flow: *I poured the milk into the cups.* **2** *v* flow: *The crowd poured out of the arena.*

pow·der (pou'dər) **1** *n* a solid reduced to dust by pounding, crushing, drying, etc.: *talcum powder.* **2** *v* sprinkle: *The ground was lightly powdered with snow.*

pow·er (pou'ər) **1** *n* strength: *Bulldozers have great power.* **2** *n* authority: *Parliament has power to make new laws.* **3** *n* energy that can do work: *gas power, electric power.* **4** *v* provide with power: *a snowmobile is powered by gas.* –**pow'er·ful,** *adj,* –**pow'er·less,** *adj.* **in power,** having control or authority: *the government in power.*

pow·wow (pou'wou') *n* a gathering of First Nations people for celebration, with dancing, singing, and other social activities.

prac·tice (prak'tis) *n* something done many times to become good at it: *hockey practice, piano practice.*

prac·ti·cal (prak'tə kəl) **1** *adj* able to be put into practice: *a practical plan.* **2** *adj* having good sense: *Practical people are not the kind of people who spend their time and money foolishly.*

prac·ti·cal·ly (prak'ti klē) **1** *adv* really: *She practically runs the whole factory.* **2** *adv Informal.* nearly: *We are practically home.*

prac·tise (prak'tis) *v* do something again and again so as to learn to do it well: *She practised her piano lesson until she could play it perfectly.* **prac·tised, prac·tis·ing.**

CONFUSABLES … practice

practice is a noun:
I have a hockey practice after school.

practise is a verb:
I will practise my trumpet solo until I get it right.

prai·rie (prer'ē) **1** *n* a large area of level or rolling land with grass but few or no trees. **2 the Prairies,** *pl.n* the great, almost treeless plain that covers much of central and southern Manitoba, Saskatchewan, and Alberta.

praise (prāz) **1** *n* saying that a thing or person is good: *When he won the race, his friends heaped praise upon him.* **2** *v* express approval of: *Everyone praised the winning team for its fine play.* **praised, prais·ing.**

prance (prans) **1** *v* spring about on the hind legs. Horses prance when they feel lively. **2** *v* move in a lively way: *The children pranced about in their new Halloween costumes.* **pranced, pranc·ing.**

prank (prangk) *n* a playful trick: *On April Fool's Day people play pranks on each other.*

prat·tle (prat'əl) *v* talk in a foolish way. **prat·tled, prat·tling.**

pray (prā) *v* speak in a worshipful way. **prayer** (prer) *n* words used in praying.

CONFUSABLES ….. pray

pray means "ask God":
We can only pray they get back safely.

prey means "victim":
The lion tracked its prey for days.

pre– *a prefix meaning* before, *as in* prehistoric.

preach (prēch) **1** *v* speak on a religious subject. **2** *v* give advice, especially in an annoying way: *My uncle is forever preaching about getting lots of exercise.*

pre·cau·tion (pri kosh′ən) *n* care taken beforehand: *Locking doors is a precaution against thieves.*

pre·cede (prē sēd′) *v* go before; come before: *A band preceded the first float in the Canada Day parade.* **pre·ced·ed, pre·ced·ing.**

pre·ced·ing *adj* going before; previous: *Look at the preceding page.*

pre·cious (presh′əs) *adj* very valuable. Gold and silver are often called the precious metals.

pre·cip·i·ta·tion (pri sip′ə tā′shən) *n* rain or snow: *There were 45 centimetres of precipitation in Edmonton last year.*

pre·cise (pri sīs′) *adj* exact: *The precise distance was 1.73 km.* **–pre·cise′ly,** *adv.*

pre·co·cious (pri kō′shəs) *adj* developed earlier than usual: *This precocious child could read well at the age of four.*

pred·a·tor (pred′ə tər) *n* an animal that lives by hunting and killing other animals for food: *Lions and hawks are predators.* **–pred′a·to·ry,** *adj.*

pre·dic·a·ment (pri dik′ə mənt) *n* an unpleasant, difficult, or dangerous situation: *She was in a predicament when she missed the last train to Penticton.*

pre·dict (pri dikt′) *v* tell beforehand; prophesy: *The weather channel predicts rain for tomorrow.* **–pre·dic′tion,** *n.*

pref·ace (pref′is) *n* an introduction to a book.

pre·fer (pri fər′) *v* like better; choose rather: *She prefers dogs to cats.* **pre·ferred, pre·fer·ring.** **–pref′er·ence** (pref′ə rəns), *n.*

pref·er·a·ble (pref′ə rə bəl) *adj* more desirable: *She decided that going out was preferable to staying home.* **pref·er·a·bly** (pref′ə rə blē) *adv* by choice: *She wants a bike, preferably a dirt bike.*

pre·fix (prē′fiks) *n* a syllable word put at the beginning of a word to change its meaning or make another word, as in *pre*historic, *un*like. ▶See the *Grammar and Usage Mini-Guide.*

preg·nant (preg′nənt) *adj* soon to give birth.

pre·his·tor·ic (prē′his tô′rik) *adj* belonging to times before histories were written: *Fossils give us information about prehistoric animals.*

prej·u·dice (prej′ə dis) *n* a strong opinion about something, formed unfairly or without knowing the facts. **–prej′u·diced,** *adj.*

pre·ma·ture (prē′mə chūr′ *or* prem′ə chūr′) *adj* before the proper time: *His premature arrival spoiled our plan to surprise him.*

❧ pre·mier (prē′myər) *n* in Canada, a prime minister of a province.

pre·pare (pri per′) *v* make ready; get ready: *She does her homework while her father prepares supper.* **pre·pared, pre·par·ing.** **–prep·a·ra′tion,** *n.*

prep·o·si·tion (prep′ə zish′ən) *n* a type of word that is used to show relationships of position, direction, time, etc. between the other words in the sentence. In the sentence *The man with the ice cream for sale stands at the corner in the afternoon,* the words *with, for, at,* and *in* are prepositions.

pre·scribe (pri skrīb′) *v* order medicine. **pre·scribed, pre·scrib·ing.** **–pre·scrip′tion** (pri skrip′shən), *n.*

pres·ent (prez′ənt *for 1-4,* pri zent′ *for 5 and 6*) **1** *adj* being in the proper place: *Every member of the class was present.* **2** *adj* at this time: *the present premier.* **3** *n* now: *That is enough for the present.* **4** *n* a gift; something given: *a birthday present.* **5** *v* give: *They presented flowers to their teacher.* **6** *v* perform: *Our class presented a play.*

pres·ence (prez′əns) *n* being present in a place.

pres·en·ta·tion (prez′ən tā′shən) *n* giving or delivering: *the presentation of a gift or a speech.*

present tense in grammar, a verb tense that expresses an action that is happening or a condition that exists now. In the sentence *I am at school,* the verb *am* is in the present tense.

presence of mind, ability to think quickly when taken by surprise.

pre·serve (pri zərv′) **1** *v* keep from harm or change; keep safe. **2** *v* prepare food to keep it from spoiling. Boiling with sugar, salting, smoking, and pickling are different ways of preserving food. **3** *n* a place where wild animals, fish, or plants are protected. **pre·served, pre·serv·ing.** **–pres·er·va′tion,** *n.*

pre·side (pri zīd′) *v* hold the place of authority: *The mayor of Toronto presides over all council meetings.* **pre·sid·ed, pre·sid·ing.**

pres·i·dent (prez′ə dənt) **1** *n* the chief officer of a company, college, society, club, etc. **2** *n* Often, **President,** the highest officer of a republic.

press (pres) **1** *v* push steadily: *Press the elevator button. Press all the juice from the orange.* **2** *v* make smooth: *You press clothes with an iron.* **3** *n* a machine for pressing: *a printing press.* **4** *n* newspapers, magazines, and the people who work for them: *The results of the Kanata Music Festival were reported by the press.*

pres·sure (presh′ər) *n* a pushing force.

pre·tend (pri tend′) **1** *v* make believe: *Let's pretend that we are pilots.* **2** *v* claim falsely: *She pretends to like you, but talks about you behind your back.* **–pre·tence′** (pri tens′ or prē′tens), *n*.

pret·ty (prit′ē) **1** *adj* attractive: *a pretty face, a pretty tune.* **2** *adv* fairly: *It is pretty late.* **pret·ti·er, pret·ti·est.**

pre·vent (pri vent′) **1** *v* keep from: *Illness prevented him from doing his work.* **2** *v* keep from happening: *Rain prevented the golf tournament.*

pre·view (prē′vyū′) *n* an advance view: *a preview of a movie.*

pre·vi·ous (prē′vē əs) *adj* the one before; earlier: *She did better in the previous competition.* **–pre′vi·ous·ly,** *adv*.

prey (prā) *n* an animal hunted for food: *Mice and birds are the prey of cats.*

prey on, hunt and kill for food: *Cats prey on mice.*

price (prīs) *n* the amount for which a thing is sold: *The price of this CD is $9.99.*

price·less *adj* beyond price; very valuable: *priceless paintings by the Group of Seven.*

prick (prik) **1** *n* a little hole made by a sharp point. **2** *v* make such a hole: *I pricked my thumb with a safety pin!*

prick·le *v* feel a tingle: *Her skin prickled when she saw the spider.* **prick·led, prick·ling.**

prick·ly **1** *adj* with many sharp points: *a prickly rosebush, a prickly porcupine.* **2** *adj* sharp and stinging: *a prickly feeling.*

prick up your ears, listen carefully.

pride (prīd) **1** *n* a good opinion of yourself: *to take pride in having done well.* **2** *n* too high an opinion of yourself: *Even though she had made a mistake, her pride kept her from admitting it.*

priest (prēst) *n* a person authorized to perform religious ceremonies.

pri·ma·ry (prī′mer′ē or prī′mə rē) *adj* first in time; first in order; first in importance: *Children go to primary school before they go to secondary school. The primary reason for this phone call is to invite you to my party.*

primary colour one of three colours that can be mixed to make any other colour. In painting, the primary colours are red, yellow, and blue.

primary stress the strongest stress in the pronunciation of a word. In the word *tel′e·phone′* there is primary stress on the first syllable *tel* and secondary stress on the third syllable *phone*.

prime (prīm) **1** *adj* first in importance. **2** *adj* first in quality: *prime Alberta beef.*

prime minister the chief minister in some governments. The prime minister of Canada is the first minister of the Federal Government.

prime number a number not exactly divisible by any whole number other than itself and 1. The numbers 2, 3, 5, 7, and 11 are prime numbers; 4, 6, and 9 are not prime numbers.

prince (prins) *n* a high-ranking male member of a royal family.

prin·cess (prin′ses) *n* a high-ranking female member of a royal family.

prin·ci·pal (prin′sə pəl) **1** *adj* most important: *Yellowknife is the principal city of the Northwest Territories.* **2** *n* the chief person, such as the head of a school.

CONFUSABLES ... principal

principal means "first in importance": "*The principal reason for your good marks is that you studied hard,*" said the principal of the school.

principle means "fact": *The principle of gravity explains why we fall down instead of up.*

prin·ci·ple (prin′sə pəl) **1** *n* a fact or belief on which other ideas are based: *Science is based on the principle that things can be explained.* **2** *n* a rule of conduct: *I make it a principle to save some money each week.*

Making a print

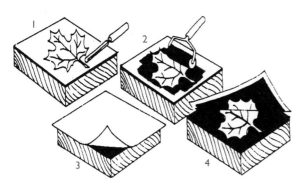

1. A design is cut into a block.
2. Ink is applied to the raised parts left in the block.
3. A sheet of paper is pressed onto the inked block.
4. When the paper is pulled off, it shows the block design in reverse.

print (print) **1** *v* make words, pictures, etc. on paper, using a printing machine: *to print a book, to print a computer document.* **2** *n* words, letters, etc. reproduced in ink by type: *This book has clear print.* **3** *v* make letters the way they look in print instead of in writing: *Print your name clearly.* **4** *n* cloth with a pattern in it: *a print dress.* **5** *n* a mark made by pressing or stamping: *He saw prints of an otter's feet in the sand.*

print·out (prin'tout') *n* the output of a computer, printed by the **printer** connected to the computer.

in print, of books, etc., still available from the publisher.

out of print, no longer sold by the publisher.

pris·on (priz'ən) *n* a building in which criminals are kept. –**pris'on·er** (priz'ə nər), *n*.

pri·vate (prī'vit) **1** *adj* not public; personal: *my private opinion.* **2** *adj* secret: *I hide my diary because it's private.* –**pri'va·cy,** *n*, –**pri'vate·ly,** *adv*.

in private, 1 not publicly: *My father spoke to the principal in private.* **2** secretly: *The children met in private to plan a surprise birthday party for their mother.*

priv·i·lege (priv'ə lij) *n* a special right or favour: *Our father has given us the privilege of using his power tools.*

prize (prīz) *n* a reward won or offered in a competition: *I won a prize for my project at the Science Fair.*

prob·a·ble (prob'ə bəl) **1** *adj* likely to happen: *Cooler weather is probable after this shower.* **2** *adj* likely to be true: *Something he ate is the probable cause of his pain.*

prob·a·bil·i·ty (prob'ə bil'ə tē) *n* chance: *There is a good probability of rain in Burnaby today.*

prob·a·bly *adv* more likely than not.

prob·lem (prob'ləm) *n* a question, especially a difficult question.

pro·ceed (prə sēd') *v* go on: *Please proceed with your story. The train proceeded to Timmins at the same speed as before.*

pro·ce·dure (prə sē'jər) *n* a method for doing things: *What is the procedure for playing this computer game?* **pro·cess** (prō'ses *or* pros'es) *n* a set of actions in a special order: *By what process is wool made into cloth?* **pro·ces·sion 1** *n* persons marching or riding: *A wedding procession drove noisily along the street.* **2** *n* an orderly moving forward: *We formed lines to march in procession onto the platform.*

pro·claim (prə klām') *v* make known publicly and officially: *The government proclaimed that July 1 would be called Canada Day.* –**proc'la·ma'tion** (prok'lə mā'shən), *n*.

prod·i·gy (prod'ə jē) *n* a marvel; a wonder: *An infant prodigy is a child remarkably brilliant in some way.* **pl prod·i·gies.**

pro·duce (prə dyūs' *or* prə dūs' *for 1 and 2,* prod'yūs *or* prō'dūs *for 3)* **1** *v* make; manufacture: *This factory produces bicycles.* **2** *v* show: *Produce your student card when you buy tickets.* **3** *n* fruit and vegetables: *She owns a produce market.* **pro·duced, pro·duc·ing.**

prod·uct (prod'əkt) **1** *n* a result of work or of growth: *factory products, farm products.* **2** *n* the result of multiplying two or more numbers together: *The product of 5 and 8 is 40.*

pro·duc·tion (prə duk'shən) *n* the act of producing: *Their business is the production of computers and printers.*

pro·fes·sion (prə fesh'ən) *n* an occupation requiring special education, such as law, medicine, or teaching.

pro·fes·sion·al 1 *adj* having to do with a profession: *professional qualifications.* **2** *adj* making a business of something that others do for pleasure: *a professional baseball player, professional musicians.*

pro·file (prō′fīl) *n* a side view, especially of a person's face.

prof·it (prof′it) *n* money gained: *If we spend $5 making cookies, we can sell them for $8 and make $3 profit.*

pro·gram (prō′gram) **1** *n* a written list of events: *a concert program, a theatre program, a hockey program.* **2** *n* a performance, especially a radio or television show. **3** *n* a set of instructions in computer language. **4** *v* enter in a program: *I programmed our VCR to tape the hockey game.* **programmed, programming.** Another spelling for **program** is **programme.**

pro·gress (prō′gres *or* prog′res) **1** *n* improvement: *Kolya's writing showed excellent progress.* **2** *n* moving forward; going ahead: *to make rapid progress on a journey.*

pro·hib·it (prō hib′it) *v* forbid by law: *Picking flowers in the park is prohibited.*

This piece of land **projects** into the ocean.

pro·ject (prō′jekt *or* proj′ekt *for 1,* prə jekt′ *for 2, 3, and 4*) **1** *n* an undertaking; activity: *Michel is busy with several projects.* **2** *v* throw forward: *A catapult projects stones.* **3** *v* cause to fall on a surface: *Movies are projected on the screen. The tree projects a shadow on the grass.* **4** *v* stick out: *The rocky point projects far into the water.*

pro·jec·tile (prə jek′tīl *or* prə jek′təl) *n* any object that is thrown with force, such as a rocket, stone, or bullet.

pro·jec·tion (prə jek′shən) *n* a part that sticks out: *rocky projections on the face of a cliff.*

prom·ise (prom′is) **1** *n* the words that say a person will do or not do something: *A person of honour always keeps a promise.* **2** *v* make a promise: *She promised to meet us in Rankin Inlet.* **3** *n* hope of success: *This pupil shows promise in music.* **prom·ised, prom·is·ing.**

prom·is·ing *adj* likely to turn out well: *a promising student.*

pro·mote (prə mōt′) **1** *v* raise in importance: *My mother has been promoted to store manager.* **2** *v* help to success: *TV ads promote new products.* **pro·mot·ed, pro·mot·ing. –pro·mo′tion,** *n.*

prompt (prompt) **1** *adj* on time: *Be prompt to class.* **2** *adj* done at once: *I expect a prompt answer.*

prone (prōn) **1** *adj* inclined: *We are prone to think evil of people we don't like.* **2** *adj* lying face down: *He is prone on his bed.*

prong (prong) *n* one of the pointed ends of a fork, antler, etc.

pro·noun (prō′noun) *n* a type of word that is used instead of a noun to refer to the noun without naming it. In the sentence *Marlo smiled because she was happy,* the pronoun *she* is used to refer to *Marlo* without repeating her name. Other examples of pronouns are: *it, I, yours, what, these, either.*

pro·nounce (prə nouns′) **1** *v* make the sounds of: *Pronounce your words clearly.* **2** *v* declare: *The doctor pronounced her cured.* **pro·nounced, pro·nounc·ing.**

pro·nun·ci·a·tion (prə nun′sē ā′shən) *n* the way of sounding words: *Most dictionaries give the pronunciation of each entry word.*

proof (prūf) *n* a way of showing the truth: *Is what you say a guess or do you have proof?*

proof·read (prū′frēd′) *v* read very carefully, looking for mistakes. **Proofread** is often shortened to **proof. proof·read, proof·read·ing.**

prop (prop) **1** *v* hold up by placing a support under or against. **2** *n* a support: *Many branches are heavy with apples and need a prop.* **propped, prop·ping.**

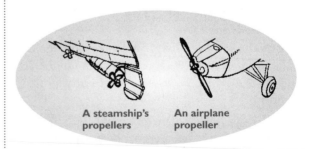

A steamship's **propellers**   An airplane **propeller**

pro·pel (prə pel′) *v* drive forward: *to propel a boat by oars.* **pro·pelled, pro·pel·ling.**

pro·pel·ler *n* a device with turning blades, for propelling boats and aircraft.

prop·er (prop'ər) *adj* correct: *Night is the proper time to sleep.* –**prop'er·ly,** *adv.*

proper noun a noun naming a particular person, place, or thing. *David, Winnipeg,* and *Monday* are proper nouns. *Boy, city,* and *day* are common nouns.

> **Grammar ✓Check.. proper noun**
> Use a capital letter at the beginning of a **proper noun**: the Peace Tower, Mr. Bart Simpson, Lassie.

prop·er·ty (prop'ər tē) **1** *n* any thing owned: *This house is the property of Mr. Drury.* **2** *n* land; buildings, houses, etc.: *He owns some property in Flin Flon.* pl **prop·er·ties.** **3 properties,** *pl.n* the furniture, etc. used in staging a play, motion picture, or television scene. This is often shortened to **props.**

proph·e·sy (prof'ə sī') *v* guess what will happen in the future: *The sailor prophesied a severe storm.* **proph·e·sied, proph·e·sy·ing.**

proph·e·cy (prof'ə sē) *n* something told about the future. pl **proph·e·cies.**

proph·et 1 *n* a person who guesses what will happen in the future. **2** *n* a person who believes his preaching to be inspired by God: *Every religion has its prophets.*

pro·por·tion (prə pôr'shən) **1** *n* the relation of one thing to another in size, number, amount, or degree: *Mix water and orange juice in the proportion of three to one by adding three cans of water to each can of orange juice.* **2** *n* a part: *A large proportion of British Columbia is mountainous.*

pro·pose (prə pōz') *v* suggest: *I propose that we should paint my room yellow.* **pro·posed, pro·pos·ing.**

pro·pos·al *n* a plan; suggestion: *Mom liked my proposal for repainting my room.*

pro·pri·e·tor (prə prī'ə tər) *n* an owner, especially of a business.

prose (prōz) *n* the normal form of spoken or written language; not poetry: *Stories can be told in poetry or prose.*

pros·pect (pros'pekt) **1** *n* anything expected or looked forward to: *The prospect of a vacation in New Brunswick is pleasant.* **2** *v* search: *to prospect for gold.*

pros·per (pros'pər) *v* be successful; have good fortune. –**pros·per'i·ty** (pros per'ə tē), *n,* –**pros'per·ous** (pros'pə rəs), *adj.*

pro·tect (prə tekt') *v* shield from harm; defend: *Protect your skin from the sun.* –**pro·tec'tion,** *n.*

pro·test (prə test') **1** *v* object: *The boys protested against having to stop their game.* **2** *v* object to: *She protested the umpire's decision.*

proud (proud) **1** *adj* thinking well of yourself: *She was too proud to cry when she hurt herself.* **2** *adj* thinking too well of yourself: *He was too proud to bother listening to a child.* –**proud'ly,** *adv.*

prove (prūv) *v* show to be true or certain: *Please prove the answer you gave.* **proved, prov·ing.**

prov·erb (prov'ərb) *n* a short, wise saying used for a long time by many people. *Don't count your chickens before they're hatched* is a proverb.

pro·vide (prə vīd') *v* supply what is needed: *Parents provide for their children.* **pro·vid·ed, pro·vid·ing.**

pro·vid·ed *conj* on the condition that; if: *She will go provided her friends can go also.*

prov·ince (prov'əns) *n* one of the ten divisions of Canada: *Prince Edward Island became a province in 1873.* –**pro·vin'cial,** *adj.*

provincial park ❀ a tract of land established as a preserve for wildlife and as a recreation area by a provincial government: *Clearwater Provincial Park in Manitoba is a beautiful place.*

pro·voke (prə vōk') *v* make angry: *Jeanette provoked him with her teasing.* **pro·voked, pro·vok·ing.** –**prov'o·ca'tion** (prov'ə kā'shən), *n.*

prowl (proul) *v* go about slowly and secretly, hunting for something to eat or steal: *Many wild animals prowl at night.*

prune (prūn) *v* cut out useless parts from: *The farmer pruned his apple trees in winter.* **pruned, prun·ing.**

pry (prī) **1** *v* look with curiosity: *She is always prying into other people's affairs.* **2** *v* raise or move by force: *Pry up that stone with a pickaxe.* **pried, pry·ing.**

psy·chi·a·try (sī kī'ə trē) *n* the branch of medicine dealing with the treatment of mental problems. –**psy·chi'a·trist**, *n.*

psy·chol·o·gy (sī kol'ə jē) *n* the science that deals with human behaviour and the way the mind works. –**psy·chol'o·gist**, *n.*

A common puffin—about 30 cm long including the tail

A willow ptarmigan—about 40 cm long including the tail

ptar·mi·gan (tär'mə gən) *n* a grouse that has feathered feet and is found in mountainous and cold regions. *pl* **ptar·mi·gans** or **ptar·mi·gan.**

pu·ber·ty (pyū'bər tē) *n* the time when a boy or girl becomes sexually capable of becoming a parent. During this time bodily changes begin to take place, such as the growth of a beard in boys and the development of breasts in girls.

pub·lic (pub'lik) **1** *adj* concerning the people as a whole; not private: *public schools, public transit.* **2** *n* all the people: *to inform the public.* –**pub'lic·ly**, *adv.*

pub·li·cize (pub' lə sīz') *v* give information to attract the attention of the public. **pub·li·cized, pub·li·ciz·ing.** –**pub·lic'i·ty**, *n.*

pub·lish (pub'lish) *v* prepare a book, newspaper, magazine, etc. for sale. –**pub'lish·er**, *n.*

pub·li·ca·tion (pub'lə kā'shən) *n* anything that is published: *This magazine is a weekly publication.*

puck (puk) *n* a hard, black, rubber disk used in the game of hockey.

pud·dle (pud'əl) *n* a small pool of any liquid: *a puddle of oil, a puddle of rain water.*

puff (puf) **1** *n* a short, quick blast: *a puff of wind, a puff of smoke.* **2** *v* breathe fast and hard: *She puffed as she climbed the stairs.* **3** *v* swell with air: *He puffed out his cheeks.*

puff·y *adj* puffed out; swollen: *Her eyes are puffy from crying.*

puf·fin (puf'ən) *n* a mostly black-and-white sea bird of the northern Atlantic and Pacific coasts. It has a short, triangular bill that is often brightly coloured.

pu·ja (pū'jə) *n* Hindu worship, with prayers, offerings, and the lighting of lamps.

pull (púl) **1** *v* move something by grasping it and drawing it toward yourself: *Pull the door open; don't push it.* **2** *v* move, usually with effort or force: *to pull a sleigh uphill.* **3** *v* *Informal.* perform; carry through: *Don't pull any tricks.*

pull·o·ver *n* a sweater put on by pulling it over your head.

pull down, destroy: *They pulled down the old school.*

pull out, leave: *The train pulled out of the station.*

pull over, move a vehicle to the side of the road and stop.

pull through, get through a difficult situation.

pull yourself together, get control of yourself.

pulp (pulp) **1** *n* the soft, fleshy part of any fruit or vegetable. **2** *n* a mixture of ground-up wood, rags, or other material from which paper is made: *The pulp and paper industry is very important in British Columbia.*

pulse (puls) *n* the regular beat of your heart: *The nurse took the man's pulse by holding his wrist and counting the beats.*

pump (pump) **1** *n* a machine for forcing liquids or gases into or out of things: *a water pump, an oil pump.* **2** *v* move something by a pump: *to pump water from a well into a pail. Pump air into the bicycle's tires.*

pump·kin (pump'kin) *n* a large, roundish, orange-yellow fruit, used for making pies and as a vegetable: *The children made a pumpkin jack-o'-lantern for Halloween.*

pun (pun) *n* the humorous use of a word where it can have different meanings. *One berry to another: "If you hadn't been quite so fresh, we wouldn't be in this jam."*

punch (punch) **1** *v* hit with your fist. **2** *n* a quick thrust or blow. **3** *v* herd or drive cattle: *He punched cows in Alberta for a living.* **4** *n* a tool for making holes. **5** *v* pierce a hole in: *I punched some paper and put it in a binder.* **6** *n* a drink made of different liquids mixed together.

punch line the last words of a joke that makes it funny: *He can't tell jokes because he gets the punch line wrong.*

punc·tu·al (pungk′chū əl) *adj* prompt; on time: *She is always punctual for meetings.*

punc·tu·ate (pungk′chū āt′) *v* use periods, commas, and other marks to help make the meaning clear. **punc·tu·at·ed, punc·tu·at·ing.** –**punc′tu·a′tion,** *n.*

Grammar ✓ Check ... punctuation

Here are the main **punctuation** marks used in English:

apostrophe '	hyphen -
brackets [ ]	parentheses ( )
colon :	period .
comma ,	question mark ?
dash —	quotation marks " "
ellipsis ...	semicolon ;
exclamation mark !	slash /

---

punc·ture (pungk′chər) **1** *n* a hole made by something pointed. **2** *v* make such a hole in: *A nail punctured my bicycle tire.* **punc·tured, punc·tur·ing.**

pun·ish (pun′ish) *v* cause a person pain, loss, or discomfort for some fault or offence: *Our courts punish people when they do wrong.* –**pun′ish·ment,** *n.*

pu·ny (pyū′nē) *adj* weak; smaller than usual. **pu·ni·er, pu·ni·est.**

pup (pup) **1** *n* a young dog; a puppy. **2** *n* a young fox, wolf, coyote, etc.

pu·pa (pyū′pə) *n* a stage between the larva and the adult in the development of many insects. In the pupa stage the insect is enclosed in a case called a **cocoon.** *pl* **pu·pae** (pyū′pē) or **pu·pas.**

pu·pil (pyū′pəl) **1** *n* a person who is learning in school or is being taught by someone: *The music teacher takes private pupils.* **2** *n* the opening in the centre of your eye that looks like a black spot.

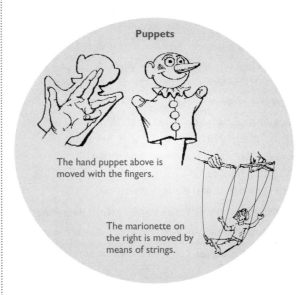

Puppets

The hand puppet above is moved with the fingers.

The marionette on the right is moved by means of strings.

pup·pet (pup′it) *n* a toy figure made to look like a person or animal and moved by wires, strings, or hands.

pur·chase (pər′chəs) **1** *v* buy: *My Dad purchased a new computer.* **2** *n* the thing bought: *That canoe was a good purchase.* **pur·chased, pur·chas·ing.** –**pur′chas·er,** *n.*

pure (pyūr) *adj* not mixed with anything else: *pure gold, pure water, pure orange juice.* **pur·er, pur·est.** –**pu′ri·ty,** *n.*

pu·ri·fy *v* make pure: *Filters are used to purify water.*

pur·pose (pər′pəs) **1** *n* a plan; an aim: *His purpose was to pass his exams.* **2** *n* the end for which a thing is made, done, used, etc.: *What is the purpose of this machine?*

pur·pose·ly *adv* on purpose: *Did you leave the door open purposely?*

on purpose, not by accident: *He tripped me on purpose.*

purse (pərs) **1** *n* a little case for carrying money. **2** *n* a handbag: *She put her keys and gloves in her purse.*

pur·sue (pər sū′) *v* chase: *The dogs pursued the rabbit.* **pur·sued, pur·su·ing.** –**pur·su′er,** *n.*

pur·suit *n* a chase: *The dog was in hot pursuit of the cat.*

pus (pus) *n* a thick, yellowish-white fluid found in an infected place in your body.

push (púsh) **1** *v* move something away by pressing against it: *Push the door; don't pull it.* **2** *v* press hard: *We pushed with all our strength.* **3** *v* Informal. urge the sale of: *The supermarkets push turkeys at Thanksgiving.* **4** *n* a shove: *Give the door a push.*
push around, *Informal.* bully.
push off, *Informal.* go away.

put (pút) **1** *v* place; lay in some place or position: *I put sugar in my tea. Put away your toys. She is putting on her tuque.* **2** *v* express: *The teacher puts things clearly.* **put, put·ting.**
put off, delay: *Don't put off going to the dentist.*
put up with, have patience with.

pu·trid (pyū′trid) *adj* rotten; foul: *The meat became putrid in the hot sun.*

puz·zle (puz′əl) **1** *n* a hard problem: *How to get all my things into one closet is a puzzle.* **2** *n* a problem to be done for fun: *This puzzle has seven pieces of wood to fit together.* **3** *v* make unable to understand something; confuse: *How the cat got out puzzled us.* **puz·zled, puz·zling.**
puzzle out, find out by thinking or trying hard: *to puzzle out the answer.*

py·ja·mas (pə jam′əz *or* pə jȧ′məz) *pl.n* garments for sleeping, consisting of a loose top and a pair of loose pants. Another spelling is **pajamas.**

> **WORD HISTORY** . . . . **pyjamas**
>
> **Pyjamas** comes from Persian *paejamah*, from *pae*, meaning "leg" and *jamah*, meaning "garment."

One of the huge stone pyramids of Egypt

pyr·a·mid (pēr′ə mid′) **1** *n* a solid with a square base and triangular sides that meet at a point. **2 the Pyramids,** *pl.n* the huge, massive stone pyramids, serving as royal tombs, built by the ancient Egyptians.

py·thon (pī′thon) *n* a large snake of Asia, Africa, and Australia that kills its prey by squeezing.

q or **Q** (kyū) *n* the seventeenth letter of the English alphabet or the sound that it stands for. In English, *q* usually occurs in the combination *qu*, as in *quick* and *quarter*. **pl q's** or **Q's.**

quad·ri·lat·er·al (kwod′rə lat′ə rəl) *n* ►See Appendix.

quad·ru·ped (kwod′rə ped′) *n* an animal that has four feet.

quad·ru·ple (kwod rū′pəl) *n* four times as much.

quake (kwāk) **1** *v* shake; tremble: *She quaked with fear.* **2** *n* an earthquake. **quaked, quak·ing.**

qual·i·fy (kwol′ə fī′) *v* make yourself fit for a certain task: *Can you qualify for the basketball team?* **qual·i·fied, qual·i·fy·ing. –qual′i·fied,** *adj.*
qual·i·fi·ca·tion (kwol′ə fə kā′shən) *n* everything that makes a person fit for some task: *Good eyesight is a necessary qualification for a pilot.*

qual·i·ty (kwol′ə tē) **1** *n* something special about a person, animal, or thing that makes it what it is: *One quality of iron is hardness; one quality of sugar is sweetness.* **2** *n* how good (or bad) something is: *That is a poor quality of cloth.* **pl qual·i·ties.**

quan·ti·ty (kwon′tə tē) **1** *n* an amount: *Equal quantities of nuts and raisins were used in the cake.* **2** *n* a large amount: *The baker buys flour in quantity.* **pl quan·ti·ties.**

quar·an·tine (kwòr′ən tēn *or* kwòr′ən tēn′) **1** *v* isolate from others to prevent the spread of an infectious disease. **2** *n* the period of isolation: *Our dog was in quarantine while it was tested for rabies.* **quar·an·tined, quar·an·tin·ing.**

quar·rel (kwò′rəl) **1** *n* an angry argument. **2** *v* fight with words: *The children were quarrelling when their parents came home.*
quar·relled or **quar·reled,**
quar·rel·ling or **quar·rel·ing.**
quar·rel·some *adj* fond of quarrelling.

quar·ter (kwòr′tər) **1** *n* one of four equal parts; one-fourth: *a quarter of an apple. A quarter of an hour is 15 minutes.* **2** *v* divide into fourths: *She quartered the apple.* **3** *n* a coin of Canada and the United States worth 25 cents.
4 quarters, *pl.n* a place to live or stay in: *The baseball team has winter quarters in Florida.*
5 *n* one of four equal periods of play in football, basketball, etc.

quar·ter·back *n* in football, the player who calls the signals.

quar·tet (kwòr′tet′) *n* a group of four musicians singing or playing together.

qua·sar (kwā′zàr) *n* a distant, starlike object in outer space. Quasars give out light as well as strong radio waves.

qua·ver (kwā′vər) *v* sing or say in a shaky voice.

A quay can be a place for motor boats to get gas.

quay (kē) *n* a landing place where ships load and unload.

quea·sy (kwē′zē) *adj* having a feeling that you might throw up: *The boat ride across the Northumberland Strait made Carlos feel queasy.* **quea·si·er, quea·si·est. –quea′si·ness,** *n.*

queen (kwēn) **1** *n* a female ruler of a nation: *Queen Elizabeth II.* **2** *n* the wife of a king. **3** *n* among bees, ants, etc., a female that lays eggs: *There is usually only one queen in a hive of bees.*

queer (kwēr) *adj* strange; peculiar: *There's a queer noise coming from my computer.*

quench (kwench) *v* put an end to; stop: *to quench a thirst, to quench a fire.*

que·ry (kwē′rē) **1** *n* a question. *pl* **que·ries. 2** *v* ask. **3** *v* express doubt about: *to query an answer.* **que·ried, que·ry·ing.**

quest (kwest) *n* an expedition in search of something: *a quest to find gold in the Yukon.*

ques·tion (kwes′chən) **1** *n* something asked for information. **2** *v* ask for information: *The police questioned the witness of the accident.* **3** *v* to doubt: *I question the truth of many of Jan's stories.*

ques·tion·a·ble *adj* doubtful; uncertain: *Whether your statement is true is questionable.*

question mark the punctuation mark (?) put after a written question.

ques·tion·naire *n* a printed set of questions: *The questionnaire asked my age and what kind of cereal I liked best.*

beside the question, off the subject of the discussion.

no question, without a doubt.

out of the question, impossible.

queue (kyū) **1** *n* a line of people, automobiles, etc.: *There was a long queue in front of the movie theatre.* **2** *v* form or stand in a long line: *We had to queue to get tickets.*

WORD HISTORY . . . . queue

Queue comes originally from the Latin word *cauda*, meaning "tail." A lineup of people looks like a long tail.

---

quib·ble (kwib′əl) **1** *n* a small complaint: *We had a few quibbles about the cafeteria menu.* **2** *v* argue about small details: *We quibbled about the best way to wrap the gift.*

quick (kwik) **1** *adj* fast and sudden: *The cat made a quick jump.* **2** *adj* coming soon; prompt: *a quick reply.* **3** *adj* not patient; hasty: *a quick temper.* **4** *adj* learning quickly; clever: *a quick mind, a quick ear.* –**quick′ly,** *adv,* –**quick′ness,** *n.*

quick·sand (kwik′sand′) *n* soft, wet sand that will not hold heavy weight.

qui·et (kwī′ət) **1** *adj* with little noise: *quiet footsteps.* **2** *n* stillness: *to read in quiet.* –**qui′et·ness,** *n.*

qui·et·en *v* make quiet.

quieten down, become quiet.

quilt (kwilt) *n* a cover for a bed, usually made of two pieces of cloth with a soft pad between, held in place by lines of stitching.

quin·tu·plet (kwin tup′lit, kwin tyū′plit, *or* kwin tū′plit) *n* one of five children born at the same time from the same mother.

quip (kwip) **1** *n* a clever remark. **2** *v* say something clever or amusing. **quip·ped, quip·ping.**

quit (kwit) **1** *v* stop: *They quit work at five.* **2** *v* leave: *His brother is quitting school this June.* **quit** or **quit·ted, quit·ting.**

quits *adj* on equal terms: *After the money was returned, the boys were quits.*

quit·ter *n Informal.* a person who shirks or gives up easily.

call it quits, abandon an attempt to do something: *Since we could not manage to set up camp in the rain, we finally called it quits and hiked back to Ingonish.*

quite (kwīt) **1** *adv* completely: *I am quite alone.* **2** *adv* really: *Her illness was quite a shock.* **3** *adv* very; rather; somewhat: *It is quite hot.*

quiv·er (kwiv′ər) **1** *n* a case to hold arrows. **2** *v* shiver: *The dog quivered with excitement.*

quiz (kwiz) *n* a short test: *Each week our teacher gives us a spelling quiz.*

quote (kwōt) *v* repeat the exact words of: *The teacher quoted the Constitution of Canada.* **quot·ed, quot·ing.** –**quo·ta′tion,** *n.*

quotation mark one of a pair of marks ("") used to show the beginning and end of a quotation.

Grammar ✓*Check* **. quotation marks**

Always use **quotation marks** at the beginning and end of somebody's exact words: "I never saw him before in my life," cried the witness.

---

quo·tient (kwō′shənt) *n* a number obtained by dividing one number by another: *If you divide 26 by 2, the quotient is 13.*

Qu'ran (kū·ràn′) *n* the holy book of Islam, containing the message God gave to Muhammad. **Koran** is another spelling.

r or **R** (är) *n* the eighteenth letter of the English alphabet or the sound that it stands for. The sound of *r* is heard twice in *rear*. *pl* **r's** or **R's.**
the three R's, reading, writing, and arithmetic.

rab·bi (rab′ī) *n* a teacher of the Jewish law and religion. *pl* **rab·bis.**

A cottontail rabbit—about 32 cm long excluding the tail

rab·bit (rab′it) *n* a burrowing mammal with soft fur, long ears, and long hind legs.

ra·bies (rā′bēz) *n* a disease that dogs and other animals get. People can get rabies if they are bitten by a **rabid** animal.

A raccoon—about 60 cm long excluding the tail

rac·coon (rə kūn′) *n* a small, greyish-brown animal with a bushy tail and a dark patch around its eyes. Most of the time raccoons live in trees and are active at night.

race (rās) **1** *n* a contest of speed: *a horse race, a car race.* **2** *v* run a race with: *I'll race you to the corner.* **3** *n* a group of living things that share the same heritage: *the human race, the race of birds.* **raced, rac·ing.**

rac·ism (rā′siz əm) *n* the mistaken belief that another group of people is not as good as your group because of their different appearance or heritage. —**rac′ist,** *n* or *adj.*

rack (rak) **1** *n* a frame to keep things on: *a towel rack, a hat rack, a baggage rack.* **2** *n* an instrument once used for torturing people by stretching them.
rack your brains, think as hard as you can.

rack·et (rak′it) *n* loud noise.

Racquets for tennis, badminton, and squash

rac·quet (rak′it) *n* a light, wide bat made of network stretched on a frame.

ra·di·ate (rā′dē āt′) **1** *v* give out rays of: *The sun radiates light and heat.* **2** spread out from a centre: *Roads radiate from the city in every direction.* **ra·di·at·ed, ra·di·at·ing.**
ra·di·ance *n* brightness: *the radiance of the sun, the radiance of a smile.* —**ra′di·ant,** *adj.*
ra·di·a·tion (rā′dē ā′shən) *n* the heat, light, or other energy radiated from something.
ra·di·a·tor 1 *n* a device for heating a room. **2** *n* a device for cooling the engine of a car.
ra·di·oac·tive (rā′dē ō ak′tiv) *adj* giving off energy as a result of the breaking up of atoms.

ra·di·o (rā′dē ō′) **1** *n* sending and receiving sounds through the air over a long distance: *We can listen to music broadcast by radio.* **2** *n* a device for making it possible to hear these sounds: *His radio cost $60.* *pl* **ra·di·os. 3** *v* send out by radio: *The ship radioed a call for help.* **ra·di·oed, ra·di·o·ing.**

ra·di·us (rā′dē əs) *n* a line going straight from the centre to the outside of a circle or a sphere: *Any spoke of a wheel is a radius.* pl **ra·di·i** (rā′dē ī) or **ra·di·us·es.**

raf·fle (raf′əl) *n* a lottery in which many people each pay a small sum for a chance to win a prize.

raft (raft) *n* logs or boards fastened together to make a floating platform.

rag (rag) **1** *n* a torn piece of cloth: *Use clean rags to rub this mirror bright.* **2 rags,** *pl.n* tattered or worn-out clothes: *The prince disguised himself as a beggar dressed in rags.*

rag·ged (rag′id) *adj* rough; uneven: *an old dog's ragged coat, a ragged edge.*

rage (rāj) *n* violent anger: *Mad with rage, Alistair dashed into the fight.*

raid (rād) **1** *n* a sudden attack. **2** *v* attack suddenly: *The enemy raided our camp.*

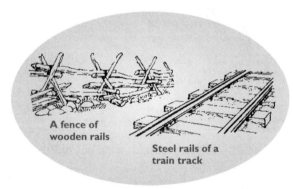

A fence of wooden rails

Steel rails of a train track

rail (rāl) **1** *n* a long bar of wood or of metal: *fence rails, stair rails. Bars laid along the ground for a railway track are called rails.* **2** *n* a railway: *We travelled across Canada by rail and by car.*

rail·way (rāl′wā′) **1** *n* a track with parallel steel rails for trains. **2** *n* a system of transportation that uses trains. **Railroad** is another name for this.

rain (rān) **1** *n* water falling in drops from the clouds. **2** *v* to fall in drops of water: *It rained all day.* –**rain′y,** *adj.*

rain·bow (rān′bō′) *n* an arch of coloured light in the sky when the sun shines through rain: *The seven colours of the rainbow are red, orange, yellow, green, blue, indigo, violet.* **rain·coat** *n* a waterproof coat worn for protection from rain.

rain·fall *n* the amount of water in the form of rain, sleet, or snow that falls within a given time

and area: *The yearly rainfall in Vancouver is much greater than that in Regina.* Another word for this is **precipitation.**

rain forest a large area of trees where there is very heavy rainfall throughout the year.

rainy day, a possible time of need in the future: *to save money for a rainy day.*

CONFUSABLES ..... rain

rain means "fall in drops":
  It may rain tonight.
reign means "rule":
  Queen Victoria reigned for sixty-four years.
rein means "strap":
  Hold on to the reins when riding a horse.

raise (rāz) **1** *v* lift up: *Children in school raise their hands to answer.* **2** *v* help to grow: *The farmer raises chickens and corn. Parents raise their children.* **3** *v* an increase: *a raise in pay.* **raised, rais·ing.**

raise the roof, *Slang.* make a big disturbance.

CONFUSABLES ..... raise

raise means "lift up." It is always followed by a noun: *I raise my hand.*
rise means "go up":
  If I raise my hand, my hand will rise.

rai·sin (rā′zən) *n* a sweet, dried grape.

rake (rāk) *n* a long-handled tool with a row of spikes at one end, used for smoothing the soil or gathering leaves, etc.

ral·ly (ral′ē) *n* a meeting of many people: *a political rally, a sports-car rally.* pl **ral·lies.**

ram (ram) **1** *n* a male sheep. **2** *v* strike head on: *One ship rammed the other ship.* **3** *v* push hard: *He rammed his hockey gear into a bag and rushed off.* **rammed, ram·ming.**

Ram·a·dan (rȧ′mə dȧn′ or rȧ′mə dȧn′) *n* in Islam, the month set aside for prayer and fasting, during which Muslims do not eat or drink from dawn until sunset.

ram·ble (ram′bəl) **1** *n* wander about: *We rambled here and there through the woods.* **2** *v* talk or write about first one thing and then another with no clear connections. **ram·bled, ram·bling.**

A ramp onto
a highway

ramp (ramp) *n* a slope connecting two different levels: *The library has an entrance ramp for wheelchairs.*

ranch (ranch) *n* a large farm for raising cattle, sheep, or horses. –**ranch′er,** *n.*

range (rānj) **1** *n* the distance between limits: *a range of colours to choose from.* **2** *v* vary between limits: *The prices of these bicycles range from $250 to $1000.* **3** *n* grassland for cattle, sheep, etc. **4** *v* wander over: *Buffaloes once ranged the plains.* **5** *n* a row or line: *a mountain range.* **ranged, rang·ing.**

rang·er *n* a person employed to take care of a large forest.

rank (rangk) **1** *n* a row or line of people or things, especially soldiers. **2** *v* arrange in order: *Rank the provinces in order of size.*

ran·sack (ran′sak) *v* search thoroughly, especially to rob: *The thief ransacked the house for jewellery.*

ran·som (ran′səm) *n* the price demanded to set a prisoner free: *to kidnap for ransom.*

rap (rap) **1** *n* a light, sharp knock: *a rap on the door.* **2** *v* knock sharply. **rapped, rap·ping.**

CONFUSABLES ...... rap

rap means "knock":
I heard a rap on the door.
wrap means "cover":
Help me to wrap the present.

rap·id (rap′id) **1** *adj* very quick. **2 rapids,** *pl.n* a part of a river where the water rushes very quickly, often over rocks. –**rap′id·ly,** *adv.*

rare (rer) **1** *adj* not usually found or seen: *Pelicans are rare birds in Canada.* **2** *adj* not happening often: *Earthquakes are rare in Alberta.* –**rare′ly,** *adv.* **3** *adj* of meat, not cooked much: *a rare steak.* **rar·er, rar·est.**

rar·ing (rer′ing) *adj Informal.* very eager: *raring to go, raring for a fight.*

ras·cal (ras′kəl) *n* a mischievous child: *My dad says we are rascals.*

rash (rash) **1** *adj* taking too much risk: *It is rash to cross the street without looking both ways.* **2** *n* many small red spots on your skin.

rasp·ber·ry (raz′ber′e) *n* a small fruit that grows on bushes: *Raspberries are usually red or black.* *pl* **rasp·ber·ries.**

rat (rat) *n* a long-tailed rodent that looks like a big mouse.

smell a rat, suspect a trick: *When they told me school was cancelled today, I smelled a rat.*

rate (rāt) **1** *n* speed: *walk at a slow rate.* **2** *n* a price: *On Tuesday, movie tickets will cost half the regular rate.* **3** *v* give an opinion of: *rate a performance.* **4** *v* be regarded: *She rates high as a musician.* **rat·ed, rat·ing.**

rat·ing *n* a grade given according to quality: *an excellent rating.*

at any rate, anyway; in any case.

rath·er (raтн′ər) **1** *adv* more willingly: *I would rather go today than tomorrow.* **2** fairly; quite: *After working so long Brian was rather tired.*

ra·ti·o (rā′shō) *n* the relation of one quantity to another. *The teacher has students and computers in the ratio of 10 to 3* means that she has ten students for every three computers. *pl* **ra·ti·os.**

ra·tion **1** *n* a share: *a ration of food.* **2** *v* share out: *We rationed the food among the four of us.*

ra·tion·al (rash′ə nəl) **1** *adj* reasonable: *Soraya was too angry to speak in a rational way.* **2** *adj* based on reason: *a rational explanation.*

rat·tle (rat′əl) **1** *n* a number of short, sharp sounds: *the rattle of empty bottles.* **2** *v* talk or say quickly: *She rattled off the names of her friends.* **3** *v Informal.* upset: *Melody was so rattled that she forgot her speech.* **rat·tled, rat·tling.**

rave (rāv) **1** *v* talk wildly: *An excited, angry person raves.* **2** *v* talk with too much enthusiasm: *Katie raved about the concert.* **raved, rav·ing.**

rav·en·ous (rav′ə nəs) *adj* very hungry.

ra·vine (rə vēn′) *n* a long, deep, narrow valley.

raw (ro) **1** *adj* not cooked: *raw meat.* **2** *adj* with the skin off: *a raw spot on your heel.*

raw material something in its natural state, before being made into something else: *raw material. Wood is the raw material from which furniture is made.*

a raw deal, unfair treatment.

ray (rā) *n* beam of light or other energy that **radiates** from something: *the rays of the sun, X rays.*

ra·zor (rā′zər) *n* a device for shaving: *an electric razor.*

RCMP ►See Appendix.

re– *a prefix meaning:* **1** again, as in *reappear, rediscover, re-enter.* **2** back, as in *repay, replace.*

USING WORDS ...... re-

Think twice before you use words like *again* or *back* with a **re-** verb, because **re-** may already have that meaning. For example, in the sentence *He replaced the book back on the shelf,* "back" is not necessary because *replaced* already means "put back."

---

reach (rēch) **1** *v* arrive at: *We reached Kitimat yesterday.* **2** *v* stretch out and touch: *I cannot reach the top of the wall.* **3** *v* communicate with: *You can reach me by e-mail.* **4** *n* the distance reachable: *The top shelf is beyond my reach.*

re·act (rē akt′) *v* act in response: *Dogs react to kindness by wagging their tails.* –**re·ac′tion,** *n.*

read (rēd) **1** understand things that are written: *We read books.* **2** *v* speak written words out loud: *Please read it to me.* **read** (red), **read·ing. read·er 1** *n* a person who reads. **2** *n* a book for learning and practising reading.

read·y (red′ē) **1** *adj* prepared: *Dinner is ready. We were ready to start at nine.* **2** *adj* willing: *Mia is ready to forgive.* **read·i·er, read·i·est.** –**read′i·ly,** *adv,* –**read′i·ness,** *n.*

re·al (rēl) **1** *adj* not made up; true: *real pleasure, the real reason.* **2** *adj* genuine; not fake: *the real thing, real diamonds.* –**re·al′i·ty** (rē al′ə tē), *n.* **real estate** land and the buildings on it. **re·al·is·tic** (rē′ə lis′tik) **1** *adj* like the real thing; lifelike. **2** *adj* seeing things as they really are; practical. **re·al′ly** (rē′ə lē *or* rē′lē) **1** *adv* in fact: *Are you really getting a new bike?* **2** *adv* very: *really helpful.*

USING WORDS ...... real

Real is an adjective: *real friends.* **Really** is an adverb: *really happy, really well.* People sometimes use **real** when they mean **really** in sentences like these: *I'm feeling really happy.* Be *really* careful to avoid using **real** in this way in your writing.

---

re·al·ize (rē′ə līz′) *v* understand clearly; be fully aware of: *The teacher realizes now how hard you worked.* **re·al·ized, re·al·iz·ing.** –**re·al·i·za′tion,** *n.*

reap (rēp) *v* cut grain or gather a crop from: *The farmer reaps the field.*

A cobra rears its head to warn that it is about to bite.

rear (rēr) **1** *n* the back part: *The kitchen is in the rear of the house.* **2** *v* help to grow: *The parents were very careful in rearing their children.* **3** *v* raise; lift up: *The snake reared its head.* **4** *v* of an animal, rise on its hind legs: *The horse reared in fright.*

rea·son (rē′zən) **1** *n* a cause: *Tell me your reasons for not liking her.* **2** *n* an explanation: *Sickness is the reason for her absence.* **3** *v* think things out; solve new problems: *Human beings can reason.* **rea·son·a·ble 1** *adj* sensible. **2** *adj* not too much: *a reasonable price.* –**rea′son·a·bly,** *adv.* **stand to reason,** be understandable: *It stands to reason that Elias would resent your insults.*

re·as·sure (rē′ə shūr′) *v* give confidence: *Barbara reassured me that her cat was friendly and would not bite, so I let it sit on my shoulder.* **re·as·sured, re·as·sur·ing.**

reb·el (reb′əl *for 1,* ri bel′ *for 2*) **1** *n* a person who resists authority instead of obeying: *The rebels organized a protest march.* **2** *v* refuse to obey. **re·belled, re·bel·ling.** –**re·bel′lious** (ri·bel′yəs), *adj.* **re·bel·lion** (ri bel′yən) *n* organized resistance against authority: *Louis Riel led a rebellion in Manitoba in 1885.*

re·call (ri kol′ *for 1,* rē′kol′ *for 2*) **1** *v* remember: *I can recall my third birthday.* **2** *n* ordering back: *The manufacturer ordered a recall of some cars because of faulty brakes.*

re·ceive (ri sēv′) *v* take something sent or offered: *I received many presents on my birthday.* **re·ceived, re·ceiv·ing.**

re·ceipt (ri sēt′) *n* a written statement that something (usually money) has been received: *Get a receipt to show you have paid.*

re·ceiv·er *n* someone or something that receives: *a football receiver, a telephone receiver.*

re·cep·tion (ri sep′shən) **1** *n* the act of receiving: *My sister's calm reception of the bad news surprised us.* **2** *n* a manner of receiving: *We were given a warm reception on arriving in the Yukon.* **3** *n* a gathering to receive and welcome people: *Our school gave a reception for our new principal.* **4** *n* the quality of the sound in a radio or of the sound and picture received by a television set.* **re·cep·tion·ist** *n* a person employed in an office to welcome and help people.

re·cent (rē′sənt) **1** *adj* done, made, or happening not long ago: *recent events.* **2** *adj* not long past; modern: *a recent period of history.* **–re′cent·ly,** *adv.*

re·cess (rē′ses) *n* a time during which work stops: *Our school has a fifteen-minute recess in the morning and afternoon.*

rec·i·pe (res′ə pē) *n* a set of directions for making food: *Please give me your recipe for chocolate chip cookies.*

re·cite (ri sīt′) *v* say over; repeat: *Timothy can recite that poem from memory.* **re·cit·ed, re·cit·ing.**

re·cit·al *n* a public performance of music, dance, etc.

reck·less (rek′lis) *adj* taking dangerous risks: *reckless driving, a reckless adventure.*

reck·on (rek′ən) **1** *v* count: *Reckon the total cost before you decide to buy.* **2** *v* consider: *Graham is reckoned a fine speller.* **3** *v Informal.* think; suppose.

reckon on, count on: *Sandy didn't reckon on breaking her leg when she decided to try skiing.*

re·claim (ri klām′) **1** *v* bring back to a useful condition: *The farmer reclaimed the swamp by draining it.* **2** *v* get from used things: *to reclaim rubber from old tires.* **3** *v* get back: *Wayne had difficulty reclaiming the money he had lent.*

rec·la·ma·tion (rek′lə mā′shən) *n* restoration to a useful, good condition: *the reclamation of deserts by irrigation.*

re·cline (ri klīn′) *v* lean back; lie down: *The tired shopper reclined on the bench.* **re·clined, re·clin·ing.**

rec·og·nize (rek′əg nīz′) *v* know again: *You have grown so much that I didn't recognize you.* **rec·og·nized, rec·og·niz·ing.**

rec·og·ni·tion (rek′əg nish′ən) **1** *n* being recognized: *By a good disguise he escaped recognition.* **2** *n* favourable attention: *The actor soon won recognition from the public.*

rec·om·mend (rek′ə mend′) **1** *v* speak in favour of: *Can you recommend this book?* **2** *v* advise: *The doctor recommended that she stay in bed.* **–rec′om·men·da′tion,** *n.*

re·cord (ri kòrd′ *for 1 and 3,* rek′ərd *for 2 and 4*) **1** *v* put into writing to keep for future use: *Record your thoughts in a diary.* **2** *n* a written account: *The secretary kept a record of what was said at the meeting.* **3** *v* put music or sounds on a disc or tape. **4** *n* a remarkable performance, especially the best achievement in a sport: *Who holds the record for the high jump?*

re·cord·er (ri kòr′dər) **1** *n* a machine: *a tape recorder, a video cassette recorder (VCR).* **2** *n* a wooden musical instrument like a flute.

off the record, not to be recorded or quoted: *The Prime Minister was speaking off the record.*

re·cov·er (rē′kuv′ər) *v* get back something lost or sent away: *to recover your health, to recover a lost wallet, to recover a space capsule.* *pl* **re·cov·er·ies. –re·cov′er·y** (ri kuv′ə rē), *n.*

rec·re·a·tion (rek′rē ā′shən) *n* play or amusement: *Walking, gardening, and reading are quiet forms of recreation.* **–rec′re·a′tion·al,** *adj.*

re·cruit (ri krūt′) **1** *n* a newly enlisted member of the armed forces, or any other group: *The nature club needs recruits.* **2** *v* get new members: *to recruit volunteers.*

rec·tan·gle (rek′tang′gəl) *n* a four-sided figure with four right angles. ▶ See Appendix. **–rec·tan′gu·lar,** *adj.*

re·cu·per·ate (ri kū′pə rāt′) *v* regain your health; get well. **re·cu·per·at·ed, re·cu·per·at·ing.**

re·cur (ri kər′) *v* occur again; be repeated: *Leap year recurs every four years.* **re·curred, re·cur·ring.**

re·cy·cle (rē sī′kəl) *v* reprocess used material so that it can be used again: *Old cars can be recycled for steel.* **re·cy·cled, re·cy·cling.**

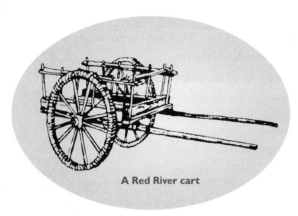

A Red River cart

red (red) *n* the colour of blood. **red·der,
red·dest.**

red·den *v* blush: *Joan's face reddened with shame.*

red-hand·ed *adj* in the act of a crime or
mischief: *The robber was caught red-handed.*

Red River cart ❧ a strong two-wheeled cart
pulled by oxen or horses.

see red, *Informal.* become very angry.

re·duce (ri dyūs′ *or* ri dūs′) *v* make less: *He is
trying to reduce his weight.* **re·duced, re·duc·ing.**

re·duc·tion (ri duk′shən) *n* the amount by
which a thing is reduced: *The reduction in cost
was $5.*

re·dun·dant (ri dun′dənt) *adj* not needed;
extra: *In the sentence* Take your feet off of the
table, *the word* of *is redundant.*

reed (rēd) *n* a kind of tall grass with a hollow
stalk that grows in wet places.

CONFUSABLES ..... reed

reed means "tall grass":
Reeds often grow in wetlands.

read means "get the meaning of":
Read the sentence.

reef (rēf) *n* a ridge of rocks or sand at the
surface of the sea: *The ship was wrecked on the
hidden reef off the coast of Lake Erie.*

reel (rēl) **1** *n* a frame like a spool, for winding
thread, rope, wire, film, a line for fishing, etc.
2 *n* a lively dance: *a Cape Breton reel.*

re·fer (ri fər′) **1** *v* relate: *The rule against
running in the hall refers to everyone.* **2** *v* send for
information: *Our librarian is referring us to many
good books.* **3** *v* turn for information or help: *A
person refers to a dictionary to find the meanings of
words.* **re·ferred, re·fer·ring.**

ref·er·ee (ref′ə rē′) *n* a person to whom
something is referred for decision, usually in
games or sports. **ref·er·ence** (ref′ə rəns) **1** *n* the
act of directing attention: *This essay contains
many references to larger history books.*
2 *n* something used for information: *A
dictionary is a reference book.* **3** *n* a statement
about someone's character or ability: *Lise had
good references from people for whom she babysat.*

re·fine (ri fīn′) *v* make pure: *Sugar, oil, and
metals are refined before they are used.*
re·fined, re·fin·ing.

**The reflection of trees
and mountains in a lake**

re·flect (ri flekt′) **1** *v* throw back light, heat,
sound, etc.: *The sidewalks reflect heat on a hot day.*
2 *v* give back a picture of: *The mirror reflects my
face.* **3** *v* think carefully: *Take time to reflect
before doing important things.* **–re·flec′tion,** *n.*

re·flex (rē′fleks) *n* an automatic action of your
body: *Sneezing and shivering are reflexes.*

re·frig·er·ate (ri frij′ə rāt′) *v* make or keep
cold: *Milk must be refrigerated.* **re·frig·er·at·ed,
re·frig·er·at·ing.**

re·frig·er·a·tor *n* an appliance for keeping food
and drinks cool.

ref·uge (ref′yūj) *n* shelter from danger: *The cat
took refuge in a tree.*

ref·u·gee (ref′yə jē′ *or* ref′yə jē′) *n* a person
who flees for refuge or safety, especially to a
foreign country.

re·fund (ri fund′ *for 1,* rē′fund *for 2*) *v* pay
back: *If these shoes do not wear well, the store will
refund your money.* **2** *n* the money paid back.

re·fuse (ri fyūz′) **1** *v* say "no" to; reject: *She
refuses the offer.* **2** *v* say you will not do it, give it,
etc.: *He refuses to answer.* **re·fused, re·fus·ing.**

re·fus·al *n* saying you will not: *Gerald's refusal to
play angered the other boys.*

re·gard (ri gȧrd′) **1** *v* consider: *She is regarded as the best doctor in town.* **2** *v* look closely at: *The cat regarded me anxiously when I picked up her kittens.* **3** *n* good opinion: *The teacher has high regard for Ron's ability.* **4 regards,** *pl.n* good wishes: *Hans sends his regards.*

re·gard·ing *prep* about: *A letter regarding the boy's behaviour was sent to his parents.*

in regard to or **with regard to,** about: *The teacher spoke to me in regard to being late.*

re·gard·less (ri gȧrd′lis) *adj* paying no attention to: *Regardless of grammar, she said, "Him and I have went."*

re·gion (rē′jən) *n* any large area: *the Yukon region, a mountainous region.* —**re′gion·al,** *adj.*

reg·is·ter (rej′is tər) **1** *n* a list; a record: *A register of attendance is kept in our school.* **2** *v* write in a list; record: *Register the names of the new pupils.*

reg·is·tra·tion (rej′i strā′shən) *n* the act of registering.

re·gret (ri gret′) **1** *v* feel sorry for or about: *We regretted that Maxine missed the field trip to the Halifax Citadel.* **2** *n* the feeling of being sorry. **re·gret·ted, re·gret·ting.** —**re·gret′ful** (ri gret′fəl), *adj.*

reg·u·lar (reg′yə lər) **1** *adj* usual: *Our regular sleeping place is the bedroom.* **2** *adj* according to a rule: *A period is the regular ending for a sentence.* **3** *adj* happening again and again at the same time: *Saturday is a regular holiday.* **4** *adj* even in size, spacing, or speed: *regular teeth, regular breathing.* —**reg′u·lar·ly,** *adv.*

reg·u·la·tion (reg′yə lā′shən) *n* a rule or law: *traffic regulations.*

re·hearse (ri hərs′) *v* practise for a performance: *We rehearsed our parts for the school play.* **re·hearsed, re·hears·ing.**

re·hears·al (ri hėr′səl) *n* a performance beforehand for practice.

reign (rān) **1** *n* the period of power of a ruler: *The queen's reign lasted 50 years.* **2** *v* to rule: *A king reigns over his kingdom.*

rein (rān) *n* a long, narrow strap for guiding an animal. Usually, **reins.**

re·in·car·na·tion (rē in kȧr nā′shən) *n* in certain religions, the teaching that each individual soul is continually **reincarnated**, or born over and over again in different bodies, living a new life each time until the goal of perfection is reached.

rein·deer (rān′dēr′) *n* a large deer, with antlers, living in northern regions. The caribou is a North American reindeer. *pl* **rein·deer.**

re·in·force (rē′in fȯrs′) *v* make stronger: *to reinforce an army, to reinforce a wall.* **re·in·forced, re·in·forc·ing.** —**re′in·force′ment,** *n.*

re·ject (ri jekt′ *for 1,* rē′jekt *for 2*) **1** *v* refuse to take, use: *Kyle rejected our offer of help. All the bruised apples were rejected.* **2** *n* anything not good enough: *The rejects were sold at a lower price.* —**re·jec′tion,** *n.*

re·joice (ri jois′) *v* be glad: *Our parents rejoice at our success.* **re·joiced, re·joic·ing.**

re·late (ri lāt′) **1** *v* tell: *The traveller related her adventures in the Northwest Territories.* **2** *v* connect in meaning: *"Better" and "best" are related to "good."* **3** *v* be connected in any way: *We are interested in what relates to ourselves.* **re·lat·ed, re·lat·ing.**

re·lat·ed *adj* connected in any way.

re·la·tion 1 *n* a connection in meaning: *Part of your answer has no relation to the question.* **2** *n* a person who belongs to the same family, such as a father, brother, aunt, nephew, cousin, etc.; a relative. **re·la·tion·ship** *n* connection.

rel·a·tive (rel′ə tiv) **1** *n* a person who belongs to the same family. **2** *adj* depending for meaning on a relation to something else: *East is a relative term; for example, Saskatoon is east of Victoria but west of Winnipeg.* —**rel′a·tive·ly,** *adv.*

re·lax (ri laks′) **1** *v* loosen up: *Relax your muscles to rest them.* **2** *v* rest from work: *Take a vacation and relax.* —**re′lax·a′tion,** *n.*

re·lay (ri lā′ *or* rē′lā) *v* take and carry farther: *Messengers will relay your message across Canada.* **re·layed, re·lay·ing.**

re·lay race (rē′lā) a race in which each member of a team runs, swims, etc. only a part of the distance, then another takes over.

re·lease (ri lēs′) **1** *v* let go: *Release the catch and the box will open.* **2** *v* set free: *release an animal from a cage.* **3** *n* make available: *release a movie, release information.* **re·leased, re·leas·ing.**

re·lent (ri lent′) *v* become less harsh: *My dad relented and let me stay up late.*

re·lent·less *adj* not relenting: *The storm raged with relentless fury.*

rel·e·vant (rel′ə vənt) *adj* connected to the point: *a relevant question.* **–rel′e·vance,** *n.*

re·lieve (ri lēv′) **1** *v* make less; make easier; reduce the pain of: *What will relieve a headache?* **2** *v* free a person on duty by taking his or her place. **re·lieved, re·liev·ing. –re·lief′** (ri lēf′), *n.*

WORD HISTORY . . . . relieve

Relieve comes from the prefix *re-* meaning "again," and the Latin *levare*, meaning "lighten." When you relieve someone of a burden, you lighten his or her load.

---

re·li·gion (ri lij′ən) **1** *n* belief in and worship of a God or gods. **2** *n* a system of: *the Christian religion, the Hindu religion.* **–re·li′gious,** *adj.*

rel·ish (rel′ish) **1** *n* something to add flavour to food. Olives and pickles are relishes. **2** *n* a kind of pickle usually made of chopped cucumbers. **3** *v* enjoy: *That cat relishes cream. Clive did not relish the idea of staying after school.*

re·luc·tant (ri luk′tənt) *adj* unwilling: *I am reluctant to go out in very cold weather.* **–re·luc′tance,** *n.*

re·ly (ri lī′) *v* depend; trust: *Rely on your friends.* **re·lied, re·ly·ing.**

re·li·a·ble (ril̄ī′ə bəl) *adj* dependable; can be trusted: *a reliable source of information.*

re·main (ri mān′) **1** *v* stay: *We shall remain at Lake Timagami till September.* **2** *v* keep on: *The town remains the same year after year.* **3** *v* be left: *A few apples remain on the tree.*

re·main·der 1 *n* the part left over: *After studying for an hour, she spent the remainder of the afternoon playing tennis.* **2** *n* in arithmetic, the number left over after dividing one number by another.

re·mark (ri màrk′) **1** *v* say: *Mother remarked that Clint's hands were dirty.* **2** *n* something said in a few words: *The Prime Minister made a few remarks.*

re·mark·a·ble *adj* special; unusual: *a remarkable memory.* **–re·mark′a·bly,** *adv.*

rem·e·dy (rem′ə dē) **1** *n* anything used to help cure illness: *A hot drink is a cold remedy.* **2** *n* anything intended to put something right: *The movie was a remedy for the children's boredom.* *pl* **rem·e·dies. –re·me′di·al** (ri mē′ dē əl), *adj.*

re·mem·ber (ri mem′ber) **1** *v* call back to mind: *I can't remember that man's name.* **2** *v* keep in mind: *Remember to take your lunch.*

re·mem·brance 1 *n* memory. **2** *n* a keepsake. **Remembrance Day** November 11, the day set aside to honour the memory of those killed in war.

re·mind (ri mīnd′) *v* make remember: *This picture reminds me of a story I heard.*

re·mind·er *n* something to help you remember.

re·mote (ri mōt′) **1** *adj* far away: *Dinosaurs lived in the remote past.* **2** *adj* out of the way: *You must travel by snowmobile to reach that remote village in the Northwest Territories.* **re·mot·er, re·mot·est.**

remote control 1 control from a distance: *Some model airplanes can be flown by remote control.* **2** a device that does this: *the TV remote control.* This is usually just called **the remote.**

re·move (ri mūv′) *v* take off; take away: *Remove your jacket.* **re·moved, re·mov·ing. –re·mov′al,** *n.*

ren·dez·vous (ron′də vū′) *n* an appointment to meet at a certain place or time: *We made a rendezvous to meet at the bus stop at 4 p.m.*

re·new (ri nyū′ *or* ri nū′) *v* give or get for a new period: *to renew a library book.*

re·new·able *adj* able to be replaced: *Trees are a renewable resource, but oil will run out.*

ren·o·vate (ren′ə vāt′) *v* make like new: *to renovate a house.* **ren·o·vat·ed, ren·o·vat·ing. –ren·o·va′tion,** *n.*

rent (rent) **1** *n* payment for the use of a place to live. **2** *v* pay for the use of something: *to rent a video.*

rent·al *n* something rented.

re·pair (ri per′) *v* put in good condition again; mend: *He repairs shoes.*

re·peat (ri pēt′) **1** *v* say again: *to repeat a word.* **2** *v* do again: *to repeat an error.* **3** *v* tell to anyone else: *Promise not to repeat this.* **4** *n* the thing repeated: *We saw the repeat on television.* **–rep′e·ti′tion** (rep′ə tish′ən), *n.*

Grammar ✓*Check* ... **repetition**

When you repeat words in your writing, the effect can be boring. Try to find synonyms (words with similar meanings) in a thesaurus.

re·place (ri plās′) **1** *v* take the place of: *Jerome replaced Jay as captain.* **2** *v* put in place again: *Replace the books on the shelves.* **re·placed, re·plac·ing. –re·place′ment** (ri plās′mənt), *n.*

re·ply (ri plī′) **1** *v* answer: *I asked Tara how she felt and she replied that she was tired.* **2** *n* an answer: *When can I expect a reply?* **re·plied, re·ply·ing.** *pl* **re·plies.**

re·port (ri pȯrt′) **1** *n* an account or statement of facts: *a school report, a report of a traffic accident.* **2** *v* give an account of something: *The radio reports the news and weather.*

re·port·er *n* a person who gathers news for a newspaper, magazine, radio or TV station, etc.

rep·re·sent (rep′ri zent′) **1** *v* stand for; be a symbol of: *The stars on this map represent Canadian cities.* **2** *v* act in place of: *We chose Fiona to represent our class at the student council meeting.*

rep·re·sent·a·tive *n* a person chosen to act or speak for others.

re·proach (ri prōch′) *n* blame or scold: *Mother reproached me for breaking a plate.*

re·proach·ful *adj* full of reproach: *a reproachful look.*

A green sea turtle—upper shell about 1 m long. This reptile has a hard shell, like one big scale.

rep·tile (rep′tīl) *n* a cold-blooded animal covered with scales. Snakes, lizards, turtles, alligators, and crocodiles are reptiles.

re·pub·lic (ri pub′lik) *n* a nation headed by a president: *The United States and Mexico are republics.*

rep·u·ta·tion (rep′yə tā′shən) *n* what people think and say about a person or thing: *The two brothers had a bad reputation for playing pranks on their friends.*

re·quest (ri kwest′) **1** *v* ask for: *Lydia requested permission to go to the washroom.* **2** *n* the act of asking: *a polite request.*

re·quire (ri kwīr′) **1** *v* need: *Do you require more money?* **2** *v* demand: *The rules required all club members to be over 12.* **re·quired, re·quir·ing. –re·quire′ment,** *n.*

res·cue (res′kyū) **1** *v* save from danger: *The dog rescued the child from drowning.* **2** *n* saving from danger: *The firefighter was praised for his brave rescue of the children in the burning house.* **res·cued, res·cu·ing. –res′cu·er,** *n.*

re·search (ri sərch′ *or* rē′sərch) **1** *n* a careful search for facts; investigation: *I did a lot of research for my report on recycling.* **2** *v* investigate.

re·sem·ble (ri zem′bəl) *v* be like; look like: *Twins resemble each other.* **re·sem·bled, re·sem·bling. –re·sem′blance,** *n.*

re·sent (ri zent′) *v* feel hurt and angry at: *She resented being called a baby.* **–re·sent·ful,** *adj,* **–re·sent′ment,** *n.*

re·serve (ri zərv′) **1** *v* save for later: *Runners reserve some strength for the last lap of a race.* **2** *n* something kept back for future use: *a reserve of energy.* **3** *n* public land set apart for a special purpose: *a nature reserve.* **4** *n* a piece of land set apart, usually by treaty, for First Nations people. **re·served, re·serv·ing.**

res·er·va·tion (rez′ər vā′shən) *n* an arrangement to keep a thing for a person: *My parents made reservations for rooms at a hotel.*

re·served *adj* kept by special arrangement: *reserved seats.* **res·er·voir** (rez′ər vwȧr′) *n* a place where water is stored for use: *This reservoir supplies the entire city.*

res·i·dence (rez′ə dəns) *n* the place where a person lives.

res·i·dent *n* a person living or staying in a place, not a visitor: *The residents of the town are proud of its new library.*

re·sign (ri zīn′) *v* give up a job or position: *The manager of the football team resigned.* **–res′ig·na′tion** (rez′ig nā′shən), *n.*

resign yourself, give in unwillingly but without complaint: *Keith had to resign himself to a week in bed when he broke his leg.*

re·sist (ri zist′) *v* struggle successfully against: *The dog resisted all my attempts to catch him. A healthy person resists disease.* **–re·sist′ance,** *n.*

re·solve (ri zolv′) *v* make up your mind: *We resolved to practise more in the future.* **re·solved, re·solv·ing. –res′o·lu′tion** (rez′ə lü′shən), *n.*

re·sort (ri zȯrt′) **1** *v* turn for help: *I had to resort to yelling to get my sister out of my room.* **2** *n* a person or thing you turn to for help. **3** *n* a place people go to for relaxation and recreation: *There are many summer resorts in Northern Ontario.*

Trees that can be used for lumber are one of Canada's best natural resources.

re·source (ri zȯrs′ *or* rē′zȯrs′) **1** *n* any supply that will meet a need: *resources of money, resources of strength.* **2 natural resources,** *pl.n* the things provided by nature that add to a country's wealth: *Canada's natural resources include fish, lumber, oil, and minerals.*

re·source·ful (ri zȯrs′fəl *or* ri sȯrs′fəl) *adj* good at thinking of ways to do things: *That resourceful boy made a chair from two old car tires.*

re·spect (ri spekt′) **1** *n* honour: *We should show respect to older people.* **2** *v* feel or show honour for: *We must respect the customs of different cultures.*

re·spect·a·ble *adj* worthy of respect: *Respectable citizens obey the laws.* **re·spect·ful** *adj* showing respect; polite: *Sven was always respectful, even to people he didn't like.* **re·spec·tive·ly** *adv* in the order mentioned: *Bob, Dick, and Eli are six, eight, and ten years old respectively.*

re·spond (ri spond′) *v* reply: *Carmen responded to my question by shaking her head.* –**re·sponse′,** *n.*

re·spon·si·ble (ri spon′sə bəl) **1** *adj* obliged to care for: *All pupils are responsible for the books given to them.* **2** *adj* deserving credit or blame: *Who's responsible for this mess on the floor?* **3** *adj* trustworthy; reliable: *The class chose a responsible person to take care of the money from the bake sale.* pl **re·spon·si·bil·i·ties.** –**re·spon′si·bil′i·ty** (ri spon′sə bil′ə tē), *n.*

rest (rest) **1** *v* be still; relax: *My grandfather rests for an hour every afternoon.* **2** *n* freedom from work, disturbance, etc.: *I needed a short rest after mowing the lawn.* **3** *n* in music, a pause. **4** *n* what is left: *The sun shone in the morning but it rained for the rest of the day.*

rest·less *adj* unable to rest: *The dog was restless, as if it sensed some danger.*

res·tau·rant (res′tə ront′) *n* a place to buy and eat a meal.

re·store (ri stȯr′) *v* bring back; put back as it was: *Restore the book to the bookcase.* **re·stored, re·stor·ing.**

re·strain (ri strān′) *v* hold something back: *She could not restrain her curiosity to see what was in the box. He restrained the puppy when guests arrived at the door.*

re·strict (ri strikt′) *v* keep within limits: *Our swim club is restricted to people 12 years old or under.* –**re·stric′tion,** *n.*

re·sult (ri zult′) **1** *n* whatever happens because of something: *The result of his fall was a broken leg.* **2** *v* have as a result: *Eating too much can result in an upset stomach.*

re·sume (ri zūm′) *v* begin again; go on: *Resume reading where we left off.* **re·sumed, re·sum·ing.**

re·tain (ri tān′) *v* keep: *Walter tripped and fell into the pool, but he retained his sense of humour and laughed about it.*

re·tire (ri tīr′) **1** *v* give up work: *Most people expect to retire at 65.* –**re·tire′ment,** *n.* **2** *v* go to bed: *We retire early, usually about 10 p.m.* **re·tired, re·tir·ing.**

re·tort (ri tȯrt′) **1** *v* reply quickly or sharply: *"It's none of your business," she retorted.* **2** *n* a sharp or clever reply: *"Why are your teeth so sharp?" asked Red Riding Hood. "The better to eat you with," was the wolf's retort.*

re·treat (ri trēt′) *v* move back: *Seeing the bear, the camper retreated rapidly. She retreated to her cottage in Muskoka on weekends.*

beat a retreat, run away: *We dropped the apples and beat a hasty retreat when the farmer began to chase us.*

re·trieve (ri trēv′) *v* get back again: *to retrieve a lost purse.* **re·trieved, re·triev·ing.**

re·turn (ri tərn′) **1** *v* go back; come back: *We return to class after lunch.* **2** *n* going or coming back: *We look forward all winter to our return to the cottage.* **3** *v* bring back; give back: *Please return this book to the library.* **4** *adj* having something to do with a return: *a return ticket.*

re·un·ion (rē yūn′yən) *n* coming together again: *a family reunion at Thanksgiving.*

re·veal (ri vēl′) *v* make known something secret: *Promise never to reveal my secret.*

re·venge (ri venj′) *n* hurting someone to get even for having been hurt.

re·verse (ri vərs′) **1** *n* the opposite: *She is so stubborn, she did the reverse of what I ordered.* **2** *v* turn the other way: *Just reverse and walk back the way you came.* **3** *n* an arrangement of gears set so as to move backward: *Put the car in reverse to back out of the garage.* **4** *n* the back: *The answers are on the reverse of the page.* **re·versed, re·vers·ing.**

re·view (ri vyū′) **1** *v* study again: *Please review this lesson for tomorrow.* **2** *n* studying again: *Before the examinations we have a review of the term's work.* **3** *n* a critical account of a book, play, movie, etc., giving its good points and its faults: *Avivah wrote a review of the movie for the school magazine.* **4** *v* prepare such a critical account: *to review a book.*

re·vise (ri vīz′) *v* read carefully and correct or improve: *Lorraine has revised the poem she wrote.* **re·vised, re·vis·ing.** –**re·vi′sion** (ri vizh′ən), *n.*

re·vive (ri vīv′) *v* bring back or come back to life: *He was nearly drowned, but we revived him.* **re·vived, re·viv·ing.**

re·volt (ri vōlt′) **1** *v* rebel. **2** *v* to cause to feel disgust: *Cruelty to animals revolts most people.* –**re·volt′ing,** *adj.*

rev·o·lu·tion (rev′ə lū′shən) *n* a complete, often violent, overthrow of a government.

re·volve (ri volv′) *v* move in a circle: *It takes a year for the earth to revolve once around the sun.* **re·volved, re·volv·ing.** –**rev′o·lu′tion** (rev′ə lü′shən), *n.*

re·ward (ri wȯrd′) **1** *n* a return made for something done: *Actors say that applause is the best reward.* **2** *n* a money payment. Rewards are sometimes given for the return of lost property.

A black rhinoceros of Africa—about 175 cm high at the shoulder and about 3 m long

rhi·noc·er·os (rī nos′ə rəs) *n* a large, thick-skinned animal of Africa and Asia with one or two upright horns on its snout. **Rhino** is a short form of this word. *pl* **rhi·noc·er·os·es** or **rhi·noc·er·os.**

WORD HISTORY . . . . rhinoceros

Rhinoceros gets its name from two Greek words: *rhis,* meaning "nose," and *keras,* meaning "horn."

---

rhyme (rīm) **1** *v* sound alike in the last part. *Long* and *song* rhyme. *Go to bed* rhymes with *sleepyhead.* **2** *n* a word or line having the same last sound as another. *Cat* is a rhyme for *mat. Hey! diddle, diddle* and *The cat and the fiddle* are rhymes. **3** *v* poetry with some of the lines ending in similar sounds. **rhymed, rhym·ing.**

rhythm (riŦH′əm) *n* a regular repetition of a beat: *the rhythm of dancing, the rhythm of music.* –**rhyth′mic,** *adj.*

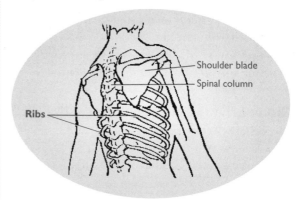

Shoulder blade
Spinal column
Ribs

rib (rib) *n* one of the curved bones round your chest.

rib·bon (rib′ən) *n* a strip of cloth used for trimming or tying: *I wrapped the present and tied a ribbon round it.*

rice (rīs) *n* the seeds of a cereal plant that grows in warm climates: *Rice is an important food in India, China, and Japan.*

rich (rich) **1** *adj* having a lot of something, usually money: *Canada is rich in water.* **2** *adj* producing a lot: *a rich soil, a rich mine.* **3** *adj* containing plenty of butter, eggs, etc.: *a rich cake.* **–rich'ness,** *n.*

rich·es *pl.n* wealth; a lot of money, land, goods, jewellery, etc.

rid (rid) *v* make free of something not wanted: *What will rid a house of rats?* **rid** or **rid·ded, rid·ding.**

get rid of, 1 get free from: *I can't get rid of this cold.* **2** to do away with: *Poison will get rid of the rats in the barn.*

good riddance, an exclamation showing relief that something or somebody has been got rid of.

rid·dle (rid'əl) *n* a puzzling question, usually meant to be funny. *Example: When is a door not a door? When it is ajar.*

ride (rīd) **1** *v* sit on something and make it go: *to ride a horse, to ride a bicycle.* **2** *v* be carried along by something: *to ride on a train, to ride in a car.* **3** *n* a big amusement machine, such as a merry-go-round, Ferris wheel, roller coaster, etc.: *Most children enjoy the rides on the midway.* **rode, rid·den, rid·ing. –rid'er,** *n.*

ridge (rij) **1** *n* a long, narrow chain of hills or mountains. **2** *n* any raised narrow strip: *the ridges in ploughed ground.*

rid·i·cule (rid'ə kyūl') *v* laugh at; make fun of: *My little sister cries if we ridicule her.* **rid·i·culed, rid·i·cul·ing.**

ri·dic·u·lous (ri dik'yə ləs) *adj* deserving ridicule; silly: *It would be ridiculous to walk backward all the time.*

Rid·van (rid'vən) *n* an important festival of the Bahai religion, taking place in the spring. It lasts 12 days in honour of the 12 days that Baha Ullah spent in the Garden of Ridvan during his exile.

rig (rig) **1** *v* supply a ship with masts, sails, ropes, etc.: *The sailor rigged the boat ready for sailing.* **2** *v* put together using odds and ends: *The children rigged up a tent with a rope and a blanket.* **3** *v* arrange in an unfair way: *The race was rigged.* **rigged, rig·ging.**

Left   Right

right (rīt) **1** *adj* good; just; lawful: *Peggy did the right thing when she told the truth.* **2** *adj* correct; true: *the right answer.* **3** *adj* of the side that is turned to the east when the main side faces north; opposite of left: *You have a right hand and a left hand.* **4** *n* something that is due to a person: *Each member of the club has a right to vote.*

right angle an angle of 90°: *The angles in a square are right angles.*

right away, immediately: *My brother promised to call home right away.*

right now, immediately: *Stop that right now!*

CONFUSABLES ..... right

right means "correct":
That is the right answer.

write means "make letters":
Write with a pencil.

rig·id (rij'id) **1** *adj* stiff; not bending: *Hold your arm rigid.* **2** *adj* strict; not changing: *In our home, it is a rigid rule to wash your hands before eating.*

rig·ma·role (rig'mə rōl') *n* foolish talk or activity; nonsense.

rim (rim) *n* an edge or border around something: *the rim of a wheel, the rim of a glass.*

rind (rīnd) *n* a hard or thick outer covering: *We do not eat the rind of melons.*

ring (ring) **1** *n* a circle: *You can tell the age of a tree by counting the rings in its trunk.* **2** *n* a thin circle of metal or other material: *a wedding ring, a key ring.* **3** *n* the sound of a bell. **4** *v* make a sound like a bell: *Did the telephone ring?* **rang, rung, ring·ing.**

rink (ringk) **1** *n* a sheet of ice for playing hockey or for skating. **2** *n* a smooth floor for roller skating. **3** *n* a sheet of ice for curling. **4** *n* a curling team of four players: *Canada's best rinks curled in the bonspiel.*

rinse (rins) *v* wash with clean water: *Rinse all the soap out of your hair after you wash it.* **rinsed, rins·ing.**

ri·ot (rī′ət) **1** *n* a violent disturbance by a crowd: *The guards stopped several riots in the prison.* **2** *v* behave in a wild, disorderly way. **3** *n Informal.* a very amusing person or performance: *Bjorn was a riot at the party.*

rip (rip) **1** *v* tear apart; tear off: *to rip the paper off a present.* **2** *n* a torn place: *Please sew up this rip in my sleeve.* **ripped, rip·ping.**

ripe (rīp) *adj* fully grown and ready to be eaten: *ripe fruit.* **rip·er, rip·est. –rip′en,** *v.*

rip·ple (rip′əl) **1** *n* a very small wave: *Throw a stone into calm water and watch the ripples spread in rings.* **2** *v* make small waves on: *A breeze rippled the quiet water of the pond.*

rise (rīz) **1** *v* stand up; go up: *Please rise from your seat. The kite rises in the air. The sun rises in the east.* **2** *v* get up from sleep: *She rises at six o'clock every morning.* **3** *v* slope upward: *Hills rise in the distance.* **4** *n* an increase: *a rise in the cost of bus fares.* **rose, ris·en, ris·ing.**

risk (risk) **1** *n* a chance of harm or loss; danger: *If you don't wear a bike helmet, you are taking a big risk.* **2** *v* take a risk: *You risk your life diving into shallow water.* **–risk′y,** *adj.*

ri·val (rī′vəl) **1** *n* a person who tries to equal or do better than another: *The two girls were rivals in class.* **2** *adj* competing: *rival teams.* **–ri′val·ry,** *n.*

riv·er (riv′ər) *n* a large stream of water that flows into a lake, ocean, etc.

riv·et (riv′it) **1** *n* a metal bolt: *Rivets fasten heavy steel beams together.* **2** *v* fasten firmly; fix firmly: *Their eyes were riveted on the TV.* **riv·et·ing** *adj* so interesting that you can't look away: *The story was so riveting that I couldn't put the book down.*

road (rōd) *n* a way between places: *The road from Sarnia to Chatham is jammed with cars.*

roam (rōm) *v* wander: *A herd of deer roamed through the forest.*

roar (rôr) **1** *v* make a loud, deep sound: *The lions roared.* **2** *n* a loud, deep sound: *a roar of laughter, a roar of applause.*

roast (rōst) **1** *v* cook in an oven or over a fire: *We roasted meat and potatoes.* **2** *n* an outdoor meal, where food is cooked over a fire: *a corn roast, a marshmallow roast.*

rob (rob) *v* take away from by force: *Thieves robbed the bank of thousands of dollars.* **robbed, rob·bing. –rob′ber,** *n,* **–rob′ber·y,** *n.*

robe (rōb) **1** *n* a long, loose outer garment. **2** *n* a bathrobe or dressing gown.

ro·bot (rō′bot) *n* a machine that does human work or looks like a human being.

rock (rok) **1** *n* a large piece of stone. **2** *v* move backward and forward, or from side to side: *My chair rocks.* **3** *v* shake violently: *The earthquake rocked the houses.* **4** *n* a kind of music with a strong beat. **rocking chair** a chair that can rock back and forward. **rock·y 1** *adj* full of rocks: *a rocky beach.* **2** *adj* shaky: *a rocky table.*

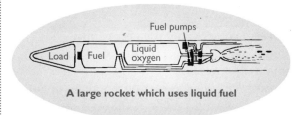
A large rocket which uses liquid fuel

rock·et (rok′it) *n* a machine shaped like a tube open at one end and filled with something that burns quickly and makes a jet of gas that pushes the tube forward. Some rockets, used for fireworks, explode into sparks. Large rockets are used for sending things into outer space.

rod (rod) *n* a thin, straight bar of metal or wood: *a lightning rod, a fishing rod.*

ro·dent (rō′dənt) *n* a mammal with teeth good for gnawing. Rats, mice, and squirrels are rodents.

ro·de·o (rō′dē·ō *or* rō dā′ō) *n* a contest of skill in roping cattle, riding horses, etc.: *The Calgary Stampede is the best rodeo I've ever seen. pl* **ro·de·os.**

rogue (rōg) *n* a tricky or dishonest person.

role (rōl) *n* an actor's part in a play, motion picture, etc.: *Cheryl wished to play the leading role in the school play.* Another spelling is **rôle.** **role model** *n* a person who is admired and imitated.

A roller skate

An inline skate

roll (rōl) **1** *v* move along by turning over and over: *Wheels roll. A ball rolls.* **2** *v* wrap: *Myles rolled himself up in a blanket.* **3** *n* something rolled up: *a roll of film, a roll of toilet paper.* **4** *v* move with a side-to-side motion: *The ship rolled in the waves.* **5** *v* make deep, loud sounds: *Thunder rolls.* **6** *n* a list of names: *I will call the roll to find out who is absent.* **7** *n* a kind of bread or cake: *a sweet roll.*

roll·er 1 *n* a cylinder used for painting, smoothing, pressing, crushing, etc. **2** *n* a long, rounded wave: *Huge rollers broke on the beaches of Terence Bay.* **roller coaster** a railway set up for amusement with small cars that roll, climb, dip sharply, turn, etc. **roller skates** skates with small wheels: *Roller skates are used on floors, roads, sidewalks, etc.* **Rollerblades** *a trademark for* roller skates that have four wheels in a line, one behind the other. Another name for these is **inline skates.**

ro·mance (rō mans′ *or* rō′mans) **1** *n* a love story. **2** *n* a love affair. –**ro·man′tic,** *adj.*

Roman	I	V	X	L	C	D	M
Arabic	1	5	10	50	100	500	1000
Examples		XXIII=23, MDCCLXI=1761					

Roman numerals

Roman numerals a system of numerals used by the ancient Romans. ▶See Appendix.

romp (romp) **1** *v* play in a rough way. **2** *n* rough, lively play: *A pillow fight is a romp.*

roof (rūf) **1** *n* the top covering of a building. **2** *n* something like a roof in shape or position: *the roof of a cave, the roof of a car, the roof of your mouth.*
raise the roof, *Informal.* make a disturbance.

rook·ie (rūk′ē) *n Slang.* a beginner, such as a new player on a team.

room (rūm) **1** *n* a part of a building with walls of its own: *a dining room, a classroom.* **2** *n* space available for something: *The concert was so crowded that we had no room to move. There is room for one more in the boat.*
roommate *n* a person who shares a room with another or others. **room·y** *adj* having plenty of room. **room·i·er, room·i·est.**

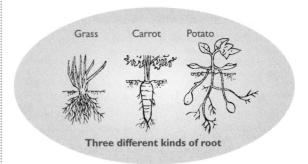

Grass Carrot Potato

Three different kinds of root

root (rūt) **1** *n* the part of a plant that grows down into the soil. **2** *n* something like a root: *the root of a tooth, the roots of your hair.* **3** *n* a word from which other words are made: *"Room" is the root of "roomy."*
root for, cheer or support a team or a member of a team.
root out, get rid of completely.
take root, become firmly fixed.

rope (rōp) **1** *n* a strong, thick line usually made of twisted strands. **2** *v* to tie or fasten with a rope. **3** *v* catch a horse, calf, etc. with a lasso. **roped, rop·ing.**
know the ropes, *Informal.* know the rules of an activity.

Rosh Ha·sha·nah (rōsh′ hȧ′shȧ nȧ′) the Jewish New Year, falling usually in late September or in early October.

rot (rot) **1** *v* decay; spoil: *So much rain will make the fruit rot.* **2** *n* the process of rotting; decay. **rot·ted, rot·ting.**
rot·ten 1 *adj* decayed; spoiled: *a rotten egg.* **2** *adj* foul; disgusting: *a rotten smell.* **3** *adj Slang.* bad; nasty: *rotten luck, to feel rotten.*

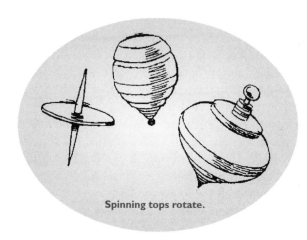
Spinning tops rotate.

ro·ta·te (rō′tāt *or* rō tāt′) *v* move around a centre: *Wheels and spinning tops rotate.* **ro·tat·ed, ro·tat·ing.** –**ro·ta′tion** (rō tā′shən), *n.*

rough (ruf) **1** *adj* not smooth: *the rough bark of trees.* **2** *adj* stormy: *rough weather.* **3** *adj* not gentle: *rough manners.* **4** *adj* not completed; done as a first try: *a rough drawing, a rough idea.* **5** *adj Informal.* unpleasant; hard; severe: *She was in for a rough time.* –**rough′ness,** *n.*
rough·en *v* make rough or become rough.
rough·ing *n* the rough treatment of another player in hockey, football, and other games: *He got a penalty for roughing.* **rough·ly 1** *adv* in a rough manner. **2** *adv* approximately: *The distance from Québec City to Vancouver is roughly five thousand kilometres.*
rough it, live without comforts: *Roughing It in the Bush is a famous book about pioneer life.*

round (round) **1** *adj* shaped like a ball or a ring: *a round hoop, round cheeks.* **2** *adv* in a circle: *Wheels go round.* **3** *v* go round: *The ship rounded Cape Horn.* **4** *prep* so as to make a turn to the other side of: *Liam walked round the corner.* **5** *n* a section of a sport: *a round in a boxing match, a round of golf.* **6** *n* a short song sung by several persons beginning one after the other: *Three Blind Mice is a round.* **7** *v* approximate to the nearest unit, ten, hundred, etc.: *Round 3478 to the nearest thousand and you get 3000.*
round·a·bout *adj* not direct: *a roundabout route. I heard about it in a roundabout way.*
round number a number in even tens, hundreds, thousands, etc. **round trip** a trip to a place and back again.
round out, complete: *to round out a paragraph.*
round up, drive or bring together: *The cowhands rounded up the cattle.*

route (rūt *or* rout) **1** *n* a way to go: *Will you go to Corner Brook by the coastal route?* **2** *n* a fixed area given to a person making deliveries, sales, etc.: *a newspaper route.*
rou·tine (rū tēn′) *n* a fixed, regular method of doing things: *Getting up and going to bed are parts of your daily routine.*

row (rō *for 1 and 2,* rou *for 3*) **1** *n* a line of people or things: *The children stood in a row in front of the row of chairs. Corn is planted in rows.* **2** *v* move a boat by means of oars: *We rowed to Reindeer Island.* **3** *n* a noisy quarrel; a loud disturbance: *The three children had a row over the bicycle. What's all this row about?*
row·dy *adj* rough and noisy. **row·di·er, row·di·est.**

roy·al (roi′əl) *adj* having to do with kings or queens: *a royal command.*
Royal Canadian Mounted Police the federal police force of Canada. **roy·al·ty** *n* a royal person; royal persons: *Kings, queens, princes, and princesses are royalty.*

rub (rub) **1** *v* move one thing back and forth against another: *Rub your hands with soap.* **2** *v* clean, smooth, or polish by moving one thing firmly against another: *Rub out your error with an eraser.* **3** *n* the act of rubbing: *Give the table a rub with this cloth.* **rubbed, rub·bing. rub the wrong way,** annoy.

rub·ber (rub′ər) **1** *n* an elastic substance. **2** *adj* made of rubber: *rubber tires.* **3** *n* overshoe.

rub·bish (rub′ish) **1** *n* useless stuff; garbage; trash: *Pick up the rubbish and put it in a bag.* **2** *n* nonsense: *Don't talk rubbish.*

rub·ble (rub′əl) *n* rough, broken stones, bricks, etc.: *the rubble left by an earthquake.*

rude (rūd) *adj* not polite: *It is rude to interrupt.* **rud·er, rud·est.** –**rude′ness,** *n.*

ruf·fle (ruf′əl) **1** *v* make rough or uneven: *A breeze ruffled the water of Frobisher Lake.* **2** *n* a strip of cloth gathered together along one edge and used for trimming. **3** *v* disturb; annoy: *Nothing can ruffle her calm temper.* **ruf·fled, ruf·fling.**

rug (rug) **1** *n* a heavy floor covering: *a fur rug, a rag rug.* **2** *n* a thick, warm cloth used as a covering: *Troy wrapped the woollen rug around himself and felt much warmer.*

rug·ged (rug′id) **1** *adj* rough and uneven: *rugged ground.* **2** *adj* sturdy and vigorous; able to do and endure much: *The Canadian pioneers were rugged people.*

ru·in (rū′ən) **1** *n* a building, wall, etc. that has fallen to pieces: *That ruin was once a beautiful castle.* **2** *v* bring to ruin; spoil: *The rain has ruined my new dress.*

rule (rūl) **1** *n* a statement of what to do and what not to do: *Obey the rules of the game.* **2** *v* to control; govern: *The majority rules in a democracy.* **ruled, rul·ing.**

rul·er 1 *n* a person who rules. **2** *n* a straight strip of wood, metal, etc. marked in units such as centimetres, used for drawing straight lines or measuring.

as a rule, usually; normally.

rule out, decide against; exclude.

rum·ble (rum′bəl) **1** *n* a deep, heavy, continuous sound: *We hear the distant rumble of thunder.* **2** *v* make such a sound: *The train rumbled along the track.* **rum·bled, rum·bling.**

rum·mage (rum′ij) *v* search thoroughly by moving things about: *I rummaged in a drawer for my gloves.* **rum·maged, rum·mag·ing.**

ru·mour (rū′mər) *n* a story talked of as news without any proof that it is true: *The rumour spread that our teacher was leaving.* Another spelling is **rumor.**

run (run) **1** *v* go faster than walking: *A horse can run faster than a person.* **2** *v* give out liquid: *My nose runs when I have a cold.* **3** *v* continue: *The hit musical ran for two years.* **4** *v* be a candidate for election: *Lynn Grout will run for mayor.* **5** *v* manage; operate: *to run a business, to run a machine.* **6** *n* the act of running: *to go for a run.* **7** *n* a point scored in baseball or cricket. **8** *n* an enclosed place for animals: *a chicken run.* **9** *n* a place where stitches have become undone: *a run in a stocking.* **ran, run, run·ning.**

run·a·way *n* a person, horse, etc. that runs out of control: *The rancher caught the runaway and brought it back to the stable.* **run·down** *n* a brief summary: *Give me a rundown on what happened at the game.* **run-down** *adj* tired; sick: *I feel run-down today, so maybe I'm catching a cold.* **run-in** *n Informal.* a sharp disagreement; argument; quarrel. **run·ner 1** *n* a person or animal that runs: *A deer is a good runner.*

2 *n* either of the narrow pieces on which a sleigh or sled slides, or the blade of a skate. **3** ❦ **runners** *pl.n* running shoes. **4** *n* a long, narrow strip: *We have a runner of carpet in our hall.*

run·ner-up *n* the person, player, or team that takes second place in a contest.

run-off 1 *n* a running off of water, as during the spring thaw or after a heavy rain: *The streams are swollen from the run-off.* **2** *n* a final, deciding race or contest. **run·way** *n* a level surface on which aircraft land and take off.

in the long run, in the end.

run across or **into,** meet by chance.

run down, say bad things about.

run out of, have no more: *to run out of milk, to run out of ideas.*

run over, ride or drive over: *The careless driver ran over my dog.*

runt (runt) *n* an animal, person, or plant that is smaller than the usual size.

ru·ral (rū′rəl) *adj* having to do with the country rather than a town or city.

rush (rush) **1** *v* move with speed: *The river rushed past.* **2** *v* act with great haste: *Mitchell rushes into things without knowing anything about them.* **3** *n* a hurry: *I can't stop to talk, I'm in a rush.* **4** *n* a great or sudden effort of many people to go somewhere or get something: *Few people got rich in the Yukon gold rush.*

rush hour the time when many people are going to or from work.

rust (rust) *n* the brownish coating that you can see on iron or steel after it has got wet.

rust·y 1 *adj* covered with rust: *a rusty knife.* **2** *adj* weak from lack of use: *Dad says his hockey playing is rusty because he hasn't played in a long time.*

rus·tle (rus′əl) **1** *n* a sound like leaves moved by the wind. **2** *v* make this sound: *Leaves rustled in the breeze.* **3** *v Informal.* steal cattle or horses. **rus·tled, rus·tling.**

ruth·less (rūth′lis) *adj* having no pity; showing no mercy; cruel.

s or **S** (es) *n* the nineteenth letter of the English alphabet, or the sound that it stands for. The sound of *s* in *soap* is different from the sound of *s* in *his*. *pl* **s's** or **S's.**

sab·bath (sab′əth) *n* the day of the week used for rest and worship: *Sunday is the Christian sabbath, Saturday is the Jewish sabbath, and Friday is the Muslim sabbath.*

sack (sak) *n* a large bag made of coarse cloth or strong paper: *Sacks are used for holding wheat.*

sa·cred (sā′krid) *adj* connected with religion; holy: *sacred writings, sacred music.*

sacred pipe a pipe smoked by many First Nations people as part of certain ceremonies.

sac·ri·fice (sak′rə fīs′) **1** *v* give up: *We decided to sacrifice part of the garden for a swimming pool.* **2** *n* the giving up of one thing for another. **sac·ri·ficed, sac·ri·fic·ing.**

sad (sad) *adj* not happy; full of sorrow: *You feel sad if your best friend moves away.* **sad·der, sad·dest.** –**sad′den,** *v,* –**sad′ly,** *adv,* –**sad′ness,** *n.*

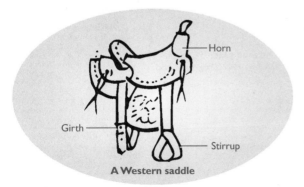

A Western saddle

sad·dle (sad′əl) *n* a seat for a rider on a horse's back, on a bicycle, etc.

sa·fa·ri (sə fä′rē) *n* a long trip or expedition, usually in Africa, to hunt or photograph wild animals.

safe (sāf) **1** *adj* free from harm or danger: *Keep money in a safe place. We feel safe with the dog in the house.* **2** *adj* careful: *a safe driver, a safe move.* **3** *n* a box that can be locked, used for keeping valuable things safe. **4** *adj* in baseball, reaching a base safely. **saf·er, saf·est.**

safe·ty **1** *n* freedom from harm or danger. **2** *adj* giving safety: *a safety belt, a safety lamp.*

safety pin a pin with a guard over the point.

sag (sag) **1** *v* bend down in the middle: *The table tennis net is sagging.* **2** *v* droop; sink: *The tired child's shoulders sagged.* **sagged, sag·ging.**

sail (sāl) **1** *n* a piece of cloth that catches the wind to make a ship move on the water. **2** *v* travel on a ship: *He sailed to Vancouver on a cruise ship.* **3** *v* manage a ship or boat: *The children are learning to sail.*

sail·board *n* a long narrow board with a sail, used in the sport of windsurfing. –**sail′board′ing,** *n.* **sail·boat** *n* a boat that is moved by sails. **sail·or** *n* a person whose work is handling a sailboat or other ship.

set sail, begin a trip by water.

saint (sānt) *n* a very holy person.

sake (sāk) **1** *n* benefit: *Don't do anything special for our sakes.* **2** *n* purpose: *They moved to the country for the sake of peace and quiet.*

for your own sake, to help yourself.

sal·ad (sal′əd) *n* vegetables or fruit, sometimes moulded in jelly, mixed with eggs, seafood, chicken, or other cold meats. Salads are usually cold.

A spotted salamander—about 15 cm long including the tail

sal·a·man·der (sal′ə man′dər) *n* an animal that looks like a lizard, but is related to frogs and toads.

sa·la·mi (sə lä′mē) *n* a spicy sausage, often flavoured with garlic.

sal·a·ry (sal′ə rē) *n* fixed pay for regular work: *Teachers are paid salaries.* pl **sal·a·ries.**

sale (sāl) **1** *n* the act of selling: *The sale of their old home made them sad.* **2** *n* selling at lower prices than usual: *This store is having a sale on jeans.*

sales·per·son *n* a person whose work is selling goods or services: *The salespeople in that shoe store were very helpful.*

for sale, to be sold: *That car is for sale.*

on sale, for sale at lower prices than usual: *All the winter boots are on sale now.*

CONFUSABLES ...... **sale**

sail means "travel on water":
The ship sails on Monday.

sale means "the act of selling" or "selling for a lower price than usual":
There is a sale on at that store.

---

sa·li·va (sə lī′və) *n* the liquid produced in your mouth. It helps you to chew and digest your food.

salm·on (sam′ən) *n* a large fish with pinkish flesh: *Canada has both Atlantic and Pacific salmon.* pl **salm·on** or **salm·ons.**

salt (solt) *n* a white substance found in the earth and in sea water: *Salt is used to season and preserve food.* –**salt′y,** *adj.*

sa·lute (sə lūt′) **1** *v* show respect in a formal manner by raising your hand to your head, by firing guns, by dipping flags, etc.: *The soldier saluted the officer.* **2** *n* the act of saluting. **sa·lut·ed, sa·lut·ing.**

sal·vage (sal′vij) **1** *v* save from fire, flood, shipwreck, etc.: *After the fire was put out we managed to salvage some of our furniture.* **2** *n* anything salvaged. **sal·vaged, sal·vag·ing.**

same (sām) *adj* exactly alike; not different: *Her name and mine are the same. We came back the same way we went.*

all the same, of no importance: *It's all the same to me whether you go or stay.*

sam·ple (sam′pəl) **1** *n* one thing to show what the others are like: *The display samples in the computer store are not for sale.* **2** *v* test a part of: *We sampled the cake and found it very good.* **sam·pled, sam·pling.**

sand (sand) **1** *n* tiny grains of rock: *the sands of the seashore, the sands of the desert.* **2** *v* spread sand over: *to sand an icy road.* –**sand′y,** *adj.*

sand bar a ridge of sand in a river or along a shore, made by tides or currents in the water.

san·dal (san′dəl) *n* a kind of open shoe made of a sole and straps.

sand·wich (sand′wich) *n* two or more slices of bread with meat, jelly, cheese, or some other filling between them.

sane (sān) *adj* having a healthy mind; not crazy. **san·er, san·est.** –**san′i·ty,** *n.*

san·i·tar·y (san′ə ter′ē) *adj* free from dirt and disease: *Food should be kept in a sanitary place.*

sap (sap) *n* the liquid that moves through a plant, carrying water, food, etc., as blood does in animals: *Maple sugar is made from the sap of sugar maple trees.*

sap·ling *n* a young tree.

sar·casm (sàr′kaz əm) *n* sneering remarks that mean the opposite of what they say.

sar·cas·tic (sàr kas′tik) *adj* using sarcasm: *"Don't hurry!" was the coach's sarcastic comment as Julian began to dress at his usual slow rate.*

sar·dine (sàr dēn′) *n* a small fish, often preserved in oil and packed into cans. pl **sar·dines** or **sar·dine.**

packed in like sardines, very much crowded.

A sari is made from one long piece of cloth, wound and folded around.

sa·ri (sà′rē) *n* a traditional outfit worn by women, mainly in India and Pakistan.

sash (sash) **1** *n* a wide ribbon, worn around the waist or over one shoulder. **2** *n* the frame that holds the glass in a window or door.

sas·ka·toon (sas′kə tün′) *n* a bush growing mainly in Western Canada, with large, sweet, purple berries: *Saskatoons are delicious in pies or made into jam.*

WORD HISTORY . . . . saskatoon

Saskatoon comes from a Cree word meaning "fruit of the tree of many branches."

❀ **Sas·quatch** (sås′kwoch) *n* according to legend, a very large, hairy, humanlike creature that lives wild in the mountains of the Pacific Coast. It is also known as **Bigfoot.**

sat·el·lite (sat′ə līt′) **1** *n* a heavenly body that revolves around a planet: *The moon is a satellite of the earth.* **2** *n* an object sent into space to revolve around the earth or other heavenly body: *a weather satellite.*

sat·in (sat′ən) *n* a cloth with one very smooth, glossy side.

sat·is·fy (sat′is fī′) **1** *v* give enough to: *Mick ate a sandwich to satisfy his hunger.* **2** *v* make contented: *Are you satisfied now?* **sat·is·fied, sat·is·fy·ing.** −**sat′is·fac′tion,** *n.*

sat·is·fac·to·ry (sat′is fak′tə rē) *adj* good enough; adequate: *a satisfactory answer, satisfactory work.* −**sat′is·fac′to·ri·ly,** *adv.*

sat·u·rate (sach′ə rāt′) *v* soak thoroughly: *During the fog, the air was saturated with moisture.* **sat·u·rat·ed, sat·u·rat·ing.**

sauce (sos) *n* something, usually liquid, served with a food to make it taste better: *chocolate sauce, cranberry sauce.*

sau·cer (sos′ər) *n* a shallow dish to put a cup on.

sau·na (son′ə) *n* a steam bath where the steam is usually made by pouring water over hot stones.

sau·sage (sos′ij) *n* chopped meat, seasoned and usually stuffed into a thin tube or skin.

sav·age (sav′ij) **1** *adj* wild or rugged: *Burton likes savage mountain scenery.* **2** *adj* fierce: *The savage dog attacked the sheep.*

USING WORDS . . . . savage

People used to call members of other societies **savages**. Nowadays, this usage is considered incorrect and inappropriate.

---

sa·van·na (sə van′ə) **1** *n* a treeless plain. **2** *n* tropical or subtropical grassland with a few trees. **3** *n* especially in the Maritimes, a swamp. **Savannah** is another spelling.

save (sāv) **1** *v* make safe from harm: *The firefighter saved the girl's life.* **2** *v* store up: *to save loonies, to save computer files.* **3** *v* make less: *to save time, to save trouble, to save expense.* **4** *n* the goalie's act of preventing a score by the other team. **saved, sav·ing.**

sav·ings *pl.n* money saved.

sa·vour (sā′vər) **1** *n* a taste or smell: *The soup has a savour of onion.* **2** *v* enjoy the taste or smell of: *Belle savoured the soup with pleasure.* Another spelling is **savor.**

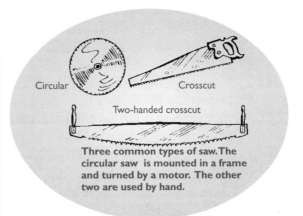

Circular   **Crosscut**

Two-handed crosscut

Three common types of saw. The circular saw is mounted in a frame and turned by a motor. The other two are used by hand.

saw (so) **1** *n* a tool for cutting, made of a thin blade or a disk with sharp teeth on the edge. **2** *v* cut with a saw: *to saw wood.* **sawed, sawed** or **sawn, saw·ing.**

saw·dust *n* the tiny bits of wood that come from sawing. **saw·mill** *n* a building where machines saw timber into planks.

say (sā) **1** *v* speak: *My parents taught me always to say "Please" and "Thank you."* **2** *v* tell: *Say what you think.* **3** *v* give an opinion: *It is hard to say which dress is prettier.* **4** *n* the chance to say something: *Everyone will have a say before the meeting ends.* **said, say·ing.**

say·ing *n* a wise statement that is often repeated: *"Haste makes waste" is an old saying.*

go without saying, be obvious: *It goes without saying that people need food to keep alive.*

scab (skab) *n* the crust that forms over a wound as it heals.

scald (skold) *v* burn with hot liquid or steam: *She scalded herself with hot water.*

scale (skāl) **1** *n* a series of marks on a line, to use in measuring: *A thermometer has a scale.* **2** *n* the size of a map or model compared with what it represents: *The scale of this map of Canada is one centimetre to one kilometre on the ground.* **3** Usually, **scales**, *pl.n* an instrument for measuring mass. **4** *n* in music, a series of tones: *Alana practises scales on the piano.* **5** *n* one of the thin plates that make the skin of some fishes and reptiles. –**scal′y**, *adj.* **6** *v* climb: *They scaled the wall with ladders.* **scaled, scal·ing.**

scalp (skalp) *n* the skin on the top and back of the head that is usually covered with hair.

scam·per (skam′pər) **1** *v* run or move away quickly: *The mice scampered when the cat came.* **2** *v* run about playfully: *The dogs were scampering in the yard.*

scan (skan) **1** *v* look at closely: *His mother scanned his face to see if he looked ill.* **2** *v* *Informal.* glance at: *I scanned the headlines in the newspaper.* **3** *v* use a scanner: *She scanned the photograph and then printed out copies for all her friends.* **scanned, scan·ning.**

scan·ner *n* a device for a computer that reads numbers, codes, or pictures.

scan·dal (skan′dəl) *n* a shameful action that shocks people. –**scan′dal·ous**, *adj.*

scape·goat (skāp′gōt′) *n* a person made to take the blame for something: *I'm the oldest, so if my sisters mess up the house, I'm the scapegoat.*

scar (skär) **1** *n* the mark left by a healed cut: *a scar on your knee.* **2** *n* any mark like this: *See the scars your shoes have made on the chair.* **3** *v* make a scar on: *Jude accidentally scarred the door with a hammer.* **scarred, scar·ring.**

scarce (skers) *adj* hard to get; rare; not plentiful: *Very old stamps are scarce.* **scarc·er, scarc·est.** –**scar′ci·ty**, *n.*

scarce·ly *adv* barely; only just: *We could scarcely see the ship through the thick fog.*

make yourself scarce, *Informal.* go away.

scare (sker) **1** *v* frighten: *Martin yelled "Boo" and that scared us.* **2** *n* a fright. **scared, scar·ing.**

scare·crow *n* a figure dressed in old clothes, put in a field to frighten birds away from growing crops. **scared** *adj* afraid: *Were you scared during the thunderstorm?* **scar·y** *adj Informal.* causing fright: *Emily tells scary stories on Halloween.*

scarf (skärf) *n* a piece of cloth worn round your neck, shoulders, or head. *pl* **scarves** (skärvz) or **scarfs.**

scat·ter (skat′ər) **1** *v* throw here and there; sprinkle: *The farmer scattered corn for the chickens. Scatter sand on the icy sidewalk.* **2** *v* go in different directions: *The geese scattered in fright when the car honked at them.*

scat·ter·brain *n* a thoughtless, disorganized person.

scav·en·ger (skav′ən jər) **1** *n* any creature that feeds on dead animals: *Vultures and jackals are scavengers.* **2** *n* a person who searches through discarded objects looking for something of value.

scav·en·ger hunt a game in which players search for things on a list. The first person to bring all the things back is the winner.

scene (sēn) **1** *n* a view; picture: *The white sailboats in the blue waters of the Bay of Fundy made a pretty scene.* **2** *n* a show of anger or bad temper in front of others: *The little boy kicked and screamed and made such a scene that his parents were ashamed of him.* **3** *n* a part of an act of a play: *The king comes to the castle in Act 1, Scene 2.*

scen·er·y (sē′nə rē) **1** *n* the general appearance of a place: *Ashley enjoys mountain scenery very much.* **2** *n* the painted hangings, screens, etc. used in a theatre to represent places: *The scenery is painted to look like a garden.*

sce·nic *adj* having something to do with natural scenery: *a scenic highway, the scenic beauty of Lake Louise.*

behind the scenes, not publicly, secretly: *A lot of planning for the festival was done behind the scenes.* **the scene of the crime,** *Informal.* the place where something happened.

scent (sent) **1** *n* a smell: *The scent of roses filled the air.* **2** *n* a smell left in passing: *The dogs followed the fox by its scent.* **3** *n* perfume: *She used too much scent.*

CONFUSABLES .... scent

scent means "smell":
The scent of roses filled the room.

sent means "did send":
I sent a birthday card to you yesterday.

cent means "penny":
There are one hundred cents in a dollar.

sched·ule (skej′əl *or* shej′əl) **1** *n* a list of events and times: *a hockey schedule, a TV schedule.* **2** *v* plan something for a definite time: *Schedule your appointment for 4 p.m.* **sched·uled, sched·ul·ing.**
on schedule, at the correct time: *The bus came on schedule.*

scheme (skēm) **1** *n* a plot: *a scheme for getting out of class.* **2** *v* plan; plot: *The bandits were scheming to rob a bank.* **schemed, schem·ing.**

school (skūl) **1** *n* a place for teaching and learning: *Children go to school to learn.* **2** *n* a large group of the same kind of fish or water animal swimming together: *a school of herring, a school of porpoises.*

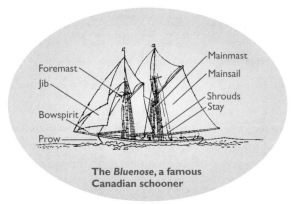

The *Bluenose*, a famous
Canadian schooner

schoon·er (skū′nər) *n* a ship with two or more masts: *The Bluenose was a famous schooner built in Nova Scotia in 1921.*

sci·ence (sī′əns) *n* knowledge based on observed facts and experiments. Biology is a natural science. Engineering is an applied science. **–sci′en·tif′ic,** *adj,* **–sci′en·tist,** *n.*
science fiction stories that combine science and fantasy: *Science fiction stories are often about life in the future or in other galaxies and make much use of the latest discoveries in science.*

scis·sors (siz′ərz) *pl.n* a tool with two sharp blades for cutting.

scoff (skof) *v* make fun to show that you do not believe something: *We scoffed at the idea of drowning in shallow water.*

scold (skōld) *v* blame with angry words: *His mother scolded him for tearing his jacket.*

scoop (skūp) **1** *n* a tool like a tiny shovel: *an ice-cream scoop.* **2** *v* take up as a scoop does: *The children scooped up the snow with their hands.*

scorch (skȯrch) **1** *v* burn slightly: *The muffin tastes scorched.* **2** *v* dry up: *The grass is scorched by so much hot sunshine.*

score (skȯr) **1** *n* the record of points made in a game, contest, or test: *The final score was 9 to 2 in favour of our baseball team.* **2** *v* make points: *She scored two runs in the second inning. I scored 10 out of 10 on the spelling quiz.* **3** *v* keep a record of the number of points made in a game or contest: *The teacher will appoint someone to score for both sides.* **4 the score,** *n Informal.* the truth about anything or things in general; the facts: *The new boy doesn't know the score yet.* **scored, scor·ing.** **–score′less,** *adj,* **–scor′er,** *n.*

scorn (skȯrn) **1** *v* look down upon: *Irene scorned him because he was a sneak and a liar.* **2** *n* a feeling that a person or act is mean or low: *Isaac felt scorn for the students who cheated.* **–scorn′ful,** *adj.*

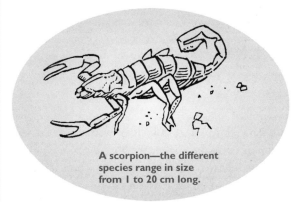

A scorpion—the different
species range in size
from 1 to 20 cm long.

scor·pi·on (skȯrp′yən) *n* a small animal related to spiders, with a poisonous stinger at the end of its tail.

scoun·drel (skoun′drəl) *n* a very bad person: *The scoundrel who set fire to the barn has been caught.*

scour (skour) **1** *v* clean by hard rubbing: *Scour that diry frying pan, please.* **2** *n* the act of scouring. **3** *v* search thoroughly: *They scoured the forest for the lost child.*

scout (skout) **1** *n* a person who is sent out to get information: *a football scout.* **2** *v* hunt around to find something: *Go and scout for firewood.*

scowl (skoul) **1** *v* look angry or sullen by lowering your eyebrows: *The angry man scowled at his son.* **2** *n* a frown.

scram·ble (skram′bəl) **1** *v* make your way by climbing, crawling, etc.: *The girls scrambled up the steep, rocky hill.* **2** *v* struggle with others for something: *The boys scrambled to get the football.* **3** *v* mix together: *scrambled eggs.* **scram·bled, scram·bling.**

scrap (skrap) **1** *n* a small piece; a small part left over: *Put the scraps of paper in the recycling bin.* **2** *v* break up: *They scrapped the old cars and recycled the steel.* **3** *v* throw something away because it is useless or worn out: *to scrap a poor plan.* **4** *n* junk. **5** *n* *Informal.* a fight. **scrapped, scrap·ping.**

scrap·book *n* a book in which pictures or clippings are pasted and kept.

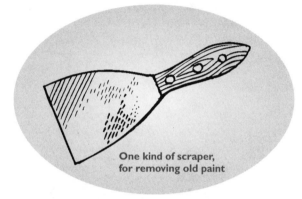

One kind of scraper,
for removing old paint

scrape (skrāp) **1** *v* rub clean with something sharp or rough: *to scrape ice from a car.* **2** *v* scratch: *to scrape your knee, to scrape a table.* **3** *n* a scraped place: *I have a scrape on my elbow.* **4** *n* a difficulty: *Adventurous people often get into scrapes.* **scraped, scrap·ing.** **–scrap′er,** *n.*
scrape along, through, or **by,** barely get through: *He thought he had failed the arithmetic quiz, but he just scraped through.*

scratch (skrach) **1** *v* mark or cut lightly with fingernails, claws, or something sharp: *Your shoes have scratched the gym floor. The cat scratched him. Don't scratch your mosquito bites.* **2** *n* a mark made by scratching or cutting: *There are deep scratches on this desk. That scratch on your hand will soon heal.* **3** *v* strike out; draw a line through.
from scratch, from the beginning: *Ross lost his notes and so had to start his project again from scratch.*
up to scratch, up to standard: *We expected the car that we rented to be in good shape, but it was not up to scratch.*

scrawl (skrol) **1** *v* write or draw poorly or carelessly. **2** *n* poor, careless handwriting.

scream (skrēm) **1** *v* make a loud, sharp, cry: *Alexandra screamed when she saw the child fall.* **2** *n* a loud, sharp, piercing cry.

screech (skrēch) **1** *v* cry out sharply in a high voice; shriek: *"Help! help!" she screeched.* **2** *n* a shrill, harsh noise: *the screech of brakes.*

screen (skrēn) **1** *n* a surface on which movies, television or computer images, etc. are seen. **2** *n* wire mesh stretched in a frame: *Screens on the windows keep out flies.*

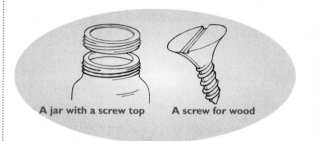

A jar with a screw top   A screw for wood

screw (skrū) **1** *n* a kind of nail with a ridge twisted evenly around it: *Turn the screw to the right to tighten it.* **2** *v* turn as you turn a screw; twist: *Screw the hinge onto the door. Screw the lid on the jar.*

screw·driv·er (skrū′drī′vər) *n* a tool for turning screws.

scrib·ble (skrib′əl) **1** *v* write or draw carelessly. **2** *v* make marks that do not mean anything. **3** *n* something scribbled. **scrib·bled, scrib·bling.**

script (skript) **1** *n* handwriting. **2** *n* the words of a play, of an actor's part, of a radio or television announcer's message, etc.

An ancient
Roman scroll

scroll (skrōl) **1** *n* a roll of paper, especially one with writing on it. **2** *v* in computing, move the words or pictures on the screen up or down.

scrub (skrub) **1** *v* clean by rubbing hard: *Mariel scrubbed the floor with a brush and hot water.* **2** *n* a scrubbing: *Give your hands a good scrub.* **scrubbed, scrub·bing.**

Atlantic sea horses—
about 10 cm long

A scrumptious apple pie

scrump·tious (skrump'shəs) *adj* very tasty; delicious: *a scrumptious apple pie.*

scu·ba (skū'bə) *n* portable breathing equipment used by underwater swimmers. *Scuba* comes from the initials of *s*elf-*c*ontained *u*nderwater *b*reathing *a*pparatus.

scuf·fle (skuf'əl) *n* a confused but not violent struggle: *The children got their faces dirty in the scuffle.* **scuf·fled, scuf·fling.**

sculp·ture (skulp'chər) *n* a statue made of marble, stone, wood, clay, wax, etc. –**sculp'tor,** *n.*

scum (skum) *n* a layer that appears on the surface of some liquids: *The scum had to be skimmed from the top of the boiling maple syrup. Green scum floated on top of the water.*

sea (sē) **1** *n* the great body of salt water that covers almost three quarters of the earth's surface. **2** *n* a large body of water smaller than an ocean: *the Mediterranean Sea.*

sea·board *n* the land near the sea: *St. John's is on the Atlantic seaboard.* **sea·food** *n* any fish or shellfish that you can eat. **sea horse** a tiny fish with a head like a horse. A sea horse swims upright. **sea level** the level of the surface of the sea. Mountains, plains, ocean beds, etc. are measured as so many metres above or below sea level. **sea lion** a large seal that lives on the Pacific Coast. **sea shell** the shell of a sea creature, such as a clam. **sea·shore** *n* the land along the sea. **sea·sick** *adj* dizzy and sick to the stomach because of being on a ship. **sea·way 1** *n* a way over the sea. **2** *n* a deep passage to the open sea: *Ocean liners reach Toronto by sailing up the St. Lawrence Seaway.* **sea·weed** *n* any plant that grows in the sea.

A scythe is good for cutting long grass.

scythe (sīŦH) *n* a long, slightly curved blade on a long handle, used for cutting grass, etc.

A harp seal–
adult about 170 cm long

seal (sēl) **1** *v* close very tightly: *She sealed the package with tape.* **2** *n* a sea mammal with large flippers, usually living in cold regions. *pl* **seals** or **seal.**

seam (sēm) *n* join where edges come together: *the seams of a coat, the seams of a carpet.*

CONFUSABLES ..... **seam**

seam means "join":
There is a seam down the side of my jeans.

seem means "appear":
Why do you seem so sad?

---

search (sɜrch) **1** *v* look for: *We searched all day for the lost kitten.* **2** *n* searching: *Drew found his book after a long search.*

search·light *n* a powerful light that can throw a bright beam in any direction.

sea·son (sē′zən) **1** *n* one of the four periods of the year; spring, summer, fall, or winter. **2** *n* any period of time when something special always happens: *the harvest season, the baseball season.* **3** *v* add flavour to: *Season your egg with salt and pepper.*

seat (sēt) **1** *n* something to sit on. Chairs, benches, and stools are seats. **2** *v* to place on a seat; to take a seat: *Sean seated himself in the most comfortable chair.*

seat belt a belt attached to the seat of a vehicle, used to hold a person in place in case of accident.

se·clud·ed (si klū′did) *adj* shut off from others; undisturbed: *a secluded cottage.*

sec·ond (sek′ənd) **1** *adj* or *adv* next after the 1st; 2nd: *the second seat from the front (adj). She finished second in the competition (adv).* ►See Appendix. **2** *adj* another: *Alain ate a second piece of pizza.* **3** *n* a unit for measuring time. There are sixty seconds in one minute, sixty minutes in one hour, and twenty-four hours in one day. *Symbol:* s

sec·ond·ar·y *adj* next after the first in order, place, time, or importance: *Reading fast is secondary to reading well.* **secondary stress** a stress that is weaker than the strongest stress in a word (primary stress). In the word *ab·bre′vi·a′tion* there is secondary stress on the second syllable and primary stress on the fourth syllable. **second hand** a hand on a clock or watch, pointing to the seconds. It moves around the whole dial once in a minute. **sec·ond-hand 1** *adj* obtained from another: *second-hand information.* **2** *adj* used: *second-hand clothes.*

sec·ond·ly *adv* in the second place.

se·cret (sē′krit) **1** *adj* known only to a few: *a secret sign, a secret cave.* **2** *n* something secret or hidden: *Can you keep a secret?* –**se′cre·cy,** *n*, –**se′cret·ly,** *adv.*

sec·tion (sek′shən) *n* a part: *She divided the orange into sections. The city of Calgary has a business section and a residential section.*

se·cure (si kyūr′) **1** *adj* free from care or fear: *Give your dog lots of attention so it will feel secure.* **2** *adj* firmly fastened: *The boards of this bridge do not look secure.* **3** *v* keep safe against loss, attack, escape, etc.: *Secure your keys in your pocket.* **se·cured, se·cur·ing.** –**se·cu′ri·ty,** *n.*

sed·i·ment (sed′ə mənt) **1** *n* solid matter that falls to the bottom of a liquid; dregs. **2** *n* earth, stones, etc. left by water, wind, or ice: *Each year the Nile River in Egypt overflows and leaves sediment on the land.*

see (sē) **1** *v* look at: *See that black cloud.* **2** *v* have the power of sight: *The blind do not see.* **3** *v* understand: *I see what you mean.* **4** *v* find out: *See what you can do for her.* **5** *v* meet; visit: *I went to see a friend.* **saw, seen, see·ing.**
see to, look after; take care of.

USING WORDS .... **saw/seen**

Saw and **seen** are both forms of the verb *see*. **Saw** is the past tense and **seen** is the past participle. Sometimes, people use **seen** when they should use **saw** in sentences like this one: *I saw some strange sights.*

Remember that **seen** cannot stand as a verb on its own. It needs an auxiliary helping verb, like *have, has, is, are, was,* or *were: I have seen some strange sights. A shadowy figure was seen in the alley.*

---

seed (sēd) *n* the thing from which a new plant grows: *We planted seeds in the garden.*
pl **seeds** or **seed.**

seed·ling *n* a young plant grown from seed.

seek (sēk) *v* try to find; try to get: *The boys are seeking a good camping place. Help me seek for my lost glove. Frances sought advice from the guidance counsellor.* **sought, seek·ing.**

seem (sēm) *v* appear to be: *This apple seemed good but was rotten inside. It seems likely to rain.*

see·saw (sē′so′) **1** *v* or *n* teeter-totter. **2** *v* move up and down or back and forth.

seg·ment (seg′mənt) *n* a part cut off, marked off, or broken off: *an orange segment, a segment of a chocolate bar.*

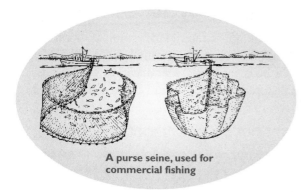

A purse seine, used for commercial fishing

seine (sān) *n* a fishing net that hangs straight down in the water.

seize (sēz) **1** *v* take hold of suddenly; grab: *When Simone lost her balance, she seized my arm.* **2** *v* take possession of by force; capture: *The soldiers seized the city.* **seized, seiz·ing.**

sel·dom (sel′dəm) *adv* rarely; not often.

se·lect (sə lekt′) *v* choose: *His uncle let him select his own birthday present.*

se·lec·tion **1** *n* a choice: *The book on space travel was her selection.* **2** *n* a range of things from which you may select: *The bookstore offered a good selection of children's books.*

self— a prefix meaning of, by, or to yourself or itself: *self-addressed, self-control, self-propelled.* **self-cen·tred** *adj* occupied with your own interests. **self-con·fi·dent** *adj* believing in your own ability. **self-con·scious** (self′kon′shəs) *adj* very aware of how you appear to others; embarrassed; shy. **self-es·teem** *n* a good opinion of yourself. **self-im·por·tant** *adj* having or showing too big an opinion of your own importance. **self-in·ter·est** *n* concern with your wants before the wants and needs of others. **self-re·spect** *n* respect for yourself; proper pride. **self-sat·is·fied** *adj* pleased with yourself.

self·ish (sel′fish) *adj* caring too much for yourself and too little for others: *Selfish people put their own interests before the interests of others.* –**self′ish·ness,** *n.*

self·less *adj* unselfish.

sell (sel) *v* exchange for money: *Bryce is going to sell his old bike. The bakery sells bread.* **sold, sell·ing.**

semi— a prefix meaning: **1** half, as in *semicircle.* **2** partly or incompletely, as in *semisweet.*

sem·i·co·lon (sem′ē kō′lən) *n* a mark of punctuation (;) that shows a break not so complete as that shown by a period.

sem·i·fi·nal (sem′ē fī′nəl) *n* one of the games played to decide who plays in the final one: *Our lacrosse team was defeated in the semifinal.*

send (send) **1** *v* make someone or something go from one place to another: *to send a child to summer camp, to send an e-mail.* **2** *v* ask for something: *Send for help at once. Send out for pizza.* **sent, send·ing.**

sen·ior (sēn′yər) **1** *adj* older: *a senior citizen.* **2** *n* an older person: *Davis is his brother's senior by two years.* **3** *adj* at a higher level; for a higher age: *the senior swim team.*

sense (sens) **1** *n* one of the special powers of the body by which people and animals become aware of the world around them: *The five senses are sight, smell, taste, hearing, and touch.* **2** *v* feel; understand: *My friend sensed that I was tired.* **3** *n* judgment; intelligence: *She had the good sense to keep out of foolish quarrels.* **4** *n* a meaning: *The word star has more than one sense.* **sensed, sens·ing.**

sen·sa·tion (sen sā′shən) **1** *n* a feeling: *Ice gives a sensation of coldness. Shannon says she has a sensation of dizziness when she climbs ladders.* **2** *n* a strong or excited feeling: *The first landing on the moon caused a sensation.*

sen·sa·tion·al **1** *adj* exciting: *The player's sensational catch made the crowd cheer wildly.* **2** *adj* trying to cause excitement: *a sensational newspaper story.*

sense·less **1** *adj* unconscious. **2** *adj* foolish; stupid: *That was a senseless thing to do.*

sen·si·ble *adj* wise: *She is much too sensible to do anything so foolish.* –**sen′si·bly,** *adv.*

sen·si·tive **1** *adj* sensing easily: *Your eyes are sensitive to light.* **2** *adj* easily affected: *The mercury in the thermometer is sensitive to changes in temperature.* **3** *adj* easily hurt: *He was very sensitive about his failure to score in the final game.*

sen·sor (sen′sər) *n* a device for measuring changes in a body's temperature, pulse rate, breathing, etc.

in a sense, in some manner.

make sense, have a meaning: *The statement "Cow cat bless Monday" doesn't make sense.*

sen·tence (sen′təns) **1** *n* a group of words that make a complete thought. *Boys and girls* is not a sentence. *The boys and girls are here* is a sentence. **2** *v* pronounce punishment on: *The judge sentenced the thief to five years in prison.* **3** *n* the punishment itself: *a five-year sentence.* **sen·tenced, sen·tenc·ing.**

Grammar √Check .... sentences

There are four types of **sentences:**

Declarative sentences make a statement:
I am wearing red socks.

Interrogative sentences ask a question:
Do you like my red socks?

Exclamatory sentences express emotion:
What beautiful red socks!

Imperative sentences make commands:
Look at my red socks.

Confederation Bridge spans the Northumberland Strait, which separates Prince Edward Island from mainland Canada.

sep·a·rate (sep′ə rāt′ *for 1* and *2,* sep′ə rit *for 3*) **1** *v* keep apart. **2** *v* divide or be divided into single parts or groups: *Separate your books from mine. After school the children separated in all directions.* **3** *adj* apart from others: *in a separate room, separate seats.* **sep·a·rat·ed, sep·a·rat·ing.** –**sep′a·rate·ly,** *adv.* –**sep′a·ra′tion,** *n.*

se·quel (sē′kwəl) *n* a story, play, or movie continuing an earlier one about the same people.

se·quence (sē′kwəns) *n* the coming of one thing after another: *Arrange the names in alphabetical sequence.*

se·rene (sə rēn′) *adj* peaceful; calm: *a serene smile.* –**se·ren′i·ty,** *n.*

se·ries (sē′rēz) *n* a number of similar things in a row: *a series of wins, a series of numbers. A series of rooms opened off the long hall.* pl **se·ries.**

se·ri·al *n* a story presented one part at a time in a magazine or newspaper, or on radio or television.

se·ri·ous (sē′rē əs) **1** *adj* thoughtful; not smiling or fooling: *a serious face. Are you joking or serious?* **2** *adj* important; important because it may do much harm: *a serious matter, a serious injury.* –**se′ri·ous·ly,** *adv,* –**se′ri·ous·ness,** *n.*

ser·mon (sər′mən) **1** *n* a public talk on religion or something connected with religion: *Ministers preach sermons in church.* **2** *n* a serious talk about conduct or duty: *The children got a sermon on table manners from their parents.*

ser·pent (sər′pənt) *n* a snake.

serve (sərv) **1** *v* work for: *Firefighters serve the public.* **2** *v* bring food to: *The waiter in the new restaurant served us very quickly.* **3** *v* in tennis and similar games, put the ball in play by hitting it. **4** *n* a serving of the ball. **served, serv·ing.** –**serv′er,** *n.*

serv·ant *n* a person employed in a household.

serv·ice 1 *n* a helpful act: *Our neighbours did many services for us when Mom was sick.* **2** *n* duty or employment: *He did thirty years' service with the railway.* **3** *n* the manner of serving food: *fast service.* **4** *v* make fit for service: *The mechanic serviced our car.* **5** *n* the act or manner of putting the ball in play in tennis and similar games. **6** *n* a religious meeting or ceremony. **serv·iced, serv·ic·ing. service station** a place for selling gasoline, oil, etc. and for car repairs.

ser·vi·ette (sər′vē et′) *n* a cloth or paper napkin used while eating. **serv·ing** *n* a helping of food.

at your service, ready to do what someone wants.

serve you right, be just what you deserve: *The punishment serves him right.*

set (set) **1** *v* put; place: *Set the box over here.* **2** *v* put in the right place: *Set the table for dinner. The doctor will set Toby's broken leg.* **3** *v* fix: *The teacher set a time limit for the examination.* **4** *v* sink: *The sun sets in the west.* **5** *n* a group; a number of things or persons belonging together: *a set of dishes, a set of numbers.* **6** *n* a device for receiving or sending by radio, television, telephone, etc.: *a TV set.* **7** *n* the scenery for a play, movie, etc. **set, set·ting.**

set·ting 1 *n* the place or time of a play or story. **2** *n* the background: *a scenic mountain setting.*

set aside, put away for later: *Set your books aside.*

set off, 1 explode: *to set off firecrackers.* **2** start to go: *to set off for home.*

set out, begin to move, start.

set·tle (set′əl) **1** *v* agree upon: *Have you settled on a day for the picnic?* **2** *v* take up residence in a new country or place: *Our cousin is going to settle in the Northwest Territories.* **3** *v* place in or come to a comfortable position: *The cat settled itself in the chair for a nap.* **set·tled, set·tling.**

set·tle·ment *n* a place where a community has been set up: *Québec City is one of Canada's oldest settlements.* **set·tler** *n* a person who settles in a new region: *The early settlers in Canada faced many hardships.*

settle down, 1 live a quieter life. **2** become quiet and pay attention.

sev·en (sev′ən) ►See Appendix.

sev·er·al (sev′rəl) *adj* more than two or three but not many.

se·vere (sə vēr′) **1** *adj* sharp; violent: *a severe headache, a severe storm.* **2** *adj* serious; grave: *a severe manner, a severe illness.* **3** *adj* difficult: *The new pilot had to pass a series of severe tests.* **se·ver·er, se·ver·est. –se·vere′ly,** *adv,* **–se·ver′i·ty,** *n.*

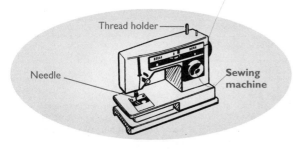

Thread holder
Needle
Sewing machine

sew (sō) *v* work with a needle and thread: *You can sew by hand or with a machine.* **sewed, sewn** or **sewed, sew·ing. –sew′ing,** *n.*

sew·er (sū′ər) *n* a pipe to take away waste matter. Sewers are usually underground.

sew·age *n* the waste matter that passes through sewers.

sex (seks) **1** *n* the fact of being male or female: *What sex is that kitten?* **2** *n* action by which a male and a female produce young. The full name for this is **sexual intercourse. –sex′u·al,** *adj.*

sex·ist *adj* mistakenly believing that the other sex is weaker, less important, or less able to do things than the sex that you are: "Girls can't play baseball" and "Boys can't write poetry" are sexist remarks.

shab·by (shab′ē) *adj* much worn; run-down: *shabby clothes, a shabby old house.* **shab·bi·er, shab·bi·est.**

shack (shak) *n* a roughly built hut or cabin.

shade (shād) **1** *n* a partly dark place, not in the sunshine: *We sat in the shade of a big tree.* **2** *n* something that shuts out some light: *a window shade, a shade for a lamp.* **3** *v* keep light from: *A big hat shades your eyes.* **4** *n* lightness or darkness of colour: *I like all shades of blue.* **5** *v* in drawing and painting, mark with different degrees of darkness: *The artist shaded the picture of the ball to make it look more real.* **shad·ed, shad·ing.**

shad·ow (shad′ō) *n* the shade made by some person, animal, or thing. **shad·y 1** *adj* in the shade: *a shady spot under a tree.* **2** *adj* giving shade: *a shady tree.* **3** *adj Informal.* dishonest: *a shady character.*

shaft (shaft) **1** *n* a deep, narrow space: *an elevator shaft, a mine shaft.* **2** *n* the long, straight handle of a hammer, golf club, etc. **3** *n* a ray or beam of light.

shag·gy (shag′ē) *adj* covered with a thick, rough mass of hair: *a shaggy dog.* **shag·gi·er, shag·gi·est.**

shake (shāk) **1** *v* move quickly backward and forward, up and down, or from side to side: *to shake a rug. The baby shook the rattle. He shook his fist in anger. Shake the dice.* **2** *v* clasp hands in greeting: *to shake hands.* **3** *v* tremble: *He is shaking with cold.* **4** *n* the act of shaking: *A shake of her head was her only answer.* **5** *n* a drink made by shaking ice cream, milk, etc. together. **shook, shak·en, shak·ing.**

shak·y 1 *adj* shaking: *a shaky voice.* **2** *adj* liable to break: *a shaky porch.*

shake hands, take a person's hand in your hand and move it up and down.

shake off, get rid of.

shake up, 1 shake hard. **2** stir up. **3** upset badly: *He was shaken up after the car crash.*

shall (shal) an auxiliary (helping) verb used: **1** *v* in questions with *I* or *we* to ask what a person is to do: *Shall we go? Shall we wait?* **2** *v* in statements with *you, he, she,* or *they,* to show that a person has to do something: *You shall pay attention. He shall stay in his room for an hour.* **3** *v* with *I* and *we* to indicate simple future time: *I shall go tomorrow if I cannot make it today. past tense* **should.**

shal·low (shal′ō) *adj* not deep: *shallow water, a shallow dish.*

sham (sham) **1** *n* a fraud; pretence: *Her goodness is all a sham.* **2** *adj* false. **3** *v* pretend: **shammed, sham·ming.**

sha·man (shä′mən) *n* in many traditional cultures, a person who uses special powers to cure illness, influence events for good or evil, etc.

shame (shām) **1** *n* a painful feeling of having done something wrong: *The child blushed with shame when she was caught lying.* **2** *n* a fact to be sorry about; pity: *What a shame you can't come to the party!* **shamed, sham·ing.**
shame·faced *adj* showing embarrassment.
shame·ful *adj* causing shame.
shame·less *adj* without shame.

sham·poo (sham pū′) **1** *v* wash the hair, scalp, a rug, etc. with a soapy liquid. **2** *n* a liquid used for shampooing.
sham·pooed, sham·poo·ing.

shan·ty (shan′tē) **1** ❧ *n* a roughly built hut or cabin. **2** *n* a song that used to be sung by sailors in rhythm with the movements made working on a sailing ship. *pl* **shan·ties.**

shape (shāp) **1** *n* the outline or form of a person or thing: *An apple is different in shape from a banana.* **2** *v* form into a shape: *Randall shapes clay into toy animals.* **3** *n* condition: *The athlete exercised to keep herself in good shape.*
shaped, shap·ing.
shape·less *adj* without a definite shape: *a shapeless lump of mud.*

share (sher) **1** *n* a part belonging to one person: *The father gave each child an equal share of ice cream.* **2** *v* use together; enjoy together: *to share a room, to share a joke, to share answers.*
3 *v* divide into parts for sharing: *Lance shared his candy with his sister. Share the work in this project.* **shared, shar·ing.**

shark (shärk) *n* a large ocean fish, which can be ferocious.

sharp (shärp) **1** *adj* with a thin cutting edge or a fine point: *a sharp knife, a sharp pin.* **2** *adj* not rounded: *a sharp corner on a box, a sharp pencil, a sharp turn.* **3** *adj* very cold: *sharp weather, a sharp morning.* **4** *adj* severe; biting: *sharp words.* **5** *adj* acting strongly on the senses: *a sharp taste, a sharp noise, a sharp pain.*

6 *adj* being aware of things quickly: *a sharp eye, sharp ears, a sharp mind.* –**sharp′ly,** *adv,* –**sharp′ness,** *n.*

sharp·en *v* make sharp: *Sharpen the pencil. Sharpen your wits.*

shat·ter (shat′ər) **1** *v* break into pieces: *A stone shattered the window.* **2** *v* destroy: *Our hopes for a picnic were shattered by the rain.*

shave (shāv) *v* cut hair from anything with a razor: *My father shaves every day.* **shaved, shaved** or **shav·en, shav·ing.**
a close shave, a narrow escape.

shear (shēr) *v* cut the wool or fleece from: *Nowadays, most farmers shear sheep with electric shears.* **sheared, sheared** or **shorn, shear·ing.**
shears *pl.n* any cutting instrument resembling large scissors: *grass shears, tin shears, barber's shears.*

shed (shed) **1** *n* a hut used for shelter, storage, etc.: *a tool shed, a wagon shed.* **2** *v* pour out; let fall: *The girl shed tears.* **3** *v* throw off; cast aside: *The snake shed its skin.* **shed, shed·ding.**

A domestic sheep— usually about 90 cm high at the shoulder

sheep (shēp) *n* an animal raised for meat, wool, and skin. *pl* **sheep.**

sheet (shēt) **1** *n* a large piece of thin cloth, used to sleep on or under. **2** *n* a flat, thin piece of anything: *a sheet of ice, a sheet of paper.*

shelf (shelf) *n* a thin, flat piece of wood attached to a wall to hold things such as books, dishes, etc. *pl* **shelves.**
shelve *v* put on a shelf: *to shelve books.*

shell (shel) **1** *n* the hard outside covering of nuts, eggs, certain animals, etc.: *Oysters, turtles, and beetles all have shells.* **2** *v* take out of a shell: *Grandma is shelling peas for dinner.*
shell·fish *n* a water animal with a shell. Oysters, clams, crabs, and lobsters are shellfish.
come out of your shell, stop being shy.

shel·ter (shel′tər) **1** *n* something that covers or protects: *Trees are a shelter from the sun.* **2** *v* protect: *Umbrellas shelter us from rain.* **3** *n* protection: *We took shelter from the storm in a barn.*

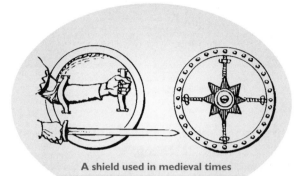
A shield used in medieval times

shield (shēld) **1** *n* a piece of armour that used to be carried for protection in battle. **2** *n* any person or thing that protects: *She wore a big hat as a shield against the sun.* **3** *v* protect; defend: *The moose shielded her calf from the grizzly bear.*

shift (shift) **1** *v* change from one place to another: *He shifted the heavy bag from one hand to the other. She tried to shift the blame to someone else.* **2** *n* a change of direction: *a shift of the wind.* **3** *n* a group of workers who work during the same period of time: *the night shift.*

shine (shīn) **1** *v* give off light: *The sun shines.* **2** *n* a light; brightness: *the shine of a lamp.* **3** *v* make bright; polish: *to shine shoes.* **shone** or **shined, shin·ing.** –**shin′y,** *adj.*

Shin·to (shin′tō) **1** *n* a follower of the ancient religion of Japan, which includes the worship of ancestors and has many gods. Shintos follow a set of seven rules that require faith, hard work, and a humble, peaceful, sincere, and thankful spirit. **2** *adj* having to do with this religion. –**Shin′to·ism′,** *n.*

ship (ship) **1** *n* any large vessel such as a steamship. **2** *n* an airship, airplane, spacecraft, etc. **3** *v* send something from one place to another by a ship, train, truck, etc. The thing sent is called a **shipment. shipped, ship·ping.**

–**ship** *a suffix meaning* the condition of being. *Friendship* means the condition of being a *friend.*

shirt (shərt) *n* a garment for the upper part of your body.
keep your shirt on, *Slang.* keep your temper.

shiv·er (shiv′ər) **1** *v* shake with cold, fear, etc. **2** *n* shaking from cold, fear, etc.

shoal (shōl) **1** *n* a shallow place in a sea, lake, or stream. **2** *n* a large number: *We saw a shoal of fish in Lake Panache.*

shock (shok) **1** *n* a sudden, upsetting disturbance: **2** *v* cause surprise, horror, or disgust: *The pictures of the airplane crash shocked me.* **3** *n* a disturbance produced by electricity passing through your body. –**shock′ing,** *adj.*

shoe (shū) *n* an outer covering for your foot.
shoe·lace *n* a cord for fastening a shoe.

shoot (shūt) **1** *v* send with force at a target: *He shot the puck into the open net. A bow shoots an arrow.* **2** *v* move suddenly and rapidly: *A motorcycle shot past. Flames shoot up from a fire.* **3** *v* grow quickly: *The corn is shooting up in the warm weather.* **4** *v* take a picture with a camera. **5** *n* a new part growing: *See the new shoots on that bush.* **shot, shoot·ing.**
shooting star a meteor as seen when it enters the earth's atmosphere.

shop (shop) **1** *v* visit stores to look at or to buy things: *We shopped all morning.* **2** *n* a place where things are sold or repaired. **shopped, shop·ping.**
shop·lift·ing *n* stealing goods from a store while pretending to be a customer.
shopping mall a large number of stores, usually under one roof, with its own parking lot.

shore (shȯr) *n* the land at the edge of a sea, lake, etc.

short (shȯrt) **1** *adj* not long: *a short time, short hair.* **2** *adj* not tall: *a short person, short grass.* **3** *adj* not enough: *I'm always short of money.* –**short′en,** *v.*
short·age *n* too small an amount: *There is a shortage of grain because of poor crops.*
short·ly *adv* soon: *I will be with you shortly.*
short-sight·ed *adj* not able to see far.
short story a short piece of fiction with only a few characters.
cut short, end suddenly.
fall short, fail to reach.
for short, to make shorter: *Patrick was called Pat for short.*
in short, briefly.
make short work of, deal with quickly.
run short, not have enough.

shot (shot) **1** *n* the sound of a gun: *They heard two shots.* **2** *n* attempt to hit: *a good shot, a practice shot.* **3** *n* *Informal.* an injection of medicine. **4** *n* *Informal.* a try: *I think I'll have a shot at snowboarding.* *pl* **shots.**
not by a long shot, not at all.

should (shůd) the past tense of **shall**, used: **1** *v* to mean that someone ought to do something: *Everyone should learn to swim.* **2** *v* to express a belief: *She should be there by now.*

shoul·der (shōl′dər) **1** *n* the part of your body to which your arm is attached. **2** *n* the edge of a road, often unpaved: *Don't drive on the shoulder.*
put your shoulder to the wheel, make a great effort.

shout (shout) **1** *v* call out loudly: *Somebody shouted "Fire!"* **2** *n* a loud call.

shove (shuv) **1** *v* to push hard: *We had to shove to get on the bus.* **2** *n* a hard push. **shoved, shov·ing.**

shov·el **1** *n* a tool with a broad blade for lifting and throwing snow, earth, etc.: *a snow shovel.* **2** *v* use a shovel.

show (shō) **1** *v* let be seen; be in sight: *The little girl showed us her paintings. The hole in his sock shows above his shoe.* **2** *v* guide: *Show him the way out.* **3** *v* explain to: *The teacher showed the children how to do the problem.* **4** *n* an entertainment, such as a stage play or movie.
showed, shown or **showed, show·ing.**
show off, try to attract attention: *Kareem is always showing off.*
show up, put in an appearance: *She showed up late for the party.*

show·er (shou′ər) **1** *n* a brief fall of rain, or anything like a fall of rain: *a shower of hail, a snow shower, a shower of tears, a shower of sparks.* **2** *n* a party at which gifts are presented on some special occasion. **3** *n* a wash in which water pours down on your body from above in small jets: *Keir takes a shower every morning.* **4** *v* wash in this way.

shred (shred) **1** *n* a very small piece torn off or cut off: *The wind tore the sail to shreds.* **2** *v* tear or cut into small pieces: *shredded paper.*
shred·ded or **shred, shred·ding.**

shriek (shrēk) **1** *n* a loud, sharp, shrill sound: *the shriek of a whistle.* **2** *v* make such a sound.

shrill (shril) *adj* high and sharp in sound: *Seagulls make shrill noises.* –**shril′ly,** *adv.*

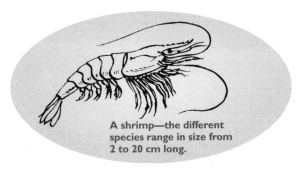
A shrimp—the different species range in size from 2 to 20 cm long.

shrimp (shrimp) *n* a small shellfish with a long tail. *pl* **shrimps** or **shrimp.**

shrink (shringk) *v* become smaller or make smaller: *Beryl's wool sweater shrank when it was washed. Hot water shrinks wool.* **shrank** or **shrunk, shrunk** or **shrunk·en, shrink·ing.**

shriv·el (shriv′əl) *v* dry up; wither: *The hot sunshine shrivelled the grass.* **shriv·elled** or **shriv·eled, shriv·el·ling** or **shriv·el·ing.**

shrug (shrug) **1** *v* raise your shoulders to show you don't know or don't care. **2** *n* this kind of movement. **shrugged, shrug·ging.**

shud·der (shud′ər) **1** *v* shiver with horror, fear, cold, etc. **2** *n* a shiver.

shuf·fle (shuf′əl) **1** *v* walk without lifting your feet. **2** *v* mix cards, etc. so as to change the order. **shuf·fled, shuf·fling.**

shut (shut) **1** *v* close something by pushing or pulling a lid, door, etc. into place: *He shut the doors and windows. Shut your eyes.* **2** *adj* closed: *The door is shut.* **shut, shut·ting.**
shut down, stop a machine: *to shut down a computer.*
shut out, defeat a team without allowing it to score.
shut up, *Informal.* stop talking.

shut·tle (shut′əl) *n* a vehicle that runs back and forth: *a space shuttle, a shuttle bus to the airport.*

shy (shī) *adj* uncomfortable with people; timid: *Zack is shy and dislikes parties. A deer is a shy animal.* **shy·er** or **shi·er, shy·est** or **shi·est.** –**shy′ness,** *n.*

sick (sik) **1** *adj* ill. **2** *adj* wanting to vomit. **3** *adj* weary; tired: *She is sick of watching TV.* **sick·ness** *n* illness; disease.

side (sīd) **1** *n* a surface or line marking the edge of something: *the sides of a square, a side of a box.* **2** *n* a surface that is not the front, back, top, or bottom: *the side of the house.* **3** *n* one surface or edge of something: *the south side of the street, a pain in your left side, to write on one side of a piece of paper.* **4** *n* a team: *The children chose sides for a game of softball.* **5** *adj* having to do with one side: *a side door, a side view.* **sid·ed, sid·ing.**

side·track *v* put aside; turn aside: *The teacher refused to be sidetracked by questions on other subjects.* **side·ways 1** *adv* to one side: *to walk sideways.* **2** *adv* with one side toward the front: *to stand sideways.*

side by side, beside one another.

side with, support, especially in an argument: *The sisters always side with each other.*

take sides, place yourself with one person against another.

siege (sēj) *n* the surrounding of a place by an army trying to capture it.

Two kinds of sieve

sieve (siv) *n* a fine net that lets small pieces pass through, but not larger pieces: *Shaking flour through a sieve breaks up lumps.*

sift *v* put through a sieve: *Sift sugar onto the top of the cake.*

sigh (sī) **1** *v* draw in and let out a long, deep breath because you are sad, tired, relieved, etc. **2** *n* the act of sighing: *a sigh of relief.*

sight (sīt) **1** *n* the power of seeing: *Birds have better sight than dogs.* **2** *n* something impressive, startling, or strange to see: *Niagara Falls is one of the sights of the world. What a sight!*

sight·see·ing *n* going around to see places of interest: *a weekend of sightseeing in Toronto.*

catch sight of, see: *I caught sight of her.*

CONFUSABLES ..... sight

sight means "view":
  A snowy day can be a beautiful sight

site means "place":
  The hospital will be built on this site.

sign (sīn) **1** *n* a mark used to represent something: *The sign for add is +.* **2** *v* write your name. Your name written by you is your **signature. 3** *n* a motion used to mean something: *A nod is a sign of agreement.* **4** *n* a board with information on it: *a stop sign.* **5** *n* an indication: *There were no signs of life about the house.* **6** *v* use sign language.

sig·nif·i·cant *adj* full of meaning: *July 1, 1867, is a significant date for Canadians.* **–sig·nif′i·cance,** *n.*

sign language a language for people who cannot hear, that uses hand movements instead of spoken words. ▶See **language.**

sig·nal (sig′nəl) **1** *n* a message: *A red light is a signal of danger. The raising of the flag was a signal to advance.* **2** *v* make a signal to: *He signalled the car to stop by raising his hand.* **sig·nalled** or **sig·naled, sig·nal·ling** or **sig·nal·ing.**

Sikh (sēk) **1** *n* a follower of a religion that began in the 1500s, based on the Guru Granth Sahib, a holy book containing the writings of ten great gurus or prophets. Sikhs believe in one God. **2** *adj* having to do with the Sikhs or their religion. **–Sikh′ism,** *n.*

si·lence (sī′ləns) **1** *n* the absence of sound: *The teacher asked for silence.* **2** *v* make silent: *The nurse silenced the baby's crying.* **si·lenced, si·lenc·ing. –si′lent,** *adj.*

in silence, without saying anything.

Grammar ✓Check .. silent letters

English spelling is full of **letters** that are **not spoken**.

• The letter -*e* is silent at the end of words like *hide* and *tape,* but you can tell it is there because it makes the other vowel sound long.

• The letters *g, k, p,* and *w* are sometimes silent when they are followed by another consonant at the beginning of words like *know* and *wrong.*

One way to remember these letters when you are spelling is to say the silent letters in your head whenever you read the word: *k-now.*

sil·hou·ette (sil′ū et′) *n* a dark outline against a lighter background. **sil·hou·et·ted, sil·hou·et·ting.**

sil·ly (sil′ē) *adj* without sense; foolish; ridiculous. **sil·li·er, sil·li·est.**

A silo beside a barn

si·lo (sī′lō) *n* an airtight building or pit in which green food, called **silage,** for farm animals is kept. *pl* **si·los.**

sil·ver (sil′vər) **1** *n* a shiny precious metal used for making coins, jewellery, cutlery, etc. **2** *adj* having the colour of silver: *a silver slipper.*

sim·i·lar (sim′ə lər) *adj* alike: *A creek and a brook are similar.* –**sim′i·lar′i·ty,** *n.*

sim·i·le (sim′ə lē) *n* a comparison of two things using the words "like" or "as." *Examples: muscles like iron, a child as brave as a lion.*

sim·ple (sim′pəl) **1** *adj* easy to do or understand: *a simple problem.* **2** *adj* not divided into parts; not complex: *An oak leaf is a simple leaf. "Scott closed the door" is a simple sentence.* **3** *adj* plain: *She usually eats simple food.* **sim·pler, sim·plest.**
sim·pli·fy *v* make plainer or easier.
sim·ply 1 *adv* in a simple way: *She explained the rules simply and clearly.* **2** *adv* only: *The baby did not simply cry; he yelled.* **3** *adv* absolutely: *simply perfect.*

Grammar ✓Check . simple sentence

A **simple sentence** contains one subject, and one verb. It may also include words that modify the subject or verb: *Johanna sang. Michael ran home. The house next door was sold last week.*

sim·u·late (sim′yə lāt′) **1** *v* pretend: *Colette simulated sleep so that nobody would disturb her.* **2** *v* imitate: *This computer software simulates the flight of an airplane.* **sim·u·lat·ed, sim·u·lat·ing.**
sim·ul·ta·ne·ous (sī′məl tā′nē əs *or* sim′əl tā′nē əs) *adj* happening at the same time: *simultaneous events.* –**si′mul·ta′ne·ous·ly,** *adv.*

sin (sin) **1** *n* a bad deed: *Lying, stealing, dishonesty, and cruelty are sins.* **2** *v* do a bad deed. **sinned, sin·ning.**

since (sins) **1** *prep* from a past time till now: *We have been up since five.* **2** *conj* because: *Since you feel tired, you should rest.*

sin·cere (sin sēr′) *adj* honest: *Leif made a sincere effort to pass his exams.* **sin·cer·er, sin·cer·est.** –**sin·cer′i·ty** (sin ser′ə tē), *n.*

sing (sing) **1** *v* make music with your voice: *He sings on television.* **2** *v* make pleasant, musical sounds: *Birds sing.* **sang** or **sung, sung, sing·ing.** –**sing′er,** *n.*

singe (sinj) *v* burn a little, especially hair or cloth. **singed, singe·ing.**

sin·gle (sing′gəl) **1** *adj* only one: *The spider hung by a single thread.* **2** *adj* for only one: *The sisters share one room with two single beds in it.* **3** *adj* not married: *She remained single all her life.*
sin·gu·lar *adj* referring to one: *"Boy" is singular; "boys" is plural.*
single out, pick out: *The teacher singled Georgina out for her excellent work.*

Grammar ✓Check ..... singular

Some words look plural, but are really **singular**. Here are some examples: *athletics, news, measles,* and *mathematics.*

sin·is·ter (sin′i stər) *adj* bad; evil; dishonest: *a sinister plan.*

sink (singk) **1** *v* fall slowly: *The sun sinks in the west.* **2** *v* go under water, or make go under water: *The ship is sinking.* **3** *n* a shallow basin with a drain: *The dishes are in the kitchen sink.* **sank** or **sunk, sunk, sink·ing.**

sip (sip) **1** *v* drink little by little: *Lana sipped her tea.* **2** *n* a very small swallow: *She took a sip.* **sipped, sip·ping.**

sir (sər) **1** *n* a polite name to use when speaking to a man: *Excuse me, sir.* **2 Sir,** *n* the title of a knight.

si·ren (sī′rən) *n* a device that makes a loud wailing sound: *We heard the sirens of the fire trucks.*

sis·ter (sis′tər) *n* a daughter of the same parents: *I have one sister and two brothers.* –**sis′ter·ly,** *adj.*

sit (sit) **1** *v* rest on your bottom: *Hannah sat on the bench.* **2** *v* watch children when parents are away; babysit: *She used to sit for the woman next door.* **sat, sit·ting.**

sit·ter *n* babysitter.

site (sīt) *n* the position or place of something: *The site for the new school has not yet been chosen.*

sit·u·a·tion (sich′ū ā′shən) *n* position: *What would you do in the same situation?*

six (siks) ►See Appendix.

size (sīz) **1** *n* the amount of surface or space a thing takes up: *The two boys are the same size.* **2** *n* one of a series of measures: *I want the larger size, please.*

size up, *Informal.* form an opinion of.

siz·zle (siz′əl) *v* make a hissing sound, like fat does when it is hot. **siz·zled, siz·zling.**

skate (skāt) **1** *n* a boot with a metal blade attached to the sole, for gliding over ice. **2** *n* a roller skate, which has wheels for rolling over the ground. **3** *v* move on skates. **skat·ed, skat·ing.**

skate·board (skāt′bȯrd′) *n* a small, narrow board with a pair of roller-skate wheels at each end used for moving along streets, sidewalks, etc.

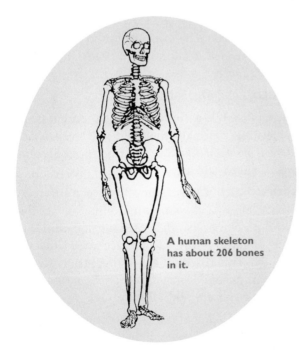

A human skeleton has about 206 bones in it.

skel·e·ton (skel′ə tən) *n* the bones of a body, fitted together.

sketch (skech) **1** *n* a rough drawing or plan. **2** *v* make a sketch or plan.

ski (skē) **1** *n* one of a pair of long, slender boards that fasten onto boots to let a person glide over snow. *pl* **skis. 2** *v* travel on skis. **skied, ski·ing.**

skid (skid) **1** *v* slide sideways while moving: *The car skidded on the slippery road.* **2** *n* an uncontrolled slide: *The car went into a skid on the icy road.* **skid·ded, skid·ding.**

skill (skil) *n* an ability gained by practice: *It takes skill to tune a piano.* −**skil·ful** or −**skill·ful,** *adj,* −**skilled,** *adj.*

skim (skim) **1** *v* remove from the top: *The cook skims the fat from the cold soup.* **2** *v* read quickly, missing some parts: *It took me an hour to skim the book.* **skimmed, skim·ming.**

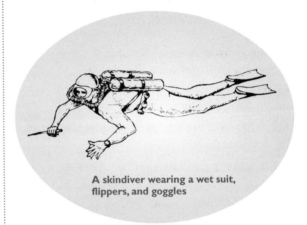

A skindiver wearing a wet suit, flippers, and goggles

skin (skin) **1** *n* the outer covering of the bodies of human beings and animals: *Cows have thick skins.* **2** *n* any outer covering, like on fruit and vegetables. **3** *v* take the skin off: *Clark skinned his knees when he fell.* **skinned, skin·ning.**

skin diving swimming underwater carrying air tanks to let you breathe.

by the skin of your teeth, only just.

skip (skip) **1** *v* move along by stepping and hopping first with one foot, then with the other, sometimes over a rope. **2** *v* send bouncing along a surface: *We like to skip stones on Peskowesk Lake.* **3** *v* pass over: *Devra skips the hard words when she reads.* **4** *v Informal.* stay away from: *to skip class.* **skipped, skip·ping.**

skirt (skərt) *n* a woman's or girl's garment that hangs from the waist.

skit (skit) *n* a short, humorous play for acting: *Our class did a skit on learning to ride a bike.*

skull (skul) *n* the bones of your head.

A striped skunk—
about 40 cm long
excluding the tail

skunk (skungk) *n* a black, bushy-tailed animal about the size of a cat, usually with white stripes along the back. Skunks give off a very strong, unpleasant smell when frightened or attacked.

sky (skī) *n* the space high above the earth, that looks like a huge dome covering the world. *pl* **skies.**
sky·line *n* the outline of buildings as seen against the sky: *the Vancouver skyline.*
sky·scrap·er *n* a very tall building: *New York is famous for its skyscrapers.*

slab (slab) *n* a broad, flat, thick piece: *a marble slab, a slab of meat.*

slack (slak) **1** *adj* not tight or firm; loose: *The rope hung slack.* **2** *adj* careless or slow: *a slack worker, a slack pace.* –**slack'en,** *v.*

slam (slam) **1** *v* shut or hit with force and noise: *He slammed the door. The car slammed into a truck.* **2** *n* a bang: *Theo threw his books down with a slam.* **slammed, slam·ming.**

slang (slang) *n* words, phrases, meanings, etc. not considered acceptable for use in formal speech and writing.

slant (slant) **1** *v* slope: *The letters in this sentence slant to the right.* **2** *n* a slope: *Has your roof a sharp slant?*

slap (slap) **1** *n* a blow with an open hand or with something flat. **2** *v* strike in this way: *He slapped at the fly with a magazine.* **slapped, slap·ping.**
✿ **slap·shot** *n* in hockey, a fast, not always accurate, shot. **slap·stick** *n* comedy full of rough play.

slaugh·ter (slot'ər) **1** *n* the killing of animals for food: *to fatten hogs for slaughter.* **2** *v* kill animals for food: *Millions of cattle are slaughtered every year.*

slave (slāv) *n* a person who is the property of another: *Slaves were bought and sold like horses.* –**slav'er·y,** *n.*

slay (slā) *v* kill, especially in battle: *Jack slew the giant.* **slew, slain, slay·ing.**

CONFUSABLES ..... slay

slay means "kill":
The knight said he would slay the dragon.
sleigh means "sled":
Oh what fun it is to ride in a one-horse open sleigh!

sled (sled) *n* a vehicle with runners, for use on ice or snow.

sleep (slēp) **1** *v* rest your body and mind: *We sleep at night.* **2** *n* a resting of your body and mind occurring naturally and regularly: *Many people need eight to ten hours of sleep a day.* **slept, sleep·ing.** –**sleep'less,** *adj,* –**sleep'y,** *adj.*

sleet (slēt) *n* partly frozen rain.

sleeve (slēv) *n* the part of a garment that covers your arm.
up your sleeve, ready for use when needed.

sleigh (slā) *n* a carriage or cart on runners for use on snow or ice.

slen·der (slen'dər) **1** *adj* long and thin: *A pencil is slender.* **2** *adj* small: *a slender meal, a slender chance.*

sleuth *n Informal.* detective.

slice (slīs) **1** *n* a thin, flat, broad piece cut from something, especially food: *a slice of bread, a slice of meat, a slice of cake.* **2** *v* cut into slices: *Slice the bread.* **sliced, slic·ing.**

slide (slīd) **1** *v* move smoothly over a surface: *to slide on ice.* **2** *n* a smooth, sloping surface for sliding: *a playground slide.* **3** *n* a small, thin sheet of glass on which things are placed, to look at under a microscope. **4** *n* a small transparent photograph: *Slides are put in a projector and shown on a screen.* **slid, slid·ing.**

slight (slīt) *adj* not much; not important: *I have a slight headache.* –**slight'ly,** *adv.*

slim (slim) **1** *adj* thin: *a slim wrist.* **2** *adj* small: *a slim chance.* **slim·mer, slim·mest.**

slime (slīm) *n* soft, sticky mud or something like it. –**slim'y,** *adj.*

slip (slip) **1** *v* move smoothly and quietly: *Aurora slipped out of the room.* **2** *v* slide suddenly: *He slipped on the icy sidewalk. The knife slipped and cut him.* **3** *n* a mistake: *She makes slips in pronouncing words.* **4** *n* a narrow strip of paper, wood, etc. **slipped, slip·ping.**

slip·per·y 1 *adj* causing or likely to cause slipping: *The steps are slippery with ice.* **2** *adj* not to be depended on; tricky.

slip·shod *adj* careless; untidy.

give someone the slip, *Informal.* get away from someone: *The deer gave the hunter the slip.*

slip of the tongue, a remark made by mistake.

slip up, *Informal.* make a mistake or error.

slit (slit) **1** *v* cut or tear along a line: *Madison used a paper knife to slit the envelope open.* **2** *n* a straight, narrow cut. **slit, slit·ting.**

sliv·er (sliv′ər) *n* a long, thin piece that has been split off or cut off; splinter.

slob·ber (slob′ər) *v* let liquid run out from your mouth; drool.

slob *n Slang.* an untidy, or clumsy person.

✤ **slob ice** small pieces of ice crowded together.

slo·gan (slō′gən) *n* a word or phrase used to advertise: *Safety First is our slogan.*

slope (slōp) **1** *v* go up or down at an angle; slant: *The land slopes toward the sea.* **2** *n* any line, surface, land, etc. that goes up or down at an angle: *If you roll a ball up a slope, it will roll down again.* **sloped, slop·ing.**

**A three-toed sloth—
about 48 cm long**

sloth (sloth *or* slōth) *n* a very slow-moving animal from South America that lives in trees: *Sloths hang upside down from tree branches.*

slouch (slouch) *v* stand, sit, or move in an awkward, drooping way: *The weary man slouched along.*

slough (slū) **1** *n* a body of fresh water formed by rain or melted snow: *Wild ducks nest on the prairie sloughs.* **2** *n* a soft, deep, muddy place.

slough off, (sluf of) cast off: *The snake sloughed off its old skin.*

slow (slō) **1** *adj* not fast or quick: *a slow journey.* **2** *adj* going at less than proper speed: *a slow runner.* **3** *v* make slow or become slow: *to slow down a car, slow up.*

slug (slug) **1** *n* a slow-moving animal like a snail, but without a shell. **2** *n* a small disc or other shaped piece of metal: *It is illegal to use slugs instead of coins in a parking meter.* **3** *v Informal.* hit hard. **slugged, slug·ging.**

slug·gish *adj* without energy: *a sluggish stream, a sluggish mood.*

slum·ber (slum′bər) **1** *v* to sleep. **2** *n* a sleep: *The baby awoke from her slumber.*

slump (slump) **1** *v* drop heavily: *He fainted and slumped to the floor.* **2** *v* move, walk, sit, etc. in a drooping manner: *The bored students slumped in their seats.* **3** *n* a heavy or sudden fall: *a slump in prices.*

slur (slər) **1** *v* speak unclearly: *Many people slur "How do you do?"* **2** *n* an insulting remark. **slurred, slur·ring.**

slush (slush) **1** *n* partly melted snow. **2** *n* silly, sentimental, talk, writing, etc.

sly (slī) *adj* cunning; tricky: *The sly cat stole the meat while the cook's back was turned.*

sly·er or **sli·er, sly·est** or **sli·est. –sly′ly,** *adv.*

on the sly, in a sly way; secretly.

small (smol) *adj* little: *A cottage is a small house.*

smart (smärt) **1** *v* feel or cause sharp pain: *Her eyes smarted from the smoke. The cut smarts.* **2** *adj* clever; bright: *Avalia is a smart girl.* **3** *adj* fresh and neat: *the smart uniform of a good soldier.* **4** *adj* fashionable: *Sherry has a smart new dress.* **–smart′ly,** *adv,* **–smart′ness,** *n.*

smart·en *v* improve in appearance: *The new rug smartens up Leroy's bedroom.*

smarten up, *Informal.* work better: *The coach told the team to smarten up.*

smash (smash) **1** *v* break or be broken into pieces with violence and noise: *The boy smashed a window with a stone.* **2** *v* crash: *The car smashed into the tree.* **3** *n* a crash: *the smash of two cars.* **4** *n* a great success: *the play was a smash.*

S
s

smear (smēr) **1** *v* rub or spread oil, grease, paint, etc. **2** *n* a mark left by smearing: *smears of paint on the floor.*

smell (smel) **1** *n* scent; odour: *the smell of roses.* **2** *v* detect smells: *We smell with our noses.* **3** *v* give out a bad smell: *That wet dog smells.* **smelled** or **smelt, smell·ing.**

smell·y *adj* having a strong or unpleasant smell: *Rotten fish are smelly.*

smile (smīl) **1** *v* show pleasure, amusement, etc. by an upward curve of the mouth. **2** *n* the act of smiling: *I gave the girl a friendly smile.* **smiled, smil·ing.**

smog (smog) *n* air pollution: *Car exhaust fumes are one of the major causes of smog.*

WORD HISTORY . . . . smog

Smog is a combination of **sm**oke and f**og**. Another word like this is **brunch**, a combination of **br**eakfast and l**unch**.

Can you think of any more words like this?

---

smoke (smōk) **1** *n* a cloud of gases from something burning. *The smoke from the campfire made our eyes water.* **2** *v* give off smoke: *The fireplace smokes.* **3** *v* breathe in the smoke from tobacco and blow it out again. **4** *v* preserve a piece of meat, fish, etc. by putting it into smoke. **smoked, smok·ing.**

smok·y 1 *adj* giving off a lot of smoke: *a smoky fire.* **2** *adj* full of smoke: *a smoky room.*

smooth (smūᴛʜ) **1** *adj* even; not rough: *smooth stones.* **2** *adj* without lumps: *smooth gravy.* **3** *adj* easy; pleasant; polite: *That salesperson is a smooth talker.* **4** *v* make smooth: *She smoothed out the ball of crushed paper and read what was on it.*

smudge (smuj) **1** *n* a dirty mark; a smear. **2** *v* smear: *The child's drawing was smudged.* **smudged, smudg·ing.**

smug (smug) *adj* self-satisfied. **smug·ger, smug·gest.**

smug·gle (smug′əl) *v* bring in or take out secretly: *They were sentenced to several years in prison for smuggling drugs into Canada. She tried to smuggle her puppy into the house.* **smug·gled, smug·gling. –smug′gler,** *n.*

snack (snak) *n* a light meal.

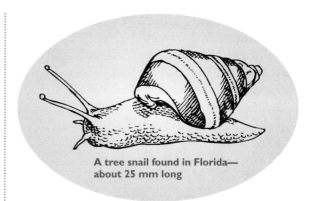
A tree snail found in Florida—
about 25 mm long

snail (snāl) *n* a small, soft-bodied animal that crawls very slowly. Most snails have shells on their backs into which they can hide for protection.

Snake: a prairie rattlesnake—
about 120 cm long

snake (snāk) *n* a long, slender reptile with no legs: *Some snakes are poisonous.*

snap (snap) **1** *v* make or cause to make a sudden, sharp sound: *This wood snaps as it burns. The teacher snapped her fingers to get our attention.* **2** *n* a quick, sharp sound: *The small box shut with a snap.* **3** *v* break suddenly: *The violin string snapped.* **4** *v* make a sudden, quick bite: *The dog snapped at the child's hand.* **5** *v* take a photograph of. **6** *n Slang.* an easy job, piece of work, etc. **snapped, snap·ping.**
cold snap, a few days of cold weather.

snarl (snàrl) **1** *v* growl sharply: *The dog snarled at the stranger.* **2** *n* a sharp, angry growl. **3** *v* speak harshly in a sharp, angry tone.

snatch (snach) *v* grab suddenly: *The hawk snatched the mouse and flew away.*

sneak (snēk) **1** *v* move or behave in a sly or secret way. **2** *n* a sneaking, cowardly person. **–sneak′y,** *adj.*

sneak·er *n* a light shoe for sports like tennis, or for general casual wear.

sneeze (snēz) *v* expel air suddenly and violently through your nose and mouth. **sneezed, sneez·ing.**

sniff (snif) **1** *v* draw air through your nose in short breaths that can be heard: *The woman who had a cold was sniffing.* **2** *v* smell with sniffs: *The dog sniffed at the stranger.* **3** *n* the act or sound of sniffing: *He cleared his nose with a loud sniff.*

snif·fle *v* sniff again and again.

sniv·el (sniv′əl) *v* whine.

snip (snip) **1** *v* cut with a small, quick stroke: *She snipped the thread.* **2** *n* the act of snipping: *With a few snips Beatrice cut out a paper doll.* **3** *n* a small piece cut off: *Pick up the snips of cloth.* **snipped, snip·ping.**

snooze (snüz) *Informal.* **1** *v* take a nap: *The dog snoozed on the porch in the sun.* **2** *n* a nap. **snoozed, snooz·ing.**

snore (snȯr) *v* breathe during sleep with a harsh, rough sound: *People often snore when sleeping on their backs.* **snored, snor·ing.**

snort (snȯrt) *v* force breath violently through your nose.

snout (snout) *n* the nose and mouth of an animal. Pigs, dogs, and crocodiles have snouts.

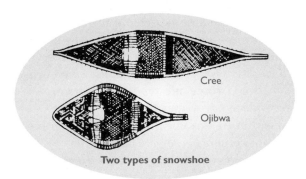

Cree

Ojibwa

Two types of snowshoe

snow (snō) **1** *n* frozen water in soft, white flakes that fall to earth: *Rain falls in summer; snow falls in winter.* **2** *v* fall as snow: *It snowed all week in the Northwest Territories.* **–snow′y,** *adj.*

snow·board *n* a wide board that you stand on to go downhill on snow. **–snow′board′ing,** *n.*

snow·bound *adj* shut in by snow; snowed in.

snow·flake *n* a small, feathery piece of snow.

❦ **snow·mo·bile** (snō′mə bēl′) *n* a small, open motor vehicle for travelling over snow and ice, with skis at the front.

snow·plough *n* a machine for clearing away snow from streets. Another spelling is **snowplow.**

snow·shoe *n* a light, wooden frame with strips of leather stretched across it: *Snowshoes keep you from sinking in deep, soft snow.*

snug (snug) *adj* warm; sheltered: *The cat has found a snug corner behind the stove.* **snug·ger, snug·gest.**

snug·gle *v* cuddle.

so (sō) **1** *adv* in such a way: *The chair is broken and has been so for a long time. Do not walk so fast.* **2** *adv* very: *You are so kind.* **3** *conj* therefore: *The dog seemed hungry, so we fed it.* **4** *conj* in order that: *Go away so I can rest.*

or so, more or less: *It came a day or so ago.*

soak (sōk) **1** *v* make or become very wet: *The rain soaked my clothes.* **2** *v* let stay in water or other liquid until wet through: *Soak the clothes before you wash them.*

soap (sōp) *n* a substance used for washing, usually made of fat and lye.

soap·stone *n* a heavy, soft stone that feels a bit like soap: *Inuit carvings are often made of soapstone.*

soar (sȯr) **1** *v* fly upward to a great height: *The eagle soared above the Purcell Mountains.* **2** *v* rise beyond what is usual: *Prices are soaring.*

CONFUSABLES ····· **soar**

soar means "fly":
An eagle can soar above the trees.

sore means "painful":
My finger is sore.

---

sob (sob) *v* cry with short, quick breaths: *The child sobbed herself to sleep.* **sobbed, sob·bing.**

so·ber (sō′bər) **1** *adj* not drunk. **2** *adj* quiet; serious: *Owen looked sober at the thought of missing the picnic.*

so·ci·e·ty (sə sī′ə tē) **1** *n* human beings living as a group: *Canadian society benefits from a wide variety of ethnic backgrounds.* **2** *n* a group of persons joined together for a common purpose or by common interests: *The Canadian Cancer Society sells daffodils to raise money for cancer research.* **pl so·ci·e·ties.**

so·cia·ble *adj* liking company; friendly.

so·cial *adj* having to do with human beings in their relations to each other: *social conditions, social problems.* **social studies** school subjects, including history and geography, that deal with the development of peoples, and the parts of the world in which they live.

sock (sok) *n* a close-fitting, knitted covering for your foot and lower leg.

so·fa (sō′fə) *n* a couch; chesterfield.

soft (soft) **1** *adj* not hard; not stiff; not rough: *Feathers, cotton, and wool are soft.* **2** *adj* quiet: *a soft voice.* **3** *adj* gentle: *a soft heart.* —**soft′en,** *v*, —**soft′ly,** *adv*, —**soft′ness,** *n*.

soft drink a cold drink that does not contain alcohol, such as ginger ale, orangeade, or root beer. **soft·ware** *n* any computer program.

sog·gy (sog′ē) **1** *adj* soaked; thoroughly wet. **2** *adj* damp and heavy: *soggy bread.* **sog·gi·er, sog·gi·est.**

soil (soil) **1** *n* earth: *Most plants grow best in rich soil.* **2** *v* make or become dirty: *She soiled her hands while changing a tire.*

so·lar (sō′lər) *adj* having to do with the sun: *a solar eclipse, solar energy.*

solar system the sun and all the planets, satellites, comets, etc. that revolve around it. ►See Appendix.

sol·dier (sōl′jər) *n* a person who serves in an army.

sole (sōl) **1** *adj* one and only; single: *the sole survivor.* **2** *n* the under surface of your foot, sock, shoe, etc.

sol·emn (sol′əm) *adj* serious: *Wynton gave his solemn promise to do better.*

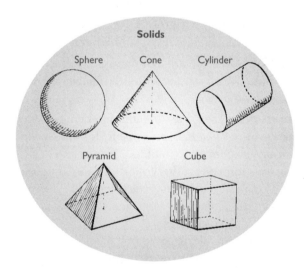

Solids

Sphere   Cone   Cylinder

Pyramid   Cube

sol·id (sol′id) **1** *adj* not a liquid or a gas: *Water becomes solid when it freezes.* **2** *adj* not hollow: *A bar of iron is solid; a pipe is hollow.* **3** *n* a figure that has length, breadth, and thickness: *A cube is a solid.*

so·lid·i·fy (sə lid′ə fī′) *v* make solid; become solid: *Extreme cold will solidify water into ice.*

so·lo (sō′lō) **1** *n* a piece of music for one voice or instrument. **2** *adj* alone: *a solo flight across the ocean.* pl **so·los.** —**so′lo·ist,** *n*.

sol·i·tar·y (sol′ə ter′ē) *adj* alone; lonely: *A solitary rider was seen in the distance. The house is in a solitary spot far away from town.*

sol·stice (sōl′stis *or* sol′stis) *n* either of the two times in the year when the sun is at its greatest distance from the equator. In the Northern Hemisphere, June 21 or 22, the **summer solstice,** is the longest day of the year and December 21 or 22, the **winter solstice,** is the shortest.

so·lu·tion (sə lū′shən) **1** *n* an answer; explanation. *What is the solution to this math problem?* **2** *n* a liquid made from putting a solid into a liquid: *Every time you put sugar in lemonade you are making a solution.*

solve (solv) *v* find the answer to; explain: *The mystery was never solved.*

some (sum) **1** *adj* a number or amount of: *Ask some friends to help you. Drink some milk.* **2** *pron* a certain number or amount: *Ya-Kee ate some and threw the rest away.* **3** *adj* a; any: *Can't you find some kind person who will help you?* **some·body** *pron* some person: *Somebody has taken my pen.* **some·day** *adv* at some future time. **some·how** *adv* in one way or another: *I'll finish this work somehow, because I promised that I would.* **some·one** *pron* some person. **some·place** *adv* somewhere.

some·thing 1 *n* some thing not named or not known: *I'm sure I've forgotten something.* **2** *n* a person of some importance: *He thinks he's something.*

some·time *adv* at one time or another: *Come to see us sometime.*

some·times *adv* now and then: *They come to visit sometimes, but not as often as they used to.*

some·where *adv* in one place or another: *Amir is somewhere in the house.*

CONFUSABLES ..... **some**

some means "a number of":
Some of us are not going to the party.

sum means "amount of money" or "total":
You owe me the sum of two dollars.

---

som·er·sault (sum′ər solt′) **1** *n* a complete roll of your body with your feet over your head. **2** *v* roll in this way.

son (sun) *n* boy or man in relation to either or both of his parents.

son-in-law *n* the husband of a person's daughter.

CONFUSABLES ...... son

son means "male child":
You are my son.

sun means "star that the earth moves round":
The sun is hot today.

---

song (song) **1** *n* something to sing: *The choir practised the song many times.* **2** *n* singing: *The canary burst into song.*

soon (sūn) **1** *adv* in a short time: *I will see you again soon.* **2** *adv* early: *Don't leave so soon!*

soot (suṫ) *n* a black powder in the smoke from burning coal, wood, oil, etc.

soothe (sūᴛʜ) *v* comfort: *The mother soothed the crying child.* **soothed, sooth·ing.**

so·phis·ti·cat·ed (sə fis′tə kā′tid) **1** *adj* experienced. **2** *adj* of machinery, more advanced: *sophisticated computers.*

sore (sȯr) **1** *adj* painful: *a sore finger.* **2** *n* a painful spot on your skin. **3** *adj Informal.* angry: *Igor is sore at missing the game.* **sor·er, sor·est.** **–sore′ly,** *adv,* **–sore′ness,** *n.*

sor·row (sȯr′ō) *n* sadness. **–sor′row·ful,** *adj.*

sor·ry *adj* sad: *I am sorry that you are sick.*

sort (sȯrt) **1** *n* a kind: *Sofia is not the sort of person to tell lies.* **2** *v* arrange: *Sort these cards according to their colours.*

soul (sōl) *n* the spiritual part of a person, thought of as separate from the body.

sound (sound) **1** *n* what can be heard: *the sound of thunder.* **2** *v* make a sound: *The wind sounds like an animal howling.* **3** *v* pronounce or be pronounced: *Sound each syllable.* **4** *v* seem: *That excuse sounds ridiculous.* **5** *adv* deeply: *She was sound asleep.* **–sound′ly,** *adv.*

sound·proof *adj* not letting sound pass through: *a soundproof room.* **sound track** a recording of the music from a movie.

soup (sūp) *n* a liquid food made by boiling meat, vegetables, fish, etc.

sour (sour) *adj* having a sharp taste like lemon juice.

source (sȯrs) *n* a person or place from which anything comes: *the source of a river. A newspaper gets news from many sources.*

south (south) **1** *n* the direction to the left as you face the setting sun. **2** *adv* or *adj* to or from the south: *They travelled south every winter (adv). There was a warm south wind (adj).* **–south′er·ly** (suᴛʜ′ər l ē), *adj,* **–south′ern** (suᴛʜ′ərn), *adj.*

south·east *n* the direction halfway between south and east. **south·paw** *n Slang.* a left-handed baseball pitcher. **South Pole** the southern end of the earth's axis. **south·ward** *adv* or *adj* toward the south: *Klaus' father drove southward toward Toronto (adv). The deck is on the southward side of the house (adj).* **Southwards** is another form for the adverb. **south·west** *n* the direction halfway between south and west.

sou·ve·nir (sū′və nēr′ *or* sū′və nēr′) *n* something given or kept to remind you of a special event: *Our aunt bought us cowboy boots as a souvenir of our holiday in Calgary.*

sow (sō *for 1,* sou *for 2*) **1** *v* plant seeds: *The farmer sows more wheat than oats.* **2** *n* a fully grown female pig. **sowed, sown** or **sowed, sow·ing.**

soy·bean (soi′bēn′) *n* a bean used in making flour, oil, etc. and as a food.

space (spās) **1** *n* the unlimited room of the universe: *Our planet Earth moves through space.* **2** *n* a limited piece of room: *Is there space in the car for another person?* **3** *v* separate by spaces: *Space your words evenly when you write.* **spaced, spac·ing.**

space·craft *n* a vehicle used for flight in outer space. **Spaceship** is another word for this.

spa·cious *adj* with plenty of room.

A girl using a spade to dig a garden

spade (spād) *n* a tool for digging.

spa·ghet·ti (spə get′ē) *n* pasta shaped into long, slender sticks.

A single span bridge

span (span) **1** *n* the part between two supports: *That bridge consists of a single span.* **2** *n* a period of time: *His span of life is nearly over.* **3** *v* extend over: *A bridge spanned the Niagara River.* **spanned, span·ning.**

spank (spangk) **1** *v* strike with an open hand, a slipper, etc. **2** *n* a slap. –**spank′ing,** *n.*

spare (sper) **1** *v* show mercy to: *He spared his enemy.* **2** *v* have available for use: *Can you spare the time?* **spared, spar·ing. 3** *adj* extra; in reserve: *a spare tire.* **spar·er, spar·est.**

spark (spàrk) **1** *n* a small bit of fire: *The burning wood threw off sparks.* **2** *n* a flash of electricity. **spar·kle 1** *v* glitter: *The diamonds sparkled.* **2** *n* a gleam; a flash of light: *I like the sparkle of her eyes.*

sparse (spàrs) *adj* thinly scattered: *a sparse population, sparse hair.* **spars·er, spars·est.** –**sparse′ly,** *adv.*

spasm (spaz′əm) *n* a sudden jerk in a muscle: *A spasm in my leg forced me to stop running.*

spawn (spon) **1** *n* the eggs of fish, frogs, shellfish, etc. **2** *v* of fish, etc., produce eggs: *Salmon spawn in the rivers of British Columbia.*

speak (spēk) **1** *v* say words: *A cat cannot speak.* **2** *v* know a language: *Do you speak French?* **spoke, spo·ken, speak·ing.**

speak·er (spē′kər) **1** *n* a person who speaks, especially one who speaks before an audience. **2** Also, **Speaker,** *n* the Speaker of the House of Commons. **3** *n* a device that makes sounds louder: *stereo speakers.*

spear (spēr) **1** *n* a weapon with a long shaft and a sharp-pointed head. **2** *v* pierce with a spear, or anything sharp: *Makoto speared a wiener with the fork.*

spe·cial (spesh′əl) **1** *adj* of a particular kind: *Have you any special colour in mind for your new coat?* **2** *adj* more than ordinary: *Today's topic is of special interest, a special friend.* –**spe′cial·ly,** *adv.*
special effects complicated pictures and sounds made for a TV program or movie, often with the help of computers. **F/X** is another name for this.
spe·cial·ty 1 *n* a special line of work, talent, etc.: *Computer programming is Natasha's specialty.* **2** *n* a product to which special attention is given: *This bakery makes a specialty of birthday cakes.* **spe·cies** (spē′sēz *or* spē′shēz) *n* a group of animals or plants that have certain things in common: *The grizzly and the black bear are two species of bear.* pl **spe·cies.**

spe·cif·ic (spə sif′ik) *adj* particular: *There was no specific reason for the quarrel.*

spec·i·men (spes′ə mən) *n* sample: *Elke collects specimens of all kinds of rocks.*

speck (spek) **1** *n* a small spot or mark: *Can you clean those specks off the window?* **2** *n* a tiny bit: *I have a speck of dirt in my eye.*

spec·ta·cle (spek′tə kəl) *n* a public show: *The Santa Claus parade was a fine spectacle.*
spec·tac·u·lar (spek tak′yə lər) *adj* making a great display: *a spectacular scene of a storm.*
spec·ta·tor (spek′tā tər) *n* a person who looks on without taking part.
spec·trum (spek′trəm) *n* the band of colours formed when a white light is broken up by being passed through water or a glass block: *A rainbow has all the colours of the spectrum: red, orange, yellow, green, blue, indigo, and violet.*

spec·u·late (spek′yə lāt′) *v* guess: *The coach refused to speculate about which team would win.* **spec·u·lat·ed, spec·u·lat·ing.** –**spec·u·la′tion,** *n.*

speech (spēch) **1** *n* the power of speaking: *Animals lack speech.* **2** *n* a public talk: *The mayor of Edmonton gave an excellent speech.*
speech·less *adj* not able to speak: *Saito was speechless with anger.*

speed (spēd) **1** *v* go fast: *The boat sped over the water.* **2** *n* a rate of movement: *The horses ran at full speed.* **sped** or **speed·ed, speed·ing.** –**speed′i·ly,** *adv,* –**speed′y,** *adj.*

spell (spel) **1** *v* write or say the letters of a word in order: *Some words are easy to spell.* **2** *n* in stories, words supposed to have magic power. **3** *n* a period of anything: *There was a long spell of rainy weather in Québec.* **spelled** or **spelt**, **spell·ing.** –**spell′ing**, *n*.

Grammar ✓*Check* ..... spelling

The **spelling** of English words can be confusing. When you have trouble remembering how to spell a word, try some of these strategies:

- Playing around with the word will help you to remember it: say it out loud, picture the letters in your head, write it down in fancy lettering.

- Think of a memory trick to help you remember hard words. For example, you can remember than *cereal* starts with *c* by remembering the sentence *I like cream in my cereal.*

- Make your own dictionary of words you misspell often, and check it whenever you write anything.

- For words with silent letters or double letters, pronounce *all* the letters in your head: *k-now, mis-spell*

- Look for similar spelling patterns: *sight/night/fright/light; bite/kite/quite.*

- Look for a smaller word inside a big word: *ar**gum**ent; t**rage**dy.*

---

spend (spend) **1** *v* pay out: *Catalina spent ten dollars today.* **2** *v* use: *Don't spend any more time on that lesson.* **spent, spend·ing.**

sphere (sfēr) *n* a round solid figure; a ball or globe. –**spher′i·cal**, (sfer′ə kəl) *adj*.

spice (spīs) **1** *n* seasoning from plants, used to flavour food: *Pepper is a common spice.* **2** *v* add flavour to. **spiced, spic·ing.** –**spic′y**, *adj*.

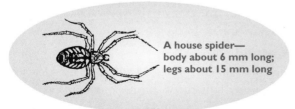

A house spider— body about 6 mm long; legs about 15 mm long

spi·der (spī′dər) *n* a small animal with eight legs and no wings: *Many spiders spin webs to catch insects for food.*

spike (spīk) **1** *n* a large, strong nail. **2** *n* a sharp-pointed piece: *The soccer players wore shoes with spikes on the soles.* **spiked, spik·ing.**

spill (spil) **1** *v* let liquid, or any loose pieces of something, fall: *to spill milk, to spill salt.* **2** *v* fall out: *Water spilled from the pail.* **spilled** or **spilt**, **spill·ing.**

A spinning wheel.
The large wheel causes the smaller one to turn, and this twists bits of wool, silk, cotton, etc. into thread.

spin (spin) **1** *v* turn or make turn quickly: *The wheel spun round.* **2** *v* twist into thread. **3** *n* a quick turn. **4** *n* a short drive: *Get your bicycle and come for a spin with me.* **spun, spin·ning. spin out,** make long and slow: *Try not to spin out your story.*

spine (spīn) **1** *n* backbone. **2** *n* a stiff, sharp-pointed growth on plants or animals. –**spi′nal**, *adj*.

spine·less 1 *adj* having no backbone: *All insects are spineless.* **2** *adj* without courage: *Spineless people do not stand up for their beliefs.* **3** *adj* having no spines: *a spineless cactus.*

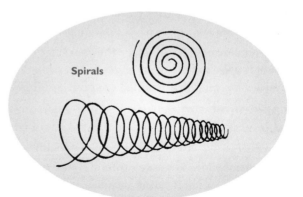

Spirals

spi·ral (spī′rəl) **1** *n* a winding and gradually widening coil. **2** *adj* coiled: *a spiral staircase.*

spir·it (spēr′it) **1** *n* the soul. **2** *n* a ghost. **spir·it·ed** *adj* full of energy: *a spirited argument.* **spir·i·tu·al** *adj* having to do with the soul. **out of spirits,** sad; gloomy.

spit (spit) **1** *v* throw something from your mouth: *to spit out saliva, to spit out a cherry stone.* **2** *n* a rod on which meat is roasted. **3** *n* a narrow point of land running into the water. **spat** or **spit, spit·ting.**

spite (spīt) **1** *n* grudge: *The child scribbled on his sister's book out of spite.* **2** *v* annoy: *Tobias hid the video game to spite his brother.* **spit·ed, spit·ing. –spite′ful,** *adj.*
in spite of, regardless of: *The children went to school in spite of the snowstorm.*

splash (splash) **1** *v* make water, mud, etc. fly about: *The baby likes to splash in the tub.* **2** *n* the sound of splashing: *a loud splash.*

splen·did (splen′did) *adj* magnificent; excellent: *splendid jewels, a splendid piece of work.*

splen·dour (splen′dər) *n* a magnificent show; glory. **Splendor** is another spelling.

splint (splint) *n* a piece of wood, metal, etc. to hold a broken bone in place.

splin·ter **1** *n* a thin, sharp piece of wood, bone, glass, etc.: *Noam got a splinter in his finger.* **2** *v* break into splinters: *The mirror splintered.*

split (split) **1** *v* break or cut from end to end: *We are splitting wood for the stove.* **2** *v* divide: *The two friends split the cost of the pizza between them.* **3** *n* a break; crack: *Frost caused the split in the rock.* **split, split·ting.**
split hairs, be too fussy: *It is splitting hairs to complain of having just 59 minutes instead of an hour in the pool.*

spoil (spoil) **1** *v* damage or be damaged: *The rain spoiled the picnic. The banana spoiled because I kept it too long.* **2** *v* damage the character of: *Some people say that giving children everything they want spoils them.* **spoiled** or **spoilt, spoil·ing.**

spokes·per·son (spōks′pər′sən) *n* a person who speaks for others: *He was the spokesperson for our class.* pl **spokes·peo·ple** (spōks′pē′pəl).

sponge (spunj) **1** *n* a sea animal that lives attached to rocks. **2** *n* the skeleton animal, used for soaking up water. **3** *n* a similar thing made artificially of rubber or plastic. **sponged, spong·ing. –spon′gy,** *adj.*

spon·sor (spon′sər) **1** *n* a person or group that supports or pays for something. **2** *n* pledge money to an organization: *Will you sponsor me for the walk for the United Way?*

spon·ta·ne·ous (spon tā′nē əs) *adj* happening naturally: *The audience burst into spontaneous cheers at the end of the song.*

spoon (spūn) *n* a small, shallow bowl at the end of a handle: *Spoons are used to take up or stir food or drink.* **–spoon′ful,** *n.*

sport (spȯrt) *n* a game needing some skill and exercise: *Baseball and football are outdoor sports; bowling and basketball are indoor sports.*

spot (spot) **1** *n* a mark, stain, or speck: *You have paint spots on your jeans. That spot on her hand is a bruise.* **2** *n* a small part unlike the rest: *His shirt is blue with white spots.* **3** *n* a place: *From this spot you can see the lake.* **4** *v Informal.* pick out: *I spotted my sister in the crowd.* **spot·ted, spot·ting. –spot′less,** *adj.*

sprain (sprān) **1** *v* injure a joint or muscles by a sudden twist: *to sprain your ankle.* **2** *n* an injury caused this: *a bad sprain.*

sprawl (sprol) *v* lie or sit with your arms and legs spread out: *The people sprawled on the beach in their bathing suits.*

spray (sprā) **1** *n* liquid in small drops: *We were wet with the sea spray.* **2** *v* scatter a liquid in small drops.

spread (spred) **1** *v* stretch out: *to spread rugs on the floor, to spread your arms.* **2** *v* scatter: *Shona spread the news.* **3** *v* cover with a thin layer: *She spread each slice with butter.* **4** *n* a covering: *Peanut butter is a spread.* **5** *n* the area of land owned by a rancher: *He has a big spread near Lethbridge.* **spread, spread·ing.**

spring (spring) **1** *v* leap or jump: *The boy sprang to his feet.* **2** *v* fly back or away as if by elastic: *A bent branch will spring back into place.* **3** *n* a device that returns to its original shape after being pulled: *Some mattresses have wire springs.* **4** *n* the season after winter. **5** *n* water flowing up from the earth. **sprang** or **sprung, sprung, spring·ing.**

sprin·kle (spring′kəl) **1** *v* scatter in drops or tiny bits: *Daliah sprinkled sand on the icy sidewalk.* **2** *n* a small quantity: *The cook put a sprinkle of nuts on the cake.* **sprin·kled, sprin·kling.**

sprin·kler *n* a device used to spray water; a lawn sprinkler.

sprint (sprint) *v* run fast for a short distance.

sprout (sprout) **1** *v* begin to grow: *Seeds sprout.* **2** *n* a bud of a plant.

spurt (spərt) **1** *v* flow suddenly: *Blood spurted from the wound.* **2** *n* a sudden rushing forth: *a spurt of energy, a spurt of flame. Spurts of flame broke out all over the building.*

spy (spī) **1** *n* a person paid to get secret information. **2** *v* act as a spy; be a spy. **3** *v* catch sight of: *She was the first to spy the whale on the coast of the Queen Charlotte Islands.* *pl* **spies. spies, spied, spy·ing.**

squab·ble (skwob′əl) *n* a noisy quarrel: *Children's squabbles annoy their parents.*

squad (skwod) *n* a small group of people working together: *a squad of soldiers.*

squan·der (skwon′dər) *v* spend foolishly; waste: *Takake squanders money on video games.*

square (skwer) **1** *n* a flat figure with four equal sides and four right angles. **2** *adj* having this shape: *a square box.* **3** *n* an open space in a city or town, often with streets on four sides, and sometimes planted with grass, trees, etc. **4** *adj* honest: *You will get a square deal at this store.* **5** *v* multiply a number by itself: *4 squared makes 16.* **squared, squar·ing.**

A pumpkin is a kind of squash.

squash (skwosh) **1** *v* crush: *The boy squashed the bug.* **2** *n* a vegetable that grows on vines on the ground. *pl* **squash** or **squash·es.**

squat (skwot) **1** *v* crouch on your heels. **2** *adj* low and broad: *Toads have squat faces.* **squat·ted** or **squat, squat·ting.**

squeak (skwēk) **1** *v* make a short, sharp, high sound: *A mouse squeaks.* **2** *n* such a sound. –**squeak′y,** *adj.*
narrow squeak, *Informal.* a narrow escape.
squeak by or **through,** barely succeed in doing something: *I just squeaked through the test.*

squeal (skwēl) **1** *v* make a long, sharp, high sound: *A pig squeals when it is hurt.* **2** *n* such a sound. **3** *v* *Informal.* inform on another.

squeeze (skwēz) **1** *v* press hard: *Don't squeeze the kitten or you will hurt it.* **2** *v* force by pressing: *I can't squeeze another thing into my hockey bag.* **3** *n* a crush: *It's a tight squeeze to get five people in that little car.* **squeezed, squeez·ing.**

squint (skwint) *v* look with your eyes partly closed.

squire (skwīr) *n* in medieval times, a young man in training to be a knight.

squirm (skwərm) *v* wriggle: *The restless child squirmed in her chair.*

A grey squirrel— about 23 cm long excluding the tail

squir·rel (skwərl) *n* a small bushy-tailed animal that usually lives in trees.

squirt (skwərt) **1** *v* force out liquid through a narrow opening: *to squirt water through a tube.* **2** *n* a jet of liquid: *Nikolai dodged a squirt of water from the hose.*

stab (stab) **1** *v* pierce or wound with a pointed weapon. **2** *n* *Informal.* an attempt: *It was a difficult puzzle but she made a stab at it.* **stabbed, stab·bing.**

sta·ble (stā′bəl) **1** *n* a building where horses or cattle are kept and fed. **2** *adj* firm; steady.

stack (stak) **1** *n* a pile of anything: *a stack of wood, a stack of hay, a stack of newspapers.* **2** *v* pile in a stack: *to stack books.*

sta·di·um (stā′dē əm) *n* rows of seats around a large, open space for games, concerts, etc. *pl* **sta·di·ums** or **sta·di·a** (stā′dē ə).

staff (staf) **1** *n* a long stick: *The flag hangs on a staff.* **2** *n* a group of workers: *Our school has a staff of 20 teachers.*

stag (stag) *n* a full-grown male deer.

A stagecoach of the 1800s

stage (stāj) **1** *n* one step in a process: *Frogs pass through a tadpole stage.* **2** *n* the raised platform in a theatre. **3** *v* put on a stage: *The play was very well staged.* **staged, stag·ing.**

stage·coach *n* a large, four-wheeled, horse-drawn coach once used for carrying passengers and mail.

stag·ger (stag'ər) **1** *v* sway or walk unsteadily. **2** *v* confuse or astonish greatly: *We were staggered by the news of the air disaster.*

stain (stān) **1** *v* soil; spot: *The tablecloth is stained where food has been spilled.* **2** *n* a spot; a dirty mark.

stair (ster) **1** *n* one of a series of steps for going from one level to another. **2** Also, **stairs,** *pl.n* a set of such steps.

CONFUSABLES ····· stair

stair means "step":
She climbed the stairs.

stare means "look":
She stared at herself in the mirror.

stake (stāk) **1** *n* a stick or post pointed at one end for driving into the ground. **2** *v* mark the edge of: *The miner staked his claim in the Northwest Territories.* **3** *n* the money risked on a gamble. **staked, stak·ing.**

at stake, to be risked: *Her swimming record is at stake.*

CONFUSABLES ····· stake

stake means "stick":
He put a stake in the ground.

steak means "thick slice of beef or fish":
We are cooking steaks on the barbecue.

stale (stāl) *adj* not fresh; not new: *stale bread, a stale joke.* **stal·er, stal·est.**

stalk (stok) **1** *n* the main stem of a plant. **2** *v* hunt silently: *The cougar stalked the deer.* **3** *v* walk proudly: *The actor stalked off the stage.*

stall (stol) **1** *n* a place in a stable for one animal. **2** *n* a small place for selling things: *stalls at a farmer's market.* **3** *v* come to a stop because of too heavy a load or too little fuel: *The truck stalled on the steep hill.* **4** *v* *Informal.* delay: *You have been stalling long enough.*

stal·lion (stal'yən) *n* a male horse.

stam·i·na (stam'ə nə) *n* lasting strength: *A long-distance runner needs stamina.*

stam·mer (stam'ər) *v* repeat the same sound while trying to speak.

stamp (stamp) **1** *n* a small piece of sticky paper put on letters, etc., to show that a charge has been paid. **2** *v* put a stamp on: *to stamp a letter.* **3** *v* bring down your foot with force: *Mikael stamped on the spider.*

stam·pede (stam pēd') **1** *n* a sudden scattering of an excited herd of cattle, horses, people, etc. **2** *n* a rodeo, often with other amusements usually found at a fair: *The Calgary Stampede begins with a huge parade.*

stand (stand) **1** *v* be on or rise to your feet: *Don't stand if you are tired, but sit down.* **2** *v* bear; put up with: *Those plants cannot stand cold; they die in the winter.* **3** *n* a table for a small business: *a newspaper stand, a fruit stand.* **stood, stand·ing.**

stand-in *n* substitute: *Will you be my stand-in at the next school council meeting?*

stand by, help; support: *to stand by a friend.*

stand for, represent: *What does the abbreviation St. stand for?*

stand out, be noticeable: *Mei-Lee's science project stood out from all the rest.*

stand up to, face bravely: *The young boy stood up to the bully.*

stand·ard (stan'dərd) *n* an accepted level of quality, size, etc.: *to set a high standard.*

stan·za (stan'zə) *n* a verse of a poem.

sta·ple (stā'pəl) **1** *adj* main; important: *Bread is a staple food in Canada.* **2** *n* a small, U-shaped piece of wire which bends to hold the papers together. **3** *v* fasten with a staple or staples. **sta·pled, sta·pling.**

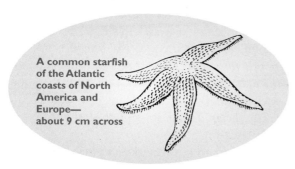

A common starfish of the Atlantic coasts of North America and Europe— about 9 cm across

star (stär) **1** *n* a heavenly body appearing as a bright point in the night sky. —**star′ry,** *adj.* **2** *n* a famous person who plays the lead in a performance: *a movie star.* **3** *adj* best; excellent: *the star player on a football team.* **4** *v* be a leading performer: *She has starred in many movies.* **starred, star·ring.**

star·fish *n* a star-shaped sea animal: *Starfish are not fish.*

star·board (stär′bərd) *n* the right side of a ship or aircraft, when facing forward.

starch (stärch) **1** *n* a white, tasteless food substance. *Potatoes, wheat, rice, and corn contain much starch.* **2** *n* a preparation of this used to stiffen clothes, etc.

stare (ster) *v* look long with your eyes wide open: *The little girl stared at the toys in the window.* **stared, star·ing.**
stare someone in the face, be very obvious: *Yoichi's spelling mistake was staring him in the face.*

start (stärt) **1** *v* begin: *to start reading a book.* **2** *n* a beginning. **3** *v* move suddenly: *Serena started in surprise.* **4** *n* a sudden movement: *I woke up with a start.* **5** *n* a beginning ahead of others: *They gave me a start because I was slower.*

star·tle *v* frighten suddenly; surprise: *The dog jumped at the girl and startled her.*

starve (stärv) **1** *v* weaken or die because of hunger. **2** *v* *Informal.* feel very hungry. **starved, starv·ing.** —**star·va′tion,** *n.*

state (stāt) **1** *n* the condition of a person or thing: *The house is in a bad state of repair.* **2** *n* nation; country. **3** *n* one of several parts of a nation: *The State of Alaska is one of the United States.* **4** *v* tell in speech or writing: *State your opinion of the new school rules.* **stat·ed, stat·ing.** —**state′ment,** *n.*

stat·ic (stat′ik) *n* crackling noises on radio and TV caused by electrical disturbances in the air.

sta·tion (stā′shən) **1** *n* a place used for a definite purpose: *a police station, a TV station.* **2** *n* a regular stopping place: *Neimah met her grandmother at the train station.*

sta·tion·ar·y (stā′shə ner′ē) *adj* not moving; not movable: *A parked car is stationary.*

sta·tion·er·y (stā′shə ner′ē) *n* writing paper, cards, and envelopes.

sta·tis·tics (stə tis′tiks) *n* numerical facts about people, the weather, etc.: *population statistics.*

stat·ue (stach′ū) *n* a figure of a person or animal made of stone, wood, metal etc.

stay (stā) **1** *v* remain: *Stay still. The cat stayed out all night.* **2** *v* live for a while: *Irina is staying with her aunt while her mother is ill.*

stead·y (sted′ē) **1** *adj* regular: *steady progress.* **2** *adj* firmly fixed: *Hold the ladder steady.* **stead·i·er, stead·i·est.** —**stead′i·ly,** *adv.*

steak (stāk) *n* a thick slice of meat or fish.

steal (stēl) *v* take something that does not belong to you: *Robbers stole the money.* **stole, sto·len, steal·ing.**

stealth·y (stel′thē) *adj* done in a secret manner: *The cat crept in a stealthy way toward the bird.*

steam (stēm) **1** *n* water in the form of gas: *Boiling water gives off steam.* **2** *v* give off or be covered with steam: *The cup of coffee was steaming.* **3** *v* cook by steam: *to steam vegetables.* **let off steam,** *Informal.* relieve your feelings.

steel (stēl) *n* iron mixed with carbon. It is very strong: *Most tools are made from steel.*

steep (stēp) *adj* almost straight up and down: *The hill is steep.*

steer (stēr) **1** *v* guide: *to steer a car.* **2** *n* of cattle, a full-grown neutered male, raised for beef.

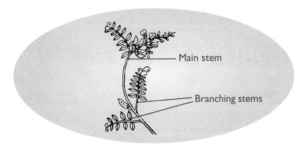

Main stem

Branching stems

stem (stem) *n* the main part of a plant, usually above the ground: *The trunk of the tree and the stalks of corn are stems.*

stench (stench) *n* a very bad smell; stink: *the stench of gas.*

sten·cil (sten′səl) **1** *n* a thin sheet of metal, paper, etc. with letters or designs cut through it. **2** *v* make with a stencil: *to stencil a design on a wall.* **sten·cilled, sten·cil·ling.**

step (step) **1** *n* a movement made by lifting your foot and putting it down again in a new position. **2** *v* walk: *Step over here, please.* **3** *n* a place for your foot: *A rung of a ladder is a step.* **4** *n* one action in a process: *The first step is to gather all your materials.* **stepped, step·ping.**

step·child *n* a child of a person's husband or wife by a former marriage: *a stepson, a stepdaughter.*

step·par·ent *n* someone married to a mother or father after the death or divorce of a natural parent: *a stepmother, a stepfather.*

watch your step, be careful: *Watch your step when you bike down that steep hill.*

ster·e·o (ster′ē ō′) *n Informal.* a radio, CD player, etc., with two or more speakers.

ster·ile (ster′īl *or* ster′əl) *adj* free from germs: *Surgical instruments must be sterile.* **–ster′i·lize′** (ster′ə līz′), *v.*

stern (stərn) *adj* severe; strict: *a stern face, a stern warning.*

stew (styū *or* stū) **1** *v* cook by slow boiling. **2** *n* food cooked by slow boiling: *beef stew.* **3** *v Informal.* worry: *She is stewing over her homework.*

stew·ard (styū′ərd *or* stū′ərd) *n* a person in charge of food and drink on a plane, ship, etc.

stick (stik) **1** *n* a long, thin piece of wood. **2** *n* something like a stick in shape: *a stick of candy, a hockey stick.* **3** *v* push: *Phuong stuck his fork into the potato. Don't stick your head out of the car window.* **4** *v* fasten: *Stick a stamp on the letter.* **–stick′y,** *adj.* **5** *v* be unable to go, or do: *Our car stuck in the mud. I am stuck on the last question.* **stuck, stick·ing.**

stick by, remain faithful to: *Shai sticks by his friends when they are in trouble.*

stick out, be obvious.

stick up, *Slang.* rob.

stick up for, *Informal.* defend.

stiff (stif) *adj* not easy to bend or move: *I have a stiff knee. The old hinges on the barn door are stiff.* **–stiff′en,** *v.*

sti·fle (stī′fəl) **1** *v* stop the breath of: *The smoke stifled the firefighters.* **2** *v* keep back: *to stifle a yawn.* **sti·fled, sti·fling.**

still (stil) **1** *adj* without moving or making noise: *The lake is still today.* **–still′ness,** *n.* **2** *conj* yet: *Though my sister has new dolls, still she loves her old one best.* **3** *adv* now as before: *Was the store still open?*

A honeybee ready to sting

Stinger

sting (sting) **1** *v* jab with a sharp point: *Bees, wasps, and hornets sting.* **2** *n* a sharp pain. **3** *v* hurt like a sting: *Hot mustard stings your tongue.* **stung, sting·ing.**

stin·gy (stin′jē) *adj* mean about spending money: *Gustav tried to save money without being stingy.* **stin·gi·er, stin·gi·est. –stin′gi·ness,** *n.*

stink (stingk) **1** *n* a bad smell. **2** *v* have a bad smell: *Decaying fish stink.* **stank** *or* **stunk, stunk, stink·ing.**

stir (stər) **1** *v* move: *The wind stirs the leaves.* **2** *v* mix by moving around with a spoon, fork, stick, etc.: *Mom stirs the sugar in her tea with a spoon.* **3** *v* excite: *Don't stir up the other children to mischief.* **4** *n* a movement: *There was a stir in the bushes.* **stirred, stir·ring.**

stitch (stich) **1** *n* in sewing, knitting, etc., the loop of thread, etc. made by a needle: *The doctor will remove the stitches tomorrow.* **2** *v* make stitches in: *She stitched the hem of her skirt.*

stock (stok) **1** *n* things for use or for sale: *This store keeps a large stock of toys.* **2** *n* cattle or other farm animals: *The farm was sold with all its stock.* **3** *v* keep a supply of: *Our camp is well stocked with everything we need.* **4** *n* water in which meat, vegetables, or fish has been cooked.
stock·ing *n* a close-fitting knitted covering for your foot and leg.

stom·ach (stum′ək) *n* the large muscular bag in your body where food goes.

stone (stōn) **1** *n* rock. **2** *n* a small piece of rock. **3** *n* a jewel: *a precious stone.* **4** *n* a hard seed: *peach stones, plum stones.* –**ston′y**, *adj.*

stool (stūl) *n* a seat without back or arms.

stoop (stūp) **1** *v* bend forward: *Brittany stooped to pick up the money.* **2** *n* a forward bend of your head and shoulders: *My uncle walks with a slight stoop.* **3** *v* lower oneself: *He stooped to cheating.*

stop (stop) **1** *v* keep from or finish moving, doing, etc.: *I stopped the boys from teasing the cat.* **2** *n* a halt: *We made a stop for lunch.* **3** *n* a place where a stop is made: *a bus stop.* **stopped, stop·ping.**

store (stȯr) **1** *n* a place where things are for sale: *a clothing store.* **2** *v* put away for use later: *The squirrel stores away nuts. We stored our skis during the summer.* **stored, stor·ing.**
stor·age *n* a place for storing: *She has put her furniture in storage.*

sto·rey (stȯr′ē) *n* a level of a building: *They are now building the second storey of our new house.* *pl* **sto·reys.**

storm (stȯrm) **1** *n* a strong wind, usually accompanied by rain, snow, hail, or thunder and lightning: *In deserts there are sand storms.* **2** *v* rush violently: *Vladimir stormed out of the room.* –**storm′y**, *adj.*

sto·ry (stȯr′ē) **1** *n* a telling of some happenings: *The man told the story of his life.* **2** *n* a telling, either true or made-up, intended to interest the reader or hearer: *fairy stories, ghost stories, stories of adventure, funny stories.* **3** *n* Informal. a falsehood: *That boy is a liar; he tells stories.* *pl* **sto·ries.**

stout (stout) **1** *adj* fat and large: *I could run faster if I weren't so stout.* **2** *adj* strongly built: *Fort York has stout walls.*

stove (stōv) *n* a device for cooking and heating: *There are wood, coal, gas, oil, and electric stoves.*

stow·a·way (stō′ə wā′) *n* a person who hides on a ship, airplane, etc. to get a free trip.

strag·gle (strag′əl) *v* spread out in an untidy, scattered way: *Weeds straggled all over the yard.*

straight (strāt) **1** *adj* without a bend or curve: *a straight line, a straight path, straight hair.* **2** *adv* in a line; directly: *Walk straight. She went straight home.* **3** *adj* honest: *a straight answer.* **4** *adj* showing no emotion: *To keep a straight face.* –**straight′en**, *v.*
straight·for·ward *adj* honest: *a straightforward answer.* –**straight′for′ward·ly**, *adv*, –**straight′for′ward·ness**, *n.*

CONFUSABLES ... straight

straight means "not bent": *Pull back your shoulders and stand straight as an arrow.*
strait means "channel of water": *The Hudson Strait joins Hudson Bay to the Atlantic Ocean.*

---

strain (strān) **1** *v* draw tight; stretch: *The weight strained the rope.* **2** *n* a force that stretches: *The strain on the rope made it break.* **3** *n* an injury caused by too much effort: *The doctor said that the pain in my ankle was the result of a strain.* **4** *v* press through a material that allows only liquid to pass through it: *The cook strained the soup to remove all the lumps.* –**strain′er**, *n.*

strait (strāt) *n* a channel connecting two larger bodies of water.

strand (strand) **1** *v* place or leave in a helpless position: *He was stranded far from home with no money.* **2** *n* a thread or string: *a strand of hair, a strand of pearls.*

strange (strānj) **1** *adj* unusual; peculiar: *What a strange experience!* **2** *adj* not known before: *Moira is moving to a strange place.* **strang·er, strang·est.** –**strange′ly**, *adv*, –**strange′ness**, *n.*
stran·ger *n* a person not known before.

stran·gle (strang′gəl) *v* kill by squeezing the throat: *Hercules strangled a snake with each hand.* **stran·gled, stran·gling.**

strap (strap) **1** *n* a narrow strip of material that bends easily: *She adjusted the shoulder straps of her backpack.* **2** *v* fasten with a strap: *We strapped the canoe onto the roof of the car.* **strapped, strap·ping.**

strat·e·gy (strat′ə jē) **1** *n* the planning and directing of military movements and operations. **2** *n* a plan for an activity: *I have a new strategy for playing that computer game.* *pl* **strat·e·gies.**

straw (stro) **1** *n* the stalks of grain after drying. **2** *n* a tube for sucking up drinks.

stray (strā) **1** *v* wander: *Our dog has strayed off somewhere.* **2** *adj* lost: *A stray cat is crying at the door.* **3** *n* anything that is lost: *That cat is a stray that we took in.*

streak (strēk) **1** *n* a long, thin mark: *Jefferson has a streak of dirt on his face.* **2** *v* *Informal.* move very fast: *She streaked past the others and over the finish line.*

stream (strēm) **1** *n* a small river. **2** *n* any steady flow: *a stream of lava, a stream of words.* **3** *v* move steadily: *Passengers streamed out of the train onto the platform.*

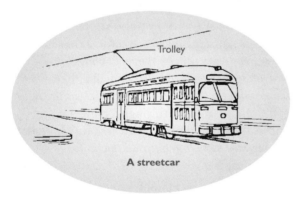

Trolley

A streetcar

street (strēt) *n* a road in a city or town, usually with buildings on both sides.

street·car *n* a large, electrically powered passenger vehicle that runs on rails on city streets.

strength (strength) *n* the quality of being strong; power: *Because of his strength he could lift great weights.* –**strength′en,** *v.*

stress (stres) **1** *v* treat as important; emphasize: *The principal stressed the importance of safety rules.* **2** *n* a mark (′) to show the spoken force of a syllable. Many words have two stresses, a heavy stress (′) and a light stress (′), as in *sub′mar·ine′.* **3** *n* pressure; strain.

stretch (strech) **1** *v* make longer: *to stretch an elastic band.* **2** *v* reach out: *She stretched out a hand for the candy.* **3** *v* extend from one place to another: *The forest stretches right to the coast of British Columbia.*

strict (strikt) **1** *adj* very careful in following a rule or in making others follow it: *Our teacher is strict but fair.* **2** *adj* harsh; severe: *Cinderella's stepmother was very strict with her.*

stride (strīd) *v* walk with long steps: *The tall man strides rapidly down the street.* **strode, strid·den, strid·ing.**

strike (strīk) **1** *v* hit: *The car struck a fence.* **2** *v* sound: *The clock strikes twelve times at noon.* **3** *v* occur to: *She smiled as an amusing thought struck her.* **4** *v* find oil, etc.: *The miner struck gold in the Yukon.* **5** *v* a stopping work in protest: *The factory workers were on strike for a week.* **struck, struck** or **strick·en, strik·ing.**

strike out, in baseball, fail to hit three times: *The batter struck out.*

string (string) **1** *n* very thin rope: *The package is tied with red string.* **2** *n* a cord with things on it: *She wore a string of beads around her neck.* **3** *v* put something on a string: *The child is stringing beads.* **4** *n* a length of wire on a musical instrument: *the strings of a violin.* **strung, string·ing.**

stringed instrument a musical instrument with strings: *A violin, a piano, a harp, and a guitar are stringed instruments.*

strip (strip) **1** *v* take off: *The boy stripped the skin from a banana.* **2** *n* a long, narrow, flat piece of something: *a strip of wallpaper.* **stripped, strip·ping.**

A tiger—about 2 m long excluding the tail. Its stripes are black on a yellow background.

stripe (strīp) *n* a long, narrow band of colour: *A tiger has stripes.*

stroke (strōk) **1** *n* a hit: *The house was hit by a stroke of lightning.* **2** *n* a single movement that is often made again and again: *Miriam stroked the cat. Simeon swims a fast stroke.* **3** *n* a mark made by a pen, pencil, etc.: *She writes with a heavy down stroke.* **4** *n* a sudden attack of certain illnesses: *sunstroke.*

stroll (strōl) **1** *v* take a quiet walk. **2** *n* a slow walk: *We went for a stroll in the park.*

strong (strong) **1** *adj* having much force or power: *A strong wind blew down the trees.* **2** *adj* able to last: *a strong rope.* **3** *adj* not weak or faint: *strong perfume.*

struc·ture (struk′chər) *n* anything composed of parts put together: *The city hall is a large stone structure. The human body is a wonderful structure.*

strug·gle (strug′əl) **1** *v* try hard against difficulties: *The swimmer struggled against the tide.* **2** *n* great effort; hard work: *Making him eat vegetables is a struggle.* **3** *n* fighting: *The struggle between the two countries went on for years.* **strug·gled, strug·gling.**

stub·born (stub′ərn) *adj* not giving in: *The stubborn girl refused to listen to reasons for not going out in the snowstorm.*

stu·dent (styū′dənt *or* stū′dənt) *n* a person who is studying in a school, college, or university: *Our school has 300 students.*

stud·y (stud′ē) **1** *v* try to learn: *Ursula studied her spelling lesson for half an hour.* **2** *v* examine carefully: *We studied the map of New Brunswick to find the shortest way to Fredericton.* **stud·ied, stud·y·ing.**

stu·di·ous (styū′dē əs *or* stū′dē əs) *adj* fond of study: *That studious boy likes school.*

stu·di·o (styū′dē ō *or* stū′dē ō) **1** *n* the workroom of a painter, photographer, etc. **2** *n* a place where movies are made. **3** *n* a place from which a radio or television program is broadcast. *pl* **stu·di·os.**

stuff (stuf) **1** *n* a thing or things: *The doctor rubbed some kind of stuff on the burn. Wade was told to move his stuff out of the room.* **2** *v* pack full; fill: *Yu-See stuffed the pillow with feathers.* **3** *v* eat too much: *He stuffed himself with candy.*

stuff·y **1** *adj* filled up: *A cold makes my head feel stuffy.* **2** *adj* not having fresh air: *a stuffy room.*

stump (stump) **1** *n* the lower end of something left after the main part is cut off: *a tree stump, the stump of a dog's tail.* **2** *v* Informal. make unable to answer: *The unexpected question stumped him.*

stun (stun) **1** *v* knock unconscious. **2** *v* shock: *Ramona was stunned by the news of her friend's car accident.* **stunned, stun·ning.**

stu·pen·dous (styū pen′dəs *or* stū pen′dəs) *adj* amazing; marvellous; immense: *Niagara Falls is a stupendous sight.*

stu·pid (styū′pid *or* stū′pid) **1** *adj* not intelligent: *a stupid person.* **2** *adj* silly: *a stupid thing to do.* **–stu·pid′i·ty,** *n.*

style (stīl) **1** *n* fashion: *Micah dresses in the latest style.* **2** *n* a way of doing something: *I like that style of haircut you have.*

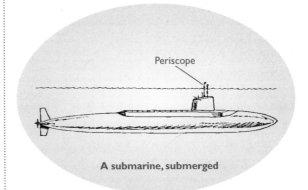

Periscope

A submarine, submerged

sub– *a prefix meaning* under or below, as in *subarctic, subway, submarine, subtitle.*

sub·ma·rine (sub′mə rēn′ *or* sub′mə rēn′) *n* a boat that can go under water.

sub·merge (səb mərj′) *v* put or go under water: *A big wave submerged us. The submarine submerged and secretly entered the harbour.* **sub·merged, sub·merg·ing.**

sub·urb (sub′ərb) **1** *n* a district just outside or near a city or town. **2 the suburbs,** *n* houses near a city or town. **–sub·ur′ban,** *adj.*

sub·way *n* an electric railway mainly underground.

sub·ject (sub′jikt *or* sub′jekt) **1** *n* something thought about, discussed, etc.: *I tried to change the subject during our talk.* **2** *n* a person who is under the power of another: *The people are the subjects of the king.* **3** *n* in grammar, the word or words for whatever does the action of the verb. ▶See the *Grammar and Usage Mini-Guide.*

sub·mit (səb mit′) **1** *v* surrender. **2** *v* hand in: *We submitted our homework for Ms. Martenson to check.* **sub·mit·ted, sub·mit·ting.**

sub·stance (sub′stəns) *n* what a thing is made of: *Ice and water are the same substance in different forms.*

sub·sti·tute (sub′stə tyūt′ *or* sub′stə tūt′) **1** *n* something or someone in place of another: *A substitute taught our class today.* **2** *v* put in the place of another: *We substituted honey for sugar in these cookies.* **sub·sti·tut·ed, sub·sti·tut·ing.** –**sub′sti·tu′tion,** *n.*

sub·tle (sut′əl) *adj* faint; not obvious: *a subtle smile, a subtle difference.* –**sub′tly,** *adv.*

sub·tract (səb trakt′) *v* take away: *Subtract 2 from 10 and you have 8.* –**sub·trac′tion,** *n.*

suc·ceed (sək sēd′) **1** *v* turn out well; do well: *Sunita's plans succeeded. Our baseball team succeeded in its effort to get to the finals.* **2** *v* take the place of: *John Abbott succeeded John A. Macdonald as prime minister of Canada.* –**suc·ces′sor,** *n.*

suc·cess (sək ses′) **1** *n* a good result: *Success in hockey comes from skill and practice.* **2** *n* a person or thing that does well. –**suc·cess′ful,** *adj.*

such (such) *adj* so great, so bad, so good, etc.: *He is such a joker!*

such as, for example: *members of the cat family, such as lions and tigers.*

suck (suk) **1** *v* draw into your mouth: *to suck through a straw.* **2** *v* hold in your mouth and lick: *The child sucked a lollipop.* –**suc′tion,** *n.*

sud·den (sud′ən) *adj* not expected; quick: *a sudden attack.* –**sud′den·ly,** *adv.*

suede (swād) *n* soft leather that feels like velvet.

suf·fer (suf′ər) *v* feel pain, sadness, injury, etc.: *to suffer from a headache.* –**suf′fer·ing,** *n.*

suf·fi·cient (sə fish′ənt) *adj* enough. –**suf·fi′cient·ly,** *adv.*

suf·fix (suf′iks) a syllable or syllables put at the end of a word to change its meaning or to make another word, as *-ly* in *badly, -ness* in *goodness,* and *-ful* in *spoonful.*

suf·fo·cate (suf′ə kāt′) *v* keep from breathing; die for lack of air: *The cat suffocated in the smoke-filled garage.* **suf·fo·cat·ed, suf·fo·cat·ing.** –**suf′fo·ca′tion,** *n.*

Sugar cane

sug·ar (shug′ər) *n* a sweet substance made from sugar cane or sugar beets.

sug·gest (sə jest′ *or* səg jest′) *v* offer an idea: *She suggested a swim, and we all agreed.* –**sug·ges′tion,** *n.*

su·i·cide (sū′ə sīd′) *n* a person who kills himself or herself on purpose.

commit suicide, kill yourself on purpose.

suit (sūt) **1** *n* a set of clothes to be worn together: *a suit of jacket and pants.* **2** *v* be good for; be best for: *A cold climate suits apples and wheat. Which date suits you best?*

suit·a·ble *adj* right for the occasion: *A simple outfit is suitable for school wear.*

suit yourself, do as you want.

sulk (sulk) *v* be silent because of a bad or angry mood. –**sulk′y,** *adj.*

sul·len (sul′ən) *adj* sulky.

sum (sum) **1** *n* an amount of money: *Leah paid a huge sum for that bicycle.* **2** *n* the total: *The sum of 2, 3, and 4 is 9.*

sum up, tell briefly: *to sum up the main points of the discussion.*

sum·ma·rize (sum′ə rīz′) *v* give the main points of: *to summarize the story in a single paragraph.* **sum·ma·rized, sum·ma·riz·ing.** –**sum′ma·ry,** *n.*

sum·mer (sum′ər) *n* the warmest season, between spring and fall.

sum·mit (sum′it) *n* the highest point: *the summit of the mountain.*

sum·mon (sum′ən) *v* send for: *The fire alarm summons the fire department.*

sun (sun) *n* the star around which the earth and the other planets revolve. The sun lights and warms the earth. –**sun′ny,** *adj.*

sun·burn *n* a burning of your skin by the sun's rays: *A sunburn is often red and painful.* –**sun′burnt′,** *adj.* **sun·dance** a sacred dance ceremony among some First Nations peoples, held once a year by a highly respected person who had received certain gifts from the thunderbird. Only specially invited people could take part. **sun·di·al** *n* an instrument for telling the time of day by the position of a shadow cast by the sun. **sun·rise** *n* the time when the sun comes up. **sun·set** *n* the time when the sun goes down.

sun·dae (sun′dā′) *n* ice cream with syrup, crushed fruit, nuts, etc. on it.

su·per– (sū′pər) *a prefix meaning* more than or above: *superhuman, supermarket.*

su·per·nat·u·ral (sū′pər nach′ə rəl) *adj* not part of the natural world; unexplained.

su·perb (sů pərb′) *adj* excellent: *a superb performance.*

su·per·in·tend·ent (sū′pər in ten′dənt) *n* a person who is in charge, directs, or manages: *a superintendent of schools, a superintendent of an apartment building.*

su·pe·ri·or (sə pēr′ē ər) **1** *adj* better: *Our players had to compete with a superior team.* **2** *adj* higher in position: *a superior officer.* –**su·pe′ri·or′i·ty,** *n.*

su·per·la·tive (sə pər′lə tiv) **1** *adj* of the highest or best kind: *You are a superlative baseball player.* **2** *n* in grammar, the third of three levels of comparison. ►See the *Grammar and Usage Mini-Guide.*

> ### Grammar ✓Check... **superlative**
> You can usually make an adjective or adverb **superlative** in one of two ways:
> - for short words, add **est** to the root word: *hardest, fastest.*
> - for longer words, add **most** before the word: *most beautiful, most thrilling.*

su·per·sti·tion (sū′pər stish′ən) *n* a belief that something can bring good or bad luck: *A common superstition is that 13 is an unlucky number.* –**su′per·sti′tious,** *adj.*

su·per·vise (sū′pər vīz′) *v* look after and direct workers or activities: *Children are supervised by teachers.* **su·per·vised, su·per·vis·ing.** –**su′per·vi′sion,** *n,* –**su′per·vi′sor,** *n.*

sup·per (sup′ər) *n* an evening meal.

sup·ply (sə plī′) **1** *v* provide: *The school supplies books for the students.* **sup·plied, sup·ply·ing. 2** *n* a lot of things ready for use: *I like to have a supply of paper for drawing. pl* **sup·plies.**

sup·port (sə pȯrt′) **1** *v* hold up: *Walls support the roof.* **2** *v* encourage; help: *Support your local hockey team.* **3** *n* encouragement; help: *We need the support of our friends.* –**sup·port′er,** *n.*

sup·pose (sə pōz′) **1** *v* imagine: *Suppose we are late, what will the teacher say?* **2** *v* believe; guess: *I suppose she will come as usual.* **sup·posed, sup·pos·ing.**

supposed to, expected to: *I was supposed to call her, but I forgot.*

su·preme (sə prēm′) *adj* highest; greatest: *a supreme ruler, supreme courage.*

sure (shůr) *adj* certain: *Are you sure you locked the door?* **sur·er, sur·est.**

for sure, *Informal.* certainly. **Surely** means the same thing.

Surfboard

Surfing

surf (sərf) **1** *n* the waves breaking on the shore. **2** *v* travel on such a wave.

sur·face (sər′fis) **1** *n* the outside or top of anything: *An egg has a smooth surface. The surface of the road is icy.* **2** *n* any face or side of a thing: *A cube has six surfaces.* **3** *n* the outward appearance: *He seems rough, but you will find him very kind under the surface.* **4** *v* rise to the surface of the water: *The submarine surfaced.* **sur·faced, sur·fac·ing.**

sur·geon (sər′jən) *n* a doctor who performs operations. –**sur′ger·y,** *n,* –**sur′gi·cal,** *adj.*

sur·name (sər′nām′) *n* the family name: *Kahn is the surname of Nathan Kahn.*

sur·plus (sər′pləs) *adj* extra: *Surplus wheat is put in storage.*

sur·prise (sər prīz′) **1** *n* something unexpected: *Mother always has a surprise for me on my birthday.* **2** *v* do something unexpected: *I surprised my sister by letting her borrow my new jacket.* **sur·prised, sur·pris·ing.**

sur·pris·ing *adj* causing surprise: *Our team made a surprising win.*

sur·ren·der (sə ren′dər) **1** *v* give up: *The escaped prisoner finally surrendered to the police.* **2** *n* the act of surrendering.

sur·round (sə round′) *v* shut in on all sides: *A high fence surrounds the fort.*

sur·round·ings *pl.n* surrounding things: *A tiger's stripes seem to make it disappear into its surroundings.*

sur·vey (sər vā′ *for 1,* sər′vā *for 2 and 3*) **1** *v* look over: *The buyers surveyed the things in the garage sale.* **2** *n* a general look; an inspection: *We made a quick survey of the room.* **3** *n* a gathering of information: *a survey of public opinion. pl* **sur·veys.**

sur·vive (sər vīv′) *v* remain alive: *Only ten of the crew survived the shipwreck. The crops survived the drought.* **sur·vived, sur·viv·ing.** –**sur·viv′al,** *n,* –**sur·viv′or,** *n.*

sus·pect (sə spekt′ *for 1,* sus′pekt *for 2*) **1** *v* think likely: *I suspect that some accident has delayed him.* **2** *n* a person suspected of doing something wrong.

sus·pi·cion (sə spish′ən) *n* a feeling that something is wrong: *Wei-Wei had a suspicion that her friend was unhappy.* **sus·pi·cious** (sə spish′əs) **1** *adj* making you suspect something: *suspicious behaviour.* **2** *adj* feeling suspicion: *The dog is suspicious of strangers.*

sus·pend (sə spend′) **1** *v* hang down by attaching to something above: *The lamp was suspended from the ceiling.* **2** *v* stop for a while: *In many places in Canada, we suspend road construction during the winter.* **3** *v* remove for a while: *He was suspended from school for a week for bad conduct.* –**sus·pen′sion,** *n.*

sus·pense (sə spens′) *n* the condition of being uncertain or worried: *The mystery story kept me in suspense until the end.*

swal·low (swol′ō) **1** *v* take into your stomach through your throat: *We swallow all our food and drink.* **2** *v Informal.* believe too easily: *Marco will swallow any story.*

swamp (swomp) **1** *n* wet, soft land. **2** *v* fill with water and sink: *The waves swamped the boat.* **3** *v* make or become helpless: *This is too much work! I'm swamped!*

Trumpeter swans—about 150 cm long including the tail; wingspread about 275 cm

swan (swon) *n* a large water bird with a long curved neck. Swans are either white or black.

swap (swop) *Informal.* **1** *v* exchange or trade: *Thor swapped his baseball bat for a hockey stick.* **2** *n* an exchange or trade. **swapped, swap·ping.**

swarm (swȯrm) **1** *n* a large group of insects, animals, people, etc. moving about together: *Swarms of children were playing in the park.* **2** *v* be crowded; crowd: *The swamp is swarming with mosquitoes.*

sway (swā) *v* swing slowly back and forth or from side to side: *The trees swayed in the wind.*

swear (swer) **1** *v* make a promise: *A witness at a trial has to swear to tell the truth.* **2** *v* use bad language. **swore, sworn, swear·ing.**

sweat (swet) **1** *n* moisture coming through your skin. **2** *v* give out moisture: *We sweat when it is very hot. A pitcher of ice water sweats on a hot day.* **3** *v Informal.* work very hard. **sweat** or **sweat·ed, sweat·ing.**

sweat lodge a building used by some First Nations peoples of the Pacific coast for ceremonies meant to cleanse the person's body, mind, and soul using steam. Often these ceremonies were part of the process of becoming an adult and would lead to receiving a vision or finding a spirit guide.

sweep (swēp) **1** *v* clean with a broom or brush. **2** *v* move swiftly: *Fire swept through the forest.* **3** *n* a winning of all the games in a series, match, contest, etc.; complete victory. **swept, sweep·ing.**

sweet (swēt) **1** *adj* having a taste like sugar: *Pears are much sweeter than lemons.* **2** *adj* pleasant: *a sweet child, a sweet smile, sweet music, a sweet voice.* **3** **sweets,** *pl.n* candy or other sweet things. –**sweet'en,** *v,* –**sweet'ly,** *adv,* –**sweet'ness,** *n.*

sweet·grass *n* a herb used by many First Nations people, which smells sweet when dried. It is usually burned to create fragrant smoke during prayer.

swell (swel) **1** *v* make or grow larger: *Rain swelled the river until it flooded the area all around. His wrist is swollen where he bumped it.* **2** *adj Slang.* excellent: *We had a swell time at the party.* **swelled, swelled** or **swol·len, swell·ing. swell·ing** *n* a swollen part.

swerve (swərv) *v* turn aside: *The car swerved to avoid hitting the dog.* **swerved, swerv·ing.**

swift (swift) *adj* very fast: *a swift canoe, a swift answer.* –**swift'ly,** *adv,* –**swift'ness,** *n.*

A girl swimming

swim (swim) **1** *v* move along in the water by using arms, legs, fins, etc.: *Fish swim. Most children like to swim.* –**swim·mer,** *n.* **2** *v* be dizzy: *The heat and noise made my head swim.* **swam, swum, swim·ming.**

swin·dle (swin'dəl) *v* cheat. *Honest businesses do not swindle their customers.* **swin·dled, swin·dling.**

swine (swīn) **1** *n* a pig. **2** *n* a coarse, beastly person. *pl* **swine.**

swing (swing) **1** *v* move back and forth: *He swings his arms as he walks.* **2** *n* a seat hung from ropes or chains, in which you may sit and swing. **3** *v* move in a curve: *She swung the bat at the ball.* **4** *n* a swinging movement: *One swing of the axe split the log.* **swung, swing·ing.**

swipe (swīp) **1** *n Informal.* a sweeping stroke: *Elijah made two swipes at the golf ball without hitting it.* **2** *v Slang.* steal.

swirl (swərl) *v* move with a spin; whirl: *dust swirling in the wind.*

switch (swich) **1** *n* a device for turning something on or off: *an electric switch.* **2** *v* change by using a switch: *Switch off the light.* **3** *v* exchange: *to switch places.*

sword (sòrd) *n* a weapon, usually metal, with a long, sharp blade fixed in a handle or hilt.

syl·la·ble (sil'ə bəl) *n* a separate sound in a word. The word *Canadian* has four syllables.

> **Grammar** ✓ *Check* ..... **syllable**
>
> When you have to divide a word at the end of a line, always divide it between **syllables**: *di-vide, syl-la-bles.* Never divide proper names or words of one syllable.

sym·bol (sim'bəl) *n* something that stands for something else: *The olive branch is a symbol of peace. The mark + is the symbol for add.*

sym·pa·thy (sim'pə thē) *n* a sharing of another person's feelings: *When Harry lost his kitten, I felt sympathy for him.* *pl* **sym·pa·thies.** –**sym'pa·thet'ic,** *adj,* –**sym'pa·thize',** *v.*

symp·tom (simp'təm) *n* a sign: *Fever is a symptom of illness.*

syn·a·gogue (sin'ə gog') *n* a building used by Jews for religious worship and teaching.

syn·o·nym (sin'ə nim') *n* a word that means the same or nearly the same as another word: *"Little" is a synonym of "small."*

syn·the·sis (sin'thə sis) *n* a combination of parts into a whole: *Plastics are produced by the synthesis of various chemicals.* –**syn'the·size',** *v.* **syn·thet·ic** (sin thet'ik) *adj* made artificially by combining chemicals; not natural: *Nylon is a synthetic fibre.*

syr·up (sēr'əp *or* sər'əp) *n* a sweet, thick liquid: *Maple syrup is made from the sap of maple trees.*

sys·tem (sis'təm) **1** *n* a set of parts forming a whole: *a railway system, the digestive system.* **2** *n* a method: *We have a system for organizing our CDs.* –**sys'tem·at'ic,** *adj,* –**sys'tem·at'i·cal·ly,** *adv.*

t or **T** (tē) *n* the twentieth letter of the English alphabet or the speech sound that it stands for. We hear the sound of *t* at the beginning and end of the word *tot*. *pl* **t's** or **T's**.

ta·ble (tā'bəl) **1** *n* a piece of furniture with a smooth, flat top on legs. **2** *n* a list: *a table of contents in the front of a book, the multiplication table, a timetable.*

ta·ble·spoon *n* a large spoon (about 15 mL) used for serving food and for measuring.

tab·let (tab'lit) *n* a small, flat piece of medicine, candy, etc.: *vitamin tablets.*

ta·boo (tə bū') *adj* forbidden by tradition: *Eating human flesh is taboo in most societies.*

tack (tak) **1** *n* a short, sharp-pointed nail with a broad, flat head: *carpet tacks.* **2** *v* fasten with tacks: *Mahmuda tacked the calendar over her desk.*

tack·le (tak'əl) **1** *n* equipment: *Fishing tackle means the rod, line, hooks, etc.* **2** *v* try to deal with: *We all have our own problems to tackle.* **3** *v* grab: *Nobaru tackled the thief and held him till help arrived.* **tack·led, tack·ling.**

tact (takt) *n* the ability to say and do the right things so as to avoid hurting people's feelings: *My friend showed tact in not talking about my failure to get into the school choir.* —**tact'ful,** *adj.*

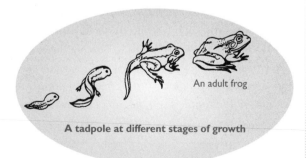

A tadpole at different stages of growth

tad·pole (tad'pōl') *n* a very young frog or toad, when it has a tail and lives in water.

tag (tag) **1** *n* a piece of card fastened to something: *Each coat in a store has a price tag.* **2** *n* a children's game in which one child who is "it" chases the rest of the children to touch one of them. The one touched is then "it" and must chase the others.

tail (tāl) **1** *n* in some animals, the part that hangs from the end of the body: *My dog wags its tail.* **2** *n* something like an animal's tail: *the tail of a kite.* **3** *v* follow close behind: *Some children tailed me all the way home.*

tails, the reverse side of a coin.

> ### CONFUSABLES ...... tail
>
> **tail** means "end part of an animal": *a horse's tail*
> **tale** means "story": *a fairy tale*

tai·lor (tā'lər) **1** *n* a person whose business is making or repairing clothes, especially men's clothes. **2** *v* make clothes, especially to fit a particular person. **3** *v* adjust: *My mother tailors her cooking to suit our likes and dislikes.*

take (tāk) **1** *v* get hold of; accept: *Take my hand. Take my advice.* **2** *v* make use of: *Akbar hates to take medicine. We took a train to go to Fredericton.* **3** *v* choose: *Take the shortest way home.* **4** *v* carry: *Please take the waste basket away and empty it.* **5** *v* subtract: *If you take 2 from 7, you have 5.* **6** *v* do; make: *Take a walk. Take my photograph.* **took, tak·en, tak·ing.**

take·out *n* food that you buy at a **takeout,** and take away to eat somewhere else.

take after, be like: *She takes after her mother.*

taken aback, suddenly surprised or startled.

take off, 1 leave the ground: *Three airplanes took off at the same time.* **2** rush away: *Gunther took off at the first sign of trouble.* **3** *Informal.* give a funny imitation of.

take over, 1 seize control. **2** continue: *I took over from my brother and finished cutting the grass.*

take part, be involved in.

take place, happen.

take to, 1 form a liking for: *Conchita took to swimming right away.* **2** go to: *The cat took to the woods and became wild.*

take your time, do not hurry.

tale (tāl) *n* a true or false story: *Grandfather loves to tell us tales of growing up in Québec.*

tal·ent (tal'ənt) *n* special natural ability: *Luciana has a talent for music.* —**tal'ent·ed,** *adj.*

talk (tok) **1** *v* use words; speak: *The baby is learning to talk.* **2** *n* conversation. **3** *n* an informal speech: *The coach gave the team a talk about team spirit.* **4** *v* persuade by talk: *We talked Carson into joining the club.*

talk·a·tive *adj* fond of talking.

talking stick among some First Nations peoples, a carved stick which gives the person holding it the right to speak. Sometimes an eagle feather is used.

talk back, *Informal.* answer rudely or disrespectfully.

talk down to, speak to in a superior tone.

tall (tol) **1** *adj* high: *Toronto has many tall buildings.* **2** *adj* in height: *My little sister is one metre tall.*

tal·ly (tal′ē) **1** *n* a mark made for a certain number of objects in keeping score: *Each tally represents one person.* pl **tal·lies.** **2** *v* count; find the total: *Will you tally the score, please?* **3** *v* agree: *Your version of the accident tallies with mine.* **tal·lied, tal·ly·ing.**

tal·on (tal′ən) *n* the claw of a bird of prey: *Eagles have talons.*

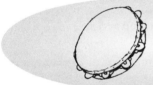

A tambourine is played by hitting it with your hand, or shaking it.

tam·bou·rine (tam′bə rēn′) *n* a small drum with jingling metal disks around the side.

tame (tām) **1** *adj* not wild: *A tame rabbit is a nice pet.* **tam·er, tam·est.** **2** *v* make tame; train: *to tame a horse.* **tamed, tam·ing.**

tam·per (tam′pər) *v* meddle in a bad way: *Do not tamper with the lock or it will break.*

tan (tan) **1** *n* the brown colour of skin caused by being in the sun. **2** *v* make or become brown by being in sun: *If you lie in the sun, you will tan.* **tanned, tan·ning.**

tang (tang) *n* a strong taste: *the tang of mustard.* –**tang′y,** *adj.*

tan·gi·ble (tan′jə bəl) **1** *adj* capable of being touched or felt by touch: *Books are tangible; stories are not.* **2** *adj* real; actual; definite: *There has been a tangible improvement in your work.*

tan·gle (tang′gəl) **1** *v* twist together in a confused mess: *The kitten had tangled the ball of yarn.* **2** *n* a confused mess. **tan·gled, tan·gling.**

tank (tangk) **1** *n* a large container for liquid or gas: *an empty gasoline tank.* **2** *n* an armoured vehicle used by soldiers.

tank·er *n* a ship, aircraft, or truck with tanks for carrying oil, gasoline, etc.

tan·trum (tan′trəm) *n Informal.* a noisy fit of bad temper.

Tao·ism (tau′iz əm) *n* a religion that began in China, based on the teachings of Laotse who wrote the Tao Te Ching. Taoism teaches people to aim for harmony and balance through a humble, simple, honest, and unselfish lifestyle. –**Tao′ist,** *n* or *adj.*

tap (tap) **1** *v* strike lightly: *Jameel tapped on the window.* **2** *n* a device for turning on and off a flow of liquid from a pipe: *Most sinks have taps for hot and cold water.* **3** *v* make a hole in to let out liquid: *They tapped the sugar maples when the sap began to flow.* **tapped, tap·ping.**

on tap, ready for use: *My mother always keeps some stamps on tap so that she won't run out.*

tape (tāp) **1** *n* a long, narrow strip of something: *audio tape, video tape, sticky tape, a measuring tape, duct tape.* **2** *v* fasten with tape; wrap with tape: *She taped her hockey stick.* **3** *v* record on tape: *The TV program was taped for later.* **taped, tap·ing.**

tape re·cord·er *n* a machine that records and plays back sound on plastic tape.

tar (tàr) **1** *n* a thick, black, sticky substance made from wood or coal: *Tar is used to cover and patch roads.* **2** *v* cover or smear with tar. **tarred, tar·ring.**

tar sands sand mixed with a tarlike substance, found especially in northern Alberta. The tar sands can be processed to give petroleum or oil.

Tarantula: one of the world's largest spiders—body about 8 cm long

ta·ran·tu·la (tə ran′chə lə) *n* a large, hairy spider, whose bite is painful but usually not serious.

tar·get (tär′git) *n* something aimed at: *The target for the fund-raising drive was $10 000.*

tar·nish (tär′nish) **1** *v* make or become dull; lose shine: *Salt will tarnish silver.* **2** *n* the dull covering, especially on silver: *I took the tarnish off with silver polish.*

tar·pau·lin (tär pol′ən) *n* a sheet of waterproof canvas.

tart (tärt) **1** *adj* having a sharp taste; sour: *Some apples are tart.* **2** *n* a piece of pastry filled with fruit, jam, etc.

task (task) *n* a piece of work: *Jarmila's task is to set the table.*

taste (tāst) **1** *n* flavour: *Sweet, sour, salt, and bitter are four important tastes.* **2** *v* try the flavour of something by eating or drinking a bit: *The chef tastes everything to see if it is right.* **3** *n* the sense by which the flavour of things is noticed: *Her sense of taste is unusually good.* **4** *n* the ability to appreciate what is good and what is bad in clothes, manners, art, etc.: *Zora's choice of music shows excellent taste.* **tast·ed, tast·ing.**
taste·less *adj* without taste: *tasteless food.*
tast·y *adj* of food or drink, tasting good.

tat·tered (tat′ərd) *adj* torn or ragged: *a tattered pair of jeans.*

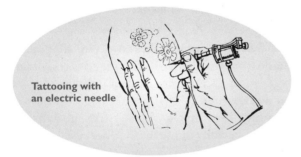

Tattooing with an electric needle

tat·too (ta tü′) **1** *v* mark the skin with designs by pricking it and putting in colours: *She had a butterfly tattooed on her ankle.* **tat·tooed, tat·too·ing.** **2** *n* a design tattooed on the skin. *pl* **tat·toos.**

taught (tot) *v* the past tense and past participle of **teach.**

CONFUSABLES .... taught

taught means "did teach":
  She taught me good manners.
taut means "tight":
  Pull the string taut.

taunt (tont) **1** *v* make fun of; mock. **2** *n* a bitter or insulting remark; mocking; jeering.

taut (tot) *adj* pulled tight: *a taut rope.*

tax (taks) **1** *n* money paid by people to the government for services like health care and education. **2** *v* put a tax on. **3** *v* put a burden on: *Reading in a poor light taxes your eyes.*

tax·i (tak′sē) **1** *n* a car and driver that you pay to use. *pl* **tax·is.** **2** *v* of an aircraft, move across the ground: *The airplane taxied onto the runway.* **tax·ied, tax·i·ing.**

tea (tē) *n* a drink made by pouring boiling water over dried leaves: *a cup of tea.*

tea·spoon *n* a small spoon (about 5 mL) used to stir tea, coffee, etc. and for measuring.

teach (tēch) *v* help to learn; show how to do; make understand. **taught, teach·ing.** –**teach′er,** *n,* –**teach′ing,** *n.*

team (tēm) **1** *n* a group of people working together, especially in a game: *a football team, a debating team.* **2** *n* two or more dogs or other animals working together. **3** *v* join together in a team: *Everybody teamed up to clean the classroom after the party.*
team·mate *n* another member of a team.
team·work *n* working together: *Teamwork makes hard jobs easier.*

tear (tēr for 1, ter for 2 and 3) **1** *n* a drop of salty water coming from your eye. –**tear′ful,** *adj.* **2** *v* pull apart; rip: *Reed tore the page in half.* **3** *n* a torn place: *Nadia has a tear in her shirt.* **tore, torn, tear·ing.**
in tears, crying.

tease (tēz) **1** *v* annoy; make fun of: *Don't tease the cat by pulling its tail. The other boys teased Ramesh about his new haircut.* **2** *n* a person who teases. **teased, teas·ing.**

tech·ni·cal (tek′nə kəl) *adj* having to do with the special facts of a science or art.
tech·nique (tek nēk′) *n* a special method of doing something: *a new technique for removing tonsils.*
tech·nol·o·gy (tek nol′ə jē) *n* the application of scientific knowledge to practical uses: *Engineering is a branch of technology.* –**tech·nol·o′gi·cal,** *adj.*

te·di·ous (tē′dē əs) *adj* tiring and boring: *A long talk that you cannot understand is tedious.*

teem (tēm) **1** *v* be full: *The swamp teemed with mosquitoes.* **2** *v* pour heavily: *It teemed all day.*

CONFUSABLES .... teem

teem means "be full":
The river is teeming with fish.
team means "people working together":
My hockey team won the tournament.

---

teen·ag·er (tē′nā′jər) *n* a person between 13 and 19 years old. **Teen** is another word for this.
teen·age *adj* having to do with teenagers: *teenage students, a teenage magazine.* **teens** *pl.n* the years of life from 13 to 19: *Dov is in his teens.*

tee·ny (tē′nē) *adj Informal.* tiny.

A teepee

tee·pee (tē′pē) *n* a cone-shaped tent once used by the First Nations peoples of the plains, made of animal skins or canvas over a frame of wooden poles. **Tipi** is another spelling.

teeth (tēth) *n* plural of **tooth.**
teethe (tēᴛн) *v* grow teeth, cut teeth.
by the skin of your teeth, just barely: *Tate caught the bus by the skin of his teeth.*

tel·e·phone (tel′ə fōn′) **1** *n* a device for speaking over distances. A short form for this is **phone. 2** *v* make a telephone call to.
tel·e·phoned, tel·e·phon·ing.

tel·e·scope (tel′ə skōp′) *n* a device for making distant objects appear nearer and larger.

tel·e·vi·sion (tel′ə vizh′ən) *n* a device for receiving pictures on a screen. **–tel′e·vise′,** *v.*

tell (tel) **1** *v* put in words; say; give information by talking: *Tell us a story. Tell the truth. Tell us about it.* **2** *v* order: *I told you to do your work.* **told, tell·ing.**
tell·tale *n* a person who tells tales on others.
tell on, tell tales about: *No child likes anyone to tell on him or her.*
tell time, know what time it is on the clock.

tem·per (tem′pər) *n* the way you feel or behave: *She has a sweet temper. He has a bad temper.*
tem·per·a·men·tal (tem′prə men′təl) *adj* easily irritated; sensitive.
lose your temper, become very angry.

tem·per·a·ture (tem′prə chər) *n* the degree of heat or cold: *The temperature of freezing water is 0°C.*

tem·ple (tem′pəl) *n* a building used for the service or worship of a god or gods: *Greek temples were beautifully built.*

tem·po·rar·y (tem′pə rer′ē) *adj* lasting for a short time only: *The campers made a temporary shelter out of branches.* **–tem′po·rar′i·ly,** *adv.*

tempt (tempt) **1** *v* make, or try to make a person do something, especially something wrong: *The sight of the food tempted the hungry woman to steal.* **2** *v* attract strongly: *The candy tempts me.* **–temp·ta′tion,** *n.*

ten (ten) ▶See Appendix.

ten·ant (ten′ənt) *n* a person paying rent to use land or buildings belonging to another person: *That building has apartments for 100 tenants.*

tend (tend) **1** *v* be likely: *Businesses tend to use more and more computers.* **–tend′en·cy,** *n.* **2** *v* take care of: *A nurse tends sick people.*

ten·der (ten′dər) **1** *adj* not hard or tough: *Stones hurt the little child's tender feet.* **2** *adj* loving: *The mother spoke tender words to her baby.* **3** *adj* sensitive; painful. **–ten′der·ness,** *n.*

tense (tens) **1** *adj* stretched tight: *a tense rope.* **2** *adj* strained: *tense nerves.* **3** *n* in grammar, a form of the verb that shows the time of the action or state expressed by the verb. *He obeys* is in the present tense. *He obeyed* is in the past tense. **tens·er, tens·est.**
ten·sion 1 *n* a stretched condition: *The tension of the bow gives speed to the arrow.* **2** *n* a strained atmosphere.

tent (tent) *n* a movable shelter, usually made of nylon or canvas held up by poles and ropes.

A sea anemone is an animal which catches food with its tentacles.

ten·ta·cle (ten′tə kəl) *n* a long, slender growth on the head or around the mouth of an animal, used to touch, hold, or move: *An octopus has eight tentacles.*

term (tərm) **1** *n* a word that has a special meaning in a particular subject: *The word "software" is a computer term.* **2** *n* a set period of time: *Fall term begins in September for most schools.*

ter·mi·nal 1 *n* the end part: *A railway terminal is the station, sheds, tracks, etc. at the end of the line.* **2** *n* a device for making an electrical connection: *the terminals of a battery.* **3** *n* a video display unit or keyboard where you can enter or get information from a computer or communications system.

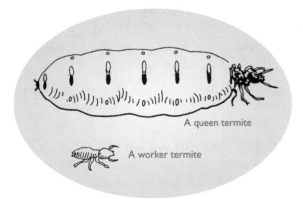

A queen termite

A worker termite

ter·mite (tər′mīt) *n* a kind of insect that has a soft, pale body. Termites feed on wood and can be very destructive to buildings, furniture, etc.

ter·rar·i·um (tə rer′ē əm) *n* a glass container in which plants or small land animals are kept. *pl* **ter·rar·i·ums** or **ter·rar·i·a** (tə rer′ē ə).

ter·res·tri·al (tə res′trē əl) *adj* of land, not water or air: *Cows, lions, and elephants are terrestrial animals.*

ter·ri·ble (ter′ə bəl) **1** *adj* causing great fear; awful: *The terrible storm in Québec destroyed many homes.* **2** *adj* very bad: *Teri has a terrible temper.* –**ter′ri·bly,** *adv.*

ter·ri·fy (ter′ə fī′) *v* frighten very much: *Terrified by the sight of the bear, Shiseo ran into the cabin.* **ter·ri·fied, ter·ri·fy·ing.**

ter·rif·ic (tə rif′ik) **1** *adj* causing great fear: *A terrific earthquake shook Japan.* **2** *adj* Slang. very good: *a terrific party.*

ter·ri·to·ry (ter′ə tòr′ē) **1** *n* land: *Much territory in the northern part of Africa is desert.* **2** 🍁 *n* **Territory,** in Canada, a region with its own elected government and administered by a commissioner appointed by the federal government: *Yukon Territory, Northwest Territories.* *pl* **ter·ri·to·ries.**

ter·ror (ter′ər) *n* great fear. –**ter′ror·ize′,** *v.* **ter·ror·ism** *n* the use of terror and violence to control people. –**ter′ror·ist,** *n.*

test (test) **1** *n* an examination: *The teacher gave us a test in arithmetic. A test showed that the water from our well was pure.* **2** *v* put to a test of any kind: *Test the wall with your finger to see if the paint is dry.*

tes·ti·fy (tes′tə fī′) *v* give evidence; tell what happened: *The police officer testified in court that the speeding car had crashed into the truck.* **tes·ti·fied, tes·ti·fy·ing.**

tes·ti·mo·ny *n* what is said when giving evidence: *A witness gave testimony that Mr. Kinski was at home all day.*

text (tekst) *n* the main part of the reading matter in a book: *This history book contains 300 pages of text and about 50 pages of questions.* **text·book** *n* a book for regular study by students.

tex·ture (teks′chər) *n* the feel or look of a substance: *Flour has a smooth texture.*

than (ᴛʜan) *conj* compared to: *Fernando is taller than his sister. You play the guitar better than I do.*

thank (thangk) **1** *v* say that you are grateful: *Toula thanked her teacher for helping her.* **2 thanks,** *pl.n* I thank you. –**thank′ful,** *adj,* –**thank′ful·ly,** *adv,* –**thank′ful·ness,** *n.*

thank·less *adj* not likely to get thanks: *Giving advice is sometimes a thankless act.*

Thanksgiving Day a day set apart as a holiday on which to give thanks, especially for the harvest: *In Canada, Thanksgiving Day is the second Monday in October.*

thank you 1 *n* the usual polite expression to show that you are grateful: *All he wants is a simple thank you.* **2 thank-you,** *adj* showing thanks: *I sent Mrs. Lao a thank-you note.*

have yourself to thank, be to blame: *You have yourself to thank if you eat too much.*

thanks to, because of: *Thanks to your efforts, we won the game.*

that (ᴛʜat) **1** *adj* or *pron* **That** is used to point out something. We use **this** for the thing nearer us and **that** for the thing farther away from us: *Let's buy this book but not that one.* *pl* **those.** **2** *conj* **That** is also used to connect a group of words: *I know that 6 and 4 add up to 10.* **3** *pron* which; who; whom: *Look at the present that I brought you. The girl that is in this photo is my sister.*

that's that is.

that's that, *Informal.* that is settled or decided.

USING WORDS . . . . . . that

That, **which**, and **who** or **whom** can all be used to introduce a clause.

Use **that** to refer to people, animals, or things: *A boy that I know broke his leg. The cat that climbed the tree got stuck. I found the nickel that I lost.*

Which is used only for things and animals, never for people: *The shoe, which fit perfectly, was made of glass.*

Who and **whom** are used for people, and sometimes for animals (especially pets): *My dog, who thinks he is human, likes to sit in the front seat of our car.*

---

thaw (tho) **1** *v* melt anything frozen: *Salt was put on the sidewalk to thaw the ice.* **2** *v* become free of frost, ice, etc.: *The pond thaws in April.* **3** *n* weather above the freezing point (0°C): *The spring thaw came late this year.*

the (ᴛʜə) *definite article.* **The** is used when referring to a certain thing or things: *The tree in our garden is a maple. The apples in the basket are McIntoshes.*

the·a·tre (thē′ə tər) *n* a place where plays or movies are shown. **Theater** is another spelling.

the·at·ri·cal (thē at′rə kəl) **1** *adj* having to do with the theatre. **2** *adj* exaggerated; artificial: *a theatrical way of speaking.*

theft (theft) *n* stealing.

theme (thēm) **1** *n* the main topic: *Protecting Manitoba's provincial parks was the speaker's theme.* **2** *n* the main melody in a piece of music.

then (ᴛʜen) **1** *adv* at that time: *My grandfather talks of his childhood, and says that prices were much lower then.* **2** *adv* next: *First comes spring, then summer.* **3** *adv* therefore: *If Hiroko broke the window, then she should pay for it.*

the·o·ry (thēr′ē) *n* an explanation based on thought: *There are several theories about the way in which the fire started.* *pl* **the·o·ries.** –**the′o·ret′i·cal** (thē′ə ret′ə kəl), *adj.*

there (ᴛʜer) **1** *adv* in that place: *Sit there.* **2** *adv* to that place: *We are going there tomorrow.* **3** *adv* **There** is used in sentences in which the verb comes before its subject: *There are three new houses on our street.*

there·a·bouts *adv* near that place or time or amount: *She lives in downtown Victoria, on Fort Street or thereabouts.* **there·fore** *adv* as a result of that: *Regan went to a party and therefore did not study her lessons.*

ther·mal (thər′məl) *adj* having to do with heat: *Steaming water comes from the underground thermal springs in Alberta.*

ther·mom·e·ter (thər mom′ə tər) *n* an instrument for measuring temperature.

ther·mo·stat *n* an automatic device for adjusting temperature: *Most furnaces are controlled by thermostats.*

the·sau·rus (thə sȯr′əs) *n* a book that gives different words that have almost the same meaning.

WORD HISTORY . . . . thesaurus

Thesaurus comes from a Greek word, *thesauros,* meaning "treasure house."
A thesaurus is a treasure house of words.

these (т͟нēz) *adj* or *pron* the plural of **this.**

they (т͟нā) *pron* things already spoken about: *I had three books yesterday, but I don't know where they are now.*

their (т͟нer) *adj* a possessive form of **they:** belonging to them: *That's their farm.*

theirs *pron* a possessive form of **they:** the one or ones belonging to them: *Our house is white; theirs is brown.*

them *pron* the objective form of **they:** *The books were a present but I don't really like them.*

them·selves **1** *pron* a form used instead of **them** when talking about the subject of the sentence: *The children dressed themselves every day.* **2** *pron* a form of **they** or **them** used to make a statement stronger: *The teachers themselves said that the test was too hard.*

they'd **1** they had. **2** they would.

they'll they will.

they're they are.

they've they have.

CONFUSABLES ..... **their**

their means "belonging to them": *their house*

there means "in that place": *Put it over there.*

they're means "they are": *They're arriving today.*

---

thick (thik) **1** *adj* filling much space from one side to the other; not thin: *Dundurn Castle has thick stone walls.* **2** *adj* set close together: *Althea has thick hair.* **3** *adj* like glue or syrup: *Thick liquids pour slowly.* –**thick′en,** *v,* –**thick′ly,** *adv,* –**thick′ness,** *n.*

thick skin, the ability to take criticism without being upset.

through thick and thin, in good times and bad: *A true friend stays loyal through thick and thin.*

thief (thēf) *n* a person who steals.

thin (thin) **1** *adj* filling little space from one side to the other; not thick: *The ice on Covehead Bay is too thin for skating.* **2** *adj* not set close together: *Stig has thin hair.* **3** *adj* like water: *This gravy is too thin.* **4** *adj* slender: *a thin person.* **5** *v* make thin; become thin: *to thin paint.*

thin·ner, thin·nest. thinned, thin·ning. –**thin′ly,** *adv,* –**thin′ness,** *n.*

thin skin, not having the ability to take criticism without being upset.

thing (thing) **1** *n* any object you can see or hear or touch or taste or smell: *All the things in the house were burned.* **2** *n* any fact, event, or idea: *It was a good thing to do.* **3** **things,** *pl.n* personal belongings: *I packed my things and took the bus to Charlottetown.*

think (thingk) **1** *v* use your mind: *You must learn to think clearly.* **2** *v* have an opinion: *Do you think it will rain?* **thought, think·ing.**

think over, consider carefully.

think up, plan.

third (thərd) ▶See Appendix.

thirst (thərst) *n* a desire for something, usually something to drink: *The traveller in the desert suffered from thirst.* –**thirst′y,** *adj.*

thir·teen (thərt′tēn′) ▶See Appendix.

thir·ty (thər′tē) ▶See Appendix.

this (т͟нis) *adj* or *pron* **This** is used to point out something. We use **that** for the thing farther away from us and **this** for the thing nearer us: *Shall we buy this book or that one? pl* **these.**

thong (thong) **1** *n* a narrow strip of leather, especially one used as a fastening. **2** *n* a kind of sandal held on by a narrow piece of leather, plastic, etc. between two toes.

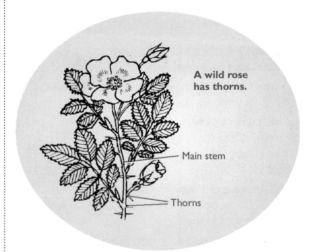

A wild rose has thorns.

— Main stem

— Thorns

thorn (thȯrn) *n* a sharp point on a stem or branch: *Roses have thorns.* –**thorn′y,** *adj.*

thor·ough (thər′ō) **1** *adj* complete: *Please make a thorough search for the lost money.* **2** *adj* doing all that should be done: *The doctor was very thorough in her examination of the sick child.* –**thor′ough·ly,** *adv.*

those (т͟нōz) *adj* or *pron* the plural of **that.**

though (ᴛʜō) *conj* in spite of the fact that: *We take our medicine, though we do not like it.*

thought (thot) **1** *n* what a person thinks: *Kar-Ling's thought was to have a picnic.* **2** *n* the act of thinking: *Thought helps us solve problems.* **3** *n* care: *Show some thought for others.* **4** *v* the past tense and past participle of **think:** *We thought it would snow yesterday.*
–**thought'ful,** *adj,* –**thought'less,** *adj.*

thou·sand (thou'zənd) ►See Appendix.

thread (thred) **1** *n* cotton, silk, etc. spun out into a fine string. **2** *v* put a thread through: *Mette threaded a hundred beads.*

threat (thret) *n* a warning of possible harm or unpleasantness: *Those black clouds are a threat of rain.* –**threat'en,** *v.*

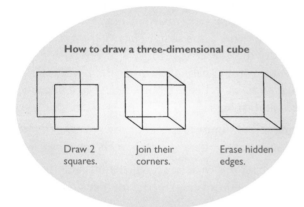

How to draw a three-dimensional cube

Draw 2 squares.   Join their corners.   Erase hidden edges.

three (thrē) ►See Appendix.
three-di·men·sion·al (thrē'di men'shə nəl) *adj* having the three dimensions of height, width, and depth: *A cube is a three-dimensional object.* This is sometimes shortened to **3D.**

thresh (thresh) *v* separate the grain or seeds from wheat, etc.: *Nowadays most farmers use a machine called a thresher to thresh their wheat.*

thrift (thrift) *n* care in using up money or things: *By thrift she managed to buy several presents.* –**thrift'y,** *adj.*

thrill (thril) **1** *n* a shivering, exciting feeling: *I get a thrill from an exciting movie.* **2** *v* give a shivering, exciting feeling to: *Stories of adventure thrilled her.*
thrill·er *n* an exciting movie, book, or TV show.

thrive (thrīv) *v* grow strong: *Most flowers will not thrive without sunshine.* **throve** or **thrived, thrived** or **thriv·en** (thriv'ən), **thriv·ing.**

throat (thrōt) *n* the inside of your neck.

throb (throb) *v* beat strongly: *The long climb up the hill made her heart throb. Xavier's wounded arm throbbed with pain.* **throbbed, throb·bing.**

throne (thrōn) *n* the chair on which a king, queen, or other person of high rank sits during ceremonies.

throng (throng) **1** *n* a crowd. **2** *v* come together in a crowd: *Many people thronged to see the TV star.*

through (thrū) **1** *prep* from end to end of; from one place to the other: *Luis worked as a lifeguard through the summer. The ball flew through the air.* **2** *prep* because of: *They became successful through working long and hard.* **3** *adj* finished: *I will soon be through.*
through·out (thrū out') *prep* in every part of: *Canada Day is celebrated throughout Canada.*

throw (thrō) **1** *v* toss: *The catcher threw the ball.* **2** *n* a toss: *That was a good throw from left field to the catcher.* **threw, thrown, throw·ing.**
throw away or **out,** put in the garbage.
throw up, *Informal.* vomit.

CONFUSABLES ..... **threw**

threw means "hurled":
He threw the ball.

through means "from end to end":
It went through the window.

thrust (thrust) *v* push hard: *Tibor thrust his hands into his pockets.* **thrust, thrust·ing.**

thud (thud) *n* a dull sound: *The book hit the floor with a thud.*

thumb (thum) **1** *n* the short, thick finger of your hand. **2** *v* turn pages quickly: *Georges thumbed through the book and gave it back to me.*
thumb·tack *n* a tack with a broad, flat head.
all thumbs, very clumsy, awkward, etc.
thumbs down, a sign of disapproval or rejection.
thumbs up, a sign of approval or acceptance.
under the thumb of, under the power of: *The bully tried to keep us all under his thumb.*

thump (thump) **1** *v* hit with something heavy: *Oman thumped the table with his fist.* **2** *n* a heavy hit, or the sound it makes: *She gave me a thump on the back because she thought I had something stuck in my throat.*

A thunderbird is often used as the top section of a totem pole.

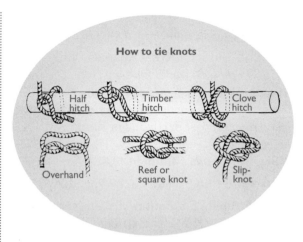

How to tie knots

Half hitch   Timber hitch   Clove hitch

Overhand   Reef or square knot   Slip-knot

thun·der (thun′dər) **1** *n* the loud noise that comes after a flash of lightning. **2** *v* make a noise like thunder: *The applause thundered through the room.* **–thun′der·ous,** *adj.*

thun·der·bird *n* in the tradition of some First Nations peoples, a spiritual power that causes thunder, lightning, rain, and other natural events. The symbol for it is a huge bird, which is often found in the art of First Nations people.

tick (tik) **1** *n* a sound like that made by a clock. **2** *n* a mark (√) used in checking.

tick·et (tik′it) *n* a card or piece of paper showing that something has to be paid, or has been paid: *a parking ticket, a bus ticket.*

tick·le (tik′əl) *v* touch lightly, causing shivers or laughter. **tick·led, tick·ling.** **–tick′lish** (tik′lish), *adj.*

tid·bit (tid′bit′) *n* a very pleasing bit of food, news, etc.

tide (tīd) *n* the rise and fall of the ocean, caused by the attraction of the moon and the sun. **High tide** comes about every 12½ hours, with **low tide** coming about halfway between each high tide.

tid·al *adj* having to do with tides: *A tidal river is affected by the ocean's tide.* **tidal wave** a large wave caused by strong winds or an earthquake.

CONFUSABLES ...... tide

tide means "rise and fall of the ocean":
  It is high tide.

tied means "knotted":
  I tied my shoelaces.

ti·dy (tī′dē) *adj* neat and in order: *a tidy room.* **ti·di·er, ti·di·est. –ti′di·ly,** *adv,* **–ti′di·ness,** *n.* **tidy up,** make something neater.

tie (tī) **1** *v* fasten with string or rope: *Please tie the newspapers in a bundle for recycling.* **2** *v* make a bow or knot: *to tie shoelaces.* **3** *n* a shaped, folded piece of cloth worn under a shirt collar and knotted in front. **4** *n* equality in points, votes, etc.: *The game ended in a tie, 3 to 3.* **5** *v* make the same score: *The two teams tied.* **tied, ty·ing.**

tie up, 1 stop: *The stalled truck tied up traffic for half an hour.* **2** be very busy: *I can't go tomorrow; I'm all tied up.*

tier (tēr) *n* one of a series of rows arranged one above another: *tiers of seats in a hockey arena.*

ti·ger (tī′gər) *n* a large, wild cat of Asia that has dull-yellow fur striped with black.

tight (tīt) **1** *adj* put together firmly: *a tight knot.* **2** *adj* fitting closely: *tight shoes.* **–tight′en,** *v,* **–tight′ly,** *adv.* **sit tight,** *Informal.* keep the same position, opinion, etc.

tile (tīl) **1** *n* a thin piece of baked clay, plastic, etc., used for covering roofs, walls, ceilings, and floors. **2** *v* cover with tiles: *to tile a bathroom floor.* **tiled, til·ing.**

till (til) **1** *prep* up to the time of: *We played till eight o'clock.* **2** *conj* up to the time when: *Walk till you come to a white house.* **3** *v* plough: *Farmers till the land.* **4** *n* a drawer for money.

tilt (tilt) *v* tip or lean to one side: *You tilt your cup when you drink. This table tilts.*

tim·ber (tim′bər) **1** *n* wood for building. **2** *n* trees that are growing and suitable for cutting. **timber line** on mountains and in the polar regions, a line beyond which trees will not grow because of the cold.

time (tīm) **1** *n* the past, present, and future: *We measure time in years, months, days, hours, minutes, and seconds.* **2** *n* a part of time: *A minute is a short time.* **3** *n* an occasion: *This time we will succeed.* **4** *n* some point in time: *What time is it?* **5** *n* an experience during a certain time: *Everyone had a good time.* **6** *v* measure the time of: *Hamish timed the horse for each kilometre.* **timed, tim·ing. 7 times,** *prep* multiplied by: *Four times three is twelve. Symbol:* ×

time line *n* a long line marked with important dates in a period of time. **time-out** *n* a short break in doing something, especially in a game: *In the third period the coach called for a time-out.*

time·ta·ble *n* a list that shows the times when things are to happen.

behind the times, out of date.

for the time being, for now.

from time to time, now and then.

in good time, at the right time.

in no time, quickly.

on time, at the right time.

time after time or **time and again,** again and again.

tim·id (tim'id) *adj* easily frightened; shy.

tin (tin) **1** *n* a soft, silver-white metal. **2** *n* any container made of tin: *a tin of beans.*

tin·gle (ting'gəl) *v* have a prickly feeling, especially from excitement: *Muhammad tingled with delight on his first trip in an airplane.* **tin·gled, tin·gling.**

tin·sel (tin'səl) *n* glittering metal in thin strips: *Tinsel is used to decorate Christmas trees.*

ti·ny (tī'nē) *adj* very small. **ti·ni·er, ti·ni·est.**

–tion *a suffix meaning:* **1** the act of. *Addition* means the act of *adding.* **2** the condition of being. *Exhaustion* means the condition of being *exhausted.* **3** the result of. *Reflection* means the result of *reflecting.*

tip (tip) **1** *n* the end part: *the tips of the fingers.* **2** *n* a small present of money in return for service: *Mr. Catania gave the waiter a tip.* **3** *n* a useful suggestion: *Dad gave me a helpful tip about pitching the tent on soft ground.* **4** *v* tilt: *Li-Ying tipped the chair backward.* **5** *v* give a small present of money to: *Did you tip the babysitter?* **tipped, tip·ping.**

tip·toe (tip'tō') *v* walk quietly on your toes. **tip·toed, tip·toe·ing.**

tire (tīr) **1** *v* use up strength: *The long walk tired Joie.* **tired, tir·ing. 2** *n* a circular rubber tube fitted around the rim of a wheel.

tired *adj* needing to rest: *The team was tired but kept playing as hard as ever.* **tire·less** *adj* never becoming tired: *a tireless worker.* **tire·some** *adj* tiring because not interesting: *a tiresome speech.*

tired of, bored with: *I'm tired of hearing about their vacation trip to Charlottetown.*

tis·sue (tish'ū) **1** *n* a mass of cells forming some part of an animal or plant: *brain tissue.* **2** *n* a thin, soft paper: *toilet tissue.*

ti·tle (tī'təl) **1** *n* the name of a book, poem, picture, song, etc. **2** *n* a name showing a person's rank, occupation, or condition in life: *Queen, Captain, Doctor, Professor, Mr., and Ms. are titles.*

> ## Grammar ✓Check . . . . . title
> Use a capital letter for all the important words in a **title**. You do not have to capitalize small words like *the, in, of, to,* unless they come at the beginning of the title: *To my Mother; In Search of the Wild Chimpanzee.*

to (tū) **1** *prep* in the direction of: *Go to the right.* **2** *prep* as far as; until: *This apple is rotten to the core.* **3** *prep* for the purpose of; for: *The park wardens came to the rescue.* **4** *prep* compared with: *The score was 9 to 5.* **5** *prep* belonging with; of: *the key to my home.*

A common toad—
usually about 9 cm long

toad (tōd) *n* a small animal like a frog, but living mostly on land. It has rough, dry skin often covered with warts.

toad·stool *n* a mushroom, especially a poisonous mushroom.

T t

toast (tōst) **1** *n* bread browned by heat. **2** *v* brown by heat: *We toasted marshmallows.* **3** *v* wish good luck to.

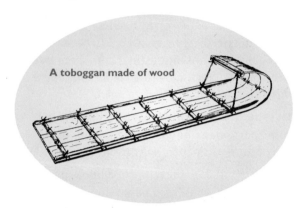

A toboggan made of wood

to·bog·gan (tə bog'ən) *n* a long flat sled without runners. The toboggan was originally used by First Nations people to carry belongings.

WORD HISTORY .... **toboggan**

Toboggan comes from the Algonquian word *tobagun*, meaning "handsled." The aboriginal peoples of North America introduced the toboggan to French settlers.

---

to·day (tə dā') **1** *n* this day; the present time: *Today is Wednesday.* **2** *adv* on or during this day: *What are you doing today?*

tod·dler (tod'lər) *n* a young child just learning to walk.

to—do (tə dü') *n* Informal. fuss: *There was a great to-do when the new puppy arrived.* *pl* **to-dos.**

toe (tō) *n* one of the five end parts of your foot.

to·fu (tō'fū) *n* a food made from cooked soybeans. **Bean curd** is another name for this.

to·geth·er (tə ɡeᴛʜ'ər) *adv* with each other: *The girls were walking together.*

toil (toil) **1** *n* hard work. **2** *v* work hard: *to toil with your hands for a living.*

toi·let (toi'lit) *n* a bowl with water at the bottom to flush the bowl clean. Waste matter from your body is disposed of in a toilet.

to·ken (tō'kən) **1** *n* a sign of something: *This picture is a token of our wonderful trip to Fredericton.* **2** *n* a piece of metal, plastic, etc. like a coin, used instead of money on buses, trains, etc.

told (tōld) *v* the past tense and past participle of **tell.**

tol·er·ate (tol'ə rāt') *v* put up with: *I tolerate my sister's teasing because I know she loves me.* **tol·er·at·ed, tol·er·at·ing.** –**tol'er·ant,** *adj.*

tol·er·ance *n* willingness to be patient toward people whose ways differ from your own.

toll (tōl) *n* a tax or fee paid: *We pay a toll when we use that highway.*

tom·a·hawk (tom'ə hok') *n* an axe used in earlier times by some First Nations people.

to·ma·to (tə mā'tō) *n* a juicy, pulpy, usually red fruit eaten as a vegetable, either raw or cooked. *pl* **to·ma·toes.**

tomb (tūm) *n* a grave for a dead body, often above ground.

tomb·stone *n* a stone that marks a tomb or grave.

to·mor·row (tə mȯr'ō) **1** *n* the day after today. **2** *adv* on the day after today.

ton (tun) **1** *n* a non-metric measure of mass, equal to about 1000 kg. **2** *n* Informal. a lot.

tone (tōn) **1** *n* a way of speaking or writing: *We disliked the angry tone of Yu-Wen's voice.* **2** *n* a normal, healthy condition: *muscle tone.* **3** *n* a shade of colour: *The room is painted in tones of brown.* **toned, ton·ing.**

tone down, soften: *Tone down your voice.*

tone up, give more strength to: *Cycling tones up the muscles in your legs.*

tongue (tung) *n* the movable fleshy part in your mouth.

tongue-tied *adj* unable to speak because of shyness, embarrassment, etc.

hold your tongue, keep silent.

on the tip of your tongue, almost remembered: *The name of that song is on the tip of my tongue.*

to·night (tə nīt') **1** *n* this night or evening. **2** *adv* on this night or evening: *Do you think it will snow tonight?*

tonne (tun) *n* a metric unit for measuring mass, equal to 1000 kg. *Symbol:* t

---

USING WORDS ..... **tonne**

When you are measuring the mass of something, it is important to use the correct unit name, **tonne**: *a tonne of wheat.*

But in expressions where the exact amount doesn't matter, use **ton**: *tons of fun.*

ton·sil (ton′səl) *n* either of the two small bits of flesh at the back of your throat.

ton·sil·li·tis (ton′sə lī′tis) *n* a diseased condition of your tonsils, making them red, swollen, and painful.

too (tū) **1** *adv* more than enough: *The summer passed too quickly.* **2** *adv* also: *The dog is hungry, and thirsty too.*

CONFUSABLES ...... too

too means "too much" or "also":
These problems are too hard. He stayed too.

to means "toward":
Go to the right.

two means "one more than one":
I have two ears.

---

tool (tūl) *n* a knife, hammer, saw, shovel, etc. used in doing work.

✿ **toon·ie** (tū′nē) *n* the Canadian two-dollar coin. **Twonie** is another spelling.

tooth (tūth) **1** *n* one of the hard, bonelike parts in your mouth, used for biting and chewing. **2** *n* something like a tooth. Each one of the projecting parts of a comb, rake, or saw is a tooth. *pl* **teeth.**

tooth·ache *n* a pain in your tooth or teeth.

top (top) **1** *n* the highest point or part: *the top of a mountain.* **2** *n* the upper surface: *the top of the table.* **3** *n* the highest place: *Our team is at the top of the league.* **4** *adj* having to do with the top: *the top shelf, the top team in baseball, top speed.* **5** *v* be higher or greater than: *Bet you can't top that score!* **6** *n* a toy that spins on a point. **topped, top·ping.**

top·ic (top′ik) *n* a subject that people think, write, or talk about: *The topic of our group's project is "The Cost of Keeping a Pet."*

to·rah (tôr′ə) in Judaism, the first five books of the Bible, containing the laws given to Moses by God, and the very beginning of Jewish history.

torch (tôrch) *n* a light that can be carried around: *A piece of pine wood makes a good torch.*

tor·ment (tôr ment′) *v* cause very great pain to: *Headaches tormented Ichiro.*

tor·na·do (tôr nā′dō) *n* a violent and destructive wind. A tornado moves forward as a whirling funnel. *pl* **tor·na·does** or **tor·na·dos.**

tor·rent (tôr′ənt) **1** *n* a violent, rushing stream of water: *a mountain torrent.* **2** *n* any violent, rushing stream: *a torrent of lava from a volcano.* –**tor·ren′tial,** *adj.*

tor·toise (tôr′təs) *n* a turtle, especially a land turtle. *pl* **tor·tois·es** or **tor·toise.**

tor·ture (tôr′chər) **1** *n* the act of making people or animals suffer very severe pain. **2** *v* cause very severe pain to: *It is cruel to torture animals.* **tor·tured, tor·tur·ing.**

toss (tos) **1** *v* throw lightly: *Militsa tossed the ball to the baby.* **2** *v* throw about; roll about: *The ship is tossed by the waves. He tossed on his bed all night.* **3** *v* flip a coin to decide something: *to toss for first place.*

to·tal (tō′təl) **1** *adj* whole; complete: *total darkness. The total cost of the hotel room and breakfast will be $90.* **2** *n* the whole amount: *Add the numbers to get the total.* –**to′tal·ly,** *adv.*

Haida totem poles in southern British Columbia

to·tem (tō′təm) **1** *n* in many different cultures, an animal or other natural object taken as the symbol of a group of related families. Among some First Nations peoples, the totem was considered to be the ancestor of the group. **2** *n* an image of this animal or object, carved, painted, woven into cloth, used in jewellery, etc. **totem pole** a large upright log carved and painted with totems, traditionally put up by many of the peoples of the northern Pacific coast. Totem poles could be read upward or downward and were a way of recording the ancestors of a clan or the important events in the clan's history. They could also be used to mark graves or land boundaries.

touch (tuch) **1** *v* put your hand or some other part of your body on or against and feel: *Misha touched the pan to see whether it was still hot.* **2** *v* be against: *Your sleeve is touching the butter.* **3** *n* the sense by which you feel things by handling them. **4** *n* communication: *A newspaper keeps you in touch with the world. François has been out of touch with us since his family moved away.* **5** *v* affect with some feeling: *The poor woman's sad story touched our hearts.*

touch·down *n* in football, a score made by a player holding the ball on or behind the opponents' goal line. **touch·y** *adj* easily upset: *Hosein is tired and very touchy today.*

touch down, land an airplane.

tough (tuf) **1** *adj* strong: *Donkeys are tough animals and can carry big loads.* **–tough'en,** *v.* **2** *adj* hard to break, cut, tear, or chew: *The steak was so tough I couldn't eat it.* **3** *adj* difficult: *a tough exam.*

tour (tūr) **1** *v* travel from place to place: *Many people tour Canada by car every summer.* **2** *n* a holiday trip: *The family made a tour through Europe.* **3** *v* go through a building, etc. to see its different parts, exhibits, etc.: *The children will tour the museum.*

tour·ist *n* a person travelling for pleasure.

tour·na·ment (tər'nə mənt) *n* a series of contests testing the skill of many persons: *a soccer tournament.*

tow (tō) *v* pull by a rope, chain, etc.: *The tug is towing three barges.*

to·ward (tə wȯrd') *prep* in the direction of: *Eliot walked toward the north.* Another word that means the same is **towards.**

tow·el (tou'əl) *n* a piece of cloth or paper for drying something.

tow·er (tou'ər) *n* a high building or frame that may stand alone or be part of another building.

town (toun) *n* a large group of houses and other buildings: *A town is usually smaller than a city but larger than a village.*

tox·in (tok'sən) *n* a poison, especially one produced by plants or animals.

tox·ic *adj* poisonous: *Fumes from an automobile exhaust are toxic.*

toy (toi) *n* something for a child to play with.

trace (trās) **1** *n* a sign of something from the past: *The explorer found traces of an ancient city at Fort Selkirk.* **2** *n* a footprint or other mark: *We saw traces of rabbits and squirrels on the snow.* **3** *n* a little bit: *Traces of gold were found along the banks of Kluane Lake.* **4** *v* follow a trail: *He traced the river to its source. She traced her family back through eight generations.* **5** *v* copy by following the lines of: *He put thin paper over the map of Canada and traced it.* **traced, trac·ing.**

track (trak) **1** *n* a line of metal rails for trains to run on. **2** *n* a mark left: *The dirt road showed many automobile tracks.* **3** *n* a path: *A track runs through the woods to the farmhouse. a race track.*

track and field the group of athletic contests done on a running track and a field next to it, including running, jumping, pole-vaulting, and throwing.

keep track of, keep within your sight, knowledge, or attention: *The noise of the crowd made it difficult to keep track of what was going on.*

make tracks, *Informal.* go very fast; run away.

track down, find by following signs or clues.

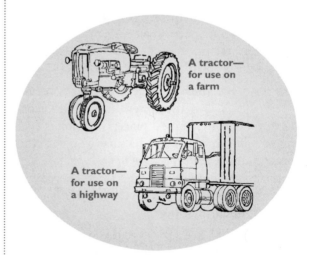

A tractor— for use on a farm

A tractor— for use on a highway

trac·tor (trak'tər) *n* a powerful machine used to pull wagons, ploughs, trailers, etc. on a farm, or on a highway.

trade (trād) **1** *n* buying and selling: *Canada has much trade with foreign countries.* **2** *v* make an exchange: *The boys traded seats.* **3** *n* a kind of work, especially one requiring skill with tools: *My big brother is learning the carpenter's trade.* **trad·ed, trad·ing. –trad'er,** *n.*

trading post a store of a trader, especially in a remote place: *The Hudson's Bay Company operates trading posts in the North.*

tra·di·tion (trə dish′ən) *n* beliefs, customs, stories, etc. passed from one generation to another. **–tra·di·tion·al,** *adj.*

traf·fic (traf′ik) *n* the people, cars, trucks, etc. coming and going along roads.

trag·e·dy (traj′ə dē) *n* a very sad happening or story. *pl* **trag·e·dies. –trag′ic,** *adj.*

trail (trāl) **1** *n* a path across a wild or unsettled region: *The prospector had followed mountain trails in the Northwest Territories for days.* **2** *n* a track or smell: *The dogs found the trail of the rabbit.* **3** *v* hunt by track or smell: *The dogs trailed the rabbit.* **4** *v* follow or pull along behind: *The dog trailed its master constantly.*

trail·er *n* a vehicle made to be pulled along by a car, truck, etc.; a mobile home: *We have a trailer that we take to Bonne Bay every summer.*

train (trān) **1** *n* a connected line of railway cars pulled by an engine. **2** *v* teach or learn a skill: *Rupinder wants to train to be a nurse.* **3** *v* make fit by exercise and diet: *The runners trained for races.* **–train′er,** *n,* **–train′ing,** *n.*

trai·tor (trā′tər) *n* a person who betrays a trust, a duty, a country, or a friend.

tramp (tramp) **1** *v* walk heavily: *Ward tramped across the floor in his heavy boots.* **2** *n* a long, steady walk: *The children took a tramp together over the hills.* **3** *n* a person who goes about on foot, living by begging, doing odd jobs, etc.

tram·ple *v* walk heavily on; crush: *The cattle broke through the fence and trampled the crops.*

A trampoline for gymnastics

tram·po·line (tram′pə lēn′ *or* tram′pə lēn′) *n* a piece of canvas or other sturdy fabric attached by springs to a metal frame, for bouncing on.

trance (trans) *n* a state of dreaminess a bit like sleep.

tran·quil (trang′kwəl) *adj* calm; quiet.

trans– *a prefix meaning* across, over, or through, as in *transatlantic.*

trans-Can·a·da *adj* extending from one end of Canada to the other: *the Trans-Canada Highway.*

trans·fer (trans′fər) **1** *v* move from one person or place to another. **2** *n* a ticket allowing a passenger to continue his or her journey on another streetcar, bus, train, etc. **trans·ferred, trans·fer·ring.**

trans·form (trans fôrm′) *v* change in form or appearance: *The blizzard transformed the bushes into glittering mounds of snow.* **–trans′for·ma′tion,** *n.*

trans·fu·sion (trans fyū′zhən) *n* the transfer of blood into a person or animal.

trans·late (tranz′lāt *or* tranz lāt′) *v* change from one language into another. **trans·lat·ed, trans·lat·ing. –trans·la′tion,** *n.*

trans·mit (tranz mit′) **1** *v* pass along: *Rats transmit disease.* **2** *v* send out signals by radio or television. **trans·mit·ted, trans·mit·ting. –trans·mis′sion,** *n.*

trans·par·ent (trans per′ənt) *adj* clear enough to see through: *Window glass is transparent.*

trans·plant (trans plant′ *for 1,* trans′plant *for 2*) **1** *v* plant again in a different place: *We start the flowers indoors and then transplant them to the garden.* **2** *n* the transfer of a body part from one person or animal to another: *a heart transplant.*

trans·port (trans pôrt′ *for 1,* trans′pôrt *for 2*) **1** *v* carry from one place to another: *Wheat is transported from the farms to the mills.* **2** *n* carrying from one place to another: *Trucks are used for transport.* **–trans′por·ta′tion,** *n.*

trap (trap) **1** *n* a device for catching animals, lobsters, birds, etc. **2** *v* catch in a trap: *The bear was trapped.* **trapped, trap·ping. –trap′per,** *n.*

trap·line *n* a series of traps set by a trapper who regularly goes over the line to remove trapped animals.

tra·peze (trə pēz′) *n* a short, horizontal bar hung by ropes like a swing, used in gymnasiums and circuses.

trash (trash) *n* worthless stuff; garbage: *Put the trash in the can.*

trav·el (trav′əl) **1** *v* go from one place to another. **2** *n* going from one place to another: *My grandmother loves travel.* **trav·elled** or **trav·eled, trav·el·ling** or **trav·el·ing.** **trav·el·ler** *n* a person who travels. **Traveler** is another spelling.

Two kinds of travois

tra·vois (trə vwä′ *or* trav′wä) **1** ❧ *n* a simple wheelless vehicle used in earlier times by First Nations people of the plains. It was made of two poles joined at one end, pulled by a dog or a horse. The poles held a platform or a net for carrying the load. **2** *n* a dog sled. *pl* **tra·vois.**

trawl (trol) **1** *n* a bag-shaped net dragged along the bottom of the sea to catch fish. **2** *v* to fish with such a net. **3** *n* a line supported by floats, with many short lines with baited hooks attached to it. **4** *v* to fish with such a line. **trawl·er** *n* a boat used in trawling.

tray (trā) *n* a flat container with a low rim around it.

treach·er·ous (trech′ə rəs) *adj* not to be trusted: *The treacherous soldier carried reports to the enemy. Thin ice is treacherous.*

tread (tred) **1** *v* step: *Don't tread on the cat's tail!* **2** *n* the sound of treading: *the tread of marching feet.* **3** *n* the part of stairs or a ladder that a person steps on: *The stair treads were covered with rubber.* **4** *n* the pattern on the surface of a tire: *The tread on the back tires is almost gone.* **trod, trod·den** or **trod, tread·ing.** **tread water,** keep upright in water, by slowly moving your legs as if cycling.

trea·son (trē′zən) *n* the act of betraying a country: *Helping the enemies of your country is treason.*

treas·ure (trezh′ər) **1** *n* valuable things: *The pirates buried treasure along the coast.* **2** *v* value highly: *Anita treasures that bear more than all her other toys.* **treas·ured, treas·ur·ing.** **treas·ur·er** *n* a person in charge of money: *The treasurer of a club pays its bills.*

treat (trēt) **1** *n* anything that gives pleasure: *Halloween treats. Being in the country is a treat to her.* **2** *v* entertain by giving food, drink, or amusement: *He treated his friends to ice cream.* **3** *v* behave toward: *My father treats our new car with care.* **4** *v* deal with to cure: *The dentist treated my toothache.*

treat·ment 1 *n* a way of behaving: *fair treatment.* **2** *n* something used to cure: *The doctor tried a new treatment for my skin problem.*

trea·ty 1 *n* an agreement made between two or more groups of people. **2** ❧ *n* an agreement made long ago between the British monarch and a group of First Nations people. The First Nations people gave up some of their land; in return, they received payment and certain rights, and some land was set aside for the use of that particular First Nation. Separate treaties were made with many First Nations; their descendants are called **treaty Indians**.

tree (trē) *n* a large plant with a woody trunk and, usually, branches and leaves.

tree line a limit on mountains and in northern regions beyond which trees will not grow because of cold, etc. The tree line marks the southern boundary of the Barrens.

trek (trek) **1** *v* travel slowly: *The settlers trekked hundreds of kilometres across the Prairies on foot.* **2** *n* a journey, especially a slow or difficult one: *It was a long trek over the Rockies.* **trekked, trek·king.**

A wooden trellis, supporting climbing plants

trel·lis (trel′is) *n* a frame of light strips of wood or metal crossing one another.

trem·ble (trem′bəl) *v* shake because of fear, excitement, cold, etc. **trem·bled, trem·bling.**

tre·men·dous (tri men′dəs) **1** *adj* dreadful; very severe: *The army suffered a tremendous defeat.* **2** *adj Informal.* enormous; very great: *That is a tremendous house for a family of three.* **3** *adj Informal.* especially good: *We saw a tremendous movie yesterday.* **trem·or 1** *n* a trembling: *a nervous tremor in your voice.* **2** *n* a shaking movement: *An earthquake is an earth tremor.*

trench (trench) *n* a ditch: *They dug a trench around the tent to carry off the rain water.*

trend (trend) **1** *n* the general direction: *the upward trend of prices.* **2** *n* a current style in fashion.

trend·y *adj* following the latest fashions or trends: *trendy clothes.*

tres·pass (tres′pas) *v* go on somebody's property without permission.

tri– *a prefix meaning* three, as in *triangle* and *tricycle.*

tri·an·gle (trī′ang′gəl) *n* a flat shape with three sides and three angles. ►See Appendix. **–tri·an′gu·lar,** *adj.*

tri·al (trī′əl) **1** *n* examining and deciding a case in court. **2** *n* trying or testing: *The engineers gave the machine another trial to see if it would work.*

tribe (trīb) *n* a group of people with the same customs under the same leaders: *nomadic tribes.* **–trib′al,** *adj.*

trick (trik) **1** *n* something done to fool or cheat. **2** *v* deceive; cheat. **3** *n* a clever act: *a magic trick.* **–trick′er·y,** *n.*

trick·y *adj* difficult to handle: *Our back door has a tricky lock.*

trick·le (trik′əl) **1** *v* flow in a small stream: *Tears trickled down his cheeks.* **2** *n* a small flow of liquid. **trick·led, trick·ling.**

trig·ger (trig′ər) **1** *n* any lever that releases a spring, catch, etc. when pulled or pressed. **2** *v* set off: *The explosion was triggered by a spark.*

trim (trim) **1** *v* make neat by cutting away parts: *to trim your hair.* **trimmed, trim·ming.** **2** *adj* neat; in good condition. **trim·mer, trim·mest. 3** decorate: *The children were trimming the Christmas tree.*

trim·mings *n* ornaments; extras: *We ate turkey with all the trimmings.*

trin·ket (tring′kit) *n* any small, fancy article, or bit of jewellery.

tri·o (trē′ō) **1** *n* a group of three singers or players performing together. **2** *n* any group of three. *pl* **tri·os.**

trip (trip) **1** *n* a journey: *We took a trip to Europe.* **2** *v* stumble or make someone stumble: *Isaiah tripped on the stairs. Her opponent tripped her with a hockey stick.* **tripped, trip·ping.**

Tri·pi·ta·ka (trip′i tä′kə) *n* the holy writings of the Buddhist religion.

tri·ple (trip′əl) **1** *adj* three times as much or as many. **2** *v* make or become three times as much or as many.

tri·plet (trip′lit) *n* one of three children born at the same time to the same mother.

tri·umph (trī′umf) **1** *n* a victory. **2** *v* gain victory: *Our team triumphed over theirs.* **–tri·um′phant,** *adj.*

triv·i·a (triv′ē ə) *n* unimportant details: *My friend told me lots of trivia about his favourite hockey team.* **–triv′i·al,** *adj.*

trol·ley (trol′ē) *n* an electric streetcar or bus that gets its power from overhead wires. *pl* **trol·leys.**

troop (trūp) **1** *n* a group or band of persons: *A troop of protesters marched to City Hall.* **2 troops,** *pl.n* soldiers: *The government sent troops to help clear the roads after the big storm.*

USING WORDS . . . . . troop

Troop and **troupe** can both be used for a group or band of people.
However, **troupe** is usually used for groups of performers, such as actors or singers.
Troop is used to describe soldiers and other organized groups.

tro·phy (trō′fē) *n* a prize, cup, etc. awarded to a victorious person or team. *pl* **tro·phies.**

trop·ics (trop′iks) *pl.n* the regions near the equator. The hottest parts of the earth are in the tropics. **–trop′i·cal,** *adj.*

trot (trot) *v* run, but not fast: *The child trotted along after his mother. The horse trotted quietly along.* **trot·ted, trot·ting.**

trou·ble (trub′əl) **1** *n* difficulty: *That boy makes trouble for his teachers.* **2** *v* cause trouble to; disturb: *Praveena is troubled by headaches.* **3** *n* effort: *Take the trouble to do careful work.* **trou·bled, trou·bling.**

trou·ble·some *adj* causing trouble: *a troublesome person, troublesome headaches.*

trough (trof) *n* a long, narrow container for holding food or water for animals.

troupe (trūp) *n* a group of actors, singers, or acrobats.

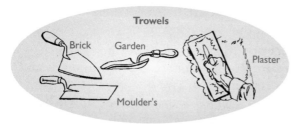

Trowels

Brick Garden Plaster Moulder's

trow·el (trou′əl) **1** *n* a tool with a flat blade, used for spreading or smoothing. **2** *n* a garden tool with a curved blade, used for taking up plants, loosening dirt, etc.

truce (trūs) *n* a stop in fighting by agreement: *A truce was declared between the two armies.*

truck (truk) **1** *n* a strongly built vehicle for carrying heavy loads: *There are many trucks on the highways nowadays.* **2** *v* carry on a truck: *Vegetables are trucked to market.*

true (trū) **1** *adj* not false: *It is true that 6 and 4 add up to 10.* **2** *adj* real: *true gold, true kindness.* **3** *adj* faithful: *my true friend.* **tru·er, tru·est.** **–truth,** *n,* **–truth′ful,** *adj.*

tru·ly 1 *adv* in a true way: *Tell me truly what you think.* **2** *adv* really; in fact: *The city of Victoria was truly a beautiful sight.*

come true, happen as expected; become real.

A trumpet is a wind instrument.

trum·pet (trum′pit) **1** *n* a brass musical instrument with a tube that is bell-shaped at one end. **2** *v* make a sound like a trumpet: *The elephant trumpeted in fright.*

trunk (trungk) **1** *n* the main stem of a tree, not the branches and the roots. **2** *n* the main part of your body, apart from your head or arms or legs. **3** *n* the enclosed storage compartment in a car. **4** *n* a big box used usually for storing or moving things. **5** *n* an elephant's nose.

trust (trust) **1** *n* a firm belief in someone or something. **2** *v* believe firmly in someone or something: *I trust my friends to tell me the truth.*

trust·wor·thy *adj* reliable: *The class chose a trustworthy student for treasurer.*

try (trī) **1** *v* make an effort: *If at first you don't succeed, try, try again.* **2** *v* test: *Try this candy and see if you like it.* **3** *v* investigate in a law court: *The man was tried and found guilty of robbery.* **tried, try·ing.**

try on, put on to test the fit, looks, etc.

try out, 1 test: *Try out this new video game.* **2** be tested: *Roman tried out for the hockey team.*

T–shirt (tē′shərt′) *n* a light shirt with, usually, short sleeves and no collar.

tub (tub) **1** *n* a large, open container for water; a bathtub. **2** *n* a round container for holding soft food like margarine.

tube (tyūb *or* tūb) **1** *n* a long pipe of metal, glass, rubber, etc.: *Tubes are mostly used to hold or carry liquids or gases.* **2** *n* a small container of soft metal or plastic, used for holding toothpaste, ointment, etc.

tuck (tuk) **1** *v* push into some narrow space: *She tucked her purse under her arm.* **2** *v* push the edge of something into place: *Tuck your shirt in.* **3** *n* a fold sewn in cloth.

tug (tug) **1** *v* pull hard: *I tugged the rope and it came loose.* **2** *n* a hard pull: *The baby gave a tug at my hair.* **tugged, tug·ging.**

tug-of-war *n* a contest between two teams pulling at the ends of a rope.

tu·i·tion (tyū ish′ən *or* tū ish′ən) *n* money paid for instruction at a private school, for music lessons, etc.

tum·ble (tum′bəl) **1** *v* fall and roll over: *The child tumbled down the stairs.* **2** *v* turn over and over: *to tumble clothes in a dryer.* **tum·bled, tum·bling.**

tum·ble-down *adj* ready to fall down; not in good condition: *a tumble-down shack.* **tum·bler 1** *n* an acrobat. **2** *n* a large drinking glass.

tu·na (tū′nə *or* tyū′nə) *n* a large sea fish, valued for food. *pl* **tu·na** or **tu·nas.**

tun·dra (tun′drə) *n* a large, flat, treeless plain in the arctic regions. The ground beneath the surface of the tundra is frozen even in summer.

tune (tyūn *or* tūn) **1** *n* a piece of music. **2** *v* correct the sound of a musical instrument: *to tune a piano.* **3** adjust a radio or television set to a channel. **tuned, tun·ing.**

tune-up *n* putting into good running order: *Mrs. Hill took her car in for an engine tune-up.*

tun·nel (tun′əl) **1** *n* any underground passage. **2** *v* make a tunnel. **tun·nelled** or **tun·neled, tun·nel·ling** or **tun·nel·ing.**

Two styles of tuque

❧ **tuque** (tūk) *n* a tight-fitting, knitted cap, knotted at one end.

A turban

tur·ban (tər′bən) *n* a scarf wound around your head or around a cap.

turf (tərf) *n* grass with its roots; sod.

A wild turkey—about 120 cm long including the tail
Wattle

tur·key (tər′kē) *n* a large bird raised for food. *pl* **tur·keys.**

turn (tərn) **1** *v* move round, or make move round, as a wheel does. **2** *n* a motion like that of a wheel: *At each turn the screw goes in further.* **3** *v* take a new direction: *The road turns to the north here.* **4** *n* a change of direction: *A turn to the left brought him in front of us.* **5** *n* a change in condition: *The sick patient has taken a turn for the better.* **6** *n* a chance to do something: *It is his turn to read.*

turn·out *n* a gathering of people for a special event: *There was a good turnout at the school dance.*

take turns, play, go, etc. one after another in proper order.

turn down, refuse: *to turn down a plan.*

turn off, shut off: *Turn off the lights.*

turn on, start.

turn out, 1 make: *That factory turns out good shoes.* **2** result: *How did the game turn out?*

tur·ret (tər′it) *n* a small tower, often on the corner of a building.

tur·tle (tər′təl) *n* a slow-moving animal with a hard shell into which it can draw its head and legs. Turtles live in fresh water, in salt water, or on land; those living on land are often called tortoises.

tusk (tusk) *n* a very long, pointed tooth that sticks out. Elephants and walruses have tusks.

tu·tor (tyū′tər *or* tū′tər) *n* a private teacher.

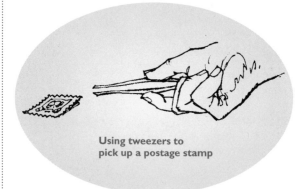
Using tweezers to pick up a postage stamp

tweez·ers (twē′zərz) *pl.n* small pincers or tongs for pulling out hairs, picking up small objects, etc.

twelve (twelv) ▶See Appendix.

twen·ty (twen′tē) ▶See Appendix.

twice (twīs) **1** *adv* two times: *Twice two is four.* **2** *adv* doubly: *twice as much.*

twig (twig) *n* a very small branch.

twi·light (twī′līt′) *n* the faint light in the sky before the sun rises and after it sets.

twin (twin) *n* one of two children born at the same time to the same mother.

twine (twīn) **1** *n* strong thread or string. **2** *v* wind or wrap around: *The vine twines around the tree.* **twined, twin·ing.**

twinge (twinj) *n* a sudden, sharp pain.

twin·kle (twing′kəl) **1** *v* shine with quick little gleams: *The stars twinkle.* **2** *n* a sparkle: *a merry twinkle in your eye.* **twin·kled, twin·kling.**

twirl (twərl) **1** *v* spin; whirl. **2** *n* a spin: *a twirl in a dance.*

twist (twist) **1** *v* turn; wind: *Yi-Su twisted the ring on her finger.* **2** *v* have a winding shape: *The path twists in and out among the rocks.* **3** *n* a curve: *The road is full of twists and turns.* **4** *v* force out of shape: *His face was twisted with pain.* **twist·er** *n* a tornado, whirlwind, etc.

twitch (twich) **1** *v* move with a quick jerk: *to twitch your nose.* **2** *n* a quick, jerky movement of some part of the body.

twit·ter (twit′ər) *n* make a sound like birds do; chirp.

two (tū) ▶See Appendix.

type (tīp) **1** *n* a kind or group alike in some way: *I don't like that type of dog.* **2** *n* printed letters or figures: *a small or large type.*

typ·i·cal *adj* very much like others of its kind: *The typical Thanksgiving dinner always includes turkey.* **ty·po** *n* a small mistake in something printed out: *I noticed a typo where I had keyed in* ilon *instead of* lion. **Typographical error** is the full form.

ty·phoon (tī fūn′) *n* a violent tropical storm, like a hurricane.

ty·rant (tī′rənt) *n* a person who uses power cruelly or unfairly.

An umbrella to keep the rain off

u or **U** (yū) *n* the twenty-first letter of the English alphabet, or the sound that it stands for. The sound of *u* in *run* is different from the sound of *u* in *rule.* *pl* **u's** or **U's.**

UFO *abbreviation for* unidentified flying object. This is any thing in the sky that cannot be identified as an aircraft from Earth.

ugh (ùh *or* u) *interj* an exclamation to show disgust or horror.

ug·ly (ug'lē) *adj* unpleasant to look at: *an ugly house, an ugly face.* **ug·li·er, ug·li·est.** –**ug'li·ness,** *n.*

ul·ti·mate (ul'tə mit) *adj* last; final: *Most people who drive too fast never consider that the ultimate result might be death in an accident.* –**ul'ti·mate·ly,** *adv.*

ul·tra·son·ic (ul'trə son'ik) *adj* having to do with sounds that human ears cannot hear. Bats make ultrasonic noises that echo off buildings, trees, etc. This helps bats to "see" these things in the dark.

ul·tra·vi·o·let (ul'trə vī'ə lit) *adj* having to do with invisible light waves in sunlight. Ultraviolet rays give you sunburn.

An ulu

❀ **u·lu** (ū'lū) *n* a knife traditionally used by Inuit women. It has a crescent-shaped blade and a handle of bone, ivory, or wood that fits your hand. It is still very much used today.

um·brel·la (um brel'ə) *n* a light, folding frame covered with cloth or plastic, carried as a protection against rain or sun.

WORD HISTORY . . . . **umbrella**

Umbrella comes from the Italian word *ombrella,* meaning "shade." The first umbrellas were used to protect people from the sun, not the rain.

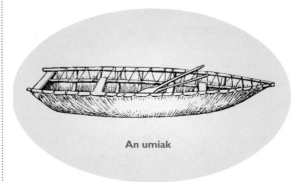

An umiak

❀ **u·mi·ak** (ū'mē ak) *n* a large, flat-bottomed boat made of skins stretched over a wooden frame. Umiaks are traditionally used by Inuit women. The Inuktitut spelling is **umiaq.**

um·pire (um'pīr) *n* a person who rules on the plays in a game: *The umpire called the last ball a foul.*

un– *a prefix meaning* the opposite of, or do the opposite of, as in *unhappy* or *unlock.*

u·nan·i·mous (yū nan'ə məs) *adj* in complete agreement; agreed to by everybody: *The children were unanimous in their wish to go to the beach.* –**u·nan'i·mous·ly,** *adv.*

un·can·ny (un kan'ē) *adj* strange and mysterious; weird: *The trees seemed to have uncanny shapes in the darkness.*

un·cle (ung′kəl) **1** *n* a brother of a person's father or mother. **2** *n* the husband of a person's aunt.

un·con·scious (un kon′shəs) **1** *adj* not able to feel or think: *Hiram was knocked unconscious when the car struck him.* **2** *adj* not aware: *I was unconscious of being followed by our dog.* **3** *adj* not meant: *unconscious rudeness.*

un·con·scious·ly *adv* without knowing what you are doing: *I unconsciously wiggle my foot when I am doing my homework.*

un·cov·er (un kuv′ər) **1** *v* take a cover off. **2** *v* make known: *The plot was uncovered when the secret message was found.*

un·daunt·ed (un dȯn′tid) *adj* not afraid: *The kitten was undaunted by the size of the Newfoundland dog.*

un·de·cid·ed (un′di sī′did) **1** *adj* not decided; not settled: *The winner is undecided if a game ends in a tie.* **2** *adj* not having your mind made up: *I'm undecided about which book to buy.*

un·der (un′dər) **1** *prep* or *adv* below; beneath: *The book fell under the table* (prep). *The swimmer went under* (adv). **2** *prep* less than: *The cost of the ticket is under ten dollars.*

under– *a prefix meaning:* **1** below, as in *underline.* **2** beneath, as in *underwear.* **3** not enough, as in *underweight.*

un·der·cov·er (un′dər kuv′ər) *adj* working or done in secret: *The jeweller was an undercover agent for the police.*

un·der·dog (un′dər dog′) *n* a person who is expected to lose: *We've been the underdogs for the last few years, but this year we think our team is going to win.*

un·der·es·ti·mate (un′dər es′tə māt′) *v* put at too low a value, amount, etc.: *Kezia lost the match because she underestimated her opponent's skill.* **un·der·es·ti·mat·ed, un·der·es·ti·mat·ing.**

un·der·foot (un′dər fu̇t′) **1** *adv* under your feet; on the ground. **2** *adv* in the way: *That cat is always underfoot.*

un·der·ground (un′dər ground′) **1** *adv* beneath the surface of the ground: *Miners work underground.* **2** *adj* beneath the surface of the ground: *an underground water pipe.* **3** *adv* into hiding: *The thieves went underground after the bank robbery.*

un·der·hand (un′dər hand′) **1** *adj* secret; not honest. **2** *adv* secretly. **3** *adj* or *adv* with an upward movement of your hand: *an underhand pitch* (adj), *to throw a ball underhand* (adv).

un·der·line (un′dər līn′) *v* draw a line under: *Underline your spelling mistakes.* **un·der·lined, un·der·lin·ing.**

> **Grammar ✓Check .... underline**
>
> **Underline** the titles of books, magazines, newspapers, movies, TV shows, plays, musical compositions, and works of art. If you are writing on a computer, you can use *italics* instead of underlining.

un·der·neath (un′dər nēth′) *prep* or *adv* below; under: *We can sit underneath this tree* (prep). *He was pushing up from underneath* (adv).

un·der·priv·i·leged (un′dər priv′ə lijd) *adj* having fewer advantages than most people have.

un·der·side (un′dər sīd′) *n* the part underneath: *The underside of the stone was covered with ants.*

un·der·stand (un′dər stand′) **1** *v* get the meaning of: *Now I understand the teacher's question.* **2** *v* know how to deal with: *A good teacher understands children.* **un·der·stood, un·der·stand·ing.**

un·der·stand·ing **1** *n* knowledge: *a clear understanding of the problem.* **2** *adj* sympathetic: *an understanding friend.*

un·der·stud·y (un′dər stud′ē) *n* a person who can substitute for an actor. *pl* **un·der·stud·ies.**

un·der·take (un′dər tāk′) **1** *v* try; attempt: *Don't undertake what you can't finish.* **2** *v* promise: *I will undertake to feed your dogs while you are away.* **un·der·took, un·der·tak·en, un·der·tak·ing.**

un·der·wa·ter (un′dər wot′ər) **1** *adj* growing or used below the surface of the water: *underwater plants. A submarine is an underwater ship.* **2** *adv* below the surface of the water: *Juana stayed underwater for two minutes.*

un·der·wear (un′dər wer′) *n* clothes worn next to your skin, under your outer clothes.

un·der·weight (un′dər wāt′) *adj* of a person or animal, with a mass that is too small compared to height and shape: *You are a little underweight, but it is nothing to worry about.*

un·do (un dü′) **1** *v* unfasten; untie: *Please undo the package.* **2** *v* cancel or reverse: *We mended the roof, but a heavy storm undid our work.* **un·did, un·done, un·do·ing.**

un·earth (un ərth′) **1** *v* dig up: *to unearth a buried city.* **2** *v* discover; find out: *to unearth a secret plan.*

un·eas·y (un ē′zē) *adj* restless; worried. **un·eas·i·er, un·eas·i·est. –un·eas′i·ly,** *adv,* **–un·eas′i·ness,** *n.*

un·e·ven (un ē′vən) **1** *adj* not level: *uneven ground.* **2** *adj* not equal; one-sided: *an uneven contest.*

un·fa·mil·iar (un′fə mil′yər) **1** *adj* not well known; strange: *That face is unfamiliar to me.* **2** *adj* not knowing: *Medgar is unfamiliar with the Greek language.*

un·fit (un fit′) **1** *adj* not suitable: *Grass is unfit for humans to eat.* **2** *adj* not good enough: *They say she is unfit for the job of class president.* **3** *adj* not healthy: *I feel unfit so I'm going to exercise more.*

un·fold (un fōld′) **1** *v* open the folds of; spread out: *to unfold a map.* **2** *v* show; explain: *to unfold the plot of a story.* **3** *v* open; develop: *Buds unfold into flowers.*

un·for·tu·nate (un fòr′chə nit) *adj* having bad luck: *an unfortunate accident.*

An ancient Roman idea of a unicorn. It was thought to have the body of a horse and the feet of an elephant.

u·ni·corn (yū′nə kòrn′) *n* an imaginary animal like a horse, but with a long horn in the middle of its forehead.

u·ni·form (yū′nə fòrm′) **1** *adj* always the same; not changing: *The earth turns around at a uniform rate.* **2** *adj* all alike: *All the toy blocks have a uniform size.* **3** *n* the special clothes worn by the members of a group when on duty: *Soldiers, police officers, and nurses wear uniforms.*

un·ion (yūn′yən) **1** *n* something formed by combining two or more members or parts: *The provinces and territories of Canada form a union.* **2** *n* a group of workers joined together to protect their interests.

u·nit (yū′nit) **1** *n* a single thing, person, or group. **2** *n* a standard amount used for measuring: *A metre is a unit of length; a minute is a unit of time; a kilogram is a unit of mass.*

u·nite (yū nīt′) *v* join together; make one; combine: *All the tennis clubs in Fredericton will unite to plan the provincial tournament.* **u·nit·ed, u·nit·ing.**

u·nique (yū nēk′) *adj* one of a kind: *Each snowflake has a unique pattern.*

USING WORDS . . . . . unique

A thing is either **unique** or it isn't. It can't be *more unique* or *less unique*. Instead of *more unique,* choose something like *more unusual.*

u·ni·sex (yū′nə seks′) *adj* suitable for either sex: *unisex clothes.*

u·ni·verse (yū′nə vərs′) *n* everything there is including Earth, the stars, and all of space: *Our world is only a small part of the universe.* **–u′ni·ver′sal·ly,** *adv.*

u·ni·ver·sal (yū′nə vər′səl) *adj* having to do with everyone or everything: *Food is a universal need.* **u·ni·ver·si·ty** (yū′nə vər′sə tē) *n* a school people go to after secondary school. Universities give advanced courses in many subjects such as literature, history, and science, and also often teach law, medicine, business, etc.

un·known (un nōn′) **1** *adj* not known; not familiar; strange; unexplored: *an unknown country, an unknown number.* **2** *n* a person or thing that is unknown: *The main actor in this movie is an unknown.*

un·less (un les′) *conj* except if: *We shall drive to Charlottetown unless it rains.*

un·like (un līk′) **1** *adj* not like; different: *The two brothers are quite unlike.* **2** *prep* different from: *Unlike most birds, penguins cannot fly.* **un·like·ly** not likely; not probable: *Ty is unlikely to win the race.*

un·mis·tak·a·ble (un′mi stā′kə bəl) *adj* clear; plain; obvious.

un·nec·es·sar·y (un nes′ə ser′ē) *adj* not necessary; needless. —**un·nec′es·sar′i·ly,** *adv*.

The kitten is unravelling the knitted scarf.

un·rav·el (un rav′əl) **1** *v* separate the threads of: *The kitten unravelled my knitting.* **2** *v* come apart: *My knitted gloves are unravelling at the wrist.* **3** *v* bring or come out of a puzzling state; clear up: *to unravel a mystery.* **un·rav·elled** or **un·rav·eled, un·rav·el·ling** or **un·rav·el·ing.**

un·ru·ly (un rü′lē) *adj* hard to control: *an unruly group of children.*

un·set·tled (un set′əld) **1** *adj* not in proper order: *Our house was all unsettled when we were painting the walls.* **2** *adj* liable to change: *The weather is unsettled this week.* **3** *adj* not inhabited: *Large parts of Canada are still unsettled.*

un·stressed (un strest′) *adj* not pronounced with force: *In the word "successful" the first and last syllables are unstressed.*

un·til (un til′) **1** *conj* up to the time when: *Celia waited until the sun had set.* **2** *conj* before: *He did not leave until evening.*

un·wield·y (un wēl′dē) *adj* hard to handle or manage: *The armour worn by knights seems unwieldy to us today.*

up (up) **1** *adv* to or in a higher place: *The bird flew up.* **2** *prep* to or at a higher place on or in something: *The cat ran up the tree.* **3** *adj* out of bed: *Please get up or you will be late (adv). The children were up at dawn (adj).* **4** *adv* completely: *My eraser is almost used up.* **5** *adv* at an end; over: *Your time is up now.*

up·ward *adv* toward a higher place: *Andrina climbed upward till she reached the apple.*

up to, 1 doing: *Tabitha is up to some mischief.* **2** capable of doing: *Do you feel up to going out so soon after being sick?* **3** *Informal.* before a person as something to be done: *It's up to you to decide.*

up·date (up′dāt′) *v* bring up to date: *The computer files at our school are updated once a month.* **up·dat·ed, up·dat·ing.**

up-to-date *adj* newest; most recent: *an up-to-date copy of a computer file.*

up·on (ə pon′) *prep* on.

up·per (up′ər) *adj* higher: *your upper lip, the upper floor.*

upper case capital letters. For example, T is upper case, but t is **lower case.**

upper hand, control; advantage: *During the first two periods, the visiting team had the upper hand.*

up·right (up′rīt′) **1** *adj* standing up straight: *Put your chair into an upright position.* **2** *adv* straight up: *Hold yourself upright.* **3** *adj* good; honest: *an upright citizen.*

up·ris·ing (up′rī′zing) *n* a rebellion: *The revolution began with small uprisings in several towns, then spread throughout the country.*

up·roar (up′rȯr′) *n* a noisy or violent disturbance: *The city was in an uproar when lions escaped from the zoo.*

up·set (up set′ *for 1-3,* up′set′ *for 4*) **1** *v* knock over: *Colm upset his glass of water.* **2** *v* disturb: *The shock upset Calvin's nerves.* **3** *adj* disturbed: *an upset stomach.* **4** *n* a defeat: *The hockey team suffered an upset.* **up·set, up·set·ting.**

up·shot (up′shot′) *n* result: *The upshot of all the delays was that we had to cancel the game.*

upside down 1 having at the bottom what should be on top: *The slice of bread and butter fell upside down on the floor.* **2** in or into complete disorder: *The children turned the whole house upside down.*

up·stairs (up′sterz′) *adv* or *adj* on or of an upper floor: *She lives upstairs (adv). He is waiting in an upstairs hall (adj).*

ur·ban (ər′bən) *adj* having to do with cities or towns: *an urban district, the urban population.*

ur·chin (ər′chin) *n* a mischievous child.

urge (ərj) **1** *n* an impulse: *I felt an urge to get out of the room.* **2** *v* try to persuade; plead with: *My grandmother urged all of us to stay longer.* **urged, urg·ing.**

ur·gent *adj* demanding immediate attention: *an urgent message.*

u·rine (yût′ən) *n* the liquid waste from your body when you go to the toilet. –**u′ri·nate′,** *v.*

us (us) *pron* the objective form of **we:** *My father went with us to the zoo.*

use (yūz *for 1,* yūs *for 2-4*) **1** *v* put something to work: *We use our legs in walking.* **2** *n* using: *the use of tools.* **3** *n* usefulness: *a thing of no practical use.* **4** *n* the purpose that a thing is used for: *to find a new use for something.* **used, us·ing.** –**use′ful** (yūs′fəl), *adj,* –**use′ful·ly,** *adv,* –**use′ful·ness,** *n,* –**use′less** (yūs′lis), *adj.*

us·a·ble (yū′zə bəl) *adj* that can be used; fit for use. **used** (yūzd) *adj* not new: *a used bike.*

u·ser-friend·ly *adj* easy to use: *a user-friendly computer program.* **u·su·al** (yū′zhū əl) *adj* in common use; ordinary: *Snow is usual in most of Canada during winter.* –**u′su·al·ly,** *adv.*

u·ti·lize (yū′tə līz′) *v* make use of: *We can utilize this old radio at camp.*

used to, 1 accustomed to: *Polar bears are used to cold weather.* **2** formerly did: *I used to go to a different school.*

use up, consume all of: *to use up your money.*

A computer keyboard

A ballpoint pen   A pencil

Writing utensils

u·ten·sil (yū ten′səl) *n* an instrument or tool used for some special purpose: *Pens are writing utensils. Pots and pans are kitchen utensils.*

ut·most (ut′mōst′) *adj* greatest possible: *Clean water is of the utmost importance to health.* **Uttermost** is another word for this.

ut·ter (ut′ər) **1** *adj* complete; total: *utter surprise, utter darkness.* –**ut′ter·ly,** *adv.* **2** *v* speak: *Dalit uttered her words slowly.* –**ut′ter·ance,** *n.*

v or **V** (vē) *n* the twenty-second letter of the English alphabet, or the sound that it stands for. We hear the sound of *v* twice in *vivid*. *pl* **v's** or **V's.**

va·cant (vā′kənt) **1** *adj* empty; not occupied: *a vacant chair, a vacant house, a vacant space.* –**va′can·cy,** *n*. **2** *adj* empty of thought; blank: *a vacant smile.*

va·ca·tion (vā kā′shən) *n* holidays: *The family spent their vacation in St. John's.*

vac·cine (vak sēn′ *or* vak′sin) *n* a preparation, often made of weakened viruses of a disease, used to protect people from that disease: *flu vaccine.* –**vac′ci·nate′** (vak′sə nāt′), *v*, –**vac′ci·na′tion,** *n*.

WORD HISTORY . . . . **vaccine**
Vaccine comes from the Latin word *vaccinus*, which means "having to do with cows." The first vaccine ever made came from the virus of a mild disease called "cowpox." This vaccine helped to protect people against smallpox, a much more serious illness.

vac·u·um (vak′yūm) **1** *n* an empty space without even air in it. **2** *v* clean with a vacuum cleaner: *My brother vacuumed the rugs yesterday.* **vacuum cleaner** a machine for cleaning carpets, curtains, floors, etc. by sucking up the dirt.

vague (vāg) *adj* not definite; not clear: *In a fog everything looks vague. Mrs. Duval's vague statement confused them.* **va·guer, va·guest.**

vain (vān) **1** *adj* having too much pride in your looks, ability, etc.: *Letitia is vain about her long hair.* **2** *adj* useless; unsuccessful: *I made vain attempts to reach her by telephone.* –**vain′ly,** *adv*. **van·i·ty** (van′ə tē) *n* too much pride in one's looks, ability, etc.
in vain, without success: *He tried in vain to lift the heavy chair.*

val·en·tine (val′ən tīn′) **1** *n* a greeting card or small gift sent or given on Saint Valentine's Day, February 14. **2** *n* a sweetheart that you choose on this day.

val·i·ant (val′yənt) *adj* brave; courageous: *a valiant knight, a valiant effort.*

val·our *n* bravery; courage. Another spelling for this is **valor.**

val·id (val′id) **1** *adj* based on facts; true: *a valid argument.* **2** *adj* legal: *A contract made by a child is not valid.*

val·ley (val′ē) *n* low land between hills or mountains: *Most large valleys have rivers running through them.*
pl **val·leys.**

val·ue (val′yū) **1** *n* worth; importance: *the value of education, the value of milk as a food.* **2** *n* the proper price: *They bought the house for less than its value.* **3** *v* think highly of: *We all value her opinion.* **val·ued, val·u·ing.**

val·u·a·ble (val′yə bəl) **1** *adj* being worth something: *a valuable friend.* **2** *adj* worth much money: *a valuable ring.* **3** Usually, **valuables,** *pl.n* articles of value: *My grandmother keeps her jewellery and other valuables in a safe.*

valve (valv) *n* a movable part that controls the flow of a liquid or gas through a pipe by opening and closing the passage. A tap is one kind of valve. You have valves in your heart that control blood flow.

vam·pire (vam′pīr) **1** *n* an imaginary creature believed to be the ghost of a corpse that comes back to life at night and sucks the blood of people while they sleep. **2** *n* a bat that lives by sucking blood from animals.

van (van) **1** *n* a covered truck for moving furniture, etc. **2** *n* a vehicle like a small bus.

van·dal (van′dəl) *n* a person who destroys or damages things on purpose, especially beautiful or valuable things: *Vandals have carved their names on that tree, and it will probably die from the damage.* –**van′dal·ism′,** *n*.

vane (vān) *n* a pointer that turns to show which way the wind is blowing.

va·nil·la (və nil′ə) *n* a food flavouring used in sweet things like ice cream.

van·ish (van′ish) *v* disappear: *The sun vanished behind a cloud.*

van·quish (vang′kwish) *v* conquer; defeat.

var·y (ver′ē) *v* change; make different: *The driver can vary the speed of a car. The weather varies.* **var·ied, var·y·ing.**

var·i·a·ble (ver′ē ə bəl) **1** *adj* changeable: *The weather is more variable in Fredericton than it is in Regina.* **2** *n* anything that can vary: *Temperature is a variable.* **var·ied** (ver′ēd) *adj* of different kinds: *a varied assortment of candies.*

va·ri·e·ty (və rī′ə tē) **1** *n* a number of different kinds: *This shop has a variety of toys.* **2** *n* a kind or sort: *Which varieties of cake did you buy?*

var·i·ous (ver′ē əs) **1** *adj* different: *There are various opinions on the best way to train a pet.* **2** *adj* several: *I have looked at various bikes, and have decided to buy this one.*

vase (vāz, vȧz, *or* voz) *n* a container for holding flowers.

vast (vast) *adj* extremely large: *vast deserts. A billion dollars is a vast amount of money.* –**vast′ly,** *adv.*

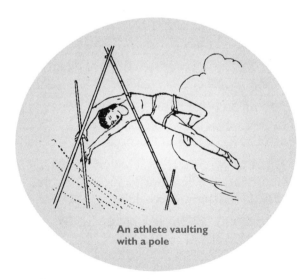

An athlete vaulting with a pole

vault (volt) **1** *n* a place for storing valuable things: *Vaults are often made of steel.* **2** *v* leap over using your hands or a pole: *Fran vaulted the fence.*

VCR *abbreviation for* video cassette recorder.

veal (vēl) *n* the meat of a calf.

Ve·das (vā′dəz) *pl.n* the most ancient holy writings of Hinduism.

veer (vēr) *v* change direction; turn: *The wind veered to the south.*

veg·e·ta·ble (vej′tə bəl) *n* a part of a plant used for food.

veg·an (vej′ən *or* vē′gən) *n* a person who eats no meat, fish, or animal products like milk or eggs. **veg·e·tar·i·an** (vej′ə ter′ē ən) *n* a person who eats vegetables but no meat or fish.

veg·e·ta·tion *n* plants: *There is not much vegetation in deserts.*

ve·hi·cle (vē′ə kəl) *n* anything used to move people or things on land or in space: *a space vehicle. Cars, sleds, trucks, and bikes are all vehicles.*

veil (vāl) *n* a piece of very thin material worn to protect or hide a person's face.

vein (vān) *n* one of the tubes that carry blood to your heart from all parts of your body.

CONFUSABLES ······ **vein**

vein means "tube in your body for blood":
Blood travels through your veins to your heart.

vain means "proud":
That boy is very vain about his looks.

---

vel·vet (vel′vit) *n* cloth with a thick, soft pile. –**vel′vet·y,** *adj.*

Ve·ne·tian blind (və nē′shən blīnd) a window blind made of horizontal pieces of wood, plastic, or metal. These pieces can be turned to change the amount of light that can get through.

venge·ance (ven′jəns) *n* punishment in return for a wrong: *The prince swore vengeance against the men who kidnapped his sister.*
with a vengeance, with great force: *It was raining with a vengeance.*

ven·i·son (ven′ə sən) *n* the meat of a deer.

ven·om (ven′əm) *n* the poison of snakes, spiders, etc. –**ven′om·ous,** *adj.*

vent (vent) *n* a hole; opening: *Johan used a pencil to make air vents in the box top so the frog could breathe.*

ven·ti·late *v* change the air in: *We ventilate a room by opening windows.* –**ven′ti·la′tion,** *n.*

ven·tril·o·quist (ven tril′ə kwist) *n* a person who can make his or her voice seem to come from somewhere else, such as a puppet.

ven·ture (ven′chər) **1** *n* a risky act: *A lucky venture in a mining company made her a rich woman.* **2** *v* dare: *No one ventured to interrupt the teacher.* **ven·tured, ven·tur·ing.**

ve·ran·da (və ran′də) *n* a large covered porch along one or more sides of a house. **Verandah** is another spelling.

verb (vərb) *n* in grammar, a word that shows action or state of being. The sentence *She walked* shows the past tense of the action *walk*.

ver·bal **1** *adj* having to do with words: *A description is a verbal picture.* **2** *adj* in spoken words: *a verbal message.* –**ver′bal·ly,** *adv.*

Grammar ✓ *Check* . . . . . **verb**

The right **verb** can add a sense of action to a sentence. Use verbs that say exactly what you mean: *He went home* is not bad, but if you replace *went* with *walked, staggered, raced, trotted, drove, slunk, tottered,* or *flew,* the sentence will come alive.

---

ver·dict (vər′dikt) *n* the decision of a jury: *The jury returned a verdict of "not guilty."*

ver·i·fy (ver′ə fī′) *v* prove to be true: *The driver's report of the accident was verified by two women who were there and had seen it happen.* **ver·i·fied, ver·i·fy·ing.**

verse (vərs) **1** *n* poetry. **2** *n* a group of lines of poetry: *Sing the first verse of "O Canada."*

ver·sa·tile (vər′sə tīl′ or vər′sə təl) *adj* able to do many things well: *Carmelle is a very versatile girl; she plays tennis, works with computers, and writes good plays.*

ver·sion (vər′zhən) *n* a description from a particular point of view: *Each of the three boys gave his own version of the quarrel.*

ver·sus (vər′səs) *prep* against: *We sometimes play baseball with girls versus boys.*

A robin is a vertebrate, and the worm it eats is an invertebrate.

ver·te·brate (vər′tə brit) *n* any creature that has a backbone. Fish, reptiles, birds, and mammals are all vertebrates. Worms are **invertebrates.**

ver·ti·cal (vər′tə kəl) *adj* straight up and down. A person standing up straight is in a vertical position. A person lying down is in a **horizontal** position.

ver·y (ver′ē) *adv* much; extremely: *The sunshine is very hot in July.*

ves·sel (ves′əl) **1** *n* a ship. **2** *n* a container. Cups, bowls, bottles, barrels, and tubs are vessels. **3** *n* a tube carrying blood or some other fluid. Veins and arteries are blood vessels.

vest (vest) *n* a short sleeveless jacket opening at the front.

vet·er·an (vet′ə rən) **1** *n* a person who has served in the armed forces. **2** *n* a person with much experience.

vet·er·i·nar·i·an (vet′ rə ner′ē ən) *n* a doctor who treats animals. **Vet** is a short form for this.

vi·a (vī′ə *or* vē′ə) *prep* by way of: *We travelled from Regina to Edmonton via Saskatoon.*

vi·a·duct (vī′ə dukt′) *n* a bridge for carrying a road or railway over a valley, a part of a city, etc.

vi·brate (vī′brāt) *v* move or cause to move quickly back and forth: *A piano string vibrates and makes a sound when a key is struck.* **vi·brat·ed, vi·brat·ing.** –**vi·bra′tion,** *n.*

vice– a *prefix meaning* substitute or deputy, as in *vice-principal* or *vice-president.*

vice ver·sa (vīs′vər′sə) a Latin phrase meaning the other way round: *Edwin blamed Roald, and vice versa (Roald blamed Edwin).*

vi·cin·i·ty (və sin′ə tē) *n* a region near or about a place; a neighbourhood: *There are no parks in this vicinity.* *pl* **vi·cin·i·ties.**

vi·cious (vish′əs) *adj* having bad habits; savagely fierce: *a vicious dog.*

vic·tim (vik′təm) *n* a person or animal mistreated, injured, or destroyed: *victims of war, victims of a disease, victims of an accident.*

vic·tor (vik′tər) *n* a winner. –**vic·to′ri·ous** (vik tò′rē əs), *adj,* –**vic′to·ry** (vik′tə rē), *n.*

Victoria Day in Canada, a national holiday falling on the Monday before or on the 24th of May, the birthday of Queen Victoria.

vict·ual (vit′əl) *n* Usually, **victuals** *pl.n* food.

vid·e·o (vid′ē ō′) **1** *n* the visual part, not the sound, of a film or television program. **2** *n* a videotape, especially of a movie.

video cassette a videotape in a cassette, for recording video programs.

video cassette recorder a device for recording and playing back television programs on a video cassette. **VCR** is a short form of this.

vid·e·o·disk *n* a disk on which pictures and sounds have been recorded. This can be played back on a TV or computer screen.

video game an electronic game in which a player controls the action on a screen. A place where people can play these games is called a **video arcade.**

vid·e·o·tape *n* magnetic tape that records sound and pictures for television.

view (vyū) **1** *n* something seen: *The view from Victoria is beautiful.* **2** *v* see; look at: *They viewed the scenery with pleasure.* **3** *n* an opinion: *A child's view of school is different from a teacher's.*

view·point *n* a point of view: *A heavy rain that is good from the viewpoint of farmers may be bad from the viewpoint of tourists.*

in view of, considering; because of.

vig·our (vig′ər) *n* healthy energy: *Olof exercised with vigour.* **Vigor** is another spelling. –**vig′or·ous,** *adj,* –**vig′or·ous·ly,** *adv.*

vile (vīl) **1** *adj* disgusting: *Old garbage has a vile smell.* **2** *adj* evil. **vil·er, vil·est.**

vil·lage (vil′ij) *n* a small group of houses and other buildings.

vil·lain (vil′ən) *n* a very wicked person: *The villain stole the box and put the blame on me.* –**vil′lain·ous,** *adj,* –**vil′lain·y,** *n.*

vin·dic·tive (vin dik′tiv) *adj* bearing a grudge: *Ivan is so vindictive that he never forgives anybody.*

vine (vīn) *n* a plant with long, slender stems that grow along the ground or up a wall, tree, or other support: *Ivy is a vine. Grapes and pumpkins grow on vines.*

vine·yard (vin′yərd) *n* a place planted with grapevines. **vin·e·gar** (vin′ə gər) *n* a sour liquid used to flavour and preserve food.

WORD HISTORY . . . . vinegar

Vinegar came into English in the Middle Ages from a French word made up of *vin,* meaning "wine," and *aigre,* meaning "sour."

---

vi·nyl (vī′nəl) *n* a tough, shiny plastic used to make floor and furniture coverings, toys, and other articles.

vi·o·lent (vī′ə lənt) *adj* done with strong, rough force: *a violent kick, violent language.* –**vi′o·lent·ly,** *adv,* –**vi′o·lence,** *n.*

vir·tu·al (vər′chū əl) *adj* real, but not in name or according to definition: *We won the battle with so great a loss of soldiers that it was a virtual defeat.* –**vir′tu·al·ly,** *adv.*

virtual reality surroundings that seem real but are made by a computer system.

vir·tue (vər′chū) *n* a particular kind of goodness: *Justice and kindness are virtues.* **vir·tu·ous** *adj* good: *virtuous behaviour.*

vi·rus (vī′rəs) *n* a tiny creature that causes certain infectious diseases.

vi·sa (vē′zə) *n* an official stamp on a passport giving a person permission to visit a particular country.

vi·sion (vizh′ən) **1** *n* the power of seeing; the sense of sight: *The woman wears glasses because her vision is poor.* **2** *n* something seen in the imagination, in a dream, etc.: *The beggar had visions of great wealth.*

vis·i·bil·i·ty *n* the distance at which things can be seen: *Fog and rain decreased visibility to about twelve metres.* **vis·i·ble** *adj* that can be seen: *The shores of New Brunswick were barely visible through the fog.* –**vis′i·bly,** *adv.*

vision quest (vizh′ən kwest′) a traditional part of becoming an adult in many First Nations cultures. The young person spends long periods of time fasting and thinking alone in the wilderness or visiting the sweat lodge for ceremonies, as a way of preparing to receive a vision and find his or her spirit guide. **Solo quest** is another word for this.

vis·u·al *adj* having to do with sight or vision: *The police officer used diagrams and films as visual aids to help us learn the safety rules.*

vis·u·al·ize *v* have a mental picture of: *I can visualize my father's reaction when he hears that I've wrecked my bike.*

vis·it (viz′it) **1** *v* go to see: *Would you like to visit Québec?* **2** *n* a short stay: *My aunt paid us a visit last week.*

vis·i·tor *n* a person who is visiting; guest.

vi·tal (vī′təl) **1** *adj* having to do with or necessary to life: *Eating is a vital function.* **2** *adj* very important: *It is vital to call home if you are going to be late.* **3** *adj* full of life and spirit: *That successful sports club is a very vital organization.* –**vi·tal′i·ty**, *n*, –**vi′tal·ly**, *adv.*

vi·ta·min *n* a substance necessary for normal growth, found especially in milk, raw fruits and vegetables, wheat, etc.

viv·id (viv′id) **1** *adj* brilliant: *Dandelions are a vivid yellow.* **2** *adj* lively: *Her description of the party was so vivid that I almost felt I had been there.* **3** *adj* strong: *I have a vivid memory of the fire.*

vo·cab·u·lar·y (vō kab′yə ler′ē) *n* all the words used by a person or group of people: *Reading will increase your vocabulary. The vocabulary of computer science has grown a lot.* *pl* **vo·cab·u·lar·ies.**

voice (vois) *n* the sound you make in speaking, singing, laughing, etc.: *The voices of the children could be heard coming from the yard.*

vo·cal (vō′kəl) **1** *adj* having to do with your voice: *Your tongue is a vocal organ.* **2** *adj* inclined to talk freely: *Wai-Ho became vocal when he got angry.*

This volcano is not very active, but it is not yet extinct.

vol·ca·no (vol kā′nō) *n* an opening in the earth's crust through which steam, ashes, and lava are forced out. *pl* **vol·ca·noes** or **vol·ca·nos.** –**vol·can′ic** (vol kan′ik), *adj.*

vol·ume (vol′yūm) **1** *n* a book, or a book forming part of a set: *You can find what you want to know in the ninth volume of this encyclopedia.* **2** *n* the space filled by something: *The box has a volume of one cubic metre.* **3** *n* loudness of sound: *Turn down the volume!*

vol·un·teer (vol′ən tēr′) **1** *n* a person who offers to help without being asked or paid. **2** *v* offer help: *When a search party was needed, many people volunteered.* –**vol′un·tar′i·ly** (vol′ən ter′ə lē), *adv,* –**vol′un·tar′y,** *adj.*

vom·it (vom′it) *v* throw up what has been eaten.

vote (vōt) **1** *n* a formal expression of choice: *In an election, the person receiving the most votes is elected.* **2** *n* give a vote: *Mrs. Matsushita voted for the new mayor.* **vot·ed, vot·ing.** –**vot′er,** *n.*

vow (vou) **1** *n* a solemn promise: *a vow of secrecy.* **2** *v* make a vow: *Cora vowed not to tell the secret to anyone.*

vow·el (vou′əl) *n* one of the letters *a, e, i, o, u* and sometimes *y.*

voy·age (voi′ij) *n* a journey by water, through the air, or through space. **voy·aged, voy·ag·ing.** –**voy′ag·er,** *n.*

❧ **vo·ya·geur** (voi′ə zhər′) *n* a boatman, especially a French Canadian, in the service of the early fur-trading companies.

vul·gar (vul′gər) *adj* rude; coarse: *vulgar words.*

Turkey vultures— about 75 cm long

vul·ture (vul′chər) *n* a large bird of prey, a bit like an eagle, that eats the flesh of dead animals.

w or **W** (dub'əl yū') *n* the twenty-third letter of the English alphabet or the sound that it stands for. The sound of *w* is heard in the word *wolf*. *pl* **w's** or **W's.**

USING WORDS . . . . the 5 W's

The five **W's** are **who**, **what**, **when**, **where**, and **why**. Reporters use the five W's to help them organize the information in their news stories. They ask questions using the five W's and then answer the questions in their writing. That way they are sure they have included all the most important information.

---

wad (wod) *n* a small, soft piece of something: *Omer used wads of cotton to plug his ears.*

wad·dle (wod'əl) *v* walk with short steps and an awkward, swaying motion, as a duck does. **wad·dled, wad·dling.**

wade (wād) *v* walk through water: *We waded the little stream, but the dog had to swim to the other side.* **wad·ed, wad·ing.**

wa·fer (wā'fər) *n* a very thin biscuit or candy: *a soda wafer, a mint wafer.*

waf·fle (wof'əl) *n* a light, crisp pancake with a pattern of squares on it.

wag (wag) *v* move from side to side: *The dog wagged its tail.* **wagged, wag·ging.**

wage (wāj) *n* money paid for work: *Rachel's wages are $9.50 an hour.*

wag·on (wag'ən) *n* a four-wheeled vehicle, especially one for carrying loads.

wail (wāl) **1** *v* cry loud and long because of sadness or pain: *The baby wailed.* **2** *n* a long cry of sadness or pain.

waist (wāst) *n* the part of your body between your ribs and your hips.

wait (wāt) **1** *v* stay or stop doing something till someone comes or something happens: *Let's wait outside.* **2** *n* the act of waiting: *We had a long wait at the doctor's office.*

wake (wāk) **1** *v* stop or make someone stop sleeping: *I usually wake at dawn. The noise will wake the baby.* **Waken** is another word for this. **2** *n* a track left behind anything: *Floods came in the wake of the storm.* **woke** or **waked, wak·ing.**

walk (wok) **1** *v* go on foot: *Walk over to the library with me.* **2** *n* the act of walking, especially for pleasure or exercise: *The children went for a walk in the park.*

walk·a·thon *n* a walk to raise money for charity.

wall (wol) **1** *n* the side of a house, room, etc. **2** *n* stone, brick, or other material built up to enclose or protect: *Cities used to be surrounded by high walls to keep out enemies.*

wal·let (wol'it) *n* a small, flat case for carrying money, cards, etc. in your pocket.

wal·low (wol'ō) **1** *v* roll about: *The pigs wallowed in the mud.* **2** *n* a place where an animal wallows: *There used to be many buffalo wallows on the prairies.*

wall·pa·per (wol'pā'pər) *n* paper, usually with a pattern, for decorating walls.

wal·rus (wol'rəs) *n* a large sea animal of the arctic regions, like a seal with long tusks. *pl* **wal·rus** or **wal·rus·es.**

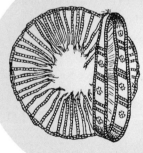

Wampum

The circular piece is the wampum record of the founding of the Iroquois League of Five Nations. It has an outer ring of shells with 50 separate strings representing the 50 chiefs of the League. The other piece is a standard Iroquois wampum belt.

wam·pum (wom'pəm) *n* beads made from shells, which eastern First Nations people used to use for money, for decoration, in ceremonies, or in wampum belts. In a wampum belt, beads were arranged in patterns which told a story.

wand (wond) *n* a slender stick: *The magician waved his wand and a rabbit popped out of the hat.*

wan·der (won′dər) *v* move about without any special purpose: *We wandered through the stores without buying anything.* –**wan′der·er,** *n.*

The moon waxes and wanes.

Waxing moon   Full moon   Waning moon

wane (wān) *v* become smaller gradually: *The moon wanes after it has become full.* The opposite is **wax. waned, wan·ing.**

on the wane, growing less; waning: *The power of the president was on the wane.*

want (wont) *v* wish for: *Zoe wants to become an engineer.*

war (wȯr) *n* fighting carried on by armed forces between countries or groups of people. **war·ri·or** *n* a soldier.

ward (wȯrd) **1** *n* a room for patients in a hospital. **2** *n* a district of a city or town. **3** *n* a person under the care of a guardian.
ward·en *n* an official who looks after something and makes sure rules are kept: *a fire warden, a park warden.*
ward off, keep away or turn aside: *Jared warded off the blow with his arm.*

ward·robe (wȯr′drōb′) **1** *n* clothes: *Lai-Sheung is shopping for her spring wardrobe.* **2** *n* a closet or piece of furniture for holding clothes.

ware·house (wer′hous′) *n* a building where goods are kept.

warm (wȯrm) **1** *adj* more hot than cold: *warm sunshine.* **2** *adj* showing affection, enthusiasm, etc.: *a warm welcome.* **3** *v* make or become warm. –**warmth,** *n.*

warm-blood·ed *adj* having warm blood that stays about the same temperature regardless of the surroundings: *The normal temperature of warm-blooded animals is between 36°C and 44°C.*

warm up, exercise for a few minutes before beginning a game, contest, etc.

warn (wȯrn) *v* tell about something that needs attention or action: *We were warned that we had to wear safety goggles while touring the steel mill.* –**warn′ing,** *n.*

warp (wȯrp) *v* bend or twist out of shape: *This old floor has warped so that it is not level.*

wart (wȯrt) *n* a small, hard lump on your skin.

war·y (wer′ē) *adj* on guard against danger; careful: *Ilya gave wary answers to all of the stranger's questions.* **war·i·er, war·i·est.** –**war′i·ly,** *adv,* –**war′i·ness,** *n.*

was (wuz) *v* a past tense of **be,** used with *I, he, she, it,* or any singular noun: *I was late for school again yesterday.*
was·n't (wuz′ənt) was not.

wash (wosh) **1** *v* clean with water: *to wash your face, to wash dishes.* **2** *n* washing or being washed: *This floor needs a good wash.* **3** *n* clothes washed or to be washed: *Maureen hung the wash on the line.* **4** *v* carry or be carried by water: *Wood is often washed ashore by waves.* **5** *n* a liquid for special use: *a mouth wash, a hair wash.*
wash·er 1 *n* a machine for washing clothes. **2** *n* a flat ring of metal, rubber, leather, etc., used with bolts or nuts, to make joints tight.
wash·ing *n* clothes, etc. washed or to be washed: *to put washing in the dryer.* **wash·out** *n Slang.* a failure; disappointment: *The party was a complete washout.* **wash·room** *n* a room with a toilet and sink, especially inside a public building: *Most gas stations have washrooms for their customers.*

wasp (wosp) *n* a flying insect that has black and yellow stripes and a stinger.

waste (wāst) **1** *v* make poor use of: *We try not to waste food.* **2** *n* a failure to use well: *Buying those boots was a waste of money; they are already starting to wear out.* **3** *n* things to be thrown away: *Garbage is waste.* **wast·ed, wast·ing.**
waste·ful *adj* using or spending too much.

CONFUSABLES ······waste

waste means "garbage":
Put your candy wrapper in the waste basket.

waist is a part of your body:
Let me measure your waist.

watch (woch) **1** *v* look at: *Are you watching the show on television?* **2** *v* look with care: *The boy watched for a chance to cross the busy street.* **3** *v* keep guard over; guard: *The dog watches over its owner's house.* **4** *n* a device for telling time, small enough to be worn on your wrist, or carried in a pocket.

watch·ful *adj* watching carefully.

watch out, be on guard: *Watch out! The tree is falling!*

The leaves of a water lily plant float on the surface of the water.

wa·ter (wot'ər) **1** *n* the liquid that falls as rain and makes up the seas, lakes, and rivers. **2** *v* sprinkle or fill with water: *to water plants. Strong sunlight will make your eyes water.*

wa·ter·col·our *n* paint mixed with water instead of oil. **Watercolor** is another spelling.

wa·ter·fall *n* a river or stream as it falls from a higher place. **wa·ter-logged** *adj* completely soaked with water. **wa·ter·proof** *adj* that will not let water through: *An umbrella should be waterproof.* **wa·ter-ski** *v* glide over the water on water skis while being towed by a boat.

wa·ter·tight 1 *adj* so tight that no water can get in or out. **2** *adj* leaving no chance for misunderstanding; perfect: *a watertight argument.*

wa·ter·y 1 *adj* full of water; wet: *watery soil, watery eyes.* **2** *adj* containing too much water: *watery soup.*

throw cold water on, discourage: *Mother will throw cold water on your plan to camp by yourself.*

wave (wāv) **1** *n* a moving ridge of water: *Waves crashed against the rocks.* **2** *n* any movement like this, especially of light, heat, or sound. **3** *v* move up and down or back and forth: *to wave a flag, to wave your hand.* **waved, wav·ing.** **–wav′y,** *adj.*

wax (waks) **1** *n* a yellowish substance made by bees, or any substance like this. **2** *v* rub with wax or something like wax: *We wax that floor once a month.* **3** *v* grow bigger: *The moon waxes till it becomes full, and then it wanes.*

way (wā) **1** *n* a manner; a method; a custom: *Konosuke is wearing his hair in a new way. Scientists are trying to find new ways to prevent disease. Don't mind her teasing; it's only her way.* **2** *n* a direction: *Look this way.* **3** *n* a road; path: *The hunter found a way through the forest.* **4** *n* a habit or custom.

give way, break down: *Several people were hurt when the bridge gave way.*

in the way or **in someone's way,** being an obstacle: *Put your bag under your desk so it won't be in the way.*

out of the way, far from where most people live or go.

we (wē) *pron* the speaker plus whoever is being spoken to or spoken about: *We will all go in the same car.*

weak (wēk) **1** *adj* easily broken: *a weak board in a floor. The building collapsed because the foundation was weak.* **2** *adj* having bodily strength: *Hayden realized he was too weak to move the rock.* **3** *adj* lacking strength of some kind: *a weak character, weak coffee.* **–weak′en,** *v.*

weak·ness 1 *n* lack of strength. **2** *n* a weak point; a slight fault. **3** *n* fondness: *Athena has a weakness for candy.*

wealth (welth) *n* riches; many valuable possessions. **–wealth′y,** *adj.*

weap·on (wep'ən) *n* any device meant to injure or kill.

wear (wer) *v* have on your body: *She wears jeans quite often.* **wore, worn, wear·ing.** **–wear′er,** *n.*

wear off, slowly disappear or stop working: *When the medicine wore off my throat started to hurt again.*

wear out, 1 become useless from long wearing: *I liked this shirt, but it's worn out now.* **2** make or become very tired: *Babysitting a small child can really wear you out.*

CONFUSABLES ...... wear

wear means "put on":
Wear your blue socks.

where means "in what place":
Where are my blue socks?

---

wea·ry (wēr'ē) *adj* tired: *weary feet.* **wea·ri·er, wea·ri·est. –wea′ri·ly,** *adv,* **–wea′ri·ness,** *n.*

A long-tailed weasel— about 30 cm long excluding the tail

wea·sel (wē′zəl) *n* a small, quick animal with a long, slender body and short legs.

weath·er (weᴛʜ′ər) *n* conditions outside: *hot weather, windy weather, wet weather.*
under the weather, *Informal.* sick.

weave (wēv) *v* make from threads or strips: *People weave thread into cloth and straw into hats.* **wove** or **weaved, wo·ven, weav·ing.**

web (web) **1** *n* something woven. A spider spins a web. **2** *n* the skin joining the toes of swimming birds and water animals like otters. **Web site** a place on the part of the Internet computer network called the **World Wide Web,** or **the Web** for short.

wed (wed) *v* marry. **wed·ded, wed·ded** or **wed, wed·ding.**

wed·ding *n* a marriage ceremony.

we'd (wēd) **1** we had. **2** we would.

wedge (wej) *n* a piece of something thin at one end: *a wedge of pie.*

weed (wēd) **1** *n* a useless or unwanted plant: *Weeds choked out the vegetables and flowers.* **2** *v* take weeds out of: *Please weed the front garden now.*

week (wēk) **1** *n* seven days, one after another. **2** *n* the time from Sunday through Saturday: *This is the last week of holidays.* **3** *n* the working days of a seven-day period: *A school week is usually five days.*
week·day *n* any day of the week except Saturday and Sunday. **week·end** *n* Saturday and Sunday.
week·ly 1 *adj* happening once a week: *a weekly trip to the supermarket.* **2** *adv* every week: *My sister is paid weekly.*

CONFUSABLES ..... **week**

week means "seven days":
She was in bed for a week.

weak means "not strong":
After her illness, she felt weak.

weep (wēp) *v* cry; shed tears. **wept, weep·ing.**

weigh (wā) *v* find the mass of: *I weighed myself this morning on the bathroom scales.*

weight 1 *n* how heavy a thing is: *Gas has hardly any weight at all. Your weight is a little less on top of a mountain than at sea level.* **2** *n* a heavy thing: *A weight keeps the papers in place.*

weight·less *adj* being free from the pull of gravity: *In outer space, all things are weightless.*

pull your weight, do your share: *We will finish the job quickly if we all pull our weight.*

CONFUSABLES ...... **weight**

weight means "pulling force": *My backpack was a heavy weight on my shoulders.*

wait means "stop till something happens": *Wait here until I get back.*

weird (wērd) *adj* eerie; strange: *We were awakened by a weird shriek.*

wel·come (wel′kəm) **1** *v* greet kindly: *We went to the airport to welcome our visitors.* **2** *n* a kind reception: *a warm welcome.* **3** *v* receive gladly: *We welcome new ideas and suggestions.* **4** *adj* gladly received: *a welcome visitor, a welcome rest.* **wel·comed, wel·com·ing.**

wel·fare (wel′fer′) *n* a condition of being or doing well: *Uncle Charles asked about the welfare of everyone in our family.*
on welfare, receiving money from the government to provide a basic standard of living: *There was a poor harvest, and many families were on welfare.*

well (wel) **1** *adv* in a good way: *The job was well done.* **bet·ter, best. 2** *adv* thoroughly: *Shake the medicine well before taking it.* **3** *adj* in good health: *He is well.* **4** *interj* an expression used to show surprise or merely to fill in: *Well! well! Here's Britt. Well, I'm not sure.* **5** *n* a hole dug in the ground to get water, oil, gas, etc.
well-be·haved *adj* showing good manners.
well-known *adj* famous. **well-off** *adj* in a good condition; fairly rich: *Your whole family is healthy, so you should consider yourself well-off. Adele's family is well-off but not wealthy.*
well-to-do *adj* quite rich.
as well, 1 also. **2** equally.
as well as, 1 in addition to. **2** as much as.

we'll (wēl) we will; we shall.

went (went) *v* the past tense of **go.**

were (wər) *v* the past tense plural of the verb **be.**
weren't were not.

we're (wēr) we are.

were·wolf (wer'wùlf' *or* wər'wùlf') *n* in stories, a person who has been changed into a wolf, or who can change into a wolf. *pl* **were·wolves.**

Wes·ak (wes'ak) *n* the Buddhist New Year festival, held in May.

west (west) **1** *n* the direction of the sunset. **2** *adv* or *adj* to or from the west: *Walk west three blocks (adv). A west wind is blowing (adj).* –**west'er·ly,** *adj,* –**west'ern,** *adj.*
West·ern·er *n* a native or inhabitant of the Western provinces.
west·ward *adv* or *adj* toward the west.
Westwards is another name for this.

wet (wet) **1** *adj* covered or soaked with water: *wet hands, a wet sponge.* **2** *adj* not dry: *Don't touch the wet paint.* **3** *adj* rainy: *wet weather.* **wet·ter, wet·test.**
wet blanket *Informal.* a person who has a discouraging or depressing effect.
wet·land *n* a marsh or swamp, often protected for wildlife. **Wetlands** is another name for this.

we've (wēv) we have.

whack (wak *or* hwak) **1** *n Informal.* a sharp, noisy blow. **2** *v Informal.* strike with such a blow: *The batter whacked the ball out of the park.*

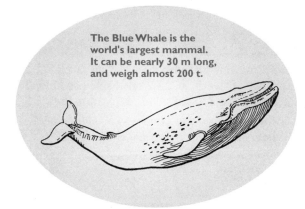

The Blue Whale is the world's largest mammal. It can be nearly 30 m long, and weigh almost 200 t.

whale (wāl *or* hwāl) *n* an animal like a huge fish and living in the sea. Whales breathe air. *pl* **whales** or **whale.**

wharf (wȯrf *or* hwȯrf) *n* a platform for ships to load and unload. *pl* **wharves** or **wharfs.**

what (wut *or* hwut) **1** *pron* or *adj* a word used in asking questions about persons or things: *What is your name (pron)? What time is it (adj)?* **2** *pron* that which: *I know what you mean.*
what·ev·er 1 *pron* anything that: *Do whatever you like.* **2** *pron* no matter what: *Do it, whatever happens.* **what's 1** what is: *What's the latest news?* **2** what has: *What's been going on here lately?*
what if, what would happen if: *What if it rains on the day of the soccer match?*

wheat (wēt *or* hwēt) *n* the grain of a cereal grass, used to make flour.

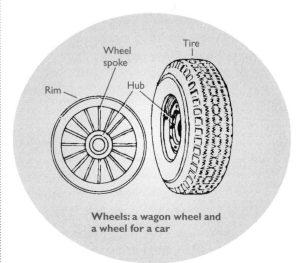

Wheels: a wagon wheel and a wheel for a car

wheel (wēl *or* hwēl) **1** *n* a round frame or disk that turns on its centre. **2** *v* turn: *He wheeled around suddenly.* **3** *v* move on wheels: *The worker was wheeling bricks in a wheelbarrow.*
wheel·bar·row *n* a small vehicle for carrying loads, with one wheel and two handles.
wheel·chair *n* a chair on wheels, used by people who cannot walk, or cannot walk very well.
at the wheel, 1 at the steering wheel. **2** in control.

when (wen *or* hwen) **1** *adv* at what time: *When does school close?* **2** *conj* at the time that: *Stand up when your name is called.*
when·ev·er *conj* or *adv* at any time that: *Please come whenever you wish (conj). She played chess whenever possible (adv).*

where (wer *or* hwer) **1** *adv* in, to, or from what place: *Where do you live? Where are you going? Where did you hear that story?* **2** *conj* in the place that: *Your coat is where you left it.*
wher·ev·er *conj* or *adv* in whatever place: *Edward goes wherever he wishes (conj). Wherever did I put my glasses (adv)?*

weth·er (weᴛʜ′ər *or* hweᴛʜ′ər) **1** *conj* a word used in expressing a choice: *Melissa does not know whether to go camping or not.* **2** *conj* if: *He asked whether he should finish the work.*

CONFUSABLES .... whether

whether means "if":
I wonder whether it will rain.

weather means "outside conditions":
What is the weather like today?

---

which (wich *or* hwich) a word used: **1** *adj* or *pron* in talking about one or more things: *Which student won the prize (adj)? I don't know which dress to wear (adj). Which seems the best plan to you (pron)? Tell me which way is best (pron).* **2** *pron* in connecting a group of words with some other word in the sentence: *Read the book which is on the desk.*

which·ev·er 1 *pron* or *adj* any one: *Take whichever you want (pron). Buy whichever hat you like (adj).* **2** *pron* or *adj* no matter which: *Whichever you take will be all right (pron). Whichever side wins, I shall be satisfied (adj).*

while (wīl *or* hwīl) **1** *n* a time: *Thomas kept us waiting a long while.* **2** *conj* during the time that: *While I was speaking, Eleni said nothing.*
worth while, worth time, attention, or effort: *All this fussing about such a small matter is hardly worth while.*

whim (wim *or* hwim) *n* a sudden fancy or notion: *She has a whim for gardening, but it won't last.*

whim·per (wim′pər *or* hwim′pər) **1** *v* cry with soft sounds, in the way that a sick child or a dog does. **2** *n* a whimpering cry.

whine (wīn *or* hwīn) **1** *v* make a soft, complaining sound: *The dog whined to go out with us.* **2** *v* complain: *Some people are always whining about little things.* **whined, whin·ing.**

whip (wip *or* hwip) **1** *n* a thing to beat with. **2** *v* beat with a whip. **3** *v* move or pull suddenly: *Fritz whipped off his coat.* **4** *v* beat cream, eggs, etc.: *Whip the cream until it is thick.* **whipped, whip·ping.**

whirl (wərl *or* hwərl) **1** *v* go round and round: *The leaves whirled in the wind.* **2** *n* a whirling movement: *The dancer suddenly made a whirl.*
whirl·pool *n* water whirling round and round.
whirl·wind *n* a whirling storm of wind.

whisk·er (wis′kər *or* hwis′kər) **1** Usually, **whiskers,** *pl.n* the hair growing on a man's face, especially on his cheeks and chin. **2** *n* a long, stiff hair growing near the mouth of a cat, rat, etc.

whis·per (wis′pər *or* hwis′pər) **1** *v* speak very softly. **2** *n* a very soft, low spoken sound.

whis·tle (wis′əl *or* hwis′əl) **1** *v* make a clear, shrill sound by forcing breath through your teeth or lips. **2** *n* the sound made by whistling. **3** *n* an instrument for making whistling sounds. **whis·tled, whis·tling.**

white (wīt *or* hwīt) **1** *n* the colour of snow. **2** *adj* having this colour or one like it: *Grandmother has white hair.* **3** *n* a part that is white or whitish: *Take the whites of four eggs.* **4** *adj* pale: *He turned white with fear.* **whit·er, whit·est. –whit′en,** *v.*

❧ **white·out** *n* a winter weather condition in which blowing snow completely fills your view.

who (hū) a word used: **1** *pron* in talking about one or more persons: *Who is your friend? Who told you? We know who is coming.* **2** *pron* in connecting a group of words with some other word in the sentence: *The girl who spoke to you is my best friend.*

who'd who would: *Who'd like to go along?*
who·ev·er 1 *pron* any person that: *Whoever wants the book may have it.* **2** *pron* no matter who: *Whoever else goes hungry, he won't.*
who'll who will; who shall.
whom *pron* the objective form of **who.**
who's who is.
whose *pron* the possessive form of **who.**

Grammar ✓Check ...... who

In formal English, **who** is used only as the subject of a verb, just as you would use *he* or *she*: *Who went to the store? She went to the store.*

Whom is used the same way as *him* or *her*: *Whom did you meet? Did you meet him?*

Always use **whom** after a preposition like *to, with, by, from,* or *of.*

CONFUSABLES ..... whose

whose means "belonging to whom":
Whose is this jacket?

who's means "who is":
Who's going to the movie?

whole (hōl) **1** *adj* complete: *Saul gave us a whole set of dishes. Three thirds make a whole.* **2** *adj* in one piece: *The dog swallowed the piece of meat whole.*

whole number a number that does not contain a fraction. **whole·some 1** *adj* good for your health: *Milk is a wholesome food.* **2** *adj* healthy-looking: *She has a wholesome face.* **whol·ly** *adv* completely.

on the whole, 1 considering everything. **2** mostly.

whoop (hūp *or* hwūp) *n* a loud cry or shout.

whooping cough (hū′ping kof′) an infectious disease that children get, which causes coughing fits with a gasp at the end.

why (wī *or* hwī) *adv* for what reason: *Why did the baby cry?*

wick (wik) *n* the string part of an oil lamp or candle that you light.

wick·ed (wik′id) *adj* bad; evil: *a wicked witch, wicked deeds.* **–wick′ed·ness,** *n.*

wide (wīd) **1** *adj* filling much space from side to side; not narrow: *a wide street.* **2** *adj* measuring a certain distance from side to side: *The door is 90 cm wide.* **3** *adv* as much as possible: *Open your mouth wide.* **wid·er, wid·est. –wide′ly,** *adv,* **–wid′en,** *v.*

wide-a·wake *adj* fully awake; with eyes wide open. **width** (width) *n* how wide a thing is: *The width of the room is three metres.*

wid·ow (wid′ō) *n* a woman whose husband is dead and who has not married again.

wid·ow·er *n* a man whose wife is dead and who has not married again.

wie·ner (wē′nər) *n* a reddish sausage, usually made of pork and beef: *Wieners in buns are called hot dogs.*

wife (wīf) *n* a married woman, especially when thought of in connection with the man she is married to: *Lotte is Oliver's wife.* pl **wives.**

wig (wig) *n* an artificial covering of hair, or of something like hair, for a head: *a doll's wig. The bald man wore a wig.*

wig·gle (wig′əl) *v* move with short, quick movements from side to side: *The restless child wiggled in her chair.* **wig·gled, wig·gling.**

wig·gly *adj* wavy: *Klein drew a wiggly line under his name.*

An Algonquian wigwam

wig·wam (wig′wom) *n* one kind of home used by First Nations people from the Atlantic to the Prairies, made from poles covered with bark, reed mats, or animal skins.

wild (wīld) **1** *adj* not tamed; not cultivated: *A coyote is a wild animal. The wild rose is the floral emblem of Alberta.* **2** *adj* violent; not calm: *a wild storm.*

wil·der·ness (wil′dər nis) *n* a region with few or no people living in it. **wild·flow·er** *n* any flower that grows in the woods, fields, etc.

wild·life *n* wild animals as a group, usually those native to a particular area: *northern wildlife.*

will (wil) an auxiliary (helping) verb used: **1** *v* to show a promise: *I will be there at 4 o'clock.* **2** *v* to refer to future happenings: *The train will arrive late in Edmonton.* **3** *v* to ask for something: *Will you please hand me that book?* past tense **would. 4** *n* the power of your mind to decide and do: *a strong will.* **5** *n* a legal statement of a person's wishes about what should be done with his or her property after he or she is dead.

will·ing *adj* cheerfully ready: *a willing helper.* **–will′ing·ly,** *adv,* **–will′ing·ness,** *n.*

wilt (wilt) *v* become limp; wither: *Flowers wilt when they do not get enough water.*

wil·y (wī′lē) *adj* tricky; cunning; crafty; sly: *The wily fox got away.* **wil·i·er, wil·i·est.**

win (win) **1** *v* be successful over others: *We all hope our team will win.* **2** *n* a success: *We had five wins and no defeats.* **3** *v* get by effort, ability, or skill: *to win fame, to win a prize.* **won, win·ning. –win′ner,** *n.*

A windmill for pumping water

The large blade keeps the wheel turned so as to catch the wind.

wind (wind *for 1,* wīnd *for 2-4*) **1** *n* moving air: *The wind bends the branches.* –**wind′y,** *adj.* **2** *v* change direction; turn: *A creek winds through the woods.* **3** *v* wrap around something: *The mother wound her arms about the child.* **4** *v* make some machine go by turning some part of it: *to wind a clock.* **wound, wind·ing.**

🌿 **wind·break** *n* a row or clump of trees planted to afford protection from the wind.

wind·break·er *n* a short jacket with close-fitting cuffs and waistband, for outdoor wear.

🌿 **wind chill** the cooling effect of wind combined with low temperature.

wind·fall 1 *n* fruit blown down by the wind. **2** *n* an unexpected piece of good luck.

wind instrument a musical instrument sounded by blowing air into it. Trumpets, saxophones, and flutes are wind instruments.

wind·mill *n* a mill or machine worked by the wind turning blades: *Windmills are used to pump water.*

win·dow 1 *n* an opening in a wall, or vehicle to let in light or air. **2** *n* on a computer screen, the box where you read or enter information.

wind·shield *n* a sheet of glass, etc. in a vehicle to keep off the wind. **wind·surf·ing** *n* the sport of gliding over water on a board with a sail.

wind up, end: *We expect to wind up the project tomorrow.*

> **WORD HISTORY . . . . window**
>
> **Window** came from the Old Norse word *vindauga,* from *vindr,* meaning "wind," and *auga,* meaning "eye." A window is a bit like an eye, isn't it?

wine (wīn) *n* an alcoholic drink made from the juice of grapes or other fruits.

A sphinx moth— wingspread about 11 cm

wing (wing) **1** *n* one of the two parts of a bird, insect, or bat used in flying. **2** *n* anything like a wing in shape or use: *the wings of an airplane.* **3** *n* either of the spaces to the right or left of the stage in a theatre. –**wing′less,** *adj.*

take wing, fly away: *The bird took wing when the cat came near.*

under the wing of, under the protection of.

wink (wingk) *v* close and open one eye on purpose as a hint or signal: *My father winked at me to sit still.*

win·ter (win′tər) *n* the coldest of the four seasons, between fall and spring. –**win′try,** *adj.*

wipe (wīp) **1** *v* rub in order to clean or dry: *We wipe our shoes on the mat.* **2** *v* take away by rubbing: *Wipe away your tears.* **wiped, wip·ing.**

wipe out, destroy completely: *The pollution in the river wiped out all the fish.*

wire (wīr) **1** *n* metal made into a thread: *telephone wire.* **2** *adj* made of wire: *a wire fence.* **3** *v* put in electrical wires. **wired, wir·ing.**

wise (wīz) *adj* having or showing knowledge and good judgment: *a wise judge, wise advice.* **wis·er, wis·est.**

wis·dom (wiz′dəm) *n* knowledge and good judgment based on experience.

–wise *a suffix meaning* in a certain manner. *Likewise* means in a *like* manner.

wish (wish) **1** *v* have a desire; express a hope: *I wish that I had enough money to buy that computer game.* **2** *n* a wishing; a desire: *What is your wish?* **3** *n* an expression of a desire for someone's happiness, good fortune, etc.: *Please give her my best wishes.*

wit (wit) **1** *n* the power to express cleverly ideas that are amusing: *Her wit kept us all laughing.* **2** *n* the power of understanding: *People with quick wits learn easily.* –**wit′ty,** *adj.*

witch (wich) *n* a person supposed to have magic power. –**witch′craft′,** *n.*

with (with) **1** *prep* in the company of: *Come with me.* **2** *prep* having, wearing, using, carrying, etc.: *a dog with big paws.* **3** *prep* because of: *The child is shaking with cold.* **4** *prep* against: *We fought with that gang.*

with·in 1 *prep* inside of: *within reach.* **2** *adv* on the inside; inside: *The house has been painted within and without.* **with·out 1** *prep* with no; not having: *A cat walks without noise. She walked past without noticing us.* **2** *adv* on the outside: *The house is painted without and within.*

do or **go without,** not have something: *Either cook your own supper or go without.*

with·draw (with dro′) **1** *v* pull back: *Ishmael quickly withdrew his hand from the hot stove.* **2** *v* take back; remove: *to withdraw money from your bank.* **3** *v* go away: *Janet withdrew from the room.* **with·drew, with·drawn, with·draw·ing. –with·draw′al,** *n.*

with·er (wiᴛʜ′ər) *v* dry up; fade: *Flowers wither after they are cut.*

wit·ness (wit′nis) **1** *n* a person who saw something happen. **2** *v* see: *William witnessed the accident.* **3** *n* a person who gives evidence.

wiz·ard (wiz′ərd) **1** *n* a person supposed to have magic power. **2** *n* Informal. a clever person; expert: *My friend is a wizard at computer games.*

wob·ble (wob′əl) *v* shake: *The front wheel on her bike wobbles.* **wob·bled, wob·bling. –wob′bly,** *adj.*

woe (wō) *n* great sadness. **–woe′ful,** *adj.*

A timber wolf—
about 70 cm high at the shoulder

wolf (wulf) **1** *n* a wild animal like a large dog. **2** *v* eat greedily: *The hungry boy wolfed down the food.* *pl* **wolves.**

cry wolf, give a false alarm.

A wolverine—
about 17 cm long including the tail

wol·ver·ine (wul′və rēn′) *n* a strong, meat-eating animal related to the skunk. Wolverines live in the forests of northern Canada.

wom·an (wum′ən) *n* an adult female human being. *pl* **wom·en** (wim′ən).

won·der (wun′dər) **1** *n* a strange and surprising thing or event: *No wonder Donald is sick; he ate four chocolate bars.* **2** *n* the feeling caused by something strange and surprising: *The baby looked with wonder at the Christmas tree.* **3** *v* wish to know: *I wonder what time it is.* **won·der·ful 1** *adj* causing wonder: *The explorer had wonderful adventures.* **2** *adj* excellent: *We had a wonderful time at the Canada Day picnic.*

won't (wōnt) will not.

wood (wud) **1** *n* the hard substance beneath the bark of trees and shrubs. **2** Often, **woods,** *pl.n* an area with a large number of growing trees.

wood·chuck *n* a small, thick-bodied North American animal with short legs and a bushy tail; groundhog. **wood·en 1** *adj* made of wood. **2** *adj* stiff as wood; awkward: *The actor gave a wooden bow and left the stage.*

wood·y 1 *adj* covered with trees: *a woody hillside.* **2** *adj* like wood: *Turnips become woody when they are left in the ground too long.*

wool (wul) **1** *n* the soft hair or fur of sheep and some other animals. **2** *n* something like wool: *Glass wool for insulation is made from fibres of glass.* **3** *n* yarn or cloth made of wool.

wool·len *adj* made of wool: *a woollen suit.* **Woolen** is another spelling. **wool·ly 1** *adj* like wool. **2** *adj* covered with wool or something like it. **Wooly** is another spelling.

pull the wool over someone's eyes, *Informal.* deceive or trick someone.

word (wərd) **1** *n* a sound or a group of sounds that has meaning and is a unit of speech: *She answered with one word, "No."* **2** *n* a command: *We have to wait till she gives the word.* **3** *n* a promise: *The boy kept his word.* **4** *v* put into words: *Angus worded his message clearly.*

word processor a computer for producing printed material like letters or reports.

word·y *adj* using too many words.

eat your words, take back what you have said.

work (wərk) **1** *n* the effort of doing or making something: *It was hard work but Maia enjoyed it.* **2** *n* employment. **3** *n* something made or done, especially something creative: *The artist considers that picture to be her greatest work.* **4** *v* work for pay: *Most people must work to live.* **5** *v* act; operate: *This pump will not work. The plan worked well.* **worked, work·ing.** –**work'er,** *n.*

work·a·hol·ic *n Informal.* a person who cannot stop working and has no time for anything else.

work·out *n Informal.* a practice: *The team had a good workout before the game.*

work out, 1 plan: *Work out your idea before you get started.* **2** solve; find out. **3** practise: *The coach makes us work out before every game.*

work up, excite; stir up.

world (wərld) **1** *n* the earth: *Ships can sail around the world.* **2** *n* all of certain animals or things of the earth: *the insect world.* **3** *n* a special interest: *the world of music.* **4** *n* all people: *The whole world knows it.* **5** *n* another planet, especially when considered inhabited.

world·wide *adj* spread throughout the world. The **World Wide Web** is a system of linked places (sites) on the Internet computer network. It is called **the Web** for short. You can see it written as **www** in Web site addresses.

on top of the world, in high spirits.

out of this world, *Informal.* great; wonderful: *The party decorations are out of this world!*

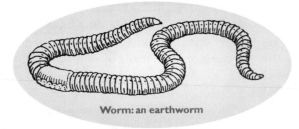

Worm: an earthworm

worm (wərm) *n* a small crawling animal: *Most worms have soft bodies and no legs.*

worn (wôrn) *v* the past participle of **wear.**

worn-out 1 *adj* used until no longer fit for use: *You should throw those worn-out shoes away.* **2** *adj* very tired.

wor·ry (wər'ē) **1** *v* feel or make anxious: *My sister worries about little things. The problem worried him.* **2** *n* an uneasy feeling: *Worry kept us awake.* **wor·ries, wor·ried, wor·ry·ing.**

worse (wərs) *adj* more bad: *Andrew is bad enough, but his brother is much worse.* –**wor'sen,** *v.*

worst *adj* most bad: *None of them are good, but she's the worst of the lot.*

wor·ship (wər'ship) **1** *n* great honour and respect given to a god. **2** *v* pay great respect to. **wor·shipped** or **wor·shiped, wor·ship·ping** or **wor·ship·ing.** –**wor'ship·per** or **wor'ship·er,** *n.*

worth (wərth) **1** *adj* good enough for; deserving of: *Charlottetown is a city worth visiting.* **2** *n* value; importance: *We sold our car for less than its worth. We should read books of real worth.* **3** *adj* equal in value to: *My old bike is worth at least $50.* –**worth'less,** *adj,* –**wor'thy** (wėr'ᴛʜē), *adj.*

worth·while (wərth' wīl' or wərth'hwīl') *adj* worth time, attention, or effort: *Daniel ought to spend his time on some worthwhile reading.*

would (wud) *v* the past tense of **will.**

would·n't would not.

wound (wünd) **1** *n* an injury caused by cutting, stabbing, shooting, etc.: *The man has a knife wound in his arm.* **2** *v* injure by cutting, stabbing, shooting, etc.

wow (wou) *Slang.* **1** *interj* an exclamation of delight, admiration, etc. **2** *v* dazzle or impress: *My mother really wowed us with her new outfit.*

wrap (rap) *v* cover by winding or folding something around: *Megan wrapped herself in a shawl.* **wrapped, wrap·ping.**

wrapped up in, devoted to; thinking of: *He is wrapped up in his work.*

wrath (rath) *n* very great anger; rage. –**wrath'ful,** *adj.*

wreath (rēth) *n* a ring of flowers or leaves twisted together. *pl* **wreaths** (rēᴛʜz).

wreathe (rēᴛʜ) **1** *v* make into a wreath. **2** *v* decorate with wreaths. **3** *v* make a ring around: *Mist wreathes the hills.*

wreck (rek) **1** *n* what is left of anything that has been destroyed or much injured: *The wreck of a ship was tossed onto the shores of Georgian Bay by the waves.* **2** *v* destroy; ruin: *to wreck a car in an accident.*

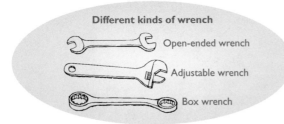

Different kinds of wrench

Open-ended wrench

Adjustable wrench

Box wrench

wrench (rench) **1** *n* a violent twist: *Toshihiko gave his ankle a wrench when he jumped off the bus.* **2** *v* twist or pull violently: *Florencia wrenched the knob off when she was trying to open the door.* **3** *n* a tool to hold and turn nuts, bolts, etc.

wres·tle (res′əl) *v* try to throw or force an opponent to the ground: *The two brothers were wrestling.* **wres·tled, wres·tling.** –**wres′tler,** *n,* –**wres′tling,** *n.*

wrig·gle (rig′əl) **1** *v* twist and turn: *Children wriggle when they are restless.* **2** *n* the act of wriggling: *With one wriggle, Ryan was under the bed.* **wrig·gled, wrig·gling.**

wring (ring) *v* twist with force; squeeze hard: *Wring the water from your wet hair.* **wrung, wring·ing.**

wring out, squeeze to remove water from: *He wrung out his wet socks.*

wrin·kle (ring′kəl) **1** *n* an irregular crease: *I must press out the wrinkles in this dress.* **2** *v* make a wrinkle or wrinkles in: *Ildiko wrinkled her forehead.* **wrin·kled, wrin·kling.**

wrist (rist) *n* the joint connecting your hand and arm.

write (rīt) **1** *v* make letters or words with pen, pencil, chalk, etc.: *You can read and write.* **2** *v* make up stories, books, etc. **wrote, writ·ten, writ·ing.**

writ·er *n* a person whose occupation is writing; author. **writ·ing 1** *n* written form: *Put your ideas in writing.* **2** *n* handwriting: *Her writing is hard to read.* **3** *n* something written; a letter, report, etc.

write down, put into writing: *Many early folk songs were never written down.*

write out, write in full: *The reporter made quick notes during the interview and then wrote out her report later.*

write up, write in detail.

wrong (rong) **1** *adj* not right; bad: *Stealing is wrong.* **2** *adj* not true; not correct: *Matt gave the wrong answer.* **3** *adj* out of order: *Something is wrong with the car.* **4** *adv* in a wrong manner; ill; badly: *You've done it all wrong.* **5** *n* anything not right such as injury or injustice: *The criminal had committed many wrongs.*

go wrong, turn out badly: *Everything went wrong today.*

in the wrong, at fault; guilty.

x or **X** (eks) **1** *n* the twenty-fourth letter of the English alphabet, or the sound that it stands for. The sound of *x* at the beginning of the word *xylophone* is different from the sound of *x* at the end of the word *fox*. **2** *n* **x** is used to indicate a certain place on a map: *X marks the spot.* **3** *n* **x** is used to symbolize a kiss. *pl* **x's** or **X's.**

Xmas (kris′məs) *n Informal.* Christmas.

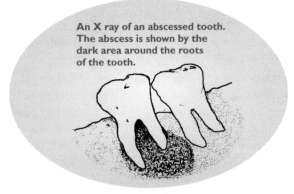

An **X** ray of an abscessed tooth. The abscess is shown by the dark area around the roots of the tooth.

X ray **1** *n* a ray that can go through things that ordinary rays of light cannot. X rays are used to photograph the inside of a person's body. **2** *n* a picture made by using X rays. **X-ray** *v* photograph with X rays: *The doctor X-rayed my wrist to see if any bones were broken.*

X's and O's a game in which two players take turns in marking X and O. The winner is the first person who can mark three X's or O's across, down, or diagonally. **Tick-tack-toe** is another name for this game.

A xylophone

xy·lo·phone (zī′lə fōn′) *n* a musical instrument consisting of two rows of wooden bars of varying lengths, which are sounded by striking them with wooden hammers.

y or **Y** (wī) *n* the twenty-fifth letter of the English alphabet, or the sound that it stands for. The sound of *y* is heard at the beginning of the word *yes*. *pl* **y's** or **Y's.**

This kind of yacht is called a yawl. It has two masts.

yacht (yot) *n* a sailing or motor-driven boat for pleasure trips or for racing.

yak (yak) *n* a large, long-haired animal of central Asia, related to the North American buffalo and to cattle.

yam (yam) *n* a kind of sweet potato: *We often have candied yams with ham.*

yank (yangk) *Informal.* **1** *v* pull with a sudden motion; jerk: *You almost yanked my arm off!* **2** *n* a sudden pull: *Dwight gave the door a yank.* **yank out,** take out with a jerk.

yap (yap) *v* bark in a snappish way; yelp: *That little dog yaps at strangers.* **yapped, yap·ping.**

yard (yàrd) **1** *n* a piece of ground near or around a house, barn, school, etc.: *My sister is in the yard cutting grass.* **2** *n* a piece of enclosed ground for some special purpose or business: *a chicken yard, a railway yard.* **3** *n* a non-metric measure of length equal to about 90 cm: *The football player ran 40 yards for a touchdown.*

yarn (yàrn) **1** *n* any thread, especially for knitting: *This yarn is soft enough for baby clothes.* **2** *n Informal.* a tale; story: *The old sailor made up exciting yarns.*

yawn (yon) **1** *v* open your mouth wide and breathe in deeply because of sleepiness or boredom. **2** *n* the act of yawning.

year (yēr) **1** *n* the period of time equal to 12 months or 365 days; January 1 to December 31. Leap year has 366 days. **2** *n* the exact period of the earth's revolution around the sun, equal to 365 days, 5 hours, 48 minutes, 46 seconds.

year·book *n* a book or report published every year: *Yearbooks often report events of the year.*
year·ling *n* an animal one year old: *a yearling colt.*
year·ly **1** *adj* happening once a year: *a yearly camping trip.* **2** *adv* every year: *A new calendar is printed yearly.*

year in, year out, always: *Christopher has always worked hard, year in, year out.*

yearn (yərn) *v* feel a desire: *Jennifer yearns for home.* –**yearn'ing,** *n.*

yeast (yēst) *n* the substance that causes bread dough to rise. Yeast consists of very small plants that grow quickly in a liquid containing sugar.

yell (yel) **1** *v* cry out with a strong, loud sound: *Ramesh yelled with pain.* **2** *n* a strong, loud cry.

yel·low (yel'ō) **1** *n* the colour of gold, butter, or ripe lemons. **2** *v* become yellow: *Paper yellows with age.* **3** *adj Informal.* cowardly.

yelp (yelp) **1** *n* a quick, sharp bark or cry: *the yelps of a small puppy.* **2** *v* make such a bark or cry: *I yelped when the rock fell on my toe.*

yes (yes) *adv* a word used to indicate that one can or will, or that something is true: *"Yes, five and two are seven," said Tyler. Will you go? Yes.* *pl* **yes·es.**

yes·ter·day (yes'tər dā') **1** *n* the day before today: *Yesterday was cold.* **2** *adv* on the day before today: *Our guests left yesterday.*

yet (yet) **1** *adv* up to the present time: *Our homework is not yet finished.* **2** *adv* now; at this time: *Don't go yet.* **3** *conj* but: *The work is good, yet it could be better.*

as yet, up to now: *As yet we have no news of the missing puppy.*

yield (yēld) **1** *v* produce: *The soil of Saskatchewan yields good crops.* **2** *n* the product: *This year's yield from the silver mine was very large.* **3** *v* give way: *The door yielded to his touch. I yielded to temptation and ate all the candy.*

yo·del (yō′dəl) *v* sing or call with sudden changes from low to high sounds.

yo·ga (yō′gə) *n* in Hinduism, a way of joining your soul with God through certain mental and physical exercises.

yo·gurt (yō′gərt) *n* a thickened food made from milk: *Yogurt can be eaten plain or with fruit or sugar.*

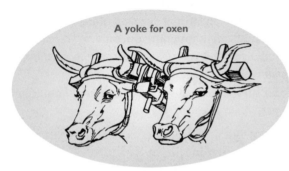
A yoke for oxen

yoke (yōk) *n* a wooden frame that fits around the neck of two work animals to fasten them together for pulling a plough or vehicle.

yolk (yōk) *n* the yellow part of an egg.

Yom Kip·pur (yom′ ki pūr′) an annual Jewish day of fasting and atoning for sins, celebrated on the tenth day after the Jewish New Year. It falls in late September or early October.

yon·der (yon′dər) *adj* within sight, but not near: *On yonder hill stands a ruined castle.*

yore (yȯr) **of yore,** *adv* of long ago: *in days of yore.*

A York boat

❋ **York boat** formerly, a type of heavy freight canoe developed by the Hudson's Bay Company at York Factory on Hudson Bay.

you (yū) **1** *pron* the person or persons spoken to: *Are you ready?* **2** *pron* anybody: *You never can tell.*

you'd 1 you had: *You'd better go quickly.* **2** you would: *You'd like this story.*

you'll you will: *You'll be surprised when I tell you.*

your a possessive form of **you.**

you're you are.

yours *pron* the one or ones belonging to you: *My hands are clean; yours are dirty.*

your·self *pron* a form used instead of **you** when referring back to the subject of the sentence: *Did you hurt yourself?*

you've you have.

> **USING WORDS . . . . . .your**
>
> **Your** and **yours** are both possessive forms of *you.*
>
> **Your** is used before a noun: *Don't forget your bag.*
>
> **Yours** is a pronoun and stands alone: *Is this yours?*
>
> **You're** is not possessive. It is a short form of *you are: You're going to be late.*

young (yung) **1** *adj* in the early part of life; not old: *A puppy is a young dog.* **2** *n* young offspring: *An animal will fight to protect its young.* **3** *adj* having the looks or qualities of a young person: *My sister looks and acts young for her age.* **4 the young,** *n* young people.

young·er (yung′gər), **young·est** (yung′gist).

young·ster *n* a child: *She is a lively youngster.*

youth (yūth) **1** *n* the time between childhood and adulthood. **2** *n* a young man. *pl* **youths. 3** *n* young people. **4** *n* the first or early stage of anything: *Space travel is still in its youth.* **–youth′ful,** *adj,* **–youth′ful·ly,** *adv,* **–youth′ful·ness,** *n.*

yowl (youl) *v* howl: *That dog is always yowling.*

yo–yo (yō′yō) *n* a small, wheel-shaped toy made up of two disks joined by a central peg to which is attached a long string. The string is held by one hand, and the toy is spun out and reeled in on the string. *pl* **yo-yos.**

yup·pie (yup′ē) *n Informal.* a fairly young adult who lives in a city, has a well-paying job, and likes to buy expensive things: *The yuppies next door built a new deck for their house.* The word is short for **young urban professional.**

z or **Z** (zed) *n* the twenty-sixth and last letter of the English alphabet, or the sound that it stands for. The sound of *z* in *seizure* is different from the sound of *z* in *zoo*. *pl* **z's** or **Z's.**

za·ny (zā′nē) *adj* foolish; comical: *Jordan's zany stories make everyone laugh.*

zeal (zēl) *n* enthusiasm.

A zebra— about 125 cm high at the shoulder

ze·bra (zē′brə *or* zeb′rə) *n* a wild animal of Africa, related to the horse, but striped with dark bands on white.

Zen (zen) *n* a Japanese branch of Buddhism that emphasizes thinking over a riddle or problem. This leads the person to a solution that results in greater understanding.

zen·ith (zē′nith) **1** *n* the point in the heavens directly overhead. **2** *n* the highest or greatest point.

ze·ro (zē′rō) **1** *n* the figure 0: *There are three zeros in 40 006.* **2** *n* nothing: *The other team's score was zero.* *pl* **ze·ros** or **ze·roes.**
zero gravity in space, a condition in which gravity does not operate; weightlessness.

> **WORD HISTORY .... zero**
>
> Zero comes from the Arabic word *sifr*, meaning "empty."

zest (zest) *n* keen enjoyment: *The hungry girl ate with zest.*

zig·zag (zig′zag′) **1** *adj* with short, sharp turns from one side to the other: *go in a zigzag direction.* **2** *v* move in a zigzag way. **3** *n* a zigzag line. **zig·zagged, zig·zag·ging.**

zinc (zingk) *n* a bluish-white metal very little affected by air and moisture. Zinc is used in electric batteries, in paint, in medicine, and for coating some metals.

zip (zip) **1** *n* a sudden, brief hissing sound. **2** *v Informal.* proceed with energy: *I zipped down to the store on my bicycle.* **3** *v* fasten or close with a zipper: *Elisha zipped up his jacket before leaving.* **zipped, zip·ping.**
zip·per *n* a sliding fastener for clothes, purses, boots, etc.

zo·di·ac (zō′dē ak′) *n* an imaginary belt of the heavens divided into 12 equal parts, called signs, named after 12 groups of stars.

zone (zōn) **1** *n* any special region: *a hospital zone, a time zone, the equatorial zone.* **2** *v* set an area apart for a special purpose, especially in a city or town: *This area is zoned for apartment buildings.* **zoned, zon·ing.**

zoo (zū) *n* a place where animals are kept and shown: *We saw lions and tigers in the zoo.*
zo·ol·o·gy (zū ol′ə jē *or* zō ol′ə jē) *n* the study of animals: *Zoology is a branch of biology.*
–**zo′o·log′i·cal** (zū′ə loj′ə kəl *or* zō′ə loj′ə kəl), *adj,*
–**zo·ol′o·gist** (zū əl′ə jist *or* zō əl′ə jist), *n.*

zoom (zūm) *v* move suddenly: *The airplane zoomed up into the clouds.*
zoom lens especially in television or movie cameras, a type of lens that can be quickly adjusted from close-ups to wide-angle shots.

Zo·ro·as·tri·an (zôr′ō as′trē ən) *n* a follower of an ancient religion which teaches that the supreme God is in an unending struggle with the spirit of evil. People are involved in this struggle and do their part by following the moral laws of God. The holy writings of this religion are called the Avesta, and the main prophet was Zoroaster. –**Zo′ro·as′tri·an·ism′,** *n.*

zuc·chi·ni (zū kē′nē) *n* a kind of dark-green squash shaped like a cucumber.

Appendix

Provinces and Territories

	Capital	Area	Population (1996, to nearest hundred)
Newfoundland & Labrador (NF) WEB SITE www.gov.nf.ca	St. John's	405 720 km^2	551 800
Prince Edward Island (PE) WEB SITE www.gov.pe.ca	Charlottetown	5 660 km^2	134 600
Nova Scotia (NS) WEB SITE www.gov.ns.ca	Halifax	55 490 km^2	909 300
New Brunswick (NB) WEB SITE www.gov.nb.ca	Fredericton	73 440 km^2	738 100
Québec (QC) WEB SITE www.gov.qc.ca	Québec	1 540 680 km^2	7 138 800
Ontario (ON) WEB SITE www.gov.on.ca	Toronto	1 068 580 km^2	10 753 600
Manitoba (MB) WEB SITE www.gov.mb.ca	Winnipeg	649 950 km^2	1 113 900
Saskatchewan (SK) WEB SITE www.gov.sk.ca	Regina	652 330 km^2	990 200
Alberta (AB) WEB SITE www.gov.ab.ca	Edmonton	661 190 km^2	2 696 800
British Columbia (BC) WEB SITE www.gov.bc.ca	Victoria	947 800 km^2	3 724 500
Yukon Territory (YT) WEB SITE www.gov.yk.ca	Whitehorse	483 450 km^2	30 800
Northwest Territory (NT) WEB SITE www.gov.nt.ca	Yellowknife	3 426 320 km^2	64 400
Nunavut	Iqaluit	—	—
CANADA WEB SITE canada.gc.ca	Ottawa	9 970 610 km^2	28 846 800

Map of Canada

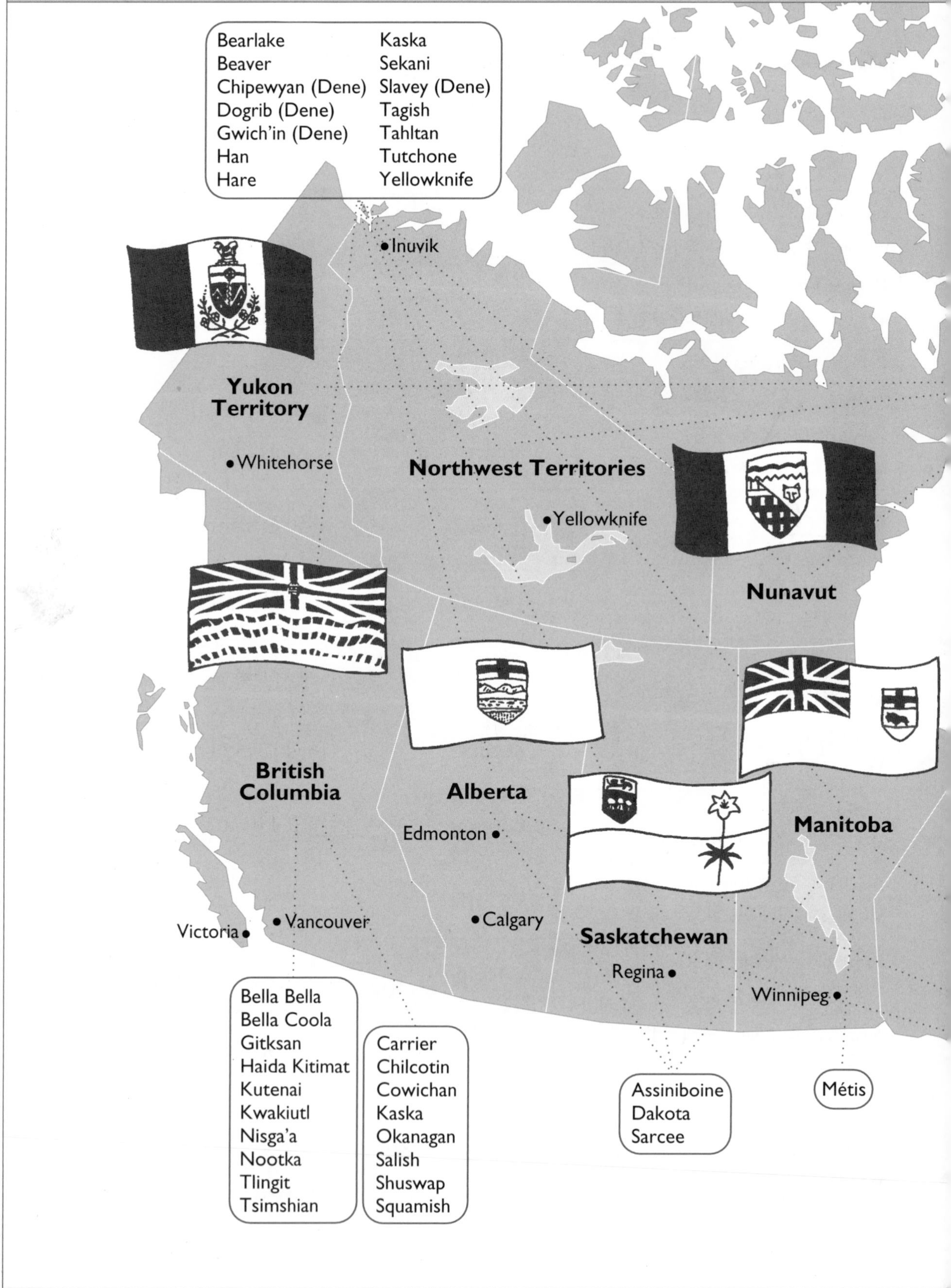

Bearlake	Kaska
Beaver	Sekani
Chipewyan (Dene)	Slavey (Dene)
Dogrib (Dene)	Tagish
Gwich'in (Dene)	Tahltan
Han	Tutchone
Hare	Yellowknife

•Inuvik

Yukon Territory

•Whitehorse

Northwest Territories

•Yellowknife

Nunavut

British Columbia

Alberta

Edmonton •

Manitoba

•Vancouver

Victoria •

•Calgary

Saskatchewan

Regina •

Winnipeg •

Bella Bella	
Bella Coola	
Gitksan	Carrier
Haida Kitimat	Chilcotin
Kutenai	Cowichan
Kwakiutl	Kaska
Nisga'a	Okanagan
Nootka	Salish
Tlingit	Shuswap
Tsimshian	Squamish

Assiniboine
Dakota
Sarcee

Métis

CANADA: Provinces and Aboriginal Peoples

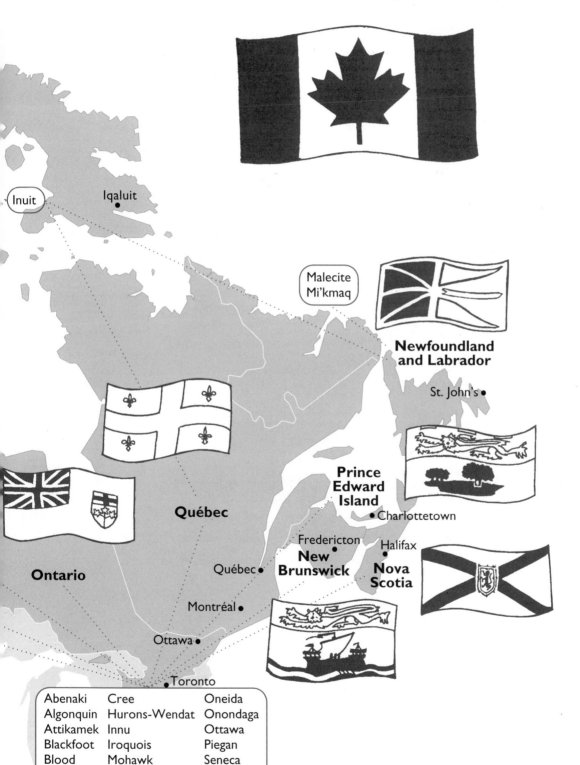

Inuit

Iqaluit

Malecite
Mi'kmaq

**Newfoundland
and Labrador**

St. John's •

**Prince
Edward
Island**

• Charlottetown

Fredericton
•

Halifax
•

Québec

**New
Brunswick**

**Nova
Scotia**

Ontario

Québec •

Montréal •

Ottawa •

• Toronto

Abenaki	Cree	Oneida
Algonquin	Hurons-Wendat	Onondaga
Attikamek	Innu	Ottawa
Blackfoot	Iroquois	Piegan
Blood	Mohawk	Seneca
Cayuga	Ojibwa	Tuscarora

Main Source: Indian and Northern Affairs Canada

Did You Know?—Superlative Canadian Facts

Largest City

    by area   Timmins, ON   3004 square kilometres

    by population   Montréal, QC   1 016 400 people

Smallest City

    by area   L'Ile-Dorval, QC   0.18 square kilometres

    by population   L'Ile-Dorval, QC   2 people

Largest Island	Baffin Island, Nunavut	507 451 square kilometres
Northernmost Point	Cape Columbia, Ellesmere Island, NT	
Southernmost Point	Middle Island, Lake Erie, ON	
Easternmost Point	Cape Spear, NF	
Westernmost Point	Yukon-Alaska boundary	
Highest City	Kimberley, BC	1 128 metres
Highest Community	Lake Louise, AB	1 540 metres
Northernmost Ice-free Port	Stewart, BC	
Longest River	Mackenzie River, NT	4 241 kilometres
Largest Lake (totally in Canada)	Great Bear Lake, NT	31 328 square kilometres
Deepest Lake	Great Slave Lake, NT	614 metres
Highest Mountain	Mt. Logan, YT	5 959 metres
Highest Waterfall	Della Falls, BC	440 metres
Greatest Waterfall	Horseshoe Falls, ON	5 365 cubic metres/second
Longest Bridge	Confederation Bridge, NB/PE	12.9 kilometres
Longest Tunnel	Rogers Pass, BC	14.6 kilometres

Emblems of Provinces and Territories

	Flower	Bird
Newfoundland & Labrador	Pitcher Plant	Atlantic Puffin
Prince Edward Island	Lady's Slipper	Blue Jay
Nova Scotia	Mayflower	Osprey
New Brunswick	Purple Violet	Black-capped Chickadee
Québec	White Lily	Snowy Owl
Ontario	White Trillium	Common Loon
Manitoba	Prairie Crocus	Great Grey Owl
Saskatchewan	Western Red Lily	Prairie Grouse
Alberta	Wild Rose	Great Horned Owl
British Columbia	Dogwood	Stellar's Jay
Yukon Territory	Fireweed	Common Raven
Northwest Territory	Mountain Avens	Gyrfalcon
Nunavut	—	—

Prime Ministers of Canada

Sir John A. Macdonald	Conservative	1867–1873, 1878–1891
Alexander Mackenzie	Liberal	1873–1878
Sir John Abbot	Conservative	1891–1892
Sir John Thompson	Conservative	1892–1894
Sir Mackenzie Bowell	Conservative	1894–1896
Sir Charles Tupper	Conservative	1896
Sir Wilfrid Laurier	Liberal	1896–1911
Sir Robert Borden	Conservative/Unionist	1911–1920
Arthur Meighen	Unionist/Conservative	1920–1921, 1926
Mackenzie King	Liberal	1921–1930, 1935–1948
Richard B. Bennett	Conservative	1930–1935
Louis St. Laurent	Liberal	1948–1957
John Diefenbaker	Progressive Conservative	1957–1963
Lester Pearson	Liberal	1963–1968
Pierre Trudeau	Liberal	1968–1979, 1980–1984
Joe Clark	Progressive Conservative	1979–1980
John Turner	Liberal	1984
Brian Mulroney	Progressive Conservative	1984–1993
Kim Campbell	Progressive Conservative	1993
Jean Chrétien	Liberal	1993–

Titles of Elected Representatives in Canada

MHA	Member of the House of Assembly	in Newfoundland and Labrador
MLA	Member of the Legislative Assembly	in most Canadian provinces and territories
MNA	Member of the National Assembly	in Québec
MP	Member of Parliament	in the Federal Government, Ottawa
MPP	Member of the Provincial Parliament	in Ontario

Some Endangered Species in Canada

Mammals	Frogs and Reptiles	Birds	
Caribou	Cricket Frog	Whooping Crane	Mountain Plover
Cougar	Leopard Frog	Eskimo Curlew	Piping Plover
Marmot	Blue Racer Snake	Northern Bobwhite	King Rail
Marten	Lake Erie Water Snake	Harlequin Duck	Loggerhead Shrike
Swift Fox	Leatherback Turtle	Peregrine Falcon	Henslow's Sparrow
Bowhead Whale		Acadian Flycatcher	Sage Thrasher
Right Whale	**Fish**	Sage Grouse	Kirtland's Warbler
Beluga Whale	Nooksack Dace	Burrowing Owl	Prothonotary Warbler
Wolverine	Salish Sucker	Spotted Owl	
	Aurora Trout		
	Acadian Whitefish		

Countries of the World

Country	Nationality	Adjective	Official Language	Currency
Afghanistan	Afghan	Afghan	Pushtu	afghani
Albania	Albanian	Albanian	Albanian	lek
Algeria	Algerian	Algerian	Arabic	dinar
Argentina	Argentine	Argentinian	Spanish	peso
Armenia	Armenian	Armenian	Armenian	dram
Australia	Australian	Australian	English	dollar
Austria	Austrian	Austrian	German	schilling*
Azerbaijan	Azerbaijani	Azerbaijani	Azerbaijani	manat
Bahamas	Bahamian	Bahamian	English	dollar
Bangladesh	Bangladeshi	Bangladeshi	Bangla	taka
Barbados	Barbadian	Barbadian	English	dollar
Belarus	Belarusian	Belarusian	Byelorussian	ruble
Belgium	Belgian	Belgian	Dutch/French	franc*
Bolivia	Bolivian	Bolivian	Spanish	Boliviano
Bosnia and Herzegovina	Bosnian and Herzegovinian		Serbo-Croatian	dinar
Brazil	Brazilian	Brazilian	Portuguese	real
Bulgaria	Bulgarian	Bulgarian	Bulgarian	lev
Cambodia	Cambodian	Cambodian	Khmer	new riel
Canada	Canadian	Canadian	English/French	dollar
Chile	Chilean	Chilean	Spanish	peso
China	Chinese	Chinese	Mandarin Chinese	yuan
Colombia	Colombian	Colombian	Spanish	peso
Costa Rica	Costa Rican	Costa Rican	Spanish	colón
Croatia	Croat	Croatian	Serbo-Croatian	kuna
Cuba	Cuban	Cuban	Spanish	peso
Czech Republic	Czech	Czech	Czech/Slovak	koruna
Denmark	Dane	Danish	Danish	krone
Ecuador	Ecuadorian	Ecuadorian	Spanish	sucre
Egypt	Egyptian	Egyptian	Arabic	pound
El Salvador	Salvadoran	Salvadoran	Spanish	colón
Ethiopia	Ethiopian	Ethiopian	Amharic	birr
Finland	Finn	Finnish	Finnish/Swedish	markka*
France	French	French	French	franc*
Germany	German	German	German	Deutsche Mark*
Ghana	Ghanaian	Ghanaian	English	cedi
Greece	Greek	Greek	Greek	drachma
Guatemala	Guatemalan	Guatemalan	Spanish	quetzal
Guyana	Guyanese	Guyanese	English	dollar
Haiti	Haitian	Haitian	French	gourde
Honduras	Honduran	Honduran	Spanish	lempira
Hungary	Hungarian	Hungarian	Hungarian	forint
Iceland	Icelander	Icelandic	Icelandic	króna
India	Indian	Indian	Hindi	rupee
Indonesia	Indonesian	Indonesian	Bahasa Indonesia	rupiah
Iran	Iranian	Iranian	Farsi (Persian)	rial
Iraq	Iraqi	Iraqi	Arabic/Kurdish	dinar
Ireland, Republic of	Irish	Irish	Irish/English	pound*
Israel	Israeli	Israeli	Hebrew/Arabic	shekel
Italy	Italian	Italian	Italian	lira*
Jamaica	Jamaican	Jamaican	English	dollar
Japan	Japanese	Japanese	Japanese	yen
Kazakhstan	Kazakhstani	Kazakhstani	Kazakh	tenge
Kenya	Kenyan	Kenyan	English/Swahili	shilling
Korea, North	Korean	Korean	Korean	won

Country	Nationality	Adjective	Official Language	Currency
Korea, South	Korean	Korean	Korean	won
Kuwait	Kuwaiti	Kuwaiti	Arabic	dinar
Lebanon	Lebanese	Lebanese	Arabic/French	pound
Libya	Libyan	Libyan	Arabic	dinar
Lithuania	Lithuanian	Lithuanian	Lithuanian	litas
Malaysia	Malaysian	Malaysian	Malay	ringgit
Mexico	Mexican	Mexican	Spanish	peso
Morocco	Moroccan	Moroccan	Arabic	dirham
Mozambique	Mozambican	Mozambican	Portuguese	metical
Namibia	Namibian	Namibian	Afrikaans/German/English	dollar
Netherlands	Dutch	Dutch	Dutch/Frisian	guilder*
New Zealand	New Zealander	New Zealander	English	dollar
Nicaragua	Nicaraguan	Nicaraguan	Spanish	córdoba
Nigeria	Nigerian	Nigerian	English	naira
Norway	Norwegian	Norwegian	Norwegian	krone
Pakistan	Pakistani	Pakistani	Urdu	rupee
Panama	Panamanian	Panamanian	Spanish	balboa
Paraguay	Paraguayan	Paraguayan	Spanish	guaraní
Peru	Peruvian	Peruvian	Spanish/Quechua	nuevo sol
Philippines	Filipino	Filipino	English/Pilipino	peso
Poland	Polish	Polish	Polish	zloty
Portugal	Portuguese	Portuguese	Portuguese	escudo*
Romania	Romanian	Romanian	Romanian	leu
Russia	Russian	Russian	Russian	ruble
Rwanda	Rwandan	Rwandan	French/Kinyarwanda	franc
Saudi Arabia	Saudi	Saudi	Arabic	riyal
Serbia and Montenegro	Serb, Montenegrin	Serb, Montenegrin	Serbo-Croatian	dinar
Singapore	Singaporean	Singaporean	Chinese/Malay/Tamil	dollar
Slovakia	Slovak	Slovak	Slovak	koruna
Somalia	Somali	Somali	Somali	shilling
South Africa	South African	South African	See below**	rand
Spain	Spanish	Spanish	Spanish	peseta*
Sri Lanka	Sri Lankan	Sri Lankan	Sinhala/Tamil	rupee
Sweden	Swedish	Swedish	Swedish	króna
Switzerland	Swiss	Swiss	German/French/Italian	franc
Syria	Syrian	Syrian	Arabic	pound
Taiwan	Chinese	Chinese	Chinese	dollar
Tajikistan	Tajik	Tajikistan	Tajik	ruble
Tanzania	Tanzanian	Tanzanian	Swahili/English	shilling
Thailand	Thai	Thai	Thai	baht
Tunisia	Tunisian	Tunisian	Arabic	dinar
Turkey	Turk	Turkish	Turkish	lira
Uganda	Ugandan	Ugandan	English	shilling
Ukraine	Ukrainian	Ukrainian	Ukrainian	hryvna
United Arab Emirates	Emiri	Emirian	Arabic	dirham
United Kingdom	British	British	English/Welsh/Scottish	pound
United States	American	American	English	dollar
Uruguay	Uruguayan	Uruguayan	Spanish	peso
Uzbekistan	Uzbek	Uzbek	Uzbek	som
Venezuela	Venezuelan	Venezuelan	Spanish	bolívar
Vietnam	Vietnamese	Vietnamese	Vietnamese	dong
Zimbabwe	Zimbabwean	Zimbabwean	English	dollar

* This currency will become **euro**, in 2002.
** Afrikaans, English, Ndebele, Pedi, Sotho, Swazi, Tsonga, Tswana, Venda, Xhosa, Zulu

Abbreviations

A.D.	in the year of our Lord	N	north	
adj	adjective	N.B.	nota bene (note well)	
adv	adverb	NHL	National Hockey League	
a.m.	ante meridiem (midnight to noon)	p. or pp.	page or pages	
anon.	anonymous	p.m.	post meridiem (noon to midight)	
Ave.	avenue	prep	preposition	
B.C.	before Christ	pron	pronoun	
B.C.E.	before the Common Era	Prof.	professor	
C.E.	Common Era	P.S.	postscript	
Co.	company	PTA	parent-teacher association	
C.O.D.	cash on delivery	RCMP	Royal Canadian Mounted Police	
conj	conjunction	Rd.	road	
D.D.S.	doctor of dental surgery	Rev.	reverend	
Dr.	doctor	rpm	revolutions per minute	
D.S.T.	daylight saving time	RSVP	please reply	
E	east	S	south	
e.g.	for example	Sr.	senior	
etc.	and similar things	S.S.	steamship	
i.e.	that is	St./Ste.	saint	
interj	interjection	St.	street	
Jr.	junior	TD	touchdown	
L.	lake	TOC	table of contents	
Ltd.	limited	v	verb	
M.D.	doctor of medicine	vol.	volume (of a book)	
Mt.	mount (mountain)	vs.	versus (against)	
n	noun	W	west	

Months

January	Jan.	July	Jul.
February	Feb.	August	Aug.
March	Mar.	September	Sept.
April	Apr.	October	Oct.
May	May	November	Nov.
June	Jun.	December	Dec.

Days

Monday	Mon.
Tuesday	Tue.
Wednesday	Wed.
Thursday	Thu.
Friday	Fri.
Saturday	Sat.
Sunday	Sun.

Numbers

	Cardinal Number	Ordinal Number	Roman Numeral
1	one	first	I
2	two	second	II
3	three	third	III
4	four	fourth	IV
5	five	fifth	V
6	six	sixth	VI
7	seven	seventh	VII
8	eight	eighth	VIII
9	nine	ninth	IX
10	ten	tenth	X
11	eleven	eleventh	XI
12	twelve	twelfth	XII
13	thirteen	thirteenth	XIII
14	fourteen	fourteenth	XIV
15	fifteen	fifteenth	XV
16	sixteen	sixteenth	XVI
17	seventeen	seventeenth	XVII
18	eighteen	eighteenth	XVIII
19	nineteen	nineteenth	XIX
20	twenty	twentieth	XX
50	fifty	fiftieth	L
100	hundred	hundredth	C
1000	thousand	thousandth	M
1 000 000	million	millionth	$\overline{M}$

Polygons

3 angles, 3 sides
triangle

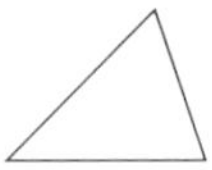

4 angles, 4 sides
quadrilateral

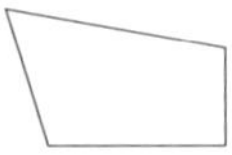

5 angles, 5 sides
pentagon

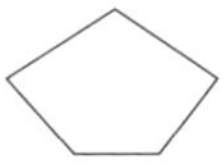

6 angles, 6 sides
hexagon

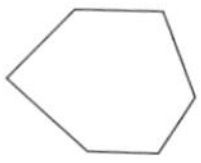

7 angles, 7 sides
septagon

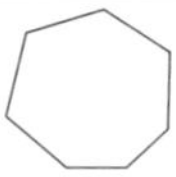

8 angles, 8 sides
octagon

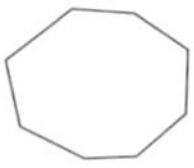

9 angles, 9 sides
nonagon

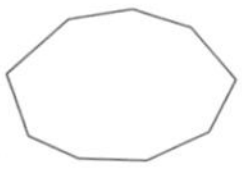

10 angles, 10 sides
decagon

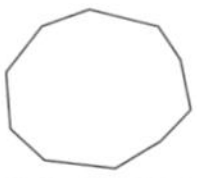

SI Units

Name	Symbol	Quantity
metre	m	length
kilogram	kg	mass
second	s	time
tonne	t	mass (= 1000 kg)

SI Prefixes

Name	Symbol	Multiplying Factor
giga-	G	1 000 000 000
mega-	M	1 000 000
kilo-	k	1 000
hecto-	h	100
deca-	da	10
deci-	h	0.1
centi-	c	0.01
milli-	m	0.001
micro-	m	0.000 001
nano-	n	0.000 000 001

Units Used with SI

Name	Symbol	Quantity
litre	L	volume or capacity
hectare	ha	area (= 10 000 m^2)
tonne	t	mass (= 1000 kg)

Conversion Factors from Metric

1 centimetre	= 0.39 inches
1 metre	= 39.4 inches
1 kilometre	= 0.62 miles
1 kilogram	= 2.20 pounds
1 litre	= 1.76 pints

Conversion Factors to Metric

1 inch	= 2.54 cm
1 yard	= 91.44 cm
1 mile	= 1.61 km
1 pound	= 0.45 g
1 gallon	= 4.55 L (U.S. 3.79 L)

The Solar System

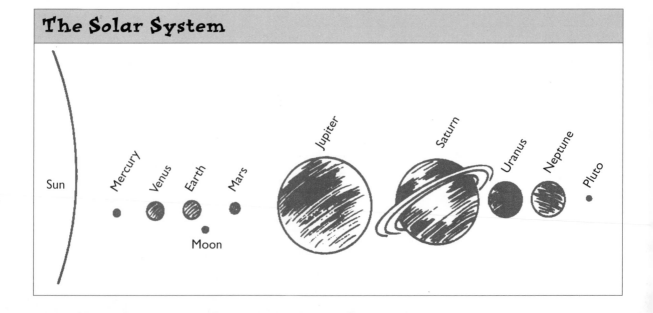

Canada's Food Guide to Healthy Eating

Enjoy a variety of foods from
each food group every day.
Young children can choose
the lower number of servings.
Teenagers can choose
the higher number.
Most other people
are in between.

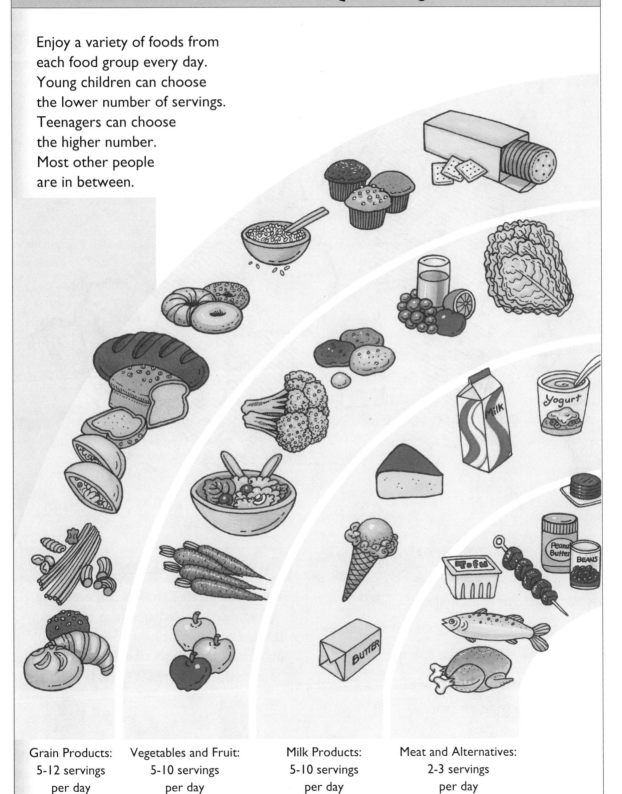

Grain Products:
5-12 servings
per day

Vegetables and Fruit:
5-10 servings
per day

Milk Products:
5-10 servings
per day

Meat and Alternatives:
2-3 servings
per day

Standard Time Zones Across Canada

Standard Time Zones were invented by Sir Sandford Fleming in 1878.
His system was adopted worldwide in 1884.

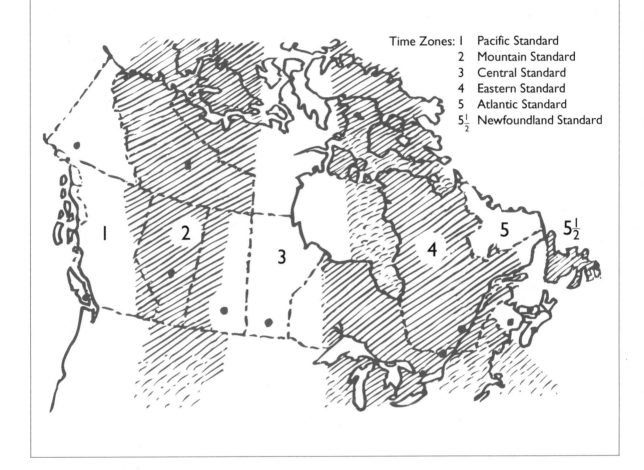

Time Zones: 1 Pacific Standard
2 Mountain Standard
3 Central Standard
4 Eastern Standard
5 Atlantic Standard
$5\frac{1}{2}$ Newfoundland Standard

O Canada

O Canada! Our home and native land!

True patriot love in all thy sons command.

With glowing heart we see thee rise,

The True North strong and free!

From far and wide, O Canada,

We stand on guard for thee.

God keep our land glorious and free!

O Canada, we stand on guard for thee.

O Canada, we stand on guard for thee!

Canada's National Flag

The Maple Leaf, Canada's National Flag, was adopted by Parliament in 1964.
It must be flown daily at all federal buildings, at airports, and at all military bases inside and outside Canada.

Grammar and Usage Mini-Guide . . . .

Abbreviation

An abbreviation is a shortened form of a word or phrase. Abbreviations are useful in informal writing, or in lists or tables. In formal writing, it is usually better to spell out the whole word, but a few abbreviations are acceptable in formal writing as well. They are:

- Mrs., Mr., Ms., and Dr. before someone's name
- St. for Saint in place names
- times, such as 7:00 p.m., A.D. 500

Active and Passive Voice

Active and passive voice are two ways of talking about something that happened.

- In the **active** voice, you tell who did something: *The firefighters extinguished the fire.*
- In the **passive** voice, you tell what happened, but you don't have to mention who did it: *The fire was extinguished.*

Passive voice is useful if you do not know who did something (*My purse was stolen!*), or if the doer of the action is not very important (*The room was decorated for the party.*). Otherwise, it is usually better to use the active voice.

Adjective

An adjective describes a noun or a pronoun: *loud*; *blue*; *two.* Adjectives can come before the word they describe: *a **tall** boy.* They can also come after a linking verb like *is, was,* or *seem*: *He is **tall**.*

Agreement of Subject and Verb

A verb should always agree with its subject.

- Singular subjects (one) take singular verbs: *John laughs loudly. Each of the games was played in the arena.*
- Plural subjects (more than one) take plural verbs: *John and Marta laugh loudly. The games were played in the arena.*

Your dictionary can help you choose the right verb form.

Adverb

An adverb describes a verb (*He ran **quickly**.*), an adjective (*a **really** dark blue car*), or another adverb (*He ran **very** quickly.*). Adverbs usually tell how, when, where, or in what manner.

Antonym

An antonym is a word that means the opposite of another word. **Hot** and **cold** are antonyms. So are **up** and **down**. Many antonyms are made by adding a prefix such as *dis-, mis-,* or *un-* to the word: *disappear; misunderstand; unroll.*

Apostrophe [']

Use an apostrophe:

- to show that something belongs to someone: *Jane's boat*
- in a contraction: *don't, can't*
- to show the plural of letters or symbols: *There are three a's in Saskatchewan and two 0's in 2008.*

Auxiliary (Helping) Verb

▶ See **Verb**.

Bias

Biassed language is language that talks about some group of people in an insulting way. Avoid making generalizations about men, women, racial groups, older people, or people with a disability. Mention a person's sex, race, age, or disability only if it is important to the meaning of what you are writing or saying.

Bibliography

A bibliography is a list of all the works used in a project, or in research. Place it on a separate page at the end. All bibliography entries should include the name of the author(s), the title of the work, and the publisher's name, with the date and place. Arrange the entries alphabetically, by author's name. Here are some example entries.

- *For a book:*
  Love, Ann, and Jane Drake. *Farming.* Toronto: Kids Can Press, 1996.
- *For a magazine article:*
  Jarzen, David. "Pollen Power." *Owl 22* (Mar. 1997)
- *For an Internet document:*
  [Author]. [Year]. [*Title of Document*]. Available: [address] [date accessed]

Capital Letter

Use capital letters for:

- the first word in a sentence: *My mother told me to be home in time for supper.*
- names of people or pets: *Jean Okalik, Sparky*
- the main words in a title: <u>*The Boy in the Drawer*</u>
- days of the week, months, and holidays: *Tuesday; September; Ramadan*
- names of companies, schools, or organizations: *Nike; St. Peter School; the United Way*

Clause

A clause is a group of words that has a subject and a verb. A sentence may have one clause (*I like watching television.*) or more than one clause (*When I have nothing better to do I like watching television, but I'd rather play hockey.*).

- A **main clause** makes a complete thought by itself: *I like watching television.*
- A **subordinate clause** does not make a complete thought by itself: *When I have nothing better to do*
- ▶ See also **Simple Sentence; Compound Sentence.**

Colon [:]

A colon warns you that something follows. Use colons:

- to introduce a list: *Canada has two official emblems: the maple leaf and the beaver.*
- to express time: *8:45; 20:00*
- after the salutation of a business letter: *Dear Ms. Rosen:*

Comma [,]

A comma shows a slight pause in a sentence. Use as few commas as possible while keeping your meaning clear. You need a comma:

- between items in a series: *Jim, Walter, and Aviva sit next to each other.*
- between sentences joined by *and, or, nor, for, but, so,* or *yet*: *Rula thought hard, but no solutions came to mind.*
- between the day and the year in a date: *January 14, 2005*
- between a city and a province or country: *Ottawa, Ontario; Liverpool, England*
- after the salutation of a personal letter: *Dear Sam,*

Comparative

When you compare things, you can make changes to the positive form of an adjective.

- **positive** (*strong*), used for regular descriptions: *She is a strong swimmer.*
- **comparative** (*stronger*), used to compare two things: *She is the stronger of the two swimmers.*

When you compare more than two things, you use the superlative form.

- **superlative** (*strongest*), used for more than two things: *She is the strongest of all the swimmers.*

Compound Sentence

A compound sentence has two main clauses joined by a comma and *and, or, nor, for, but, so,* or *yet*. Each clause has its own subject and its own verb: *I want to go skating, but my skates aren't sharp.*

- ▶ See also **Simple Sentence.**

Compound Word

A compound word is a word that is made up of two other words: *chalkboard, weightlifter,* and *handshake* are compound words. Some compound words are written as one word (*handbook*). Others are written with a hyphen (*hand-held*), and some are written as two words (*hand brake*). If you are not sure of the correct form, look the word up in a dictionary.

Conjunction

A conjunction is a word that connects other words, phrases, or clauses. The two main types of conjunctions are:
- co-ordinating conjunctions (*and, or, nor, for, but, so, yet*)
- subordinating conjunctions (*whenever, after, if, since, because, before, unless*)

Connecting Word

Use connecting words to link your ideas. This will make your writing flow from one idea to the next. Here are some useful connecting words and phrases: *afterward, although, as if, as long as, as much as, as soon as, even if, even though, first, in addition to, in order that, in spite of, similarly, since, so that.*

Contraction

A contraction is a shortened form of two words, such as *can't, won't, wouldn't.* Contractions are fine in informal writing and speech. In more formal writing, it is usually better to spell out the words: *cannot, will not, would not.*

▶ See also **Apostrophe**.

Dash (—)

A dash marks a strong break in a sentence, or emphasizes certain words: *Did you ever see the film—but no, it was made before you were born. Jack works hard—when he has to.* Sometimes, two dashes are used to set off a phrase or clause: *It wasn't until Friday—or it may have been Saturday—that I discovered the note in my backpack.* When you use dashes this way, remember to include the second dash.

Dialogue

Dialogue is conversation. To make dialogue sound like real spoken language, you can use incomplete sentences and some slang words that would not normally be acceptable in written work. Put quotation marks around each person's words and start a new paragraph every time someone starts to speak:

"Let's put a bell around the cat's neck, so we know when she is coming," said the first mouse.

"Great idea!" cried the others.

"But who," asked a small mouse from the back of the room, "will be the one to bell the cat?"

Double Negative

Using a negative word (such as *never, barely, scarcely, hardly*) in the same sentence as *not* makes a double negative. Avoid confusion by taking out or changing one of the two words:

Confusing: *I won't never go there again.*
Better: *I will never go there again.* OR *I won't go there again.*

Draft Version

You should make several draft versions of a piece of writing, until it is exactly what you want.
- Make your first draft have all the ideas that you want to include. Don't worry about things like checking spelling yet.
- In your next draft, check that all your information is correct, and organize your ideas so that they flow from one to the next.
- In the next draft, check and fix any errors in grammar, spelling, or punctuation.
- Your final version should be clean. Make sure you give it a title, and write your name on it.

Exclamation Mark [!]

An exclamation mark shows surprise, delight, or alarm. Avoid using too many exclamation marks, or your reader will get bored.

Too Many: *The room was a mess! Tables were overturned! The drawers had been pulled out! Clothes were everywhere! I understood immediately! The house had been robbed!!!!*

Better: *The room was a mess. Tables were overturned and the drawers had been pulled out. Clothes were everywhere. I understood immediately—the house had been robbed!*

Formal Language

Formal language is the careful language that is used in lectures, speeches, and essays. Some things that are allowed in informal speech or writing are not acceptable in formal writing. Here is a paragraph written in formal language:

Every Saturday morning, I go to the farmer's market. I buy vegetables, and I examine the goods that are for sale. Every stall contains unique treasures that catch my attention. I am never sure what I will find there.

To see the same paragraph written more informally, check the entry under **Informal Language**.
▶ See also **Sentence Fragment; Abbreviation**.

Homonym

Homonyms are homophones or homographs. **Homographs** are words that are **written the same** but have different meanings, such as *tear* (a drop of water from your eye) and *tear* (rip). **Homophones** are words that **sound the same** but have different meanings, such as *meat* (animal flesh) and *meet* (join up with). Words like *bank* (one side of a river) and *bank* (a place to keep money) are homophones and homographs, both at once!

Hyphen [-]

Use hyphens:
- in spelled-out numbers between 21 and 99: *twenty-six*
- in spelled-out times of the day: *the five-fifteen bus*
- to divide a word between syllables at the end of a line: *dis-satisfied; dissat-isfied; dissatis-fied*
- after some prefixes: *all-round; co-operate; ex-boyfriend; half-hearted; pre-test; pro-Canadian; re-enter; self-centred*
- in some compound words: *sister-in-law; hand-held*
▶ See also **Compound Word**.

Informal Language

Informal language is the language you use in everyday speech or casual writing. Here is an example of informal writing:

Every Sat. in the a.m., I head down to the farmer's market. I buy veggies, and then I check out the stuff for sale. Every stall grabs my attention with really cool things you can't find anywhere else. You just never know what you'll find there!

To see the same paragraph written more formally, check the entry under **Formal Language**.

Linking Verb
▶ See **Verb**.

Metaphor and Simile

Metaphors and similes are both ways of writing comparisons. A simile compares two things or ideas directly using *like* or *as*: *The icicles looked like bony fingers.* A metaphor makes the comparison indirectly, without using *like* or *as*: *Bony fingers of ice.*

Noun

A noun is a word that names a person (*boy; Jim*), place (*Canada; garden; school*), or thing (*table; river; house*). A proper noun names a specific person, place, or thing. Always capitalize a proper noun: *Jonah Allingham; Burnaby, B.C.; the Eiffel Tower.*
▶ See also **Subject/Verb Agreement**.

Paragraph

A paragraph is a group of sentences that tell about one main idea. The first line of a paragraph is usually indented. A paragraph often begins with a topic sentence that tells the main idea. The other sentences in the paragraph say something about the topic sentence. Sometimes a connecting word like *next, therefore, so, finally, however,* or *then* helps to show how a sentence is connected to the rest of the paragraph.

Parentheses [()]

Use parentheses:

- to add extra comments in a sentence: *They lived happily ever after (and so did the dog).*
- to explain something or give information: *That mask (the one with the green skin) scares some people.*

Part of Speech

Every word used in a sentence belongs to one of the eight parts of speech: **noun**, **adjective**, **verb**, **adverb**, **conjunction**, **preposition**, **pronoun**, or **interjection**. A word can take on different roles, or parts of speech, in different sentences. For example, the word *run* can act as a noun (*I went on a five-kilometre run.*) or a verb (*I run fast.*) or even an adjective (*The run organizers said it was a success.*).

Period [.]

Use a period:

- at the end of a sentence: *The sky is blue.*
- after abbreviations and initials: *J.J. Cale; Mr.; St.*

Phrase

A phrase is a group of words used together in a sentence: *for the first time; thinking fast; to be a scientist* are all phrases. A phrase cannot act as a sentence or a clause on its own.

- Some phrases can act as **adjectives**: *The book **on the table** is mine.*
- Phrases can also act as **adverbs**: *We played baseball **after supper.***

▶ See also **Clause**.

Plural

The plural form of a word shows that it talks about more than one. Nouns, pronouns, and verbs can be plural.

Plural Noun

Plural nouns usually end in -*s*: *houses, pigs, ideas.* However, some nouns have irregular plural forms.

- Some don't end in -*s*: *children, men, women, mice, geese.*
- Others have the same form for both singular and plural: *deer, moose.*
- Some words look plural, but are treated as singular: *news, measles, mathematics.*

If you aren't sure how to form the plural of a word, check the dictionary entry for the singular form of the word.

▶ See also **Pronoun; Subject-Verb Agreement.**

Possessive

Use possessive forms of nouns and pronouns to show belonging. Here is how to make a noun possessive:

- For most singular nouns, add *'s*: *Jim's idea, the cat's paw*
- For plural nouns ending in -*s*, add only an apostrophe: *the students' project, the Livakos' pet, the cars' lights*
- For plural nouns that do not end in -*s*, add *'s*: *children's games, people's pets, geese's feathers*

Possessive pronouns never need an apostrophe: *mine, yours, his, hers, ours, theirs.*

Prefix

A prefix is a word or syllable added to the beginning of a word to make a new word. For example, *dis-* added to *appear* makes *disappear.* Often, knowing what a prefix means can help you to figure out the meaning of a word. Here is a list of some common prefixes and their meanings:

anti- (against): *antifreeze*
multi- (many): *multicultural*
bi- (two): *bicycle*
dis- (not): *disagree*
in- (not): *inexpensive*
inter- (between; among): *international*
mis- (wrong): *misunderstand*
non- (not): *nonstop*
post- (after): *postscript*

re- (again): *reheat*
semi- (half): *semicircle*
trans- (across): *transplant*
tri- (three): *triangle*
un- (not): *unnecessary*
uni- (one): *uniform*

Preposition

A preposition is a word that shows the connection between a noun and some other word in the sentence. In the phrase *the pencil on the desk*, the preposition *on* connects the noun *pencil* to the word *desk*. Some words that sometimes function as prepositions are: *above, at, before, behind, by, down, for, from, in, of, on, past, since, to, under, until, with.*

Pronoun

A pronoun is a word that replaces a noun. If the noun is singular, then use a singular pronoun. If the noun is plural, use a plural pronoun. Some useful pronouns are *I, me, mine, you, yours, he, him, his, she, her, hers, it, we, us, they, them, theirs.* These are called personal pronouns. Other pronouns include words such as: *who, what, this, those, that, everyone, someone, nobody, either, neither, myself,* and *yourself.*

Proofreading Symbols

The following symbols may be used to mark changes on your writing.

∧	INSERT	The house̬on fire. (is)
ℒ	DELETE	Rattlesnakes are are very dangerous.
≡	CAPITAL	ali may be in danger!
/	LOWER CASE	We Ꞙompost all our food scraps.
¶	NEW PARAGRAPH	So that day ended badly. The next day…
⊙	ADD PERIOD	Liu wondered which way to go⊙
∧	ADD COMMA	Bring your tent͵a sleeping bag, and a flashlight.
#	ADD SPACE	Daniel#and I are leaving tomorrow.
⌒	CLOSE SPACE	Chickens can't fly, but duc⌒ks can.

Proofreading Tips

Proofreading is the last stage in the writing process, before you present your work to your audience. When you proofread, try these tips:

- Read slowly, checking each word. Sometimes it helps to start from the last word and work backward to the beginning. Use a ruler to help you keep your place.
- Make sure each sentence begins with a capital letter and has proper end punctuation.
- Check that commas, semicolons, and colons are used correctly.
- Check that all place names and proper names are spelled correctly and that they begin with a capital letter.
- Check that each paragraph is indented.
- Check for spelling errors, especially in words you often misspell. Look up any words you aren't sure of in a dictionary.

Question Mark [?]

Use a question mark at the end of a direct question: *Where is the remote?* You don't need a question mark in sentences like this: *Sasha asked where the remote was.*

Quotation Marks [" "]

When you write someone's exact words, put them in quotation marks: John said, *"I like school."* You don't need quotation marks in sentences like this: *John said that he liked school.* Also use quotation marks around the titles of short stories, newspaper articles, magazine articles, and episodes of television shows.
► See also **Dialogue**.

Run-on Sentence

A run-on sentence tries to say too much. Run-ons happen when you combine two sentences into one without proper punctuation: *The sky is clear we can go out to play.* To fix a run-on sentence, you can do one of these things:

- Separate the sentences into two sentences beginning with a capital letter and ending with a period, question mark, or exclamation mark: *The sky is clear. We can go out to play.*
- Join the sentences with a semicolon, or with a comma and a joining word: *The sky is clear; we can go out to play.* OR *The sky is clear, so we can go out to play.*
- Join the two sentences into a single sentence: *Since the sky is clear, we can go out to play.*

Semicolon [;]

Use a semicolon:
- to separate two related sentences. When you use a semicolon like this, you tell your reader that the sentence that follows is closely connected to the one before: *I love watching television after school; it relaxes me.*
- to separate items in a list if you have already used a comma: *Walter has lived in Tokyo, Japan; London, England; and Estevan, Saskatchewan.*

Sentence Types

A sentence is a group of words that expresses a complete thought. Every sentence needs a subject and a verb. There are four kinds of sentences:
- **Declarative** sentences tell something. They end with a period: *This book is heavy.*
- **Interrogative** sentences ask a question. They end with a question mark: *Why are you so happy?*
- **Exclamatory** sentences express surprise or strong feeling. They usually end in an exclamation mark: *How beautiful the sky is tonight!*
- **Imperative** sentences give a command. They may end with a period or an exclamation mark. In imperative sentences, the subject is often not written, because it is always "you": *(You) Watch out! (You) Get your jacket on.*

Sentence Fragment

A sentence fragment is a group of words that is punctuated like a sentence, but is missing either a subject or a verb, or both. We use sentence fragments all the time when we speak. In informal writing, or when you are writing dialogue, they are acceptable, but in formal writing they are not:
Who won the prize? Josh. [*Josh* is a sentence fragment because it has no verb.]
I wasn't picked for the part. Never understood why. [*Never understood why* is a sentence fragment because it has no subject.]

Simile

▶ See **Metaphor and Simile**.

Simple Sentence

A simple sentence has one main subject and one main verb: *The camel spit at me!* *Camel* is the subject, and *spit* is the verb.
▶ See also **Compound Sentence**.

Spelling

The **spelling** of English words can be confusing. Here are a few rules that work most of the time. There are exceptions, though, so check in a dictionary to be sure.
- If it sounds like *me*, write *i* before *e* except after *c: piece.*
- For plurals, add *es* to words that end in *ch, s, sh,* or *x: catches, misses, wishes, boxes.*
- When adding *ing* or *ed*, double the final consonant of a verb that ends in a single vowel plus a consonant: *sitting, ripped.*

When you have trouble remembering how to spell a word, try some of these strategies:
- Playing around with the word will help you to remember it: say it out loud, picture the letters in your head, write it down in fancy lettering.
- Think of a memory trick to help you remember hard words. For example, you can remember that *cereal* starts with *c* by

remembering the sentence *I like cream in my cereal.*

- Make your own dictionary of words you misspell often, and check it whenever you write.
- For words with silent letters or double letters, pronounce *all* the letters in your head: *k-now, mis-spell*
- Look for similar spelling patterns: *sight/night/fright/light; bite/kite/quite.*
- Look for a smaller word inside a big word: *argument, tragedy.*

Subject

The subject of a sentence names the person or thing that the sentence is about. The subject is usually near the beginning of the sentence: *Arnold rode his bicycle.* **The cat** *scratched the screen.*

Suffix

A suffix is a syllable or letters added to the end of a word to make a new word. Adding suffixes can change adjectives to verbs, verbs to nouns, etc. Here are some common suffixes that can make different word types:
Noun suffixes:
-er, -or: *teacher, instructor*
-ment: *agreement*
-ness: *awareness*
-ship: *friendship*

Adjective suffixes:
-able: *agreeable*
-er, -est: *longer, longest*
-ful: *delightful*
-less: *fearless*

Verb suffixes:
-en: *strengthen*
-ize: *crystallize*
Adverb suffix:
-ly: *quickly*

Superlative

▶ See **Comparative**.

Synonym

Synonyms are words with similar meanings. *Discuss, talk,* and *chat* are synonyms. You can use synonyms to avoid repeating the same word in a passage. You can also use them to express a particular meaning. For example, in the sentence, *We chatted on the phone for over an hour,* the word *chat* is better than *talked* or *discussed,* because it tells your reader that you were talking in an easy, familiar way. Look in a thesaurus to find synonyms.

Tense

The tense of a verb tells you when the action happened. There are three main tenses in English: past, present, and future.
Do not switch from one main tense to another. For example, this passage shifts between past and present tenses:

Pedro walks up to the door. He had been waiting for this moment for the last two years. He reaches for the knocker and lets it fall. The door opens slowly, and there stood the biggest man he had ever seen.

It needs to be rewritten in either past tense or present tense. For example, here is what it would look like in present tense:

Pedro walks up to the door. He has been waiting for this moment for the last two years. He reaches for the knocker and lets it fall. The door opens slowly, and there stands the biggest man he has ever seen.

Verb

A verb is a word that tells what a person, place, or thing is or is doing.
- Most verbs are **action verbs**: *go, sleep, take, walk, run, dream.*
- **Linking verbs** link the subject to a word that describes the subject. The most common linking verbs are *is, am, are, was,* and *were: I am sad. That animal is an iguana.*
- An **auxiliary verb** is a verb that helps another verb. In the sentence *I have been here before,* the auxiliary verb is *have.* Some verbs that work as auxiliaries are *have, be, can,* and *will.*

▶ See also **Tense; Subject-Verb Agreement.**